D1542361

NELSON SERIES IN HUMAN RESOURCES MANAGEMENT

International Human Resource Management: A Canadian Perspective

P ETER J. D OWLING
VICTORIA UNIVERSITY OF WELLINGTON
NEW ZEALAND

M ARION F ESTING
ESCP-EAP EUROPEAN SCHOOL OF MANAGEMENT
GERMANY

A LLEN D. E NGLE, S R.
EASTERN KENTUCKY UNIVERSITY
UNITED STATES

S TEFAN G RÖSCHL
ESSEC BUSINESS SCHOOL
FRANCE

SERIES EDITOR:
M ONICA B ELCOURT
YORK UNIVERSITY

NELSON / EDUCATION

NELSON EDUCATION

International Human Resource Management: A Canadian Perspective

by Peter J. Dowling, Marion Festing, Allen D. Engle, Sr., and Stefan Gröschl

Associate Vice President, Editorial Director:
Evelyn Veitch

Editor-in-Chief, Higher Education:
Anne Williams

Acquisitions Editor:
Amie Plourde

Marketing Manager:
Kathaleen McCormick

Developmental Editor:
Tracy Yan

Permissions Coordinator:
Sandra Mark

Senior Content Production Manager:
Imoinda Romain

Production Service:
Newgen

Copy Editor:
June Trusty

Proofreader:
Jennifer Knight

Indexer:
Kay Banning

Manufacturing Coordinator:
Joanne McNeil

Design Director:
Ken Phipps

Cover Design:
Wil Bache

Compositor:
Newgen

Printer:
Edwards Brothers

Library and Archives Canada Cataloguing in Publication

International human resource management : a Canadian perspective / Peter J. Dowling ... [et al.].

Includes bibliographical references and index.

ISBN 978-0-17-644097-8

1. International business enterprises–Personnel management–Textbooks.

2. Personnel management–Textbooks. I. Dowling, Peter J.
HF5549.5.E45I68 2008   658.3
C2008-901300-X

ISBN-10: 0-17-644097-6
ISBN-13: 978-0-17-644097-8

Contents

Chapter 4   Staffing International Operations for Sustained Global Growth   111

Chapter 10   International Industrial Relations   333

Chapter 11   Performance Management   361

Chapter 12 IHRM Trends: Complexity, Challenges, and Future Choices 393

About the Series

The management of human resources has become the most important source of innovation, competitive advantage, and productivity, more so than any other resource. More than ever, human resources management (HRM) professionals need the knowledge and skills to design HRM policies and practices that not only meet legal requirements but also are effective in supporting organizational strategy. Increasingly, these professionals turn to published research and books on best practices for assistance in the development of effective HR strategies. The books in the *Nelson Series in Human Resources Management* are the best source in Canada for reliable, valid, and current knowledge about practices in HRM.

The texts in this series include:

- *Managing Performance through Training and Development*
- *Management of Occupational Health and Safety*
- *Recruitment and Selection in Canada*
- *Strategic Compensation in Canada*
- *Strategic Human Resources Planning*
- *An Introduction to the Canadian Labour Market*
- *Research, Measurement, and Evaluation of Human Resources*
- *Industrial Relations in Canada*

The *Nelson Series in Human Resources Management* represents a significant development in the field of HRM for many reasons. Each book in the series is the first, and now, best-selling text in the functional area. Furthermore, HR professionals in Canada must work with Canadian laws, statistics, policies, and values. This series serves their needs. It is the only opportunity that students and practitioners have to access a complete set of HRM books, standardized in presentation, that enables them to access information quickly across many HRM disciplines. The books are essential sources of information that meet the requirements for the Canadian Council of Human Resource Associations (CCHRA) National Knowledge exam for the academic portion of the HR certification process. This one-stop resource will prove useful to anyone looking for solutions for the effective management of people.

The publication of this series signals that the field of human resources management has advanced to the stage where theory and applied research guide practice. The books in the series present the best and most current research in the functional areas of HRM. Research is supplemented with examples of the best practices used by Canadian companies that are leaders in HRM. Each text begins with a general model of the discipline and then describes the implementation of effective strategies. Thus, the books serve as an introduction to the functional area for the new student of HR and as a validation source for the more experienced HRM practitioner. Cases, exercises, and endnotes provide opportunities for further discussion and analysis.

As you read and consult the books in this series, I hope you share my excitement in being involved and knowledgeable about a profession that has such a significant impact on organizational goals and employees' lives.

Monica Belcourt, Ph.D., CHRP
Series Editor
January 2008

About the Authors

Stefan Gröschl

(Ph.D., Oxford Brookes University, England) is Associate Professor for Human Resources Management, Diversity Management, and Organizational Behaviour and co-chairs the Diversity and Performance Chair at the ESSEC Business School in Paris, France. Previous appointments include Oxford Brookes University, England, and the University of Guelph, Canada. He is a visiting professor at Royal Roads University, Canada, and a graduate faculty member at the University of Guelph.

Stefan's primary research interests focus on HR policies and practices supporting the integration of disadvantaged and/or minority employee groups into the workforce. His work has been published in national and international academic journals and the *Nelson Series in Human Resources Management*, and presented at national and international conferences of organizations such as the Administrative Sciences Association of Canada (ASAC) and the European Group for Organizational Studies (EGOS).

Peter J. Dowling

(Ph.D., The Flinders University of South Australia) is Professor of International Business in the School of Marketing & International Business at Victoria University of Wellington, New Zealand. Previous appointments include The University of Melbourne, Monash University, the University of Tasmania, and the University of Canberra. He has also held visiting appointments in the United States at Cornell University and Michigan State University and in Germany at the University of Paderborn and the University of Bayreuth. He has co-authored three books: *Strategic Management: Competitiveness and Globalisation* (3rd ed.); *Human Resource Management in Australia* (2nd ed.); and *People in Organizations: An Introduction to Organizational Behavior in Australia*. He has also written or co-authored over 70 journal articles and book chapters, and serves on the editorial boards of the *International Journal of Human Resource Management, Journal of International Business Studies, Journal of World Business, Management International Review, Journal of International Management, Journal of Management & Organization, ZfP-German Journal of Human Resource Research, Management Review, Asia Pacific Journal of Human Resources*, and *Thunderbird International Business Review*.

Peter is a past National Vice-President of the Australian Human Resources Institute, past Editor of the *Asia Pacific Journal of Human Resources* (1987–1996), and a Life Fellow of the Australian Human Resources Institute. Currently, he is a Vice President of the Australia & New Zealand International Business Academy, President-Elect of the International Federation of Scholarly Associations of Management (IFSAM), and a Senior Research Affiliate of the Center for Advanced Human Resource Studies at Cornell University. Peter is also a past President of the Australian & New Zealand Academy of Management.

Marion Festing

(Ph.D., University of Paderborn) is Professor of Human Resource Management and Intercultural Leadership at ESCP-EAP European School of Management in Berlin, Germany. Previous appointments include the University of Paderborn, Germany. Marion has gained educational, research, and work experience in France, Australia, Tunisia, Taiwan, and the United States. Her publications include *Strategisches Internationales Personalmanagement* (*Strategic International Human Resource Management* (2nd ed.), a co-authored text, *Internationales Personalmanagement* (*International Human Resource Management*) (2nd ed.), and guest-edited special issues of *Management International Review* on IHRM. She has also written or co-authored over 50 book chapters and journal articles, and published in international journals such as *Management International Review, Economic and Industrial Demography, European Management Journal*, and the *International Journal of Globalisation and Small Business*.

Marion serves on the editorial boards of *Career Development International, Journal of Management & Organization, International Journal of Globalisation and Small Business, ZfP-German Journal of Human Resource Research*, and *Zeitschrift für Management*. She was co-organizer of the 6th conference on International Human Resource Management in Paderborn in 1998, and co-chair of the IHRM track at the IFSAM conference in Berlin in 2006. Her current research interests focus on transnational HRM strategies, global careers, and global compensation.

Allen D. Engle, Sr.

(D.B.A., University of Kentucky) is a Professor of Management in the College of Business and Technology at Eastern Kentucky University. He is a national and regional professional member of World at Work (formerly the American Compensation Association) and the Society for Human Resource Management, and a long-time member of the U.S. Academy of Management. While at Eastern, he has taught courses in management (undergraduate and graduate), a number of areas within human resource administration, organizational behaviour, organizational theory, and international management (undergraduate and graduate). He has been Visiting Lecturer at the FHS Hochschule Für Technik, Wirtschaft und Soziale Arbeit, St. Gallen in Switzerland, and Visiting Professor of International Management at the University of Pécs in Hungary.

Allen's research interests are in the topic areas of compensation theory and practices, leadership and organizational change, job analysis, managerial competencies, and organizational design, particularly as these impact on multinational firms. He has published in regional, national, and international academic journals, presenting academic papers on many of the topic areas presented above at conferences in the United States, Australia, Canada, Estonia, Germany, Hungary, Ireland, Slovenia, Spain, and the United Kingdom. Allen has consulted for regional firms and presented professional seminars in the areas of performance appraisal systems, executive team-building, strategically responsive compensation systems, intercultural management issues, and organizational change.

The author team is an excellent example of collaborative work—across a great many time zones—in the new global context of the 21st century, with tricontinental representation from the Asia–Pacific, Europe, and North America.

Preface

According to the *2006 World Investment Report* issued by the United Nations, in 2005 there were a total of 77,000 transnational corporations with over 770,000 foreign affiliates. Since the 1990s, employment in foreign affiliates has increased from 24 to 62 million workers worldwide. Canada and Canadian businesses play an important role in this globalization process. In the above-mentioned UN report, Canadian companies such as Thomson, Alcan Inc.,[1] and Nortel Networks were among the world's top 100 non-financial transnational companies ranked by foreign assets, while in terms of transnationality[2] and internationality,[3] these companies ranked first, fifth, and eighth, respectively.

Looking back at Canada's history, with its strong exporting of and trade experience with its natural resources, its membership in international trade associations such as NAFTA, its recently signed first trans-Atlantic free trade agreement with the European Fair Trade Association (EFTA) countries—Iceland, Norway, Switzerland, and Liechtenstein[4]—and a Foreign Investment Protection and Promotion Agreement with India, Canada's international presence and involvement does not come as a surprise. In particular, Canada's experience of accommodating to its historically culturally diverse population could be an advantage for, or reason why, Canadian businesses such as Thomson successfully operate in cultural settings other than their own.

This textbook is based on Dowling, Festing, and Engle's fifth edition (2007) of *International Human Resource Management*. We have organized the complexities particular to HRM activities in multinational enterprises in such a way that teachers of both undergraduate and graduate students have a choice as to how they will present the material. We have tried to find a balance that is meaningful to Canadian readers and to those of the various other cultures and educational traditions, while accurately capturing the realities facing HRM professionals practising in multinational enterprises.

Each chapter opens with a vignette introducing the chapter topic with closely related real-life stories, current debates, trends, and issues. Each chapter includes chapter learning objectives, figures and tables to illustrate the text efficiently, margin definitions of key terms, a chapter summary, a list of key terms, and endnotes that provide full information on the sources cited in the chapter. Throughout each chapter, the International Human Resource Management Today (IHRM Today) boxes feature stories or cases that illustrate current, real-life examples of the textual material. The International Human Resource Management Notebook (IHRM Notebook) boxes present practical, hands-on information for HR practitioners, and highlight key points in the chapter. The end-of-chapter material provides a list of websites for readers to access to add to their understanding of the chapter topic; WWW icons in the chapter margins indicate when an URL has been provided in the Web Links section.

Further, we have linked the textual material in our book with the required professional capabilities (RPCs) necessary to earn a Certified

Human Resources Professional (CHRP) designation. Applicants for this Canada-wide designation, granted by the Canadian Council of Human Resources Associations, must now pass two national exams based on 203 required professional capabilities. RPC icons appear in the margins of the text, indicating the relevant RPCs in the list at the end of the chapter. These RPCs are listed by functional area on the Professional Assessment Resource Centre (PARC) website at www.cchra-ccarh.ca/parc//en/section_3/ss33e.asp.

As the RPCs on PARC are not numbered we have adopted the following referencing system. When we reference an RPC, we designate it with a margin icon. Each RPC is numbered and is preceded by the chapter number. For example, RPC 8.2 is the second RPC presented in Chapter 8. At the end of the chapter, we list the specific RPCs that we have identified as being relevant to the text. We hope that this linkage of our content to the RPCs will help students and practitioners preparing for the CHRP assessments.

Endnotes

1. During the writing of this textbook, the Canadian aluminum company Alcan was taken over by Rio Tinto, a U.K.-listed company that owns smelters in Australia, New Zealand, and the United Kingdom, and bauxite mines and alumina refineries in Australia and Sardinia. Rio Tinto Alcan will be one of the dominant key players in the global aluminum industry.
2. The UN *World Investment Report 2006* calculates a company's transnationality as the average of three ratios: foreign assets to total assets, foreign sales to total sales, and foreign employment to total employment.
3. The UN *World Investment Report 2006* calculates a company's internationality as the number of foreign majority-owned affiliates divided by the number of all majority-owned affiliates.
4. According to Foreign Affairs and International Trade Canada, the EFTA countries as a whole comprise Canada's eighth-largest merchandise export destination. For more information, visit www.dfait-maeci.gc.ca/tna-nac/efta-en.asp

Acknowledgments

This book is dedicated to Zoë.

For their invaluable assistance with this first international HRM textbook with a Canadian perspective, I must acknowledge and thank the many people who aided me in the process. This text would have never come to life without their input.

First, my thanks to the reviewers, who took the time to read and provide feedback on early versions of the chapters. Their helpful suggestions resulted in a number of improvements to the text, and I thank each of them:

Gerald Hunt,
  Ryerson University

Sudhir Saha,
  Memorial University

Karan Gardner,
  Georgian College

Sharon O'Sullivan,
  University of Ottawa

Second, I must thank the authors of the original text on which this book is based for their trust and support: Peter Dowling, Marion Festing, and Allen D. Engle, Sr.

Third, given that this is my first textbook, I cannot thank enough the team at Nelson: Jackie Wood, Tracy Yan, Shannon White, Amie Plourde, and Jennifer Pegg, as well as Monica Belcourt, series editor, for their assistance, guidance, patience, and support. I was very fortunate to have such a dedicated team of supporters who guided me each step of the way. Special thanks to June Trusty, my copy editor.

Finally, I thank Adri for all her support.

Gracias.
Stefan Gröschl

Chapter 1

Introduction

Chapter Learning Objectives

After reading this chapter, you should be able to:

- define key terms in international human resource management (IHRM) and consider several definitions of IHRM
- discuss the historically significant issue of expatriate assignment management and review the evolution of these assignments to reflect the increasing diversity with regard to what constitutes international work and the type and length of international assignments
- outline the differences between domestic and international human resource management, and detail a model that summarizes the variables that moderate these differences
- discuss the complexity of IHRM, the increasing potential for challenges to existing IHRM practices and current models, and an increasing awareness of the wide number of choices within IHRM practices due to increased transparency and faster and more detailed diffusion of these practices across organizational units and firms

EXPANSION PLANS: KRAFT AND IVANHOE MINES LTD. (CANADA)

At the beginning of July 2007, the international press reported a provisional agreement between the U.S. food producer Kraft and the French group Danone for Kraft to buy Danone's biscuit arm for US$7.2 billion. The likelihood of such an international deal had implications not only for the stock market, the shareholders, and the financial community, but it was also of particular concern for Danone's employees:

> Kraft yesterday sought to allay French fears over job security following confirmation it had provisionally agreed to buy the biscuit arm of Danone. Yesterday, the US food producer said it had agreed not to close any biscuit factories in France for at least three years, and existing management would be retained. Also, Kraft pledged to keep the European headquarters of its enlarged biscuit business in the Paris region for at least two years, emphasizing that it had no plans to move for the "foreseeable future."*

The fear of job loss and the increased anxiety and uncertainty among Danone's workforce in this potential takeover by Kraft highlight the sensitive and complex nature of human resource-related challenges with which the HR function might be confronted by the international expansions of the companies involved.

Other examples of internationalization reflect the equally important operational and strategic aspects with which the human resource management (HRM) function has to deal. For example, in Mongolia's largest draft investment agreement, Ivanhoe Mines Ltd. (Canada) and the United Kingdom-listed Rio Tinto are planning to jointly develop and operate a mine at Oyu Tolgoi in the Gobi desert in Mongolia.**

While the draft investment agreement and the construction of this mine were hailed as marking an important milestone by the Canadian mining company and symbolized the closure of five years of political bargaining and negotiations with the Mongolian government, Ivanhoe Mines' Canadian HRM function will be faced with a number of tough operational and strategic questions—starting from recruiting local staff, selecting the right home-country managers, training and development, compensation, and many other traditional HR practices and processes that change when put within an international context. One of our key aims of this book is the exploration of these changing characteristics of the HRM function when put within an international context—starting with this introductory chapter outlining the scope of this book.

Sources: *Jones, A., & Cameron, D. (2007, July 4). Kraft seeks to allay Danone fears. *Financial Times*, 16. **Bream, R. (2007, June 29). Mongolian mine win for Ivanhoe and Rio Tinto. *Financial Times*, 16.

Scope of the Book

The field of international HRM has been characterized by three broad approaches.[1] The first[2] emphasizes cross-cultural management: examining human behaviour within organizations from an international perspective. A second approach developed from the comparative industrial relations (IR) and HRM[3] literature and seeks to describe, compare, and analyze HRM systems in various countries. A third approach seeks to focus on aspects of HRM in multinational firms.[4] These approaches are depicted in Figure 1.1. In this book, we take the third approach. Our objective is to explore the implications that the process of internationalization has for the activities and policies of HRM. In particular, we are interested in how HRM is practised in multinational organizations.

As Figure 1.1 demonstrates, there is an inevitable overlap between the three approaches when one is attempting to provide an accurate view of the global realities of operating in the international business environment. Obviously, cross-cultural management issues are important when dealing with the cultural aspects of foreign operations. Some of these aspects will be taken up in Chapter 9, where we deal with HRM in the host-country context—indicated by (a) in Figure 1.1. Chapter 10 deals with industrial relations issues and draws on literature from the comparative IR field—(b) in Figure 1.1. While the focus of much of this book is on the established **multinational enterprise (MNE)**—a firm that owns or controls business activities in more than one foreign country—we recognize that international HRM

multinational enterprise (MNE)

a firm that owns or controls business activities in more than one foreign country

FIGURE 1.1

Interrelationships between Approaches to the Field

issues are also faced by small, internationalizing firms that have not yet reached multinational firm status, family-owned firms, and nongovernmental organizations (NGOs).[5]

Defining International HRM

Before we can offer a definition of international **HRM**, we should first define the general field of HRM. Typically, HRM refers to those activities undertaken by an organization to effectively utilize its human resources. These activities would include at least the following:

1. human resource planning
2. staffing (recruitment, selection, placement)
3. performance management
4. training and development
5. compensation (remuneration) and benefits
6. industrial relations

The question is: Which activities change when HRM goes international? A model developed by Morgan[6] (shown in Figure 1.2) is helpful. He presents IHRM on three dimensions:

 1.1

1. The broad human resource activities of procurement, allocation, and utilization. These three broad activities can easily be expanded into the six HR activities listed above.

FIGURE 1.2

A Model of IHRM

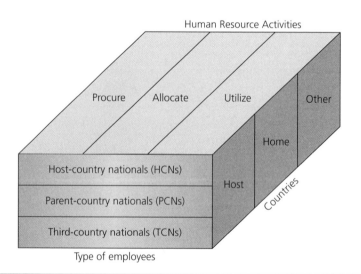

Source: Adapted from: Morgan, P. V. (1986). International Human Resource Management: Fact or Fiction? *Personnel Administrator, 31*(9), 44.

2. The national or country categories involved in international HRM activities:

- the host country where a subsidiary may be located
- the home country where the firm is headquartered
- "other" countries that may be the source of labour, finance and other inputs

3. The three categories of employees of an international firm:

- host-country nationals (HCNs)
- parent-country nationals (PCNs)
- third-country nationals (TCNs)

Thus, for example, Canada's Four Seasons Hotels and Resorts employs French citizens (HCNs) in its George V hotel in Paris, sends Canadian citizens (PCNs) to Asia–Pacific countries on assignment, and may send some of its Australian employees on assignment to its hotels in Tokyo (as TCNs). The nationality of the employee is a major factor in determining the person's "category," which in turn is frequently a major driver of the employee's compensation.

Morgan defines **international HRM** as *the interplay among the three dimensions depicted in Figure 1.2—human resource activities, type of employees, and countries of operation*. We can see that in broad terms, international HRM involves the same activities as domestic HRM (e.g., procurement refers to HR planning and staffing). However, domestic HRM is involved with employees *within only one national boundary*. Increasingly, domestic HRM is taking on some of the flavour of international HRM, as it deals more and more with a multicultural workforce. Thus, some of the current focus of domestic HRM on issues of managing workforce diversity may prove to be beneficial to the practice of international HRM. However, it must be remembered that the way in which diversity is managed within a single national context may not necessarily transfer to a multinational context without some modification.

international HRM

the interplay among human resource activities, types of employees, and countries of operation

What Is an Expatriate?

One obvious difference between domestic and international HRM is that staff are moved across national boundaries into various roles within the international firm's foreign operations—these employees have traditionally been called *expatriates*. An **expatriate** is an employee who is working and temporarily residing in a foreign country.

Some firms prefer to call such employees *international assignees*. While it is clear in the literature that PCNs are always expatriates, it is often overlooked that TCNs are expatriates, as are HCNs who are transferred into parent-country operations outside their home country.[7] Figure 1.3 illustrates how all three categories may become expatriates.

Lately, the term **inpatriate** has come into vogue to signify the transfer of subsidiary staff into the parent-country (headquarters) operations.[8] Its use has added a level of confusion surrounding the definition of an expatriate. For example, the *International Human Resource Management Reference Guide*,

expatriate

an employee who is working and temporarily residing in a foreign country

inpatriate

an employee who transfers from a subsidiary to the parent-country (headquarters) operations

FIGURE 1.3

International Assignments Create Expatriates

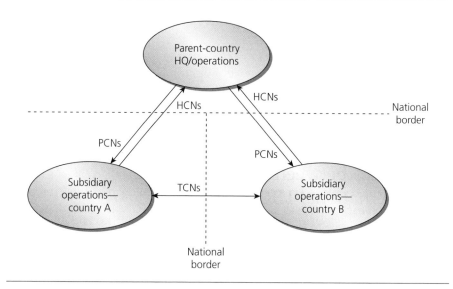

published by the Institute for International Human Resources (a division of the U.S. Society for Human Resource Management) defines an inpatriate as a "foreign manager in the U.S." A "foreign manager in the U.S." is then defined as "an expatriate in the U.S. where the U.S. is the host country and the manager's home country is outside of the U.S."[9] In other words, an inpatriate is also defined as an expatriate. A further indication of the confusion created by the use of the term *inpatriate* is that some writers in international management define an HCN as an inpatriate. For the purposes of this text, HCNs become inpatriates only when they are transferred into the parent-country operations as expatriates, as illustrated in Figure 1.3.

Given the substantial amount of jargon in international HRM, it is questionable as to whether the term *inpatriate* adds enough value to justify its use. However, companies now use the term. For example, the Finnish multinational Nokia uses *expatriate* to signify staff who are transferred out of, and *inpatriate* to signify staff transferred into, a particular country. These terms are regarded as a constant reminder to all managers that there are movements of staff that need to be managed, and not all are PCNs. For clarity, we will use the term *expatriate* throughout this text to refer to employees who are transferred out of their home base into some other area of the firm's international operations, unless we are directly quoting from another source. In doing so, we recognize that there is increasing diversity with regard to what constitutes international work, the type and length of international assignments, and the increasingly strategic role of the HR function in many organizations, which in turn influences the nature of some expatriate roles.

Stahl and Björkman have recognized this expansion in the scope of the field of IHRM in their *Handbook of Research in International Human Resource Management*, where they define the field of IHRM in the following way:

> We define the field of IHRM broadly to cover all issues related to the management of people in an international context. Hence our definition of IHRM covers a wide range of human resource issues facing MNCs in different parts of their organizations. Additionally, we include comparative analyses of HRM in different countries.[10]

We will be examining the expanding scope of the IHRM field in this book and will return to the question of a definition of the field in the final chapter.

Differences between Domestic and International HRM

In our view, the *complexity* of operating in different countries and employing different national categories of workers is a key variable that differentiates domestic and international HRM, rather than any major differences between the HRM activities performed. Dowling[11] argues that the complexity of international HR can be attributed to six factors:

1. more HR activities
2. the need for a broader perspective
3. more involvement in employees' personal lives
4. changes in emphasis as the workforce mix of expatriates and locals varies
5. risk exposure
6. broader external influences

Each of these factors is now discussed in detail to illustrate its characteristics.

More HR Activities

To operate in an international environment, a human resource department must engage in a number of activities that would not be necessary in a domestic environment: international taxation; international relocation and orientation; administrative services for expatriates; host-government relations; and language translation services.

Expatriates are subject to international taxation and often have both domestic (i.e., home-country) and host-country tax liabilities. Therefore, tax equalization policies must be designed to ensure that there is no tax incentive or disincentive associated with any particular international assignment.[12] The administration of tax equalization policies is complicated by the wide variations in tax laws across host countries and by the possible time lag between the completion of an expatriate assignment and the settlement of domestic and international tax liabilities. In recognition of these difficulties, many multinational firms retain the services of a major accounting firm for international taxation advice.

International relocation and orientation involves arranging for pre-departure training; providing immigration and travel details; providing housing, shopping, medical care, recreation, and schooling information; and finalizing compensation details such as delivery of salary overseas, determination of various overseas allowances, and taxation treatment. (The issue of expatriates returning to their home country [repatriation] is covered in detail in Chapter 8). Many of these factors may be a source of anxiety for the expatriate and require considerable time and attention to successfully resolve potential problems—certainly much more time than would be involved in a domestic transfer/relocation such as Toronto to Ottawa, London to Glasgow, or Frankfurt to Munich.

RPC 1.3

An MNE also needs to provide administrative services for expatriates in the host countries in which it operates. Providing these services can often be a time-consuming and complex activity because policies and procedures are not always clear-cut and may conflict with local conditions.

Ethical questions can arise when a practice that is legal and accepted in the host country may be at best unethical and at worst illegal in the home country. For example, a situation may arise in which a host country requires an AIDS test for a work permit for an employee whose parent firm is headquartered in Canada, where employers generally do not have the right to conduct mandatory pre-employment HIV/AIDS screening or testing, or in a country where businesses follow the International Labour Organization (ILO) *Code of Practice on HIV/AIDS*. As outlined in IHRM Notebook 1.1, the ILO's *Code of Practice* has not only had an impact on

---

IHRM Notebook 1.1

Response of Canadian Businesses Abroad to the ILO *Code of Practice on HIV/AIDS*

Under the heading "Screening for purposes of exclusion from employment or work processes," the ILO *Code of Practice on HIV/AIDS* states that "HIV/AIDS screening should not be required of job applicants or persons in employment."*

In its report on Canada's foreign policy on HIV/AIDS, the Public Health Agency of Canada (PHAC) describes a number of Canadian companies operating abroad and their responses to the ILO's *Code of Practice*. While companies such as Molson have been active through awareness and marketing campaigns, many of these responses fall within the IHRM area. Barrick Gold Corporation developed workplace and community HIV/AIDS initiatives through its subsidiary in Tanzania, supporting its employees and families through affordable housing, free condoms, counselling, and the provision of community health educators. In South Africa, mining company Placer Dome Inc., in partnership with the Employment Bureau of South Africa and the Canadian International Development Agency, developed a home-care program for its terminally ill workers with AIDS. According to PHAC's report, Placer Dome and Barrick Gold also developed plans for providing employees in their African mines with antiretroviral therapies.**

---

*International Labour Organization. (2001). The ILO *Code of Practice on HIV/AIDS* (Key Principle 4.6). Geneva.
**Foster, J., & Garmaise, D. (2003). *Meeting the Challenge: Canada's Foreign Policy on HIV/AIDS—With a Particular Focus on Africa*, Section 7.0. Public Health Agency of Canada.

Canadian business practices in Canada but has also influenced Canadian businesses abroad.

How does the corporate HR manager deal with the potential expatriate employee who refuses to meet this requirement for an AIDS test and the overseas affiliate that needs the services of a specialist expatriate from headquarters? These issues add to the complexity of providing administrative services to expatriates.

Host-government relations represent an important activity for an HR department, particularly in developing countries where work permits and other important certificates are often more easily obtained when a personal relationship exists between the relevant government officials and multinational managers. Maintaining such relationships helps resolve potential problems that can be caused by ambiguous eligibility and/or compliance criteria for documentation such as work permits. Canadian multinationals, however, must be careful in how they deal with relevant government officials, as payment or payment-in-kind such as dinners and gifts may violate Canada's Corruption of Foreign Public Officials Act (1998).

Provision of language translation services for internal and external correspondence is an additional international activity for the HR department. Morgan[13] notes that if the HR department is the major user of language translation services, the role of this translation group is often expanded to provide translation services to all foreign operation departments within the multinational.

The Need for a Broader Perspective

HR managers working in a domestic environment generally administer programs for a single national group of employees who are covered by a uniform compensation policy and taxed by one national government. Because HR managers working in an international environment face the problem of designing and administering programs for more than one national group of employees (e.g., PCN, HCN, and TCN employees who may work together in Zurich at the European regional headquarters of a Canadian-based multinational), they need to take a broader view of issues. For example, a broader, more international perspective on expatriate benefits would endorse the view that all expatriate employees, regardless of nationality, should receive a foreign service or expatriate premium when working in a foreign location.

Yet some MNEs that routinely pay such premiums to their PCN employees on overseas assignment (even if the assignments are to desirable locations) are reluctant to pay premiums to foreign nationals assigned to the home country of the firm. Such a policy confirms the traditional perception of many HCN and TCN employees that PCN employees (particularly U.S. and European PCNs) are given preferential treatment.[14] Complex equity issues arise when employees of various nationalities work together, and the resolution of these issues remains one of the major challenges in the international HRM field. (Equity issues with regard to compensation are discussed in Chapter 7.)

More Involvement in Employees' Personal Lives

A greater degree of involvement in employees' personal lives is necessary for the selection, training, and effective management of both PCN and TCN employees. The HR department or HR professional needs to ensure that the expatriate employee understands housing arrangements, health care, and all aspects of the compensation package provided for the assignment (cost-of-living allowances, premiums, taxes, and so on). Many multinationals have an "International HR Services" section that coordinates administration of the above programs and provides such services for PCNs and TCNs as handling their banking, investments, arranging for home rental while the employee is on assignment, coordinating home visits, and facilitating final repatriation.

In the domestic setting, the HR department's involvement with an employee's family is limited. The firm may, for example, provide private employee health insurance programs. Or, if a domestic transfer is involved, the HR department may provide some assistance in relocating the employee and family. In the international setting, however, the HR department must be much more involved in order to provide the level of support required and will need to know more about the employee's personal life. For example, some governments require the presentation of a marriage certificate before granting a visa to an accompanying spouse. Thus, marital status could become an aspect of the selection process, regardless of the best intentions of the firm to avoid using a potentially discriminatory selection criterion. In such a situation, the HR department should advise all candidates being considered for the position of the host country's visa requirements with regard to marital status and allow candidates to decide whether they wish to remain in the selection process.

Apart from providing suitable housing and schooling in the assignment location, the HR department may also need to assist children left behind at boarding schools in the home country.[15] In more remote or less hospitable assignment locations, the HR department may be required to develop, and even run, recreational programs. For a domestic assignment, most of these matters either would not arise or would be primarily the responsibility of the employee rather than the HR department.

Changes in Emphasis as the Workforce Mix of PCNs and HCNs Varies

As foreign operations mature, the emphases put on various human resource activities change. For example, as the need for PCNs and TCNs declines and more trained locals become available, resources previously allocated to areas such as expatriate taxation, relocation, and orientation are transferred to activities such as local staff selection, training, and management development. The latter activity may require establishment of a program to bring high-potential local staff to corporate headquarters for developmental assignments. The need to change emphasis in HR operations as a foreign subsidiary matures is clearly a factor that would broaden the responsibilities of local HR activities such as human resource planning, staffing, training and development, and compensation.

Risk Exposure

Frequently, the human and financial consequences of failure in the international arena are more severe than in domestic business. For example, while we discuss the topic in more detail in Chapter 5, expatriate failure (the premature return of an expatriate from an international assignment) and underperformance while on international assignment are potentially high-cost problems for MNEs. Direct costs (salary, training costs, and travel and relocation expenses) per failure to the parent firm may be as high as three times the domestic salary plus relocation expenses, depending on currency exchange rates and location of assignments. Indirect costs such as loss of foreign market share and damage to key host-country relationships may be considerable.

Another aspect of risk exposure that is relevant to international HRM are militant groupings and activities, and terrorism, particularly in the current political climate since the tragic 9/11 attack in New York in 2001. IHRM Today 1.1 provides an example of such a threat to employees on international assignments.

Most major multinationals must now consider political risk and terrorism when planning international meetings and assignments, and spending on protection against terrorism is increasing. Terrorism has also clearly had an effect on the way in which employees assess potential international assignment locations.[16]

The HR department may also need to devise emergency evacuation procedures for highly volatile assignment locations subject to political or terrorist violence or major epidemic or pandemic crises such as severe acute respira-

---

IHRM Today 1.1

Militants Release Hostages

On June 4, 2006, 16 oil workers (including 8 British, Canadian, and U.S. expatriates) who were kidnapped aboard the Norwegian Fred. Olsen Energy ASA oil rig by militant Ijaw youths in Nigeria regained their freedom. According to Nigeria's governor Goodluck Jonathan, multinational oil companies operating in Nigeria need to better honour and respect their memorandums of understanding entered into with Nigeria's host communities to prevent militant actions such as the kidnapping of these oil workers. While Jonathan stressed that his government would work to ensure that incidents of abduction of expatriate oil workers would no longer happen, this example reflects the importance of international HR activities such as governmental/community relationship-building and development as discussed above—especially in developing countries such as Nigeria.

Source: James, S., Nwezeh, Kingsley, & Bassey, O. (2006, June 5). Militants release hostages. *All Africa*.

tory syndrome (SARS) and avian influenza. For a comprehensive analysis of the impact of SARS on human resource management in the Hong Kong service sector, see Lee and Warner.[17]

Broader External Influences

The major external factors that influence international HRM are the type of government, the state of the economy, and the generally accepted practices of doing business in each of the various host countries in which the multinational operates. A host government can, for example, dictate hiring procedures, as has been the case until recently in Malaysia (see IHRM Today 1.2).

In developed countries, labour is more expensive and better organized than in less-developed countries, and governments require compliance with guidelines on issues such as labour relations, taxation, and health and safety. These compliance issues shape the activities of the subsidiary HR manager to a considerable extent. In less-developed countries, labour tends to be cheaper and less organized, and government regulation is less pervasive, so these factors take less time. On the other hand, the subsidiary HR manager must spend more time, however, learning and interpreting the local ways of doing business and the general code of conduct regarding activities such as gift-giving.

It is also likely that the subsidiary HR manager will become more involved in administering benefits either provided or financed by the multinational, such as housing, education, and other facilities not readily available in the local economy. Moreover, despite the absence of compliance regulations (and/or despite the absence of governmental monitoring bodies to ensure compliance), the prevalence and interest of international NGOs in such areas (e.g., Amnesty International's Business and Human Rights division) means that proactive awareness of and compliance with international labour standards are increasingly necessary.

RPC 1.5

Variables That Moderate Differences between Domestic and International HRM

Earlier in this chapter, it was argued that the *complexity involved in operating in different countries and employing different national categories of employees* is a key variable that differentiates domestic and international HRM, rather than any

---

IHRM Today 1.2

Former Malaysian Hiring Procedures

The Malaysian government during the 1970s introduced a requirement that foreign firms comply with an extensive set of affirmative action rules designed to provide additional employment opportunities for the indigenous Malays who constitute the majority of the population but who tend to be underrepresented in business and professional employment groups relative to Chinese Malays and Indian Malays.

Various statistics showing employment levels of indigenous Malays throughout the firms were required to be forwarded to the relevant government department. Many foreign investors regarded these requirements as a major reason for complaints about bureaucracy and inflexibility in Malaysia, and these complaints are one significant reason for the revision of these requirements.

major differences between the HRM activities performed. Many firms under-estimate the complexities involved in international operations, and there has been consistent evidence to suggest that business failures in the international arena are often linked to poor management of human resources. In addition to complexity, four other variables moderate (that is, either diminish or accentuate) the differences between domestic and international HRM. These four additional moderators are:

1. cultural environment
2. industry (or industries) with which the multinational is primarily involved
3. extent of reliance of the multinational on its home-country domestic market
4. attitudes of senior management

Together with the complexity involved in operating in different countries, these five variables constitute a model that explains the differences between domestic and international HRM (see Figure 1.4).

The Cultural Environment

There are many definitions of **culture**, but the term is usually used to describe a shaping process over time. This process generates relative stability, reflecting a shared knowledge structure that attenuates (i.e., reduces)

culture
a shaping process over time

FIGURE 1.4

A Model of the Variables That Moderate Differences between Domestic and International HRM

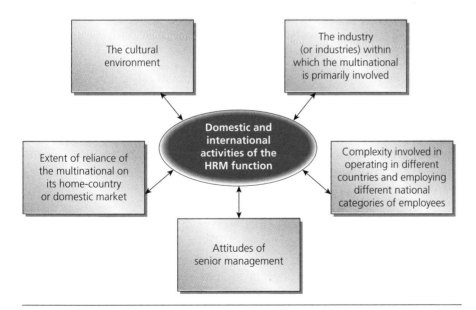

Source: Dowling, P. J. (1999). Completing the Puzzle: Issues in the Development of the Field of International Human Resource Management. *Management International Review* (Special Issue No. 3), 31.

variability in values, behavioural norms, and patterns of behaviour.[18] An important characteristic of culture is that it is so subtle a process that one is not always conscious of its effect on values, attitudes, and behaviours. One usually has to be confronted with a different culture in order to fully appreciate this effect.

Anyone travelling abroad, either as a tourist or on business, experiences situations that demonstrate cultural differences in language, food, dress, hygiene, and attitude toward time. While the traveller can perceive these differences as novel and even enjoyable, for people required to live and work in a new country, such differences can prove difficult. They may experience **culture shock**—a phenomenon experienced by people who move across cultures. The new environment requires many adjustments in a relatively short period of time, challenging people's frames of reference to such an extent that their sense of self, especially in terms of nationality, comes into question. People experience, in effect, a shock reaction to new cultural experiences that cause psychological disorientation because they misunderstand or do not recognize important cues. Culture shock can lead to negative feelings about the host country and its people and a longing to return home.[19]

Because international business involves the interaction and movement of people across national boundaries, an appreciation of cultural differences and when these differences are important is essential. Research into these aspects has assisted in furthering our understanding of the cultural environment as an important variable that moderates differences between domestic and international HRM. However, while cross-cultural and comparative research attempts to explore and explain similarities and differences, problems are associated with such research. A major problem is that there is little agreement on either an exact definition of culture or on the operationalization of this concept. For many researchers, culture has become an omnibus variable, representing a range of social, historic, economic, and political factors that are invoked *post hoc* to explain similarity or dissimilarity in the results of a study. As Bhagat and McQuaid[20] have noted:

> Culture has often served simply as a synonym for nation without any further conceptual grounding. In effect, national differences found in the characteristics of organizations or their members have been interpreted as cultural differences.

To reduce these difficulties, culture needs to be defined *a priori* rather than *post hoc* and it should not be assumed that national differences necessarily represent cultural differences.

Another issue in cross-cultural research concerns the *emic–etic* distinction.[21] **Emic** refers to culture-specific aspects of concepts or behaviour, and **etic** refers to culture-common aspects. These terms have been borrowed from linguistics: A phon*emic* system documents meaningful sounds specific to a given language, and a phon*etic* system organizes all sounds that have meaning in any language.[22]

culture shock

a phenomenon experienced by people who move across cultures into new environments requiring many adjustments in a relatively short period of time

emic

culture-specific aspects of concepts or behaviour

etic

culture-common aspects

Both the emic and etic approaches are legitimate research orientations. A major problem may arise, however, if a researcher imposes an etic approach (that is, assumes universality across cultures) when there is little or no evidence for doing so. A well-known example of an imposed etic approach is the convergence hypothesis that dominated much of U.S. and European management research in the 1950s and 1960s. This approach was based on two key assumptions.[23] The first assumption was that there were principles of sound management that held regardless of national environments. Thus, the existence of local or national practices that deviated from these principles simply indicated a need to change these local practices. The second assumption was that the universality of sound management practices would lead to societies becoming more and more alike in the future. Given that the United States was the leading industrial economy at that time, the point of convergence was the U.S. model.

To use Kuhn's[24] terminology, the convergence hypothesis became an established paradigm that many researchers found difficult to give up, despite a growing body of evidence supporting a divergence hypothesis. In an important early paper that reviewed the convergence/divergence debate, Child[25] made the point that there is evidence for both convergence and divergence. The majority of the convergence studies, however, focus on macro-level variables (for example, organizational structure and technology used by firms across cultures), and the majority of the divergence studies focus on micro-level variables (for example, the behaviour of people within firms). His conclusion was that although firms in different countries are becoming more alike (an etic or convergence approach), the behaviour of individuals within these firms is maintaining its cultural specificity (an emic or divergence approach).

As noted above, both emic and etic approaches are legitimate research orientations, but methodological difficulties may arise if the distinction between these two approaches is ignored or if unwarranted universality assumptions are made.[26] The debate on assumptions of universality is not limited to the literature in international management, as this issue has also become a topic of debate in the field of international relations and strategic studies where international management research is cited.[27] For a recent review of the convergence/divergence question, see Brewster.[28]

The Importance of Cultural Awareness

Despite the methodological concerns about cross-cultural research, it is now generally recognized that culturally insensitive attitudes and behaviours stemming from ignorance or from misguided beliefs ("my way is best" or "what works at home will work here") not only are inappropriate but often cause international business failure. Therefore, an awareness of cultural differences is essential for the HR manager at corporate headquarters as well as in the host location.[29] Activities such as hiring, promoting, rewarding, and dismissal will be determined by the practices of the host country and often are based on a value system peculiar to that country's culture. A firm may decide to head up a new overseas operation with an expatriate general manager but appoint a local as the HR department manager, a person who is familiar with the host country's HR practices. This practice can assist in avoiding problems but can still lead to dilemmas for senior managers (see IHRM Today 1.3).

In comparing home-country and host-country management and work practices, Wyatt[30] recounts a good example of the fallacy of assuming "what works at home will work here" when dealing with work situations in another culture (see IHRM Today 1.4).

Coping with cultural differences, and recognizing how and when these differences are relevant, is a constant challenge for international firms. Helping to prepare staff and their families for working and living in a new cultural environment has become a key activity for HR departments in those multinationals that appreciate (or have been forced, through experience, to appreciate) the impact that the cultural environment can have on staff performance and well-being. We will address key issues relating to cultural differences and staff preparation and adjustment in later chapters of this text.

Hofstede's Framework of National Culture

Before leaving the issue of culture and cultural differences, it is appropriate to acknowledge the important contribution to international management literature of the cultural typologies proposed over 25 years ago by Hofstede in his classic book *Culture's Consequences: International Differences in Work-Related Values*, which proposed that national culture can be set out as a measurable set of constructs.[31] While a more detailed discussion is beyond the scope of this chapter, a very considerable amount of literature has been generated since the initial publication of Hofstede's book, much of it examining the

IHRM Today 1.3

Local Recruitment Practices

Despite their transition between the old-style Maoist and a market-driven model, many Chinese management principles continue to be based, at least to some extent, on concepts such as "guanxi" (relationships based on exchange of favours), "renqing" (human obligations), and "mianzi" (face; reputation). Based on the guanxi principle, it has been common for Chinese managers to select applicants based on their family background and social connections rather than their educational background and professional skills. In a number of other developing countries such as Indonesia, local employees feel an obligation to employ their extended family if they are in a position to do so.

This may lead to a situation where staff are hired who do not posses the required technical competence. While this could be seen as a successful example of adapting to local expectations and customs, from a Western perspective these employment practices would be seen as nepotism, negative practices that are not in the best interests of the enterprise because the best people have not been hired for the job.

Source: Yu, J., & Gröschl, S. (2004). *The impact of Chinese culture on human resource management practices in Sino-foreign hotels operating in China.* EuroCHRIE 2004 Conference, Ankara, Turkey.

Exporting Home-Country Work Practices

HR department staff of a large firm in Papua New Guinea were concerned over a number of accidents involving operators of very large, expensive earthmoving vehicles. The expatriate managers investigating the accidents found that local drivers involved in the accidents were chewing betel nut, a common habit for most of the coastal peoples of Papua New Guinea and other Pacific islands.

Associating the betel nut with depressants such as alcohol, the expatriate managers banned the chewing of betel nut during work hours. In another move to reduce the number of accidents, free coffee was provided at loading points, and drivers were required to alight from their vehicles at these locations. What the managers did not realize was that betel nut, like their culturally acceptable coffee, is, in fact, a stimulant, although some of the drivers were chewing it to cover up the fact that they drank beer before commencing work. As Wyatt points out, many indigenous workers used betel nut as a pick-me-up in much the same way as the expatriates used coffee.

methodological limitations of the cultural dimensions proposed by Hofstede (individualism/collectivism, power distance, masculinity/femininity, and uncertainty avoidance).[32] Some of this literature includes conceptual critiques of Hofstede's work, with a relatively recent paper by McSweeney generating a considerable amount of debate.[33] For a broader review of the contribution of Hofstede's work to the field of international management, see Hoppe,[34] Gerhart and Fang,[35] and Leung et al.[36]

Industry Type

Porter[37] suggests that the industry (or industries, if the firm is a conglomerate) in which a multinational firm is involved is of considerable importance because patterns of international competition vary widely from one industry to another. At one end of the continuum of international competition is the **multidomestic industry**, one in which competition in each country is essentially independent of competition in other countries. Traditional examples include retailing, distribution, and insurance. At the other end of the continuum is the **global industry**, one in which a firm's competitive position in one country is significantly influenced by its position in other countries. Examples include the commercial aircraft, semiconductor, and copier industries. The key distinction between a multidomestic industry and a global industry is described by Porter as follows:

> The global industry is not merely a collection of domestic industries but a series of linked domestic industries in which the rivals compete against each other on a truly worldwide basis. . . . In a multidomestic industry, then, international strategy collapses to a series of domestic strategies. The issues that are uniquely international revolve around how to do business abroad, how to select good countries in which to compete (or assess country risk), and

multidomestic industry

an industry in which competition in each country is essentially independent of competition in other countries

global industry

an industry in which a firm's competitive position in one country is significantly influenced by its position in other countries

mechanisms to achieve the one-time transfer of know-how. These are questions that are relatively well developed in the literature. In a global industry, however, managing international activities like a portfolio will undermine the possibility of achieving competitive advantage. In a global industry, a firm must in some way integrate its activities on a worldwide basis to capture the linkages among countries.

The role of the HRM function in multidomestic and global industries can be analyzed using Porter's value-chain model.[38] In Porter's model, HRM is seen as one of four support activities for the five primary activities of the firm. Since human resources are involved in each of the primary and support activities, the HRM function is seen as cutting across the entire value chain of a firm. If the firm is in a multidomestic industry, the role of the HR department will most likely be more domestic in structure and orientation.

At times there may be considerable demand for international services from the HRM function (for example, when a new plant or office is established in a foreign location and the need for expatriate employees arises), but these activities would not be pivotal—indeed, many of these services may be provided via consultants and/or temporary employees. The main role for the HRM function would be to support the primary activities of the firm in each domestic market to achieve a competitive advantage through either cost/efficiency or product/service differentiation. If the multinational is in a global industry, however, the "imperative for coordination" described by Porter would require an HRM function structured to deliver the international support required by the primary activities of the multinational.

The need to develop coordination raises complex problems for any multinational. As Laurent[39] has noted:

> In order to build, maintain, and develop their corporate identity, multinational organizations need to strive for consistency in their ways of managing people on a worldwide basis. Yet, and in order to be effective locally, they also need to adapt those ways to the specific cultural requirements of different societies. While the global nature of the business may call for increased consistency, the variety of cultural environments may be calling for differentiation.

In IHRM Notebook 1.2, Laurent outlines the steps required for the development of a truly international conception of human resource management.

In offering this proposal, Laurent acknowledges that these are difficult steps that few firms have taken:

> They have more to do with states of mind and mindsets than with behaviors. As such, these processes can only be facilitated and this may represent a primary mission for executives in charge of international human resource management.[40]

Implicit in Laurent's analysis is the idea that by taking the steps he describes, a multinational attempting to implement a global strategy via coordination of

Key Steps for Development of an International Conception of HRM

1. An explicit recognition by the parent organization that its own peculiar ways of managing human resources reflect some assumptions and values of its home culture.

2. An explicit recognition by the parent organization that its peculiar ways are neither universally better nor worse than others but are different and likely to exhibit strengths and weaknesses, particularly abroad.

3. An explicit recognition by the parent organization that its foreign subsidiaries may have other preferred ways of managing people that are neither intrinsically better nor worse, but could possibly be more effective locally.

4. A willingness by headquarters to not only acknowledge cultural differences, but also to take active steps in order to make them discussable and therefore usable.

5. The building of a genuine belief by all parties involved that more creative and effective ways of managing people could be developed as a result of cross-cultural learning.

activities would be better able to work through the difficulties and complex tradeoffs inherent in such a strategy. Increasingly, multinationals are taking a more strategic approach to the role of HRM and are using staff transfers and training programs to assist in coordination of activities. We discuss these issues in more detail in subsequent chapters of the book.

Reliance of the Multinational on Its Home-Country Domestic Market

A pervasive but often ignored factor that influences the behaviour of multinationals and resultant HR practices is the extent of reliance of the multinational on its home-country domestic market. When for example, we look through lists of very large firms (such as those that appear in *Fortune* and other business magazines), it is frequently assumed that a global market perspective would be dominant in the firm's culture and thinking. However, size is not the only key variable when looking at a multinational—the extent of reliance of the multinational on its home-country domestic market is also very important. In fact, for many firms, a small home market is one of the key drivers for seeking new international markets.

The United Nations Conference on Trade and Development (UNCTAD), in its annual survey of foreign direct investment, calculates what it refers to as an "index of transnationality," which is an average of ratios of foreign assets to total assets, foreign sales to total sales, and foreign employment to total employment.[41] The "top ten" multinationals are shown in Table 1.1. Based on this index of transnationality, the most foreign-oriented multinational is Thomson Corporation (Canada), with an average of 97 percent of the three ratios (foreign assets to total assets, foreign sales to total sales, and foreign employment to total employment) located outside of Canada.

TABLE 1.1

World Top 10 Nonfinancial Transnational Corporations, Ranked by UNCTAD Transnational Index

TRANSNATIONAL INDEX	RANKING BY FOREIGN ASSETS	COMPANY NAME	HOME ECONOMY	INDUSTRY
1	70	Thomson Corporation	Canada	Media
2	88	CRH Plc	Ireland	Lumber and other building material dealers
3	19	Nestlé SA	Switzerland	Food and beverages
4	2	Vodafone Group Plc	United Kingdom	Telecommunications
5	56	Alcan Inc	Canada	Metal and metal products
6	57	Koninklijke Ahold	USA/Netherlands	Retail
7	47	Philips Electronics	Netherlands	Electrical and electronic equipment
8	99	Nortel Networks	Canada	Telecommunications
9	38	Unilever	United Kingdom/ Netherlands	Diversified retail
10	5	British Petroleum Company Plc	United Kingdom	Petroleum exploration, refining, distribution

Source: The data in this table is based on the World Investment Report, 2006; *FDI from Developing and Transition Economies: Implications for Development*, United Nations Conference on Trade and Development (UNCTAD), 2006.

The only U.S. firm in the 30 multinationals ranked by the transnational index is the AES Corporation (electricity, gas, and water), ranked 22nd. McDonald's Corporation is ranked 35th. The reason for this lower ranking of U.S. firms in terms of the transnational index is as obvious as it is important—*the size of the domestic market* for U.S. firms. A very large domestic market (for U.S. firms, this is in effect the North American Free Trade Agreement [NAFTA] market) influences all aspects of how a multinational organizes its activities. For example, it will be more likely to use an international division as the way it organizes its international activities (see Chapter 2) and even if it uses a global product structure, the importance of the domestic market will be pervasive.

A large domestic market will also influence the attitudes of senior managers toward their international activities and will generate a large number of managers with an experience base of predominantly or even exclusively domestic market experience. Thus, multinationals from small advanced economies like Switzerland (population 7.5 million), Ireland (4 million), Australia (20 million) and the Netherlands (16.5 million) and medium-sized advanced economies like Canada (33 million), the United Kingdom (60 million), and France (61 million) are in a quite different position to multinationals based in the United States, which is the largest advanced economy in the world with a population of 300 million. U.S. multinationals also enjoy the advantage of a dominant position in the NAFTA market (Canada, the United States, and Mexico), which has a total market population of 439 million.

If the UNCTAD data is rank-ordered only on the ratio of foreign assets to total assets (i.e., excluding the ratios of foreign sales to total sales, and foreign employment to total employment) the listing shown in Table 1.2 demonstrates the effect of large-scale domestic sales and domestic employment on the transnational index ranking in Table 1.1, with four U.S. firms listed and only two firms from the transnational index (the British companies Vodafone Group and British Petroleum) remaining. In other words, the removal of domestic sales from the transnational index significantly reinterprets the data that is presented in Table 1.1. It is therefore worth keeping in mind that the frequent criticism of U.S. companies, U.S. senior managers, and U.S. business schools as inward-looking and ethnocentric may perhaps be true to some extent, *but it is equally true* that a focus on domestic U.S. sales and revenue is also an entirely rational response to the overwhelming importance of the North American market for many of these businesses.

TABLE 1.2

World Top 10 Nonfinancial Transnational Corporations, Ranked Only by Foreign Assets

RANKING BY FOREIGN ASSETS	TRANSNATIONAL INDEX	COMPANY NAME	HOME ECONOMY	INDUSTRY
1	68	General Electric	USA	Electrical and electronic equipment
2	4	Vodafone Group Plc	United Kingdom	Telecommunications
3	67	Ford Motors	USA	Motor vehicles
4	90	General Motors	USA	Motor vehicles
5	10	British Petroleum Company Plc	United Kingdom	Petroleum exploration, refining, distribution
6	38	Exxon Mobil	USA	Petroleum exploration, refining, distribution
7	25	Royal Dutch/ Shell Group	United Kingdom/ Netherlands	Petroleum exploration, refining, distribution
8	62	Toyota Motor Corporation	Japan	Motor vehicles
9	20	Total	France	Petroleum exploration, refining, distribution
10	10	France Telecom	France	Telecommunications

Source: The data in this table is based on the World Investment Report, 2006; *FDI from Developing and Transition Economies: Implications for Development*, United Nations Conference on Trade and Development (UNCTAD), 2006.

The demands of a large domestic market present a challenge to the globalization efforts of many U.S. firms. As Cavusgil[42] has noted in an important book on internationalizing business education, the task of internationalizing business education in the United States is a large one. So too is the task facing many U.S. firms in terms of developing global managers—an issue to which we will return in Chapter 6.

Attitudes of Senior Management toward International Operations

The point made by Laurent earlier in this chapter that some of the changes required to truly internationalize the HR function "have more to do with states of mind and mindsets than with behaviors" illustrates the importance of a final variable that may moderate differences between international and domestic HRM: the attitudes of senior management toward international operations. It is likely that if senior management does not have a strong international orientation, the importance of international operations may be underemphasized (or possibly even ignored) in terms of corporate goals and objectives. In such situations, managers may tend to focus on domestic issues and minimize differences between international and domestic environments.

Not surprisingly, senior managers with little international experience (and successful careers built on domestic experience) may assume that there is a great deal of transferability between domestic and international HRM practices. This failure to recognize differences in managing human resources in foreign environments—regardless of whether it is because of ethnocentrism, inadequate information, or a lack of international perspective—frequently results in major difficulties in international operations. The challenge for the corporate HR manager who wishes to contribute to the internationalization of the firm is to work with top management in fostering the desired "global mindset." This goal requires, of course, an HR manager who is able to think globally and to formulate and implement HR policies that facilitate the development of globally oriented staff.[43]

Applying a Strategic View of International HRM

Our discussion up to this point has suggested that a broader or more strategic view of IHRM is required to better explain the complexity and challenges of managing IHRM issues. An example of a theoretical framework that has been derived from a strategic approach using a multiple methodological approach is that of De Cieri and Dowling.[44] Their framework is depicted in Figure 1.5 and assumes that multinational firms operate in the context of worldwide conditions, including the external contexts of industry, nation, region, and inter-organizational networks and alliances. An example of the latter would be the impact of the removal of internal trade barriers and integration of national markets following the recent expansion of the membership of the European Union. These external factors exert direct influence

FIGURE 1.5

A Model of Strategic HRM in Multinational Enterprises

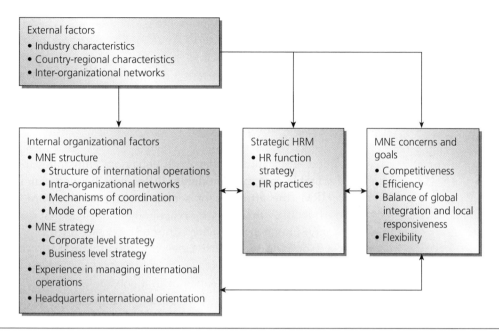

Source: Adapted from: De Cieri, H., & Dowling, P. J. (1999). Strategic Human Resource Management in Multinational Enterprises: Theoretical and Empirical Developments. In P. M. Wright et al. (Eds.), *Research in Personnel and Human Resource Management: Strategic Human Resources in the 21st Century* (Supplement 4). Stamford, CT: JAI Press.

on internal organizational factors, HRM strategy and practices, and multinational concerns and goals.

The internal organizational factors are shown in Figure 1.5 in order of most "tangible" to most "intangible." *MNE structure* refers to both the structure of international operations and intra-organizational networks, along with mechanisms of coordination that are discussed in more detail in Chapter 2. The life cycle stage of the firm and the industry in which it operates are important influences on HRM strategy and practices in multinationals, as are the various international modes of operation and levels of firm strategy.

 1.6

The most intangible organizational factors are experience in international business and the international orientation of headquarters. Following developments in the literature (such as that of Taylor, Beechler, and Napier,[45] who take an integration of resource dependence and resource-based perspective), the model suggests that there are reciprocal relationships among organizational factors, strategic HRM, and multinational concerns and goals.

With regard to HR strategy and practices, reciprocal relationships between strategic issues and HRM strategy and practices have been highlighted by research that takes a resource-based perspective.[46] In addition, several studies have shown that HR activities such as expatriate management are influenced by both external and internal factors.[47] A more strategic approach to HRM is expected to assist the firm in achieving its goals and objectives. This view is influenced by the emerging body of strategic HRM literature that examines the relationships among endogenous characteristics, HRM strategy and practices, and firm performance or competitive advantage.[48] While some research has suggested that multinationals will gain by utilizing and integrating appropriate HRM strategy and practices to enhance firm performance,[49] the evidence is inconclusive and important questions remain about the nature of this relationship.[50] The model offered by De Cieri and Dowling aims to assist in the cross-fertilization of ideas to further develop theory and empirical research in strategic HRM in multinational firms.

The Enduring Context of IHRM

As Figures 1.4 and 1.5 show, international firms compete in an increasingly complex environment, where the level of challenge of doing business can be highly variable. Internationalizing firms rely on having the right people to manage and operate their businesses and good IHRM practices that are appropriate to the context in which they occur. This combination of appropriate people and HR practices has been a constant critical success factor in international business ventures. For example, the following quotation is taken from a detailed case study of a large U.S. multinational, where the authors, Desatnick and Bennett[51] concluded:

> The primary causes of failure in multinational ventures stem from a lack of understanding of the essential differences in managing human resources, at all levels, in foreign environments. Certain management philosophies and techniques have proved successful in the domestic environment: their application in a foreign environment too often leads to frustration, failure and underachievement. These "human" considerations are as important as the financial and marketing criteria upon which so many decisions to undertake multinational ventures depend.

This study was reported in 1978 but many international managers today would concur with the sentiments expressed in this quote. In this book, we attempt to demonstrate some ways in which an appreciation of the international dimensions of HRM can assist in this process.

Summary

The purpose of this chapter has been to provide an overview of the emerging field of international HRM. We did this by first defining key terms in IHRM and considering several definitions of IHRM. We then introduced the historically significant issue of expatriate assignment management and reviewed the evolution of these assignments to reflect the increasing diversity with regard to what constitutes international work and the type and length of international assignments.

Furthermore, we outlined the differences between domestic and international human resource management by looking at six factors that differentiate international and domestic HR (more HR activities, the need for a broader perspective, more involvement in employees' personal lives, changes in emphasis as the workforce mix of expatriates and locals varies, risk exposure, and broader external influences) and detailing a model that summarizes the variables that moderate these differences.

We highlighted the complexity of IHRM, the increasing potential for challenges to existing IHRM practices and current models, and an increasing awareness of the wide number of choices within IHRM practices due to increased transparency and faster and more detailed diffusion of these practices across organizational units and firms. We concluded that the *complexity involved in operating in different countries and employing different national categories of employees* is a key variable differentiating domestic and international HRM, rather than any major differences among the HR activities performed.

We also discussed four other variables that moderate differences between domestic and international HRM: the *cultural environment*, the *industry (or industries) with which the multinational is primarily involved*, the *extent of reliance of the multinational on its home-country domestic market*, and the *attitudes of senior management*. These five variables are shown in Figure 1.4. Finally, we discussed a model of strategic HRM in multinational enterprises (Figure 1.5), which draws together a number of external environment and internal organizational factors that impact on IHRM strategy and practice and, in turn, on MNE goals.

In our discussion of the international dimensions of HRM in this book, we will be drawing on the HRM literature. Subsequent chapters will examine the context for IHRM and the international dimensions of the major activities of HRM: HR planning and business operations, recruitment and selection, performance management, training and development, compensation, and labour relations. We will provide comparative data on HRM practices in different countries, but our major emphasis is on the international dimensions of HRM confronting Canadian and other multinational firms, whether large or small, when facing the challenge of managing people in an international context.

Key Terms

culture 13

culture shock 14

emic 14

etic 14

expatriate 5

global industry 17

HRM (human resource management) 4

inpatriate 5

international HRM 5

multidomestic industry 17

multinational enterprise (MNE) 3

Web Links

www 1.1   For more information on Canada's 1998 Corruption of Foreign Public Officials Act (1998), go to Canada's Department of Justice website:

http://laws.justice.gc.ca/en/showdoc/cs/C-45.2///en?page=1

www 1.2   For an excellent website on terrorism, go to the following Columbia University site:

www.columbia.edu/cu/lweb/indiv/lehman/guides/terrorism.html

www 1.3   For the latest information on epidemic and pandemic crises, go to the World Health Organization website:

www.who.int/csr/en

RPC Icons

RPC 1.1   Leads in the development of HR initiatives that support the organization's strategic directions

RPC 1.2   Leads in the development of HR initiatives that support the organization's strategic directions

RPC 1.3   Directs the organization in ethical HR practices and application of conflict-of-interest guidelines

RPC 1.4   Establishes compensation policies and procedures based on the program and compliance with the legal framework

RPC 1.5   Recommends benefit plan most suited to organizational objectives

RPC 1.6   Selects candidates and negotiates terms and conditions of employment

Discussion Questions

1. What are the main similarities and differences between domestic and international HRM?
2. Define these terms: international HRM, PCN, HCN, and TCN.
3. Discuss at least two of the variables that moderate differences between domestic and international HR practices.

Using the Internet

1. Use sites such as **www.wfpma.com** (World Federation of Personnel Management Associations) and **www.cchra.ca/Web/CCHRA/content.aspx?f=29752** (Canadian Council of Human Resources Associations) to explore and compare some of the current practices and challenges

faced by HR managers across Canada and around the world. The World Federation of Personnel Management Associations site also provides a wide range of, and links to, HR professional associations around the world.

2. Use sites such as **www.international.gc.ca/commerce/index.aspx** (Foreign Affairs and International Trade Canada) as a starting point to explore Canada's governmental support structures and guidelines helping Canadian businesses and their HR functions that are planning to expand or are already operating outside of Canada.

Exercises

1. Go to the library and collect information and material about a multinational organization relevant to the identification and discussion of two HR activities in which this multinational firm must engage that would not be required in a domestic environment.

2. Pick an internationally operating organization and interview the HR director about why a greater degree of involvement in employees' personal lives is inevitable in many international HRM activities.

3. Each country has its own human rights and employment legislations. Some of these country-specific legislations might allow for employment practices and policies that are illegal or unethical in Canada. Discuss to what extent Canadian companies should apply HR policies and practices that support a strategy of maximum profit at the lowest cost and comply solely with local employment and human rights legislation and standards.

Case

Two Sides to Every Story

Four years ago, Pressman Company entered into a joint venture with a Polish firm to manufacture a variety of plumbing supplies, both for the internal Polish market and for export to neighbouring countries. Last week, Pressman received the resignation of Jonathan Smith, an expatriate from the home office who nine months ago was appointed general manager of the Polish subsidiary for a four-year term. In the previous 39 months, two other expatriate general managers from the home office had also decided to call it quits long before their foreign assignments expired. In addition, 13 of the 28 Canadian technicians sent to work in the Polish facility returned home early. George Stevens, a senior vice president at corporate headquarters, estimates that these expatriates' resignations and early returns have cost the company at least $4 million in direct expenses and probably three times as much in lost production and delayed schedules.

Chapter 1: Introduction

When he heard rumours of widespread discontent in the workforce and a threatened wildcat strike, Stevens decided to travel to the Polish facility to find out what was happening. In the course of interviewing five local supervisors and ten workers with the help of a translator, he repeatedly heard three complaints: First, the Canadian managers and technicians thought they "knew it all" and treated their Polish counterparts with contempt; second, the Canadian employees had unrealistic expectations of what could be accomplished within the stipulated deadlines established at corporate headquarters; and third, Canadian employees were making three times more money than their Polish counterparts and enjoyed looking down their noses at locals by driving fancy cars, living in expensive homes, and hiring an army of maids and helpers.

When he arrived back in Canada, Stevens also interviewed Jonathan Smith and five of the technicians who returned early. Some common reasons for their early resignations emerged from these interviews. First, they described their Polish colleagues as "lazy" and "just doing the minimum to get by while keeping a close eye on the clock for breaks, lunches, and go-home time." Pushing them to work harder only provoked anger. Second, they indicated that the Polish workers and managers had a sense of entitlement with little intrinsic motivation and initiative. Third, they complained of loneliness and their inability to communicate in Polish. Finally, most reported that their spouses and children were homesick and longing to return to Canada after the first month or so. As he sits in his office, George Stevens is staring blankly out the window, trying to decide what to do.

Source: Gomez-Mejia, L., Balkin, D., Cardy, R., Dimick, D., & Templer, A. (2004). *Managing Human Resources*. Toronto: Pearson Prentice Hall, 486.

Questions

1. What are the key HR-related problems in this case?
2. What could Pressman's international HR function at headquarters have done differently to avoid some of the current HR-related problems and conflicts?
3. How could headquarters' international HR department overcome these challenges?
4. What lessons could be learned from this case in terms of level of HR involvement in international expansion decisions?

Endnotes

1. H. De Cieri & P. J. Dowling. (1999). Strategic Human Resource Management in Multinational Enterprises: Theoretical and Empirical Developments. In P. Wright et al. (Eds.), *Research and Theory in SHRM: An Agenda for the 21st Century*. Greenwich, CT: JAI Press.
2. For examples of this approach, see: N. Adler. (1997). *International Dimensions of Organizational Behavior* (3rd ed.). Cincinnati, OH: South-Western; and A. Phatak. (1997). *International*

Management: Concept & Cases. Cincinnati, OH: South-Western. See also the special issue on Asia–Pacific HRM. (2000). *International Journal of Human Resource Management, 11*(2).

3. See, for example: C. Brewster & A. Hegewisch. (1994). *Policy and Practice in European Human Resource Management—The Price Waterhouse Cranfield Survey*. London: Routledge.

4. See: P. Dowling & R. Schuler. (1990), *International Dimensions of Human Resource Management* (1st ed.). Boston, MA: PWS-Kent; P. Dowling, R. Schuler, & D. Welch. (1994). *International Dimensions of Human Resource Management* (2nd ed.). Belmont, CA: Wadsworth; P. J. Dowling, D. E. Welch, & R. S. Schuler. (1998). *International Human Resource Management: Managing People in a Multinational Context* (3rd ed.). Cincinnati: South-Western.

5. T. M. Welbourne & H. De Cieri. (2001). How New Venture Initial Public Offerings Benefit from International Operations. *International Journal of Human Resource Management, 12*(4), 652–668.

6. P. Morgan. (1986). International Human Resource Management: Fact or Fiction? *Personnel Administrator, 31*(9), 43–47.

7. See H. De Cieri, S. L. McGaughey, & P. J. Dowling, Relocation. (1996). In M. Warner (Ed.), *International Encyclopaedia of Business and Management, 5*. London: Routledge, 4300–4310, for further discussion of this point.

8. For an example of the way in which the term is being used, see: M. G. Harvey, M. M. Novicevic, & C. Speier. (2000). Strategic Global Human Resource Management: The Role of Inpatriate Managers. *Human Resource Management Review, 10*(2), 153–175.

9. Curiously, the *International Human Resource Management Reference Guide* also states that the word *inpatriate* "can also be used for U.S. expatriates returning to an assignment in the U.S." This is a contradiction of the first part of the definition of an inpatriate being a "foreign manager in the U.S." and is illogical. U.S. expatriates returning to the United States are PCNs and cannot also be classed as "foreign managers in the U.S."—perhaps they are "repatriates," but they are not inpatriates. As defined, this term is of use only in the United States.

10. G. Stahl & I. Björkman (Eds.). (2006). *Handbook of Research in International Human Resource Management*. Cheltenham, UK: Edward Elgar, 1.

11. P. J. Dowling. (1988). International and Domestic Personnel/Human Resource Management: Similarities and Differences. In R. S. Schuler, S. A. Youngblood, & V. L. Huber (Eds.), *Readings in Personnel and Human Resource Management* (3rd ed.). St. Paul, MN: West Publishing.

12. See: D. L. Pinney. (1982). Structuring an Expatriate Tax Reimbursement Program. *Personnel Administrator, 27*(7), 19–25; and M. Gajek & M. M. Sabo. (1986). The Bottom Line: What HR Managers Need to Know About the New Expatriate Regulations. *Personnel Administrator, 31*(2), 87–92.

13. Morgan. International Human Resource Management: Fact or Fiction?

14. R. D. Robinson. (1978). *International Business Management: A Guide to Decision Making* (2nd ed.). Hinsdale, IL: Dryden.

15. Although less common in the United States, the use of private boarding schools is common in countries (particularly European countries) that have a colonial tradition where both colonial administrators and businesspeople would often undertake long assignments overseas and expect to leave their children at a boarding school in their home country. This is especially true of Britain, which also has a strong cultural tradition of the middle and upper classes sending their children to private boarding schools (curiously described by the British as "public" schools, even though they are all private institutions that charge fees) even if the parents are working in Britain.

16. See: T. M. Gladwin & I. Walter. (1980). *Multinationals Under Fire: Lessons in the Management of Conflict,* Chapter 4, Terrorism. New York: John Wiley; and M. Harvey. (1993). A Survey of Corporate Programs for Managing Terrorist Threats. *Journal of International Business Studies, 24*(3), 465–478. Also, see Chapter 12 of this textbook.

17. G. Lee & M. Warner. (2005). Epidemics, Labor Markets and Unemployment: The Impact of SARS on Human Resource Management in the Hong Kong Service Sector. *International Journal of Human Resource Management, 16*(5), 752–771.

18. M. Erez & P. C. Earley. (1993). *Culture, Self-Identity and Work.* Oxford: Oxford University Press.

19. J. E. Harris & R. T. Moran. (1979). *Managing Cultural Differences.* Houston: Gulf.

20. R. S. Bhagat & S. J. McQuaid. (1982). Role of Subjective Culture in Organizations: A Review and Directions for Future Research. *Journal of Applied Psychology, 67*, 653–685.

21. See: J. W. Berry. (1980). Introduction to Methodology. In H. C. Triandis & J. W. Berry (Eds.), *Handbook of Cross-Cultural Psychology, Vol. 2: Methodology.* Boston: Allyn & Bacon; H. De Cieri & P. J. Dowling. (1995). Cross-Cultural Issues in Organizational Behavior. In C. L. Cooper & D. M. Rousseau (Eds.), *Trends in Organizational Behavior* (Vol. 2). Chichester, UK: John Wiley & Sons, 127–145; and M. B. Teagarden & M. A. Von Glinow. (1997). Human Resource Management in Cross-Cultural Contexts: Emic Practices Versus Etic Philosophies. *Management International Review, 37* (Special Issue No. 1), 7–20.

22. See: H. Triandis & R. Brislin. (1984). Cross-Cultural Psychology. *American Psychologist, 39*, 1006–1016.

23. See: G. Hofstede. (1983). The Cultural Relativity of Organizational Practices and Theories. *Journal of International Business Studies, 14*(2), 75–89.

24. T. S. Kuhn. (1962). *The Structure of Scientific Revolution* (2nd ed.). Chicago, IL: University of Chicago Press.

25. J. D. Child. (1981). Culture, Contingency and Capitalism in the Cross-National Study of Organizations. In L. L. Cummings & B. M. Staw (Eds.), *Research in Organizational Behavior, 3.* Greenwich, CT: JAI Publishers.

26. For a comprehensive collection of mistakes made by multinational firms that paid insufficient attention to the cultural environment in their international business operations, see: D. A. Ricks. (1993). *Blunders in International Business.* Cambridge, MA: Blackwell. For further literature on this topic, see: P. S. Kirkbride & S. F. Y. Tang. (1994). From Kyoto to Kowloon: Cultural Barriers to the Transference of Quality Circles from Japan to Hong Kong. *Asia Pacific Journal of Human Resources, 32*(2), 100–111; M. Tayeb. (1994). Organizations and national culture: Methodology considered. *Organization Studies, 15*(3), 429–446; P. Sparrow, R. S. Schuler, & S. E. Jackson. (1994). Convergence or Divergence: Human Resource Practices and Policies for Competitive Advantage Worldwide. *International Journal of Human Resource Management, 5*(2), 267–299; M. Morishima. (1995). Embedding HRM in a Social Context. *British Journal of Industrial Relations, 33*(4), 617–643; and J. E. Delery & D. H. Doty. (1996). Modes of Theorizing in Strategic Human Resource Management: Tests of Universalistic, Contingency, and Configurational Performance Predictions. *Academy of Management Journal, 39*, 802–835.

27. S. P. Huntington. (1996, November/December). The West: Unique, Not Universal. *Foreign Affairs*, 28–46.

28. C. Brewster. (2006). Comparing HRM Policies and Practices Across Geographical Borders. In G. Stahl & I. Björkman (Eds.), *Handbook of Research in International Human Resource Management.* Cheltenham, UK: Edward Elgar, 68–90.

29. R. L. Tung. (1993). Managing Cross-National and Intra-National Diversity. *Human Resource Management, 32*(4), 461–477.

30. T. Wyatt. (1989). Understanding Unfamiliar Personnel Problems in Cross-Cultural Work Encounters. *Asia Pacific Journal of Human Resources, 27*(4), 5.

31. G. Hofstede. (1980). *Culture's Consequences: International Differences in Work-Related Values.* Newbury Park, CA: Sage.

32. There is voluminous literature on Hofstede's work. An excellent website that summarizes some of this work can be found on the International Business Center's website: http:// geert-hofstede.international-business-center.com/index.shtml. For a recent article on Hofstede's work, see: F. Chiang. (2005). A Critical Examination of Hofstede's Thesis and Its Application to International Reward Management. *International Journal of Human Resource Management, 16*(9), 1545–1563.

33. B. McSweeney. (2002). Hofstede's Model of National Cultural Differences and Their Consequences: A Triumph of Faith—A Failure of Analysis. *Human Relations, 55*(1), 89–118.

34. M. H. Hoppe. (2004). Retrospective on Culture's Consequences. *Academy of Management Executive, 18*(1), 73–93.

35. B. Gerhart & M. Fang. (2005). National Culture and Human Resource Management: Assumptions and Evidence. *International Journal of Human Resource Management, 16*(6), 971–986.

36. K. Leung, R. S. Bhagat, N. R. Buchan, M. Erez, & C. B. Gibson. (2005). Culture and International Business: Recent Advances and Their Implications for Future Research. *Journal of International Business Studies, 36*(4), 357–378.

37. M. E. Porter. (1986). Changing Patterns of International Competition. *California Management Review, 28*(2), 9–40.

38. M. E. Porter. (1985). *Competitive Advantage: Creating and Sustaining Superior Performance*. New York: The Free Press.

39. A. Laurent. (1986). The Cross-Cultural Puzzle of International Human Resource Management. *Human Resource Management, 25*, 91–102.

40. Ibid., 100.

41. This section is based on the World Investment Report, 2006; *FDI from Developing and Transition Economies: Implications for Development*. United Nations Conference on Trade and Development (UNCTAD), 2006.

42. S. Tamer Cavusgil. (1993). *Internationalising Business Education: Meeting the Challenge*. East Lansing, MI: Michigan State University Press.

43. See: C. Bartlett, S. Ghoshal, & P. Beamish. (2008). *Transnational Management: Text, Cases, and Readings in Cross Border Management*. Boston, MA: McGraw-Hill/Irwin; and V. Pucik. (1997). Human Resources in the Future: An Obstacle or a Champion of Globalization? *Human Resource Management, 36*, 163–167.

44. H. De Cieri & P. J. Dowling. (1999). Strategic Human Resource Management in Multinational Enterprises: Theoretical and Empirical Developments. In P.M. Wright et al. (Eds.), *Research in Personnel and Human Resource Management: Strategic Human Resources in the 21st Century* (Supplement 4). Stamford, CT, JAI Press.

45. S. Taylor, S. Beechler, & N. Napier. (1996). Toward an Integrative Model of Strategic International Human Resource Management. *Academy of Management Review, 21*, 959–985.

46. Taylor et al., ibid; K. Kamoche. (1997). Knowledge Creation and Learning in International HRM. *International Journal of Human Resource Management, 8*, 213–222.

47. D. Welch. (1994). Determinants of International Human Resource Management Approaches and Activities. *Journal of Management Studies, 32*; M. Harvey, M. M. Novicevis, & C. Speier. (2000). An Innovative Global Management Staffing System: A Competency-Based Perspective. *Human Resource Management, 39*(4), 381–394.

48. B. Becker & B. Gerhart. (1996). The Impact of Human Resource Management on Organizational Performance: Progress and Prospects. *Academy of Management Journal, 39*(4), 779–801; L. Dyer & T. Reeves. (1995). Human Resource Strategies and Firm Performance: What Do We Know and Where Do We Need to Go? *International Journal of Human Resource Management, 6*(3), 656–670.

49. M. Festing. (1997). International Human Resource Management Strategies in Multinational Corporations: Theoretical Assumptions and Empirical Evidence from German Firms.

Management International Review, 37 (Special Issue No. 1), 43–63; and S. J. Kobrin. (1994). Is There a Relationship Between a Geocentric Mind-Set and Multinational Strategy? *Journal of International Business Studies, 25*, 493–511.

50. P. M. Caligiuri & L. K. Stroh. (1995). Multinational Corporate Management Strategies and International Human Resource Practices: Bringing IHRM to the Bottom Line. *International Journal of Human Resource Management, 6*, 494–507; R. B. Peterson, J. Sargent, N. K. Napier, & W. S. Shim. (1996). Corporate Expatriate HRM Policies, Internationalization, and Performance in the World's Largest MNCs. *Management International Review, 36*, 215–230; P. Sparrow, R. S. Schuler, & S. E. Jackson. (1994). Convergence or Divergence: Human Resource Practices and Policies for Competitive Advantage Worldwide. *International Journal of Human Resource Management, 5*, 267–299.

51. R. L. Desatnick & M. L. Bennett. (1978). *Human Resource Management in the Multinational Company*. New York: Nichols.

The Organizational Context

Chapter Learning Objectives

After reading this chapter, you should be able to:

- discuss how international growth places demands on management
- define factors that impact on how managers of internationalizing firms respond to these management challenges, including
    - structural responses to international growth
    - control and coordination mechanisms, including cultural control
- analyze the effect of responses on human resource management approaches and activities

UPS: From Bicycle Messenger Service to $30 Billion Multinational Company

Imagine having 13 regional directors reporting to you. Those 13 have a total of 72 district managers reporting to them. And each of those 72 district managers runs an operation the size of a *Fortune* 1000 company. Now imagine that that's just your core business, and you have several other business units to oversee—a couple of them with revenues in excess of $1 billion.

This was the introduction to a *Harvard Business Review* interview with United Parcel Service (UPS) chairman Jim Kelly, discussing UPS's reinvention process in 2001. This introduction and its figures give you some indication about the size, geographical distribution, and level of internationalization of UPS and many other multinationals that we are going to meet throughout this textbook.

But how do companies that have the size and scope of UPS manage, control, and coordinate operations with more than 360,000 people in 200 countries and territories? How did UPS grow from a bicycle messenger service in Seattle in 1907 to a $30 billion multinational company? What have been some of the organizational challenges faced by managers and employees on this path of globalization? How has the HR function been affected by such international growth? These are questions we will address in the following sections.

Source: Kirby, J. (2001, November). Reinvention with Respect. *Harvard Business Review*, 117.

Introduction

This chapter builds on material covered in Chapter 1, to provide a meaningful organizational context for drawing out the international dimension of human resource management—the central theme of this book. In this chapter, we start with the premise that the human resource (HR) function does not operate in a vacuum, and that HR activities are determined by, and influence, organizational factors.

Human resource practices, policies, and processes are imbedded in the strategic, structural, and technological context of the MNE.[1] This "administrative heritage" is particularly critical for global firms, as the international organization will be called on to operate across a wide variety of competitive environments and yet somehow balance these diverse social, political, and economic contexts with the requirements of the original home context.[2] In Chapter 1, we looked at the general global environment in which firms compete. Here we focus on internal responses as firms attempt to deal with global environment challenges. Figure 2.1 illustrates the major elements encountered as a result of international growth that place demands on management.

The various elements in Figure 2.1 are not mutually exclusive. For example, geographical dispersion affects firm size, creating pressure on control mechanisms that, in turn, will influence structural change. Growth (size of the firm) will affect the flow and volume of information, which may reinforce a control response (such as what functions, systems, and processes to centralize and what to decentralize). As we will examine in Chapter 3, mode of operation involved (such as international joint ventures or mergers and acquisitions) will affect the rate of geographical dispersion. Geographical dispersion will involve more encounters with national cultures and languages, thus affecting the flow and volume of information. The demands of the host country can influence the composition of the workforce (the mix of parent-country nationals [PCNs], host-country nationals [HCNs], and third-country nationals [TCNs]).

An in-depth examination of all of these elements is beyond the scope of this book. Rather, the purpose of this chapter is to explore some of the managerial responses to these influences that concern human resource management (HRM). Our focus remains on the connection between organizational factors, management decisions, and HR consequences. To a certain extent, how the internationalizing firm copes with the HR demands of its various foreign operations determines its ability to execute its chosen expansion strategies. Indeed, early Finnish research suggests that personnel policies should lead rather than follow international operation decisions,[3] yet one could argue that most companies take the opposite approach—that is, they use

FIGURE 2.1

Management Demands of International Growth

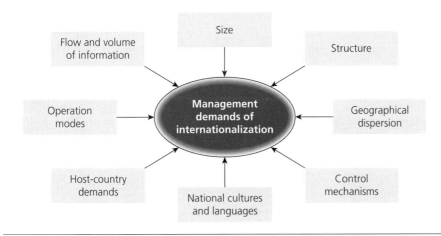

market-driven strategies. We will now follow the path that a domestic firm takes as it evolves into a global entity, and illustrate how international human resource management (IHRM) is affected by the way the internationalization process itself is managed.

The Path to Global Status

Most firms pass through several stages of organizational development as the nature and scope of their international activities grow. As they go through these evolutionary stages, their organizational structures[4] change, typically due to:

- Strain imposed by growth and geographical spread.
- Need for improved coordination and control across business units.
- Constraints imposed by host-government regulations on ownership and equity.

Multinationals are not born overnight; the evolution from a domestic to a truly global organization may involve a long and somewhat torturous process with many and diverse steps, as illustrated in Figure 2.2. Although research into internationalization has revealed a common process, it must be stressed that this process is not exactly the same for all firms. As Figure 2.2 shows, some firms may use other operation modes, such as licensing and subcontracting, instead of (or as well as) establishing their own foreign production or service facilities.

Some firms go through the various steps rapidly while others evolve slowly over many years, although recent studies have identified a speeding

Figure 2.2

Stages of Internationalization

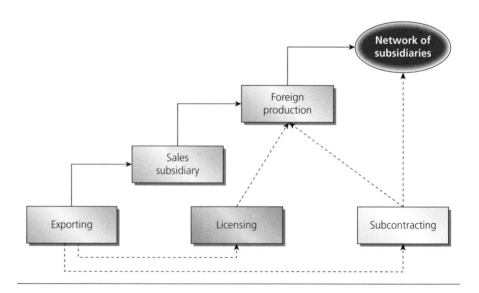

up of the process. For example, some firms are able to accelerate the process through acquisitions, thus leapfrogging over intermediate steps (that is, they move directly into foreign production through the purchase of a foreign firm, rather than initial exporting followed by establishment of a sales subsidiary, as per Figure 2.2). Nor do all firms follow the same sequence of stages as they internationalize—some firms can be driven by external factors such as host-government action (for example, be forced into a joint venture) or an offer to buy a company. Others are formed expressly with the international market in mind—often referred to as *born globals*.[5] In other words, the number of steps, or stages, along the path to multinational status varies from firm to firm, as does the time frame involved.[6] However, the concept of an evolutionary process is useful in illustrating the organizational adjustments required of a firm moving along the path to multinational status. As mentioned earlier, linked to this evolutionary process are structural responses, control mechanisms, and HRM policies, which we now examine.

Export

Exporting is typically the initial stage for manufacturing firms entering international operations. As such, it rarely involves much organizational response until the level of export sales reaches a critical point. Of course, simple exporting may be difficult for service companies (such as legal firms), so they may be forced to take an early step into foreign direct investment operations (via a branch office or joint venture).[7]

Exporting often tends to be handled by an intermediary (for example, a foreign agent or distributor), as local market knowledge is deemed critical. As export sales increase, however, an export manager may be appointed to control foreign sales and actively seek new markets. This person is commonly from the domestic operation. Further growth in exporting may lead to the establishment of an export department at the same level as the domestic sales department, as the firm becomes more committed to, or more dependent on, its foreign export sales, as Figure 2.3 shows. At this stage, exporting is controlled from the domestic-based home office, through a designated export manager. (See also IHRM Notebook 2.1.)

The role of the HR department is unclear, as indicated by the dotted arrow between these two functional areas in Figure 2.3. There is a paucity of empirical evidence about HR responses at this early internationalization stage, even though there are HR activities involved (such as the selection of export staff) and perhaps training of the foreign agency staff. As the development of policies and procedures surrounding the HR aspects of the firm's early international activities are handled by the marketing department or exporting staff, the HR department has little, if any, involvement at this stage.[8]

Sales Subsidiary

As the firm develops expertise in foreign markets, agents and distributors are often replaced by direct sales with the establishment of sales subsidiaries or branch offices in the foreign market countries. This stage may be prompted

FIGURE 2.3

Export Department Structure

IHRM Notebook 2.1

Canada's International Business Opportunities Centre

The International Business Opportunities Centre (IBOC) in partnership with Canadian trade commissioners around the world, along with Canada's embassies, high commissions, and consulates, aims at connecting foreign investors and buyers with Canadian exporting companies. Once a potential foreign buyer shows an interest in business opportunities with Canada, Canadian trade officers contact the IBOC. The latter identifies and contacts Canadian exporters matching the foreign investor needs:

Many of these business leads translate into export sales for Canadian companies—or potential future deals, new partners, new suppliers and even developing new products and services that will meet the needs of the foreign buyer.

Source: International Business Opportunities Centre. Retrieved July 25, 2007, from www.e-leads.ca/cancompanies/default-e.asp

---

by problems with foreign agents, more confidence in the international sales activity, the desire to have greater control, and/or the decision to give greater support to the exporting activity, usually due to its increasing importance to the overall success of the organization. The export manager may be given the same authority as other functional managers, as illustrated in Figure 2.4.

Exporting is still controlled at corporate headquarters, but the firm must make a decision regarding the coordination of the sales subsidiary, including staffing. If the firm wishes to maintain direct control, reflecting an ethnocentric attitude, it opts to staff the sales subsidiary from its headquarters through

FIGURE 2.4

Sales Subsidiary Structure

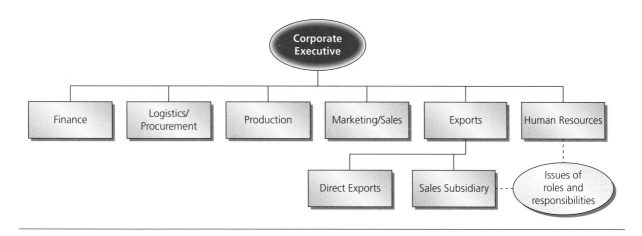

the use of parent-country nationals). If it regards country-specific factors—such as knowledge of the foreign market, language, sensitivity to host-country needs—as important, it may staff the subsidiary with host-country nationals. However, it would appear that many firms use PCNs in key sales subsidiary positions.

The decision to use PCNs leads into expatriation management issues and activities. It may be that, at this point, the HR department becomes actively involved in the personnel aspects of the firm's international operations, although there is little empirical evidence as to when, and how, HR-designated staff becomes involved.

WWW2.2

WWW2.3

International Division

For some firms, it is a short step from the establishment of a sales subsidiary to a foreign production or service facility. This step may be considered small if the firm is already assembling the product abroad to take advantage of cheap labour or to save shipping costs or tariffs, for example. Alternatively, the firm may have a well-established export and marketing program that enables it to take advantage of host-government incentives or counter host-government controls on foreign imports by establishing a foreign production facility. For some firms, though, the transition to foreign direct investment is a large step. However, having made the decision to produce overseas, the firm may establish its own foreign production facilities, or enter into a joint venture with a local firm, or buy a local firm. Regardless of the method of establishment, foreign production/service operations tend to trigger the creation of a separate international division in which all international activities are grouped, as Figure 2.5 demonstrates.

With the spread of international activities, typically the firm establishes what have been referred to as "miniature replicas," as the foreign subsidiaries

FIGURE 2.5

International Division Structure

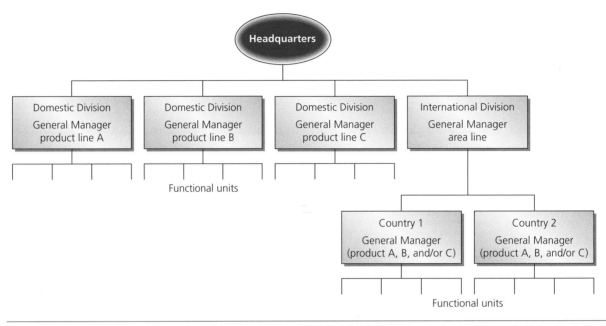

Source: Adapted from: Hill, C. (1997). *International Business: Competing in the Global Marketplace* (2nd ed.). Chicago, IL: Richard Irwin.

are structured to mirror that of the domestic organization. The subsidiary managers report to the head of the international division, and there may be some informal reporting directly to the various functional heads. For example, in reference to Figure 2.5, there may be contact regarding staffing issues between the HR managers in the two country subsidiaries and the HR manager at corporate headquarters.

Many firms at this stage of internationalization are concerned about maintaining control of the newly established subsidiary and will place PCNs in all key positions in the subsidiary. However, some firms decide that local employment conditions require local handling and place an HCN in charge of the subsidiary HR function, thus making an exception to the overall ethnocentric approach. Others may place HCNs in several key positions, including HRM, either to comply with host-government directives or to emphasize the local orientation of the subsidiary.

The role of corporate HR staff is primarily concerned with expatriate management, although there will be some formal monitoring of the subsidiary HR function through the head of the international division. Pucik[9] suggests that, initially, corporate HR activities are confined to supervising the selection of staff for the new international division, and expatriate managers perform a major role in "identifying employees who can direct the daily operations of the foreign subsidiaries, supervising transfer of managerial and technical know-how, communicating corporate policies, and keeping corporate HQ informed." As the firm expands its foreign production or service facilities into other countries, increasing the size of its foreign workforce, accompanied by a growth in the number of expatriates, more formal HR policies become necessary. The capacity of corporate HR staff to design appropriate policies may depend on how institutionalized existing approaches to expatriate management concerns have become, especially policies for compensation and pre-departure training; the more isolated the corporate HR function has been from the preceding international activities, the more difficult the task is likely to be.[10] The export department (or its equivalent) may have been in charge of international staffing issues and instigated required personnel responses, and might now consider that it has the competence to manage expatriates.

Global Product/Area Division

Over time, the firm moves from the early foreign production stage into a phase of growth through production or service, standardization, and diversification. Consequently, the strain of sheer size may create problems. The international division becomes over-stretched, making effective communication and efficiency of operation difficult. In some cases, corporate top managers may become concerned that the international division has enjoyed too much autonomy, acting so independently from the domestic operations to the extent that it operates as a separate unit—a situation that cannot be tolerated as the firm's international activities become strategically more important.

Typically, tensions will emerge between the parent company (headquarters) and its subsidiaries, stemming from the need for national responsiveness at the subsidiary unit and global integration imperatives at the parent headquarters. The demand for national responsiveness at the subsidiary unit develops because of factors such as differences in market structures, distribution channels, customer needs, local culture, and pressure from the host government. The need for more centralized global integration by headquarters comes from having multinational customers, global competitors, and the increasingly rapid flow of information and technology, and from the quest for large volume for economies of scale. As a result of these various forces for change, the multinational confronts two major issues of structure:

1. The extent to which key decisions are to be made at the parent-country headquarters or at the subsidiary units (centralization vs. decentralization).
2. The type or form of control exerted by the parent over the subsidiary unit.

The structural response, at this stage of internationalization, can be either a product/service-based global structure (if the growth strategy is through product or service diversification) or an area-based structure (if the growth strategy is through geographical expansion); see Figures 2.6a and 2.6b.

As part of the process of accommodating subsidiary concerns through decentralization, the multinational enterprise (MNE) strives to adapt its

FIGURE 2.6a

Global Product Division Structure

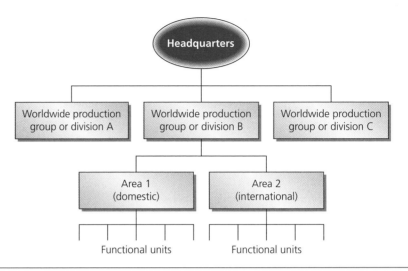

Source: Adapted from: Hill, C. (1997). *International Business: Competing in the Global Marketplace* (2nd ed.). Chicago, IL: Richard Irwin.

FIGURE 2.6b

Global Area Division Structure

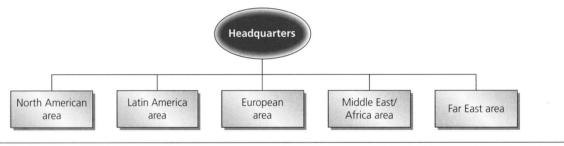

Source: Adapted from: Stopford, J., and Wells, I. (1972). *Strategy and Structure of the Multinational Enterprise*. New York: Basic Books.

HRM activities to each host country's specific requirements. This naturally impacts on the corporate HRM function. As there is an increasing devolution of responsibility for local employee decisions to each subsidiary, with corporate HR staff performing a monitoring role, intervening in local affairs occurs less frequently (see IHRM Today 2.1).

This HRM monitoring role reflects management's desire for central control of strategic planning—formulating, implementing and coordinating strategies for its worldwide markets. As well, the growth in foreign exposure combined with changes in the organizational structure of international operations results in an increase in the number of employees needed to oversee the activities between the parent firm and its foreign affiliates. Within the human

BP's Decentralized Structure

The following is an excerpt from an article by E. Crooks, "Hayward set for his first BP challenge," in the July 24, 2007, *Financial Times*, page 20.

The roots of today's BP go back to former chairman and chief executive Sir Robert Horton's "Project 1990" restructuring plan, with its emphasis on cutting back the corporate centre and giving more autonomy to individual business units. Lord Browne's BP was characterised by a combination of strict financial controls imposed from the centre and a high degree of managerial independence in operational terms.

Business unit leaders—the "Buls"—were put in charge of an operation such as an oil field or group of fields, with staff numbers ranging from a few hundred to a few thousand, set demanding financial objectives and told to get on with it. As one former executive puts it: "The business unit was pretty much a medieval lord, as far as the running of his fiefdom went." . . .

BP's much less centralized approach [than Exxon-Mobil's] to operational decision-making had many strengths: it encouraged entrepreneurialism and initiative; it smoothed the rapid integration of the companies that BP acquired in its four-year spree from 1998–2001, and it helped drive down costs to deliver outstanding financial performance. But it also had its weaknesses. . . .

Decentralized operations have inhibited BP's ability to share best practice around the group, which can be vital when investing in challenging and high-value projects. . . . They

have also hindered the board from knowing exactly what was going on on the ground. . . . The incentives for the Buls to conceal problems and the lack of effective ways for top management to check what they were being told, have been blamed for slip-ups such as BP's embarrassing failure to hit its production targets in 2002. In the worst case, top management's lack of detailed operational knowledge led to lapses in safety. An internal BP probe into the 2005 Texas City explosion found that John Manzoni, the then-head of refining and marketing, . . . should have carried out a "much deeper dive" into the true state of the refinery after "clear warning signals" from previous accidents.

Attempts at BP to pool the knowledge of its staff world-wide have had a mixed record. "Peer assist," which brings together experts to advise on an operational problem, is said to have slipped into the doldrums after the Amoco and Arco mergers at the end of the 1990s. Great Operators Teams, another plan to spread best practice, had a patchy effect. . . .

Allowing so much operational independence to the business units has encouraged them to develop their own activities, often chasing up blind alleys or duplicating initiatives.

[On July 25, 2007, the *Financial Times* reported that, at a press conference, BP's chief executive, Tony Hayward, announced that the company planned to restrict BP's business units in their operational independence—responding to operational performance problems.]

---

resource function, the development of managers able to operate in international environments generally becomes a new imperative.[11]

As the MNE grows and the trend toward a global perspective accelerates, it increasingly confronts the **"think global, act local"** paradox.[12] The increasingly complex international environment—characterized by global competitors, global customers, universal products, rapid technological change, and world-scale factories—pushes the multinational toward global

"think global, act local"
this paradox faces multinationals aiming for global integration while pushing for local responsiveness

integration while, at the same time, host governments and other stakeholders (such as customers, suppliers, and employees) push for local responsiveness. To facilitate the challenge of meeting these conflicting demands, the multinational will typically need to consider a more appropriate structure, and the choice appears to be from among the matrix, the mixed structure, the heterarchy, the transnational, or the multinational network. These options are now described and discussed.

The Matrix

In the matrix structure, the multinational is attempting to integrate its operations across more than one dimension. As shown in Figure 2.7, the international or geographical division and the product division share joint authority. Advocates of this structural form see, as its advantages, that conflicts of interest are brought out into the open and that each issue with priority in decision making has an executive champion to ensure it is not neglected. In other words, the matrix is considered to bring into the management system a philosophy of matching the structure to the decision-making process. Research on the matrix structure[13] indicates that the matrix "continues to be the only organizational form which fits the strategy of simultaneous pursuit of multiple business dimensions, with each given equal priority. . . . [The] structural form succeeds because it fits the situation." In practice, firms that have adopted the matrix structure have met with mixed success. One reason is that it is an expensive structural form in that it

FIGURE 2.7

Global Matrix Structure

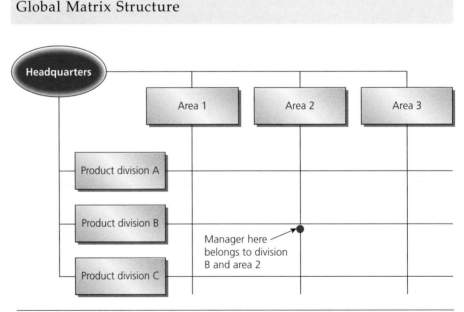

Source: Adapted from: Hill, C. (1997). *International Business: Competing in the Global Marketplace* (2nd ed.). Chicago, IL: Richard Irwin.

requires careful implementation and commitment (and often a great deal of time) on the part of top management to be successful.

In Figure 2.7, area managers are responsible for the performance of all products within the various countries that comprise their regions, while product managers are responsible for sales of their specific product ranges across the areas. For example, product A manager may be concerned with sales of product A in Europe, the Americas, and the Asia–Pacific area. Product managers typically report to a vice president (perhaps of "Global Products" or a similar title) for matters pertaining to product, and to another vice president (perhaps a "VP International") who is responsible for geographical matters. There is a similar dual reporting line for functional staff, including HR staff. Country/area HR managers may also be involved in staffing issues involving product division staff (reporting indirectly to the VP Global Products). There may be additional requirements to report to corporate HR at headquarters.

One early and public supporter of the matrix organization was Percy Barnevik, former chief executive officer of Asea Brown Boveri (ABB), the European electrical systems and equipment manufacturer.[14] ABB's decade-long efforts at matrix control were very influential in the popular and academic press, intriguing executives at a number of global firms.

Overall, efforts to successfully implement the matrix solution have been problematic. Bartlett and Ghoshal[15] comment that, in practice, particularly in the international context, the matrix has proven to be all but unmanageable. They isolate four contributing factors:

1. Dual reporting, which leads to conflict and confusion.
2. The proliferation of communication channels, which creates informational logjams.
3. Overlapping responsibilities, which produce turf battles and a loss of accountability.
4. The barriers of distance, language, time, and culture, which often make it very difficult for managers to resolve conflicts and clarify confusion.

Bartlett and Ghoshal conclude that the most successful MNEs focus less on searching for the ideal structure and more on developing the abilities, behaviour, and performance of individual managers. This assists in creating "a matrix in the minds of managers," where individual capabilities are captured and the entire firm is motivated to respond cooperatively to a complicated and dynamic environment. It seems clear that if the MNE opts for a matrix structure, particular care must be taken with staffing. As Ronen[16] notes:

> It requires managers who know the business in general, who have good interpersonal skills, and who can deal with the ambiguities of responsibility and authority inherent in the matrix system. Training in such skills as planning procedures, the kinds of interpersonal skills necessary for the matrix, and the kind of analysis and orderly presentation of ideas essential to planning within a group is most important for supporting the matrix approach.

Moreover, management development and human resource planning are even more necessary in the volatile environment of the matrix than in the traditional organizations.

Mixed Structure

RPC 2.5

In an attempt to manage the growth of diverse operations, or because attempts to implement a matrix structure have been unsuccessful, some firms have opted for what can only be described as a mixed form (see, for example, IHRM Today 2.2). In an early survey conducted by Dowling[17] on this issue, more than one-third (35 percent) of respondents indicated that they had mixed forms, and around 18 percent had product or matrix structures.

Although all structural forms that result from the evolutionary development of international business are complex and difficult to manage effectively, given an MNE's developing capabilities and experience at each new stage, mixed structures appear even more complex and harder to explain and implement, as well as control. Thus, as our discussion of the matrix structure emphasized, it is important that all employees understand the mixed framework and that attention is also given to supporting mechanisms, such as corporate identity, interpersonal relationships, management attitudes, and HR systems, particularly promotion and reward policies.

Beyond the Matrix

Early studies of headquarter–subsidiary relationships tended to stress resources, people, and information flows from headquarters to subsidiary, examining these relationships mainly in the context of control and coordination. However, in the large, mature multinational, these flows are multidirectional: from headquarters to subsidiary; from subsidiary to subsidiary; and between subsidiaries. The result can be a complex network of interrelated

IHRM Today 2.2

Mixed Structures

A number of mixed structures also seem to have emerged in response to global pressures and tradeoffs. For example, organizations that pursued area structures kept these geographical profit centres but added worldwide product managers. Colgate-Palmolive has always had strong country managers. But, as the company doubled the funding for product research, and as Colgate Dental Cream became a universal product, product managers were added at the corporate office to direct the R&D funding and coordinate marketing programs worldwide.

Similarly, product-divisionalized firms have been reintroducing the international division. At Motorola, the product groups had worldwide responsibility for their product lines. As the company competes with the Japanese in Japan, however, an international group has been introduced to help coordinate across product lines.

Source: Galbraith, J. R., & Kazanjian, R. K. (1986). Organizing to Implement Strategies of Diversity and Globalisation: The Role of Matrix Designs. *Human Resource Management, 25*(1), 50.

activities and relationships, and the multinational management literature identifies three descriptions of organizational structures—the heterarchy, the transnational, and the network firm. While they have been given different names, each form recognizes that, at this stage of internationalization, the concept of a superior structure that neatly fits the corporate strategy becomes inappropriate. The proponents of these forms are in agreement that multinationals at this stage become less hierarchical. We will take a brief look at each of these more decentralized, organic forms.

The Heterarchy

This structural form was proposed by Hedlund,[18] a distinguished Swedish international management researcher, and recognizes that a multinational may have a number of different kinds of centres apart from that traditionally referred to as "headquarters." Hedlund argued that competitive advantage does not necessarily reside in any one country (the parent country, for example). Rather, it may be found in many, so that each subsidiary centre may be simultaneously a centre and a global coordinator of discrete activities, thus performing a strategic role not just for itself, but for the MNE as a whole (the subsidiary labelled "centre" in Figure 2.8). For example, some multinationals may centralize research and development in a particular subsidiary. In a heterarchical MNE, control is less reliant on the top-to-bottom mechanisms of previous hierarchical modes and more on normative mechanisms, such as the corporate culture and a widely shared awareness of central goals and strategies.

From an HRM perspective, the heterarchy is interesting in that its success appears to rest solely on the ability of the multinational to formulate, implement, and reinforce the required human resource elements. Hedlund

RPC 2.6
RPC 2.7

FIGURE 2.8

The Networked Organization

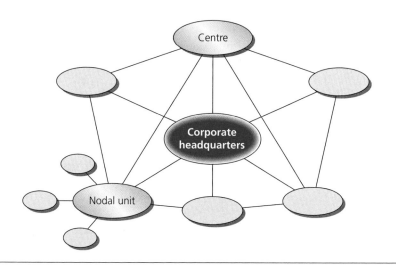

recognized that the heterarchy demands skillful and experienced personnel as well as sophisticated reward and punishment systems in order to develop the normative control mechanisms necessary for effective performance. The use of staff as an informal control mechanism is important, and we will explore this later in this chapter.

RPC 2.8

In a later article, Hedlund[19] proposed a structural model that he termed the N-form. This model builds on his heterarchy concept and integrates work from knowledge organization scholars. Hedlund argued that a new structural form is required to allow for knowledge management. His N-form takes away divisions, allows for temporary constellations and the use of project teams, and places stress on lateral communication and dialogue between units and individuals. The top-management role was presented as that of a catalyst, architect, and protector of knowledge rather than a monitor and resource allocator. The use of mechanisms, such as cross-functional teams and empowerment of lower-level employees, was advocated to further support the N-form.

The Transnational

The term *transnational* has been coined to describe an organizational form that is characterized by an interdependence of resources and responsibilities across all business units, regardless of national boundaries. The term has also become a descriptor of a particular type of multinational that tries to cope with the large flows of components, products, resources, people, and information among its subsidiaries, while simultaneously recognizing distributed specialized resources and capabilities. As such, the transnational demands a complex process of coordination and cooperation involving strong cross-unit integrating devices, a strong corporate identity, and a well-developed worldwide management perspective. In their study, Bartlett and Ghoshal[20] noted:

> Among the companies we studied, there were several that were in the process of developing such organizational capabilities. They had surpassed the classic capabilities of the *multinational* company that operates as decentralised federations of units able to sense and respond to diverse international needs and opportunities; and they had evolved beyond the abilities of the global company with its facility for managing operations on a tightly controlled worldwide basis through its centralised hub structure. They had developed what we termed *transnational* capabilities—the ability to manage across national boundaries, retaining local flexibility while achieving global integration. More than anything else this involved the ability to link local operations to each other and to the centre in a flexible way, and in so doing, to leverage those local and central capabilities.

RPC 2.9

In fact, the matrix, the heterarchy, and the transnational share a common theme regarding the human resource factor. Therefore, developing transnational managers or global leaders who can think and act across national and subsidiary boundaries emerges as an important task for top management when introducing these complex organizational forms. Staff transfers play a critical role in integration and coordination.

The Multinational as a Network

Some scholars are advocating viewing certain large and mature internationalized firms as a network, in situations where:

- Subsidiaries have developed into significant centres for investments, activities, and influence, and can no longer be regarded as at the periphery.[21] Interaction between headquarters and each subsidiary is likely to be dyadic, taking place between various actors at many different organizational levels and covering different exchanges, the outcome of which will be important for effective global performance.

- Such MNEs are loosely coupled political systems rather than tightly bonded, homogeneous, hierarchically controlled systems.[22] This runs counter to the traditional structure, where linkages are described formally via the organization's structure and standardized procedures, and informally through interpersonal contact and socialization.[23]

Figure 2.8 attempts to depict such an intricate crisscrossing of relationships. One subsidiary may act as a nodal unit linked a cluster of satellite organizations. Thus, one centre can assume responsibility for other units in its country or region. In line with this view, Ghoshal and Bartlett[24] have expanded their concept of the transnational to define the MNE as an interorganizational system. This comprises a network of exchange relationships among different organizational units, including headquarters and national subsidiaries, as well as external organizations such as host governments, customers, suppliers, and competitors with which the different units of the multinational must interact. These authors argue that a new way of structuring is not the issue—it is more the emerging management philosophy, with its focus on management processes: "The actual configuration of the processes themselves, and the structural shell within which they are embedded, can be very different depending on the businesses and the heritage of each company."[25] Ghoshal and Bartlett cite GE, ABB, and Toyota as prime examples of companies involved in developing such processes, with Intel and Corning, Philips and Alcatel, Matsushita and Toshiba regarded as companies embarking on a network-type configuration.

The management of a multi-centred networked organization is complex. Apart from the intra-organizational network (comprising headquarters and the numerous subsidiaries), each subsidiary also has a range of external relationships (involving local suppliers, customers, competitors, host governments, and alliance partners). The management of both the intra-organizational and interorganizational spheres, and of the total integrated network, is crucial to global corporate performance. It involves what has been termed a less-hierarchical structure, featuring five dimensions:

R P C 2.10

1. Delegation of decision-making authority to appropriate units and levels.
2. Geographical dispersal of key functions across units in different countries.
3. De-layering of organizational levels.
4. De-bureaucratization of formal procedures.
5. Differentiation of work, responsibility, and authority across the networked subsidiaries.[26]

Research cited by Nohria and Ghoshal focuses on the capability of networking subsidiaries to package "slack resources" (pools in capital, production, or human resources beyond those required for local purposes) to stimulate "local-for-local, local-for-global, and global-for-global innovation processes."[27] Integrated networks of these "slack resource" pools are combined by way of interpersonal contacts, mentoring relationships, and sophisticated communications networks in order to identify and distribute new products, processes, and technologies.

Beyond Networks

Doz, Santos, and Williamson[28] have coined the term *metanational* to describe firms composed of three types of units: First, locally imbedded "sensing units" are responsible for uncovering widely dispersed sources of engineering and market insights. Developing new technologies and processes can no longer be assumed to be the sole task of a conveniently located home-country headquarters research and development unit, or even an MNE-based centre of excellence. Second, "magnet" units are described as attracting these unpredictably dispersed innovative processes, creating a business plan to convert these innovations into viable services or products. Finally, a third set of units is responsible for marketing and producing adaptations of these products and services for a range of customers around the world. The metanational system is described as:

> . . . a global tournament played at three levels. It is a race to identify and access new technologies and market trends ahead of the competition, a race to turn this dispersed knowledge into innovative products and services, and a race to scale and exploit these innovations in markets around the world.[29]

The Place of the HR Function in Structural Forms

As we point out in our treatment of the various forms, there has been little direct investigation into how the HR function develops in response to structural changes as a consequence of international growth. An exception is a study of the changing role of the corporate HR function in 30 U.K. firms.[30] The authors, Scullion and Starkey, found three distinct groups that they describe as follows:

1. *Centralized HR companies*, characterized by large, well-resourced HR departments responsible for a wide range of functions. The key role for corporate HR was to establish and maintain control over worldwide top-level management positions, such as divisional and subsidiary managers, so that strategic staffing was under central control. Companies in this group operated within product-based or matrix structures.

2. *Decentralized HR companies*, characterized by devolving the HR responsibilities to a small group that confined its role to senior management at corporate HQ. This was consistent with the decentralized approach to other functions. Companies within this group operated within product or region-based structures, with only one reporting using a matrix.

3. *Transition companies*, characterized by medium-sized corporate HR departments staffed by a relatively small group at corporate headquarters. They operated in a decentralized, product-based structure, although again one company reported using a matrix structure.

Scullion and Starkey note that the varied roles of corporate HR within these three groups impacted on the way in which activities such as training and performance appraisal were handled and on the ability of corporate HR to plan for staff movements throughout the worldwide operations.

Different Countries Take Different Paths

The above discussion takes a generalist view of the growth of the internationalizing firm through the various stages to multinational status, and the corresponding organizational structures. However, it is important to note a cultural element. If, as Stopford and Wells, state, MNEs may develop global capabilities by an emphasis on product diversity, leading to worldwide product division structures, or alternatively, by an emphasis on cultural responsiveness, leading to regional or area division structures, the question arises as to what role the cultural origin of the multinational plays in the path to globalization.[31] See Figure 2.9 for a presentation of this issue. As can be seen from this figure, European firms have tended to take a different structural path than their U.S. counterparts.

Franko's study of 70 European multinationals revealed that European firms moved directly from a functional "mother–daughter" structure to a global structure with worldwide product or area divisions, or to a matrix organization without the transitional stage of an international division.[32] Human resource management practices, changing to serve the needs of the new structure, adjusted accordingly. Swedish firms have traditionally adopted the mother–daughter structure, but Hedlund's work noted that this had changed. The Swedish multinationals in his study tended to adopt a mixture of elements of the mother–daughter structure and elements of the product division, at this stage of their internationalization process.[33] It may be that there is a preference for matrix-type structures within European firms, particularly Nordic MNEs. One could suggest that this structural

FIGURE 2.9

Culture of Origin and Structural Paths to Globalization

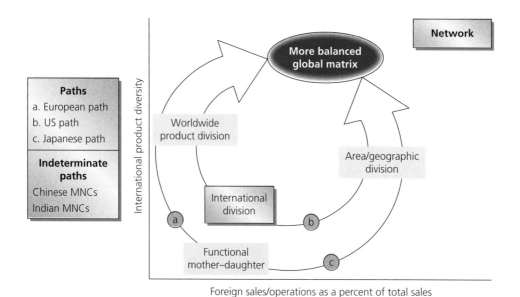

Source: Adapted from: Stopford, J., and Wells, I. (1972). *Strategy and Structure of the Multinational Enterprise*. New York: Basic Books.

form has better suited the more collaborative, group-oriented work organization found within these firms. In contrast, U.S. firms that have experimented with the matrix form appear to have met with limited success (see, for example, IHRM Today 2.3).

Japanese multinationals are evolving along similar lines to their U.S. counterparts. Export divisions have become international divisions but, according to Ronen,[34] the rate of change was slower. The characteristics of Japanese organizational culture (such as the control and reporting mechanisms and decision-making systems), the role of trading companies, and the systems of

IHRM Today 2.3

U.S. Firms and the Matrix Form

As part of a reorganization process called "Ford 2000," the Ford Motor Company abandoned its regional structure in 1993 and adopted a form of global matrix organization characterized by a multidisciplinary product team approach with networked plants across regions. In the process, the European regional headquarters was moved to the United States in an attempt to develop global decision making. In November 2001, Ford announced a restructuring and plant rationalization that effectively took the company back to a regional structure. Further restructuring, particularly of its North American operations in 2006, is underway as Ford seeks to retrieve its competitive position.

Source: *Financial Times* series (1997, October 15), The Global Company, 14, and *The Economist* (2001, November 13), 82.

management appear to contribute to the slower evolution of the international division. In some cases, despite their high degree of internationalization, Japanese firms may not adapt their structures as they become more dispersed. As mentioned previously, Ghoshal and Bartlett were able to include Japanese firms in their description of the network multinational. A 1996 study of 54 companies,[35] taken from the *Fortune* 1991 list of the world's 500 largest industrial corporations, revealed that the degree of internationalization differed between firms from the United States, Europe, and Japan. The study also reports that the U.S. multinationals in the sample gave more autonomy to their international operations than did their Japanese counterparts.

We should mention that internationalizing firms from other Asian nations may also vary in structural form and growth patterns. Korean conglomerates (*chaebols*) have had a stronger preference for growth-through-acquisitions than the "greenfield" (building) approach taken by Japanese multinationals, and this has influenced their structural responses in terms of control and coordination. The so-called Chinese "bamboo" network/family firms may face significant challenges as their international activities expand and it becomes more difficult to maintain the tight family control that characterizes overseas Chinese firms.

In 1995, only 3 mainland Chinese firms were listed in *Fortune's* top 500 global companies. This number is expanding but relatively few Chinese firms have international operations.[36] Newly emerging Chinese multinationals, such as the white goods manufacturer Haier and PetroChina, an oil and gas producer, appear to be following an acquisition path, although there is little data on how these firms are integrating foreign operations.

Some research has begun into the internationalization of Chinese MNEs. For example, Shen's 2001 study of 10 Chinese firms,[37] mostly state-owned enterprises of various sizes and from different industries, reports an incremental approach: moving into neighbouring East and South East Asia before expanding into North America. These firms were at different stages of internationalization: four had foreign sales offices, three had sales offices and subsidiaries, and three were considered global in terms of number of foreign subsidiaries (either wholly-owned or international joint ventures). Global area divisional or global functional structures were utilized. As with China, there is a similar relative paucity of information regarding Indian MNEs and their internationalization.

Some researchers have gone so far as to question the existence of a truly global firm. Doremus et al.[38] find empirical support for their contention that institutional infrastructures (the cultural heritage codified into legislation and values related to banking and financial markets, research and development capabilities and patterns of technological change, as well as governmental and managerial preferences and strategic propensities) combine to limit the ability of firms to move too far beyond their regional homes. Three regional blocks are presented for multinational firms: North America, Europe (largely German-based multinationals) and Asia (largely Japanese-based multinationals). The authors report economic data to support their contention that while each of these regional powers have some impact outside of their own regions, practically no firms operate significantly in a balanced manner across all three regions of the world (see also IHRM Today 2.4). Deep-seated differences in financial institutions, how technology is acquired and developed, and how products and services are consumed are all too divergent from each firm's region of origin for complete global cross-seeding to occur. According to Rugman, centres of regional competitive advantage may be created with some limited interventions outside of the regional core.[39]

Fashion or Fit?

The above discussion has traced the evolution of the firm from a domestic-oriented into a global-oriented firm. A note of caution should be added. Growth in the firm's international business activity does require structural responses, but the evolutionary process will differ across multinationals. Apart from the country of origin aspect, other variables—size of organization, pattern of internationalization, management policies, and so on—also play a part. As Figure 2.9 illustrated, firms undergo stages of restructuring as they attempt to grapple with environment changes that require strategic responses.

Control Mechanisms

As indicated in Figure 2.1 at the beginning of this chapter, international operations place additional stresses on control mechanisms. There is also additional stress on the firm's ability to coordinate resources and activities. As the chairman and chief executive officer of the French hotel and travel company, Accor, explained in a newspaper interview:[40]

> Accor has to be a global company, in view of the revolution in the service sector which is taking place . . . National [hotel chains]

IHRM Today 2.4

Canada's Foreign Direct Investment Abroad

While in the past the notion of regional powers was also true for Canada and its North America block, Canada's foreign direct investment abroad has become more diversified across other countries. The share of Canadian direct investments in the United States has fallen from 69 percent (20 years ago) to 52 percent (10 years ago) to 43 percent in 2006. Yet, with $223.6 billion of direct Canadian investment in the United States, the United States continues to be far ahead of the United Kingdom ($59 billion), Barbados ($38 billion), and Ireland ($24.7 billion). The European Union as a whole accounted for 27 percent of Canada's total foreign direct investment.

Furthermore, the United States continues to be the number one investor in Canada, with $273.7 billion or 61 percent of total foreign direct investment in Canada. Other important investors include the United Kingdom with $29.5 billion and France with $27.8 billion. Thus, while we can observe a slow decline of foreign direct investments between Canada and the United States, the figures indicate that there is still a very strong North American regional block structure.

Source: Statistics Canada, *The Daily* (2007, May 9). Foreign Direct Investment 2006. Retrieved July 24, 2007, from www.statcan.ca/Daily/English/070509/d070509a.htm

cannot optimise their operations. They cannot invest enough money . . . Globalisation brings considerable challenges which are often under-estimated. The principal difficulty is getting our local management to adhere to the values of the group . . . Every morning when I wake I think about the challenges of coordinating our operations in many different countries.

Figure 2.10 presents two strategies for global control. It is important to note these two strategies are not independent or divorced from each other. Rather they present a difference in emphasis.

Traditionally, multinational firms have emphasized more formal, structural forms of control. As presented earlier in the chapter, strategy is implemented via the factoring of work flows, the articulation of control by some combination of specialization characterized by functional global product division, national, regional (area) divisions, or matrix structures. Structure results in hierarchies, functional authority and increasingly prescribed job descriptions, selection criteria, training standards, and compensable factors.

FIGURE 2.10

Control Strategies for Multinational Firms

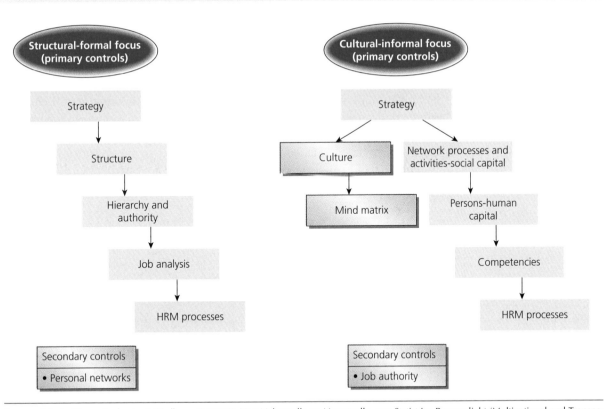

Source: Adapted from: Engle, A., & Stedham, Y. (1998). Von Nebenrolle zu Hauptrolle, von Statist ins Rampenlicht (Multinational and Transnational Strategies—Implications for Human Resource Practices). Conference Proceedings of the Sixth Conference on International Human Resource Management, Paderborn, Germany: University of Paderborn; and Engle, A., Mendenhall, M., Powers, R., & Stedham, Y. Conceptualizing the Global Competency Cube: A Transnational Model of Human Resource. *Journal of European Industrial Training, 25*(7), 15–23.

Human resource activities act to implement existing structural systems of control. Communication and relationships are formalized and prescribed and budgetary targets and "rational" explicit, quantitative criteria dominate performance management systems.[41] Complementary, yet definitely secondary, control is developed and maintained via more informal personal and social networks—the informal organization.

An alternative perspective has developed in response to perceived shortcomings in an overreliance on bureaucratic structural controls in dealing with the significant variations in distance and people experienced in the far-flung activities and operations of multinational firms and presented in Chapter 1. The unique cultural interactions and the contextual and physical distances that characterized multinational operations may have outstripped the capabilities of solely structural and formal forms of control.[42] As long ago as 1981, William Ouchi termed the phrase "clan control" to describe social control as a legitimate control system to supplement or replace traditional structural, bureaucratic control.[43] A more cultural focus emphasizes the group-level potential of corporate culture, informal social processes, personal work networks, and the investment in social capital to act as sources of more complete and nimble control in a complex multi-product, multicultural environment. On the individual level, an emphasis on people (as opposed to jobs), their competencies and skills, and the investment in human capital become the focus of more customized human resource practices and processes.[44] Formal, structural controls still exist, but they are not the primary source of control.

Results from a survey of 390 Mexican subsidiaries of U.S. MNEs by Gomez and Sanchez[45] led them to conclude that predicting the preferred combination of formal and informal controls a multinational might choose is problematic. The complexities related to subsidiary mandate and reliance on local or corporate technologies and skills, as well as the cultural distance between the corporate and host cultures, need to be considered in determining the mix of formal and informal control. Clearly, more research is called for in this topic area.[46] Returning to several of the elements in Figure 2.10, we will review informal control processes.

Control through Personal Relationships

A consistent theme in the descriptions of transnational and networked organization forms is the need to foster vital knowledge generation and diffusion through lateral communication via a network of working relationships. Networks are considered as part of an individual's or organization's **social capital**: contacts and ties, combined with norms and trust, that facilitate knowledge sharing and information exchanges between individuals, groups, and business units.[47]

As network relationships are built and maintained through personal contact, organizations need processes and forums where staff from various units can develop types of personal relationships that can be used for organizational purposes. For example, working in cross-functional and/or cross-border

social capital

contacts and ties, along with norms and trust, that facilitate knowledge sharing and information exchanges

Chapter 2: The Organizational Context

teams can assist in developing personal contacts. Training and development programs, held in regional centres or at headquarters, become an important forum for the development of personal networks that foster informal communication channels.

Control through Corporate Culture

Some advocates of more complex structural forms regard the use of cultural control as an effective informal control mechanism. Corporate culture is variously defined, but essentially it refers to a process of socializing people so that they come to share a common set of values and beliefs that then shape their behaviour and perspectives (see, for example, IHRM Notebook 2.2). It is often expressed as "our way of doing things." Cultural control may be a contentious issue for some—evidence of multinational imperialism where corporate culture is superimposed on national cultures in subsidiary operations. However, its proponents offer persuasive arguments as to its value as a management tool.[48] The emphasis is on developing voluntary adherence to corporate behavioural norms and expectations through a process of internalization of corporate values and beliefs.

WWW2.4

IHRM Notebook 2.2

Four Seasons' Golden Rule

Founded in 1960, Canadian-based Four Seasons Hotels and Resorts is one of the leading operators of luxury hotels, currently managing 75 hotels in 31 countries and with more than 31 properties in planning and under development.

Four Seasons' managers believe that human resource management is key to the firm's success. According to one senior manager, "People make the strength of this company. Procedures are not very varied or special. What we do is fairly basic." Human resource management starts and ends with the "Golden Rule," which stipulates that one should treat others as one wishes to be treated. Managers see it as the foundation of the firm's values and thus its culture. "The golden rule is the key to the success of the firm, and it's appreciated in every village, town, and city around the world. Basic human needs are the same everywhere," Sharp [Isadore Sharp, Four Seasons founder and CEO] emphasized.

Kathleen Taylor, president, Worldwide Business Operations, provided an example of how Four Seasons

went about enacting the Golden Rule as a core value: "We give employees several uniforms so they can change when the uniforms become dirty. That goes to their dignity, but it is uncommon in the hospitality industry. People around the world want to be treated with dignity and respect, and in most organizational cultures that doesn't happen."

Managers acknowledged that many service organizations make similar statements on paper. What differentiates Four Seasons is how the chain operationalizes those statements. Crowl [David Crowl, vice president, sales and marketing, Europe, the Middle East, and Africa] noted, "A service culture is about putting what we all believe in into practice. We learn it, we nurture it, and most important, we do it."

Source: Hallowell, R., Bowen, D., & Knoop, C. (2002). Four Seasons goes to Paris. *Academy of Management Executive, 16*(4), 11–12.

The literature on corporate culture recognizes the role played by HR activities in fostering corporate culture. For example, Alvesson and Berg[49] regard HRM activities as important means of establishing corporate culture identity. HR activities that build corporate culture include recruitment and selection practices, as firms hire or "buy" people who appear to hold similar values. Training and development programs, reward systems and promotion are also activities that reinforce company value systems.[50] Such reinforcement is considered to lead to more committed and productive employees who evince appropriate behaviour and therefore reduce the need for formal control mechanisms. Placement of staff is another method. Some global firms have become even more systematic in their efforts to achieve control by way of shared corporate culture. As this chapter's case will show, these efforts can become a central element in IHRM strategy.

Summary

The purpose of this chapter has been to identify the HR implications of the various options and responses that international growth places on the firm. We focused on aspects such as the organizational context in which IHRM activities take place and identified different structural arrangements as the firm moves along the path to multinational status—from export department through to more complex varieties such as the matrix, heterarchy, transnational, and networked. We also provided an outline of formal and informal mechanisms, with emphasis on control through personal networks and relationships, and control through corporate culture, drawing out HRM implications.

This was followed by our discussion as to how international growth affects the firm's approach to HRM. Firms vary from one another as they go through the stages of international development, and react in different ways to the circumstances they encounter in the various foreign markets. There is a wide variety of matches between IHRM approaches, organizational structure, and stage of internationalization. For example, almost half of the U.S. firms surveyed by Dowling[51] reported that the operations of the HR function were unrelated to the nature of the firm's international operations. Monks' study of nine subsidiaries of multinationals operating in Ireland[52] found that the majority adopted a local approach to the HR function, with headquarters involvement often limited to monitoring the financial implications of HR decisions.

We concluded that stages of development and organizational forms should not to be taken as normative. Research does suggest a pattern and a process of internationalization but firms do vary in how they adapt to international operations (we used nationality of the parent firm to illustrate this).

Through the approach taken in this chapter, we have been able to demonstrate that there is an interconnection between international HRM approaches and activities and the organizational context, and that HR managers have a crucial role to play. In order to better perform this role, it would seem important that HR managers understand the various international structural options—along with the control and coordination demands imposed by international growth.

Key Terms

social capital 56   "think global, act local" 43

Web Links

www 2.1   Foreign Affairs and International Trade (FAIT) Canada provides useful information for Canadian companies wanting to export internationally. For more information, go to:

http://www.international.gc.ca/commerce/index.aspx?lang=en

www 2.2   For more information about the Canadian Trade Commissioner Service supporting Canadian businesses in Canada and abroad, check out the FAIT site:

www.infoexport.gc.ca/ie-en/MarketReportsAndServices.jsp.

www 2.3   For information about regional and bilateral initiatives and trade agreements with Canada, go to the FAIT site:

www.international.gc.ca/tna-nac/reg-en.asp.

www 2.4   For more information about Four Seasons Hotels and Resorts and its corporate culture and policies, go to:

www.fourseasons.com/about_us

RPC Icons

RPC 2.1   Leads in the development of HR initiatives that support the organization's strategic directions

RPC 2.2   Leads in the development of HR initiatives that support the organization's strategic directions

RPC 2.3   Leads in the development of HR initiatives that support the organization's strategic directions

RPC 2.4   Contributes to improvements in the organization's structures and work processes

RPC 2.5   Contributes to improvements in the organization's structures and work processes

RPC 2.6   Contributes to improvements in the organization's structures and work processes

RPC 2.7   Leads in the development of HR initiatives that support the organization's strategic directions

RPC 2.8   Contributes to improvements in the organization's structures and work processes

RPC 2.9   Contributes to improvements in the organization's structures and work processes

RPC 2.10   Contributes to improvements in the organization's structures and work processes

RPC 2.11   Leads in the development of HR initiatives that support the organization's strategic directions

Discussion Questions

1. What are the stages that a firm typically goes through as it grows internationally, and how does each stage affect the HR function?
2. What are the specific HRM challenges in a networked firm?
3. Country of origin influences the firm's approach to organization structure. As MNEs from China and India internationalize, to what extent are their methods likely to differ from those observed for Japanese, European, and Canadian MNEs?

Using the Internet

1. Check out the website of the multinational company Thomson Corporation (**www.thomson.com/about/history**) (or a similar Canadian multinational company) and discuss its historical development. What does expansion into countries like Argentina (Thomson: 2000—La Ley, a leading legal publisher in Argentina) mean to this company's IHRM approach?
2. Read about Canada's Compass Group (**www.compass-group.com**) and its mother organization Compass Group PLC (**www.compass-group.com/aboutus**) and discuss some of the HR challenges this corporation faces employing 400,000 people worldwide. What are some of the cultural elements within Compass that could be used as control mechanisms?

Exercises

1. Compare multinational enterprises such as manufacturer Bombardier with a service-oriented organization such as Four Seasons Hotels and Resorts. How could their different industries influence the two companies and their international HR policies (e.g., staffing)?
2. Think about your last job or internship. Describe your previous employer's organizational culture. How were those cultural values and beliefs transferred to employees and managers? How successful in transferring these values and beliefs was your employer? Why?

Case

Globalizing Corporate Culture—"True Believers" in "The Toyota Way"

Mikkabi, Japan, is not the home of any renowned Buddhist temple or Shinto shrine, but it does act as a global repository for corporate philosophy and the missionary headquarters of Toyota. It is the location of the Toyota Institute.

According to the institute's general manager, Koki Konishi, "We must prevent the Toyota way from getting more and more diluted as Toyota grows overseas." With 200,000 workers in 27 plants worldwide, in addition to those employed in the 18 plants in Japan, global expansion has led to concerns about maintaining and yet adapting the MNE's core values around the world.

This institute, which is closed to the public, is designed to socialize executives in Toyota's philosophies of collective problem solving, empowering production workers to value quality so much that they will stop production lines in order to correct defects in real time, has been so successful that similar institutes are planned in Kentucky and Thailand. "Toyota is growing more quickly than the company's ability to transplant its culture to foreign markets," according to Takaki Nakanishi, Tokyo-based auto analyst for JPMorgan Securities. "This is a huge issue for Toyota, one of the biggest it will face in the coming years."

Latonda Newton, a general manager responsible for North American training and development, experienced the institute first-hand. One of a "class" of 40 managers from Japan, the United States, New Zealand, and Singapore, Newton described a week of 12- to 14-hour days at the institute. A series of opening lectures on the "Toyota Way" by president Katsuaki Wantanabe, past president Fujio Cho, and other top-level executives are combined with a daily focus on more specific concepts and practices. These practices include "genchi genbutsu"—stressing that production problems can be analyzed and solved only at the source and not behind a desk—and the continuous improvement philosophy of "kaizen." More interpersonal values are also communicated in the intense, week-long program. Topics include problem solving by factoring complex problems into smaller components, mutual respect in the workplace, consensus building, and an understanding of Toyota's richly informative, yet complex production charts, factory screens, and colour-coded graphics that make up the cross-cultural vocabulary of the "Toyota Way."

Source: Fackler, Martin. (2007, February 19). The "Toyota Way" Is Translated for a New Generation of Foreign Managers. New York Times News Service, *Lexington [Kentucky] Herald Leader*, C1 and C7.

Questions

1. How is Toyota trying to internationalize its corporate values and beliefs? What organizational level is Toyota targeting and why?
2. Find examples of other multinational companies and their methods and tools for transferring their organizational values and beliefs to managers and employees.
3. Many national and multinational companies try to create a very strong organizational or corporate culture. Ideally, managers and employees should eat and breathe Company A. In times of skilled-labour shortages and strong competition for management talents, how could a strong company culture be counterproductive and represent a barrier in the external recruitment and selection process?

Endnotes

1. For more on the potential of strategic and structural activities to impact international human resource processes and systems, see: P. Evans, V. Pucik, & J.-L. Barsoux. (2002). *The Global Challenge: Frameworks for International Human Resource Management.* Boston: McGraw-Hill, particularly Chapter 2.

2. A discussion of the "administrative heritage" that may link MNE country of origin to a predisposition for certain strategies and structural options is presented by: C. Bartlett, S. Ghoshal, & P. Beamish. (2008). in *Transnational Management: Text, Cases and Readings in Cross-Border Management*, (5th ed.). Boston: McGraw-Hill/Irwin, 333–340; T. Jackson. (2002). *International HRM: A Cross-Cultural Approach.* London: Sage Publications; and P. Buckley & P. Ghauri. (2004). Globalization, Economic Geography and the Strategy of Multinational Enterprises. *Journal of International Business Studies, V35*, 81–98.

3. M. Svard & R. Luostarinen. (1982). Personnel Needs in the Internationalising Firm. FIBO Publication No. 19. Helsinki: Helsinki School of Economics.

4. The organization's structure defines the tasks of individuals and business units within the firm and the processes that result from the intertwined tasks: identifying how the organization is divided up (differentiated) and how it is united (integrated).

5. B. M. Oviatt & P. P. McDougall. (1994). Toward a Theory of International New Ventures. *Journal of International Business Studies, 25*(1), 45–64.

6. J. Johanson & J. E. Vahlne. (1990). The Mechanism of Internationalisation. *International Marketing Review, 7*(4), 11–24; and L. Welch & R. Luostarinen. (1988). Internationalisation: Evolution of a Concept. *Journal of General Management, 14*(2), 34–55.

7. A study of U.S. service firms involved in international operations showed that wholly owned subsidiary/branch office was the most common method, although engineering and architecture firms used direct exports and consumer services used licensing/franchising: K. Erramilli. (1991). The Experience Factor in Foreign Market Entry Behaviour of Service Firms. *Journal of International Business Studies, 22*(3), 479–501. Similar results were found in a study of Australian service firms: LEK Partnership. (1994). *Intelligent Exports and the Silent Revolution in Services.* Canberra: Australian Government Publishing Service.

8. J. Ricart, M. Enright, P. Ghemawat, S. Hart, & T. Khanna. (2004). New Frontiers in International Strategy. *Journal of International Business Studies, 35*, 175–200; D. Welch & L. Welch. (1997). Pre-Expatriation: The Role of HR Factors in the Early Stages of Internationalization. *International Journal of Human Resource Management, 8*(4), 402–413.

9. See: V. Pucik. (1985). Strategic Human Resource Management in a Multinational Firm. In H. V. Wortzel & L. H. Wortzel (Eds.), *Strategic Management of Multinational Corporations: The Essentials.* New York: John Wiley, 425.

10. N. Adler. (2002). *International Dimensions of Organizational Behavior* (4th ed.), Chapter 8. Cincinnati: South-Western; M. Bloom, G. Milkovich, & A. Mitra. (2003). International Compensation: Learning How Managers Respond to Variations in Local Host Contexts. *International Journal of Human Resource Management, 14*(8), 1350–1367.

11. Pucik. Strategic Human Resource Management in a Multinational Firm.

12. C. Bartlett & S. Ghoshal. (1992). Organizing for Worldwide Effectiveness: The Transnational Solution. In R. Buzzell, J. Quelch, and C. Bartlett (Eds.), *Global Marketing Management: Cases and Readings,* 3rd ed. Reading, MA: Addison Wiley.

13. J. R. Galbraith & R. K. Kazanjian. (1986). Organizing to Implement Strategies of Diversity and Globalisation: The Role of Matrix Designs. *Human Resource Management, 25*(1), 50. See also: T. T. Naylor. (1985). The International Strategy Mix. *Columbia Journal of World Business, 20*(2); and R. A. Pitts & J. D. Daniels. (1984). Aftermath of the Matrix Mania. *Columbia Journal of World Business, 19*(2) for a discussion of the matrix structure.

14. W. Taylor. (1991, March–April). The Logic of Global Business: An Interview with ABB's Percy Barnevik. *Harvard Business Review*, 91–105. For a more complete presentation of ABB's strategic intent and structural and process qualities, see: K. Barham & C. Heimer. (1998). *ABB: The Dancing Giant*. London: Financial Times/Pitman Publishing.

15. C. A. Bartlett & S. Ghoshal. (1990, July–August). Matrix Management: Not a Structure, a Frame of Mind. *Harvard Business Review*, 138–145.

16. S. Ronen. (1986). *Comparative and Multinational Management*. New York: John Wiley, 330.

17. P. J. Dowling. (1988). International HRM. In L. Dyer (Ed.), *Human Resource Management: Evolving Roles and Responsibilities, 1*. ASPA/BNA Handbook of Human Resource Management Series. Washington, DC: BNA.

18. G. Hedlund. (1986). The Hypermodern MNC—A Heterarchy? *Human Resource Management, 25*(1), 9–35.

19. G. Hedlund. (1994). A Model of Knowledge Management and the N-form Corporation. *Strategic Management Journal, 15*, 73–90.

20. Bartlett & Ghoshal. Organizing for Worldwide Effectiveness, 66.

21. J. Birkinshaw & N. Hood. (1998). *Multinational Corporate Evolution and Subsidiary Development*. London: Macmillan Press.

22. M. Forsgren. (1990). Managing the International Multi-Centre Firm: Case Studies from Sweden. *European Management Journal, 8*(2), 261–267. Much of this work has been based on the concepts of social exchange theory and interaction between actors in a network.

23. J. I. Martinez & J. C. Jarillo. (1989, Fall). The Evolution of Research on Coordination Mechanisms in Multinational Corporations. *Journal of International Business Studies*, 489–514.

24. S. Ghoshal & C. A. Bartlett. (1990). The Multinational Corporation as an Interorganizational Network. *Academy of Management Review, 8*(2), 603–625.

25. S. Ghoshal & C. Bartlett. (1995). Building the Entrepreneurial Corporation: New Organizational Processes, New Managerial Tasks. *European Management Journal, 13*(2), 145.

26. R. Marschan. (1997). Dimensions of Less-Hierarchical Structures in Multinationals. In I. Björkman & M. Forsgren (Eds.), *The Nature of the International Firm*. Copenhagen Business School Press.

27. N. Nohria & S. Ghoshal. (1997). *The Differentiated Network: Organizing Multinational Corporations for Value Creation*. San Francisco: Jossey-Bass, 28–32.

28. Y. Doz, J. Santos & P. Williamson. (2001). *From Global to Metanational: How Companies Win in the Knowledge Economy*. Boston: Harvard Business School Press.

29. Ibid., 247.

30. H. Scullion & K. Starkey. (2000). In Search of the Changing Role of the Corporate Human Resource Function in the International Firm. *International Journal of Human Resource Management, 11*(6), 1061–1081.

31. Much of the research in this area has focused on the United States. No studies could be found that explicitly focused on Canada and Canadian multinationals and their international HR structures in response to their international growth.

32. L. Leksell. (1981). Headquarter–Subsidiary Relationships in Multinational Corporations. Stockholm: Stockholm School of Economics.

33. G. Hedlund. (1984, Fall). Organization In-Between: The Evolution of the Mother–Daughter Structure of Managing Foreign Subsidiaries in Swedish MNCs. *Journal of International Business Studies*, 109–123.

34. S. Ronen. (1986). *Comparative and Multinational Management*. New York: John Wiley.

35. R. B. Peterson, J. Sargent, N. K. Napier, & W. S. Shim. (1996). Corporate Expatriate HRM Policies, Internationalisation and Performance. *Management International Review, 36*(3), 215–230.

36. E. Yin & C. J. Choi. (2005). The Globalization Myth: The Case of China. *Management International Review, 45*(Special Issue No. 1), 103–120.

37. J. Shen. (2006). Factors Affecting International Staffing in Chinese Multinationals (MNEs). *International Journal of Human Resource Management, 17*(2), 295–315.

38. P. Doremus, W. Keller, L. Pauley, & S. Reich. (1998). *The Myth of the Global Corporation*. Princeton: Princeton University Press.

39. For additional empirical support for the idea of the regional multinational and the difficulties inherent in being a balanced global firm, see: A. Rugman & R. Hodgetts. (2001). The End of Global Strategy. *European Management Journal, 19*(4), 333–343; and E. Schlie & G. Yip. (2000). Regional Follows Global: Strategy Mixes in the World Automotive Industry. *European Management Journal, 18*(4), 343–354.

40. Interview by Andrew Jack. (1997, October 13). *Financial Times*, 14.

41. A. Engle & P. Dowling. (2006). State of Origin: Research in Global Performance Management—Progress or a Lost Horizon? Conference Proceedings of the VII World Congress of the International Federation of Scholarly Associations of Management, Berlin; G. Jones. (2007). *Organization Theory, Design and Change* (5th ed.), Chapters 4 and 5. Upper Saddle River, NJ: Pearson/Prentice-Hall; R. Marschan, D. Welch, & L. Welch. (1996). Control in Less-Hierarchical Multinationals: The Role of Personal Networks and Informal Communication. *International Business Review, 5*(2), 137–150.

42. For a discussion of a more complete form of control that is more appropriate for advanced multinational firms, via a more balanced combination of structural "anatomy," process "physiology," and cultural "psychology," see: C. Bartlett, S. Ghoshal, & P. Beamish. (2008). *Transnational Management: Text, Cases and Readings in Cross-Border Management* (5th ed.). Boston: McGraw-Hill/Irwin, 343–347.

43. W. Ouchi. (1981). *Theory Z*. New York: Avon Books.

44. A. Engle, M. Mendenhall, R. Powers, & Y. Stedham. (2001). Conceptualizing the Global Competence Cube: A Transnational Model of Human Resource Management. *European Journal of Industrial Training, 25*(7), 346–353.

45. C. Gomez & J. Sanchez. (2005). Human Resource Control in MNCs: A Study of the Factors Influencing the Use of Formal and Informal Control Mechanisms. *International Journal of Human Resource Management, 6*(10), 1847–1861.

46. A prescriptive approach to developing a hybrid, more balanced formal and informal strategy of control is provided by: F. Nilsson & N.-G. Olve. (2001). Control Systems in Multibusiness Companies: From Performance Management to Strategic Management. *European Management Journal, 19*(4), 344–358. An empirical assessment of 24 international manufacturing firms in the United Kingdom provided evidence of wide variance in the degree to which multinational firms provide forums for informal control processes; some respondents appeared to rely on more formal control systems: P. Kidger. (2002). Management Structures in Multinational Enterprises: Responding to Globalization. *Employee Relations, 24*(1), 69–85. For a theoretical discussion of the potential relationships between social capital, HRM, and corporate strategy, see: S.-C. Kang, S. Morris & S. Snell. (2007). Relational Archetypes, Organizational Learning, and Value Creation: Extending Human Resource Architecture. *Academy of Management Review, 32*(1), 236–256.

47. J. Nahapiet. & S. Ghoshal. (1998). Social Capital, Intellectual Capital, and the Organizational Advantage. *Academy of Management Review, 23*(2), 242–266; M. Hitt, L. Bierman, K. Uhlenbruck, & K. Shimizu. (2006). The Importance of Resources in the Internationalization of Professional Service Firms: The Good, the Bad and the Ugly. *Academy of Management Journal, 49*(6), 1137–1157.

48. D. Ravasi & M. Schultz. (2006). Responding to Organizational Identity Threats: Exploring the Role of Organizational Culture. *Academy of Management Journal, 49*(3), 433–458.

49. M. Alvesson & P. Berg. (1992). *Corporate Culture and Organizational Symbolism*. Berlin: Walter de Gruyter.

50. A. Engle & M. Mendenhall. (2004). Transnational Roles, Transnational Rewards: Global Integration in Compensation. *Employee Relations, 26*(6), 613–625; D. Welch & L. Welch. (2006). Commitment for Hire? The Viability of Corporate Culture as a MNC Control Mechanism. *International Business Review, 15*(1), 14–28.

51. P. J. Dowling. (1989. Hot Issues Overseas. *Personnel Administrator, 34*(1), 66–72.

52. K. Monks. (1996). Global or Local? HRM in the Multinational Company: The Irish Experience. *International Journal of Human Resource Management, 7*(3), 721–735.

Chapter 3

The Context of Cross-Border Alliances and SMEs

Chapter Learning Objectives

After reading this chapter, you should be able to:

- define cross-border mergers and acquisitions (M&As),[1] the different stages of formation, and phase-specific strategic HR requirements
- describe the formation process of international joint ventures (IJVs) and identify HR measures and roles relevant in the development of such cross-border alliances
- discuss the internationalization of small and medium-sized enterprises (SMEs)[2] and their approaches to international human resource management

Throughout the past decade, international business newspapers and journals have been full of articles about national and cross-border merger and acquisition bids and announcements. A look at the *Financial Times* (FT) on any given day gives you a marché-like feeling. Take the FT's Companies/International section of, for example, July 31, 2007; about half of all of the articles cover multimillion-dollar (or multibillion-dollar) actual or potential national mergers and international mergers:

> "Chinese carmakers moot merger"—discussing Shanghai Automotive Industrial Corporation and its memorandum of understanding with Nanjing Automobile and a possible merger of the two car manufacturer rivals.

> "Bancroft split casts doubt over Dow Jones"—discussing the potential sale of Dow Jones, owner of *The Wall Street Journal*, to Rupert Murdoch's News Corporation.

> "Fiat makes offer for its stricken parts supplier TK Aluminum"—discussing Fiat's offer to buy TK Aluminum.

> "Gosh remains interested in alliance with US carmaker"—discussing future alliances between the French-Japanese partners Renault/Nissan and any of the big three U.S. carmakers.

These headlines show the dynamics of globalization and the level of internationalization through M&As. At the same time, the news highlights a strong M&A trend in industries such as car manufacturing and natural resources industries—both sectors in which many Canadian companies have historically been strongly involved (e.g., Ontario's auto and mining industries). Some commentators view this involvement and Canada's role in international M&As as that of the prey rather than a hunter—as foreign investors snap up Canadian companies in record numbers* (e.g., the Alcan takeover by Rio Tinto and Western Oil Sands by Marathon).

At the same time, some Canadian companies have been very proactive in international M&A activities (e.g., the Toronto Stock Exchange-listed multinational enterprise Thomson Corp. acquisition of Reuters Group PLC.) The positive and significant returns to shareholders in mergers with Canadian participation** might be an incentive for more

Canadian businesses to follow Thomson Corp. onto the international stage through foreign mergers and acquisitions.

Sources: *Belcourt, M., & McBey, K. (2007). *Strategic Human Resources Planning*. Toronto: Thomson Nelson, 322. **Yce, A., & A. Ng. (2005). Effects of private and public Canadian mergers. *Canadian Journal of Administrative Sciences, 22*(2), 111–124.

Introduction

Chapters 2 and 3 complement each other and are designed to deliver insights into the most important organizational contexts of international human resource management. While in the last chapter we outlined how the international growth of MNEs places demands on management, in this chapter, the IHRM implications of other modes of international operations become our centre of interest. Consequently, we move from an internal perspective on structure, control mechanisms, and managerial responses to a global perspective that includes external partners.

This chapter discusses the role of HRM and the challenges it faces in international mergers and acquisitions. Our particular attention will be the role of small and medium-sized businesses in such cross-border activities and their approaches to international HRM.

Cross-Border Alliances

The strategic importance of alliances has increased in the course of globalization.[3] **Cross-border alliances** are cooperative agreements between two or more firms from different national backgrounds, which are intended to benefit all partners. As depicted in Figure 3.1, these comprise equity as well a non-equity arrangements.[4]

- A **non-equity cross-border alliance** "is an investment vehicle in which profits and other responsibilities are assigned to each party according to a contract. Each party cooperates as a separate legal entity and bears its own liabilities."[5] Examples include international technology alliances or strategic R&D alliances,[6] as well as cooperative agreements in different functional areas such as marketing or production.[7]
- **Equity modes** involve a "foreign direct investor's purchase of shares of an enterprise in a country other than its own."[8] These include the establishment of subsidiaries as mentioned in Chapter 2, either through Greenfield investments or acquisitions, as well as through joint ventures or mergers. The latter typically involve long-term collaborative strategies, which require the support of appropriate HR practices.[9] They represent typical cross-border equity-based alliances.

cross-border alliances

cooperative agreements between two or more firms from different national backgrounds

non-equity cross-border alliance

investment vehicle in which profits and other responsibilities are assigned to each party

equity modes

foreign direct investor's purchase of shares of an enterprise in a country other than its own

FIGURE 3.1

Equity and Non-Equity Modes of Foreign Operation

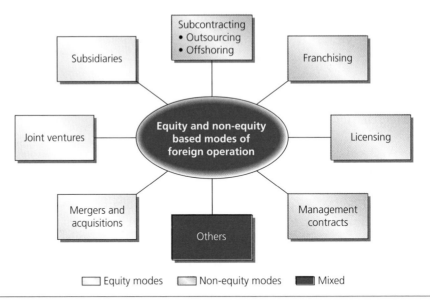

Source: Adapted from: Kutschker, M., & Schmid, S. (2004). *Internationales Management*. Munich and Vienna: R. Oldenbourg, 821.

Equity as well as non-equity cross-border alliances pose specific challenges to international human resource management. Often, these are crucial to the success of the international operation. As Schuler and Tarique note, "Some of the HR issues that are critical to the success of equity-based international or cross-border alliances may also arise in non-equity cross-border alliances, but they are often less central to the success of the alliance."[10] Hence, the difference in HRM in equity and non-equity cross-border alliances is supposed to lie in the differing extent to which specific HR measures are used.[11] However, it has to be stated that there is a research deficit with respect to HRM in non-equity cross-border alliances[12] and it is beyond the scope of this chapter to discuss implications of all foreign entry modes in detail.[13]

Cross-Border Mergers and Acquisitions

merger

result of an agreement between two companies to join their operations together

acquisition

one company buys another company intending to control the activities of the combined operations

A **merger** is the result of an agreement between two companies to join their operations together. Partners are often equals. For example, the Daimler-Chrysler merger was supposed to be a merger between equals in its first stage.[14] More information about this merger can be found in the case at the end of this chapter: "HR in the DaimlerChrysler Merger."

An **acquisition**, on the other hand, occurs when one company buys another company with the intention of controlling the activities of the combined operations.[15] This was the case when the Dutch steel company Mittal, ranked second by volume in crude steel production in 2005, initiated a hostile takeover of the Luxembourg-based Arcelor group, ranked first in the same statistic.[16]

Figure 3.2 shows that a merger usually results in the formation of a new company, while an acquisition involves the acquiring firm keeping its legal identity and integrating a new company into its own activities. The HR challenge in both cases consists of creating new HR practices and strategies that meet the requirements of the M&A.

Our focus in this book will be on cross-border mergers and acquisitions (M&As). This means that firms with headquarters located in two different countries are concerned. Many of the HRM challenges faced in mergers and in acquisitions are similar, and for this reason we will not further differentiate between these two entities. The United Nations Conference on Trade and Development (UNCTAD) defines **cross-border M&As** as follows:[17]

> Cross-border M&As involve partial or full takeover or the merging of capital, assets and liabilities of existing enterprises in a country by TNCs [transnational corporations] from other countries. M&As generally involve the purchase of existing assets and companies.

Cross-border M&As have seen tremendous growth over the last two decades, in part because of the phenomenon of globalization. "Both the value and number of cross-border M&As rose in 2005 to $716 billion (an 88% increase) and to 6,134 (a 20% increase), respectively."[18] This is depicted in Figure 3.3.

A report analyzing cross-border acquisitions from a Canadian perspective[19] concluded that, between 1997 and 2002, Canadian firms acquired 447 foreign companies worth $124 billion, while foreign companies acquired 345 Canadian companies worth $144 billion. The key players in Canadian

Ⓡ Ⓟ Ⓒ 3.1

cross-border M&A

merging or takeover of an enterprise in one country by TNCs from another country

FIGURE 3.2

The Formation Processes of M&As and HR Challenges

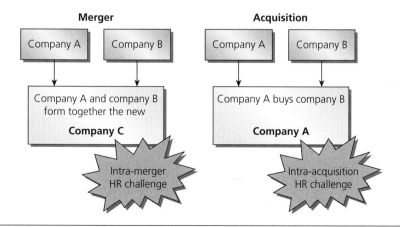

FIGURE 3.3

Mergers and Acquisitions in US$ Billions

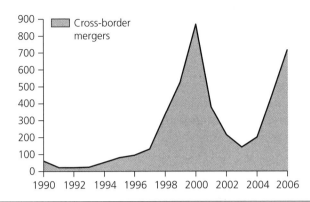

Source: UNCTAD. (2006). World Investment Report, 2006. *FDI from Developing and Transition Economies: Implications for Development.* New York and Geneva: United Nations.

outward and inward transactions were the United States and Europe, with the highest number of activities reported in the energy and minerals sector. The latest figures from the World Investment Report 2006 show that in 2005 Canadian inward cross-border mergers and acquisitions were worth $27,014 million, while at the same time, Canadian companies spent $2,505 million on outward mergers and acquistions.[20] The latest example of a potential international M&A with Canadian participation is described in IHRM Today 3.1.

W W W 3.1

One major reason to engage in mergers or acquisitions is often to facilitate the rapid entry into new markets.[21] Thus, "mergers and acquisitions are

IHRM Today 3.1

Thomson Merger with Reuters

Reuters Group PLC agreed in May 2007 to Thomson Corporation's offer for a merger worth US$17.7 billion—a partnership that could create one of the world's largest financial news providers. The legal complexity and some of the HR implications of such transactions are highlighted in the *Financial Times'* merger update on July 27, 2007:

> Thomson Corporation is hoping to secure regulatory clearance for its . . . [$17.7 billion] offer for Reuters by the first quarter of next year, the Canadian business information group said yesterday. . . . Dick Harrington, who will step down as chief executive when the Reuters acquisition completes, said reviews by the US

Department of Justice, the European Commission and the Canadian Competition Bureau would complete "hopefully in the first quarter and maybe sooner if we get a little bit lucky.". . . Mr Harrington said the company had spent about $2m in retention bonuses and was confident that "all our senior people at Thomson Financial are on board and driving the business hard."

Source: Edgecliffe-Johnson, A. (2007, July 27). Thomson hopeful on Reuters deal. *Financial Times*, "Companies/The Americas," 18.

a predominant feature of the international business system as companies attempt to strengthen their market positions and exploit new market opportunities."[22] Some of the factors that a firm takes into consideration when deciding on a target country include the growth aspiration of the acquiring company, risk diversification, technological advantages, a response to government policies in a particular country (see IHRM Today 3.2), exchange rate advantages, favourable political and economic conditions, or an effort to follow clients.[23]

WWW 3.2

A current example of such a target country is Canada, according to *The Economist*—as can be seen in IHRM Today 3.3—and in IHRM Today 3.4, we provide an example of a country that would like to be a target country.

Despite the high yearly growth rates in the area of M&As there seems to be a gap between the expected added value and the benefits realized from an M&A.[24] However, there is growing appreciation that the way the M&A is managed during the different phases (especially in the post-merger integration phase) has an impact on its performance, and in turn on the added value created.[25] M&A management has been investigated from many different perspectives. The work of Larsson and Finkelstein[26] provides an excellent overview of M&As from different research fields, including strategic management, economics, finance, organizational theory, and human resource management.[27] Of course, all sources of research are important when explaining the phenomenon of M&A success.

For the purposes of this chapter, we are going to focus solely on HR and its role in employee relations. The quality of employee relations, ranging from employee support to employee resistance, is influenced by variables such as the similarity between the management styles of the two organizations,[28] the type of cross-border combinations, the combination potential in terms of efficiency gains, or the extent of organizational integration.

IHRM Today 3.2

A Review of Canada's Merger Policies

Initiated by the Canadian government and led by Red Wilson, chairman of Montreal-based Canadian Aviation Electronics, an independent panel is reviewing Canada's competition and investment policies:

> The panel's findings are widely expected to lead to a significant relaxation of foreign ownership and competition rules in the telecommunications industry. The group is also likely to address concerns about the "hollowing-out" of corporate Canada as a result of a series of foreign takeovers of some of the most prominent

companies. The government said that the panel would examine possible reciprocity between Canada's competition and investment regimes and those in other countries, and consider tightening foreign investment rules on national security grounds. Jim Flaherty, the finance minister, said that "we must ensure our competition framework is modern and flexible."

Source: Simon, B. (2007, July 12). Canada to review mergers policy. *Financial Times*.

IHRM Today 3.3

Shopping in Canada

"Consumer spending remains strong, with house prices shattering all records in May. Unemployment at 6.1% is at a 33-year low. Even the beleaguered manufacturing industry, battered by a high dollar and competition with China, has staged a rebound. The economy is 'worrisomely good,'" says Philip Cross, chief economic analyst at Statistics Canada, the national statistical agency.

Foreign investors appear to share that opinion and are snapping up Canadian companies in record numbers. This has prompted a debate about whether corporate Canada is being "hollowed out." Many wonder whether Canada's corporate bosses are sufficiently aggressive. But even this debate is taken as a sign of economic strength: only good times allow the luxury of navel gazing.

Source: Time to put a tiger in his tank. (2007, June 23). *The Economist*, 56.

IHRM Today 3.4

Gaiatsu Wanted

In contrast to Canada (see IHRM Today 3.2 and 3.3) Japan is struggling to attract foreign investors. Currently, Japan's inward foreign direct investment amounts to only 2.4 percent of its national output. Reasons include low consumer spending, declining wages and prices, a shrinking population, lack of local managerial talents, and low productivity—a situation that does not attract many foreign investors to Japan.

In response, Japan has changed its commercial code, inviting foreign companies and investors to buy Japanese businesses. Japan hopes that this gaiatsu, or "foreign pressure," will help to re-form and restore Japanese businesses and introduce new competition—as was the case, for example, with Renault's takeover of Nissan. With the acquisition of Japanese businesses by foreign investors Japan expects to receive new ideas and approaches to change its old industry structures and business models.

Source: Gaijin at the gates. (2007, August 18). *The Economist*, 49–50.

RPC 3.2

There is evidence that employee resistance endangers M&A performance, as it may hinder synergy realization.[29] For this reason, it is important that all M&As effectively manage issues where employee resistance is encountered, so that employee support can evolve. This is a process in which the HRM function can play a major role.

RPC 3.3

A study by Birkinshaw et al.[30] found that the integration of tasks[31] between two companies is interdependent with human integration. The dimensions of human integration in this study included visibility and continuity of leadership, communication processes during integration, integrating mechanisms used, acquired personnel retained, and voluntary personnel loss.

Task and human integration interact in different phases to foster value creation in acquisitions:

> In phase one, task integration led to a satisfying solution that limited the interaction between acquired and acquiring units, while human integration proceeded smoothly and led to cultural convergence and mutual respect. In phase two, there was renewed task integration built on the success of the human integration that has been achieved, which led to much greater interdependencies between acquired and acquiring units.[32]

Figure 3.4 summarizes the impact of human integration and task integration on acquisition outcome.

Birkinshaw et al. conclude that the human integration process is especially difficult to manage and takes time. Complexity and the length of the integration process increase even more in the case of cross-border alliances.[33] One reason for this is that both of the firms undergoing acquisition processes are embedded in their own national, institutional, and cultural settings.[34] Typical problems that arise in cross-border M&As involve the following:

- Within the first year of a merger, it is not uncommon for a company's top-management level to lose up to 20 percent of its executives. Over a longer time frame, this percentage tends to increase even further.[35]

FIGURE 3.4

Impact of Human and Task Integration on Acquisition Outcome

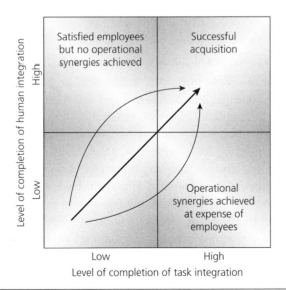

Source: Birkinshaw, J., Bresman, H., & Hakanson, L. (2000). Managing the post-acquisition integration process: How the human interaction and task integration processes interact to foster value creation. *Journal of Management Studies, 37*(3), 395–425.

- Personnel issues are often neglected.[36]
- Finally, a high number of M&As fail or do not produce the intended results.[37]

When a firm is acquired by another firm, so is its existing workforce. Considering this fact, we will describe the typical phases characterizing cross-border M&A processes and outline which HR practices are important at each of the different stages. At this point, it must be admitted that the extent to which these HR practices are carried out very much depends on the extent to which integration of the two companies is actually aspired. In the case of low integration (e.g., if the M&A is carried out mainly for portfolio reasons), both companies remain separate cultures. However, in the case of high integration, it is crucial for the M&A to meet the HR requirements of the different phases, which will be outlined in the next section.[38]

M&A Phases and HR Implications

Typically, mergers and acquisitions are characterized by different phases. Depending on the publication, these phases will have different names. However, the M&A process usually consists of the following steps:

1. A *pre-M&A phase* including a screening of alternative partners based on an analysis of their strengths and weaknesses.
2. A *due diligence* phase[39] that focuses more in depth on analyzing the potential benefits of the merger. Here, product–market combinations, tax regulations, and also compatibility with respect to HR and cultural issues are of interest.[40]
3. In the *integration planning phase*, which is based on the results of the due diligence phase, planning for the new company is carried out.
4. In the *implementation phase*, plans are put into action.

Various studies have shown that the HR department becomes increasingly involved in the phases of M&A integration as the process evolves. For example, a study conducted in Germany of 68 M&As revealed that HR issues are only seriously considered once the integration strategy has actually been defined.[41] Schmidt refers to a study of 447 senior HR executives who represented mainly large companies with more than 1,000 employees. Most participants were from North America, supplemented by representatives of companies in Europe, Latin America, and Asia. He found that those companies that involved the HR department early in the process were more successful than others with a low HR involvement.[42] Both studies showed that the strongest involvement of the HR department took place in the last two phases of the M&A process. From this study, Schmidt has derived best practices, which should be considered in the different M&A process phases. They are complemented by culture-specific aspects, which are of special importance in cross-border M&As (see IHRM Notebook 3.1).

HR Activities in the Phases of a Cross-Border M&A

Pre-M&A phase
- Identification of people-related issues
- Planning for due diligence
- Assessing people
- Working out the organizational/cultural fit
- Forming the M&A steering team
- Educating the team on the HR implications

Due diligence phase
Estimating people-related
- Transactional costs
- Ongoing costs
- Savings
- Identifying and assessing cultural issues

Integration planning phase
- Developing employee culture-sensitive communication strategies
- Designing key talent retention programs
- Planning and leading integration efforts
- Developing a new strategy for the new entity
- Helping the organization cope with change
- Defining an organizational blueprint and staffing plan

Implementation and assessment phase
- Managing ongoing change, especially cultural change
- Managing employee communications
- Advising management on dealing with people issues
- Aligning HR policies, especially total rewards
- Monitoring the process of organizational and people-related integration activities
- Ensuring the capture of synergies via incentives
- Initiating learning processes for future M&As

Source: Adapted from: Schmidt, J. A. (2001). The Correct Spelling of M&A Begins with HR. *HR Magazine*, 102–108.

Strategic HRM and the Role of the HR Function in M&As

Aguilera and Dencker[43] suggest a strategic approach to HR management in M&A processes. Based on strategic HRM literature suggesting a fit between business strategy and HR strategy, they argue that firms should match their M&A strategy with their HR strategy while relying on three conceptual tools:

> Resources are defined as tangible assets such as money and people, and intangible assets, such as brands and relationships. In the context of HRM in M&As, decisions about resources involve staffing and retention issues, with termination decisions being particularly important. Processes refer to activities that firms use to convert the resources into valuable goods and services. For example, in our case, these would be training and development programs as well as appraisal and reward systems. Finally, values are the way in which employees think about what they do and why they do it. Values shape employee's priorities and decision making.[44]

These ideas deliver starting points for developing HR strategies for the newly created entity. Hence, they give hints on how to meet the intra-merger or intra-acquisition HR challenges outlined in Figure 3.1. Taking such a strategic

 3.6

approach and aligning the HRM activities with the M&A strategy with respect to resources, processes, and values is also a challenging task for the HR manager to perform: The HR manager must develop a set of integrated HR activities that are not only in line with the business strategy but with the M&A strategy as well.[45] Based on the well-known work of Ulrich (1997),[46] the HR function can take the role of strategic partner (i.e., management of strategic human resources), an administrative expert (i.e., management of the firm's infrastructure), an employee champion (i.e., management of the employee contribution), or a change agent (i.e., management of transformation and change). In each phase of the M&A process, each role involves different activities.

The Role of Expatriates in M&As

The role of expatriates has been discussed with respect to knowledge transfer between the acquiring and the acquired company. However, the transfer of embedded knowledge is not guaranteed by each international assignment. While some studies have revealed the importance of prior working experience with a specific host country or with a particular entry mode as a success factor for expatriates involved in the integration of mergers,[47] this has not been confirmed for acquisitions. In a study by Hébert et al., prior experience did not have an impact on the performance of the acquired firm.[48]

In contrast to these findings, the above-mentioned study on M&As in Germany revealed that successful integration is dependent on managers' industry experience, experience with similar projects, and particularly in the case of cross-border alliances, level of intercultural competence.[49] An emphasis on industry experience is in line with the suggestion by Hébert et al., who state that industry experience is an important asset when staffing an acquired subsidiary with an expatriate because it can lead to a transfer of best practices.[50]

These arguments have implications for the staffing of the post-merger integration team. Hébert et al.[51] suggest that acquiring companies should not completely rely on the placement of expatriates within the top-management team of an acquired subsidiary. They suggest creating a strong team including a mix of both—expatriates and local members of top management—and that the acquisition integration be viewed as a learning process. A study by Villinger (1996) of 35 acquisitions by western MNEs in Hungary, the Czech Republic, Slovakia, and Poland on post-acquisition managerial learning[52] highlights the importance of appropriate cross-border management skills. The author emphasizes that local language skills as well as sensitivity toward cultural differences are crucial for M&A success. It is especially important to note this when companies from developing countries represent the acquired firm in the M&A process. As Villinger[53] notes:

> Interestingly, although language and communication problems are clearly pointed out as the key barrier to successful learning from both sides, there seems to be a consensus that the command of the partner's language is mainly a requirement for eastern

RPC 3.7

managers, and significantly less so for western partners. This may be surprising, as it can lead to a situation in which a hundred eastern European managers have to learn German, instead of a small number of German expatriates learning the local language. However, it may be argued that the language chosen for (future) communications will depend on the expected direction of "the flow of learning" between the two partners.

A Comparative Approach to HRM in M&A Processes

While it seems possible to identify the typical phases of M&A processes across nationalities and industries, the content of the HR measures appears to depend much on the nationality and culture of the companies involved in the M&A. Based on an analysis of two surveys of HRM practices in Canada and 12 other countries, Sparrow and Budhwar[54] develop a nine-factor empirical framework to compare the national HRM patterns across

IHRM Notebook 3.2

Canada's HRM Pattern

Based on their empirical findings, Sparrow and Budhwar developed nine factors that "seem to follow a clear logic and . . . should therefore be seen as representing underlying 'HRM recipes' to which the personnel managers from around the world sign up or not." In the first table below, Sparrow and Budhwar position Canada and the other 12 countries in the first five dimensions by categorizing the countries' scores for each factor into high and low.

	Structural Empowerment		Accelerated Resource Development		Employee Welfare Emphasis		Efficiency Orientation		Long Termism	
	High	Low	High	Low	High	Low	High	Low	High	Low
U.S.	X			X	X		X			X
Canada	X			X	X			X		X
U.K.	X			X		X		X		X
Italy		X		X		X		X		X
Japan		X		X	X		X		X	
India		X		X	X			X	X	
Australia	X		X			X	X		X	
Brazil	X		X		X			X	X	
Mexico	X		X		X			X		X
Argentina		X	X		X			X		X
Germany		X	X			X		X	X	
Korea		X	X			X	X		X	
France		X	X			X	X			X

(continued)

Canada's HRM Pattern (continued)

Sparrow and Budhwar's first five factors and their HRM patterns are presented in the following table.

Factor	HRM Pattern
Structural Empowerment	Importance is attached to increasing spans of control to promote de-layering, eradicating specialized and directed workforces, introducing flexible cross-functional teams, analyzing individual performance, rewarding employees for business productivity gains and customer service . . . promoting employee empowerment and involvement through ownership and participation, and sharing the benefits, risks and costs of organizational change.
Accelerated Resource Development	Importance is attached to the early identification of high-potential employees, establishment of multiple and parallel career paths, rewarding employees for enhancing skills and knowledge, and providing continuous training and development and basic education.
Employee Welfare Emphasis	Importance on offering personal family assistance, ensuring employees pursue good health aggressively, encouraging and rewarding external volunteer activities, and matching employee demands for flexible retirement, [promoting] a culture that empathizes equality, . . . [providing] more open access to information systems.
Efficiency Orientation	High reliance on the use of quality university hiring programs to resource the organization with an elite deemed capable of self-monitoring, . . . utilizing a non-permanent workforce who are provided with flexible benefits but inflexible retirement opportunities. Diversity is an issue and is managed through tailored programs.
Long Termism	Importance of providing full-time employment, rewarding long-term performance criteria such as innovation and creativity (rather than productivity), avoiding the use of a non-permanent workforce, providing basic education and training and open access to information systems.

Sources: Adapted from: Sparrow, P., & Budhwar, P. (1997). Competition and change: Mapping the Indian HRM recipe against world-wide patterns. *Journal of World Business, 32*(3), 230, 233.

these countries. While in IHRM Notebook 3.2 we can observe some similarities and clusters of HR profiles among Latin countries and Anglo-Saxon countries, overall the 13 countries covered "are pursuing distinctive 'HRM recipes,'" according to Sparrow and Budhwar.

In another study, Child et al.[55] highlight the following HRM policy characteristics for the different countries of their investigation (the United States, Japan, Germany, France, and the United Kingdom):

- Performance-related pay is more popular in the United States than in Japan or Germany.
- Recruitment in the United States tends to be rather short term, as compared to Germany, France, and the United Kingdom. While in

Japan the lifetime orientation is less than before, there is still a longer-term focus than in the other countries.

- Training and career planning is most extensive in the United States.

Despite the fact that there are signs of convergence in HR practices across countries due to the increasing globalization of markets, companies' cultural and institutional differences and the resulting impact on HR still seem to be important.[56] This seems to also hold true when M&A processes are concerned and especially in the post-integration phase. Child et al.[57] summarize the results of their case study research as follows:

- Convergence across nationalities in HRM policies was evident in post-acquisition moves toward performance-related pay, training, and team-based product development.
- Most acquirers also made adjustments to suit the local culture.
- American HRM reflected a short-term, individualistic national business culture.
- Japanese HRM, although adopting some American methods, generally reflected long-term, consensual, team-based, collectivist national philosophies.
- French companies have also been influenced by international HRM best practice but still tend to display an ethnocentric approach that gives precedence to managers of French origin.
- German companies were the most anxious to adopt international practices in their acquisitions, even when these conflicted with their national tendencies. For example, they force themselves to be more informal.

IHRM Notebook 3.3 summarizes more details on the post-acquisition trends in HRM practices identified in the United States, Japan, France, Germany, and the United Kingdom.

International Equity Joint Ventures

International joint ventures (IJVs), the second type of equity-based, cross-border alliance to be discussed in this chapter, have also experienced tremendous growth during the last two decades. They will continue to represent a major means of global expansion for MNEs[58] In emerging economies such as China, they represent the dominating operational mode for MNEs' market entry (see IHRM Today 3.5).[59] According to a well-known definition by Shenkar and Zeira,[60] an IJV is:

> A separate legal organizational entity representing the partial holdings of two or more parent firms, in which the headquarters of at least one is located outside the country of operation of the joint venture. This entity is subject to the joint control of its parent firms, each of which is economically and legally independent of the other.

An IJV can have two or more parent companies. Many IJVs, however, involve two parent companies. This is why we concentrate on this constellation in the following. As will be outlined later, problems will become even

international joint venture
legal entity representing holdings of parent firms located outside the country of operation

Post-Acquisition Trends in HRM Practices

	USA	Japan	Germany	France	UK
Pay	PRP*	PRP growing	PRP growing	PRP growing	PRP growing
Recruitment	Short term	Lifetime	Long term	French, long term; local, less so	Less short term than USA
Training	High; on course	On the job	Technical bias	To a ceiling	Increased; courses
Career Planning	Little	Steady and slow	Ad hoc	Highly structured	Very variable
Product development	Team-based	Team-based	Team-based		Not very team-based
Culture	Top-down	Bottom-up; consensual	Top-down	Top-down	Top-down
Appraisal	Regular and formal	Subtle, not transparent	Growing	Growing	Regular annual
Promotion	Fast and performance-based	Slow and seniority-based	Based on technical expertise	Emphasis on formal qualification; fast	Variable
Communications	Formal, need-to-know approach	Open when asked	Open and informal	Open and formal	Need-to-know approach

*Performance-related pay

Source: Child, J., Faulkner, D., & Pitkethly, R. (2001). *The management of international acquisitions*. Oxford, UK: Oxford University Press, 172.

PKF International and the Chinese Market

Eric Trait, the international director for PKF International, sees "a continuing long-term development and growth strategy in China." He believes that PKF's approach to development in the region differs from its larger competitors. "Unlike the Big Four who can afford to pump expatriate resources in and so on, we have to be more circumspect financially," Tait says. This approach has its benefits, he argues, as he sees the country as a place where people "like to get to know you over time and develop a business."

In a move that helps to assist this demand, staff members from other PKF members' firms, such as those in London and Sydney, are currently being seconded to the region. Tait says there is a widespread interest from advisers in these firms to gain this experience, but finding people with both the language skills and technical knowledge is difficult.

Source: Woods, C. *Profile–PKF International: A cautious approach to commerce*. Retrieved July 27, 2007, from www.worldaccounting intelligence.com

more complex with more than two partners. The equity division between the parent companies of the joint venture may differ. In some cases, the ratio is 50:50; in others, the dominance of one partner becomes more obvious, with a ratio of 51:49 or through various other combinations. This, of course, has implications for the control of the IJV, an issue that will be discussed later in this chapter. Figure 3.5 depicts the formation of an IJV.

In contrast to M&As, the parent companies of an IJV keep their legal identity, and an additional new legal entity representing the IJV is established. Figure 3.5 also indicates the level of complexity that an IJV represents for the human resource management function. For this reason, IJVs clearly represent an important field of research for IHRM scholars.[61] The topics of research on IHRM in IJVs are very similar to those in M&As. In both cases, partners with different institutional, cultural, and national backgrounds come together and must balance their interests. However, in IJVs, this challenge includes the following factors:

- On the one hand, HR must manage relationships at the interfaces between the IJV and the parent companies. The different partners that make up the IJV may possibly follow different sets of rules, and this can lead to critical dualities[62] within the HR function.
- On the other hand, the HR department must develop appropriate HRM practices and strategies for the IJV entity itself. HR has to recruit, develop, motivate, and retain human resources at the IJV level.

For the sake of the IJV's performance, these two challenges have to be taken into consideration during the different phases of establishing and managing the joint venture.[63] These will be described later in this chapter.

According to a literature analysis by Schuler, the main reasons for engaging in an IJV are to:[64]

FIGURE 3.5

Formation of an International Equity Joint Venture

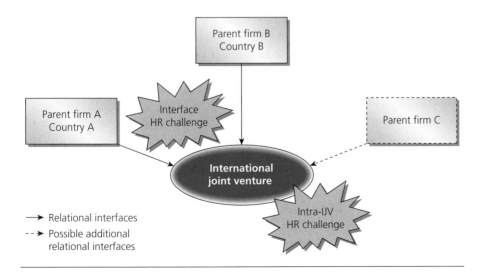

- Gain knowledge and transfer that knowledge.
- Comply with the requirements of the host government.
- Facilitate increased economies of scale.
- Gain local knowledge.
- Obtain vital raw materials.
- Spread the risks (e.g., share financial risks).
- Improve competitive advantage in the face of increasing global competition.
- Provide a cost-effective and efficient response forced by the globalization of markets.

Special emphasis should be given to the knowledge transfer or learning objective.[65] IJVs provide an excellent opportunity to learn from another company in two ways. First, each company has the chance to "learn the other partner's skills." This can include gaining know-how and process knowledge in specific functional areas such as R&D or acquiring local knowledge about a specific market or culture. Second, companies acquire working experience in cooperating with other firms. Thus, the IJV can be used as a medium for organizational learning processes as well.[66]

Unfortunately, there is evidence that many IJVs fail[67] or do not produce the expected results.[68] Major reasons for these failures can be traced back to the lack of interest in the human resource management and cross-cultural management aspects of international joint ventures.[69] These two issues will be addressed in the following sections.

IJV Development Stages and HRM Implications

Similar to the M&A processes discussed earlier, the development of IJVs can also be described in development stages. Schuler distinguishes four stages: (1) the formation, in which the partnership between the parent companies is the centre of interest; (2) the development of the joint venture itself; (3) the implementation of the joint venture; and (4) the advancement of the activities.[70] IHRM Notebook 3.4 summarizes the characteristic features of the different IJV stages and respective HR implications. It is important to remember that the different stages of development are not independent from each other. Activities in the first stage have an impact on activities in the second stage and so on. Furthermore, complexity can increase depending on the number of parent companies[71] and countries involved in the joint venture.[72]

The stages model shows that compatibility between the IJV partners is most important when it comes to mutual learning opportunities between the parent companies and the joint venture. This aspect should be focused on from the beginning of a joint venture formation process. As all learning processes include communication processes and are carried out by people, the management of the human resources at this point is critical. This encompasses all activities of the HR function including recruitment, selection, training and development, performance management, and compensation. A strategic approach requires not only a strong compatibility of the various HR activities and practices, but also strong compatibility with the IJV strategy.[73]

IJV Development Stages and HR Implications

IJV Development Stages	HR Implications
Stage 1: Formation	
• Identifying reasons • Planning for utilization • Selecting dedicated manager • Finding potential partners • Selecting likely partners • Resolving critical issues • Negotiating the arrangement	• The more important learning is, the greater the role for HRM • Knowledge needs to be managed • Systematic partner selection is essential • Be thorough for compatibility • Ensure extensive communications and use skilled negotiators • Develop integrative strategies for learning
Stage 2: Development	
• Locating the IJV • Establishing the right structure • Getting the right senior managers	• Concerns of multiple sets of stakeholders need to be considered for long-term viability and acceptance • The structure will impact on the learning and knowledge management processes • Recruiting, selecting and managing senior staff are critical
Stage 3: Implementation	
• Establishing the vision, mission, values, strategy and structure • The people sharing this and learning from each other will provide direction to the IJV	• Need to design policies and practices with local–global considerations • Developing HR policies and practices • Staffing and managing the employees
Stage 4: Advancement and beyond	
• Learning from the partner • Transferring new knowledge to the parents • Transferring new knowledge to other locations	• Partners need learning capacity • HR systems need to be established to support knowledge flow to the parent

Adapted from: Schuler, R. S. (2001). Human Resource Issues and Activities in International Joint Ventures. *International Journal of Human Resource Management, 12*(1), 1–52.

Within the different stages of IJV formation, the HR manager may take on many roles in order to meet the challenges of interaction between the parent company and the IJV:

- In the *partnership role*, HR managers should take all stakeholders' needs into account (including those of the counterparts in the other parent firm[s] and in the IJV) and demonstrate a thorough understanding of the business and the market.
- As a *change facilitator and strategy implementer*, HR managers should be able to conceptualize and implement new strategies involving trust-based communication and cooperation with relevant partners. This also requires the creation of a stable learning environment.

- As an *innovator*, the HR manager should be able to identify talent for executing IJV strategies and adapting to changes in the IJV stages.
- As a *collaborator*, the HR manager's strengths should lie in creating win–win situations characterized by sharing rather than competing between the different entities engaged in the joint venture.[74]

Of course, the HR roles are not exclusive. For the success of the IJV, it is most important that the HR manager be able to combine aspects of all roles.

The Importance of Cross-Cultural Management in International Joint Ventures

As outlined in the earlier section on the comparative approach of HR in M&As, the national, institutional, and cultural environments of a firm do indeed matter. Here, we will focus on cultural issues that play an important role in IJVs.[75] This information on comparative HRM as well as on cross-cultural HRM is relevant to both M&As and IJVs. In many studies, the implications of different cultural employee backgrounds coming together in an IJV have been in the centre of interest. In the most recent studies, there is an especially strong focus on China.[76] Such a case is described in IHRM Today 3.6, which addresses the HR-related challenges of two different institutional and cultural environments working together in a common venture. This example illustrates how cultural differences matter in collaboration, decision making, and loyalty in the Chinese–German joint venture: the Beijing Lufthansa Centre Co. Ltd. For a discussion and interpretation of the cultural differences involved in such a venture, refer to Chapter 9, where the host-country context is discussed more extensively.

IHRM Today 3.6

Chinese–German Joint Venture: Beijing Lufthansa Centre Co. Ltd.

The Joint Venture

When in 1978 the People's Republic of China opened its frontiers for foreign investors, the need for modern hotels, apartments, and office space that could meet Western requirements became obvious, Deutsche Lufthansa AG and the government of the city of Beijing decided to cooperate in the establishment of a multifunctional service centre. This was supposed to provide a logistical basis for international business travellers for whom China was an unknown territory at that time. The joint venture contract was signed in 1986, and in May 1992, the Beijing Lufthansa Centre Co. Ltd. was opened as one of the largest Chinese-German ventures.

Requirements for the Selection of the Management Team

According to the legal requirements of joint ventures in China, the management team of a joint venture is composed with *equal representation* of both parties. For the selection of the German members, their *technical abilities and industry* as well as *management know-how* were of major importance to ensure acceptance by their Chinese counterparts. Furthermore, an *understanding of Chinese culture*, combined with the ability to accept and cope with decision-making structures and the lifestyle of the foreign country were important in creating an environment of cooperation and learning. Learning opportunities were a major motive in the Chinese decision to work in a joint venture.

Another important aspect was *language*. As many of the older Chinese were not able to speak English at that time, there was often a need for a translator. All documents had to be translated into either English or Chinese. For all important meetings, there were translators. German managers took into account that this was time-consuming and that not all information might have been transferred. Consequently, it would be useful for the cooperation and the atmosphere within the joint venture if the Germans also had Chinese language capabilities.

The German management team members were told that if they were able to influence the selection of their Chinese counterparts, they needed to understand that *status and important contacts, as well as informal relationships within the administration and government* played an important role in ensuring an important contribution to the joint venture's success.

Collaboration

Although all parties should have a common interest in the success of the joint venture, *different perspectives* on specific topics can lead to conflict. This can have an impact on the choice of suppliers (foreign versus Chinese, instead of quality considerations) or on the use of company cars representing important status symbols. The use of foreign consultants was favoured by the Germans for quality reasons, while the Chinese voted for local consultants for cost reasons. The same was true in discussions concerning the need of expatriates. Chinese managers tried to avoid expensive expatriates, while the German counterparts were convinced that they needed people with specific qualifications that, according to them, could be provided only by expatriates. Again, the negotiations about these issues were very time-consuming.

With respect to *decision making*, the joint venture contract stated that the general manager was responsible for daily business and that this person be supported by a Chinese deputy. These regulations ensured that the Chinese legal and cultural environment was sufficiently respected in the decision making processes. However, in practice, this meant that the general manager could not decide anything without the Chinese deputy and decision processes became slow and complicated. This led to a change in the decision-making relationship between the general manager and the deputy, which gave more power to the deputy and ensured that the general manager could make only a limited number of decisions without the deputy.

Loyalty

In many situations, strong loyalty to the parent company presented a problem because the managers did not put the common project at the centre of interest. For example, it was reported that the Chinese managers didn't want to make decisions without consulting their parent firm, which again led to very slow decision processes. Here, the high degrees of power distance and uncertainty avoidance of the Chinese partners may have influenced this behaviour. However, this approach endangers loyalty to the joint venture and such delays also discourage local employees and management from both sides. Another issue that led to difficulties involved the way in which expatriate managers viewed their jobs in the joint venture. For them, their positions were often just another step in their careers that could possibly lead to a higher position after the assignment. In this case, loyalty to the parent company was higher than loyalty to the joint venture.

Source: Based on: Probst, H. J. (1995). Human Resources in einem deutsch-chinesischen Joint Venture—Praxiserfahrungen am Beispiel der Beijing Lufthansa Center Co. Ltd.. (Human resources in a German-Chinese joint venture—Experiences from the Beijing Lufthansa Center Co. Ltd.). *Duisburg Working Papers on East Asian Economic Studies No. 22*. Germany: The University of Duisburg-Essen.

The Top-Management Team and the Role of Expatriates in IJVs

As shown in IHRM Today 3.6, the IJV's top-management team has a high impact on the performance of the joint venture. The team's main task is to control the daily business operations of the IJV. The Lufthansa case is typical when the two parent firms of an IJV share equal equity division. Usually, both have the right to be equally represented on the management team, and control of the key management positions is a critical issue when negotiating an IJV contract. Each firm tries to protect its own interests and to keep as much control as possible by staffing key positions with its own people.[77] Kabst[78] calls these IJV positions "functional gatekeepers"—they try to protect their firm's assets in specific functional areas such as R&D, production, and marketing.

Due to the fact that the parent companies compete for these few management positions, the top-management team is usually composed of individuals from different cultural contexts. As in all multicultural teams, diversity may provide opportunities, but the individuals may also have problems working together. The critical challenge for a multicultural team heading an IJV is not only that it has to deal with different cultural expectations, but that it also has to balance various management styles and strategic objectives of the different parent firms. Li et al.[79] point out that identification with both the IJV and the parent firm can lead to significant role conflicts and divided loyalty for IJV managers: Top-management team "members serving as control agents for the parent company often face the crisis of loyalty, commitment and organizational identity."[80] As in the Beijing–Lufthansa case study, an exaggerated identification with the parent firm can affect communication and decision-making processes in the multicultural team and lead to lower commitment and, consequently, to problems in decision making and unsatisfactory results. The relative status and power positions of the parent companies gain importance at the expense of the management of the IJV.[81]

To avoid intercultural conflicts, companies have started to recruit country experts from outside the company rather than repositioning internal technical experts, as the example of a Western beverage company in IHRM Today 3.7

IHRM Today 3.7

Country Expert Expatriates

The company has been investing heavily in China's growing beverage market and has set up six joint ventures with different local partners over the last five years. It has been rapidly building its China organizations by assessing managers from the headquarters to its joint ventures in China. However, due to their lack of knowledge about the local culture and market conditions, many of these managers had problems working in the local environment and left their positions in the joint ventures much earlier than at full term. In response to the high turnover rate, the company changed its recruiting strategy and began hiring expatriates who know the country well (e.g. degree holders in Chinese studies) for joint venture assignments in China. This, however, led to an unexpected problem. The "country-expert" expatriates often took the side of the local partner whenever there were conflicts between the partners, rather than taking the side of the parent as was expected. The trust and loyalty of these country-expert expatriates was now doubted by their own parent firm.

Source: Li, J., Xin, K., & Pillutla, M. (2002). Multi-cultural leadership teams and organizational identification in international joint ventures. *International Journal of Human Resource Management*, *13*, 322.

shows. To address these problems and to increase IJV performance, Li et al. suggest taking explicit measures for improving organizational identity and identification at the IJV level.[82] Starting points for this process were discussed in the analysis of the HR implications of the IJV stages in IHRM Notebook 3.4.

International SMEs

SMEs: Strategic Importance and Barriers to Internationalization[83]

The discussion about globalization and international management is very much dominated by the well-known names of MNEs from all over the world, while the role of small and medium-sized companies (SMEs) is infrequently discussed. It is important to note that there is no common worldwide accepted definition of SMEs, and criteria as well as limits differ. Most countries use headcount (number of employees), annual turnover, annual balance sheet total, or a combination of those criteria to define small and medium-sized businesses. In Canada, governmental agencies such as Statistics Canada not only use different standards to identify what is a small business and what is a medium-sized business, but also define "business" in different ways—depending on data user needs. Sources such as Statistics Canada's *Employment Dynamics*, for example, provide information about businesses that are entities with employees—excluding self-employed people who have no employees and do not draw salaries from their businesses for themselves.[84] In most cases, Canadian small businesses are defined as companies with up to 49 employees and annual total revenues between $30,000 and $5 million, while medium-sized companies have between 50 and 500 employees and annual total revenues between $5 million and $50 million.

In contrast, for example, the European Commission (EU) standards seem much more standardized and set in terms of measures for and definitions of SMEs, as Table 3.1 shows. Depending on the issue, additional qualitative criteria such as the identity of enterprise ownership and personal responsibility for the enterprise's activities should be taken into account as well.[85]

It is often forgotten that small and medium-sized companies play an important role in the world economy, as shown by the following figures:

TABLE 3.1

EU Defining Standards for SMEs			
ENTERPRISE CATEGORY	HEADCOUNT	ANNUAL TURNOVER	ANNUAL BALANCE SHEET TOTAL
Medium-sized	<250	<€50 million	<€43 million
Small	<50	<€10 million	<€10 million

Source: European Commission (Ed.). (2005). *The new SME definition: User guide and model declaration*. Brussels: European Commission, 14.

- In 2001, just 0.2 percent of Canadian firms had 500 or more employees, while around 92 percent of all Canadian companies employed fewer than 20 workers. Between 1991 and 2001, Canadian medium-sized firms experienced the strongest growth among the different business categories—a 29 percent increase.[86]
- In the European Economic Area (EEA) and Switzerland, there are more than 16 million enterprises. Less than 1 percent comprises large enterprises; the rest are SMEs. Two-thirds of all jobs in this region are in SMEs, while one-third of all jobs are provided by large enterprises.[87] In many countries, the percentage of employees working for enterprises with fewer than 20 employees amounts to more than 80 percent.[88]
- SMEs constitute the backbone of the Asia–Pacific region, accounting for 90 percent of enterprises, between 32 and 48 percent of employment, and between 80 and 60 percent of gross domestic product in individual Asia–Pacific economies.[89]
- In the United States, more than 80 percent of total employment is with organizations with fewer than 20 employees.[90]

The strong position of SMEs in their national economies is not reflected to the same extent in the international business environment.[91] When internationalizing their operations, SMEs experience different challenges than large organizations (see IHRM Notebook 3.5). They have less experience with environmental contexts in different countries, less power to withstand the demand of host governments, fewer reputation and financial resources, and fewer resources for managing international operations.[92]

In the European Union and in many countries such as Singapore, Korea, and South Africa, SME internationalization is promoted by the policies of their home countries. As the UNCTAD World Investment Report[93] suggests:

IHRM Notebook 3.5

Access barriers for SMEs

The top 10 barriers to access to international markets as identified by an OECD survey of 978 SMEs worldwide include the following:

1. Shortage of working capital to finance exports.
2. Identifying foreign business opportunities.
3. Limited information to locate/analyze markets.
4. Inability to contact potential overseas customers.
5. Obtaining reliable foreign representation.
6. Lack of managerial time to deal with internationalization.
7. Inadequate quantity of and/or untrained personnel for internationalization.
8. Difficulty in managing competitors' prices.
9. Lack of home government assistance/incentives.
10. Excessive transportation/insurance costs.

Source: Organisation for Economic Co-operation and Development (Ed.). (2006). *Removing barriers to SME access to international markets*. Geneva: OECD. Keynote paper at OECD–APEC Global Conference, Athens, Greece, November 5–8, 2006. Retrieved February 17, 2007, from www.oecd.org/dataoecd/4/16/37818320.pdf

Policymakers need to support entrepreneurship and foster the creation of start-up MNEs, especially in knowledge-based industries. In terms of enterprise development countries make up for the lack of entrepreneurial talents and start-up candidates through the promotion of new industries and the creation of "seed companies." Spinoffs from public research institutes or from leading universities may also be encouraged, backed by relevant financial institutions.

Canada provides a number of support services for business startups and cross-border business activities, as highlighted in previous chapters. One of these support services is the Canada Border Services Agency (CBSA), which was created in 2003 to manage the access of people and goods to and from Canada. The CBSA includes a Small and Medium–Sized Enterprises Centre that provides information and help for Canadian SMEs that export and import goods.

IHRM Features in SMEs

Much of our knowledge generated in the area of IHRM applies to large organizations.[94] While there is evidence that some recruitment or compensation practices are applicable to small organizations as well, the management of people in small organizations often differs from practices and strategies of established large organizations.[95] Although our understanding of IHRM in SMEs is still limited, there are some key points that we outline in this section of the chapter.

The Importance of the Founder/Owner

Internationalization process theory, which is derived from the behavioural model of uncertainty avoidance,[96] suggests that specific features of the owner or founder of an SME have an impact on the internationalization process of this particular enterprise.[97] The "experiential market knowledge" of the managers is assumed to have a direct impact on the choice of foreign markets and thus, the internationalization process of the SME. This theoretical approach predicts that managers start the internationalization process in geographically and culturally close markets and that with increasing experience they move toward more distant markets. Consequently, in a globalizing SME, the top managers responsible for internationalization decisions should have an international background to be prepared to make those decisions.

Research on global startups or *born globals*,[98] which are characterized by an important international orientation and growth from inception, have confirmed this:[99] "The founders of international new ventures are more 'alert' to the possibilities of combining resources from different national markets because of the competencies they developed from their earlier activities."[100] Manolova et al. report that person-related factors such as international experiences/skills, international orientation, environmental perceptions, and demographic factors such as age, education, and tenure had systematic effects on the internationalization of small firms. Summarizing the results of their own study they state:[101]

> We expected that owners/founders who had international work experience, or established personal networks and relationships abroad, would possess the skills necessary to conduct international business arrangements. Consistent with this, owners/founders or managers who have more positive perceptions of the international environment will also be more likely to internationalize their own small businesses.

Recruitment, Selection, and Retention

The above-mentioned barriers to SME internationalization included a scarcity of qualified international managers. Small firms may have more difficulties than large firms in recruiting adequate international managers.[102] It has been argued that many less-qualified employees are employed by SMEs because they do not meet the recruitment requirements of large organizations and were forced to work for SMEs as their second choice. As one interviewee in the study by MacMahon and Murphy[103] stated: "You get these big multinationals who cream off the top graduates and production operatives, which leaves a small business very vulnerable in terms of the quality and availability of labor." Indeed, recruitment, selection, and staffing have been shown to be problematic for SMEs because these firms are perceived to lack legitimacy as employers with a strong international orientation.[104]

 3.9

Kühlmann[105] has analyzed the image of SMEs as employers on the external labour market in Germany. He found that image advantages of SMEs as compared to large organizations included a good working atmosphere, less anonymity, a high degree of information, and low requirements for mobility. Participants of the study perceived the following factors as disadvantages: career opportunities, employee benefits, progressiveness of the company, training programs, pay, and international working opportunities. Figure 3.6 outlines the consequences of SME employer image for internationalization. The results indicate a self-fulfilling prophecy: Potential job candidates think that SMEs do not have strong international operations and do not apply. Because the SMEs cannot recruit qualified international managers, they are not as successful in international markets as they could be. In order to attract more applicants interested in international operations, Kühlmann suggests HR marketing activities for SMEs that clearly communicate that the firm has a strong position in international markets and offers international career opportunities. If the small size of the firm makes it difficult to attract sufficient interest, he recommends cooperation with other SMEs in a similar situation.

Furthermore, research[106] has shown that selection criteria of SMEs often include a general fit with the small organization or technical capabilities rather than requirements that refer to a future position with international responsibility. Small firms often look for generalist knowledge rather than

FIGURE 3.6

SME Employer Image and Internationalization

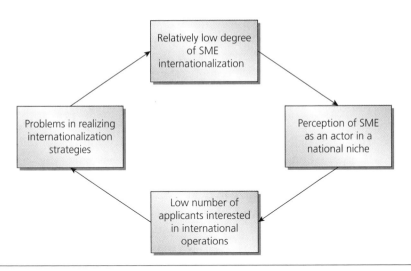

Source: Adapted from: Kühlmann, T. M. (2000). Internationalisierung des Mittelstandes als Herausforderung für die Personalauswahl und–entwicklung (Internationalization of medium-sized enterprises as a challenge for recruitment and development). In Gerhard und Lore Kienbaum Stiftung, J. Gutmann, R. Kabst (Eds.), *Internationalisierung im Mittelstand: Chancen—Risiken—Erfolgsfaktoren.* Wiesbaden: Gabler, 362.

for specialists. However, it has to be stressed that the requirements for international managers in SMEs are similar to those identified in large organizations.[107] Consequently, internationalizing SMEs should rethink their selection criteria and define a set of international competencies.[108]

With respect to retaining key employees, the perceived advantages and disadvantages of working for an SME outlined in the image study cited above are useful indicators. The advantages need to be emphasized and SMEs should also consider improving, for example, the training opportunities or career paths of their key employees. Furthermore, the importance of financial benefits should be noted. In an empirical study of 449 German SMEs with up to 1,000 employees, Weber and Kabst[109] found that financial participation programs were offered in more than 20 percent of the companies—presumably to increase the manager's identification with the firm with the aim to create long-term retention of key personnel.

Human Resource Development: The Challenge of Learning

Learning processes are of critical importance in the volatile global environment of modern business. This is especially true in cross-border alliances, which are ranked third as preferred foreign market entry strategies of SMEs, after export activities and subsidiaries.[110] Although organizational learning is a neglected area in SME research,[111] early evidence indicates that it may differ between small and large organizations.

 3.10

Training and development activities tend to be rather short-term-oriented in SMEs and are not supposed to meet long-term strategic needs.[112] The distinctive cultural features of a small organization indicate an informal learning approach using local networks and socialization[113] rather than formalized training.[114] Often, the focus is on acquiring tacit knowledge related to the specific context of the firm rather than on gaining explicit knowledge. Based on case study research, Anderson and Boocock have developed a model describing learning in the specific context of small organizations, which is shown in IHRM Notebook 3.6.

With respect to the specificities of the international environment, Brussig et al.[115] suggest that HRM should encourage staff in boundary-spanning positions,[116] (i.e., at the external interface of the SME) to pay attention to aspects relevant to internationalization decisions. On the one hand, this involves improving the capacity for perceiving relevant environmental developments —suggested training programs could include strategy and communication seminars. On the other hand, employees must be motivated to report and share their observations regularly and systematically, which requires good communication within the company. Anderson and Boocock[117] conclude that:

IHRM Notebook 3.6

Learning in Small Organizations

Individual learning processes
- Formal learning may be undertaken to meet operational, technical learning needs
- Informal learning, based on experience, develops specialized and market knowledge
- Tacit knowledge is prevalent
- Learning is not explicitly planned or evaluated

Internal organizational context
- Prior experience of key decision makers is an important influence on learning culture
- Organizational culture 'filters' the knowledge that is acquired by individuals
- Structures of communication determine how/if knowledge will be disseminated within the organization

Learning in small organizations

External organizational environment
- Formal and informal business networks provide the main source of knowledge, ideas, advice and support for 'boundary spanners'
- Local and national agencies are perceived as less relevant and are used less frequently

Source: Adapted from: Anderson, V., & Boocock, G. (2002). Small Firms and Internationalization: Learning to Manage and Managing to Learn. *Human Resource Management Journal, 12*, 18.

Those involved in HRD [human resource development] in smaller organizations . . . should resist the temptation to impose "large firm thinking" into a small organizational context. In small firms there is a complex interaction between scarce resources, reliance on the motivations and abilities of a few key individuals and a necessary focus on short-term priorities. The study suggests that "smallness" does not preclude generative learning, but the achievement of this is not universally relevant.

However, there is still a lack of knowledge about the "optimal" balance between formal and informal training in SMEs[118] and the relationship between training and firm performance is still unresolved.[119] Another problem is that training is often perceived as an "unaffordable luxury" in SMEs, particularly with regard to the training of expatriates.[120]

Expatriate Management

As the previous sections have shown, an informal approach to human resource management still dominates in SMEs[121]—especially for expatriate employees.[122] Research on this topic is relatively scarce, but an empirical study by Weber and Kabst of 449 German SMEs with up to 1,000 employees shows that expatriate assignments predominantly occur in the cases of joint ventures and wholly owned foreign subsidiaries. Sometimes also licensing agreements involve expatriates. After the challenge of recruiting people in foreign markets, the internal recruitment of employees for international jobs is perceived as the most important problem for the investigated firms. This finding is in line with the above discussion concerning problems with SME recruiting. However, a positive sign of a systematic approach to expatriate management in SMEs is that more than 16 percent of firms indicated that they send employees abroad for management development reasons (for a discussion on reasons for international assignments, see Chapter 4).

In terms of training, the most important activities were language courses, while cross-cultural training only played a minor role.[123] When SMEs needed cross-cultural training for potential expatriates, these employees were sent to external training institutions. Given the small number of expatriates, in-house training is not a viable option for most SMEs. The cultural integration of foreign acquisitions remains a challenge for SMEs.[124]

 3.11

Limited Resources of the HR Department and Outsourcing

The list of barriers to internationalization of SMEs presented earlier in IHRM Notebook 3.5 indicated that resources such as financial capital, qualified human capital to initiate and control internationalization processes, and time are scarce. This in part explains why sophisticated management strategies are lacking and the appointment of HR specialists does not occur, on the grounds that the costs cannot be justified with respect to the size of SMEs.[125] The focus of the usually small HR group in an SME is usually on administrative tasks, and most important HR decisions are made by the founder/owner of the enterprise.[126] The fact that most of the important HR activities are left to line managers is problematic for two reasons, according to Klaas et al.:[127]

> First, the complexity of many HR activities is likely to result in them becoming a significant drain on managerial time and resources. As such, HR tasks may interfere with managerial responsibilities that are directly related to revenue production. . . . Second, many HR tasks involve substantial complexity and, thus, the quality of HR decisions may well be affected in that the general managers often lack significant training and expertise in HR.

On the national level, professional employer organizations have been discussed as possible providers of HR-related services—based on a contractual agreement with the SME, the professional employer organization can become the outsourced HR department for the respective firm. This option can lead to improved managerial satisfaction in SMEs and higher quality HR decisions.[128] Thus, outsourcing of HR practices represents a potentially valuable strategy to cope with the size-related deficiencies of HRM in SMEs. However, risks of outsourcing strategically important activities should always be closely monitored.

RPC 3.12

As an alternative, we also found cooperations with large MNEs in the German automobile industry. Suppliers followed the car producers in foreign locations and benefited from the HR experience of the MNE. The latter supports small suppliers with its know-how about expatriate management, the environment of the relevant markets, and its relationships with relevant governmental institutions for gaining visa and working permits. Furthermore, information about human resource management issues in the local country is shared. Thus, a symbiosis can emerge between the interests of the MNE in facilitating the effective functioning of its suppliers abroad and the interests of SMEs that need relevant specialized information in order to prevent mistakes and reduce costs.

Summary

In this chapter, we have extended the discussion about the organizational context of MNEs conducted in Chapter 2 to other organizational forms, which pose specific problems to IHRM (i.e., cross-border alliances and globalizing SMEs). Cross-border M&As have seen a tremendous growth in the course of globalization. We have described their formation process as well as four important development phases: pre-M&A phase, due diligence phase, integration planning phase, and implementation phase. In each of the phases, specific strategic HR requirements need to be taken into account in order to effectively manage the M&A process. The role of expatriates is mainly discussed with respect to learning effects. A comparative approach to HR in M&As indicates the complexity that emerges from the institutional and cultural environments in which the firms are embedded.

The number of IJVs has increased significantly over the last few decades. In the chapter we outlined the IJV formation process, which poses considerable challenges for the HR function. Four stages are identified for the development of IJVs (formation, development, implementation, advancement and beyond), which require specific HR measures and roles. We also addressed the importance of cross-cultural management in IJVs, which is an important factor for effective cooperation across all levels of the IJV, including the top-management team. Both types of equity-based cross-border alliances are very similar, involving strategic, comparative, and cross-cultural HRM issues, as well as specified expatriate roles.

The third organization form we addressed was the case of the internationalized SME. In this case, different challenges have been identified. First, we outlined the strategic importance of SMEs in international business and examined barriers to SME internationalization. We also addressed important IHRM features distinguishing SMEs from MNEs: the founder/owner of the SME; recruitment, selection, and retention; human resource development with special emphasis on learning; expatriate management; and the limited resources of the HR department in SMEs and outsourcing opportunities.

Key Terms

acquisition 70

cross-border alliances 69

cross-border M&A 71

equity modes 69

international joint venture 81

merger 70

non-equity cross-border alliance 69

Web Links

www 3.1   Canada's Competition Bureau is an independent law enforcement agency responsible for the administration and enforcement of the Competition Act. The agency provides information and support for Canadian businesses regarding Canadian competition laws and mandatory requirements for merger pre-notifications:

www.competitionbureau.gc.ca/internet/index.cfm?itemID= 16&lg=e

www 3.2   The Investment Canada Act concerns non-Canadians who acquire control of an existing Canadian business or who want to create a new Canadian business. The Investment Canada Act can be found at:

http://strategis.ic.gc.ca/epic/site/ica-lic.nsf/en/Home

www 3.3   The Canada Border Services Agency (CBSA), created in 2003 to manage the access of people and goods to and from Canada, includes a Small and Medium–sized Enterprise Centre that provides information and help for Canadian SMEs in exporting and importing goods:

www.cbsa.gc.ca/agency-agence/who-qui-eng.html

RPC Icons

RPC 3.1   Leads in the development of HR initiatives that support the organization's strategic directions

RPC 3.2   Plans for and manages the HR aspects of organizational change (e.g., mergers, acquisitions, divestitures, and downsizing, in the context of organizational strategies and legislated requirements)

RPC 3.3   Develops and implements a communications plan that supports strategies for employee involvement

RPC 3.4   Leads in the development of HR initiatives that support the organization's strategic directions

RPC 3.5   Contributes to improvements in the organization's structures and work processes

RPC 3.6   Leads in the development of HR initiatives that support the organization's strategic directions

RPC 3.7   Contributes to the development of the organization's vision, goals, and strategies, with a focus on human capital

RPC 3.8   Contributes to the development of the organization's vision, goals, and strategies, with a focus on human capital
Guides and facilitates change in organizational culture and/or values consistent with business strategies

RPC 3.9   Monitors the HR activities of the organization, identifies problem areas, initiates responses, and resolves issues that stand in the way of business success

RPC 3.10   Monitors HR activities of the organization, identifies problem areas, initiates responses, and resolves issues that stand in the way of business success

RPC 3.11   Monitors HR activities of the organization, identifies problem areas, initiates responses, and resolves issues that stand in the way of business success

RPC 3.12   Contributes to the development of the organization's vision, goals, and strategies, with a focus on human capital

Discussion Questions

1. Describe the formation process of cross-border mergers, acquisitions, and international joint ventures. What are the major differences?
2. Describe the development phases of an M&A and the respective HR implications.
3. Outline the development phases of an IJV and the respective HR implications.
4. In which way do cultural and institutional differences impact the HR integration in M&As and in IJVs?
5. What are the barriers to internationalization for SMEs?
6. What are some of the typical challenges for HRM in internationalized SMEs?

Using the Internet

1. Use sites such as the Canada Border Services Agency's website page for SMEs at **www.cbsa.gc.ca/agency-agence/who-qui-eng.html** and find out more about the key concerns and challenges for small and medium-sized businesses when getting involved in cross-border transactions. What could their HR functions do to overcome some of these challenges?
2. Find a failure of an international merger or acquisition. Analyze the failure, its causes, and the HR role in this situation. In groups, formulate recommendations on how the HR function could have helped to prevent this failure.

Exercises

1. Think back to your last job or internship. Think about the company in terms of its size and its organizational culture and climate. Did you feel comfortable? Why or why not? Think about your values and career objectives and how these might influence your decision to choose a large organization or a small business.
2. Find somebody who worked in a company that has been acquired by or has merged with a foreign company. How did this person feel during the acquisition or merger? Why? Ask him or her what HRM activities were initiated in those organizations to deal with the employees' fears and feelings of uncertainty due to the acquisition or merger.
3. Do you think that larger organizations have more sophisticated HR practices and support structures? Why?

Case

HR in the DaimlerChrysler Merger

The Merger

The merger between Chrysler and Daimler-Benz was one of the largest in history. Both companies had started to screen the automobile industry for partners in 1997. In early 1998, Jürgen E. Schrempp, CEO of the German-based Daimler-Benz company, took the initiative and suggested a merger to Robert J. Eaton, CEO of the American-based Chrysler corporation. The merger contract was signed in May 1998.

HR in the Different Phases of the M&A

At the beginning of the merger, "soft" people skills were not an important issue to consider. Even in the second phase, when the merger was negotiated,

HR issues continued to play a minor role. Negotiations were dominated by legal and financial aspects. Due to the strict secrecy at this stage, the corporate HR directors of both companies were not informed nor involved.

In the integration planning phase in August 1998, management teams from both firms developed strategies for the merged company. These teams identified a number of issues that had to be dealt with during the post-merger integration. With respect to HR, one important challenge was to solve the remuneration problem: The German top managers earned much less than their American counterparts. The contrary was the case for the lower management levels. It was decided that the salaries for those German top managers who had international responsibility would be raised to the U.S. level. For a broader group of German managers, a component of their salary would be linked to the company's profit and its share price. At this stage, all employees were informed via various media such as letters, the companies' intranet systems, and films. Furthermore, cultural issues involved in the merger were taken into account for the first time. The new board was composed of eighteen members, including both Schrempp and Eaton as chairmen, eight board members from Chrysler, the same number from Daimler-Benz, and two from the Daimler subsidiaries Dasa and Debis.

During the post-merger integration phase, mixed teams worked on more than 1,000 projects identified by the post-merger integration coordination team. Only 43 projects were in the area of HR, including such topics as corporate culture, employee profit-sharing, leadership styles, labour relations, global job evaluation, exchange programs, and management development. The board member responsible for human resources was not included in the "Chairman's Integration Council," the core of DaimlerChrysler's management structure during the post-merger integration phase.

Within the first two years of the merger, DaimlerChrysler lost about 20 top executives, especially from the Chrysler side. There is little evidence about a systematic retention program for this level. During the information campaign for the other levels, the focus was on job security. Only two years after the merger, DaimlerChrysler executives admitted that the organization had cultural problems. Examples included inappropriate humour, political incorrectness, perceived excessive formality, sexual harassment, and improper documentation of meetings. The company offered intercultural training for executives and management exchange programs.

Long-Term Effects

In 2000, profitability at Chrysler sharply dropped and there was a 20 percent decline in the DaimlerChrysler share price. At that time, the market capitalization of DaimlerChrysler was little more than that of Daimler-Benz before the merger.

Some years later, at the beginning of 2007 and after important financial losses mainly on the Chrysler side, the media are discussing the possibility of a separation of Daimler and Chrysler. Although Chrysler had to close several production plants and had cut down around 40,000 jobs during the first years following the merger, it has to admit important economic problems for the third time after the merger endangering the overall success of the combined company.

Adapted from: Kühlmann, T., & Dowling, P. J. (2005). DaimlerChrysler: A Case Study of a Cross-Border Merger. In G. K. Stahl and M. E. Mendenhall, *Mergers and Acquisitions: Managing Cultures and Human Resources*. Stanford, CA: Stanford Business Books, 351–363.

Questions

1. Why do you think the board member responsible for human resources was not included in the Chairman's Integration Council? Can you think of any consequences for the two companies?
2. How could the HR function of the two merging companies have addressed organizational and national cultural differences before they became problems?
3. If you compare the information given about the DaimlerChrysler merger with the list of HR activities outlined in IHRM Notebook 3.1, you can analyze the strengths and the weaknesses from an HR perspective. What lessons could be learned from this process?

Endnotes

1. Our discussion about cross-border alliances has a special emphasis on equity-based alliances, including mergers and acquisition and international joint ventures. These alliances are given priority in our text due to their association with complex IHRM processes and practices, which is the main interest of study in this book.
2. SMEs represent important elements in the world economy. However, in IHRM research, they are often neglected. There is evidence that their approaches to international human resource management differ to a large extent from those of large MNEs and this is why we cover this topic in the present chapter.
3. R. S. Schuler & I. Tarique. (2006). Alliance forms and human resource issues: Implications and significance. In O. Shenkar & J. J. Reuer (Eds.), *Handbook of strategic alliances*. Thousand Oaks, CA: Sage Publications, Inc., 219–239.
4. W. F. Cascio & M. G. Serapio, Jr. (1991). Human resources systems in an international alliance: The undoing of a done deal? *Organizational Dynamics,19*, 63–74.
5. R. S. Schuler, S. E. Jackson, & Y. Luo. (2004). *Managing human resources in cross-border alliances*. London/New York: Routledge, 2.
6. UNCTAD. (2006). World Investment Report, 2006. *FDI from Developing and Transition Economies: Implications for Development*. New York/Geneva: United Nations, 126.
7. R. S. Schuler & I. Tarique. (2006). Alliance forms and human resource issues: Implications and significance. In O. Shenkar & J. J. Reuer (Eds.), *Handbook of strategic alliances*. Thousand Oaks, CA: Sage Publications, Inc.,
8. UNCTAD. (2006). World Investment Report, 2006. *FDI from Developing and Transition Economies: Implications for Development*. New York/Geneva: United Nations, 297.
9. J. Child & D. Faulkner. (1998). *Strategies of cooperation*. Oxford/London: Oxford University Press.

10. Schuler & Tarique. Alliance forms and human resource issues: Implications and significance, 220.

11. Schuler & Tarique. Alliance forms and human resource issues: Implications and significance.

12. For recent notable exceptions, see, for example: B. M. Lajara. (2002). The role of human resource management in the cooperative strategy process. *Human Resource Planning, 25*, 34–44; B. M. Lajara, F. G. Lillo, & V. S. Sempere. (2003). Human resources management: A success and failure factor in strategic alliances. *Employee Relations, 25*, 61–80; P. S. Budhwar, H. K. Luthar, & J. Bhatnagar. (2006). The dynamics of HRM systems in Indian BPO firms. *Journal of Labor Research, 27*, 339–360.

13. For an overview see: D. Welch & L. Welch. (1994). Linking operation mode diversity and IHRM. *International Journal of Human Resource Management, 5*, 911–926.

14. T. Kühlmann & P. J. Dowling. (2005). DaimlerChrysler: A case study of a cross-border merger. In G. K. Stahl & M. E. Mendenhall, *Mergers and acquisitions: Managing cultures and human resources*. Stanford, CA: Stanford Business Books, 351–364.

15. For other definitions, see also: R. S. Schuler, S. E. Jackson, & Y. Luo. (2004). *Managing human resource in cross-border alliances*. London: Routledge, 5.

16. UNCTAD. (2006). World Investment Report, 2006. *FDI from Developing and Transition Economies: Implications for Development*. New York/Geneva: United Nations, 123–225.

17. Ibid., 15.

18. Ibid., 13.

19. M. Marth. (2004). Cross-border acquisitions: A Canadian perspective. *Statistics Canada*, Catalogue No. 11-621-MIE-No 013.

20. UNCTAD. (2006). World Investment Report, 2006. *FDI from Developing and Transition Economies: Implications for Development*. Retrieved July 25, 2007, from www.unctad.org/fdistatistics.

21. Greenfield FDI refers to investment projects that entail the establishment of new production facilities such as offices, buildings, plants, and factories, as well as the movement of intangible capital (mainly services). See: UNCTAD. (2006). World Investment Report, 2006. *FDI from Developing and Transition Economies: Implications for Development*. New York/Geneva: United Nations, 15.

22. J. Child, D. Faulkner, & R. Pitkethly. (2001). *The management of international acquisitions*. Oxford, UK: Oxford University Press, 1.

23. Schuler, Jackson, & Luo. (2004). *Managing human resources in cross-border alliances*. Child, Faulkner, and Pitkethly distinguish between market drivers, cost drivers, competitive drivers, and government drivers for M&As. See: Child, Faulkner, & Pitkethly. *The management of international acquisitions*.

24. The same is true for international joint ventures. See: K. W. Glaister, R. Husan, & P. J. Buckley. (2003). Learning to manage international joint ventures. *International Business Review, 12*, 83–108.

25. Child, Faulkner, & Pitkethly. *The management of international acquisitions*.

26. R. Larsson & S. Finkelstein. (1999). Integrating strategic, organizational, and human resource perspectives on mergers and acquisitions: A case survey of synergy realization. *Organization Science, 10*, 1–26. For the special case of acquisitions, see a similar analysis by: J. Birkinshaw, H. Bresman, & L. Hakanson. (2000). Managing the post-acquisition integration process: How the human integration and task integration processes interact to foster value creation. *Journal of Management Studies, 37*, 395–425.

27. Larsson and Finkelstein (ibid.) state that the emphasis primarily was on the post-combination integration process investigating cultural and other conflicts. In the related HRM research, psychological aspects, communication, and careers were important topics.

28. This is confirmed by the work of: D. K. Datta. (1991). Organizational fit and acquisition performance: Effects of post-acquisition integration. *Strategic Management Journal,12*, 281–297. In contrast, Datta did not find an impact of differences in the evaluation and rewards systems on post-merger integration performance, although "reward systems are often employed to reinforce values, beliefs, and practices in an organization" (292).

29. Larsson & Finkelstein. Integrating strategic, organizational, and human resource perspectives on mergers and acquisitions: A case survey of synergy realization.

30. J. Birkinshaw, H. Bresman, & L. Hakanson. (2000). Managing the post-acquisition integration process: How the human integration and task integration processes interact to foster value creation. *Journal of Management Studies, 37*, 395–425.

31. Task integration was measured by the initial plans for integration, integration mechanisms used, problems encountered during integration, and task specialization during integration. See Birkinshaw, Bresman, & Hakanson, ibid.

32. Ibid, 395.

33. J. A. Krug & D. Nigh. (2001). Executive perceptions in foreign and domestic acquisitions: An analysis of foreign ownership and its effect on executive fate. *Journal of World Business, 36*(1), 85–105.

34. R. V. Aguilera & J. C. Dencker. (2004). The role of human resource management in cross-border mergers and acquisitions. *International Journal of Human Resource Management, 15*, 1355–1370.

35. See for example the study by: Krug and Nigh. (2001). Executive perceptions in foreign and domestic acquisitions: An analysis of foreign ownership and its effect on executive fate. *Journal of World Business, 36*(1), 85–105.

36. Aguilera & Dencker. The role of human resource management in cross-border mergers and acquisitions.

37. A. Delios & P. W. Beamish. (2001). Survival and profitability: The roles of experience and intangible assets in foreign subsidiary performance. *Academy of Management Journal, 44*, 028–1038.

38. Schuler et al. differentiate among four types of integration: (1) the portfolio type, which has been mentioned in the text; (2) blending (i.e., the best elements from each culture are chosen); (3) a new company creation, with a new culture that fits the new organization; (4) assimilation, where legitimacy is assigned to only one culture. See: Schuler, Jackson, & Luo. (2004). *Managing human resources in cross-border alliances*. London/New York: Routledge. 90.

39. Some experts argue that the due diligence phase is part of the first phase, which they call *pre-combination*. This is followed by a combination and integration stage and a solidification and assessment stage. See: Schuler, Jackson, & Luo. *Managing human resources in cross-border alliances*.

40. With respect to auditing human resource management, see: G. W. Florkowski & R. S. Schuler. (1994). Auditing human resource management in the global environment. *International Journal of Human Resource Management, 5*(4), 827–851.

41. C. Geighardt, S. Armutat, H. Döring, M. Festing, C. Frühe, E. Nell, & W. Werner. (2007). *Erfolgreiche M&As—Was das Personalmanagement dazu beiträgt (Successful M&As—The impact of human resource management)*. Praxispapiere 2-2007. Düsseldorf: DGFP.

42. J. A. Schmidt. (2001). The correct spelling of M&A begins with HR. *HR Magazine*, 102–108.

43. Aguilera & Dencker. The role of human resource management in cross-border mergers and acquisitions.

44. Ibid., 1357.

45. E. M. Antila. (2006). The role of HR managers in international mergers and acquisitions: A multiple case study. *International Journal of Human Resource Management, 17*, 999–1020.

46. D. Ulrich. (1997). *Human resource champions: The next agenda for adding value and delivering results*. Boston, MA: Harvard Business School Press.

47. A. Delios & P. W. Beamish. (2001). Survival and profitability: The roles of experience and intangible assets in foreign subsidiary performance. *Academy of Management Journal, 44*, 1028–1038.

48. L. Hébert, P. Very, & P. W. Beamish. (2005). Expatriation as a bridge over troubled water: A knowledge-based perspective applied to cross-border acquisitions. *Organization Studies, 26*, 1468.

49. C. Geighardt, S. Armutat, H. Döring, M. Festing, C. Frühe, E. Nell, & W. Werner. (2007). *Erfolgreiche M&As—Was das Personalmanagement dazu beiträgt (Successful M&As—The impact of human resource management)*. Praxispapiere 2-2007. Düsseldorf: DGFP.

50. Hébert, Very, & Beamish. Expatriation as a bridge over troubled water: A knowledge-based perspective applied to cross-border acquisitions, 1469.

51. Ibid., 1455–1476.

52. R. Villinger. (1996). Post-acquisition managerial learning in Central East Europe. *Organization Studies* (Walter de Gruyter GmbH & Co. KG.), *17*, 181–206.

53. Ibid., 203.

54. P. Sparrow & P. Budhwar. (1997). Competition and change: Mapping the Indian HRM recipe against world-wide patterns. *Journal of World Business, 32*(3), 224–242.

55. Child, Faulkner, & Pitkethly. (2001). *The management of international acquisitions*. Oxford UK: Oxford University Press.

56. Katz/Darbishire (2001), Streeck (2001), and Pudelko (2006) discuss converging divergences in employment systems. With respect to employment systems, they see an increasing divergence. However, in terms of workplace patterns at least, Katz and Darbishire (2001) have identified a growing convergence. This is confirmed by research by the Cranfield Network on Comparative Human Resource Management, which mainly focuses on Europe (Brewster, 2006). Brewster, Mayrhofer, and Morley (2004) give a more differentiated perspective. They distinguish between directional convergence and final convergence. The first is concerned with whether the same trends can be observed in different countries and the latter addresses the results. Their conclusion, based on the Brewster, Mayrhofer, and Morley, 2004, data, is as follows: "From a directional point of view, there seems to be a positive indication of convergence. However, when one looks at the question from a final convergence point of view, the answer is no longer a clear positive. None of the HR practices converged at the end of the decade. Rather, the maximum point of convergence is reached in the middle of the decade with signs of divergence after that" (Brewster, Mayrhofer, & Morley, 2004). Thus, the results concerning the convergence or divergence of HRM systems, including performance management systems, are mixed. There is no clear tendency, although in an empirical study concerning the convergence–divergence debate in HRM, Pudelko (2005) concludes that the majority of the HR managers investigated (they originated from Germany, the United States, and Japan) expect a convergence of HRM systems. See: H. Katz & O. Darbishire. (2001). Converging divergences: Worldwide changes in employment systems. *Industrial and Labor Relations Review (review symposium), 54*(3), 681–716; W. Streeck. (2001). High equality, low activity: The contribution of the social welfare system to the stability of the German collective bargaining regime: Converging divergences. *Industrial and Labor Relations Review (review symposium), 54*(3), 698–706; M. Pudelko. (2006). A comparison of HRM systems in the USA, Japan and Germany in their socio-economic context. *Human Resource Management Journal, 16*(2), 123–153; C. Brewster. (2006). *International human resource*

management: If there is no "best way," how do we manage? (inaugural lecture, Henley Management College, U.K.); C. Brewster, W. Mayrhofer, & M. Morley (Eds.). (2004). *Human resources: Evidence of convergence?* London: Elsevier.

57. Child, Faulkner, & Pitkethly. (2001). *The management of international acquisitions.* Oxford UK: Oxford University Press, 180.

58. Y. Gong, O. Shenkar, Y. Luo, & M.-K. Nyaw. (2005). Human resources and international joint venture performance: A system perspective. *Journal of International Business Studies, 36*, 505–518.

59. K.-B. Chan, V. Luk, & G. X. Wang. (2005). Conflict and innovation in international joint ventures: Toward a new Sinified corporate culture or "alternative globalization" in China. *Asia Pacific Business Review, 11*(4), 461–482.

60. O. Shenkar & Y. Zeira. (1987). Human resources management in international joint ventures: Directions for research. *Academy of Management Review, 12*, 547.

61. The following sources represent milestones in HRM-related IJV research: P. Lorange. (1986). Human resource management in multinational cooperative ventures. *Human Resource Management, 25*, 133–148; Shenkar & Zeira. (1987). Human resources management in international joint ventures: Directions for research. *Academy of Management Review, 12*, 546–557; D. J. Cyr. (1995). *The human resource challenge of international joint ventures.* Westport, CT/ London: Quorum Books; Schuler. (2001). Human resource issues and activities in international joint ventures. *International Journal of Human Resource Management, 12*, 1–52; Schuler, Jackson, & Luo. *Managing human resource in cross-border alliances*; Gong, Shenkar, Luo, & Nyaw. (2005). Human resources and international joint venture performance.

62. P. Evans, V. Pucik, & J.-L. Barsoux. (2002). *The global challenge: Frameworks for international human resource management.* Boston, MA: McGraw-Hill.

63. For these challenges, see: Gong, Shenkar, Luo, & Nyaw. Human resources and international joint venture performance. Similar ideas can be found in: K. W. Glaister, R. Husan, & P. J. Buckley. (2003). Learning to manage international joint ventures. *International Business Review, 12*, 83–108.

64. Schuler. (2001). Human resource issues and activities in international joint ventures. *International Journal of Human Resource Management, 12*, 4.

65. See, for example: D. J. Cyr. (1995). *The human resource challenge of international joint ventures.* Westport CT/ London: Quorum Books; P. Iles & M. Yolles. (2002). International joint ventures, HRM and viable knowledge migration. *International Journal of Human Resource Management, 13*, 624 641; H. Barkema, O. Shenkar, F. Vermeulen, & J. Bell. (1997). Working abroad, working with others: How firms learn to operate international joint ventures. *Academy of Management Journal, 40*, 426–443.

66. Glaister, Husan, & Buckley. Learning to manage international joint ventures.

67. However, changes in the ownership structure do not necessarily reflect a failure; these changes might be made to meet the necessities of a volatile global environment.

68. See, for example: S. H. Park & M. V. Russo. (1996). When competition eclipses cooperation: An event history analysis of joint venture failure. *Management Science, 42*(6), 875–891; A. B. Sim & M. Y. Ali. (2000). Determinants of stability in international joint ventures: Evidence from a developing country context. *Asia Pacific Journal of Management, 17*, 373–397.

69. For an encompassing list of reasons for failures of international joint ventures, see Schuler et al., *Managing human resources in cross-border alliances.*

70. Schuler. Human resource issues and activities in international joint ventures, 1–5.

71. See, for example: P. Beamish & A. Kachra. (2004). Number of partners and JV performance. *Journal of World Business, 39*, 107–120; D. Cyr. (1995). *The human resource challenge of international joint ventures.* Westport, CT/London: Quorum Books; Schuler & Tarique. Alliance forms and human resource issues: Implications and significance. D. R. Briscoe & R. S. Schuler. (2004). *International human resource management: Policies and practices for the global enterprise* (2nd ed.). New York: Routledge.

72. Schuler & Tarique. Alliance forms and human resource issues: Implications and significance.

73. For fit concepts in IHRM, see, for example: J. Milliman, M. A. Glinow, & N. Nathan. (1999). Organizational life cycles and strategic international human resource management in multinational companies: Implications for congruence theory. *Academy of Management Review, 16*, 318–339.

74. Schuler. Human resource issues and activities in international joint ventures, 44.

75. For conceptual work, see, for example: L. McFarlane Shore, B. W. Eagle, & M. J. Jedel. (1993). China–United States joint ventures: A typological model of a goal congruence and cultural understanding and their importance for effective human resource management. *International Journal of Human Resource Management, 4*, 67–83; and P.-X. Meschi & A. Roger. (1994). Cultural context and social effectiveness in international joint ventures. *Management International Review, 34*, 197–215.

76. For a discussion of U.S.- and Japan-affiliated banks in Korea, see: Sang H. Nam. (1995). Culture, control and commitment in international joint ventures. *International Journal of Human Resource Management, 6*, 553–567; for analyses of China–Western joint ventures, see: Y. Lu & I. Björkman. (1997). HRM practices in China–Western joint ventures: MNC standardization versus localization. *International Journal of Human Resource Management, 8*, 614–628; Lu & Björkman. (1999). The management of human resources in Chinese–Western joint ventures. *Journal of World Business, 34*, 306–324; Björkman & Lu. (2001). Institutionalization and bargaining power explanations of HRM practices in international joint ventures—The case of Chinese–Western joint ventures. *Organization Studies* (Walter de Gruyter*), 22*, 491–512; K. S. Chen & M. Wilson. (2003). Standardization and localization of human resource management in Sino-foreign joint ventures. *Asia Pacific Journal of Management, 20*, 397–408; K. Leung & J. Y. Y. Kwong. (2003). Human resource management practices in international joint ventures in mainland China: A justice analysis. *Human Resource Management Review, 13*, 85–105; E. W. K. Tsang. (1994). Human resource management problems in Sino-foreign joint ventures. *International Journal of Manpower, 15*, 4–21; Shore, Eagle, & Jedel. (1993). China–United States joint ventures: A typological model of a goal congruence and cultural understanding and their importance for effective human resource management. *International Journal of Human Resource Management, 4*, 67–83.

77. Gong, Shenkar, Luo, & Nyaw. Human resources and international joint venture performance: A system perspective; J. Li, K. Xin & M. Pillutla. (2002). Multi-cultural leadership teams and organizational identification in international joint ventures. *International Journal of Human Resource Management, 13*, 322.

78. R. Kabst. (2004). Human resource management for international joint ventures: Expatriation and selective control. *International Journal of Human Resource Management, 15*(1), 1–16.

79. Li, Xin, & Pillutla. Multi-cultural leadership teams and organizational identification in international joint ventures. See also: J. M. Frayne & M. Geringer. A social cognitive approach to examine joint venture general manager performance. *Group and Organizational Management, 19*, 240–262. For the role of HRM policies as providers of control mechanisms, see also: J. Child, D. Faulkner, & R. Pitkethly. (2001). *The management of international acquisitions.* Oxford UK: Oxford University Press.

80. Li, Xin, & Pillutla. Multi-cultural leadership teams and organizational identification in international joint ventures, 321.

81. Ibid., 320–337.

82. Ibid., 322.

83. This section is partly based on: M. Festing. (2007). Globalization of SMEs and implications for international human resource management. *International Journal of Globalisation and Small Business, 2*(1).

84. M. Tjepkema & J. Brunet. (2000). Insights on . . . frequently asked questions on small businesses. *Small Business and Special Surveys Division, 4*(1). Ottawa: Statistics Canada.

85. Institut für Mittelstandsforschung Bonn: www.ifm-bonn.org

86. Statistics Canada. (2005, February 15). Study: Business Dynamics in Canada. *The Daily.* Retrieved July 31, 2007, from www.statcan.ca/Daily/English/050215/d050215a.htm.

87. *UN-ECE Operational Activities: SME—Their role in foreign trade.* (1997). Background paper prepared by the United Nations Economic Commission for Europe (UN-ECE) Secretariat for the Black Sea Economic Cooperation Organization Workshop held November 13–14 in Kiev, Ukraine. Retrieved February 17, 2007, from the UN-ECE website: www.unece.org/indust/sme/foreignt.htm

88. Organisation for Economic Co-operation and Development (OECD). *OECD Stat Extracts.* Retrieved February 20, 2006, from http://stats.oecd.org/WBOS/default.aspx?DatasetCode=CSP6

89. *UN-ECE Operational Activities: SME—Their role in foreign trade*: www.unece.org/indust/sme/foreignt.htm

90. Organisation for Economic Co-operation and Development (OECD). *OECD Stat Extracts*: http://stats.oecd.org/WBOS/default.aspx?DatasetCode=CSP6

91. Organisation for Economic Co-operation and Development (Ed.). (2006). *Removing barriers to SME access to international markets.* Geneva: OECD. Keynote paper at OECD–APEC Global Conference, Athens, Greece, November 5–8, 2006. Retrieved February 17, 2007, from www.oecd.org/dataoecd/4/16/37818320.pdf. For empirical evidence on the United Kingdom, see: H. Matlay & D. Fletcher. (2000). Globalization and strategic change: Some lessons from the UK small business sector. *Strategic Change, 9,* 437–449.

92. For a discussion of SME barriers to internationalization in various contexts, see: S. Vachani. (2005). Problems of foreign subsidiaries of SMEs compared with large companies. *International Business Review, 14,* 415–439; M. Fujita. (1995). Small and medium-sized transnational corporations: Salient features. *Small Business Economics, 7,* 251–271; D. A. Kirby & S. Kaiser. (2003). Joint ventures as an internationalization strategy for SMEs. *Small Business Economics, 21,* 229–242; Z. J. Acs, R. Morck, J. M. Shaver, & B. Yeung. (1997). The internationalization of small and medium-sized enterprises: A policy perspective. *Small Business Economics, 9,* 7–20; P. J. Buckley. (1997). International technology transfer by small and medium-sized enterprises. *Small Business Economics, 9,* 67–78; UN-ECE Operational Activities: *SMEs—Their role in foreign trade,* retrieved February 27, 2007, from www.unece.org/indust/sme/foreignt.htm.

93. UNCTAD. (2006). World Investment Report, 2006. *FDI from Developing and Transition Economies: Implications for Development.* New York/Geneva: United Nations, 80.

94. V. Anderson & G. Boocock. (2002). Small firms and internationalization: Learning to manage and managing to learn. *Human Resource Management Journal, 12,* 5–24; A. Wilkinson. (1999). Employment Relations in SMEs. *Employee Relations, 21,* 206–217.

95. For an excellent overview, see: M. S. Cardon & C. E. Stevens (2004). Managing human resources in small organizations: What do we know? *Human Resource Management Review, 14,* 295–323; A. E. Barber, M. J. Wesson, Q. M. Roberson, & M. S. Taylor. (1999). A tale of

two job markets: Organizational size and its effect on hiring practices and job search behavior. *Personnel Psychology, 52*, 841–867; Anderson & Boocock. (2002). Small firms and internationalization: Learning to manage and managing to learn. *Human Resource Management Journal, 12*, 5–24.

96. J. Johanson & J. -E. Vahlne. (1977). The internationalization process of the firm: A model of knowledge development and increasing foreign market commitment. *Journal of International Business Studies, 8*(1), 23–32; J. Johanson & J. -E. Vahlne. (1990). The mechanism of internationalization. *International Marketing Review, 7*(4), 11–24; L. Melin. (1992). Internationalization as a strategy process. *Strategic Management Journal, 13*, 99–118.

97. This finding is comparable to board internationalization of large companies. Knowledge and experiences gained in foreign markets are supposed to positively influence the extent and quality of firm internationalization. See, for example: N. Athanassiou & D. Nigh. (2002). The impact of the top-management team's international business experience on the firm's internationalization: Social networks at work. *Management International Review, 42*, 157–181. For measurement issues of board internationalization, see: S. Schmid & A. Daniel. (2006). *Measuring board internationalization—towards a more holistic approach.* ESCP-EAP Working Paper No. 21, Berlin: ESCP-EAP European School of Management. For empirical evidence from the U.K. small-business sector, see: H. Matlay & D. Fletcher. (2000). Globalization and strategic change: Some lessons from the UK small business sector. *Strategic Change, 9*, 437–449.

98. M. Rennie. (1993). Global competitiveness: Born global. *McKinsey Quarterly, 4*, 45–52; G. A. Knight & S. T. Cavusgil. (1996). The born global: A challenge to traditional internationalization theory. *Advances in International Marketing, 8*, 11–26.

99. T. K. Madsen & P. Servais. (1997). The internationalization of born globals: An evolutionary process. *International Business Review, 6*(6), 561–583.

100. P. P. McDougall, S. Shane, & B. M. Oviatt. (1994). Explaining the formation of international new ventures: The limits of theories from international business research. *Journal of Business Venturing, 9*, 475.

101. T. S. Manolova, C. G. Brush, L. F. Edelman, & P. G. Greene. (2002). Internationalization of small firms. *International Small Business Journal, 20*, 22.

102. I. O. Williamson. (2000). Employer legitimacy and recruitment success in small businesses. *Entrepreneurship Theory and Practice*, 27–42.

103. J. MacMahon & E. Murphy. (1999). Managerial effectiveness in small enterprises: Implications for HRD. *Journal of European Industrial Training, 23*, 32.

104. M. S. Cardon & C. E. Stevens. (2004). Managing human resources in small organizations: What do we know? *Human Resource Management Review, 14*, 295–323.

105. T. M. Kühlmann. (2000). Internationalisierung des Mittelstandes als Herausforderung für die Personalauswahl und –entwicklung (Internationalization of Medium-Sized Enterprises as a Challenge for Recruitment and Development). In Gerhard und Lore Kienbaum Stiftung, J. Gutmann, & R. Kabst (Eds.), *Internationalisierung im Mittelstand: Chancen—Risiken—Erfolgsfaktoren.* Wiesbaden: Gabler, 357–371.

106. This has been confirmed in literature analysis by: Cardon & Stevens. (2004). Managing human resources in small organizations: What do we know? *Human Resource Management Review, 14*, 295323. However, this study does not focus explicitly on *international* SMEs.

107. *Globalisierung in kleinen und mittleren Unternehmen. Erfahrungen und Ansatzpunkte für das Personalmanagement (Globalization of SMEs—Experiences and recommendations for human resource management)*, Praxispapiere. Düsseldorf: DGFP (forthcoming).

108. Ibid.

109. W. Weber & R. Kabst. (2000). Internationalisierung mittelständischer Unternehmen: Organisationsform und Personalmanagement (Internationalization of medium-sized enterprises—

Organization form and human resource management). In Gerhard und Lore Kienbaum Stiftung, J. Gutmann, & R. Kabst (Eds.), *Internationalisierung im Mittelstan: Chancen—Risiken—Erfolgsfaktoren*. Wiesbaden: Gabler, 3–92.

110. Ibid.

111. Anderson & Boocock. Small firms and internationalization: Learning to manage and managing to learn.

112. R. Hill & J. Stewart. (2000). Human resource development in small organizations. *Journal of European Industrial Training, 24*, 105–117.

113. Cardon & Stevens. Managing human resources in small organizations: What do we know?

114. *Globalisierung in kleinen und mittleren Unternehmen. Erfahrungen und Ansatzpunkte für das Personalmanagement (Globalization of SMEs—Experiences and recommendations for human resource management)*, Praxispapiere. Düsseldorf: DGFP (forthcoming).

115. M. Brussig, L. Gerlach, & U. Wilkens. (2001). *The development of globalization strategies in SMEs and the role of human resource management*. Paper presented at the Global Human Resource Management Conference, Barcelona.

116. J. D. Thompson. (1967). *Organizations in action*. New York: McGraw-Hill; and A. H. Aldrich. (1979). *Organizations & environments*. Englewood Cliffs, NJ: Prentice Hall.

117. Anderson & Boocock. Small firms and internationalization: Learning to manage and managing to learn, 20.

118. Cardon & Stevens. Managing human resources in small organizations: What do we know?

119. D. J. Storey. (2004). Exploring the link among small firms, between management training and firm performance: A comparison between the UK and other OECD countries. *International Journal of Human Resource Management,15*, 112–1330.

120. J. MacMahon & E. Murphy. (1999). Managerial effectiveness in small enterprises: Implications for HRD. *Journal of European Industrial Training, 23*, 29.

121. B. Kotey & P. Slade. (2005). Formal human resource management practices in small growing firms. *Journal of Small Business Management, 43*, 16–40; D. J. Storey. (2004). Exploring the link among small firms between management training and firm performance: A comparison between the UK and other OECD Countries. *International Journal of Human Resource Management,15*, 112–133; J. S. Hornsby & D. F. Kuratko. (2003). Human resource management in U.S. small businesses: A replication and extension. *Journal of Developmental Entrepreneurship, 8*, 73–92.

122. For an exception, see: H. Harris & L. Holden. (2001). Between autonomy and control: Expatriate managers and strategic HRM in SMEs. *Thunderbird International Business Review, 43*(1), 77–100.

123. W. Weber & R. Kabst. (2000). Internationalisierung mittelständischer Unternehmen: Organisationsform und Personalmanagement (Internationalization of medium-sized enterprises—Organization form and human resource management). In Gerhard und Lore Kienbaum Stiftung, J. Gutmann, & R. Kabst (Eds.), *Internationalisierung im Mittelstand: Chancen—Risiken—Erfolgsfaktoren*. Wiesbaden: Gabler, 3–92.

124. *Globalisierung in kleinen und mittleren Unternehmen. Erfahrungen und Ansatzpunkte für das Personalmanagement (Globalization of SMEs—Experiences and recommendations for human resource management)*, Praxispapiere. Düsseldorf: DGFP (forthcoming).

125. N. Kinnie, J. Purcell, S. Hutchinson, M. Terry, M. Collinson, & H. Scarbrough. (1999). Employment relations in SMEs—Market-driven or customer-shaped? *Employee Relations, 21*, 218–235; B. S. Klaas, J. McClendon, & T. W. Gainey. (2000). Managing HR in the small and medium enterprise: The impact of professional employer organizations. *Entrepreneurship Theory and Practice*, 107–124.

126. T. M. Kühlmann. (2000). Internationalisierung des Mittelstandes als Herausforderung für die Personalauswahl und –entwicklung (Internationalization of Medium-Sized Enterprises as a Challenge for Recruitment and Development). In Gerhard und Lore Kienbaum Stiftung, J. Gutmann, & R. Kabst (Eds.), *Internationalisierung im Mittelstand. Chancen—Risiken—Erfolgsfaktoren*. Wiesbaden: Gabler, 357–371.

127. B. S. Klaas, J. McClendon, & T. W. Gainey. (2000). Managing HR in the small and medium enterprise: The impact of professional employer organizations. *Entrepreneurship Theory and Practice*, 107.

128. Ibid., 107–124.

Chapter 4

Staffing International Operations for Sustained Global Growth

As outlined in the Chapter 3 vignette, we can observe more and more international mergers, acquisitions, and alliances, highlighting the continuous trend of the internationalization of companies. With expansion beyond national borders and the forging of partnerships with foreign organizations, businesses and managers move into more complex and uncertain environments, as the following appeal for help from a Dutch national in a forum provided by Canadian immigration law firm Campbell Cohen (CanadaVisa.com) illustrates:

> Hi there,
>
> Looking for some help. I am a Dutch citizen and a Canadian Permanent Resident. I have lived in Canada for the past 6 years. I work for the Canadian company Provincial Aerospace in Newfoundland. I am being sent on contract (for anywhere between 3 and 12 years) to Curacao (the Netherlands Antilles). There I will be working for Provincial Airlines N.V., which will be a Netherlands Antillean company, wholly owned by the Canadian company Provincial Aerospace. Will I be considered to be working for a Canadian company? In other words, can I stay for longer than 3 years and keep my Permanent Residency in Canada? I will not be paying income taxes in Canada anymore, but in the Netherlands Antilles.
>
> Thanks for your help,
>
> Dutch PR holder

This appeal for help provides an indication of the complexities facing managers when they are sent on foreign assignments and the ambiguity and uncertainty that confront these managers—particularly when the home-country office and its management provide limited support and help. The quoted message illustrates the importance of the HR function and highlights the need for HRM to play a leading role in the staffing of international operations by supporting and guiding managers involved in assignments in foreign countries—and by that we mean not only in terms of clarifying the nationality of the company for which a person will actually be working.

Introduction

This chapter defines the role of HRM in sustaining international business operations and growth. We examine the various approaches taken to staff international operations and the allocation of human resources to the firm's various international operations to ensure effective strategic outcomes. The pivotal role of international assignments is outlined.

We conclude with a discussion of the role of the HR function within this context, examining in particular the issue of centralization and decentralization of the HR function and its activities.

Approaches to Staffing

Internationalizing firms confront staffing issues that are either not present in a domestic environment or are complicated by the international context in which these activities take place. Take, for example, this scenario. A Canadian MNE wishes to appoint a new finance director for its Irish subsidiary. It may decide to fill the position by selecting from finance staff available in its parent operations (that is, a PCN), or to recruit locally (a HCN), or to seek a suitable candidate from one of its other foreign subsidiaries (a TCN).

The IHRM literature uses four terms to describe MNE approaches to managing and staffing their subsidiaries. These terms are taken from the seminal work of Perlmutter,[1] who claimed that it was possible to identify among international executives three primary attitudes—*ethnocentric*, *polycentric*, and *geocentric*— toward building a multinational enterprise, based on top-management assumptions on which key product, functional, and geographical decisions were made. To demonstrate these three attitudes, Perlmutter used aspects of organizational design such as decision making, evaluation and control, information flows, and complexity of organization. He also included "perpetuation," which he defined as "recruiting, staffing, development." A fourth attitude—*regiocentric*—was added later.[2] We will consider the connection between these four categories and staffing practices, and examine the advantages and disadvantages of each approach.

Ethnocentric

In an **ethnocentric** system, few foreign subsidiaries have any autonomy, and strategic decisions are made at headquarters. Key positions in domestic and foreign operations are held by headquarters' personnel. Subsidiaries are managed by staff from the home country (PCNs). There are often sound business reasons for pursuing an ethnocentric staffing policy:

- A perceived lack of qualified host-country nationals (HCNs).
- The need to maintain good communication, coordination, and control links with corporate headquarters. For firms at the early stages of internationalization, an ethnocentric approach can reduce the perceived high risk. When a multinational acquires a firm in another country, it may wish to initially replace local managers with PCNs to ensure that the new subsidiary complies with overall corporate objectives and policies, or because local staff may not have the required level of competence. Thus, an ethnocentric approach to a particular foreign market situation could be perfectly valid for a very experienced multinational. Having your own person, in whom you

 4.1

ethnocentric

subsidiary activities controlled primarily by home-country operation; key managers are PCNs

can place a degree of trust to "do the right thing," can moderate the perceived high risk involved in foreign activities. This has been referred to by Bonache, Brewster, and Suutari as "assignments as control."[3]

An ethnocentric policy, however, has a number of disadvantages, according to Zeira:[4]

- It limits the promotion opportunities of HCNs, which may lead to reduced productivity and increased turnover among that group.
- The adaptation of expatriate managers to host countries often takes a long time, during which PCNs often make mistakes and poor decisions.
- When PCN and HCN compensation packages are compared, the often considerable income gap in favour of PCNs is often viewed by HCNs as unjustified.
- For many expatriates, a key overseas position means new status, authority, and an increase in standard of living (see IHRM Today 4.1). These changes may affect expatriates' sensitivity to the needs and expectations of their host-country subordinates. These needs and expectations can be very different from those encountered in the home country, and international managers have to understand this, as IHRM Today 4.2 illustrates.

Expatriates are also very expensive to maintain in overseas locations. A recent study by PricewaterhouseCoopers[5] reports that the average expatriate assignment cost per annum is US$311,000, with a range of between US$103,000 and US$396,000. It is interesting to note that the average expatriate management cost amounts to US$22,378 as compared to the management of an average employee of US$3,000 (see IHRM Today 4.3).

IHRM Today 4.1

No Nicer Place Than Canada

While it is true that many expatriates who go on international assignments will experience an increase in standards of living, Canadian expatriates most likely will not—as they have already some of the highest standards of living at home. Several surveys have ranked Canadian cities in top places in terms of quality of life. A global survey by Mercer Human Resource Consulting ranked Calgary number one in the world in terms of quality and availability of hospital and medical supplies and the level of air pollution and infectious diseases. In Mercer's 2006–2007 quality of life index measuring political, socioeconomic and environ-mental aspects, health and safety, education, transportation, and public services, Vancouver came 3rd, Toronto was 15th, and Ottawa finished 18th, followed by Montreal as 22nd and Calgary as 24th. And for the fourth year in a row (2002–2005), Vancouver was ranked the most livable city for British expatriates by *The Economist*.

Sources: Lazaruk, Susan. (2005, October 4). *The Economist* magazine names Vancouver most livable city for Brit expats. *The Canadian Press*; and Galt, Virginia. (2007, April 2). No place cleaner than Calgary, global survey says. *The Globe and Mail*.

What Works at Home Does Not Necessarily Work Abroad: Impressions from Working in Poland

Rainer van Daak was born in Frankfurt, Germany. Currently, he is working as an international sales manager for a German international electronics company in Warsaw, Poland. He summarizes some aspects of his working experience in Poland:

> All my colleagues here are Polish. In my company, I'm the only foreigner in Poland, and also the only one in the whole of Eastern Europe! A lot of people want to work for the parent company in the US and I know people who have gone to Australia or Singapore.
>
> I think people are afraid to come to Eastern Europe because salaries are lower. But I can recommend working in Poland. It's a good experience. There are jobs here and a lot more people can speak English these days.
>
> The working culture is different though. People are not so punctual and projects tend to start at the last minute. I think Germans like

> to be ready in advance. You can be a German-style manager and push everyone or you can be a friend.
>
> People don't take things from your experience. They have their own way of doing things. You can try to suggest doing things a different way and switching back if it doesn't work. But they don't even want to try. It's really hard for a manager.
>
> Polish people are really smart and Polish universities are really good. You see this in the field of electronics. International companies come here to hire Polish developers. Poles are very inventive. They haven't always had access to parts so they improvise and look at things differently.

Source: *Europeans on the Move—Portraits of 31 Mobile Workers.* (2006). European Commission. Luxemburg: Office for Official Publications of the European Communities.

Polycentric

In the **polycentric** approach, the MNE treats each subsidiary as a distinct national entity with some decision-making autonomy. Subsidiaries are usually managed by local nationals (HCNs), who are seldom promoted to positions at headquarters, and PCNs are rarely transferred to foreign subsidiary operations. The main advantages of a polycentric policy, some of which address shortcomings of the ethnocentric policy identified above, are:

RPC 4.2

polycentric

each subsidiary treated as a distinct national entity; usually managed by HCNs

- Employing HCNs eliminates language barriers, avoids the adjustment problems of expatriate managers and their families, and removes the need for expensive cultural awareness training programs.
- Employment of HCNs allows a multinational company to take a lower profile in sensitive political situations.
- Employment of HCNs is less expensive, even if a premium is paid to attract high-quality applicants.
- Gives continuity to the management of foreign subsidiaries. This approach avoids the turnover of key managers that, by its very nature, results from an ethnocentric approach.

The Cost of Employing Expatriates

The chart below compares the cost of employing a Canadian manager in the United Kingdom to employing a U.K. manager. The example involves a manager, based in Ontario, who earns about $85,000 per year, with a $17,000 bonus, who is to be sent on a three-and-a-half-year assignment to London, England. He is married, with one school-aged child who attends private school. This manager receives an automobile allowance, as well as one trip home per year. The company pays for the relocation, household goods storage, and tax return preparations. As shown in the chart below, the cost of sending this manager on an international assignment is nearly a million dollars, compared to the approximately $300,000 it would cost to employ a U.K.-based manager.

Cost Element	Cost ($)
Base salary	297,000
Bonus	59,500
Gross income	357,000
Cost-of-living allowance	92,800
Housing allowance	135,000
Education allowance	61,500
Automobile allowance	55,300
Home leave (1 per year)	32,400
Relocation, storage, and tax return	76,300
Additional tax expenses	175,500
Total cost	**985,800**

Source: Belcourt, Monica, Bohlander, George, and Snell, Scott. (2007). *Managing Human Resources*. Toronto: Thomson Nelson.

A polycentric policy, however, has its own disadvantages:

- Bridging the gap between HCN subsidiary managers and PCN managers at corporate headquarters. Language barriers, conflicting national loyalties, and a range of cultural differences (for example, personal value differences and differences in attitudes toward business) may isolate the corporate headquarters staff from the various foreign subsidiaries. The result may be that a multinational firm could become a "federation" of independent national units with nominal links to corporate headquarters.
- Career paths of HCN and PCN managers. Host-country managers have limited opportunities to gain experience outside their own country and cannot progress beyond the senior positions in their own subsidiary. Parent-country managers also have limited opportunities to gain overseas experience. As headquarters positions are held only by PCNs, the senior corporate management group will have limited exposure to international operations and, over time, this will constrain strategic decision making and resource allocation.

Of course, in some cases the host government may dictate that key managerial positions must be filled by its nationals. Alternatively, the multinational may wish to be perceived as a local company as part of a strategy of local responsiveness. Having HCNs in key, visible positions assists this.

Geocentric

In a **geocentric** system, the MNE takes a global approach to its operations, recognizing that each part (subsidiaries and headquarters) makes a unique contribution with its unique competence. It is accompanied by a worldwide integrated business, and nationality is ignored in favour of ability. This is a major goal that the European telecommunications company Vodafone would like to achieve. As a company speaker said:

> We want to create an international class of managers. In our view, the right way to do it is to have people close to one another, sharing their different approaches and understanding how each different part of the company faces specific business challenges in the same overall scenario. We want to develop a group of people who understand the challenges of being global on the one hand and are still deeply rooted in the local countries on the other. Our target is to develop an international management capability that can leverage our global scale and scope to maintain our leadership in the industry.[6]

There are three main advantages to this approach:

- It enables a multinational firm to develop an international executive team that assists in developing a global perspective and an internal pool of labour for deployment throughout the global organization.
- It overcomes the "federation" drawback of the polycentric approach.
- It supports cooperation and resource sharing across units.

As with the other staffing approaches, disadvantages are associated with a geocentric policy:

- Host governments want a large number of their citizens employed and may utilize immigration controls in order to force HCN employment if enough people and adequate skills are available or require training of a HCN over a specified time period to replace a foreign national.
- Many Western countries require companies to provide extensive documentation if they wish to hire a foreign national instead of a local national. Providing this documentation can be time-consuming, expensive, and at times futile. Of course, the same drawback applies to an ethnocentric policy. A related issue, which will be discussed later, is the difficulty of obtaining a work permit for the accompanying spouse or partner.
- A geocentric policy can be expensive to implement because of increased training and relocation costs. A related factor is the need to

R P C 4.3

geocentric
MNE takes global approach to operations, recognizing unique competence of foreign subsidiary

have a compensation structure with standardized international base pay, which may be higher than national levels in many countries.

- Large numbers of PCNs, TCNs, and HCNs need to be sent abroad in order to build and maintain the international team required to support a geocentric staffing policy. To successfully implement a geocentric staffing policy, therefore, requires longer lead time and more centralized control of the staffing process. This necessarily reduces the independence of subsidiary management in these issues, and this loss of autonomy may be resisted by the subsidiary.

Welch[7] has identified IHRM barriers that may impede a multinational from building the staffing resources required to sustain the geocentric policy that is implicit in globalization literature. The barriers—staff availability, time and cost constraints, host government requirements, and ineffective HRM policies—reflect the issues surrounding the geocentric approach listed in the literature reviewed above. While there may be a genuine predisposition among top managers at headquarters regarding the staffing of its global operations, leveraging critical resources in order to build the necessary international team of managers may prove to be a major challenge.

Regiocentric

 4.4

regiocentric

foreign subsidiary reflects the geographic strategy and structure of the MNE

The **regiocentric** approach reflects the geographic strategy and structure of the MNE. Like the geocentric approach, it utilizes a wider pool of managers but in a limited way. Staff may move outside their countries but only within the particular geographic region. Regional managers may not be promoted to headquarters positions but enjoy a degree of regional autonomy in decision making.[8] For example, a Canadian-based firm could create three regions: Europe, the Americas, and Asia–Pacific. European staff would be transferred throughout the European region (say a Briton to Germany, a French national to Belgium, and a German to Spain). Staff transfers to the Asian–Pacific region from Europe would be rare, as would transfers from the regions to headquarters in Canada.

The advantages of using a regiocentric approach are:

- It allows interaction between executives transferred to regional headquarters from subsidiaries in the region and PCNs posted to the regional headquarters.
- It reflects some sensitivity to local conditions, since local subsidiaries are staffed almost totally by HCNs.
- It can be a way for a multinational to gradually move from a purely ethnocentric or polycentric approach to a geocentric approach.[9]

There are some disadvantages in a regiocentric policy:

- It can produce federalism at a regional rather than a country level and constrain the organization from taking a global stance.
- While this approach does improve career prospects at the national level, it only moves the barrier to the regional level. Staff may

advance to regional headquarters but seldom to positions at the parent headquarters.

IHRM Notebook 4.1 summarizes the advantages and disadvantages of using the three categories of staff—PCNs, HCNs and TCNs.

 4.5

IHRM Notebook 4.1

The Advantages and Disadvantages of Using PCNs, TCNs, and HCNs

Parent-Country Nationals

Advantages

- Organizational control and coordination is maintained and facilitated.
- Promising managers are given international experience.
- PCNs may be the best people for the job because of special skills and experiences.
- There is assurance that the subsidiary will comply with company objectives, policies, etc.

Disadvantages

- The promotional opportunities of HCNs are limited.
- Adaptation to host country may take a long time.
- PCNs may impose an inappropriate HQ style.
- Compensation for PCNs and HCNs may differ.

Third-Country Nationals

Advantages

- Salary and benefit requirements may be lower than for PCNS.
- TCNs may be better informed than PCNs about the host-country environment.

Disadvantages

- Transfers must consider possible national animosities (e.g., India and Pakistan).
- The host government may resent hiring of TCNs.
- TCNs may not want to return to their own countries after assignment.

Host-Country Nationals

Advantages

- Language and other barriers are eliminated.
- Hiring costs are reduced, and no work permit is required.
- Continuity of management improves, since HCNs stay longer in positions.
- Government policy may dictate hiring of HCNs.
- Morale among HCNs may improve as they see career potential.

Disadvantages

- Control and coordination of HQ may be impeded.
- HCNs have limited career opportunity outside the subsidiary.
- Hiring HCNs limits opportunities for PCNs to gain foreign experience.
- Hiring HCNs could encourage a federation of national rather than global units.

A Philosophy toward Staffing

In summary, based on top-management attitudes, a multinational can pursue one of several approaches to international staffing. It may even proceed on an *ad hoc* basis,[10] rather than systematically selecting one of the four approaches discussed above. A danger with this approach, according to Robinson[11] is that:

> The firm will opt for a policy of using parent-country nationals in foreign management positions by default, that is, simply as an automatic extension of domestic policy, rather than deliberately seeking optimum utilization of management skills.

This option is really a policy by default; there is no conscious decision or evaluation of appropriate policy. The "policy" is a result of corporate inertia, inexperience, or both. The major disadvantage here (apart from the obvious one of inefficient use of resources) is that the firm's responses are reactive rather than proactive, and a consistent human resources strategy that fits its overall business strategy is difficult to achieve.

While the various attitudes have been a useful way of demonstrating the various approaches to staffing foreign operations, it should be stressed that:

- The above categories refer to managerial attitudes that reflect the sociocultural environment in which the internationalizing firm is embedded, and are based on Perlmutter's study of U.S. firms.
- These attitudes may reflect a general top-management attitude, but the nature of international business often forces adaptation on implementation. That is, a firm may adopt an ethnocentric approach to all of its foreign operations, but a particular host government may require the appointment of its own people in the key subsidiary positions; so, for that market, a polycentric approach is mandatory. In such instances, a uniform approach is not achievable.
- As will be outlined in further detail later, the strategic importance of the foreign market, the maturity of the operation, and the degree of cultural distance between the parent and host country influence the way in which the firm approaches a particular staffing decision.[12] In some cases, a MNE may use a combination of approaches. For example, it may operate its European interests in a regiocentric manner and its Southeast Asian interests in an ethnocentric way until there is greater confidence in operating in that region of the world.
- The approach to policy on executive nationality tends to reflect organizational needs. For instance, if the multinational places a high priority on organizational control, then an ethnocentric policy will be adopted. However, there are difficulties in maintaining a uniform approach to international staffing. Therefore, strategies in different countries may require different staffing approaches.

Because of these operating realities, it is sometimes difficult to precisely equate managerial attitudes toward international operations with the structural forms we presented in Chapter 2. The firm external and internal contingencies facing the particular internationalizing firm influence its staffing choices. These include context specificities, company-specific variables, local unit specificities, and IHRM practices.

Context Specificities

The local context of the headquarters as well as of the subsidiary can be described by cultural and institutional variables (for a detailed description of cultural and institutional variables in the host-country context see Chapter 9). Cultural values may differ to a great extent between the headquarters and the host-country context. For example, Tarique, Schuler, and Gong see the cultural similarity between parent country and subsidiary country as a moderator in the relationship between MNE strategy and subsidiary staffing.[13] Gong has found that MNEs tend to staff cultural-distant subsidiaries with PCNs and that this has a positive effect on labour productivity.[14] The institutional environment includes, for example, the legal environment or the education system.[15] The latter may be directly linked to staff availability on the local labour market (see IHRM Today 4.4).

Furthermore, the country-specific contextual factors in the parent country may lead to a country-of-origin effect; i.e., MNEs may try to transfer management practices from their home country to foreign locations. Another effect is the host-country effect, which implies that subsidiaries are influenced by their local environment.[16] In addition, the type of industry in which the firm is active may have an impact as well.

Company-Specific Variables

Company-specific variables are mainly depicted from the framework on strategic HRM in multinational enterprises introduced in Chapter 1. The most relevant variables are MNE structure and strategy, international experience, corporate governance, and organizational culture that describe the MNE as a whole.[17]

Local Unit Specificities

As the staffing approach may vary with the cultural and institutional environment, it may also be dependent on the specificities of the local unit. An important factor here is the establishment method of the subsidiary; i.e., whether it is a merger, an acquisition, or a shared partnership.[18] Furthermore, the strategic role of a subsidiary, its strategic importance for the MNE as a whole and the related questions of the need of control and the locus of decision may play important roles for staffing decisions.[19]

IHRM Practices

Selection, training and development, compensation, and career management (including expatriation as well as repatriation) in a broader firm context—covered in the second part of this book—play an important role in the

Staff Shortages in China

The following newspaper extract reflects the staffing challenges of multinational organizations such as HSBC when operating in environments lacking skilled and qualified staff.

HSBC has added to concern about the hiring crunch facing multinationals in China, saying there are not enough suitable candidates on the ground to back expansion drives. Richard Yorke, chief executive of HSBC China, said finding enough experienced staff and training them adequately was the toughest issue he faced. "This [recruitment] is the largest blockage that we face," Mr. Yorke said yesterday as HSBC and other foreign banks opened locally incorporated subsidiaries to operate in the Chinese retail market. "It is a question of managing high rates of growth in the business in an environment of low general levels of experience."

His comments highlight the battle for talent in the financial services industry in China, a result of rapid expansion of domestic and international companies in a sector that has been gradually opened up to competition under Beijing's accession to the World Trade Organization. Investment by multinationals in China in recent years has squeezed the pool of available staff, making it harder for companies to hire and retain good workers in industries, including engineering, cars and finance. In surveys of foreign executives in China, staffing has often been listed as a bigger problem than copyright violations or government relations.

HSBC expects to hire 1,000 people this year. Its present headcount is 3,000. Citigroup plans to hire a similar number. Standard Chartered said it did not have a specific target for this year. It grew its headcount from 1,200 to 2,200 last year. The hiring crunch has been exacerbated by big local banks that are also aiming to expand in the richer-client and wealth-management segments of the market, which have tended to be the focus of foreign banks. Over the past year, the big four accountancy firms have been embarking on an even more ambitious recruitment drive to cope with the wave of new listings by Chinese companies, while investment management firms have also been expanding at a rapid rate.

Source: Dyer, Geoff. (2007, April 3). HSBC highlights China staffing woes. *The Financial Times*, 17.

development of effective policies required to sustain a preferred staffing choice.

These four groups of factors are supposed to systematically affect staffing practices. Due to situational factors, individual staffing decisions might be made in an unexpected way. Further, it has to be acknowledged that there are interdependencies between the determining variables outlined in Figure 4.1. However, for analytical reasons, only the impact on the staffing choices, which is in the centre of interest in this chapter, is discussed. Figure 4.1 illustrates the suggested linkages.

 4.8

The model in Figure 4.1 may be helpful in drawing together the various contextual, organizational, and HR-related issues in determining staffing choices. For example, a firm that is maturing into a networked organization (company specificity) will require IHRM approaches and activities that will

FIGURE 4.1

Determinants of Staffing Choices

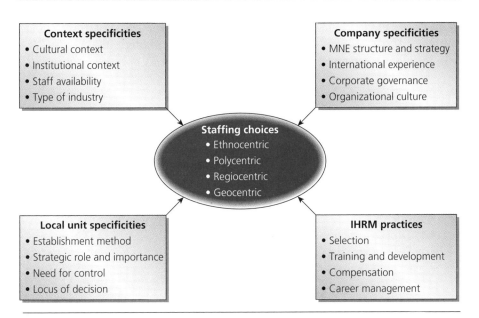

Context specificities
- Cultural context
- Institutional context
- Staff availability
- Type of industry

Company specificities
- MNE structure and strategy
- International experience
- Corporate governance
- Organizational culture

Staffing choices
- Ethnocentric
- Polycentric
- Regiocentric
- Geocentric

Local unit specificities
- Establishment method
- Strategic role and importance
- Need for control
- Locus of decision

IHRM practices
- Selection
- Training and development
- Compensation
- Career management

Source: Based on: Welch, D. (1994). Determinants of international human resource management approaches and activities: A suggested framework. *Journal of Management Studies, 31*(2), 150; De Cieri, H., & Dowling, P. J. (2006). Strategic international human resource management in multinational enterprises: Developments and directions. In G. K. Stahl and I. Björkman (Eds.), *Handbook of research in international human resource management*. Cheltenham, UK: Edward Elgar, 15–35; Thompson, Y., & Keating, M. (2004). An empirical study of executive nationality staffing practices in foreign-owned MNC subsidiaries in Ireland. *Thunderbird International Business Review, 46*(6), 771–797; and Festing, M., Eidems, J., & Royer, S. Strategic issues and local constraints in transnational compensation strategies: An analysis of cultural, institutional and political influences. (2007, April). *European Management Journal, 25*(2), 118–131.

enhance its ability to develop a flexible global organization that is centrally integrated and coordinated yet locally responsive—a geocentric approach. However, a key assumption underlying the geocentric staffing philosophy is that the multinational has sufficient numbers of high-calibre staff (PCNs, TCNs, and HCNs) constantly available for transfer anywhere, whenever global management needs dictate.[20]

As we discussed earlier, it is not easy to find or nurture the required numbers of high-quality staff (firm-specific and situation variables), nor assign them to certain operations due to host-country requirements (context specificities). For example, a study by Richards[21] of staffing practices and subsidiary performance of U.S. multinationals in the United Kingdom and Thailand found a link among perceptions of subsidiary performance, subsidiary location, and staffing. Subsidiaries in Thailand appeared to perform better with an HCN in charge than a PCN.

Many studies investigating the determinants of staffing policies have been conducted in MNEs stemming from developed countries. Recently, a study of Chinese MNEs has confirmed that Western models are generally applicable to Chinese MNEs as well.[22] However, the author points out that the same categories sometimes have different meanings. It is interesting to note that in this study, culturally determined factors such as trust and personal moral merits have proved to be of special importance for staffing decisions. Overall, it seems that the different determinants of staffing choices outlined above all have an important impact, although the model as a whole is yet to be empirically tested.

Transferring Staff for International Business Activities

The above discussion demonstrates the options for staffing key positions in foreign operations. We will now look at the HR consequences of these approaches, and the broader implications in terms of:

- Reasons for using international assignments.
- Types of international assignments.
- Role of expatriates and non-expatriates.
- Role of inpatriates.

Reasons for International Assignments

Given the difficulties surrounding international assignments, it is reasonable to question why multinationals persist in using expatriates. Certainly, there are ebbs and flows associated with the number of staff moved internationally. Frequently, predictions are made that expatriates will become like dinosaurs, as firms implement localization strategies, replacing expatriates with HCNs as a way of containing employment costs. For example, in a 2005 survey of 203 companies by the consulting firm PricewaterhouseCoopers,[23] participants expected their use of expatriates would continue to grow in response to pressures for internationally mobile staff. This trend was despite the global environment volatility and may be regarded as evidence of a continuing commitment to international business operations.[24] Another survey of global trends in international assignments, by the consulting firm GMAC,[25] confirmed this trend. It indicated that 47 percent of participating firms expected an increase in the number of expatriates, compared to 39 percent in its 2004 survey.[26] The increase is expected for short-term as well as for long-term assignments.[27] Why? As a practitioner involved in expatriate management explains:[28]

> As I talk to people, they say they wish they could shrink the expatriate population because of the expense in terms of benefits, services and support. And as long as I've been in this business, people say they are going to scale down on expats but it never happens. Until we have people all over the world with the skills they need, employers are going to have to continue to send expatriates.

The international management and IHRM literature has consistently identified three key organizational reasons for the use of various forms of international assignments: position filling, management development, and organization development.

Position Filling

The organization has a need and, depending on the type of position and the level involved, will either employ someone locally or transfer a suitable candidate. The 2002 global survey by the consulting firm GMAC Global Relocation Services[29] asked respondents to indicate their primary objectives for international assignments. The most common reason was to fill a skills gap, followed by the launch of a new endeavour, and technology transfer. In the 2004 survey, firms ranked "to fill a skills gap" as the primary reason, followed by launch of a new endeavour and building management expertise. Likewise, Wong's study[30] of two Japanese department stores in Hong Kong found that short-term job filling was the main reason for using expatriate staff rather than for long-term development and socialization of individuals. However, this seems to have changed. Interestingly, a 2006 study by PricewaterhouseCoopers[31] revealed that the problem of staff availability had decreased in the previous five years. Instead, the costs of staff were an important driver, at least for European organizations.

Management Development

Staff can be moved into other parts of the organization for training and development purposes, and to assist in the development of common corporate values. For this reason, we see headquarters staff transferred to subsidiary operations, or subsidiary staff transferring into the parent operations or to other subsidiary operations. Assignments may be for varying lengths of time and may involve project work as well as a trainee position. The perceived link between international experience and career development can be a motivation for staff to agree to such transfers.

Organization Development

In organization development, strategic objectives of the operation come into play: the need for control; the transfer of knowledge, competence, procedures, and practices to various locations; and the exploitation of global market opportunities, as we outlined in Chapter 1. As a result, organizational capabilities enabling a firm to compete in global markets might be developed.[32] Indeed, a 2002 PricewaterhouseCoopers report[33] found that greater staff mobility assisted in supporting a global corporate culture and assisted the cross-fertilization of ideas and practices. One participant from an insurance firm is quoted as saying: "To create a truly global organization, we will have to embed a culture of cross-border mobility into the organization's genetic code, which will take 10 years." International assignments allow staff to gain a broader perspective, as they become familiar with more than one operation (see IHRM Today 4.5).

Types of International Assignments

Employees are transferred internationally for varying lengths of time, depending on the purpose of the transfer and the nature of the task to be performed. Companies tend to classify types according the length or duration of the assignment:

short-term assignments

up to three months

extended assignments

up to one year

long-term assignments

one to five years

- *Short term:* Up to three months. **Short-term assignments** are usually for troubleshooting, project supervision, or as a stopgap measure until a more permanent arrangement can be found.
- *Extended:* Up to one year. **Extended assignments** may involve activities similar to those for short-term assignments.
- *Long term:* **Long-term assignments** vary from one to five years, involving a clearly defined role in the receiving operation (such as being the managing director of a subsidiary). The long-term assignment has also been referred to as a *traditional expatriate assignment.*

IHRM Notebook 4.2 illustrates some of the differences between short-term and traditional expatriate assignments. It should be noted that definitions of short-term and long-term assignments vary and depend up organizational choices.

Within these three broad assignment categories, it is possible to find what are termed *non-standard assignments:* commuter assignments, rotational assignments, contractual assignments, and virtual assignments.

Commuter Assignments

Commuter assignments are special arrangements in which the person concerned commutes from the home country on a weekly or biweekly basis to the place of work in another country. Cross-border workers or daily commuters are not included. Usually, the family of the assignee stays in the home country. For example, the person lives in Windsor, Ontario, but works in Detroit. In 2001,

Differences between Traditional and Short-Term Assignments

	Traditional Assignments	**Short-Term Assignments**
Purpose	• Filling positions or skills gaps • Management development • Organizational development	• Skills transfer/problem solving • Management development • Managerial control
Duration	Typically 12–36 months	Typically up to 6 months or 12 months
Family's position	Family joins the assignee abroad	Assignee is unaccompanied by the family
Selection	Formal procedures	Mostly informal, little bureaucracy
Advantages	• Good relationships with colleagues • Constant monitoring	• Flexibility • Simplicity • Cost-effectiveness
Disadvantages	• Dual-career considerations • Expensive • Less flexibility	• Taxation • Side effects (alcoholism, high divorce rate) • Poor relationships with local colleagues • Work permit issues

Source: Adapted from: Tahvanainen, M., Welch, D., and Worm, V. (2005). Implications of Short-Term International Assignments. *European Management Journal, 23*(6), 669.

more than half of the 82 companies representing 13 nationalities that were investigated in a study by PricewaterhouseCoopers expected a further increase in the use of commuter assignments.[34]

Rotational Assignments

Rotational assignments involve employees commuting from the home country to a place of work in another country for a short, set period, followed by a break in the home country. Rotational assignments are used for workers on oil rigs or in other hardship locations, for example. Again, the family usually remains in the home country. Out of all non-standard assignments, companies expected the lowest growth rates for this type of assignment.[35]

Contractual Assignments

Contractual assignments are used in situations where employees with specific skills vital to an international project are assigned for a limited duration of six to twelve months. Research and development (R&D) is one area that is using multinational project teams and lends itself to short-term contractual assignments in conjunction with longer-term assignments and virtual teams.[36] According to the above-mentioned study by PricewaterhouseCoopers, contractual assignments play only a slightly more important role than rotational assignments.

Virtual Assignments

In a virtual assignment, the employee does not relocate to a host location but manages, from home base, international responsibilities for a part of the organization in another country. In the case of virtual assignments, the manager heavily relies on communications technologies such as telephone, e-mail, and video conferences. Furthermore, frequent visits in the host country are necessary. The PricewaterhouseCoopers[37] survey found that 28 percent of the surveyed firms anticipated an increasing use of virtual assignments, compared with 17 percent in a similar survey two years previously. A total of 65 percent of respondents who use virtual assignments reported having seen an increase in the number of virtual assignments used by their company and the same proportion indicated an expected increase in the next two years. The main reasons given by responding firms for experimenting with the virtual assignment were similar to that of other non-standard forms of international assignments: the shortage of mobile staff prepared to accept longer term postings, and for cost containment reasons.

Some of these arrangements assist in overcoming the high costs of international assignments. However, non-standard assignments are not always effective substitutes for the traditional expatriate assignment. As the PricewaterhouseCoopers 2000 report's authors point out:

> There are real concerns about the viability of commuter arrangements over an extended period of time due to the build up of stress resulting from intensive travel commitments and the impact on personal relationships.[38]

Most of the research into assignment issues has been around the long-term assignment type, mainly because it forms the bulk of international assignments. In contrast, short-term and extended assignments have received limited research attention.[39] The situation is similar in terms of non-standard assignments. For example, Welch, Worm, and Fenwick[40] comment: "While non-standard assignments have long been used in conjunction with, or instead of, traditional expatriate assignments, this has yet to translate into a comparable body of academic inquiry." Their study of the use of virtual assignments by Australian and Danish firms has suggested that, while there are certain advantages of operating virtually (such as not having to relocate a family unit), there are disadvantages that may affect successful work outcomes. These are: (1) role conflict, dual allegiance, and identification issues and (2) interpersonal and work relationships.

Role Conflict, Dual Allegiance, and Identification Issues

Role conflict, dual allegiance, and identification issues can arise between the person in the home location and the virtual work group in the foreign location. For example, to whom does the virtual assignee "belong"—to the home location where the person physically resides for most of the time or to the foreign unit? How much time should be devoted to the "virtual" work responsibilities versus the "real" work?

Interpersonal and Work Relationships

Given that much of the work is done through electronic media, the potential for cultural misunderstandings increases, and the geographical distance means normal group interaction is not possible. Communication is mainly through conference calls, videoconferencing, and e-mails, and depends on good skills in using these media. Frequent visits between the two locations are required to support the working of this arrangement, as not everything can be settled virtually. Face-to-face meetings are still required.

Virtual assignments tend to be used for regional positions—such as European marketing manager, where the person is mainly coordinating a number of countries' marketing activities but is based at a regional centre. The 2000 PricewaterhouseCoopers study found that virtual assignments were more common in Europe, with no companies indicating the use of such arrangements in the Asia–Pacific region. Geographical distance in terms of flight hours and time zones were the main difficulties encountered in operating virtually between operations in Europe and the Asia–Pacific.

The Roles of an Expatriate

As mentioned previously, the reasons for using expatriates are not mutually exclusive. They do however underpin expectations about the roles that staff play as a consequence of being transferred from one location to another country. These roles are delineated in Figure 4.2.

FIGURE 4.2

The Roles of an Expatriate

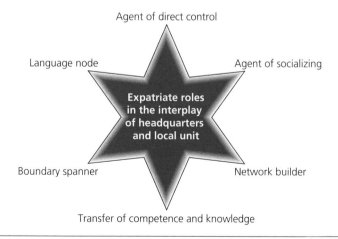

Agent of direct control

Language node

Agent of socializing

Expatriate roles in the interplay of headquarters and local unit

Boundary spanner

Network builder

Transfer of competence and knowledge

The Expatriate as an Agent of Direct Control

The use of staff transfers can be regarded as a bureaucratic control mechanism,[41] where the primary role is that of ensuring compliance through direct supervision. Harzing[42] found that German companies tend toward this form of control. She labels expatriates who are such agents as "bears," arguing that the analogy reflects the level of dominance of this type of expatriate control. To a certain extent, using expatriates for control reflects an ethnocentric predisposition, but this can be important in ensuring subsidiary compliance, enabling strategic objectives for local operations to be achieved.

The Expatriate as an Agent of Socialization

The role of the expatriate as an agent of socialization is related to the use of corporate culture as an informal control mechanism that we examined in Chapter 2. There is an implicit expectation that expatriates assist in the transfer of shared values and beliefs (see IHRM Today 4.6).

Harzing likens expatriates who transfer corporate values to "bumblebees." However, as Fenwick et al.[43] point out, there has been little empirical investigation as to how effective expatriates have been as agents of socialization. In fact, attempts to instill corporate values and norms ritualized in the form of certain expected behaviours often have negative results at the subsidiary level.

International assignments do assist in knowledge sharing and competence transfer, and encourage adoption of common work practices, aspects of which may comprise elements of corporate culture. Staff in the various organizational units may be exposed to different viewpoints and perspectives that will shape their behaviour and may reinforce their feeling of belonging. In their study, Goodall and Roberts[44] relate a reaction by a Chinese employee in the Chinese operation of a European oil company. Her time in the parent's operation in Europe enabled her to appreciate how the company valued its name and reputation, and she was able to better understand the company's code of conduct and attitude toward occupational health and safety.

Expatriates as Network Builders

As we discussed in Chapter 2, international assignments are viewed as a way of developing social capital:[45] fostering interpersonal linkages that can be used for informal control and communication purposes. Naturally, as employees move between various organizational units, their network of personal relationships changes, leading to Harzing's analogy of expatriates as "spiders" to describe this role. How these employees are utilized is person-dependent. People tend to nurture and protect their networks, to be very selective about the way they use their connections, and to evaluate the potential damage to key individuals in their networks if the connection was to be used inappropriately. In their study of project teams and networks, Schweiger et al.[46] provide the following example of how international assignments assisted network development:

Toyota's Senseis

In a rare interview,* Toyota's president Katsuaki Watanabe explains how Toyota transfers its corporate values and beliefs to its international operations and outlines some of the challenges.

> It takes time to develop Toyota people, who are trained on the job rather than in a classroom. Only when employees start working at Toyota do they learn from their superiors what values and skills they need in order to do their jobs. Most of our plants outside Japan were set up in the past ten years, so even senior employees overseas have relatively little experience with the Toyota Way. Toyota develops T-type people.** As you may know, the vertical stroke of the T stands for the fact that employees must intensify or deepen what they do, and the horizontal stroke indicates that they must learn other jobs. Creating T-type personnel is a time-consuming process. However, in many countries outside Japan it's tough to employ people for the long term. The moment we start operations, employee turnover begins. So we are learning how to retain people.
>
> We used to transmit the Toyota Way through the mother plant system, whereby a Japanese plant served as the parent of each new overseas plant we set up. That Japanese plant was responsible for training people in the overseas plant and instilling the Toyota Way in them. Because of the rate at which we are growing overseas, we have done away with that system. We now send people from Japan, coordinators, to instill our philosophy and concepts in our overseas companies. When a new company is established, the coordinator will serve as a teacher, or sensei, for its employees. After some years a second-generation coordinator will serve as a coach rather than a mentor. After several more years a third-generation coordinator will act as an adviser rather than a coach. The coordinators are critical to training people in the Toyota Way, but we have only about 2,000 coordinators. Our people in Japan take turns serving as coordinators every three to five years. Given the size of our business, we need three times as many coordinators as we have at present.

Sources: *Stewart, Thomas A., & Raman, Anand P. (2007, July–August). Lessons from Toyota's long drive. *Harvard Business Review*, 74–83.
**See: Hansen, Morten T., & von Oetinger, Bolko. (2001, March). Introducing T-Shaped Managers: Knowledge Management's Next Generation. *Harvard Business Review*.

I depended heavily on the contacts I had developed over the years. The time spent in international assignments was invaluable. I knew important people in several key operations. I knew how they operated and what was important to them. They also knew that I was credible and would help them when the opportunity arose.

Further, as Marschan et al.[47] explain: "People may be introduced to each other but not form the type of relationship on which productive networks are built." Take the case of Laura, an American expatriate, who has worked in India for several years and built up a strong network comprising subsidiary staff, key host-government officials, clients, suppliers, and the like. She is now being transferred to the Canadian operations and Angelo, from the Italian subsidiary, is taking her place. Laura may take Angelo around and introduce him to key individuals in this personal network, but it will not guarantee that Angelo will be readily accepted into that network of critical contacts.

W W W 4.2

W W W 4.3

While short-term assignments may not allow the expatriate to develop as wide a range of contacts in one location as a traditional assignment allows, over time they can increase the number and variety of networks, giving opportunity for the transfer of ideas and competence.[48] Duration of the assignment, therefore, will have an impact on the person's ability to develop networks.

Expatriates as Boundary Spanners

Boundary spanning refers to activities, such as gathering information, that bridge internal and external organizational contexts. Expatriates are considered boundary spanners because they can collect host-country information, act as representatives of their firms in the host country, and can influence agents. For example, attending a social function at a foreign embassy can provide the expatriate with an opportunity to network, gather market intelligence, and promote the firm's profile at a high level. Networking activity emerged as a way in which expatriates from various nationalities operating in Hong Kong were able to engage in boundary-spanning activities.[49]

Expatriates as Language Nodes

In Chapter 2, we discussed how many multinational firms operate through language standardization—or a common corporate language—usually English. Marschan-Piekkari et al.[50] found that Finnish expatriates working for the elevator company Kone sometimes became what they termed *language nodes*. They give as an example a Finn (whom they refer to as "Mr. X") who learned to speak Spanish while working as an expatriate in the firm's South American operations. On repatriation back to the Finnish headquarters, Mr. X found that he had become "the man in Finland who speaks Spanish." Kone employees from the firm's Spanish-speaking operations, including Mexico, would call Mr. X, preferring to conduct queries and gain information from him in Spanish and to check information sent to them in English.

Transfer of Competence and Knowledge

Overall, international assignments are seen as an effective way of accomplishing multiple objectives. In fact, one could argue that there are elements of competence and knowledge transfer in all of the roles we have identified. However, evidence as to the effectiveness of expatriates in conducting their numerous roles is sparse. Factors that may affect effectiveness include:

- The creation of an environment of openness and support for cross-fertilization of ideas and implementation of "best practice."
- The need for knowledge and information to travel dyadically, that is, between the expatriate and the host location, and back to the expatriate's home location, if the multinational is to benefit from

international assignments as a mechanism for competence and knowledge transfer.

- Despite the recognition of the importance of personal networks in knowledge and information transfer, staffing decisions often are made without regard to their effect on network relationships. In many cases, there is no strategic approach controlling these effects.
- There is a link between the duration of the assignment and the effective transfer of knowledge and competences. Some knowledge and competence may be transferred quickly, while other skills and knowledge (particularly where a high level of tacitness is present) may take longer.
- Naturally, much of what is transferred depends on the expatriate concerned, in terms of ability to teach others and motivation to act as an agent of knowledge and competence transfer. For example, Goodall and Roberts[51] quote the experience of a Colombian HCN working for a European oil company:

> It is important that there is really a transfer of technology between expat and Colombian. And during the last two years, nothing is learned. The expat goes and then they bring another expat. . . . There should be more of a formal commitment to training, a follow-up. They [expatriates] should be evaluated on coaching with Columbians.

A final point: Bolino and Feldman[52] make an interesting observation that when expatriates are assigned for position filling due to a lack of appropriate local staff, such expatriates are often forced to take over some of the responsibilities of their colleagues due to differences in knowledge and competence levels. Consequently, they argue that expatriates often spend significant time on less challenging tasks to help out co-workers, and train them. In such cases, while the expatriates may assist in skills transfer, over time their own level of competence may decrease as they are not developing their own expertise. Thus, when expatriates return to their home operation, they may find that their knowledge is obsolescing.

The Role of Non-Expatriates

The above discussion centred on the international assignment. What has tended to be overlooked is that a considerable amount of international business involves what can be called non-expatriates: people who travel internationally yet are not considered expatriates as they do not relocate to another country. That is, non-expatriates are international business travellers[53]—people for whom a large proportion of their role involves constant international visits to foreign markets, subsidiary units, international projects, and the like. Non-expatriates are popularly termed "road warriors," "globetrotters," "frequent fliers," or even "flexpatriates."[54]

International travel is an essential component of their work, as in the case of international sales staff whose job is almost totally composed of international travel and managers whose job entails numerous periodic visits to international operations. International sales representatives attend trade fairs, visit foreign agents and distributors, demonstrate new products to potential clients, and negotiate sales contracts. Various staff will visit foreign locations to deal with host-country government officials, alliance partners, subcontracting firms, and foreign suppliers.

In spite of e-mails and videoconferencing, international business travel is increasing.[55] People still prefer to conduct certain business activities, hold meetings, and interact face to face. As Mintzberg et al.[56] note:

> Why do so many effective international managers get into airplanes rather than pick up telephones when they need to communicate seriously? As we move from written communication (letters, e-mail) to strictly oral (telephones) to face-to-face forms, communication appears to become richer and more nuanced.

However, international business travel can make heavy demands on staff. For example, the Norwegian firm Moelven, a global player in the timber industry, when initially developing its operations in the Russian market through importing in the early 1990s, had to become highly involved in building personal relationships with key individuals in Russia:

> One manager from the purchasing department responsible for imports commented: "Personal contacts were so important that during the first three years [of] dealing with the Russians, I had between 50 and 100 trips to Russia, talking to suppliers and maintaining the personal networks."[57]

Apart from the resource implications, there are issues relating to the management of international business travellers that do not seem to be addressed in the IHRM literature. This may be due to the fact that this category of staff does not include expatriates on traditional or non-standard assignments. The international component of their work is performed within the context of their "normal" duties. Regardless, there are several important issues that should be considered. There is a high level of stress involved for those whose job responsibilities contain a large proportion of international business travel. In one of the few articles on this issue, DeFrank et al.[58] identify the following factors as stressors:

- *Home and family issues*—such as missing important anniversaries and school events. The more frequent the travel, the greater the potential for family and marital relationships to be strained.
- *Work arrangements*—the "domestic" side of the job still has to be attended to even though the person is travelling internationally. Modern communications allow work to accompany them, so the business traveller is expected to deal with home-base issues via modem while remote from the office. When the travellers return to the home office, they may face crises, backlogs of paperwork, and so forth.

- *Travel logistics*—airline connections, hotel accommodations, and meeting schedules.
- *Health concerns*—poor diet, lack of physical exercise, lack of sleep, coping with jet lag, and exposure to disease and other illnesses (such as SARS and deep-vein thrombosis).
- *Host-culture issues*—as international business is conducted in other cultural settings, the person is still expected to be able to operate in unfamiliar environments and handle cultural differences effectively. However, the limited empirical and anecdotal evidence suggests that non-expatriates do not receive the same level of cross-cultural training as expatriates—if any.

The above list contains the negatives associated with international business travel. However, there are positives. People involved in this side of international business will relate the excitement and thrills of conducting business deals in foreign locations, the lifestyle (top hotels, business-class travel, duty-free shopping), and its general exotic nature as the reasons why they enjoy international business travel, despite its very real negatives.

Non-expatriate business travellers also perform many of the roles of expatriates in terms of being agents for socialization, network builders, boundary spanners, and language nodes. From the limited evidence available, however, it would seem that the management of staff using these forms of arrangements falls to the functional or line managers involved, rather than the HR department as such.

The Role of Inpatriates

If organizations work on a global scale, they need sufficient qualified staff to meet the requirements of globalization. As we discussed above, a shortage of multicultural managers possessing global leadership competencies may limit the opportunities of an MNE to gain competitive advantage. To support this process, a new term for the management development of a specific type of HCNs called *inpatriation* has recently occurred.

As we outlined in Chapter 1, **inpatriates** are mainly distinguished from expatriates by definition. They include HCNs and TCNs on international assignments from a foreign location to the headquarters of the MNE. Inpatriates are supposed to serve as "linking pins" between the different organizational units of an MNE. According to Reiche, they are "expected to share their local contextual knowledge with HQ staff in order to facilitate effective corporate activities in these local markets. At the same time they are socialized in the HQ corporate culture and learn firm-specific routines and behaviors that enable them to master future management tasks within the organization. As a result, inpatriates seem to act both as knowledge senders and receivers."[59] Collings and Scullion[60] have identified the following key drivers for recruiting inpatriate managers:

inpatriates
HCNs or TCNs from a foreign location who are assigned to MNE headquarters

- Desire to create a global core competency and a cultural diversity of strategic perspectives in the top-management team,[61] thus increasing the capability of organizations to "think global and act local."
- Desire to provide career opportunities for high-potential employees in host countries (i.e., HCNs and TCNs).
- The emergence of developing markets that often represent difficult locations for expatriates in terms of quality of life and cultural adjustment.

Inpatriates represent a phenomenon that can be observed in addition to the traditional expatriation to an increasing extent.[62] For example, the German MNE Bosch employed 519 inpatriates in January 2006. While this number is still small compared to the current number of expatriates (1,059), it is nevertheless significant given that 15 years ago, Bosch assigned only 300 expatriates to foreign locations.[63] It indicates the tremendous process of internationalization that has taken place within this company and that is associated with a need of international managers in all parts of the organization—being able to realize bilateral knowledge transfer between the foreign unit represented by the inpatriate and the headquarters. However, the strategy of inpatriation also underlines that the strategic importance of headquarters is still prevailing, indicating that knowledge of the culture, the structure, and the processes specific to headquarters are still important requirements for vertical career advancement. Despite inpatriation, career opportunities for HCNs and TCNs are often limited: Usually, the assignment to headquarters aims at training the manager for a top-management position back home in the foreign subsidiary. Especially if firms aim at open-sky policies[64] (i.e., offering career opportunities independently from the nationality), inpatriation can only be a first step, reflecting a rather ethnocentric approach. Harvey and Buckley[65] conclude that in this case "inpatriation may be a dangerous process."

While it might be more difficult for inpatriates than for PCNs to realize a vertical career in headquarters, they experience the same integration and repatriation problems as expatriates during and after their international assignment. Consequently, they may not reach the same return on investment for their international assignment as expatriates. This can be guaranteed only if career opportunities for inpatriated HCNs or TCNs exist as well at headquarters. In this case, inpatriation can be an important step in realizing a geocentric orientation within the MNE and thus an open sky for HCN and TCN managers.

Return on Investment of International Assignments

From an organizational perspective, international assignments are a very risky and costly way of developing employees.[66] Consequently, the question arises whether they are worth it. This question gains even more importance as companies are becoming more cost-sensitive when managing expatriates.[67]

Traditionally, the success of an international assignment has been measured using expatriates' failure rates (including premature return from an

 4.9

assignment or unexpected quitting during, as well as after, an assignment),[68] the financial costs associated with the assignment, and the performance of the expatriate.[69] The PricewaterhouseCoopers 2005 survey on international assignments reveals that companies have an increasing interest in measuring the value of international assignments in a more differentiated way.[70] PricewaterhouseCoopers suggests use of a return on investment (ROI) approach. This concept has only recently been applied to international assignments and expatriate management activities.[71] According to McNulty and Tharenou (2004: 88)

> . . . expatriate ROI should be defined as a calculation in which the financial and non-financial benefits to the MNC are compared to the financial and non-financial costs of the international assignment, as appropriate to the assignment's purpose.[72]

While the expenses associated directly with the assignment (such as salary or relocation costs) may be relatively easy to quantify, it is more complex to estimate the administrative costs of running an international assignment.[73] McNulty and Tharenou suggest analysis of all IHRM support activities, including assignment planning, expatriate selection, administration of the relocation program, expatriate compensation, training and development, family support practices, performance management, repatriation, and retention in the context of the assignment purpose with respect to costs and benefits in order to calculate expatriate ROI. Even more complexity is expected when management development outcomes are assessed. Here, the focus should be on the extent to which the assignee has developed a global mindset and/or on the quality of the acquired global leadership skills.[74]

IHRM Notebook 4.3 shows the indicators that can be used to calculate a ROI on a single international assignment. It should be noted here that a "one best" ROI formula for international assignments does not exist, because the objectives pursued with each assignment are likely to be different.[75]

For determining expatriate ROI, McNulty and Tharenou recommend an approach comprising four steps:[76]

1. Identifying financial and non-financial costs and benefits.
2. Linking the costs and benefits to the purpose of the long-term assignment.
3. Identifying the appropriate antecedents from a system's perspective.
4. Conducting the calculation at an appropriate time within the context of the assignment's purpose.

In a 2005 study, Johnson,[77] as well as the GMAC *Global Relocation Trends* survey,[78] found that only 14 percent of the investigated companies measured expatriate ROI. If ROI was measured, half of the investigated companies in the GMAC survey indicated that they defined it as "accomplished assignment objectives at expected cost."[79] It is interesting to note that according to the PricewaterhouseCoopers 2006 survey report, the costs of managing an international assignment program represent 7 percent of the total costs, including compensation, long-term benefits, and allowances.[80]

Indicators for Calculating Return on International Assignment Investment

Investment	Return
Direct costs of the assignment	**Quantifiable assignment objectives, e.g.**
• Employee's salary	• Open a new office (finding a location, establishing an office, hiring and training local employees)
• Taxes	• Increase a company's sales by a specified amount over a certain period of time
• Housing	**Non-quantifiable assignment objectives with respect to organization development, e.g.**
• Shipment of household goods	
• Education assistance for dependants	• Strengthening the corporate culture in the local entity
• Spouse support	• Improving the relationship with a joint venture partner
• Cross-cultural training	• Providing knowledge transfer between headquarters and foreign location
• Goods and service allowance	
• Repatriation logistics	
• Reassignment costs	
Administrative costs of running an international assignment program	**Non-quantifiable assignment objectives with respect to management development, e.g.**
• Home-based HR support (assignment planning, selection and compensation management)	• Understanding an international market critical to the business
• Assignment location or host-based HR support	• Networking in another country to build a new client base
• Post-assignment placement costs	• Integrating into the local work environment
• Post-assignment career tracking costs	• Providing effective feedback to subordinates in a manner appropriate to the local culture
Adjustment costs	• Making presentations to an international audience in a foreign language
• Settling in services	
• Spouse and family support	• Working well across multiple time zones and cultures
• Cross-cultural and language adjustments	
• Destination familiarization and house-hunting trips	

Source: Adapted from: McNulty, Y. M., & Tharenou, P. (2004). Expatriate return on investment. *International Studies of Management and Organization, 34*(3), 68–95; and Johnson, L. (2005). Measuring International Assignment Return on Investment. *Compensation Benefits Review, 37*(2), 50–54.

As we outlined above, international management development has become the major goal associated with international assignments. In this case, all investment is focused on retaining the internationally experienced manager in the company with a long-term career perspective. But as expatriation represents an important transition point in the career of an employee, it includes several career risks. "Expatriation, as a specific time period in one's career, might be conducive to a change of organization, particularly when the individual does not feel that an international assignment is beneficial to his or her career within the expatriation organization."[81] Therefore it is important to focus research on how companies can retain expatriated employees.

Stahl and Cerdin[82] outlined that organizations not providing effective IHRM support practices tend to end up with dissatisfied managers who are likely to leave the company. Surveys have shown that the turnover of repatriated assignees amounts up to percentages between 14 and 23.[83] Considering that the PricewaterhouseCoopers 2006 study revealed important performance increases during and after an international assignment, these turnover rates mean important losses for the firms not able to amortize their investments in the human capital of their international managers. This indicates the importance of post-assignment career tracking as an issue for MNEs (see IHRM Today 4.7).

IHRM Today 4.7

Canadian Expats Coming Home

An article in *The Globe and Mail* in 2006 described some of the issues and challenges with which Canadian expatriates are faced when coming home from international assignments:

Canadians returning from postings abroad often discover, to their dismay, that it is not always easy coming home. Many find their career progression has stalled—they have been out of sight, out of mind while colleagues in the home office moved ahead. Their networks have frayed. The corporate culture has changed. There can also be the financial shock of high domestic housing prices after several years away.

Then there is the "reverse culture shock." Human resources manager Laurel McLean of Calgary-based Enbridge Inc. tells of an employee, newly repatriated from Colombia, who emerged from the firm's Edmonton office and looked around, bewildered, for his car. "He was used to having somebody out there waiting for him and taking him here, there and wherever he wanted to go. All of a sudden, he was responsible for his own transportation," Ms. McLean says. He remembered that he had driven to work, but had no idea where he had parked. Ms. McLean heard a similar story from a family just returned from Kazakhstan: "They walked into a supermarket and froze. They had to restrain themselves from buying bunches of stuff . . . Over there [in Kazakhstan], if there was fresh produce, you

bought everything you could, because it might not be there next week."

It is not uncommon for expatriate employees to come back to Canada wondering "now what?" says Stephen Cryne, executive vice-president of the Canadian Employee Relocation Council, a research and advisory organization whose members include employers that transfer employees and firms that provide relocation services. The council found, in a 2005 survey of almost 100 major Canadian employers, that only 27 percent had programs "to facilitate an appropriate career position upon repatriation." And most of those employers wait until the end of the employees' foreign assignments to offer repatriation assistance, the prevailing attitude being, "Don't worry, Charlie, we'll find something for you," Mr. Cryne says.

Ms. McLean, who has conducted research at the University of Calgary on the repatriation practices of Canadian energy companies, says studies indicate that more than 25 percent of repatriated employees leave within a year of returning home. In the course of her research, Ms. McLean found that "a lot of people go out thinking they are really going to boost their career and for most of them, they gain a lot personally from it, but not as much career-wise as they would have anticipated."

(continued)

Canadian Expats Coming Home (continued)

There is no question that the foreign experience is broadening and enriching, Mr. Cryne says. However, not all employers are taking advantage of that experience. "A lot of people feel they have sacrificed for the company, and they are not being rewarded when they return," Ms. McLean says. "But, you know, there is some give and take to that. They are treated pretty well when they are on assignment, so there are a lot of gains to it as well." Ms. McLean says she has avoided the high attrition rate at Enbridge by staying in close touch with her company's expatriate employees, visiting each foreign location at least once a year and advising employees of the importance of career-planning and staying connected throughout their posting. "When people have been out of sight for seven or eight years, they kind of become frozen in time [in the eyes of the managers back home]," says Ms. McLean, who helps returning Enbridge employees update their résumés. "If you left as a senior engineer and came back having managed an engineering department of 100 people overseas, the people back home won't necessarily recognize that, they won't recognize the growth and the change."

Executive recruiter Jeff Rosin, managing director for Canada for Korn/Ferry International, says there are relatively few openings at the top for repatriated employees to move into. And while they might be given bigger titles on their return home, their scope of operation is often smaller. Adds Ms. McLean: "It's a huge challenge for companies because how do you replicate that kind of experience in the domestic organization?"

Source: Galt, Virginia. (2006, February 22). It's not easy to come home again: Employees can find it tough to return from stints abroad. *The Globe and Mail* (Report on Business: Globe Careers Special Report), C6.

The Role of the Corporate HR Function

Having considered the approaches to staffing and examining international assignments and the role of expatriates and non-expatriates, we now turn our attention to the role played by the corporate HR function in managing people in a multinational context.

 4.10

Much of the IHRM literature is focused on whom to place in control of foreign operations and activities. However, like other functional areas, HR professionals in multinationals face strategic choices. First, can we manage our people like a global product? The concept of a global internal labour market does imply some belief that it is possible to deploy human resources in much the way as other resources. However, comparative HRM and cross-cultural management literature suggests that standardizing work practices and HRM activities is not the same as product standardization. In contrast, globalization occurs at the level of the particular function.[84]

Second, what HR matters require central control and what can be delegated to subsidiary HR managers? The answer partly depends on organizational and administrative imperatives and the economic and political imperatives of the host location. For example, the desire for control and coordination may stress a geocentric approach to staffing that requires standardized policies to encourage equal treatment of all staff on international assignments (that is, an administrative imperative). Legal constraints, cost considerations, and host-government directives may require compromises in terms of staffing (economic and political imperatives).

Scullion and Starkey[85] remark that there has been little empirical research into the corporate HR function's role and how it may change over time.[86] As we discussed in Chapter 2, a firm that is internationalizing must make structural and processual changes, and we indicated ways in which the HR department may need to respond. We outlined Scullion and Starkey's finding from a study of 30 British-owned international companies where they identified centralized, decentralized, and transition HR companies. The roles of the various HR departments in these three organizational categories reflect the structural differences, which are summarized in Table 4.1. As you would expect, there is a direct link between the structure of the company and the roles of the HR function. However, there is a common approach to the management of key executive staff across the three organizational types, suggesting the need for coordination and integration of international activities that, in turn, requires greater central control over key managerial staff.

A related aspect in terms of centralization and decentralization is the nature of the activities performed by the HR function. Table 4.1 indicates a primary concern of corporate HR departments—to be able to deploy staff throughout the worldwide operations of the multinational—and this is a major driver of centralization, whether supported by formal mechanisms or not. Multinationals may also centralize training and development programs. For example, Motorola, a U.S. multinational, has its own "university"; Lufthansa, the German airline, and Ikea, the Swedish furniture retailer, have their own "business schools"). Hiring of HCNs tends to be devolved to the local level, given the need for adherence to local hiring practices.

Another driver is the level of sophistication within the firm regarding its international business operations. The more mature the firm, the more likely it has

TABLE 4.1

Various Roles of Corporate HR

CENTRALIZED HR COMPANIES	DECENTRALIZED HR COMPANIES	TRANSITION HR COMPANIES
• Large well-resourced HR departments • Key role: management of all high-grade management positions worldwide • Key activities: planning international assignments and performance management globally, identifying high-potential staff	• Small HR departments • Key role: managing elite corporate managers • Key activities: influencing operating units to support international assignments, supporting decentralized HR	• Medium-sized HR departments • Key role: management and career development of senior managers and expatriates • Key activities: persuading divisional managers to release key staff using informal and subtle methods, strategic staffing

Source: Adapted from: Scullion, H., & Starkey, K. (2000). In Search of the Changing Role of the Corporate Human Resource Function in the International Firm. *International Journal of Human Resource Management, 11*(6), 1061–1081.

centralized those HR activities that it considers to be strategic. The position of the corporate HR function is also dependent on its profile within the top executive team. For many firms, despite the impact that international growth has on a firm's HR activities, the precise nature and extent of that impact on corporate performance is not well understood by many senior managers. Possible explanations are:

- HR managers become involved in strategic decisions only when there is a critical mass of expatriates to be managed.
- Senior management is more likely to recognize HR issues when international assignments become of significant strategic value, and therefore are more likely to leverage the required resources.
- There is often a considerable time lag before HR constraints on international expansion come to the attention of senior corporate management.
- As we discussed in Chapter 1, a global perspective, through a broader view of issues, enables the development of more effective corporate policies. The need for a global perspective applies to staff in the corporate HR department, at the regional HR level, and in divisional and business units. HR managers could undertake international assignments themselves to gain appreciation of both global corporate and local unit concerns. The use of international assignments can be supplemented with frequent meetings of corporate and subsidiary HR managers. Smaller firms with limited resources may find it impossible to finance international assignments, but they may be able to identify other ways to globally orientate HR staff, such as an annual visit to key overseas subsidiaries.

In line with the above issues, Novicevic and Harvey[87] argue that corporate HR staff need to redefine their traditional role as bureaucratic administrators and become "influencers" over areas of subsidiary practices, such as encouraging career ladders to assist in global staffing decisions and designing performance appraisal and compensation systems and policies that support lateral integration and informal communication. These types of activities, it is suggested, will enhance what these authors call *homogenization of best practices*, while endeavouring to maintain specific capabilities and responsiveness at the local subsidiary level, thus ensuring the relevance of the corporate HR function. This describes what is meant if a company moves from international human resource management, which essentially means managing an international workforce to global human resource management, including all HR activities worldwide.[88]

Summary

This chapter has expanded on the role of staffing international operations for sustaining international business operations. We have outlined the various approaches to staffing international operations—ethnocentric, polycentric, geocentric, and regiocentric—and discussed their advantages and disadvantages. In addition, we presented a model delineating factors that may determine the choice of these options: context specificities, company characteristics, features of the local unit, and IHRM practices.

We showed that the primary reasons for using international assignments include position filling, management development, and organization development. There are indicators that the importance of management development increases. We distinguished and discussed various types of international assignments, including short, extended, and long-term (traditional), and non-standard forms such as commuter, rotational, contractual, and virtual assignments, and presented the implications for the firm as well as for the individual.

Our discussion of the roles of expatriates highlighted the complexity of this topic. An expatriate can act as an agent for direct control, as an agent for socialization, as a network builder, as a boundary spanner, and as a language node. These various expatriate roles help to explain why expatriates are utilized and illustrate why international assignments continue to be an important aspect of international business from the organization's perspective.

We emphasized that non-expatriates are also critical to international business operations. International business travellers present their own challenges, such as the effect of frequent absences on family and home life, the possible negative health effects, and other stress factors. The management of such individuals, though, does not appear to fall within the domain of the HR department.

Another important development in IHRM was addressed in our discussion about inpatriates. This is a group of employees who differ from expatriates only by definition, because it includes only those employees who are sent to headquarters by foreign locations and not those who are assigned by headquarters.

In line with the increasing need of companies to control costs and develop cost–benefit assessment processes, we pointed out the importance and the possibility of measuring expatriate return on investment (ROI). Furthermore, building on sections in Chapters 1 and 2, we acknowledged the importance of the role of the corporate HR function as the firm grows internationally.

Key Terms

ethnocentric 113

extended assignments 126

geocentric 117

inpatriates 135

long-term assignments 126

polycentric 115

regiocentric 118

short-term assignments 126

Web Links

www 4.1   The GMAC Global Relocation Services website provides more information about global relocation trends and challenges:

     www.gmacglobalrelocation.com/home.asp

www 4.2   Expatriates.com is a site that was created by and for expatriates:

     www.expatriates.com

www 4.3 The Canuckabroad website is a resource for Canadian expatriates abroad or for Canadians planning to travel:

www.canuckabroad.com

RPC Icons

RPC 4.1	Leads in the development of HR initiatives that support the organization's strategic directions
RPC 4.2	Leads in the development of HR initiatives that support the organization's strategic directions
RPC 4.3	Leads in the development of HR initiatives that support the organization's strategic directions
RPC 4.4	Leads in the development of HR initiatives that support the organization's strategic directions
RPC 4.5	Develops an organization or unit design to fit a given set of business objectives and environmental factors
RPC 4.6	Develops an organization or unit design to fit a given set of business objectives and environmental factors
RPC 4.7	Develops an organization or unit design to fit a given set of business objectives and environmental factors
RPC 4.8	Identifies the organization's HR needs
RPC 4.9	Evaluates the effectiveness of HR strategies using various measurement, assessment, and accountability approaches
RPC 4.10	Contributes to the development of the organization's vision, goals, and strategies—with a focus on human capital

Discussion Questions

1. Outline the main characteristics of the four approaches to international staffing.
2. Which factors determine the choice of a staffing approach? Would an MNE choose the same staffing approach worldwide? Put your arguments in the context of the model outlining determinants of staffing choices (Figure 4.1).
3. What are the reasons for using international assignments?
4. What is the role of inpatriates? Do inpatriates guarantee a geocentric staffing policy?
5. Why is it important to measure return on investment of international assignments? Which indicators can be used?
6. As a newly appointed project manager of a research team, you think that you will be able to mange the project virtually from your office in Calgary, even though the other six members are located in Rome, Italy. This will solve a personal dilemma, as your family does not want to be relocated. The project has a six-month deadline. What factors should you need to consider in order to make this virtual assignment effective?

Using the Internet

1. Check the discussion forums of Meetup Inc.'s website for Canadian expatriates (**http://canadian.meetup.com**) and find out some of the key challenges and issues that Canadian expatriates face while abroad.
2. Browse through the online magazine *The Canadian Expat* (**www.thecanadianexpat.com**) and identify some of the topics and themes about which Canadian expats are concerned that are (or can be) influenced and managed by the HR function.

Exercises

1. Read again about the Dutch PR's situation at the beginning of the chapter and think about some of the areas and aspects that should have been managed by his company's HRM team. How could the HR function help its Dutch employee?
2. Think about your current personal situation and imagine that tomorrow you will receive an offer for an international assignment in Mombasa, Kenya. Considering your personal situation, how would this assignment and its requirements be different from a job offer in Vancouver or another city in Canada? What kind of help and support would you expect from the HR team in your organization?

Case: RBC Dexia Investor Services

Part A

In 2005, the Toronto-based Royal Bank of Canada (Canada's largest bank and the sixth largest in North America) and Dexia, a leading Belgian bank with major fund services in Luxembourg, announced plans to create a joint venture that would combine both organizations' institutional investor services into an integrated entity. In 2006, the 50/50 ownership joint venture, RBC Dexia Investor Services, was launched, with its head office in London, England, its RBC Dexia Investor Services Trust in Canada, and its RBC Dexia Investor Services Bank in Luxembourg. The new joint venture employed 4,300 people in 15 countries and, due to increased business volume, required 300 more staff in the Luxembourg offices within 18 months.

At the same time, changes took place at the top-management level, where "with little apparent warning it was announced on 16th October that Loehr would take over the responsibilities of the first CEO of RBC Dexia Investor Services Bank and holding company executive committee member

Michel Malpas. No explanation has been given for this change." Another key HR decision at the top-management level included the rotation of the chairman and CEO between Luxembourg and Toronto every two years.

Source: RBC Dexia Investor Services. (2006). *Feature Articles*. Retrieved August 10, 2007, from www.rbcdexia-is.com/documents/en/FeatureArticles/Breaking%20new%20ground.pdf

Questions

1. When two international companies like RBC and Dexia partner up in a joint venture, many positions are double-occupied. From an HR perspective, how would you approach this problem? What are your options to solve this problem?
2. What are some of the other key HR challenges in an international partnership such as that of Canada's RBC and Luxembourg's Dexia?
3. What are your options to fill the 300 additionally required jobs in Luxembourg?
4. What kind of impression could the sudden and justification-lacking announcement of changes at the top-management level have on employees?

Part B

On June 1, 2007, the job site Workopolis posted a job offer by the RBC Financial Group in Canada. Aside the usual job details, the job offer had the following note:

> RBC Dexia welcomes applicants from RBC, however, employees should be aware that RBC Dexia is not a subsidiary within the group of companies that form RBC Financial Group. An RBC employee who accepts a position at RBC Dexia must resign from RBC and join RBC Dexia as a new employee. Service history from RBC and RBC pension and benefit entitlement cannot be transferred to RBC Dexia.

Source: Workopolis. RBC Financial Group ad for senior manager. Retrieved August 8, 2007, from http://campusen.workopolis.com/work.aspx?action=Transfer&View=Content/JobSeeker/JobPostingView&jobid=9238174&lang=EN&RSS=true&OldUrl=

Questions

1. Based on the message in this note, what are the consequences for employees wanting to move from RBC to RBC Dexia?
2. With regard to service history, pensions, and benefits, what are the options for HRM to help employees wanting to move from RBC to RBC Dexia?

Endnotes

1. H. V. Perlmutter. (1969). The torturous evolution of the multinational corporation. *Columbia Journal of World Business, 4*(1), 9–18.

2. D. A. Heenan & H. V. Perlmutter. (1979). *Multinational organization development*. Reading, MA: Addison-Wesley.

3. J. Bonache, C. Brewster, & V. Suutari. (2001). Expatriation: A developing research agenda. *Thunderbird International Business Review*, (1), 3–20.

4. Y. Zeira. (1976). Management development in ethnocentric multinational corporations. *California Management Review, 18*(4), 34–42.

5. PricewaterhouseCoopers (Eds.). (2006). *Measuring the value of international assignments*. London, UK: PricewaterhouseCoopers.

6. PricewaterhouseCoopers (Eds.). (2006). *Managing mobility matters: 2006*. London, UK: PricewaterhouseCoopers.

7. D. Welch. (1994). HRM implications of globalization. *Journal of General Management, 19*(4), 52–68.

8. Heenan & Perlmutter. *Multinational organization development*.

9. A. J. Morrison, D. A. Ricks, & K. Roth. (1991, Winter). Globalization versus regionalisation: Which way for the multinational? *Organizational Dynamics*, 17–29.

10. I. Torbiörn. (2005). Staffing policies and practices in European MNCs: Strategic sophistication, culture-bound policies or ad hoc reactivity? in H. Scullion & M. Linehan (Eds.), *International human resource management: A critical text*. Houndmills, Basingstoke, Hampshire, UK: Palgrave Macmillan, 47–68.

11. R. D. Robinson. (1978). *International business management: A guide to decision making* (2nd ed.). Hinsdale, IL: Dryden, 297.

12. N. Boyacigiller. (1990). The role of expatriates in the management of interdependence, complexity and risk in multinational corporations. *Journal of International Business Studies, 21*(3), 357–381; and D. E. Welch. (1994). Determinants of international human resource management approaches and activities: A suggested framework. *Journal of Management Studies, 31*(2), 139–164.

13. I. Tarique, R. Schuler, Y. Gong. (2006). A model of multinational staffing composition. *International Journal of Human Resource Management, 17*(2), 207–224.

14. See the results of a study among Japanese subsidiaries by: Y. Gong. (2003). Subsidiary staffing in multinational enterprises: Agency, resources, and performance. *Academy of Management Journal, 45*(6), 728–739. A similar analysis has been carried out by: Y. Thompson & M. Keating. (2004). An empirical study of executive nationality staffing practices in foreign-owned MNC subsidiaries in Ireland. *Thunderbird International Business Review, 46*(6), 771–797.

15. For an institutional perspective see the national business systems approach by: R. D. Whitley. (1992). *European Business Systems: Firms and Markets in Their National Contexts*. London, UK: Sage Publications.

16. For a discussion of European staffing approaches, see: I. Torbiörn. (2005). Staffing policies and practices in European MNCs: Strategic sophistication, culture-bound policies or ad hoc reactivity. In H. Scullion & M. Linehan (Eds.), *International human resource management: A critical text*. Houndmills, Basingstoke, Hampshire, UK: Palgrave Macmillan, 47–68.

17. For a similar discussion, see: C. M. Vance & Y. Paik. (2006). *Managing a global workforce: Challenges and opportunities in international human resource management*. Armonk, NY/London, UK: M. E. Sharpe.

18. For a discussion of these factors on subsidiary HRM, see: Y. Kim & S. J. Gray. (2005). Strategic factors influencing international human resource management practices: An empirical study of

Australian multinational corporations. *International Journal of Human Resource Management, 16*(5), 809–830.

19. For the issue of subsidiary consideration, see: M. M. Novicevic & M. Harvey. (2004). Staffing architecture for expatriate assignments to support subsidiary cooperation. *Thunderbird International Business Review, 46*(6), 709–724. For a discussion of the impact of different subsidiary strategies, see: J. Bonache & Z. Fernandez. (2004). Strategic staffing in multinational companies: A resource-based approach. In C. Brewster & H. Harris. *International HRM: Contemporary Issues in Europe.* London/New York: Routledge, 163–182. For a resource dependence perspective on the emergence of international HRM strategies, see: M. Festing, J. Eidems, & S. Royer. (2007, April). Strategic issues and local constraints in transnational compensation strategies: An analysis of cultural, institutional and political influences. *European Management Journal, 25*(2), 118–131.

20. Welch. HRM implications of globalization.

21. M. Richards. (2001). U.S. multinational staffing practices and implications for subsidiary performance in the U.K. and Thailand. *Thunderbird International Business Review, 34*(2), 225–242.

22. J. Shen. (2006). Factors affecting international staffing in Chinese multinationals (MNEs). *International Journal of Human Resource Management, 17*(2), 295–315.

23. PricewaterhouseCoopers (Eds.). (2005). *International assignments: Global policy and practice key trends, 2005.* London, UK: PricewaterhouseCoopers.

24. Important destinations include China in the first place, closely followed by Central and Eastern Europe, especially from the perspective of European companies, and the Indian subcontinent. See: PricewaterhouseCoopers (Eds.). (2005). *International assignments: Global policy and practice key trends, 2005.*

25. GMAC Global Relocation Services in conjunction with U.S. National Foreign Trade Council Inc and SHRM Global Forum. (2005). *Global relocation trends: 2005 survey report.* Woodbridge, IL: GMAC.

26. GMAC Global Relocation Services in conjunction with U.S. National Foreign Trade Council Inc and SHRM Global Forum (2004). *Global relocation trends: 2003/2004 survey report.* Woodbridge, IL: GMAC.

27. PricewaterhouseCoopers. *International assignments: Global policy and practice key trends, 2005.*

28. K. Blassingame. (2001). "C" change recommended for expat. management. *Employee Benefit News, 15*(10), 12.

29. GMAC Global Relocation Services in conjunction with U.S. National Foreign Trade Council Inc and SHRM Global Forum. (2002). *Global relocation trends: 2002 survey report.* Woodbridge, IL: GMAC.

30. May M. L. Wong. (2001). Internationalising Japanese expatriate managers. *Management Learning, 32*(2), 237–251.

31. PricewaterhouseCoopers (Eds.). *Managing mobility matters, 2006.* London, UK: PricewaterhouseCoopers.

32. Based on a literature review of German IHRM studies, Harzing concludes that all key reasons for international assignments can lead to organization development "defined as the increase of the company's potential to succeed and to compete in the international market" (Harzing 2001: 368). See: A.-W. Harzing. (2001). Of bears, bumble-bees, and spiders: The role of expatriates in controlling foreign subsidiaries. *Journal of World Business, 36*(4), 366–379. With respect to IHRM, Morris et al. distinguish between integrative and creative capabilities to meet the challenges of the global market. See: S. S. Morris, A. A. Snell, & P. M. Wright. (2006). A resource-based view of international human resources: Toward a framework of integrative and

creative capabilities. In Stahl & Björkman (Eds.), *Handbook of research in international human resource management*, 433–448.

33. PricewaterhouseCoopers (Eds.). (2002). *International Assignments: Global Policy and Practice Key Trends 2002*. London, UK: PricewaterhouseCoopers.

34. PricewaterhouseCoopers (Eds.). (2001). *Managing a virtual world: Key trends 2000/2001*. London, UK: PricewaterhouseCoopers.

35. While the increase of this type of assignment during the previous two years was estimated at 11 percent, an increase within the following two years was expected by 18 percent of the investigated companies. See: PricewaterhouseCoopers. *Managing a virtual world: Key trends 2000/2001*.

36. A. Mendez. (2003). The coordination of globalized R&D activities through project teams organization: An exploratory empirical study. *Journal of World Business, 38*(2), 96–109.

37. PricewaterhouseCoopers (Eds.). (2000). *Managing a virtual world: International non-standard assignments, policy and practice*. London, UK: PricewaterhouseCoopers.

38. Ibid., 11.

39. D. E. Welch & L. S. Welch. (1994). Linking operation mode diversity and IHRM. *International Journal of Human Resource Management, 5*(4), 911–926; and M. Tahvanainen, D. Welch, & V. Worm. (2005). Implications of short-term international assignments. *European Management Journal, 23*(6), 663–673.

40. D. E. Welch, V. Worm, & M. Fenwick. (2003). Are virtual assignments feasible? *Management International Review, 43* (Special Issue No. 1), 98.

41. For a literature review and discussion on the use of staff transfers as a control mechanism, see: D. Welch, M. Fenwick, & H. De Cieri. (1994). Staff transfers as a control strategy: An exploratory study of two Australian organizations. *International Journal of Human Resource Management, 5*(2), 473–489.

42. Harzing. Of bears, bumble-bees, and spiders: The role of expatriates in controlling foreign subsidiaries.

43. M. S. Fenwick, H. L. De Cieri, & D. E. Welch. (1999). Cultural and bureaucratic control in MNEs: The role of expatriate performance management. *Management International Review, 39*, 107–124.

44. K. Goodall & J. Roberts. (2003). Only connect: Teamwork in the multinational. *Journal of World Business, 38*(2), 150–164.

45. S. S. Morris, A. A. Snell, & P. M. Wright. (2006). A resource-based view of international human resources: Toward a framework of integrative and creative capabilities. In Stahl & Björkman (Eds.), *Handbook of research in international human resource management*, 433–448.

46. D M. Schweiger, T. Atamer, & R. Calori. (2003). Transnational project teams and networks: Making the multinational more effective. *Journal of World Business, 38*, 127–140.

47. R. Marschan, D. Welch, & L. Welch. (1996). Control in less-hierarchical multinationals: The role of personal networks and information communication. *International Business Review, 5*(2), 137–150.

48. J. Birkinshaw & N. Hood. (2001, March). Unleash innovation in foreign subsidiaries. *Harvard Business Review*, 131–137.

49. K. Y. Au & J. Fukuda. (2002). Boundary spanning behaviors of expatriates. *Journal of World Business, 37*, 285–296.

50. R. Marschan-Piekkari, D. Welch, & L. Welch. (1999). Adopting a common corporate language: IHRM implications. *International Journal of Human Resource Management, 10*(3), 377–390.

51. K. Goodall & J. Roberts. (2003). Only connect: Teamwork in the multinational. *Journal of World Business, 38*, 159.

52. M.C. Bolino & D.C. Feldman. (2000). Increasing the skill utilization of expatriates. *Human Resource Management, 39*(4), 367–379.

53. D. E. Welch, L. S. Welch, & V. Worm. (2007). The international business traveller: A neglected but strategic human resource. *International Journal of Human Resource Management, 18*(2), 173–183.

54. H. Mayerhofer, L. C. Hartmann, G. Michelitsch-Riedl, & I. Kollinger. (2004). Flexpatriate assignments: A neglected issue in global staffing. *International Journal of Human Resource Management, 15*(8), 1371–1389.

55. American Express. (2002, October 9). International travellers optimistic about travel for 2003. Press release.

56. H. Mintzberg, D. Dougherty, J. Jorgensen, & F. Westley. (1996). Some surprising things about collaboration: Knowing how people connect makes it work better. *Organizational Dynamics, 25*(1), 62.

57. L. S. Welch, G. R. G. Benito, P. R. Silseth, & T. Karlsen. (2002). Exploring inward–outward linkages in firms' internationalization: A knowledge and network perspective. In S. Lundan (Ed.), *Network knowledge in international business*. Cheltenham, UK: Edward Elgar, 216–231.

58. R. S. DeFrank, R. Konopaske, & J. M. Ivancevich. (2000). Executive travel stress: Perils of the road warrior. *Academy of Management Executive, 14*(2), 58–71.

59. B. S. Reiche. (2006). The inpatriate experience in multinational corporations: An exploratory case study in Germany. *International Journal of Human Resource Management, 19*(9), 1580.

60. D. Collings & H. Scullion. (2006). Global Staffing. in Stahl & Björkman (Eds.), *Handbook of research in international human resource management*, 141–157.

61. Similar ideas can be found in: M. G. Harvey, C. Speier, & M. M. Novicevic. (2001). The role of inpatriation in global staffing. *International Journal of Human Resource Management, 10*(3), 459–476.

62. M. G Harvey, M. M. Novicevic, & C. Speier. (2000). Strategic global human resource management: The role of inpatriate managers. *Human Resource Management Review, 10*(2), 153–175.

63. G. Heismann. (2006). Einmal Karriere und zurück (Careers and Repatriation). Lufthansa Classic, *7*, 80–85.

64. M. Festing & B. Müller. (2007). Open Sky—Möglichkeiten und Grenzen der Personalentwicklung in einer globalen Unternehmenskultur (Open Sky—Essentials and limits of management development in a global corporate culture). In W. Auer-Rizzi, S. Blazejewski, W. Dorow, & G. Reber (Eds.), *Unternehmenskulturen in globaler Interaktion—Analysen, Erfahrungen, Lösungsansätze*. Wiesbaden: Gabler, 327–343.

65. M. G. Harvey & M. R. Buckley. (1997). Managing inpatriates: Building a global core competency. *Journal of World Business, 32*(1), 35–52.

66. S. Perkins. (2006). *International Reward and Recognition* (research report). London, UK: CIPD.

67. For example, the GMAC 2005 report revealed that 65 percent of the investigated companies tried to reduce international assignment expenses. See: GMAC Global Relocation Services in conjunction with U.S. National Foreign Trade Council Inc and SHRM Global Forum. *Global Relocation Trends: 2005 Survey Report.*

68. For a critical discussion on expatriate failure rates, see: A.-W. Harzing & C. Christensen. (2004). Expatriate failure: Time to abandon the concept? *Career Development International, 9*(7), 616–626.

69. D. G. Collings & H. Scullion. (2006). Strategic Motivations for international transfers: Why do MNCs use expatriates? In H. Scullion & D. G. Collings (Eds.), *Global staffing*. London/New York: Routledge, 39–56.

70. This discussion can be placed in the broader context of "HR affordability," which is reflected in an increased interest in metrics. See: C. Brewster, P. Sparrow, & H. Harris. (2005). Towards a

new model of globalizing HRM. *International Journal of Human Resource Management, 16,* 949–970.

71. Scullion & Collings (Eds.). *Global staffing.*

72. Y. M. McNulty & P. Tharenou. (2004). Expatriate return on investment. *International Studies of Management and Organization, 34*(3), 68–95. A similar definition can be found in: L. Johnson. (2005). Measuring international assignment return on investment. *Compensation Benefits Review, 37*(2), 53.

73. For a transaction cost theoretical analysis of staffing decisions, see: G. R. G Benito, S. Tomassen, J. Bonache-Perez, & J. Pla-Barber. (2005). A transaction cost analysis of staffing decisions in international operations. *Scandinavian Journal of Management, 21,* 101–126. For an agency theory-based analysis, see: Y. Gong. (2003). Subsidiary staffing in multinational enterprises: Agency, resources, and performance. *Academy of Management Journal, 45*(6), 728–739. For the use of economic theories in international human resource management, see: M. Festing. (2006). International human resource management and economic theories of the firm. In Stahl & Björkman (Eds.), *Handbook of research in international human resource management,* 449–462.

74. See, for example: J. S. Osland, A. Bird, M. Mendenhall, & A. Osland. (2006). Developing global leadership capabilities and global mindset: A review. In Stahl & Björkman (Eds.), *Handbook of research in international human resource management,* 197–222; P. Caligiuri. (2006). Developing global leaders. *Human Resource Management Review, 16*(2), 219–228; and M. Mendenhall, T. M. Kühlmann, & G. K. Stahl (Eds.). (2000). *Developing global business leaders.* Westport, CT: Greenwood Publishing Group.

75. Y. M. McNulty & P. Tharenou. (2004). Expatriate return on investment. *International Studies of Management and Organization, 34*(3), 68–95.

76. Ibid., 89.

77. L. Johnson. (2005). Measuring international assignment return on investment. *Compensation Benefits Review. 37*(2), 50–54. A similar result is reported in the *Mercer International Assignments Survey, 2005/2006.*

78. GMAC Global Relocation Services in conjunction with U.S. National Foreign Trade Council Inc and SHRM Global Forum. *GMAC global relocation trends: 2005 survey report.*

79. Ibid., p. 16.

80. PricewaterhouseCoopers (Eds.). *Measuring the value of international assignments.*

81. G. K. Stahl & J.-L. Cerdin. (2004). Global careers in French and German multinational corporations. *Journal of Management Development, 23*(9), 887.

82. Ibid., 885–902.

83. M. Festing & B. Mueller. (2007). Expatriate Careers and the Psychological Contract—An Empirical Study on the Impact of International Human Resource Management. Paper presented at the *9th Conference on International Human Resource Management,* Tallinn, Estonia; PricewaterhouseCoopers (Eds.). Measuring the value of international assignments; and GMAC Global Relocation Services in conjunction with U.S. National Foreign Trade Council Inc and SHRM Global Forum. *GMAC global relocation trends: 2005 survey report.*

84. For similar arguments, see: P. R. Sparrow. (2006). *Globalization of HR at functional level: Exploring the issues through international recruitment, selection and assessment processes.* International Programs Visiting Working Papers, Cornell University.

85. H. Scullion & K. Starkey. (2000). In search of the changing role of the corporate human resource function in the international firm. *International Journal of Human Resource Management, 11*(6), 1061–1081.

86. For a recent review, see: H. Scullion & J. Paauwe. (2005). Strategic HRM in multinational companies. In H. Scullion & M. Linehan (Eds.), *International human resource management: A critical text.* Houndmills, Basingstoke, Hampshire, UK: Palgrave Macmillan, 22–46.

87. M. Novicevic & M. Harvey. (2001). The changing role of the corporate HR function in global organizations of the twenty-first century. *International Journal of Human Resource Management, 12*(8), 1251–1268.

88. C. Brewster, P. Sparrow, & H. Harris. (2005). Towards a new model of globalizing HRM. *International Journal of Human Resource Management, 16*, 949–970; and P. R. Sparrow. (2006). *Globalization of HR at functional level: Exploring the issues through international recruitment, selection and assessment processes.* International Programs Visiting Working Papers, Cornell University.

Chapter 5

Recruiting and Selecting Staff for International Assignments

Chapter Learning Objectives

After reading this chapter, you should be able to:

- explain the myth of the global manager
- discuss the debate surrounding expatriate failure
- outline the factors moderating intent to stay or leave the international assignment
- list selection criteria for international assignments
- explain why dual-career couples can represent a barrier to staff mobility
- answer the question: Are female expatriates different?

DUAL-CAREER COUPLES: TRAILING SPOUSE'S JOB NEEDS START TO GET MORE COMPANY TIME

Ruth Whitby loves her husband, Ben—and she also loves her job. When he was transferred to Japan, Whitby, a British medical doctor, struggled for a year to get a license to practice in Japan. She eventually succeeded and built a thriving medical practice in Tokyo, only to see her diplomat husband transferred again. This time all attempts at practicing medicine in their new home of Vienna failed. Dr. Whitby, 39, now leaves her two small children, Joe, 8, and Isobel, 6, every third week to practice at a clinic in London.

Thirty years ago, a diplomat's wife like Whitby might have busied herself planning luncheons and ironing her husband's shirts. Times have changed. Almost half of spouses of overseas employees have their own jobs and their unwillingness to give these up is an increasing impediment to mobility, according to corporate surveys. In a time of cost cuts and economic downturns, overseas employers are loath to spend money finding a job for an accompanying spouse. . . .

The issue of dual career partners is quietly becoming a crisis in multinational human resources circles, but still one that many employers would rather not address. . . . A 1999/2000 survey by the accountants PricewaterhouseCoopers of 270 European employers found that almost two thirds listed the spouse or partner's career as a barrier to mobility. The authors of the study also noted that "factors rated least highly by companies when selecting people for assignments such as partner adaptability and dual career management are the most likely to be the cause of failed assignments."

"We are seeing this problem more and more," said Pam Braun, a spokeswoman for Royal Dutch Shell Group. "The dual career issue is hot. Now every partner, and more and more are men, wants to have a career." Despite these findings, and numerous other surveys showing the same trends, companies are slow to address this issue. Only 19 percent of companies participating in the Windham survey helped spouses to find jobs, 20 percent helped with career planning, and 11 percent paid a job-finding fee. A third offered no assistance at all.

"A lot of human resources managers know this dual career issue exists," said the Britain-based lecturer and career counselor Joanna Parfitt. "But they still have their heads in the sand."

Source: Excerpt from: Lang, Gretchen. (2004, March 27). Dual-career couples: Trailing spouse's job needs start to get more company time. *International Herald Tribune*. Retrieved June 21, 2005, from www.iht.com/articles/2004/03/27/rspouse_ed3__1.php

Introduction

Hiring and then deploying people to positions where they can perform effectively is a goal of most organizations, whether domestic or international. **Recruitment** is defined as searching for and obtaining potential job candidates in sufficient numbers and of good quality so that the organization can select the most appropriate people to fill its job needs. **Selection** is the process of gathering information for the purposes of evaluating and deciding who should be employed in particular jobs. It is important to note that recruitment and selection are discrete processes and both processes need to operate effectively if the firm is to successfully manage its staffing process. For example, a firm may have an excellent selection system for evaluating candidates but if there are insufficient candidates to evaluate, then this selection system is less than effective. Both processes must operate effectively for optimal staffing decisions to be made. We will return to this point later in the chapter.

Some of the major differences between domestic and international staffing are, first, that many firms have predispositions with regard to who should hold key positions in headquarters and subsidiaries (i.e., ethnocentric, polycentric, regiocentric, and geocentric staffing orientations) and second, the constraints imposed by host governments (e.g., immigration rules with regard to work visas and the common requirement in most countries to require evidence as to why local nationals should not be employed rather than hiring foreigners), which can severely limit the firm's ability to hire the right candidate. In addition, as Scullion and Collings[1] note, most expatriates are recruited *internally* rather than externally, so the task of persuading managers (particularly if they are primarily working in a domestic environment) to recommend and/or agree to release their best employees for international assignments remains a key issue for international HR managers.

In this chapter, we will explore the key issues surrounding international recruitment and selection, with a focus on selection criteria. Implicit in much of the discussion and research about selecting staff for international assignments is that there are common attributes shared by persons who have succeeded in operating in other cultural work environments—that is, the so-called global manager. Our discussion on this topic centres around four myths: that there is a universal approach to management; that all people can acquire appropriate behaviours; that there are common characteristics shared by global managers; and that there are no impediments to global staff mobility. We then consider various factors—such as expatriate failure, selection criteria, dual-career couples, and gender—that impact on the multinational's ability to recruit and select high-calibre staff for deployment internationally. For convenience, we will use the term *multinational* throughout this chapter, but it is important to remember that the issues pertain variously to all internationalizing companies, regardless of size, industry, stage in internationalization, nationality of origin, and geographical diversity. We continue to use the term *expatriate* to include all three categories transferred into headquarters' operations—PCNs (parent-country nationals), TCNs

recruitment

process of searching for and obtaining potential job candidates

selection

process of evaluating and deciding who should be given certain jobs

(third-country nationals), and HCNs (host-country nationals)—although much of the literature on expatriate selection is focused only on PCNs. While there is a growing interest and literature by European academics and practitioners in this field, the latter has been dominated by U.S. research into predominantly U.S. samples of expatriates—reflected by the numerous mentioning of U.S. sources, examples, and figures in this chapter.

Issues in Staff Selection

Global Manager Myths

Multinationals depend on being able to develop a pool of international operators from which they can draw as required. Such individuals have been variously labelled "international managers" or "global managers." The concept of a global manager appears to be based on the following myths or assumptions.

Myth 1: There Is a Universal Approach to Management

The view that there is a universal approach to management persists despite research evidence to the contrary, and many multinationals continue to transfer home-based work practices into their foreign operations without adequate consideration as to whether this is appropriate. The persistence of a belief in universal management may be evidence of a lingering ethnocentric attitude or perhaps an indicator of inexperience in international operations. However, as we discussed in Chapter 1 in relation to the convergence–divergence debate, work practices have, to a certain extent, converged through the transfer of technology and "best practice" and this process is supported by the global spread of management education programs that reflect the dominant Western approach to management. Linked to this process is the belief in the power of organizational culture as a moderator of cultural differences in the work setting.

Myth 2: People Can Acquire Multicultural Adaptability and Behaviours

effectiveness skills

ability to successfully translate managerial or technical skills into the foreign environment

coping skills

ability to become reasonably comfortable, or at least survive, in a foreign environment

Some people can adopt culturally appropriate behaviours but that does not apply all of the time in all cultural settings.[2] It depends, as we will examine later, on the individual's reaction to a particular cultural environment, as it is not always easy to put into practice what you know is the right way to behave, and some individuals have much better effectiveness and coping skills than others.[3] **Effectiveness skills** are defined as the ability to successfully translate the managerial or technical skills into the foreign environment, whereas **coping skills** enable the person to become reasonably comfortable, or at least survive, in a foreign environment. Those who are able to function adequately in other cultural settings may be regarded as having good effectiveness and coping skills. As we examine later in this chapter, cultural adjustment has been linked to expatriate performance and influences how international assignments are perceived.

Myth 3: Common Characteristics Are Shared by Successful International Managers

The body of literature on expatriate selection tends to reflect this approach, as we will explore in the next section of this chapter. It is possible to identify predictors of success, in that a person who has certain characteristics, traits, and experience is more likely to perform effectively in foreign environments than a person who does not share this profile. However, this has to be countered by other factors involved not just in the selection process, but also in the way the person responds to the foreign location. It is also unclear how the identified predictors of success should be measured.

Myth 4: There Are No Impediments to Mobility

We have mentioned that particularly large multinationals are endeavouring to develop and exploit an internal labour market from which expatriates—international managers—can be drawn. As Forster[4] points out, firms may have become more global in their operations but their people have not. The barriers to furthering a geocentric staffing policy—staff availability, time and cost constraints, and host-government requirements—reveal how the multinational's ability to deploy what may be the best person into a particular position can be curtailed. That some multinationals are experimenting with alternatives such as the virtual assignment is indicative of this constraint.

Compounding the above myths is the way in which the term *global manager* is sometimes used to describe a person who has a global "mindset," although international experience is often a prerequisite for building the global perspective required. Baruch[5] argues that there is no consistent way to characterize a global manager. He suggests that the basic qualities commonly listed—intelligence, motivation, adaptability, and entrepreneurship—are the same requirements for any successful manager today.

Profile of an Expatriate

Table 5.1 shows the current profile of an expatriate, drawn from results of a 2005 GMAC worldwide survey of 125 multinationals representing both small and large organizations. For 46 percent of respondents, the company's headquarters was located outside of the United States (a record high response from non-U.S. firms). As the results show, while the largest group of expatriates is made up of PCNs, this group is not the majority and the HCN and TCN groups are significant. Most expatriates are male (77 percent), aged 30–49 (66 percent), married (61 percent), and accompanied by a spouse (81 percent) and children (52 percent). While the majority of assignments are 1–3 years (53 percent), a total of 27 percent of assignments are classified as short term (i.e., less than one year). The primary reason for the assignment is to fill a position and, interestingly, only 12 percent of assignees had prior international experience.

Given the important roles commonly assigned to expatriates, the recruitment and selection process needs to be taken very seriously, and it is logical to assume that MNEs take great care in the selection of their international

W W W 5.1

Table 5.1

Current Expatriate Profile				
			HCN	(29%)
EXPATRIATE CATEGORY	PCN	(44%)	TCN	(27%)
Gender	Male	(77%)	Female	(23%)
Age	30–49	(66%)	20-29	(16%)
Marital status	Married	(61%)	Single	(28%)
			Partner	(11%)
Accompanied by	Spouse	(81%)	Children	(52%)
Duration	1–3 years	(53%)	Short term	(27%)
			Permanent	(20%)
Primary reason	Fill a position			
Prior international experience	12%			

Source: Adapted from: *Global Relocation Trends: 2005 Survey Report.* (2006). GMAC Global Relocation Services, National Foreign Trade Council, and SHRM Global Forum. GMAC GRS.

assignees. What is evident from the now considerable literature on the topic is that the selection of expatriates is complex. Indeed, predicting future performance potential when hiring or promoting staff is challenging at the best of times, but operating in foreign environments certainly adds another level of uncertainty. For this reason, before we take a critical look at criteria for expatriate selection, we should consider the current debate surrounding expatriate non-performance.

Expatriate Failure

There are three questions related to expatriate failure: its definition, the magnitude of the phenomenon, and the costs associated with failure. We will treat these separately before examining the reasons attributed to expatriate failure and the link to selection criteria.

What Do We Mean by *Expatriate Failure?*

The term *expatriate failure* has been defined as the premature return of an expatriate (that is, a return home before the period of assignment is completed). In such a case, an expatriate failure represents a selection error, often compounded by ineffective expatriate management policies. There has been some discussion in the literature about the usefulness of defining expatriate failure so narrowly. An expatriate may be ineffective and poorly adjusted, yet, if not recalled, the person will not be considered a failure. Because of an inability either to effectively handle the new responsibilities or to adjust to the country of assignment, performance levels may be diminished. These results will not immediately be apparent but can have long-term negative consequences in terms of subsidiary performance.

However, if the expatriate remains for the duration of the assignment, to all intents and purposes, the assignment will have been considered a success.

Thus, the premature return rate is not a perfect measure of success or failure, and may underestimate the problem. For example, in his study of 36 British-based firms, Forster[6] used the broadest definition of failure (that is, including underperformance and retention on completion of the assignment). Forster found that a high proportion of staff struggle to cope with their overseas assignments, concluding:

> If we accept that a broader definition of EFRs [expatriate failure rates] is warranted, then it can be argued that the actual figure of those who are "failing" on IAs [international assignments] could be somewhere between 8 per cent and 28 per cent of UK expatriates and their partners.

Support for broadening the definition of expatriate failure comes from a 1997/1998 Price Waterhouse[7] study of international assignment policy and practice among European multinationals (including U.S. subsidiaries). Unlike previous surveys of this kind, the study added "underperformance" to its definition of assignment failure and found:

> The rates for employees currently under-performing on assignment as a result of difficulties in adapting to their cultural surroundings are even higher. 29% of companies report a rate in excess of one in twenty, with 7% reporting a rate over one in ten.

What Is the Magnitude of the Phenomenon We Call *Expatriate Failure?*

Tung's[8] highly cited 1981 article could be said to have started the discussion about expatriate failure and, more particularly, the inability of U.S. nationals to handle an international assignment. Her results suggested that expatriate failure was of more concern to U.S. firms: 24 percent of the U.S. firms in her sample ($n = 80$) had recall rates below 10 percent, compared to 59 percent of the West European ($n = 29$) and 76 percent of the Japanese firms ($n = 35$) reporting recall rates of less than 5 percent. Later studies appear to confirm Tung's European results[9] in terms of expatriate failure. Many studies that explore expatriate failure and expatriate adjustment persist in quoting high U.S. rates of failure, variously reporting it as falling between 30 to 50 percent and even higher.

Harzing[10] has questioned the reported failure rates in the U.S. literature, claiming there is "almost no empirical foundation for the existence of high failure rates when measured as premature re-entry." More recently, Christensen and Harzing have questioned the value of the whole concept of expatriate failure, arguing that "it might well be time to abandon the concept of expatriate failure altogether and instead draw on the general HR literature to analyze problems related to turnover and performance management in an expatriate context."[11]

When we delve further into this issue to establish how large the problem actually is, we find a suggestion of a declining rate. Evidence can be gained

W W W 5.2

from two global surveys, conducted in 2002 and 2005. The first was a survey of 300 multinationals (46 percent North American, 28 percent European, and 9 percent U.K.) from a wide range of industries by U.S.-based consulting firm ORC Worldwide.[12] ORC reported that almost 56 percent of respondents did not know the return rate of their expatriates. Those who keep records indicated, on average, that less than 10 percent of their international assignments ended in early recall. The second survey, by GMAC Global Relocation Services (GMAC GRS) mentioned earlier, asked responding firms to indicate their attrition rate—that is, expatriate turnover, including early recall from an international assignment and on completion of the assignment. Again, we find that some firms (36 percent) could not answer, as they did not have the figures. Those that did have the information indicated that 21 percent left the firm during an assignment and 23 percent within one year of returning from an assignment. It would have been useful to find out why so many of the responding firms in these two surveys did not keep records on assignment failures. Perhaps this is because it is not seen as an important issue?

Respondents in the ORC Worldwide survey were also asked to define a failed assignment. Some 72 percent defined it as "early return of the expatriate." The other definitions were "unmet business objectives" (71 percent), "problems at assignment location" (49 percent), and "unmet career development objectives" (32 percent). It would appear that multinationals are recognizing that there are many aspects to a failed assignment, although it is not clear from the report if responding firms were separating out underperformance from early recall. Unmet business objectives, problems at assignment location, and unmet career development objectives may be reasons for early recall rather than a definition.

From the above discussion, though, we can draw a number of conclusions:

1. Broadening the definition of expatriate failure beyond that of premature return is warranted. Following up broad surveys with interviews with responding firms may assist in this.

2. Regardless of the definition or precise amount of "failure," its very exposure as a problem has broadened the issue to demonstrate the complexity of international assignments. In fact, one could argue that the so-called persistent myth of high U.S. expatriate failure rates has been a positive element in terms of the attention that has subsequently been directed toward expatriation practices. It has certainly provoked considerable research attention to the causes of expatriate failure.

3. The evidence about expatriate failure rates is somewhat inconclusive. Recent studies suggest that high failure rates reported in the 1980s have not persisted for U.S. nationals. Although recent reports do not break down results into nationality groups, U.S. firms form the largest group in these surveys. The European studies reported above were conducted at various intervals since Tung's original study, and do not include the same countries. Further, non-U.S. researchers have been reporting from regional or single country perspectives (see for example, Björkman and Gertsen,[13] who found expatriate failure rates

of less than five percent for Nordic firms; Dowling and Welch[14] reported similar results for Australian firms).

4. The above studies tend not to differentiate between types of expatriate assignments, the level of "international" maturity,[15] or firm size— factors that may influence failure in its broadest sense.

5. It may be that companies operating internationally have since become more aware of the problems associated with expatriate failure and have learned how to avoid them. That is, multinationals have become more sophisticated in their approach to IHRM activities. Benchmarking against other firms may have assisted in the development of an awareness of international assignment issues.

What Are the Costs of Failure?

These can be both *direct* and *indirect*. Direct costs include airfares and associated relocation expenses, plus salary and training costs. The precise amount varies according to the level of the position concerned, country of destination, exchange rates, and whether the "failed" manager is replaced by another expatriate.

The "invisible" or indirect costs are harder to quantify in money terms but can prove to be more expensive for the company. Many expatriate positions involve contact with host-government officials and key clients. Failure at this level may result in loss of market share, difficulties with host-government officials, and demands that expatriates be replaced with HCNs (thus affecting the multinational's general staffing approach). The possible effect on local staff is also an indirect cost factor, since morale and productivity could suffer.[16]

Failure also, of course, has an effect on the expatriate concerned, who may lose self-esteem, self-confidence, and prestige among peers.[17] Future performance may be marked by decreased motivation, lack of promotional opportunities, or even increased productivity to compensate for the failure. Finally, the expatriate's family relationships may be threatened. These are additional costs to organizations that are often overlooked.

Factors Moderating Performance

Naturally, the debate about the degree to which expatriate failure occurs has been accompanied by investigation and speculation about why failure occurs. Expatriates tend to have a higher profile, so reducing the rate of incidence is of some strategic importance as multinationals continue to rely on expatriates and therefore wish to encourage mobility. In Canada, there are about 68,000 Canadians on international assignments at any given time and, according to the *Canadian HR Reporter*, quoting the 2005 Canadian Employee Relocation Council (CERC) *CERC Employee Relocation Policy Survey*, 68 percent of companies operating in Canada expect the number of foreign assignments to remain steady or to continue to increase.[18]

Consequently, considerable research has been attempted to identify factors that may moderate performance and affect the decision to stay or leave an international assignment. The primary intention has been to link

FIGURE 5.1

International Assignments: Factors Moderating Performance

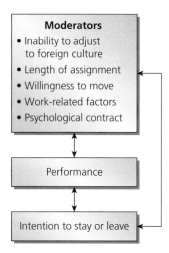

reasons for early recall to predictors of success and thereby generate selection criteria that may assist multinationals in their staffing decisions. While the focus has predominately been on cross-cultural adjustment, other factors have been identified, as shown in Figure 5.1. We will base our examination of the issue on this figure.

Inability to Adjust to the Foreign Culture

Inability to adjust to the foreign culture has been a consistent reason given for expatriate failure—and has been the subject of considerable interest to researchers. Again, we must acknowledge the pioneering contribution of Tung's study[19] in providing the impetus for this interest. Tung found national differences in the responses between the U.S. and Japanese firms. Asked to rank reasons for failure in descending order of importance, U.S. firms ranked "inability of the spouse to adjust" as the most important, whereas this was ranked fifth for the Japanese firms. For the European firms, "inability of the spouse to adjust" was the only consistent response provided.

RPC 5.1

Tung[20] noted that the relatively lower ranking of "inability of spouse to adjust" by Japanese respondents is not surprising, given the role and status to which Japanese society relegates the spouse. However, other social factors may contribute to this finding. Because of the extremely competitive nature of the Japanese education system, the spouse commonly opts to remain in Japan with the children, particularly where male offspring are concerned. The Japanese word for these unaccompanied male expatriates is *tanshin funin*, or *bachelors in exile*.[21] Thus, in many cases, the spouse is not a factor in expatriate failure. Unlike the debate around the magnitude of the problem, research over the past 20 years has shown a consistent ranking of "inability of the spouse/partner/family to adjust" as a primary cause of early recall. The GMAC GRS 2005 global survey mentioned above reported the following reasons for early return (in rank order):

1. Family concerns.
2. Accepted new position in the company.
3. Completed assignment early.
4. Cultural adjustment challenges.
5. Security concerns.
6. Career concerns.

The persistence of family concerns as a reason for early return over several decades since Tung's findings were published, despite company programs to try to alleviate the problem, indicate how difficult an international assignment can be for some. It certainly explains why so much attention has been given to expatriate adjustment, and confirms the importance of the selection process.

While there is limited evidence (at least readily accessible and in English) regarding expatriate experiences from other Asian countries, accounts indicate that expatriates from these countries may face similar adjustment problems. For example, Selmer et al.[22] report that spouses and children of Chinese expatriates in Hong Kong were normally not permitted to accompany the expatriates. While adjustment was not the focus of this study, the authors found that most of the respondents would have liked to have had their families with them, and conclude that the precarious situation of the families was not conducive to the pursuit of an international career.

Process of Adjustment

The dilemma is that adjustment to a foreign culture is multifaceted, and individuals vary in terms of their reaction and coping behaviours. The concept of an adjustment cycle or curve, depicted in Figure 5.2, is helpful in demonstrating the typical phases that may be encountered during cultural adjustment. The curve (sometimes referred to as the *U-curve*) is based on psychological reactions to the assignment and comprises certain phases.[23]

Phase 1 commences with reactions prior to the assignment—the expatriate may experience a range of positive and negative emotions such as excitement, anxiety, fear of the unknown, or a sense of adventure. There can be an upswing of mood on arrival in the assignment country that produces what has been referred to as the "honeymoon" or "tourist" phase. Then, as the novelty wears off, realities of everyday life in the foreign location begin to intrude, homesickness sets in, and a downswing may commence—a feeling that "the party is over"[24]—which can create negative appraisals of the situation and the location leading to a period of crisis—*Phase 2*. This can be a critical time, and how the individual copes with the psychological adjustment at this phase has an important outcome in terms of success or failure. There is a suggestion that "failure as an early recall" may be triggered at this point (indicated by the dotted arrow in Figure 5.2). Once past this crisis point, as the expatriate comes to terms with the demands of the

FIGURE 5.2

Phases of Cultural Adjustment

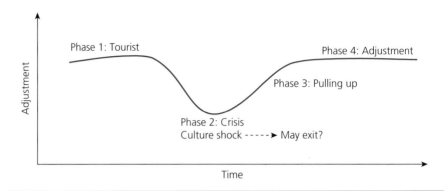

Source: Adapted from: De Cieri, H., Dowling, P. J., & K. F. Taylor. (1991). The Psychological Impact of Expatriate Relocation on Partners. *International Journal of Human Resource Management, 2*(3), 380.

new environment, there is a pulling up—*Phase 3*—as the person begins to adjust to the new environment. This levels off over time to what has been described as healthy recovery—*Phase 4*.

However, when considering the above U-curve, one should remember the following points:

- The U-curve is not normative. Some people do not experience this U-curve. Individuals will differ in their reactions to the foreign location.
- The time period involved varies, and there is no conclusive statistical support for the various phases. Black and Mendenhall[25] point out that the U-curve describes these phases but does not explain how and why people move through the various phases.
- There may be other critical points during the assignment—beyond Phase 4—that may produce downturns, negative reactions, and upswings (that is, a cyclical wave rather than a U-curve).

Despite these limitations, however, expatriates often relate experiencing these phases, and awareness of the psychological adjustment process can assist the expatriate to adopt positive coping behaviours. We should also note that family members experience the phases differently, and do not necessarily move through the various phases at the same time as each other. How accompanying family members handle cultural adjustment is important, as there can be a spillover effect—an unhappy spouse may affect the expatriate's ability to adjust, and thus impact on performance. For example, in their study of American managers in Japan, Korea, Taiwan, and Hong Kong, Black and Stephens[26] found a high correlation between spouse and expatriate adjustment. Companies can assist in the cultural adjustment of the expatriate and employee by using volunteer employees who have worked abroad as expatriates to "adopt" a visiting family and assist in the family's adjustment. Larger companies that employ expats in different parts of the world could support and assist new expats with the development of networks with colleagues in the same host country/region.

Length of Assignment

There is some evidence that length of assignment does contribute to adjustment and performance. For example, the average assignment for Japanese firms tends to be four to five years, compared with the figure shown in Table 5.1 of 1–3 years for 53 percent of the sample of the GMAC 2005 survey. A longer assignment allows the expatriate more time to adjust to the foreign situation and become productive.[27] Japanese firms often do not expect the expatriate to perform up to full capacity until the third year; the first year of the foreign assignment is seen mainly as a period of adjustment to the foreign environment.

Willingness to Move

In a situation where an employee is a reluctant expatriate or accompanied by reluctant family members, it is more likely that they may interpret negatively events and situations encountered in the new environment. In their survey of 405 U.S. managers and their spouses/partners, Brett and Stroh[28] found a significant causal relationship between the manager and the spouse's willingness to move. They conclude that managers who are most ready for international relocations are those whose spouses are also supportive of that move—a not surprising finding. Other studies support the importance of a positive outlook. For example, Hamill[29] reported that the reasons for lower British expatriate failure rates were that British managers were more internationally mobile than U.S. managers, and that perhaps British companies had developed more effective expatriate policies. Dowling and Welch[30] note that the respondents in their research perceived an expatriate posting as a desirable appointment—an opportunity to travel and live overseas—leading to a positive outlook on the foreign assignment. Willingness to relocate as a predictor of success should include the views of family members and is also associated with the perceived desirability of the location of the international assignment.

Work Environment-Related Factors

Gregersen and Black[31] studied 220 American expatriates in four Pacific Rim countries. They found a positive correlation between what they term "intent to stay in the overseas assignment" and the PCN's commitment to the local company, adjustment to interaction with HCNs, and adjustment to general living conditions. Adjustment to the work role itself however, was negatively associated with "intent to stay." Support for these factors as moderators has come from a study by Shaffer et al.[32] of expatriates working in 10 U.S. multinationals. However, Bolino and Feldman[33] extended this to include skills utilization and commitment to the organization. Their study of 268 expatriates from six Fortune 500 companies found that effective skill utilization was significantly related to job satisfaction, organization commitment, and intent to finish the international assignment.

Job autonomy is also a powerful factor influencing expatriate turnover.[34] Another moderator is the perceived level of organizational support—from home as well as from the host unit.[35] Further, once the expatriate has mastered, or nearly completed, the assigned work, other factors may surface and assume relative importance. For instance, if the work becomes less demanding and no longer so time-consuming, the expatriate may have time to pay more attention to negative cross-cultural experiences that the family is encountering. These negative experiences can become distorted when combined with lack of challenge at work and thus sow seeds for early recall or underperformance.

Selection Criteria

We now have a fuller understanding of the phenomenon called *expatriate failure* and the multifaceted nature of international assignments and why developing appropriate selection criteria has become a critical IHRM issue. It should be noted that selection is a two-way process between the individual and the organization. A prospective candidate may reject the expatriate assignment, either for individual reasons, such as family considerations, or for situational factors, such as the perceived toughness of a particular culture.

It is a challenge for those responsible for selecting staff for international assignments to determine appropriate selection criteria. Figure 5.3 illustrates the factors involved in expatriate selection, both in terms of the individual and the specifics of the situation concerned. It should be noted that these factors are interrelated. We base the following discussion on this figure.

Technical Ability

Naturally, the person's ability to perform the required tasks is an important consideration. Technical and managerial skills are therefore an essential criterion. Indeed, research findings consistently indicate that multinationals

FIGURE 5.3

Factors in Expatriate Selection

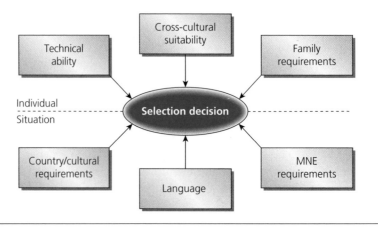

Chapter 5: Recruiting and Selecting Staff for International Assignments

place heavy reliance on relevant technical skills during the expatriate selection process.[36] For example, the ORC Worldwide 2002 survey mentioned earlier found that 72 percent of responding firms selected assignees on the basis of skills or competencies for the job. This is not surprising given that "position filling" is the most common reason for an international assignment. Reinforcing the emphasis on technical skills is the relative ease with which the multinational may assess the candidate's potential, as technical and managerial competence can be determined on the basis of past performance. Since expatriates are predominantly internal recruits, personnel evaluation records can be examined and checked with the candidate's past and present superiors. The dilemma though is that past performance may have little or no bearing on one's ability to achieve a task in a foreign cultural environment.

Cross-Cultural Suitability

As we have already discussed, the cultural environment in which expatriates operate is an important factor in determining successful performance. Apart from the obvious technical ability and managerial skills, expatriates require cross-cultural abilities that enable the person to operate in a new environment. There appears to be a consensus that desirable attributes should include cultural empathy, adaptability, diplomacy, language ability, positive attitude, emotional stability, and maturity.[37]

In practice, while intercultural competence is recognized as important, it is difficult to precisely define what this comprises, let alone assess a candidate's suitability in this regard. One has to take into consideration aspects such as the individual's personality, attitude to foreigners, ability to relate to people from another cultural group, and so on. Multinationals may indicate that, for example, relational abilities are an important expatriate selection criterion, but few will assess a candidate's relational ability through a formal procedure such as judgment by senior managers or psychological tests. As we will discuss shortly, testing procedures are not necessarily the answer.

Family Requirements

The contribution that the family, particularly the spouse, makes to the success of the overseas assignment is now well documented, as we mentioned above in relation to the impact of the accompanying spouse/partner on early return. Despite the importance of the accompanying spouse/partner, as Shaffer and Harrison[38] point out, the focus has been on the expatriate (see also IHRM Today 5.1). From the multinational's perspective, expatriate performance in the host location is the important factor. However, the interaction between expatriate and spouse/partner and family members' various adjustment experiences is now well documented.

WWW5.3

It should be pointed out that the spouse or accompanying partner often carries a heavy burden. On arrival in the country of assignment, the responsibility for settling the family into its new home falls on the spouse/partner, who may have left behind a career, along with friends and social support networks

CERC Spousal Benefits Survey

A 2006 survey organized by the Canadian Employee Relocation Council (CERC) explored how Canadian organizations provided spousal benefits for transferring employees. The survey found that 85 percent of the 40 participating companies provided some form of spousal benefits, while 15 percent did not provide any services or benefits to spouses of transferring employees. More than half of all companies provided career counselling and helped with résumé writing as spousal benefits. Other services ranged from retraining/upgrading and assistance in securing employment to some financial compensation.

A second part of CERC's survey looked at spousal benefits for spouses employed by the same company. In such cases only 63 percent of employers provided spousal benefits, while 37 percent of organizations did not provide any services to spouses of transferring employees. The services or benefits for spouses employed by the same company ranged from guaranteeing a job within the organization (90 percent) and assistance to secure employment in the company (internally: 33 percent; externally: 28 percent) to financial compensation (if employment cannot be secured) (85 percent).

Source: *CERC Spousal Benefits Survey*. (2006, February). Canadian Employee Relocation Council.

(particularly relatives). In developing countries, the employment of house servants is quite common but this is an aspect of international living to which many Westerners from developed countries have some difficulty adjusting. It is often not possible for the spouse/partner to work in the country of assignment and the well-being and education of the children may be an ongoing concern. Although the majority of spouses/partners are female, accompanying male spouses/partners face similar problems of adjustment.[39] In fact, when you add cultural adjustment problems to such a situation, it is perhaps not so surprising to find that some couples seek to return home prematurely.

Despite studies that emphasize the link between the favourable opinion of the spouse to the international assignment and expatriate adjustment, companies appear reluctant to include the spouse/partner in the selection process, treating it in a peripheral way.[40] As a survey by Price Waterhouse[41] survey found:

> Compared to our 1995 survey, the number of companies which routinely interview an employee's spouse or partner as part of the selection process has increased slightly, from 9% to 11%. However, overall, fewer companies involve the spouse or partner in the selection process under any circumstances, rising from half in 1995 to two-thirds currently. Of the companies which do interview the spouse or partner, 12% interview them on their own. Given that more than a third of the companies believe the assignments that either failed, or had been ended prematurely, due to a spouse or partner's difficulties with adapting to life in the host location, it is perhaps a little surprising that companies are not attributing more importance to assessing their suitability.

The 2002 ORC Worldwide survey did not address the involvement of the spouse/partner in the selection process, although the survey reported that assistance was provided to help the accompanying person cope with the international assignment.

Apart from the accompanying partner's career, there are family considerations that can cause a potential expatriate to decline the international assignment. Disruption to children's education is an important consideration, and the selected candidate may reject the offered assignment on the grounds that a move at this particular stage in his or her child's life is inappropriate. The care of aging or invalid parents is another consideration. While these two reasons have been noted in various studies, what has been somewhat overlooked is the issue of single parents. Given increasing divorce rates, this may become a critical factor in assignment selection and acceptance where the custody of children is involved. The associated legal constraints, such as obtaining the consent of the other parent to take the child (or children) out of the home country, and visiting/access rights, may prove to be a major barrier to the international mobility of both single mothers and single fathers.

Country/Cultural Requirements

As discussed in Chapter 1, international firms are usually required to demonstrate that an HCN is not available before the host government will issue the necessary work permit and entry visa for the desired PCN or TCN. In some cases, the multinational may wish to use an expatriate and has selected a candidate for the international assignment, only to find the transfer blocked by the host government. Many developed countries are changing their legislation to facilitate employment-related immigration, which will make international transfers somewhat easier—for example, the European Union Social Charter allows for free movement of citizens of member countries within the EU. It is important that HR staff keep up to date with relevant legislative changes in the countries in which the MNE is involved.

The IHRM Today 5.2 case shows how one U.S. MNE's careful planning allowed it to obtain the required number of PCN visas to successfully launch its business in Australia.

An important, related point is that generally a work permit is granted to the expatriate only. The accompanying spouse or partner may not be permitted to work in the host country. Increasingly, multinationals are finding that the inability of the spouse to work in the host country may cause the selected candidate to reject the offer of an international assignment. If the international assignment is accepted, the lack of a work permit for the accompanying spouse or partner may cause difficulties in adjustment and even contribute to failure. For these reasons, as reported above, some multinationals provide assistance in this regard.

Further, the host country may be an important determinant. Some regions and countries are considered "hardship postings": remote areas away from major cities or modern facilities or war-torn regions with high

Citibank Plans for Changing Staffing Needs

Banks, along with oil and construction companies, remain heavy users of PCN employees, because these industries require very specific (sometimes firm-specific) skills frequently not found in foreign locations. In the mid-1980s, Australia offered a once-only opportunity for foreign banks to enter the local market. Citibank already held a limited banking licence that allowed it to operate in Australia as a merchant bank and finance company. A year before the licences were to be awarded, Citibank sent one of its senior HR managers on a year-long assignment to Sydney to assess the staffing implications of an application to the Australian government for a banking licence. First, an assessment was made as to how many PCN visas would be required. Then, a detailed summary was prepared for the Australian immigration department that demonstrated the history of Citibank's investment in training Australian nationals, with career examples of HCNs who were now employed by Citibank in Australia, in other foreign locations, and in the United States. This proved to be a successful strategy: Citibank received one of the sixteen licences on offer and all of the PCN work permits it requested.

physical risk. Accompanying family members may be an additional responsibility that the multinational does not want to bear. There may be a reluctance to select females for certain Middle East or South East Asian regions, and in some countries a work permit for a female expatriate will not be issued. These aspects may result in the selection of HCNs rather than expatriates.

W W W 5.4

To overcome this problem, a group of more than 20 large multinationals (including Shell, British Airways, Unilever, PricewaterhouseCoopers, and Siemens) has established an organization called "Permits Foundation" in an attempt to promote the improvement of work permit regulations for spouses of expatriates. It also aims to raise government awareness of the connection between work permits and employee mobility.

MNE Requirements

Situational factors often have an influence on selection decisions. For example, the MNE may consider the proportion of expatriates to local staff when making selection decisions, mainly as an outcome of its staffing philosophy. However, operations in particular countries may require the use of more PCNs and TCNs than would normally be the case, as multinationals operating in parts of Eastern Europe and China are discovering. This will affect the selection ratio—that is, PCN:TCN:HCN. Other situational factors include the mode of operation involved, duration and type of assignment, and whether training of local staff is part of the job.

Mode of Operation

Selecting staff to work in an international joint venture may involve major input from the local partner, and could be heavily constrained by the negotiated agreement on selection processes.[42]

Assignment Duration and Type

Family members tend not to accompany an expatriate when the assignment is for only three to six months, so family requirements would not normally be a relevant factor in the selection decision in such cases.[43]

Amount of Knowledge Transfer Required

If the nature of the job is to train local staff, then the MNE may include training skills as a selection criterion.

Language

The ability to speak the local language is an aspect often linked with cross-cultural ability. However, we have chosen to stress language as situation-determined in terms of its importance as a factor in the selection decision. Language skills may be regarded as of critical importance for some expatriate positions but lesser in others, although some would argue that knowledge of the host-country's language is an important aspect of expatriate performance, regardless of the level of position.

Differences in language are recognized as a major barrier to effective cross-cultural communication.[44] Yet, in terms of the other selection criteria we examined above, from the multinational's perspective, language is placed lower down the list of desirable attributes. For example, the ORC Worldwide survey results rank language ability as the fifth most important selection criteria. In the past, U.S. multinationals have tended to place a relatively low importance on foreign language skills. For example, in a 1990 study of U.S. multinationals, Fixman[45] found that foreign language skills were rarely considered an important part of international business success. She comments: "Language problems were largely viewed as mechanical and manageable problems that could be solved individually." This view is also confirmed by the consistent and relatively poor performance of young Americans in polls of geographic literacy sponsored by the National Geographic Education Foundation. In the most recent 2006 poll[46] of young American adults between the ages of 18 and 24, the following results were reported:

- 50 percent of the sample thought it was "important but not absolutely necessary" to know where countries in the news are located.
- 75 percent did not know that a majority of Indonesia's population of 245 million is Muslim (making it the largest Muslim country in the world).
- 74 percent of the sample thought that English was the most commonly spoken language in the world, rather than Mandarin Chinese.

There are signs that in a post-9/11 world, the United States is beginning to refocus on some of these issues. Recently, the Committee on Education and the Workforce of the U.S. Congress[47] examined the issue of international and foreign language studies and the Chair of the Committee noted that:

Congress created Title VI in the National Defense Education Act of 1958 to address a sense of crisis caused by U.S. citizens' lack of knowledge of other countries and cultures. This program remains the federal government's leading mechanism for supporting programs that produce Americans with expertise in foreign languages and international studies, including international business. . . . Continued federal support for these programs reflects the significance and growing relevance of language and area studies, diplomacy, national security, and business competitiveness.

This level of commitment is encouraging but as we noted in Chapter 1, the task of internationalizing business education in the United States is a large one and will require considerable resources and persistence for significant progress to be made.

Another component to language as a situation factor in the selection decision is the role of the *common corporate language*. As previously discussed, many multinationals adopt a common corporate language as a way of standardizing reporting systems and procedures. This is not, perhaps, an issue for PCN selection within multinationals from the Anglo-Saxon world (Britain, the United States, Canada, Australia, and New Zealand), where the chosen corporate language remains the same as that of the home country. However, it becomes an expatriate selection issue for multinationals from non-English-speaking countries that adopt English as the corporate language, unless the posting is to a country with a shared language. For instance, a Spanish multinational, using Spanish as the corporate language, selecting a PCN to head its new subsidiary in Mexico, does not face the same language issue as a Spanish multinational, with English as its corporate language, selecting a PCN for its Canadian facility. For the latter, fluency in English would be required. Lack of fluency in the corporate language, therefore, can be a selection barrier. Prospective candidates may be eliminated from the potential pool due to a lack of at least competency in the common language.[48] Language ability therefore may limit the MNE's ability to select the most appropriate candidate.

Use of Selection Tests

 5.3

Although there is consensus among scholars and practitioners that personal characteristics (or traits) are important, there is considerable debate about how such personal characteristics can be reliably and accurately measured. Personality and psychological tests have been used in the selection process, but the effectiveness of such tests as predictors of cultural adjustment is questioned. For example, Torbiörn[49] comments that although desirable personality traits are specified and recommended, the tests or criteria to assess these traits are seldom convincingly validated. Likewise, Willis[50] states that if tests are used, they should be selected with care and regard for reliability and validity because, while some tests may be useful in suggesting potential problems, there appears to be little correlation between test scores and performance. He further adds that most of the relevant tests have been devised in the United States and, therefore, may be culture-bound. Use of such tests without careful modification on non-American nationals adds another question mark to their reliability and validity as predictors of expatriate success. It is important that HRM staff in all locations are aware of the debate surrounding the use of selection tests, particularly the culture-bound nature of psychometric tests designed for PCNs.

Another constraint is that in some countries (the United Kingdom and Australia, for instance), there is controversy about the use of psychological tests.[51] There is also a different pattern of usage across countries—the use of such tests is very low in Germany.[52] The 1997/1998 Price Waterhouse survey reported only 12 percent used formal assessment centres, and some companies "indicated through their comments that they also use psychometric tests." The majority of respondents (85 percent) mainly assessed expatriate suitability through the traditional interview process. More recent surveys have not addressed this aspect of selection.

The difficulty of predicting success, then, seems to be related to the lack of valid and reliable screening devices to identify, with certainty, managers who will succeed in a foreign assignment. The crucial variables affecting the adjustment of the individual and family are not only difficult to identify or measure, but the complex relationship between personality factors and ability to adjust to another culture is not well understood.[53]

Another drawback of expatriate selection based on traits or characteristics is the subjective nature of the scoring of abilities, especially those classified as personal and environmental characteristics. Nevertheless, models derived from this approach have value in that they provide some guidelines that can be applied during the selection process, rather than mere reliance on the potential manager's domestic record as a predictor.[54] One such model is offered by Mendenhall and Oddou[55] and outlined in IHRM Notebook 5.1.

IHRM Notebook 5.1

A Four-Dimensional Model

Mendenhall and Oddou propose a four-dimensional approach that attempts to link specific behavioural tendencies to probable overseas performance:

1. The self-oriented dimension—the degree to which the expatriate expresses an adaptive concern for self-preservation, self-enjoyment, and mental hygiene.
2. The perceptual dimension—the expertise the expatriate possesses in accurately understanding why host nationals behave the way they do.
3. The others-oriented dimension—the degree to which the expatriate is concerned about host-national co-workers and desires to affiliate with them.

4. The cultural-toughness dimension—a mediating variable that recognizes that acculturation is affected by the degree to which the culture of the host country is incongruent with that of the home country.

The evaluation of the candidate's strengths and weaknesses on these four dimensions, Mendenhall and Oddou suggest, will focus appropriate attention on cross-cultural ability and behaviour, thus complementing technical ability assessment.

Equal Employment Opportunity Issues

RPC 5.4

In the recruitment and selection process, multinationals must address the issue of equal employment opportunity (EEO) for employees in all employment locations. This involves taking into consideration the increasingly conflicting national laws on employment. As Jain, Sloane, and Horwitz[56] mention, mandatory retirement and hiring ages are illegal in some countries, while in other countries age restrictions are openly stated in job ads. While Canada's human rights legislation has been prohibiting discrimination in employment on the grounds of age for at least the past 30 years, in Germany (until the 2006 Antidiskriminierungsgesetz), many job ads explicitly stated maximum age restrictions. Based on a case of harassment and race discrimination, the complexities and challenges of home-country EEO applied abroad are illustrated in IHRM Today 5.3.

Equal employment opportunity laws are expressions of social values with regard to employment and reflect the values of a society or country.[57] With the increasing rate of female entry into the workforce, many Western countries have introduced legislation to cover sex discrimination. In Canada, women account for approximately 50 percent of the workforce and are protected by Canada's Employment Equity Act and supported through, for example, equal pay legislation. Despite some evidence of the continuous existence of a glass ceiling and barriers to top-paying jobs for Canadian women, the latter often cannot be compared with women in parts of the Middle East, Africa, Asia, and Latin America, where women are perceived to have a lower social status and are not universally employed. Multinationals must be aware

---

IHRM Today 5.3

Home-Country EEO Legislation and Its Application Abroad

The United States has a comprehensive statute (Title VII of the Civil Rights Act of 1964) to cover many EEO situations. In 1991, the U.S. Supreme Court* held that this Act does not apply outside the territorial borders of the United States. The case involved an American citizen who claimed that he had been illegally discriminated against while working overseas for a U.S. corporation. A naturalized citizen born in Lebanon, the plaintiff began working for Aramco Corporation in Texas in 1979 and was transferred by the company to work in Saudi Arabia in 1980, where he worked until he was discharged in 1984. The Court rejected the person's claim that he had been harassed and ultimately discharged by Aramco Corporation on account of his race, religion, and national origin. This decision had important implications for the status and protection of Americans working abroad for U.S. firms, and the Civil Rights Act was subsequently amended by the U.S. Congress in 1991 to extend protection to all U.S. citizens working overseas.

---

*E.E.O.C. v. Arabian American Oil Co., 111 S. Ct. 1227 (1991). For an excellent commentary on this case, see G. L. Clark, (1992), The Geography of Civil Rights, *Environment and Planning D: Society and Space, 10,* 119–121. For details on the amendment, see Civil Rights Act of 1991, §109(a), 105 Stat. 1077, codified at 42 U.S.C. §2000e(f).

of the different forms and levels of equal employment opportunity legislations and antidiscrimination laws, and ensure subsidiary compliance where appropriate in selecting expatriates.

Expatriate Selection in Practice: The Role of the Coffee Machine

As we indicated at the beginning of the section on selection criteria, most multinationals admit that technical and/or managerial skills are the dominant, sometimes only, criteria used. We have suggested that reliance on technical skills is mainly due to the fact that most international assignments are "position filling." Of the factors outlined in Figure 5.3, technical skills are perhaps the easiest to measure. It could be argued that Figure 5.3 represents a best practice or ideal selection model, which many MNEs do not in fact use. Harris and Brewster[58] have argued that expatriate selection, in reality, often tends to be an ad hoc process that they describe as the "coffee-machine" system.

Harris and Brewster suggest that executives chatting around the coffee machine (or water cooler) can start the selection process through a casual conversation about an assignment need confronting one of them. Another executive can volunteer the name of a potential expatriate, thus starting an informal short list of candidates. What happens next, according to Harris and Brewster, is that the multinational's processes are then activated to legitimize the decision that has, in effect, already been made around the coffee machine. Harris and Brewster relate that this process was the most common form of selection process they encountered in their study of U.K. firms. They then derived a typology of selection systems to explain variations found in the way expatriate selection is conducted, detailed in Table 5.2.

Harris and Brewster regard the coffee-machine scenario as an example of the informal/closed cell in their typology. It is of course possible to find examples of formal, open selection processes in firms as well as informal or closed systems. Harris and Brewster note that the process can be influenced by the maturity of the multinational, its stage in the internationalization process, and its size or industry. The type of position involved, the role of the HR function in the process, and whether the multinational is reactive rather than proactive where international assignment selection is involved remain key factors in how selection processes work in multinationals. In addition to a carefully developed selection process, IHRM Today 5.4 highlights the importance of assignment letters, while IHRM Today 5.5 summarizes current international relocation activities and policies of companies operating in Canada.

Dual-Career Couples

So far, we have focused on selecting suitable candidates for international assignments. We will now consider an emerging constraint—the dual-career couple—on the available pool of candidates, thus hindering the recruitment and selection process. The rise in dual-career couples, along with the aging population and other family-related situations, combine to make more people immobile. Employees are prepared to state the grounds for refusal

TABLE 5.2

Harris and Brewster's Selection Typology

	FORMAL	INFORMAL
Open	• Clearly defined criteria • Clearly defined measures • Training for selectors • Open advertising of vacancy (internal/external) • Panel discussions	• Less-defined criteria • Less-defined measures • Limited training for selectors • No panel discussions • Open advertising of vacancy • Recommendations
Closed	• Clearly defined criteria • Clearly defined measures • Training for selectors • Panel discussions • Nominations only (networking/reputation)	• Selectors' individual preferences determine selection criteria and measures • No panel discussions • Nominations only (networking/reputation)

Source: Harris, H., & Brewster, C. (1999). The Coffee-Machine System: How International Selection Really Works. *International Journal of Human Resource Management, 10*(3), 493. Reproduced with permission.

IHRM Today 5.4

Assignment Letters

In addition to well-developed selection processes and criteria, the Canadian Employee Relocation Council (CERC) strongly recommends letters of assignment as the basis for an agreement between employers and employees on international assignments. While the number of such agreements has doubled between 2003 and 2005, most employers have not gone beyond the standard content outlining employment conditions such as effective date and termination date, services to be performed, location, compensation, taxation, housing, medical and health coverage, home visits, and relocation supports and benefits such as maintenance of the existing home, shipping of personal goods, and cost of living allowances.

A good letter of assignment helps to clarify what happens if an international assignment does not work out and could include:

- Definition of the employment laws that apply.
- Clear statement as to who is employing the employee.
- Procedures to deal with cases of family sickness or emergencies.
- Employment opportunities for the employee if he or she has to return home early.
- Non-compete and clawback provisions.
- Procedures for dealing with cases of employees who violate host-country laws or in some manner damage the company's reputation.

As illustrated in IHRM Today 5.3, without a very detailed letter of assignment, employers and in particular their international assignees often operate in a grey area. The parties involved might not be fully aware of, for example, what employment laws they have to abide by, what their legal rights and obligations are—and worse—as the Chapter 4 opening vignette shows—who the actual employer is.

Source: Cryne, S. (2007, March 12). Avoiding the perils of foreign assignments. *Canadian HR Reporter*.

International Relocation Activities and Policies of Companies Operating in Canada

On a biannual basis, the Canadian Employee Relocation Council (CERC) conducts surveys of employee relocation policies and practices of organizations with operations in Canada. The following is the Executive Summary of the *CERC 2007 Employee Relocation Policy Survey.*

The 2007 survey confirmed that Canadian businesses remain very active in the global marketplace, with 46% relocating employees internationally. 74% of companies expect permanent international relocations to increase or remain at similar levels over the next 12 months, and 82% of respondent companies anticipate that temporary international transfers will increase or remain at similar levels over the next 12 months.

The average cost of a permanent relocation is reported at $91,125. Over 30% of firms reported average costs of over $100,000. The average cost of a temporary relocation/assignment is $77,875.

The vast majority of companies, 81%, continue to manage their international relocation through a written policy, with 15% reporting they manage international mobility through an Employment Agreement on an ad hoc basis. The number of companies providing employees with a Cost of Living Allowance, at 70%, is similar to 2005. Reversing a 2005 trend is the number of companies that provide Hardship Allowances or Foreign Service Premiums—73% and 78%, respectively, compared to 62% and 59% in 2005.

The number of companies providing reemployment assistance for the spouse has increased to 45%—following a decline to just 25% in 2005. There is a noticeable decline in the number of companies providing coverage to maintain children in the former location for education purposes.

As reported in 2005, international concerns around terrorism and security have not impacted acceptance rates for foreign postings, with just 6% of companies reporting a decrease in acceptance rates for security reasons. [T]he number of corporations with a written tax policy declined in 2007; for international assignments this dropped from 73% to 49% today. 74% of corporations with a global workforce use tax equalization as their preferred method of tax treatment of expatriates.

The major management challenges, as reported by these corporations, continue to be family and tax issues, remaining largely unchanged since 2005. As reported in previous surveys legal firms are the service of choice for obtaining visas in almost two-thirds of the organizations requiring assistance. There is a definite trend in the number of companies using the home country for payroll purposes—increasing to 68% in 2007 from 36% in 2005.

Only 29% of companies report having a formal repatriation program; 40% have a program to facilitate an appropriate career position upon repatriation—increasing from 27% in 2005. The majority of companies with a program in place did not begin the career planning process until close to the end of the assignment. Only 23% of companies track retention rates among repatriated employees.

32 of the 51 companies completing the international section of the survey responded that they have short-term international assignees; 56% of those firms expect an increase in volume in the coming year. As in 2005, the most common challenge is tracking short-term assignments for tax purposes.

Source: *CERC 2007 Employee Relocation Policy Survey*—Executive Summary. (2007). Canadian Employee Relocation Council, 11–12.

5.6

as "family concerns." That this has become more acceptable as a reason reflects a significant shift in thinking about the role of non-work aspects impinging on work-related matters.

The increase in the number of dual-career couples is a worldwide trend, one that is posing a dilemma for both companies and employees alike. This is not surprising given that accepting a traditional international assignment will impact on the career of the potential candidate's spouse or partner. The ORC Worldwide 2002 survey focused on the issue of dual careers and international assignments. A major finding was that spousal or dual-career issues were the most common reasons for rejecting international assignments reported by North American and European firms, but were rarely cited by Asian firms. Rather, concern for children and ageing parents were barriers to assignment acceptance for this group. Likewise, the GMAC GRS 2005 survey cites spouse career concerns as the third most frequent reason for assignment refusal.

Multinationals are being forced to select from a diminishing pool of candidates who may be less qualified. This has strategic implications for staffing policies, and may be a reason why more TCNs are being utilized. As we noted when discussing the expatriate profile in Table 5.1, 27 percent of expatriates were TCNs in the 2005 GMAC survey. While cost containment remains a major driver of localization (that is, replacing expatriates with HCNs), staff availability is also a factor.[59] Reflecting this global trend, the impact of the accompanying spouse/partner's career orientation on the international assignment is an emerging area of research. It seems that career orientation not only affects the couple's willingness to move, but also may negatively affect performance and retention in the foreign location.[60] Some multinationals are endeavouring to come up with solutions to the dual-career challenge. These can be divided into two categories: finding alternative arrangements and making the assignments more "family-friendly."

Alternative Assignment Arrangements

A number of alternative assignment arrangements can be identified in international staffing: short-term assignments, commuter assignments, and other arrangements.

Short-Term Assignments

In the ORC Worldwide 2002 survey, 72 percent of responding firms used short-term assignments (compared with 26 percent in a 1996 ORC survey) as an alternative means of satisfying the international assignment need.

Commuter Assignments

In commuter assignment situations (sometimes referred to as "commuter marriages"), the spouse may decide to remain in the home country, and the couple works out ways to maintain the relationship with the help of the firm. Alternatively, couples may move to jobs in adjoining countries or within the same geographical region to make commuting (relationship-maintenance) easier. Multinationals often adjust compensation benefits to fit with agreed arrangements. The ORC survey found that 46 percent of responding firms had such arrangements (compared with 19 percent in 1996).

Other Arrangements

According to the ORC 2002 report, other arrangements include unaccompanied assignments (50 percent in 2002 compared to 23 percent in 1995), assignments replaced by business travel (57 percent), and virtual assignments (16 percent).

Little attention has been given to the advantages and disadvantages of these non-standard assignments in terms of the individual employees, their spouses, and the strategic objectives that prompt the use of international rather than local staff. While these arrangements may have short-term benefits in overcoming reluctance to move, how effective they will be in encouraging dual-career couples to accept international assignments over time is yet to be determined. Whatever type of international assignments Canadian employees select, once abroad they can get help and assistance from the Canadian government (e.g., Service Canada at www.servicecanada.gc.ca).

Family-Friendly Policies

Inter-Company Networking

The multinational might use inter-company networking in an attempt to place the accompanying spouse or partner in a suitable job with another multinational—sometimes in a reciprocal arrangement. To illustrate: A U.S. multinational may enter into an agreement with a German multinational also operating in, say, China, to find a position within their respective Chinese facilities for each other's accompanying partner (that is, "You find my expatriate's spouse a job and provide a work visa, and I will do the same for you"). Alternatively, a local supplier, distributor, or joint venture partner may agree to employ the accompanying spouse/partner.

Job-Hunting Assistance

The multinational might provide spouse/partner assistance with an employment search in the host country. This may be by funding employment agency fees, making career counselling available, or simply assisting the person in obtaining a work permit. Some multinationals may provide a fact-finding trip to the host location before the actual assignment. The 2005 GMAC GRS survey reports that 31 percent of responding firms assisted in finding the accompanying spouse/partner employment by funding job-finding and executive search fees.

Intra-Company Employment

Intra-company employment is perhaps a logical but often somewhat difficult solution. It means sending the couple to the same foreign facility, perhaps to the same department. Not all multinationals (or all couples) are comfortable with the idea of having a husband-and-wife team in the same work location, and there can often be difficulties obtaining work visas for such arrangements.

On-Assignment Career Support

Motorola[61] is an example of how a multinational may assist spouses to maintain and even improve career skills through what Motorola calls its Dual-Career Policy. This consists of a lump-sum payment for education expenses, professional association fees, seminar attendance, language training to upgrade work-related skills, and employment agency fees. Conditions are attached, such as requiring that the spouse must have been employed before the assignment. Thus, if the spouse is unable to find suitable employment, the time can be spent on career development activities.

Other examples of on-assignment assistance include providing help in establishing contacts and paying for a spouse's lost income. The idea is to maintain skills so that the spouse may find work on reentry into the home country.

These examples of family-friendly policies demonstrate that creative thinking can assist multinationals overcome the potential barrier sometimes presented by dual-career situations. It is not possible to comment with authority on how effective the above assistance schemes are in terms of overcoming the dual-career barrier. However, it is clear that multinationals are attempting to address the issue and create solutions for this barrier to mobility.

Are Female Expatriates Different?

Our final issue in terms of selection for international assignments is related to gender. The typical expatriate tends to be male: 23 percent in the GMAC GRS 2005 survey were females, 14 percent in the ORC 2002 survey. The authors of both of these surveys make the point that that the proportion of females is increasing. For example, the ORC report compares the 2002 situation to that of its 1992 survey, where only five percent of expatriates were female. You can go farther back to a 1984 article, in which Adler[62] reported a survey of international HR practices in over 600 U.S. and Canadian companies that found only three percent of the 13,338 expatriates identified were female. She found that female expatriates tended to be employed by companies with over 1,000 employees in the banking, electronics, petroleum, and publishing industries. It has been argued that as the proportion of women in the domestic workforce continues to increase, and as international experience becomes an essential criterion for career progression within multinationals, we will see more international managers who are female.

Over the past decade or so, researchers have attempted to discover why so few expatriates are female. Is it because they were unwilling to relocate? Is it attitudinal? Does it reflect a somewhat externalized belief that men in some cultures, such as certain Asian countries, do not like reporting to female managers, particularly foreign women, and therefore women should not be posted overseas, creating what has been referred to as "the glass border that supports the glass ceiling"?

A number of studies challenge some of the attitudes regarding the suitability of females for international assignments. For example, Stroh, Varma, and Valy-Durbin[63] found that U.S. and Canadian women are interested in and likely to accept international assignments, although there are variations between those with children and those without. However, the women in this study tended to believe that their firms were hesitant to ask them to accept an international assignment, although supervisors (whether male or female) did not necessarily share that belief. Further, performance of female expatriates was found initially to be affected by host-country prejudice regarding the role of women in certain countries—considered as culturally tough assignment locations. However, the longer the women were on such assignments, the less they perceived that prejudice was a barrier to effectiveness. Caligiuri and Tung,[64] in their study of female and male expatriates in a U.S.-based multinational, found that females can perform equally as well as their male counterparts regardless of a country's attitude toward women in managerial positions.

Taking a different approach in her study of Austrian female expatriates, Fischlmayr[65] used the concepts of external and self-established barriers to explore why women are underrepresented in international assignments. These are listed in Table 5.3.

Through 21 interviews with HR managers and female expatriates in Austrian multinationals from various industries and positions, Fischlmayr found that the attitudes of HR directors were a major barrier to the selection of female expatriates, although self-established barriers were also very strong. Females in Austrian companies often had to specifically request an international assignment, whereas their male colleagues were required to take international assignments. Further, some women regarded that their age was decisive in terms of others' perceptions and expectations about their behaviour. The older the woman, the easier it is to get an international assignment. Fischlmayr concludes that women are partly to blame for their underrepresentation.

TABLE 5.3

Barriers to Females Taking International Assignments

EXTERNAL BARRIERS	SELF-ESTABLISHED BARRIERS
• HR managers reluctant to select female candidates • Culturally tough locations or regions preclude female expatriates • Those selecting expatriates have stereotypes in their minds that influence decisions	• Some women have limited willingness to relocate • The dual-career couple • Women are often a barrier to their own careers by behaving according to gender-based role models

Source: Based on: Fischlmayr, I. C. (2002). Female Self-Perception as Barrier to International Careers? *International Journal of Human Resource Management, 13*(5), 773–783.

 5.8

Mayrhofer and Scullion[66] report on the experiences of male and female expatriates in the German clothing industry. They found that women were sent into a diverse number of countries, including those with an Islamic influence. Overall, there were few differences in the experiences of both gender groups, although female expatriates placed more value on integration of spouse/family issues prior to and during the assignment than did the males in the sample. Assignment lengths in this industry tended to be shorter and involved various forms of non-standard assignments, and there were generally more female managers than perhaps found in other industries. More women than men were assigned for longer assignment terms, and these authors conclude that the higher proportion of women in the industry appeared to make gender less of an issue. However, this did not apply to the top senior management positions, where women were less represented. Mayrhofer and Scullion conclude that there are still barriers to female expatriates in terms of senior expatriate positions.

A further contribution comes from a study by Napier and Taylor[67] of female expatriates from various countries working in Japan, China, and Turkey. The women fell into three categories: traditional expatriates; "trailers," who were spouses/partners of male expatriates; and "independents"—professional women who could be called "self-selected" expatriates. Napier and Taylor found that gaining credibility with local clients was a major issue. Accommodating cultural differences, maintaining a social life, and a need for appropriate interpersonal skills were important factors in coping with work demands. Networks became important in both business and social contexts. Being a minority (foreign females) meant higher visibility than they were used to and could be a positive in terms of getting access to key clients and customers.

What emerges as common across the various studies on female expatriates is that assignment location, level of organization support, spouse/partner satisfaction, and intercultural experiences are important in terms of performance. The list of moderators is similar to those we discussed in general terms earlier in this chapter. What does appear to differentiate female and male expatriates is the degree to which these moderators affect individual performance and the value placed on cultural awareness training prior to the international assignment. The dual-career issue may prove to be a greater barrier for female mobility, as males are more reluctant to accompany their spouse/partner.

Summary

This chapter has addressed key issues affecting recruitment and selection for international assignments. We have covered four myths related to the concept of a global manager—that there is a universal approach to management; that people can acquire multicultural adaptability and behaviours; that there are common characteristics shared by successful international managers; and that there are no impediments to mobility. We also analyzed the debate surrounding the definition and magnitude of expatriate failure, and discussed cultural adjustment and other moderating factors affecting expatriate intent to stay and performance (these included duration of the assignment, willingness to move, and work-related factors).

We argued for individual and situational factors to be considered in the selection decision. Our evaluation of the common criteria used revealed the difficulty of selecting the right candidate for an international assignment and the importance of including family considerations in the selection process. Further, we discussed dual-career couples as a barrier to staff mobility and reviewed the techniques multinationals are utilizing to overcome this constraint. In the final part of this chapter, we looked at female expatriates and discussed whether they face different issues than their male counterparts.

While our appreciation of the issues surrounding expatriate recruitment and selection has deepened in the past 30 years, we believe that much remains to be explored. The field is dominated by U.S. research into predominantly U.S. samples of expatriates, although there has been an upsurge in interest from European academics and practitioners. Will the factors affecting the selection decision be similar for multinationals emerging from countries such as China and India? If more multinationals are to encourage subsidiary staff to consider international assignments as part of an intraorganizational network approach to management, we will need further understanding of how valid the issues discussed in this chapter are for all categories of staff from different country locations. It is apparent, though, that staff selection remains critical. Finding the right people to fill positions, particularly key managers—whether PCN, TCN, or HCN—can determine international expansion. However, effective recruitment and selection is only the first step.

Key Terms

coping skills 156

effectiveness skills 156

recruitment 155

selection 155

Web Links

www 5.1 On the GMAC Global Relocation Services site, click on "Insight and Ideas" to locate and download the latest *Global Relocation Trends Survey Report* containing more information about international recruitment and selection:

www.gmacglobalrelocation.com

www 5.2 On the ORC Worldwide site, you will find more information about expatriates and expatriate workforce surveys:

www.orcinc.com

The Canadian Employee Relocation Council (CERC) site provides information and support for the relocation industry:

www.cerc.ca

www 5.4 For more information about the Permits Foundation, go to:

www.permitsfoundation.com

www 5.5 The Canadian government site Service Canada offers Canadians living abroad assistance and important information about taxation, customs, and many other relevant aspects of living abroad:

www.servicecanada.gc.ca

RPC Icons

RPC 5.1 Identifies potential source of qualified candidates

RPC 5.2 Selects candidates and negotiates terms and conditions of employment

RPC 5.3 Evaluates screening, selection and orientation processes, and outcomes at the organizational level

RPC 5.4 Promotes a productive culture in the organization that values diversity, trust, and respect for individuals and their contributions

RPC 5.5 Identifies potential source of qualified candidates

RPC 5.6 Leads in the development of HR initiatives that support the organization's strategic directions

RPC 5.7 Contributes to the development of the organization's vision, goals, and strategies, with a focus on human capital

RPC 5.8 Formulates organization development strategies in accordance with legislated and/or voluntary diversity and equity goals

Discussion Questions

1. What is the difference between a global manager and a global mindset?
2. Should multinationals be concerned about expatriate failure? If so, why?
3. What are the most important factors involved in the selection decision?
4. Are female expatriates different?

Using the Internet

1. While much of the debate and focus in the past and current chapters have been Canadians and Canadian companies going abroad, the Canadian government site "Invest in Canada" (**www.investincanada**

.com/Director.aspx?lang=en) provides you with some insights into how Canada tries to attract and help foreigners and their businesses to expand their operations in Canada. Select a country of your choice and compare its governmental online support systems with Canada's online services advising and guiding foreign businesses entering your selected country.

2. Browse through the online Canadians Resident Abroad *CRA Magazine* at **www.canadiansresidentabroad.com** and analyze some of the daily-life issues and challenges of employees and their families living abroad. How can home-country managers and HRM help?

Exercises

1. Put yourself in the position of a manager interviewing a candidate for an international assignment. What are the differences between an international assignment job interview and a "regular" job interview? What are the challenges?

2. Discuss with your classmates the proposition that most expatriate selection decisions are made informally, as suggested by the "coffee-machine" solution.

3. If you have not yet been on an international assignment, how would you feel about accepting the challenge of an international assignment? Think about your strengths and weaknesses when it comes to such an assignment.

4. If you have been on an international assignment, think about what went right and what went wrong. What would you do differently now?

Case

The Reinhart Case

On June 24, 1998, Edward Leonard of Creston, British Columbia, a diamond driller working for Terramundo Drilling Inc., was kidnapped by members of the Revolutionary Armed Forces of Colombia (Fuerzas Armadas Revolucionarias de Colombia—FARC) in the northeast of Colombia. Leonard's capturer wanted to negotiate a deal for gold mining shares with Greystar Resources Ltd.—a gold mining company in Vancouver and the owner of claims in Colombia's Santander province for which Terramundo and Leonard were contracted to drill core samples.

Leonard's boss, Terramundo's Norbert Reinhart, wanted to purchase his employee's freedom by paying $100,000 to the FARC guerrillas. On October 6, 1998, in a meeting with the guerrillas, Reinhart handed over the money While Reinhart was hoping to walk away with Leonard after the money was paid, the FARC realized that Reinhart was the president of Terramundo and thought that with him they had an even better hostage. After 94 days of captivity and some complicated and complex negotiations between the FARC, local contact persons, and Canadian government and company officials, Norbert Reinhart was released on January 8, 1999.

This case shows the dangers of frontier mining (which has a strong tradition in Canada) and illustrates some of the potential challenges for employees on international assignments. At the same time, the case has invited heated debate about the responsibilities of companies operating in industries and geographic regions that are dangerous for their employees and the necessity for precautions to be taken and support structures provided to protect these international assignees. (In the same year that Reinhart was taken hostage, more than 2,100 people were kidnapped in Colombia—including at least 43 foreigners.)

Source: Fennell, T., & Timmins, S. (1999, January 25). Reinhart released by Rebels. *Maclean's*.

Questions

1. Was it the right decision in the first place for Terramundo to operate in a region that was well known for being controlled by FARC guerrillas, and where kidnapping was a very common way to fund FARC activities?
2. Did Reinhart do the right thing by trying to help his employee in the way described above? What were Reinhart's alternatives?
3. What can companies operating in industries such as the mining or oil business do to protect their international assignees? What should be the role of the HRM function?
4. When sent to remote and dangerous geographic regions, should all employees (home- and host-country employees) get the same employment support and workplace safety and security support? Is the reality of the situation in line with your response?

Endnotes

1. H. Scullion & D. Collings. (2006). International recruitment and selection. In H. Scullion & D. Collings (Eds.), *Global Staffing*. London, UK: Routledge, 59–86.
2. For a recent review of the culture literature, see: K. Leung, R. Bhagat, N. Buchan, M. Erez & C. Gibson. (2005). Culture and international business: Recent advances and their implications for future research. *Journal of International Business Studies, 36*(4), 357–378.
3. F. T. Murray & A. H. Murray. (1986). Global Managers for Global Businesses. *Sloan Management Review, 27*(2), 75–80.
4. N. Forster. (2000). The Myth of the "International Manager." *International Journal of Human Resource Management, 11*(1), 126–142. See also: C. A. Bartlett & S. Ghoshal. (1997). The Myth of the Generic Manager: New Personal Competencies for New Management Roles. *California Management Review, 40*(1), 92–116.
5. Y. Baruch. (2002, January–February). No Such Thing as a Global Manager. *Business Horizons*, 36–42.

6. N. Forster. (1997). The Persistent Myth of High Expatriate Failure Rates. *International Journal of Human Resource Management, 8*(4), 430.

7. Price Waterhouse (Eds.). (1997). *International Assignments: European Policy and Practice.* Europe: Price Waterhouse.

8. R. L. Tung. (1981). Selection and Training of Personnel for Overseas Assignments. *Columbia Journal of World Business, 16*(1), 68–78; R. L. Tung. (1982). Selection and Training Procedures of U.S., European and Japanese Multinationals. *California Management Review, 25*(1), 57–71; and R. L. Tung. (1984, Fall). Human Resource Planning in Japanese Multinationals: A Model for U.S. Firms? *Journal of International Business Studies,* 139–149.

9. C. Brewster. (1988). *The Management of Expatriates* (Human Resource Research Centre Monograph Series, No. 2). Bedford, UK: Cranfield School of Management. In a pilot study, Hamill investigated the IHRM practices and policies of seven British multinationals. He found that the failure rate among British expatriates was significantly lower (less than 5 percent) than that reported for U.S. multinationals. (J. Hamill. (1989). Expatriate Policies in British Multinationals. *Journal of General Management, 14*(4), 19–33; E. Marx. (1996). *International Human Resource Practices in Britain and Germany.* London, UK: Anglo-German Foundation.

10. A-W. Harzing. (1995). The Persistent Myth of High Expatriate Failure Rates. *International Journal of Human Resource Management, 6*(2), 458.

11. C. Christensen & A.-W. Harzing. (2004). Expatriate failure: Time to abandon the concept? *Career Development International, 9*(7), 616–626.

12. *Dual Careers and International Assignments Survey.* (2002). Organizational Resource Counselors, Inc. (The organization changed its name to ORC Worldwide in 2003.)

13. I. Björkman & M. Gertsen. (1990, December). Corporate Expatriation: An Empirical Study of Scandinavian Firms. In *Proceedings of the Third Symposium on Cross-Cultural Consumer and Business Studies,* Honolulu. Danish firms did not respond to Tung's survey, but Swedish and Norwegian firms did.

14. P. J. Dowling & D. Welch. (1988). International Human Resource Management: An Australian Perspective. *Asia-Pacific Journal of Management, 6*(1), 39–65. Although precise records were not kept, the four companies estimated failure rates of less than 5 percent.

15. For example, Enderwick and Hodgson explain that the absence of "expatriate failure" in their study of New Zealand firms may be due to their early stages in internationalization. See: P. Enderwick & D. Hodgson. (1993). Expatriate Management Practices of New Zealand Business. *International Journal of Human Resource Management, 4*(2), 407–423.

16. M. E. Mendenhall & G. Oddou. (1988, September–October). The Overseas Assignment: A Practical Look. *Business Horizons,* 78–84

17. M. Mendenhall & G. Oddou. (1985). The Dimensions of Expatriate Acculturation: A Review. *Academy of Management Review, 10,* 39–47.

18. S. Cryne. (2007, March 12). Avoiding the perils of foreign assignments. *Canadian HR Reporter.*

19. Tung. Selection and Training Procedures.

20. Ibid.

21. Tanshin Funin: Bachelors in Exile. (1990, December). *Focus Japan,* 4.

22. J. Selmer, B. P. Ebrahimi, & L. Mingtao. (2002). Career Management of Business Expatriates from China. *International Business Review, 11*(1), 17–33.

23. For a review and assessment of the U-curve, see: J.S. Black & M. Mendenhall. (1991). The U-Curve Adjustment Hypothesis Revisited: A Review and Theoretical Framework. *Journal of International Business Studies, 22*(2), 225–247.

24. H. De Cieri, P. Dowling, & K. Taylor. (1991). The Psychological Impact of Expatriate Relocation on Partners. *International Journal of Human Resource Management, 2*(3), 377–414;

M. Kauppinen. (1994). *Antecedents of Expatriate Adjustment: A Study of Finnish Managers in the United States*. Helsinki: Helsinki School of Economics Press.

25. Black & Mendenhall. The U-Curve Adjustment Hypothesis Revisited.

26. J. S. Black & G. K. Stephens. (1989). The Influence of the Spouse on American Expatriate Adjustment and Intent to Stay in Pacific Rim Overseas Assignments. *Journal of Management, 15*(4), 529–544. See also M. Kauppinen, *Antecedents of Expatriate Adjustment*, for support of this finding.

27. Tung. Selection and Training Procedures.

28. J. M. Brett & L. K. Stroh. (1995). Willingness to Relocate Internationally. *Human Resource Management, 34*(3), 405–424.

29. Hamill. Expatriate Policies in British Multinationals.

30. P. J. Dowling & D. Welch. International Human Resource Management: An Australian Perspective. One U.S. personnel director interviewed by the authors pointed out that attributing expatriate recall to "failure of spouse to adjust" was at times a simplistic explanation. He postulated that, apart from the probability of the expatriate blaming his wife for his own failure to adjust, some astute spouses may see the expatriate's poor performance and trigger the early recall to limit damage to the expatriate's career.

31. H. B. Gregersen & J. S. Black. (1990). A Multifaceted Approach to Expatriate Retention in International Assignments. *Group & Organization Studies, 15*(4), 461–485.

32. M. S. Shaffer, D. A. Harrison, & K. M. Gilley. (1999). Dimensions, Determinants, and Differences in the Expatriate Adjustment Process. *Journal of International Business Studies, 30*(3), 557–581.

33. M. C. Bolino & D. C. Feldman. (2000). Increasing the Skill Utilization of Expatriates. *Human Resource Management, 39*(4), 367–379.

34. See, for example: M. Birdseye & J. Hill. (1995). Individual, Organizational/Work and Environmental Influences on Expatriate Turnover Tendencies: An Empirical Study. *Journal of International Business Studies, 26*(4), 787–813; and E. Naumann. (1993). Organizational Predictors of Expatriate Job Satisfaction. *Journal of International Business Studies, 24*(1), 61–79.

35. M. Kraimer, S. J. Wayne, & R. A. Jaworski. (2001). Sources of Support and Expatriate Performance: The Mediating Role of Expatriate Adjustment. *Personnel Psychology, 54*, 71–92.

36. A. L. Hixon. (1986). Why Corporations Make Haphazard Overseas Staffing Decisions. *Personnel Administrator, 31*(3), 91–94; M. E. Mendenhall, E. Dunbar, & G. Oddou. (1987). Expatriate Selection, Training and Career-Pathing: A Review and a Critique. *Human Resource Planning, 26*(3), 331–345; J. McEnery & G. DesHarnais. (1990). Culture Shock. *Training and Development Journal, 44*(4), 43–47; I. Björkman & M. Gertsen. (1993). Selecting and Training Scandinavian Expatriates: Determinants of Corporate Practice. *Scandinavian Journal of Management, 9*(2), 145–164. E. Marx. (1996). *International Human Resource Practices in Britain and Germany*; Price Waterhouse (Eds.), *International Assignments: European Policy and Practice*. Europe: Price Waterhouse.

37. P. Caligiuri. (2000). The Big Five Personality Characteristics as Predictors of Expatriate's Desire to Terminate the Assignment and Supervisor-Rated Performance. *Personnel Psychology, 53*, 67–88.

38. M. A. Shaffer & D. A. Harrison. (2001). Forgotten Partners of International Assignments: Development and Test of a Model of Spouse Adjustment. *Journal of Applied Psychology, 86* (2), 238–254.

39. M. Harvey. (1985, Spring). The Executive Family: An Overlooked Variable in International Assignments. *Columbia Journal of World Business*, 84–93. See also: A. Thompson. (1986). Australian Expatriate Wives and Business Success in South East Asia. *Euro-Asian Business Review, 5*(2), 14–18; and J. E. Harris. (1989). Moving Managers Internationally: The Care and Feeding of Expatriates. *Human Resource Planning, 12*(1), 49–53.

40. J. S. Black & G. K. Stephens. (1989). The Influence of the Spouse on American Expatriate Adjustment and Intent to Stay in Pacific Rim Overseas Assignments. *Journal of Management, 15*(4), 541; see also: H. De Cieri, P. J. Dowling, & K. F. Taylor. (1991). The Psychological Impact of Expatriate Relocation on Partners. *International Journal of Human Resource Management, 2*(3), 377–414; and Brewster, *The Management of Expatriates*.

41. Price Waterhouse (Eds.). *International Assignments: European Policy and Practice*. Europe: Price Waterhouse.

42. S. N. As-Saber, P. J. Dowling, & P. W. Liesch. (1998). The Role of Human Resource Management in International Joint Ventures: A Study of Australian–Indian Joint Ventures. *International Journal of Human Resource Management, 9*(5), 751–766.

43. D. Welch & L. Welch. (1994). Linking Operation Mode Diversity and IHRM. *International Journal of Human Resource Management, 5*(4), 911–926.

44. D. Victor. (1992). *International Business Communication*. New York: Harper Collins.

45. C. Fixman. (1990, September). The Foreign Language Needs of U.S.-Based Corporations. *ANNALS*, AAPSS, *51*, 25.

46. *National Geographic–Roper Public Affairs 2006 Geographic Literacy Study*. A copy of this report is available on the National Geographic website: www.nationalgeographic.com

47. News update provided by the U.S. Congress Education & the Workforce Committee. Retrieved May 4, 2006, from www.house.gov/ed_workforce/press109/first/04apr/t6042205.htm. See also the report *International Education and Foreign Language Studies in Higher Education* (ISBN 0160749123) published by this Congress committee in 2005.

48. R. Marschan-Piekkari, D. Welch, & L. Welch. (1999). Adopting a Common Corporate Language. *International Journal of Human Resource Management, 10*(3), 377–390.

49. I. Torbiörn. (1982). *Living Abroad: Personal Adjustment and Personnel Policy in the Overseas Setting*. New York: John Wiley.

50. H. L. Willis. (1984). Selection for Employment in Developing Countries. *Personnel Administrator, 29*(7), 55.

51. See, for example: P. Sparrow & J-M. Hiltrop. (1994). *European Human Resource Management in Transition*. Hemel Hempstead, Herts: Prentice Hall International; P. J. Dowling. (1988). Psychological Testing in Australia: An Overview and an Assessment. In G. Palmer (Ed.), *Australian Personnel Management: A Reader*. Sydney: Macmillan.

52. Marx found that only 4.4 percent of the Germany companies in her survey used such tests, compared with 15.2 percent in the U.K. firms. See: Marx. *International Human Resource Practices in Britain and Germany*.

53. Hixon. Why Corporations Make Haphazard Overseas Staffing Decisions.

54. G. M. Baliga & J. C. Baker. (1985). Multinational Corporate Policies for Expatriate Managers: Selection, Training, Evaluation. *Advanced Management Journal, 50*(4), 31–38. For a review and discussion of cross-cultural adjustment, see also: J. S. Black. (1990). The Relationship of Personal Characteristics with the Adjustment of Japanese Expatriate Managers. *Management International Review, 30*(2), 119–134.

55. M. Mendenhall & G. Oddou. The Dimensions of Expatriate Acculturation. For a review of the Type A literature, see: V. A. Price. (1982). *Type A Behaviour Pattern: A Model for Research and Practice*. New York: Academic Press.

56. H. C. Jain, P. J. Sloane, & F. M. Horwitz. (2003). *Employment Equity and Affirmative Action: An International Comparison*. Armonk, NY: M. E. Sharpe.

57. For a review of this area, see: H. C. Jain, P. J. Sloane, & F. M. Horwitz. Ibid.

58. H. Harris & C. Brewster. (1999). The Coffee-Machine System: How International Selection Really Works. *International Journal of Human Resource Management, 10*(3), 488–500.

59. M. G. Harvey. (1995). The Impact of Dual-Career Families on International Relocations. *Human Resource Management Review, 5*(3), 223–244.

60. G. K. Stephens & S. Black. (1991). The Impact of Spouse's Career-Orientation on Managers during International Transfers. *Journal of Management Studies, 28*(4), 425.

61. *Managing Expatriates' Return* (Report Number 1148-98-RR).(1996). New York: The Conference Board.

62. N. J. Adler. (1984). Women in International Management: Where Are They? *California Management Review, 26*(4), 78–89.

63. L. K. Stroha, A. Varma, & S. J. Valy-Durbin. (2000). Why Are Women Left at Home: Are They Unwilling to Go on International Assignments? *Journal of World Business, 35*(3), 241–255.

64. P. A. Caligiuri & R. L. Tung. (1999). Comparing the Success of Male and Female Expatriates from a US-Based Multinational Company. *International Journal of Human Resource Management, 10*(5), 763–782.

65. I. C. Fischlmayr. (2002). Female Self-Perception as Barrier to International Careers? *International Journal of Human Resource Management, 13*(5), 773–783.

66. W. Mayrhofer & H. Scullion. (2002). Female Expatriates in International Business: Empirical Evidence from the German Clothing Industry. *International Journal of Human Resource Management, 13*(5), 815–836.

67. N. K. Napier & S. Taylor. (2002). Experiences of Women Professionals Abroad: Comparisons Across Japan, China and Turkey. *International Journal of Human Resource Management, 13*(5), 837–851.

Chapter 6

International Training and Development

Chapter Learning Objectives

After reading this chapter, you should be able to:

- discuss the importance of the role of training in supporting expatriate adjustment and on-assignment performance
- identify the components of effective pre-departure training programs such as cultural awareness, preliminary visits, and language skills, along with relocation assistance and training for trainers
- explain the effectiveness of pre-departure training
- define the developmental aspect of international assignments
- describe the process of training and developing international management teams
- identify trends in international training and development

While not all of the approximately 68,000 Canadians who are currently on international assignments encounter the extreme conditions described in the following excerpt from a newspaper article, many expatriates experience culture shock, have language and other communication problems, face long-term separation from their loved ones, and encounter many other professional and personal challenges. Many of those assignees often wish they had been better trained and prepared for their international assignments.

> As legions of cockroaches defiantly scurried out of boxes stored in the kitchen of his new apartment, Michael Twohey began to think he'd made a big mistake leaving Canada for a posting in China.
>
> "I had never seen bugs that large. I spent the whole night killing cockroaches," recalls Mr. Twohey, who is now manager for professional programs for York University's English Language Institute in Toronto. A few sleepless nights later, he thought he had the roach problem under control, when the invasion of the monster rats began.
>
> At that point, he was ready to drop out of what would eventually be a two-year assignment teaching English and grab the first available transportation out of Chongqing, a sprawling city on the upper end of China's Yangtze River. "I had to ask the basic question: 'Why am I here'? The first couple of days you find yourself excited by everything. Then the realization hits you in the face. You're not here on a holiday; you're here to work. That's always unsettling.

Source: Excerpt from: Immen, W. (2003, November 12). Ready to work abroad? *The Globe and Mail*, "Advice."

Introduction

Reflecting the general literature on this topic, the focus of this chapter is on the traditional expatriate assignment. However, whenever possible, we will discuss training and development aspects relating to short-term assignments, non-standard assignments, and international business travellers.

Basically, in this chapter, we will consider the role of training in preparing and supporting personnel on international assignments and examine how the international assignment is a vehicle for both training and development, as reflected in the reasons why international assignments continue to play a strategic role in international business operations.

In order to compete successfully in a global market, more firms are focusing on the role of human resources as a critical part of their core competence and source of competitive advantage. As Kamoche[1] comments: "We suggest that the human resource refers to the accumulated stock of knowledge, skills, and abilities that the individuals possess, which the firm has built up over time into an identifiable expertise." **Training** and **development** activities are part of the way in which the multinational builds its stock of human resources—its human capital. An indication of the importance of this is the increasing number of multinationals that have established their own "universities" or "schools." The Motorola, McDonald's, and Disney corporate universities are good examples of these in-house training centres. Several European, Japanese, and Korean firms have similar arrangements, such as the Lufthansa Business School and the Ericsson Management Institute.

The international assignment in itself is an important training and development tool:

- Expatriates are trainers, as part of the transfer of knowledge and competence between the various units—a major rationale for the use of international assignments. Whether implicitly or explicitly stated, they are expected to assist the multinational train and develop HCNs—that is, train their replacements.
- Expatriates are also expected to ensure that systems and processes are adopted, and inevitably they will be engaged in showing how these systems and processes work, as well as monitoring effective performance of HCNs.
- One of the reasons for international assignments is management development. A move into another area—job rotation—is a useful way for employees to gain a broader perspective. It assists in developing capable people who form the required pool of global operators, as discussed in earlier chapters.

Therefore, the way in which an MNE anticipates and provides suitable training for international assignments is an important first step. This is reflected in the growth of interest in, and provision of, pre-departure training to prepare expatriates and accompanying family members for international assignments.

Figure 6.1 is a schematic representation of the structure of this chapter. It shows the link between international recruitment and selection, which we covered in Chapter 5, and training and development activities. Most expatriates are internal hires, selected from within the multinational's existing operations although, as indicated by the dotted arrow in Figure 6.1, some expatriates may be hired externally for an international assignment. We will now consider the various elements related to expatriate training and development in the context of managing and supporting international assignments.

 6.1

FIGURE 6.1

International Training and Development

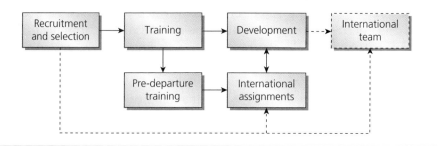

The Role of Expatriate Training

Given that the primary selection criterion for most MNEs is technical ability, it is not surprising to find that most of the literature is devoted to expatriate pre-departure training activities that are mainly concerned with developing cultural awareness. Attention to this aspect has been fuelled by the reported link between expatriate failure rates and cultural adjustment discussed in Chapter 5. Therefore, once an employee has been selected for an expatriate position, pre-departure training is considered to be the next critical step in attempting to ensure the expatriate's effectiveness and success abroad, particularly when the destination country is considered culturally tough. In Figure 6.1, pre-departure training is indicated as a subset of general training. Effective cultural training, it is advocated, assists individuals to adjust more rapidly to the new culture. As Earley[2] points out, "A major objective of intercultural training is to help people cope with unexpected events in a new culture."

The limited, predominately U.S.-based research into this area reveals that a large number of U.S. multinationals have been reluctant to provide even a basic level of pre-departure or cross-cultural training, although this is slowly changing.

Particular interest in the area began with Tung's[3] study on expatriation practices, including the use of pre-departure training programs. While throughout the 1980s and 1990s the provision of such programs to international assignees was very limited (see IHRM Today 6.1), over the past few years MNEs have started to invest more heavily into the preparation of their employees departing on international assignments, possibly in part due to the growth in numbers of providers of pre-departure training that multinationals can access.

Global trend surveys conducted by the consulting firm GMAC Global Relocation Services (in conjunction with the U.S. National Foreign Trade Council and the SHRM Global Forum) concluded that data on provision of cross-cultural training (CCT) were somewhat consistent between its 2002 and 2004 surveys, as shown in Table 6.1. The majority of firms in these surveys are U.S.-based (79 percent in the 2004 survey).

Pre-Departure Training Initiatives in the '80s and '90s

Tung's results showed that U.S. multinationals tended to use training programs for expatriates less frequently than European and Japanese firms (32 percent compared with 69 percent and 57 percent, respectively). The U.S. attitude toward the provision of pre-departure training appeared to persist through the 1980s. For example, a 1984 study of 1,000 U.S. multinationals found that only 25 percent offered extensive pre-departure training programs,* while a 1989 study of U.S. firms found that only 13 percent of respondents indicated that they would offer expatriates a pre-departure program.**

Among the various reasons cited by firms in these studies was that top management did not believe pre-departure training was necessary or effective.[†] So, while the potential benefits of cultural awareness training are widely acknowledged, such training was downgraded or not offered by a large number of U.S. multinationals.[‡]

A 1997 survey of European firms (including subsidiaries of non-European multinationals) found only 13 percent of responding firms always provided expatriates with access to cultural awareness courses, although a further 47 percent provided briefings for culturally "challenging" postings (compared with 21 percent in a 1995 survey).[§]

*Baker, J. C. (1984, July). Foreign Language and Departure Training in U.S. Multinational Firms. *Personnel Administrator*, 68–70.

**Feldman, D. (1989). Relocation Practices. *Personnel*, 66(11), 22–25. See also: McEnery, J., & DesHarnais, G. (1990, April). Culture Shock. *Training and Development Journal*, 43–47.

[†]Mendenhall, M., & Oddou, G. (1985). The Dimensions of Expatriate Acculturation. *Academy of Management Review, 10*, 39–47; and Zeira, Y. (1975). Overlooked Personnel Problems in Multinational Corporations. *Columbia Journal of World Business, 10*(2), 96–103.

[‡]Black, J. S., & Mendenhall, M. (1990). Cross-Cultural Training Effectiveness: A Review and a Theoretical Framework for Future Research. *Academy of Management Review, 15*(1), 113–136.

[§]Price Waterhouse. (1997/1998). *International Assignments: European Policy and Practice*. Europe: Price Waterhouse.

TABLE 6.1

Availability of Cross-Cultural Training in MNEs

	GMAC 2002	GMAC 2004
CCT available	64 per cent	62 per cent
CCT attendance optional	76	74
Provided to:		
• Employee only	2 percent	5 percent
• Employee and spouse	29	27
• Whole family	33	28
• None	36	40

Source: 2003 and 2004 *Global Relocation Trends Survey Reports*, provided by GMAC Global Relocation Services, LLC. All Rights Reserved.

While in 2003 many Canadian multinational companies expected to increase the number of international assignments and believed they had been doing an acceptable job in terms of preparing their employees for their international assignments, many Canadian-based firms admitted that improvements

W W W 6.1

W W W 6.2

in their current pre-departure programs were possible. In Immen's summary of a survey conducted by Cigna International Expatriate Benefits, Mercer Human Resource Consulting and International SOS of Canada,[4] most of the survey's participating companies did some training and counselling for their employees destined for international assignments. However, due to the urgency of some of these overseas assignments, for some organizations there was no or only little time for employee pre-departure training. In Immen's article, Virginia Hollis, vice president of global markets for Cigna and one of the analysts of the survey, explained that only a third of the participating MNEs had a system in place that tracks expatriate failures and successes—providing us with no clear and detailed numbers of Canadians failing in their overseas posts.

Previously, multinational firms placed less priority on providing pre-departure training for the spouse and family.[5] However, perhaps due to increasing recognition of the interaction between expatriate performance and family adjustment, more multinationals are now extending their pre-departure training programs to include the spouse/partner and children. This is reflected in the GMAC figures in Table 6.1 and in another survey—the 2002 survey of dual careers and international assignments by ORC Worldwide. The latter report's authors commented that provision of pre-departure training for accompanying spouses and partners continued to increase. However, as Table 6.1 shows, the percentage of firms that make CCT *optional* remains very high (74 percent in 2004), so it is possible that many expatriates still receive very little training. In a 2005 review of CCT, Littrell and Salas[6] suggest that a lack of synthesis in the area of CCT research has made it difficult for managers to implement CCT. Their review provides a number of research-based guidelines as to how MNEs can enhance the success of their CCT programs.

Components of Effective Pre-Departure Training Programs

Studies indicate that the essential components of pre-departure training programs that contribute to a smooth transition to a foreign location include cultural awareness training, preliminary visits, language instruction, and assistance with practical, day-to-day matters.[7] We will look at each of these in turn.

Cultural Awareness Programs

6.2

It is generally accepted that, to be effective, the expatriate employee must adapt to and not feel isolated from the host country. A well-designed cultural awareness training program can be extremely beneficial, as it seeks to foster an appreciation of the host-country's culture so that expatriates can behave accordingly, or at least develop appropriate coping patterns. Without an understanding (or at least an acceptance) of the host-country culture and its value and belief system, the expatriate is likely to face some difficulty during

Challenges in Foreign Countries

One of the most difficult challenges of international business is dealing with a different "hierarchy of values" that exists between foreign countries and the Western world, according to Rod Wade of Talisman Energy Inc. . . . One example of this value difference, which can be frustrating and costly when operating in foreign countries, is the absence of rule of law. "Despite its imperfections, we take this for granted in our society," said Wade, the general manager of inter-national operations, business support and development with Talisman. "It is shocking to experience a society or culture that does not have a functioning rule of law. And by functioning rule of law I mean the ability of a citizen, a company, to seek and receive some semblance of justice and security.

While the quoted article above talks about the potential costs for the company, we must not forget that an international assignment in a cultural context that has very different forms or understandings of justice and security could also be very costly, frustrating, and even dangerous for the international assignees placed in such environments—highlighting the importance of pre-departure cultural awareness training.

Source: Macedo, R. (2006, February 14). Many challenges faced by industry in foreign countries. *The Daily Oil Bulletin.*

the international assignment. Therefore, cultural awareness training remains the most common form of pre-departure training. One aspect of differing value and belief systems in foreign countries is outlined in IHRM Today 6.2.

The components of cultural awareness programs vary according to country of assignment, duration, purpose of the transfer, and the provider of such programs. As part of her study of expatriate management, Tung[8] identified five categories of pre-departure training, based on different learning processes, type of job, country of assignment, and the time available. These were: area studies programs that include environmental briefing and cultural orientation; culture assimilators; language training; sensitivity training; and field experiences. To understand possible variations in expatriate training, Tung proposed a contingency framework for deciding the nature and level of rigour of training. The two determining factors were the degree of interaction required in the host culture and the similarity between the individual's native culture and the new culture. The related training elements in her framework involved the content of the training and the rigour of the training. Essentially, Tung argued that:

- If the expected interaction between the individual and members of the host culture was low, and the degree of dissimilarity between the individual's native culture and the host culture was low, then training should focus on task- and job-related issues rather than culture-related issues. The level of rigour necessary for effective training should be relatively low.
- If there was a high level of expected interaction with host nationals and a large dissimilarity between the cultures, then training should focus on cross-cultural skill development as well as on the new task. The level of rigour for such training should be moderate to high.

Tung's model specifies criteria for making training method decisions—such as degree of expected interaction and cultural similarity. One limitation of the model is that it does not assist the user to determine which specific training methods to use or what might constitute more or less rigorous training.

More than a decade later, Tung[9] revisited her earlier work and reported that her original recommendations held, although with some changes:

- Training should be more orientated to lifelong learning than "one-shot" programs with an area-specific focus.
- There should be more emphasis on provision of foreign language training.
- There should be emphasis on the levels of communication competence, not just verbal communication, so the person becomes bicultural and bilingual, which enables an easier transition between one culture and another.
- Cross-cultural training should assist in managing diversity.
- The preview of the expatriate position should be realistic, as this facilitates effective performance.

FIGURE 6.2

The Mendenhall, Dunbar, and Oddou Cross-Cultural Training Model

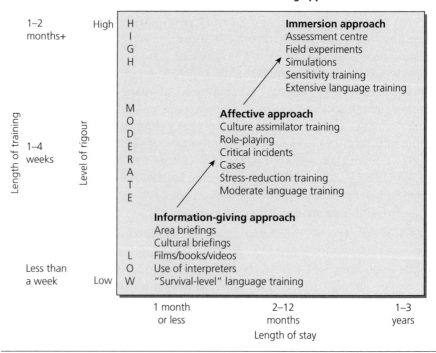

Source: Mendenhall, M., Dunbar, E., & Oddou, G. (1987). Expatriate Selection, Training and Career-Pathing: A Review and Critique. *Human Resource Management, 26*, 338. Reprinted with permission.

Mendenhall and Oddou extended Tung's model and this was refined subsequently by Mendenhall, Dunbar, and Oddou,[10] who proposed three dimensions: training methods, levels of training rigour, and duration of the training relative to degree of interaction and culture novelty (see Figure 6.2). This model provides useful guidelines for determining an appropriate program, as outlined in IHRM Notebook 6.1.

Later, Black and Mendenhall[11] concluded that the earlier model, like that of Tung's, was primarily "cultural" in nature, with little integration of the individual's new tasks and the new host culture. Black and Mendenhall therefore proposed what they described as an extensive theory-based model using Bandura's social learning theory and prior cultural awareness training models. They take three aspects of social learning theory—attention, retention, and reproduction—and show how these are influenced by individual differences in expectations and motivation, and the incentives to apply learned behaviours in the foreign location. This approach recognizes that effective training is only the first step and that the expatriate's willingness and ability to act on that training in the new environment is crucial to effective performance.

An obvious practical limitation of Black and Mendenhall's model is that insufficient time is often given as a reason why multinationals do not provide pre-departure training. It would therefore be difficult to develop appropriate pre-departure training programs in such cases. Other contextual and

IHRM Notebook 6.1

Determining Factors for Cross-Cultural Training Programs

According to Mendenhall, Dunbar, and Oddou's model, if the expected level of interaction is low and the degree of similarity between the individual's home culture and the host culture is high, the length of the training should probably be less than a week. Methods such as area or cultural briefings via lectures, movies, or books would provide the appropriate level of training rigour.*

On the other hand, if the individual is going overseas for a period of two to twelve months and is expected to have some interaction with members of the host culture, the level of training rigour should be higher and its length longer (one to four weeks). In addition to the information-giving approaches, training methods such as culture assimilators and role-playing may be appropriate.** If the individual is going to a fairly novel and different host culture and the expected degree of interaction is high, the level of cross-cultural training rigour should be high and training should last as long as two months. In addition to the less rigorous methods already discussed,

sensitivity training, field experiences, and intercultural experiential workshops may be appropriate training methods in this situation.

Sources: *Earley advocates the use of both documentary and Interpersonal methods to prepare managers for intercultural assignments (Earley, P. [1987]. International Training for Managers: A Comparison of Documentary and Interpersonal Methods. *Academy of Management Journal, 30*, 685–698). Baliga and Baker suggest that the expatriate receive training that concentrates on the assigned region's culture, history, politics, economy, religion, and social and business practices. They argue that only with precise knowledge of the varied components of their host culture can the expatriate and family grasp how and why people behave and react as they do (Baliga, G., & Baker, J. C. [1985, Autumn]. Multinational Corporate Policies for Expatriate Managers: Selection, Training, and Evaluation, *Advanced Management Journal*, 31–38).

**For further information on the use of cultural assimilators, see: Brislin, R. W. (1986). A Culture General Assimilator: Preparation for Various Types of Sojourns. *International Journal of Intercultural Relations, 10*, 215–234, and Cushner, K. (1989). Assessing the Impact of a Culture General Assimilator. *International Journal of Intercultural Relations, 13*, 125–146.

situational factors—such as cultural toughness, length of assignment, and the nature/type of the job—may have a bearing on the content, method, and processes involved in the cultural awareness training program. More importantly, monitoring and feedback should be recognized as important components of individual skill development, particularly as adjustment and performance are the desired outcomes of cultural awareness training.

RPC 6.3

Figure 6.3 draws together the components of the three models reviewed above. It stresses the importance of attention paid by the potential expatriate to the behaviours and probable outcomes of a cultural awareness training program; the individual's ability and willingness to retain learned behaviours; and the reproduction of learned behaviours as appropriate in the host location. Poor performance could be addressed by clarifying incentives for more effective reproduction of the required level of behaviour, or by providing additional cultural awareness training during the international assignment. Therefore, we combine adjustment and performance and link it to the performance management system, whereas Black and Mendenhall have adjustment and performance as separate outcomes, with adjustment leading to performance. We argue that performance affects adjustment in many instances. Further, it seems important that adjustment and performance be linked to the MNE's performance management system, as will become clearer in Chapter 11, where we address performance management systems and issues.

FIGURE 6.3

Cultural Awareness Training and Assignment Performance

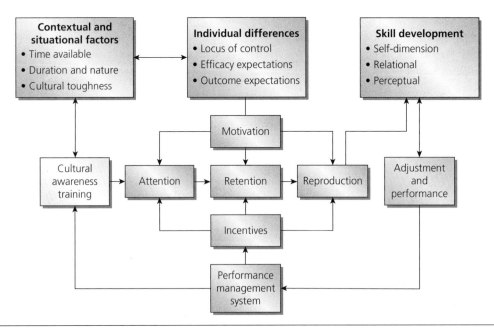

Source: Adapted from: Tung, R. (1981). Selecting and Training of Personnel for Overseas Assignments. *Columbia Journal of World Business, 16*, 68–78; Mendenhall, M., Dunbar, E., & Oddou, G. (1987). Expatriate Selection, Training and Career-Pathing: A Review and Critique. *Human Resource Management, 26*, 331–345; and Black, J. S., & Mendenhall, M. (1989). A Practical But Theory-Based Framework for Selecting Cross-Cultural Training Methods. *Human Resource Management, 28*(4), 511–539.

Preliminary Visits

One technique useful in orienting international employees is to send them on a preliminary trip to the host country. A well-planned trip overseas for the candidate and spouse provides a preview that allows them to assess their suitability for and interest in the assignment. Such a trip also serves to introduce expatriate candidates to the business context in the host location and helps encourage more informed pre-departure preparation. When used as part of a pre-departure training program, visits to the host location can assist in the initial adjustment process.

W W W 6.4

The 1997/1998 Price Waterhouse European survey mentioned previously reported that 53 percent of firms always provided preliminary visits and a further 38 percent indicated such use in certain circumstances. The average length of visit was about a week. The country of assignment was a determining factor. Visits were not provided if the country concerned was already known to the expatriate (perhaps from a previous visit either on firm-related business or as a tourist) or was perceived as being culturally similar to the home base (e.g., Zurich to Frankfurt, or New York to Toronto). Unfortunately, the 2002 and 2004 surveys by GMAC and the 2002 ORC Worldwide survey do not deal with preliminary visits. However, a study of expatriates from Germany, the United States, Korea, and Japan working in Singapore, along with Singaporean repatriates and expatriates, did include preliminary visits as part of pre-departure training. Osman-Gani[12] reports that of these five groups, only the U.S. expatriates rated preliminary visits as important, ranking such visits second, behind cross-cultural training.

Obviously, the prospective assignee may reject the assignment on the basis of the preliminary visit. As one firm in the Price Waterhouse 1997/1998 European study is reported to have admitted: "We do not provide pre-assignment visits where conditions are so poor that nobody would want to go." Most firms that utilize preliminary visits, though, weigh the cost of a preliminary visit against premature recall and underperformance risks. A potential problem is that the aim of the preliminary visit is often twofold   part of the selection decision and part of pre-departure training. The multinational could send mixed signals if it offers the preliminary visit as part of the selection process but the prospective assignee finds on arrival in the proposed country of assignment that he or she is expected to make decisions regarding suitable housing and schools. Such treatment could be interpreted as "accepting the preliminary visit equals accepting the assignment," thus negating its role in the decision-making process. When multinationals use the preliminary visit to allow the assignee (and spouse) to make a more informed decision about accepting the overseas assignment, it should be used solely for that purpose.

Combined with cultural awareness training, the preliminary visit is a useful component of a pre-departure program. Exposure to the expatriate community, if one exists in the proposed host location, can also be a positive outcome. Brewster and Pickard[13] found that an expatriate community has an influence on expatriate adjustment.

 6.5

Language Training

Language training is a seemingly obvious, desirable component of a pre-departure program. However, it is consistently ranked below that of the desirability for cultural awareness training. In trying to understand why language skills are given a lower priority, we should consider the following aspects related to language ability that need to be recognized: generally, English is the language of world business; the ability to speak the host-country's language can improve the expatriate's effectiveness and negotiating ability; and being able to speak the corporate language can give expatriates added power in the subsidiary.

Role of English as the Language of World Business

It is generally accepted that English is the language of world business, although the form of English is more "international English" than that spoken by native speakers of English.[14] India is an attractive location for foreign call centres, due in part to the availability of a large English-speaking population from which to recruit employees. The willingness of Chinese nationals to acquire English fluency is confirming the dominance of English. Multinationals from Anglo-Saxon or English-speaking countries such as the United Kingdom, the United States, Canada, Australia, and New Zealand often use the dominant role of English as a reason for not considering language ability in the selection process, and for not stressing language training as part of pre-departure programs. Tung[15] reports that a 12-country study of almost 3,000 executives found that respondents from the United States, the United Kingdom, Canada, and Australia—all English-speaking countries—deemed language skills as unimportant. This is in contrast to executives from Europe, Asia, and South America, however, who considered knowledge of a foreign language as critical to success.

A similar attitude emerged from a study of U.S. multinationals' foreign language needs. Fixman[16] found that foreign language skills were seldom included as part of cross-cultural understanding, and that language problems were largely viewed as mechanical and manageable problems that could easily be solved. As Pucik[17] comments, an exclusive reliance on English diminishes the MNE's linguistic capacity. The resultant lack of language competence has strategic and operational implications, as it limits the multinational's ability to monitor competitors and process important information. For example, translation services, particularly those external to the firm, cannot make strategic inferences and firm-specific interpretations of language-specific data. Fixman[18] raises the question of protecting important technology in international joint venture activities: "It would seem that the less one understands of a partner's language, the less likely one is to detect theft of technology." Perhaps more importantly, as Wright and Wright[19] in their study of British firms point out, to accept English as the *de facto* language of international business gives the advantage to the other person:

The other speaker controls what is communicated and what is understood. The monolingual English speaker has less room to maneuver, no possibility of finding out more than he is given. His position forces him to be reactive rather than proactive in the relationship. What he says and understands is filtered through the other speaker's competence, over which he has no control.

Disregarding the importance of foreign language skills may reflect a degree of ethnocentrism. A study by Hall and Gudykunst[20] has shown that the lower the level of perceived ethnocentrism in an MNE, the more training the MNE provides in cultural awareness and language training. Disregarding the importance of foreign language skills also reflects a degree of perhaps unconscious arrogance on the part of expatriates from English-speaking countries. However, more firms are including language training as evidenced by recent surveys. For example, the 2002 GMAC survey revealed that provision of language training to spouses and partners, as part of pre-departure training programs, had markedly increased. A total of 59 percent of the responding firms provided language training prior to departure, and 74 percent provided language training while the person was on assignment. In fact, it was the most common form of spousal assistance while on assignment—and is reflected in the 2004 GMAC survey, where 60 percent of responding firms indicated provision of language training as part of their spousal assistance package. The survey report does not indicate when this training was provided, although one respondent volunteered: "Language training is a top challenge."[21] (See also the discussion on language ability as a selection criterion in Chapter 5.)

Host-Country Language Skills and Adjustment

Clearly, the ability to speak a foreign language can improve the expatriate's effectiveness and negotiating ability. As Baliga and Baker[22] point out, it can improve managers' access to information regarding the host-country's economy, government, and market. Of course, the degree of fluency required may depend on the level and nature of the position that the expatriate holds in the foreign operation, the amount of interaction with external stakeholders such as government officials, clients, and trade officials, as well as with host-country nationals.

In a survey of 400 expatriates by Tung,[23] the importance of language skills was identified as a critical component in assignment performance. Respondents indicated that ability to speak the local language, regardless of how different the culture was to their home country, was as important as cultural awareness in their ability to adapt and perform on assignment. Knowledge of the host-country language can assist expatriates and family members gain access to new social support structures outside of work and the expatriate community.

Language skills are therefore important in terms of task performance and cultural adjustment. Its continued omission from pre-departure training can be partly explained by the length of time it takes to acquire even a rudimentary level of language competence. Hiring language competent staff to enlarge the "language pool" from which potential expatriates may be drawn is one answer, but its success depends on up-to-date information being kept on all employees, and frequent language auditing to see whether language skills are maintained.[24]

Knowledge of the Corporate Language

As previously mentioned, multinationals tend to adopt (either deliberately or by default) a common company language to facilitate reporting and other control mechanisms. Given its place in international business, quite often English becomes the common language within these multinationals. Expatriates can become language nodes, performing as communication conduits between subsidiary and headquarters, due to their ability to speak the corporate language. It also can give added power to their position in the subsidiary as expatriates—particularly PCNs—often have access to information that those not fluent in the corporate language are denied. An expatriate fluent in the parent-company language and the language of the host subsidiary can perform a gate-keeping role, whatever the formal position the expatriate may hold.

Most MNEs use staff transfers as part of their corporate training programs, with HCN recruits spending time at corporate headquarters. These training programs will normally be conducted in the corporate language. Fluency in the corporate language is, therefore, usually a prerequisite for international training assignments and may constrain the ability of subsidiary employees to attend and benefit from such training. An exception to this pattern would be an example where key new line managers from important emerging markets may be trained in their own language at corporate headquarters—a practice that the McDonald's Corporation follows at its corporate training facility in Chicago.[25] Pre-departure training programs often may need to include both the language of the host country and the corporate language.

Practical Assistance

Another component of a pre-departure training program is that of providing information that assists in relocation. Practical assistance makes an important contribution toward the adaptation of the expatriate and his or her family to their new environment. Being left to fend for oneself may result in a negative response toward the host-country's culture and/or contribute to a perceived violation of the psychological contract. Many multinationals now take advantage of relocation specialists to provide this practical assistance in, for example, finding suitable accommodation and schools.

Further language training for the expatriate and family could be provided, particularly if such training was not possible before departure. Usually, during the assignment, host-country HR staff will organize any further orientation programs and language training. However, it is important that corporate HRM staff liaise with the sending line manager as well as the HR department in the foreign location to ensure that practical assistance is provided.

Training for the Training Role

Expatriates are often used for training because of a lack of suitably trained staff in the host location. Consequently, expatriates often find themselves training HCNs as their replacements. The obvious question is how are expatriates prepared for this training role? There is little research on this question. We do know from the cross-cultural management literature that there are differences in the way people approach tasks and problems, and that this can have an impact on the learning process.[26] The ability to transfer knowledge and skills in a culturally sensitive manner perhaps should be an integral part of pre-departure training programs—particularly if training is part of the expatriate's role in the host country.

One way that MNEs could improve the quality and content of the training offered to expatriates in their role of training HCNs as their replacements would be to better utilize the knowledge transfer process when expatriates are repatriated. A 2005 paper by Lazarova and Tarique[27] examined this issue and argues that effective knowledge transfer occurs when there is a fit between individual readiness to transfer knowledge and organizational receptivity to knowledge. Specifically they propose that:

> Organizations should try to match the level of intensity of their knowledge transfer mechanisms to the type of knowledge gained abroad. Thus, highly intense extraction tools (e.g., assigning repatriates to strategic teams) should be used to acquire international knowledge with high tacitness and high specificity. . . . Such knowledge would be transferred most effectively through rich mechanisms involving frequent communication between the repatriate and other organizational members. Organizations can use low intensity extraction tools (e.g., presentations, intranet) to acquire explicit international knowledge (e.g., information on banking laws and regulations in a particular foreign market). (370)

Training and the Company Code of Conduct

As a result of high-profile cases related to ethical behaviour and corporate governance, the 2004 GMAC survey asked responding firms if they were instituting programs to train expatriates regarding the company's code of conduct. A total of 37 percent indicated that they had. However, since the form this training took and when it was delivered was not specified, it is difficult to evaluate the significance of this response.

TCN and HCN Expatriate Training

Anecdotal evidence suggests that in some firms, pre-departure training may not be provided for TCNs being transferred to another subsidiary or for HCNs transferred into the parent-country operations. Where it is provided, it may not be to the extent of that available for PCNs. This omission could create perceptions of inequitable treatment in situations where PCNs and TCNs work in the same foreign location and might affect adjustment to the international assignment. Not considering the need for training for HCNs transferred to the parent organization reflects an ethnocentric attitude.[28]

There may be a link between the amount of training, particularly cross-cultural, and assignment length. HCNs transferred to either headquarters or to another subsidiary are often on short-term, project-based assignments or assignments for management development purposes. As such, these may not be regarded as "genuine" expatriate postings, thus falling outside the ambit of the HR function. In order to design and implement TCN and HCN pre-departure training, local management, particularly in the HR department, needs to be conscious of the demands of an international assignment —just as we have discussed in terms of corporate/headquarters HR staff. Recognition of the demands of an international assignments and encouragement from headquarters are perhaps also needed, along with monitoring to ensure that sufficient subsidiary resources are allocated for pre-departure training.

Provision of Training for Non-Traditional Expatriate Assignments

In theory, all staff should be provided with the necessary level of pre-departure training, given the demands of the international assignment. Cultural adjustment is inherent in international staff transfers. Pre-departure training should also be provided for employees on short-term assignments, on non-standard assignments such as commuting, and for international business travellers. However, there is a paucity of information regarding pre-departure training for non-standard assignments.

Short-Term and Non-Standard Assignments

Given the generally low level of provision of pre-departure training to traditional expatriates, it is not surprising to find that those on short-term and non-standard assignments receive little or no preparation before departure. The oversight may be due to lack of time, which is a standard reason for non-provision of pre-departure training. This may be why multinationals are beginning to use modern technology—as outlined in IHRM Today 6.3—to overcome time and resource constraints.

International Business Travellers

Non-expatriates tend to be a forgotten group, yet for many firms they may comprise the largest contingent of employees involved in international business. International business travellers are flying into and out of foreign operations performing a myriad of tasks, including training, such as explaining new product development, or service, or process to HCN employees that will involve demonstrations, seminar presentations, and other methods of information dissemination. Such internal company interaction usually will involve the use of the corporate language. Therefore, non-expatriates need to be aware that HCNs will differ in their level of

IT-Based Training for Short-Term and Non-Standard Assignments

The GMAC 2004 survey referred to earlier asked respondents if they used CD-based and Web-based cross-cultural programs. Only 16 percent (compared to 21 percent in 2002) of responding firms used such facilities, of which:

- 65 percent used CD- and Web-based programs as additional forms of support for in-person programs (compared to 60 percent in 2002).
- 30 percent used CD- and Web-based programs as stand-alone alternatives (compared to 41 percent in 2002).
- 5 percent indicated that CD- and Web-based programs were the only form of pre-departure training offered (compared to 16 percent in 2002).

The 2004 survey does not report on the specifics of this training. However, in the 2002 survey, more detail was made available. For example, one firm explained that employees on short-term assignments were provided with access to Web-based information, while longer-term expatriates were provided with both in-person and Web-based programs. The 2002 GMAC data revealed that firms with smaller expatriate populations (1–25 and 51–100) were more likely to use CD- or Web-based cross-cultural training, than were firms with 101 or more expatriates.

competence. It is easy to equate intelligence with language fluency, with lack of fluency being perceived as a sign of stupidity. Company briefings and training sessions will need to take into account local variances in how people conduct themselves in formal situations, and approach the "classroom" situation.

International business travellers may be providing new product information to foreign agents or distributors, which naturally involves cross-cultural interaction. Competence in the local language or at least an ability to work with and through interpreters may be required. The same applies to those conducting negotiations with host-government officials, prospective clients, suppliers, and subcontractors. All of these activities are strategically important, yet there is little in the literature regarding the provision of training for these roles. From the limited, mainly anecdotal, information available, it would seem that non-expatriates learn on the job and gradually acquire the knowledge and skills to function effectively in various countries and situations.[29] For a review of international business traveller literature, see Welch and Worm.[30]

The Effectiveness of Pre-Departure Training

The objective of pre-departure training is to assist the expatriate to adjust to the demands of living and working in a foreign location. The question is: How effective is such training, and what components have been considered to be essential by those who have been provided pre-departure training?

The GMAC surveys asked firms to indicate the value of cross-cultural preparation for expatriate success, as shown in Table 6.2. For the 2004

 6.6

TABLE 6.2

Perceived Value of Cross-Cultural Preparation of Expatriates

VALUE RATING	GMAC 2002	GMAC 2004
Of great value	35%	36%
Of high value	45%	37%
Of medium value	17%	21%
Of little value	Not available	6%

Source: 2003 and 2004 *Global Relocation Trends Survey Reports*, provided by GMAC Global Relocation Services, LLC. All Rights Reserved.

survey, over two-thirds of the respondents indicated that cross-cultural training was "of great value" or "of high value." However, it should be noted that information on how the responding firms evaluated their training was not provided in either survey—a common problem with many surveys of training utilization.

Several academic studies have attempted to assess the effectiveness of pre-departure training. Eschbach, Parker, and Stoeberl[31] report the results of a study of 79 U.S. repatriates. They measured cognitive, affective, and experiential cross-cultural training and language training, provided by the company or self-initiated. The amount and type of training, based on the models of Tung and Black et al. described earlier in this chapter, was included. Expatriates with integrated cross-cultural training exhibited cultural proficiency earlier, and appeared to have greater job satisfaction, than those with lesser training. Repatriates commented that there was a need for accurate, up-to-date cultural and language training for expatriates and spouses, and many considered that preliminary visits should be used.

The second study was a meta-analysis of the cross-cultural training literature.[32] The conclusion reached was that the effectiveness of cross-cultural training was somewhat weaker than expected due to:

- Limited data, as few organizations systematically evaluate or validate the effectiveness of their training programs or make any evaluation results available to the public
- The use of a mixture of different training methods, making it difficult to evaluate which method is most effective.
- The large diversity in cultures that expatriates face.
- The interaction between individual differences between expatriates and the work environment they face. What works for one person may not work for another. Thus, the effects of cross-cultural training can be as diverse as the countries to which expatriates are assigned.

The authors add that traditional training methods may underestimate the complexity of international business life, where expatriate managers are required to perform complex jobs across multiple cultural contexts, sometimes on the same day or even in the same hour. Training programs that capture this reality are difficult to find, and many existing cross-cultural training programs have yet to prove their utility.[33]

Developing Staff through International Assignments

International assignments have long been recognized as an important mechanism for developing international expertise. The expected outcomes include two key areas:

1. *Management development:* Individuals gain international experience, which assists in career progression, while the multinational gains through having a pool of experienced international operators on which to draw for future international assignments.

2. *Organizational development:* International assignments also provide a multinational with a way of accumulating a stock of knowledge, skills, and abilities on which it can base its future growth. A global mindset is an important side benefit, as key personnel take a broader view. Further, as discussed previously, expatriates are agents of direct control and socialization, and assist in the transfer of knowledge and competence.

 6.7

We will now consider these outcomes, first from the perspective of the individual and then from the multinational's viewpoint.

Individual Development

An international assignment can be compared to job rotation, a management development tool that seeks to provide certain employees with opportunities to enhance their abilities by exposing them to a range of jobs, tasks, and challenges. It is therefore not surprising to find an implicit assumption that an international assignment has *per se* management development potential. Along with expected financial gain, perceived career advancement is often a primary motive for accepting international assignments. This is particularly the case in smaller population, advanced economies (e.g., the Netherlands, Australia, Sweden, and New Zealand) where the relatively small local economy is not big enough to generate growth, and international activities provide the opportunity for ongoing revenue growth. In such a situation, employees understand that international experience is frequently a requirement for further career advancement. However, there is a paucity of research that demonstrates the link between an international assignment and career advancement. Two exceptions are studies by Feldman and Thomas and by Naumann.[34] While these studies confirm career expectations as motives, the expatriates involved were taken from those currently on assignment. Overall, there remains a need for research that establishes career paths as a direct consequence of international assignments (see IHRM Notebook 6.2).

Lack of Research into Career Outcomes of International Assignments

There are two possible explanations for the lack of interest in the career outcomes of international assignments:

1. Companies and academics have been somewhat pre-occupied with the process of expatriation from the organization's perspective. It is important to understand the roles played by the various international HRM activities, so that proper management and support for expatriates can be provided to reduce under-performance and improve cost-effectiveness.

2. Surveys consistently report that expatriates consider career progression as a primary motive for accepting international assignments. Such a consistency of response—that is, career advancement as a reason for accepting an overseas assignment—has masked the issue of whether these career expectations are, indeed, met. In other words, we know why people accept international assignments, but we do not have a clear picture of when and how these expectations are met, and the consequences to both the individual and the multinational if the expected career outcomes are not met.

Developing International Teams

Expatriates may gain individual management development from the international assignment, as we previously discussed. The international assignment often is the training ground for the international "cadre" in Figure 6.4. International teams can be formed from those who have had international experience, although the international assignment itself may be assignment to an international team or to form an international team.

FIGURE 6.4

Developing International Teams through International Assignments

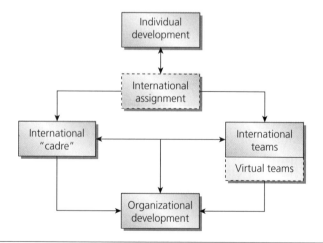

It is frequently argued that multinationals, especially in networked organizations, would benefit from using international teams as a way to:

- Foster innovation, organizational learning, and the transfer of knowledge.
- Break down functional and national boundaries, enhancing horizontal communication and information flows.
- Encourage diverse inputs into decision making, problem solving, and strategic assessments.
- Develop a global perspective.
- Develop shared values, thus assisting in the use of informal, normative control through socialization.

Research and development and international projects are common situations where teamwork is utilized and forms the basis of much of the literature on multinational teams, a subset of which is the virtual team, where members are geographically dispersed (see Figure 6.4).

To a certain extent, international assignments achieve team-building by exposing employees to various parts of the global organization. Consequently, expatriates develop local networks that often persist after completion of the assignment. These predominantly informal networks can later be activated for work situations, such as providing membership of project teams. Not everyone will wish to become part of an international "cadre," but to create an effective global pool of international operators, many multinationals are conscious that they need to provide international experience to many levels of managers, regardless of nationality. A small cadre comprising only PCNs may defeat the purpose of having a team of experienced employees who are capable of operating in multiple environments on various types of tasks and jobs. For example, Peterson[35] found that Western-based multinationals operating in Central and Eastern Europe were increasing the use of TCN and HCN expatriate transfers as a way of widening the "corporate talent pool."

While the international assignment plays an important role in both management and organizational development, its effectiveness depends on the individuals concerned, the type of multinational and contextual factors. For example, Caligiuri and Di Santo[36] argue that certain personality characteristics that have been identified as expatriate predictors of success cannot be developed through international assignments. In other words, individual characteristics such as dogmatic or authoritarian tendencies are not likely to be altered through an expatriate experience. However, Caligiuri and Di Santo do suggest that individuals can learn to be more sensitive to the challenges of working in another country—that is, become culturally aware. This knowledge and experience would prove valuable when working on an international team composed of colleagues of other nationalities.

The MNE needs to be able to provide the resources and support for those working on international teams, such as R&D projects. Managers supervising international teams, for example, will need to understand processes such as group dynamics, especially how national cultures affect group functioning. Those who have previous experience of international assignments and teams will be better placed than those who have not. Perhaps this is why some MNEs are placing greater stress on the need for international experience and are prepared to use expatriates despite the cost and difficulties often associated with international assignments. For recent reviews of the literature on developing international teams, see Gibbs,[37] Maznevski et al.,[38] and Caligiuri and Tarique.[39]

Trends in International Training and Development

There are a number of emerging and continuing trends in international training and development that we can briefly comment on. First, although the pressure from globalization continues to push MNEs toward a convergent approach to training and development, there is a continuing pressure from many countries (particularly developing countries) for *localization of training and development* initiatives of which MNEs must be mindful. Al-Dosary and Rahman[40] have reviewed the benefits and problems associated with localization of training and development. Second, there is a growing realization that although globalization is having a major impact on business processes and associated training and development efforts in MNEs, there is evidence that for competence development and learning, it is still necessary to consider *the impact and importance of the national context and institutions* on such efforts (see Geppert[41]).

Third, there is increasing awareness of the important role of *nongovernmental organizations (NGOs)* in international training and development (see Chang, and Brewster and Lee for recent reviews[42]). Fourth, with the rise of China as an economic superpower, there is increasing interest in all aspects of training and development with a focus on China (see Wang et al., Zhao, Zhang et al., Zhu, and Wang and Wang for recent reviews[43]). Finally, there is a realization in the training and development literature that the field must address global, comparative, and national level contexts for training and development, just as the international HRM field is beginning to do (see Metcalfe and Rees[44] for a recent review).

Summary

This chapter has concentrated on the issues relating to training and developing expatriates for international assignments. In the process, we have discussed the role of expatriate training in supporting adjustment and on-assignment performance, and the components of effective pre-departure training programs such as cultural awareness, preliminary visits, language skills, relocation assistance, and training for trainers.

We showed how cultural awareness training appears to assist in adjustment and performance and therefore should be made available to all categories of staff selected for overseas postings, regardless of duration and location. Further, we discussed the need for language training for the host country and in the relevant corporate language, and the impact that an international assignment may have on an individual's career.

We argued for the international assignment to be considered as an important way of training international operators and developing the international "cadre." In this sense, an international assignment is both training (gaining international experience and competence) and managerial and organizational development. Finally, we showed how international assignments are connected to the creation of international teams, and identified and discussed current trends in international training and development.

Key Terms

development 193   training 193

Web Links

www 6.1   An important aspect of preparing for international assignments, in particular when they include spouses/partners and children, is ensuring that health and safety insurance and benefits are arranged before leaving Canada. Even if the assignments are in developed countries, local health care systems might not always provide the same services or at different costs. To learn more about such benefits packages check out, for example, CIGNA International Expatriate Benefits, a health insurance company that operates worldwide:

www.cigna.com

www 6.2   Mercer LLC provides a range of global studies and surveys containing HR-related information important to organizations operating beyond their national borders:

www.mercerhr.com

www 6.3   International SOS, a worldwide health and security company, assists employees on international assignments. To learn more about the services and medical care provisions international assignees require for their overseas projects go to:

www.internationalsos.com/en/americasregion_canada.htm

www 6.4   A number of expatriate sites help expatriates with information about countries, cultures, and the challenges of day-to-day living in a particular country. Expatica, for example, provides detailed information on six European countries and five country-oriented survival guides:

www.expatica.com

RPC Icons

RPC 6.1 Contributes to the development of the organization's vision, goals, and strategies, with a focus on human capital

RPC 6.2 Leads in the development of HR initiatives that support the organization's strategic directions

RPC 6.3 Develops and delivers learning strategies to close the gap between current human capital capabilities and the future needs of the organization

RPC 6.4 Leads in the development of HR initiatives that support the organization's strategic directions

RPC 6.5 Leads in the development of HR initiatives that support the organization's strategic directions

RPC 6.6 Monitors and evaluates HR effectiveness as it relates to business success, and identifies areas that need improvement and development

RPC 6.7 Contributes to the development of the organization's vision, goals, and strategies, with a focus on human capital

Discussion Questions

1. What are some of the challenges faced in training expatriate managers?
2. How does an international assignment assist in developing a "cadre" of international operators? Why is it necessary to have such a cadre?
3. Why do some MNEs seem reluctant to provide basic pre-departure training?

Using the Internet

1. Go to the Four Seasons Hotels and Resorts website at **www .fourseasons.com** and find out about its recently opened hotels worldwide and the hotels that it plans to open in the near future. Select one hotel outside North America and discuss in a group the personal and professional challenges you would face when accepting an international assignment in such a country.
2. Browse through government support websites such as Canada's Foreign Affairs and International Trade's Centre for Intercultural Learning at **www.dfait-maeci.gc.ca/cfsi-icse/cil-cai/home-en.asp** and analyze in groups how Canada's government is helping Canadians in their preparations for international assignments.

Exercises

1. Assume that you are the HR director for a small company that has begun to make international assignments. You are considering using an external consulting firm to provide pre-departure training for

employees, as you do not have the resources to provide this in house. What components will you need covered? How will you measure the effectiveness of the pre-departure training program provided by this external consultant?

2. When discussing today's many aging workforces around the world, one is sometimes confronted with the statement or attitude that older people are less mobile, flexible, and willing to relocate and less able to learn about new cultures and languages, and are therefore less suitable for international assignments than their younger colleagues. Discuss the truth of this statement, using facts and figures rather than relying on perceptions and stereotypes.

Case

An International Career Move

John Markham is a biochemist who now works as a manager with Drugs From Bugs (DFB), an innovative international pharmaceutical firm. John has been with DFB for the past 10 years. He is married and has two children (a daughter in high school and a son in kindergarten). His wife, Anya, is a certified general accountant who works for a major accounting firm in the Toronto area. Their combined household income amounts to $150,000. The president of DFB has asked John to become the managing director of DFB's operations in Israel. The government there has just offered a number of incentives to international pharmaceutical firms that make Israel a highly desirable location in which to operate.

John is keen on increasing the business in Israel, but he has concerns about his future with the company. He has heard that life in Israel can be fascinating but also quite difficult for someone who has never lived outside Canada.

John has received a memo from Anne Monty, DFB's vice president of HR: "John, I hear there are quite a few good websites about Israel. You might want to check them out. Meanwhile, I have asked the Israeli Tourist Board to forward some material to you. Are you free for lunch next week? I look forward to hearing your thoughts. Cheers, [signed] Anne."

Source: Gröschl, S. (2007). Strategic International HRM. In M. Belcourt & K. McBey (Eds.), *Strategic Human Resources Planning*. Toronto: Thomson Nelson, 317.

Questions

1. What are the different personal and professional aspects John needs to consider before making a decision?
2. Evaluate the pre-departure suggestions provided by DFB's vice president of HR. What kind of additional help and training would you offer to John (if any)?

3. If John decides to accept the international assignment with DFB and take his wife and kids with him, what type of additional training should DFB offer to him?

Endnotes

1. K. Kamoche. (1996). Strategic Human Resource Management with a Resource-Capability View of the Firm. *Journal of Management Studies, 33*(2), 216.
2. P. C. Earley. (1987). Intercultural Training for Managers: A Comparison. *Academy of Management Journal, 30*(4), 686.
3. R. Tung. Selection and Training Procedures of U.S., European, and Japanese Multinationals. *California Management Review, 25*(1) (1982), 57–71. Tung also asked those respondents who reported no formal training programs to give reasons for omitting these programs. Again, differences were found among the three regions. The U.S. companies cited a trend toward employment of local nationals (45 percent); the temporary nature of such assignments (28 percent); the doubtful effectiveness of such training programs (20 percent); and lack of time (4 percent). The reasons given by European multinationals were the temporary nature of such assignments (30 percent); lack of time (30 percent); a trend toward employment of local nationals (20 percent); and the doubtful effectiveness of such programs. Responses from the Japanese companies were lack of time (63 percent) and doubtful effectiveness of such programs (37 percent).
4. W. Immen. (2003, November 12). Ready to work abroad? *The Globe and Mail*, "Advice."
5. K. Barham & M. Devine. (1990). *The Quest for the International Manager: A Survey of Global Human Resource Strategies* (Special Report No. 2098). London, UK: Ashridge Management Research Group. The Economist Intelligence Unit. See also: D. Welch. (1994). Determinants of International Human Resource Management Approaches and Activities: A Suggested Framework. *Journal of Management Studies, 31*(2), 139–164.
6. L. N. Littrell & E. Salas. (2005). A Review of Cross-Cultural Training: Best Practices, Guidelines, and Research Needs. *Human Resource Development Review, 4*(3), 305–334.
7. See, for example: M. Mendenhall & G. Oddou. (1986, Winter). Acculturation Profiles of Expatriate Managers: Implications for Cross-Cultural Training Programs. *Columbia Journal of World Business*, 73–79.
8. R. Tung. (1981). Selecting and Training of Personnel for Overseas Assignments. *Columbia Journal of World Business, 16*, 68–78.
9. R. L. Tung. (1998). A Contingency Framework of Selection and Training of Expatriates Revisited. *Human Resource Management Review. 8*(1), 23–37.
10. M. Mendenhall & G. Oddou. Acculturation Profiles of Expatriate Managers; M. Mendenhall, E. Dunbar, & G. Oddou. Expatriate Selection, Training and Career-Pathing: A Review and Critique. (1987). *Human Resource Management, 26*, 331–345.
11. J. S. Black & M. Mendenhall. (1989). A Practical But Theory-Based Framework for Selecting Cross-Cultural Training Methods. *Human Resource Management, 28*(4), 511–539.
12. A. M. Osman-Gani. (2000). Developing Expatriates for the Asia-Pacific Region: A Comparative Analysis of Multinational Enterprise Managers from Five Countries Across Three Continents. *Human Resource Development Quarterly, 11*(3), 213–235.
13. C. Brewster & J. Pickard. (1994). Evaluating Expatriate Training. *International Studies of Management and Organization, 24*(3), 18–35.
14. C. Wright & S. Wright. (1994). Do Languages Really Matter? The Relationship between International Business Success and a Commitment to Foreign Language Use. *Journal of Industrial*

Affairs, 3(1), 3–14. These authors suggest that international English is perhaps a better term than "poor" or "broken" English.

15. Tung. A Contingency Framework of Selection and Training of Expatriates Revisited.

16. C. Fixman. (1990, September). The Foreign Language Needs of U.S.-Based Corporations. *Annals, AAPSS,* 511.

17. V. Pucik. (1985). Strategic Human Resource Management in a Multinational Firm. In H. V. Wortzel & L. H. Wortzel (Eds.), *Strategic Management of Multinational Corporations: The Essentials*. New York: John Wiley.

18. C. Fixman. The Foreign Language Needs of U.S.-Based Corporations. 36.

19. Wright & Wright. Do Languages Really Matter? 5.

20. P. Hepner Hall & W. B. Gudykunst. (1989). The Relationship of Perceived Ethnocentrism in Corporate Cultures to the Selection, Training, and Success of International Employees. *International Journal of Intercultural Relations, 13,* 183–201.

21. *GMAC 2004 Global Survey,* 44.

22. G. Baliga & J. C. Baker. (1985). Multinational corporate policies for expatriate managers: Selection, training and evaluation. *Advanced Management Journal,* 31–38.

23. R. L. Tung & Arthur Andersen. (1997). *Exploring International Assignees' Viewpoints: A Study of the Expatriation/Repatriation Process*. Chicago IL: Arthur Andersen, International Executive Services.

24. R. Marschan, D. Welch, & L. Welch. (1997). Language: The Forgotten Factor in Multinational Management. *European Management Journal, 15*(5), 591–597; see also, Fixman. The Foreign Language Needs of U.S.-Based Corporations.

25. The first author had the opportunity a number of years ago to visit McDonald's Hamburger University in Chicago and observe training for new store managers from a number of developing markets in such countries as Eastern Europe and Russia. The training facility was able to conduct a number of simultaneous training programs with full simultaneous translation into the native language of the participants.

26. See, for example: H. Park, S.D. Hwang, & J. K. Harrison. (1996). Sources and Consequences of Communication Problems in Foreign Subsidiaries: The Case of United States Firms in South Korea. *International Business Review, 5*(1), 79–98; and A. Rao & K. Hashimoto. (1996). Intercultural Influence: A Study of Japanese Expatriate Managers in Canada. *Journal of International Business Studies, 27*(3), 443–466.

27. M. Lazarova & I. Tarique. (2005). Knowledge transfer upon repatriation. *Journal of World Business, 40,* 361–373.

28. M. Harvey. (1997). "Inpatriation" Training: The Next Challenge for International Human Resource Management. *International Journal of Intercultural Relations, 21*(3), 393–428.

29. An exception is an article by R. S. DeFrank, R. Konopaske, & J. M. Ivancevich, (2000), Executive Travel Stress: Perils of the Road Warrior, *Academy of Management Executive, 14*(2), 58–71. However, the authors devote only one paragraph to host-culture issues.

30. D. Welch & V. Worm. (2006). International business travellers: A challenge for IHRM. In G. Stahl & I. Björkman (Eds.), *Handbook of Research in International Human Resource Management*. Cheltenham, UK: Edward Elgar, 283–301.

31. D. M. Eschbach, G. E. Parker, & P. A. Stoeberl. (2001). American Repatriate Employees' Retrospective Assessments of the Effects of Cross-Cultural Training on their Adaptation to International Assignments. *International Journal of Human Resource Management, 12*(2), 270–287.

32. M. A. Morris & C. Robie. (2001). A Meta-Analysis of the Effects of Cross-Cultural Training on Expatriate Performance and Adjustment. *International Journal of Training and Development, 5*(2), 112–125. The authors define meta-analysis as "a method developed in the late 1970s to summarize and integrate research findings from multiple articles . . . to resolve conflicting

findings of multiple studies on the same topic by combining their results in a systematic fashion," 113–114.

33. J. Selmer, I. Torbiörn, & C. T. de Leon. (1998). Sequential Cross-Cultural Training for Expatriate Business Managers: Pre-departure and Post-arrival. *International Journal of Human Resource Management, 9*(5), 831–840.

34. D. C. Feldman & D. C. Thomas. (1992). Career Issues Facing Expatriate Managers. *Journal of International Business Studies, 23*(2), 271–294; and E. Naumann. (1992). A Conceptual Model of Expatriate Turnover. *Journal of International Business Studies, 23*(3), 449–531.

35. R. B. Peterson. (2003). The Use of Expatriates and Inpatriates in Central and Eastern Europe Since the Wall Came Down. *Journal of World Business, 38*, 55–69.

36. P. Caligiuri & V. Di Santo. (2001). Global Competence: What is It, and Can It Be Developed Through Global Assignments? *Human Resource Planning, 24*(3) 27–35.

37. J. Gibbs. (2006). Decoupling and coupling in global teams: Implications for human resource management. In G. Stahl & I. Björkman (Eds.), *Handbook of Research in International Human Resource Management.* Cheltenham, UK: Edward Elgar, 347–363.

38. M. Maznevski, S. Davison, & K. Jonsen. (2006). Global virtual team dynamics and effectiveness. In G. Stahl & I. Björkman (Eds.), *Handbook of Research in International Human Resource Management.* Cheltenham, UK: Edward Elgar, 364–384.

39. P. Caligiuri & I. Tarique. (2006). International assignee selection and cross-cultural training and development. In G. Stahl & I. Björkman (Eds.), *Handbook of Research in International Human Resource Management.* Cheltenham, UK: Edward Elgar, 302–322.

40. A. Al-Dosary & S. Rahman. (2005). Saudization (Localization)—A critical review. *Human Resource Development International, 8*(4), 495–502.

41. M. Geppert. (2005). Competence development and learning in British and German subsidiaries of MNCs: Why and how national institutions still matter. *Personnel Review, 34*(2), 155–177.

42. W. Chang. (2005). Expatriate training in international nongovernmental organizations: A model for research. *Human Resource Development Review, 4*(4), 440–461; C. Brewster & S. Lee. (2006). HRM in not-for-profit international organizations: Different, but also alike. In H. Larsen & W. Mayrhofer (Eds.), *European Human Resource Management.* London, UK: Routledge.

43. J. Wang, G. Wang, W. Ruona, & J. Rojewski. (2005). Confucian values and the implications for International HRD. *Human Resource Development International, 8*(3), 311–326; C. Zhao. (2005). Management of corporate culture through local managers' training in foreign companies in China: A qualitative analysis. *International Journal of Training and Development, 9*(4), 232–255; D. Zhang, Z. Zhang, & B. Yang. (2004). Learning organization in mainland China: Empirical research on its application to Chinese state-owned enterprises. *International Journal of Training and Development, 8*(4), 258–273; C. Zhu, *Human Resource Management in China: Past, Current and Future HR Practices in the Industrial Sector.* London, UK: Routledge; J. Wang & G. Wang. (2006). Exploring national human resource development: A case of China management development in a transitioning context. *Human Resource Development Review, 5*(2), 176–201.

44. B. Metcalfe & C. Rees. (2005). Theorizing advances in international human resource development. *Human Resource Development International, 8*(4), 449–465.

Chapter 7

International Compensation

Chapter Learning Objectives

After reading this chapter, you should be able to:

- explain the complexities that arise when firms move from compensation at the domestic level to compensation in an international context
- detail the key components of an international compensation program
- outline the two main approaches to international compensation and the advantages and disadvantages of each approach
- explain the special problems areas of taxation, valid international living-cost data, and the problems of managing TCN compensation
- discuss recent developments related to global compensation issues

INTERNATIONAL COMPENSATION AT RBC

Gary Dobbie, senior vice president of compensation, benefits, and employee relations at the Royal Bank of Canada (RBC) in Toronto:

> Before they move, our international transferees meet with move managers and financial advisors who know our compensation programs, at our expense, so even if they will have an adverse tax event, such as the possibility to lose residency status in their home country if they sell their home, they understand the implication of that. They come to appreciate that [the international assignment is] a personal decision. And they understand what they will gain from the assignment personally and professionally. . . . The faster they can become acclimatized and the family can get settled, the better for business, the more productive they can be in their new office.

Alison Cosadinos, senior manager of U.S. pensions and benefits for RBC, who was formerly a U.S. resident:

> When I moved to Canada, the relocation company that RBC provided helped me sell my house in the U.S., coordinated the move, and liaised with the lawyers to coordinate visa and work permit issues. It really took a lot of pressure off me to know knowledgeable experts were helping each step of the way.

These experiences of two senior RBC compensation and benefits managers illustrate the importance and implications of employers providing the right support and guidance for international assignees and ensuring that they understand their international compensatory options and compensation packages. The comments give some indication of the wide range of compensation variables and aspects to be considered in the development and design of international compensation systems and policies.

Source: Cohen, S. (2007, January 2007). Bridging the border. *Benefits Canada* magazine. Retrieved September 12, 2007, from www.benefitscanada.com/news/article.jsp?content=20070119_133431_6084

Introduction

Similar to the introductory chapter, our discussion in this chapter of international compensation illustrates and addresses the complexity of HR policies and practices when put into an international context, including:

1. Management of more activities from a broader perspective.
2. Greater involvement in the lives of far-flung employees.
3. Balancing of the needs of PCNs, HCNs, and TCNs.
4. Control of exposure to financial and political risks.
5. Increased awareness of and responsiveness to host-country and regional influences.

Global compensation practices have recently moved far beyond the original domain of expatriate pay. Compensation is increasingly seen as a mechanism to develop and reinforce a global corporate culture;[1] a primary source of corporate control, explicitly linking performance outcomes with associated costs;[2] and the nexus of increasingly strident, sophisticated, and public discourses on central issues of corporate governance in an international context.[3]

Increased *complexities* in global pay include the growing use of outsourced activities and subsequent labour pricing needs;[4] balancing centralization and decentralization of incentives, benefits, and pensions, given the technical capabilities of Web-based human resources information systems;[5] and balancing the need for more accurate and detailed performance metrics on international assignees with the realities of a cost-sensitive environment resulting from maturing global competitiveness.[6]

Increasingly, domestic pay practices of long standing have been questioned as firms move into the global arena. These overt challenges to deeply held national and corporate values and pay systems include challenges to the universal applicability of incentive pay programs[7] and what some critics view as out-of-control executive compensation programs, often driven by U.S.-based multinational pay systems.[8] Critiques of U.S.-based MNE pay for executives have recently expanded to include challenges to the effectiveness of legal and institutional forms of corporate governance and the roles, responsibilities, and pay practices of corporate boards and compensation committees, as well as the use of executive pay consultants.[9]

Greater *choice*, the growing ability to systematically identify and implement heretofore novel or unrecognized pay practices, may be seen to result from increases in the transparency of pay practices around the world due to increased global media attention and reach, changes in corporate reporting regulations, the sheer number of assignments across borders, and the impact of the World Wide Web.[10] It remains to be seen if this increased choice will translate into a predictable set of global pay practices.

These complexities, challenges, and choices facing managers involved in global compensation decisions do not change two primary areas of focus. These individuals must manage highly complex and turbulent local details while concurrently building and maintaining a unified, strategic pattern of compensation policies, practices, and values.

For multinationals to successfully manage compensation and benefits requires knowledge of employment and taxation law and the customs, environment, and employment practices of many foreign countries; familiarity with currency fluctuations and the effect of inflation on compensation; and an understanding of why and when special allowances must be supplied

global compensation
compensation that could be seen as a mechanism to develop a global corporate culture

Having A Driver: A Luxury or a Necessity?

In Canada and most other Western countries, a driver may be considered a luxury, available only to very senior managers. In developing economies, a driver is economical in terms of cost, effectiveness, and safety. Apart from the expectation that managers use drivers, parking is frequently chaotic in developing countries (especially in large cities) and the driver also performs the function of a parking attendant.

In some developing countries, it is quite common for the police to arrest drivers involved in traffic accidents and leave them in detention while responsibility and damages are assessed. Such a risk for their employees is unacceptable to most firms. Many multinationals do not allow their expatriate employees to drive at all in some developing countries and provide local drivers for both the expatriate and spouse.

and which allowances are necessary in what countries (see, for example, IHRM Today 7.1)—all within the context of shifting political, economic, and social conditions. The level of local knowledge needed in many of these areas requires specialist advice, and many multinationals retain the services of consulting firms that may offer a broad range of services or provide highly specialized services relevant to HRM in a multinational context.[11] Because of its complexity and expense, much of the discussion in this chapter addresses PCN compensation. However, issues relevant to TCNs and HCNs are also described because they are becoming more important to the success of many multinationals.[12]

Expatriate compensation—long the preoccupation of global HR executives—is increasingly seen more as a component of a more balanced, albeit complex, system of worldwide pay only.[13] National and regional differences in the meaning, practice, and tradition of pay remain significant sources of variation in the international firm. Yet these contextual sources of complexity must be balanced with strategic intent and administrative economy.[14] Rather than seeing pay as an ethnocentric extension of an essentially domestic strategy, pay systems are increasingly becoming truly global—with truly global objectives (see IHRM Today 7.2).[15]

Objectives of International Compensation

When developing international compensation policies, a firm seeks to satisfy several objectives. First, the policy should be consistent with the overall strategy, structure, and business needs of the multinational. Second, the policy must work to attract and retain staff in the areas where the multinational has the greatest needs and opportunities. Thus, the policy must be competitive and recognize factors such as incentive for foreign service, tax equalization, and reimbursement for reasonable costs. Third, the policy should facilitate the transfer of international employees in the most cost-effective manner for the firm. Fourth, the policy must give due consideration to equity and ease of administration.

Global Compensation Programs

According to the *Expatica* website, the findings of a Mercer HR Consulting survey indicate a trend toward global compensation packages among U.S.- and Europe-based multinational organizations.

"Pay strategies play an important role in the success of multinational organizations," said Mark Edelsten, a European partner at Mercer in London, England. "Increasingly, pay is being managed from a global perspective—to facilitate global expansion efforts, better manage labour costs, create internal equity, or ensure effective governance," he said.

The key areas on which international compensation policies and packages focus include pay in relation to the market, short- and long-term incentive policies, and consistent processes of job grading and levelling. Aspects related to employee training and development, and recognition and career programs are not standard elements of international compensation packages.

Source: *Expatica*. (2005, March 24). Multinationals go for global compensation programmes. Retrieved September 13, 2007, from www.expatica.com/actual/article.asp?channel_id=7&story_id=18404

The international employee will also have a number of objectives that need to be achieved from the firm's compensation policy. First, the employee will expect the policy to offer financial protection in terms of benefits, social security, and living costs in the foreign location. Second, the employee will expect a foreign assignment to offer opportunities for financial advancement through income and/or savings. Third, the employee will expect issues such as housing, education of children, and recreation to be addressed in the policy. (The employee will also have expectations in terms of career advancement and repatriation, as discussed in Chapter 8).

If we contrast the objectives of the multinational and the employee, we of course see the potential for many complexities and possible problems, as some of these objectives cannot be maximized on both sides. The "war stories" about problems in international compensation that we see in HR practitioner magazines is testimony to these complexities and problems. However, if we take away the specialist jargon and allow for the international context, are the competing objectives of the firm and the employee *fundamentally* different from that which exists in a domestic environment? We think not. We agree with the broad thrust of an article by Milkovich and Bloom,[16] which argues that firms must rethink the traditional view that local conditions dominate international compensation strategy. We will return to these issues at the end of the chapter after we have covered some of the technical aspects and complexities of compensation in an international context.

Key Components of an International Compensation Program

The area of international compensation is complex primarily because multinationals must cater to three categories of employees: PCNs, TCNs, and HCNs. In this section, we discuss key components of international compensation: base salary, foreign service inducement/hardship premium, allowances, and benefits.

base salary

in an international context, the primary component of a package of allowances

Base Salary

The term **base salary** acquires a somewhat different meaning when employees go abroad. In a domestic context, base salary denotes the amount of cash compensation that serves as a benchmark for other compensation elements (such as bonuses and benefits). For expatriates, it is the primary component of a package of allowances, many of which are directly related to base salary (e.g., foreign service premium, cost-of-living allowance, housing allowance) as well as the basis for in-service benefits and pension contributions. It may be paid in home or local-country currency. The base salary is the foundation block for international compensation whether the employee is a PCN or TCN. Major differences can occur in the employee's package depending on whether the base salary is linked to the home country of the PCN or TCN, or whether an international rate is paid. (We will return to this issue later in the chapter.)

Foreign Service Inducement/Hardship Premium

Parent-country nationals often receive a salary premium as an inducement to accept a foreign assignment or as compensation for any hardship caused by the transfer. Under such circumstances, the definition of hardship, eligibility for the premium, and amount and timing of payment must be addressed. In cases in which hardship is determined, Canadian firms could refer to the *Foreign Service Directives* issued by the Treasury Board Secretariat and accessible on the Treasury Board Secretariat website. Additional information is available on the National Joint Council website. As Ruff and Jackson[17] have noted, however, making international comparisons of the cost of living is problematic.

It is important to note, though, that these payments are more commonly paid to PCNs than TCNs. Foreign service inducements, if used, are usually made in the form of a percentage of salary, usually 5 to 40 percent of base pay. Such payments vary, depending on the assignment, actual hardship, tax consequences, and length of assignment. In addition, differentials may be considered; for example, a host-country's workweek may be longer than that of the home country, and a differential payment may be made in lieu of overtime, which is not normally paid to PCNs or TCNs.

Allowances

Issues concerning allowances can be very challenging to a firm establishing an overall compensation policy, partly because of the various forms of allowances that exist. The *cost-of-living allowance* (COLA), which typically receives the most attention, involves a payment to compensate for differences in expenditures between the home country and the foreign country (to account for inflation differentials, for example). Often this allowance is difficult to determine, so companies may use the services of organizations such as ORC

Worldwide (a U.S.-based firm)[18] or ECA International (based in Britain).[19] These firms specialize in providing COLA information on a global basis, regularly updated, to their clients. The COLA may also include payments for housing and utilities, personal income tax, or discretionary items.[20]

The provision of a *housing allowance* implies that employees should be entitled to maintain their home-country living standards (or, in some cases, receive accommodation that is equivalent to that provided for similar foreign employees and peers). Such allowances are often paid on either an assessed or an actual basis. Other alternatives include company-provided housing, either mandatory or optional; a fixed housing allowance; or assessment of a portion of income, out of which actual housing costs are paid. Housing issues are often addressed on a case-by-case basis, but as a firm internationalizes, formal policies become more necessary and efficient. Financial assistance and/or protection in connection with the sale or leasing of an expatriate's former residence are offered by many multinationals. Those in the banking and finance industry tend to be the most generous, offering assistance in sale or leasing, payment of closing costs, payment of leasing management fees, rent protection, and equity protection. Again, TCNs receive these benefits less frequently than PCNs.

There is also a provision for *home leave allowances*. Many employers cover the expense of one or more trips back to the home country each year. The purpose of paying for such trips is to give expatriates the opportunity to renew family and business ties, thereby helping them to avoid adjustment problems when they are repatriated. Although firms traditionally have restricted the use of leave allowances to travel home, some firms give expatriates the option of applying the allowances to foreign travel rather than returning home. Firms allowing use of home leave allowances for foreign travel need to be aware that expatriate employees with limited international experience who opt for foreign travel rather than returning home may become more homesick than other expatriates who return home for a "reality check" with co-workers and friends.[21]

Education allowances for expatriates' children are also an integral part of any international compensation policy. Allowances for education can cover items such as general tuition, language class tuition, enrollment fees, books and supplies, transportation, room and board, and uniforms. (While not common—at least in public schools—in Canada, it is quite common in many countries for high-school students to wear uniforms.) The level of education provided for, the adequacy of local schools, and transportation of dependants who are being educated in other locations may present problems for multinationals. PCNs and TCNs usually receive the same treatment related to educational expenses. The cost of local or boarding school for dependent children is typically covered by the employer, although there may be restrictions, depending on the availability of good local schools and on their fees. Attendance at a university may also be provided for, when deemed necessary.

Relocation allowances usually cover moving, shipping, and storage charges; temporary living expenses; subsidies for appliance or car purchases (or sales); and down payments or lease-related charges. Allowances related to perquisites (cars, club memberships, servants,[22] and so on) may also need to be considered (usually for more senior positions, but this varies according to location). These allowances are often contingent on tax-equalization policies and practices in both the home and the host countries.

Increasingly, many MNEs are also offering *spouse assistance* to help guard against or offset income lost by an expatriate's spouse as a result of relocating abroad. According to a survey by the Canadian Employee Relocation Council, however, in Canada very few companies offer these kinds of services or benefits to the spouses of their international assignees.[23]

To summarize, MNEs generally pay allowances in order to encourage employees to take international assignments and to keep employees "whole" relative to home standards. We will present more about this concept later in the chapter. In terms of housing, companies usually pay a tax-equalized housing allowance in order to discourage the purchase of housing and/or to compensate for higher housing costs. This allowance is adjusted periodically, based on estimates of both local and foreign housing costs.

Benefits

The complexity inherent in international benefits often brings more difficulties than when dealing with compensation. Pension plans are very difficult to deal with from country to country, as national practices vary considerably. Transportability of pension plans, medical coverage, and social security benefits are very difficult to normalize. Therefore, firms need to address many issues when considering benefits, including whether to:

- Maintain expatriates in home-country programs, particularly if the firm does not receive a tax deduction for it.
- Enroll expatriates in host-country benefit programs and/or making up any difference in coverage, if this is an option for the firm.
- Provide home-country or host-country social security benefits.

In some countries, expatriates cannot opt out of local social security programs. In such circumstances, the firm normally pays for these additional costs. Canadians maintaining their residency status when abroad usually continue to pay Canadian social security, while—in some cases—being able to waive the host-country social security taxes. For example, Canadians with a Canadian residency status working in the United States continue to pay into such programs as the Canadian/Quebec Pension Plan and Employment Insurance, while being able to waive the tax payable under the U.S. Federal Insurance Contributions Act. European PCNs and TCNs enjoy portable social security benefits within the European Union.

Laws governing private benefit practices differ from country to country, and firm practices also vary. Not surprisingly, multinationals have generally done a good job of planning for the retirement needs of their PCN employees, but this is generally less the case for TCNs.[24] There are many reasons for this: TCNs may have little or no home-country social security coverage; they may have spent many years in countries that do not permit currency transfers of accrued benefit payments; or they may spend their final year or two of employment in a country where final average salary is in a currency that relates unfavourably to their home-country currency. How their benefits are calculated and what type of retirement plan applies to them may make the difference between a comfortable retirement in a country of their choice and a forced penurious retirement elsewhere.

In addition to the already discussed benefits, multinationals also provide vacations and special leave. Included as part of the employee's regular vacation, annual home leave usually provides airfares for families to return to their home countries. Rest and rehabilitation leave, based on the conditions of the host country, also provides the employee's family with free airfares to a more comfortable location near the host country. In addition to rest and rehabilitation leave, emergency provisions are available in case of a death or illness in the family. Employees in hardship locations often receive additional leave expense payments and rest and rehabilitation periods.

Approaches to International Compensation

There are two main options in the area of international compensation—the *going-rate approach* (also referred to as the *market-rate approach*) and the *balance-sheet approach* (sometimes known as the *build-up approach*). In this section, we describe each approach and discuss the advantages and disadvantage inherent in each.[25]

The Going-Rate Approach

The key characteristics of the going-rate approach are summarized in Table 7.1. With this approach, the base salary for the international transfer is linked to the salary structure in the host country. The multinational usually obtains information from local compensation surveys and must decide whether local nationals (HCNs), expatriates of the same nationality, or expatriates of all nationalities will be the reference point in terms of benchmarking. For example, a Canadian bank operating in Tokyo would need to decide whether its reference point would be local Japanese salaries, salaries paid by other Canadian competitors

RPC 7.5
RPC 7.6

TABLE 7.1

Going-Rate Approach

- Based on local market rates
- Relies on survey comparisons among:
  - Local nationals (HCNs)
  - Expatriates of same nationality
  - Expatriates of all nationalities
- Compensation based on the selected survey comparison
- Base pay and benefits may be supplemented by additional payments for low-pay countries

Chapter 7: International Compensation

in Tokyo, or salaries paid by all foreign banks operating in Tokyo. With the going-rate approach, if the location is in a low-pay county, the multinational usually supplements base pay with additional benefits and payments.

The advantages and disadvantages of the going-rate approach are summarized in IHRM Notebook 7.1. The advantages are that there is equality with local nationals (very effective in attracting PCNs or TCNs to a location that pays higher salaries than those received in the home country); the approach is simple and easy for expatriates to understand; expatriates are able to identify with the host country; and there is often equity among expatriates of different nationalities.

The going-rate approach also has disadvantages, however. First, there can be variation between assignments for the same employee. This is most obvious when we compare an assignment in an advanced economy with one in a developing country, but also between assignments in various advanced economies, where differences in managerial salaries and the effect of local taxation can significantly influence an employee's compensation level using the going-rate approach. Not surprisingly, individual employees are very sensitive to this issue. Second, there can be variation between expatriates of the same nationality in different locations. A strict interpretation of the going-rate approach can lead to rivalry for assignments to locations that are financially attractive and little interest in locations considered to be financially unattractive.

Finally, the going-rate approach can pose problems on repatriation if the employee's salary reverts to a home-country level that is below that of the host country. This is not only a problem for firms in developing countries, but also for firms from many countries where local managerial salaries are well below those of Canada or the United States—the world market leader in managerial salaries[26]—as outlined in IHRM Today 7.3.

As the list in IHRM Today 7.3 shows, managers from Argentina or Australia would be very positive about a going-rate approach to compensation if they were offered senior expatriate assignments in Canada or the United States, but would have some difficulties adjusting back to local salaries on their repatriation to their home country.

IHRM Notebook 7.1

Advantages and Disadvantages of the Going-Rate Approach

Advantages	Disadvantages
• Equality with local nationals	• Variation between assignments for same employee
• Simplicity	• Variation between expatriates of same nationality in different countries
• Identification with host country	• Potential re-entry problems
• Equity among different nationalities	

Worldwide CEO Compensation Rates

A survey by Towers Perrin of total compensation for CEOs around the world reported the following results for various countries (all figures in U.S. dollars):

- United States $2,164,952
- United Kingdom $1,184,936
- Italy $1,137,326
- **Canada**   **$1,068,964**
- Singapore $1,033,274
- Mexico $1,002,357
- Belgium $ 987,387
- The Netherlands $ 862,711
- Australia $ 707,747
- China (Hong Kong) $ 651,339
- Venezuela $ 467,868
- Argentina $ 431,300

Source: Towers Perrin. *Worldwide Total Remuneration, 2005–2006*, 20. Total compensation included basic salary, variable bonus, compulsory company contributions, voluntary company contributions, perquisites, and long-term incentives. See also the Towers Perrin website (www.towers.com) for further information.

The Balance-Sheet Approach

The key characteristics of the balance-sheet approach (which is the most widely used approach for international compensation) are summarized in Table 7.2. The basic objective is to *"keep the expatriate whole"*[27] (that is, maintaining relativity to PCN colleagues and compensating for the costs of an international assignment) through maintenance of home-country living standard plus a financial inducement to make the package attractive. This approach links the base salary for PCNs and TCNs to the salary structure of the relevant home country. For example, a Canadian executive taking an international position would have his or her compensation package built on

TABLE 7.2

The Balance-Sheet Approach

- Basic objective is maintenance of home-country living standard plus financial inducement
- Home-country pay and benefits are the foundations of this approach
- Adjustments to home package to balance additional expenditure in host country
- Financial incentives (expatriate/hardship premium) added to make the package attractive
- Most common system in usage by multinational firms

the Canadian base-salary level rather than that applicable to the host country. The key assumption of this approach is that foreign assignees should not suffer a material loss due to job transfer, and this is accomplished through the utilization of what is generally referred to as the *balance-sheet approach*. According to Reynolds:

> The balance-sheet approach to international compensation is a system designed to equalize the purchasing power of employees at comparable position levels living overseas and in the home country, and to provide incentives to offset qualitative differences between assignment locations.[28]

Where costs associated with the host-country assignment (for key categories of outlays see IHRM Notebook 7.2) exceed equivalent costs in the parent country, these costs are met by both the firm and the expatriate to ensure that parent-country equivalent purchasing power is achieved.

Table 7.3 shows a typical spreadsheet for an expatriate assignment using the balance-sheet approach. In this example, a Canadian expatriate is assigned to a country called New Euphoria, which has a cost-of-living index of 150 relative to Canada and a currency exchange rate of 1.5 relative to the Canadian dollar. In addition to a foreign service premium, a hardship allowance is also payable for this location. Housing is provided by the firm, and a notional cost for this is recognized by a 7 percent deduction from the package, along with a notional tax deduction (we discuss taxation later in the chapter). The expatriate can see from this spreadsheet what components are offered in the package and how the package will be split between Canadian currency and New Euphoria currency.

The advantages and disadvantages of the balance-sheet approach are summarized in IHRM Notebook 7.3. There are three main advantages. First, the balance-sheet approach provides equity between foreign assignments and between expatriates of the same nationality. Second, repatriation of expatriates is facilitated by this emphasis on equity with the parent country, as expatriate compensation remains anchored to the compensation system in

IHRM Notebook 7.2

Key Categories of Expatriate Outlays

Four major categories of outlays incurred by expatriates are incorporated into the balance-sheet approach:

1. *Goods and services*—home-country outlays for items such as food, personal care, clothing, household furnishings, recreation, transportation, and medical care
2. *Housing*—the major costs associated with housing in the host country
3. *Income taxes*—parent-country and host-country income taxes
4. *Reserve*—contributions to savings, payments for benefits, pension contributions, investments, education expenses, social security taxes, etc.

TABLE 7.3

Expatriate Compensation Worksheet

Employee: Brian Smith
Position: Marketing Manager
Country: New Euphoria
Reason for change: New Assignment
Effective date of change   February 1, 2009

Item	Amount CDN$ PA	Paid in Canadian Dollars CDN$ PA	Paid in Local Currency NE$ PA
Base salary	200,000	100,000	150,000
Cost-of-living allowance	50,000		75,000
Overseas service premium (20%)	40,000	40,000	
Hardship allowance (20%)	40,000	40,000	
Housing deduction (7%)	−14,000	−14,000	
Tax deduction	−97,000	−97,000	
TOTAL	219,000	69,000	225,000

COLA Index = 150
Exchange Rate = 1.5   Authorized/Date

IHRM Notebook 7.3

Advantages and Disadvantages of the Balance-Sheet Approach

Advantages	Disadvantages
• Equity	• Can result in great disparities
• Between assignments	• Between expatriates of different nationalities
• Between expatriates of the same nationality	• Between expatriates and local nationals
• Facilitates expatriate re-entry	• Can be quite complex to administer
• Easy to communicate to employees	

the parent country. Third, this approach is easy to communicate, as Table 7.3 illustrates.

The balance-sheet approach has two main disadvantages. First, this approach can result in considerable disparities—both between expatriates of different nationalities and between PCNs and HCNs. Problems arise when international staff are paid different amounts for performing the same (or very similar) job in the host location, according to their different home base salary. For example, in the Singapore regional headquarters of a Canadian bank, a Canadian PCN and an Australian TCN may perform the same banking duties but the Canadian will receive a higher salary than the Australian because of the differences in Canadian and Australian base-salary levels. As noted above, differences in base-salary levels can also cause difficulties between expatriates and HCNs. Traditionally, this has referred to the problem of highly paid PCNs being resented by local HCN employees because these "foreigners" are perceived as being excessively compensated (and because they are blocking career opportunities for locals).

However, feelings of resentment and inequity can also run in the other direction. A Chinese (Hong Kong) firm that establishes a subsidiary in Canada (or acquires a Canadian business) may find that if it uses a balance-sheet approach, its expatriates may be substantially underpaid compared to local Canadian employees. While the logic of the balance sheet states that being tied to the home country assists in repatriation because the expatriate identifies with the home country, research in equity theory[29] suggests that employees do not always assess compensation issues in a detached and rational way.

The high local managerial salaries paid in the United States pose additional base-salary issues and concerns—in particular for U.S. employees working for foreign firms operating in the United States. Many non-U.S. multinationals are reluctant to pay high U.S. salaries to U.S. employees who are offered international assignments (as HCNs transferring to the firm's home-country operations, or as TCNs). U.S. employees are equally reluctant to accept the lower salaries paid in the firm's home country. Thus, the balance-sheet approach can not only produce disparities but might also act as a barrier to staff acceptance of international assignments.

A second problem with the balance-sheet approach is that while this approach is both elegant and simple as a concept, it can become quite complex to administer. Complexities particularly arise in the areas of tightly integrated private and government fund transfers—or, put more plainly, taxes and pensions.

Taxation

RPC 7.9

The taxation aspect of international compensation is probably the one that causes the most concern to HR practitioners and expatriates (both PCNs and TCNs), as taxation generally evokes emotional responses.[30] No one enjoys paying taxes, and this issue can be very time-consuming for both the firm and the expatriate. To illustrate the potential problems, an assignment abroad means that a Canadian expatriate, maintaining residency in Canada, is taxed on worldwide income in Canada and most likely in the country of assignment. In most cases, international assignees who maintain their residency with Canada or who have significant ties to Canada (causing these managers to be defined as Canadian residents) will be allowed foreign tax credits for taxes already paid in their assigned country. Nevertheless, these managers have to file an annual Canadian tax return on their worldwide earnings, while international assignees who become non-residents of Canada have to file final departure tax returns with the Canada Revenue Agency before going abroad. The dual tax cost for many Canadian and other expatriates, combined with all of the other expatriate costs, makes some multinationals think twice about making use of expatriates

Multinationals generally select one of the following approaches to handling international taxation:

- *Tax equalization*—firms withhold an amount equal to the home-country tax obligation of the PCN, and pay all taxes in the host country.
- *Tax protection*—The employee pays up to the amount of taxes he or she would pay on compensation in the home country. In such a situation, the employee is entitled to any windfall received if total taxes are less in the foreign country than in the home country. In her review of global compensation, Stuart[31] adds two other approaches: (1) ad hoc (each expatriate is handled differently, depending on the individual package agreed to with the firm) and (2) laissez-faire (employees are "on their own" in conforming to host-country and home-country taxation laws and practices). However, neither of these approaches is recommended, and we will focus on tax equalization and tax protection, as these are the most common approaches.

Tax equalization is by far the more common taxation policy used by multinationals[32] (see IHRM Today 7.4). Thus, for a PCN, tax payments equal to the liability of a home-country taxpayer with the same income and family status are imposed on the employee's salary and bonus. Any additional premiums or allowances are typically paid by the firm, tax-free to the employee. As multinationals operate in more and more countries, they are subject to widely discrepant income tax rates.

tax equalization

amount withheld equal to the home-country tax obligation for payment to host country

tax protection

employee pays up to the amount of taxes that would be due in the home country

---

It is also important to note that just focusing on income tax can be misleading, as the shares of both personal and corporate taxes are rising in Organisation for Economic Co-operation and Development (OECD) countries.[33] For example, if we look at selected maximum federal marginal tax rates (see Table 7.4), the top five highest taxation countries are the Netherlands, Belgium, France, Australia, and China. Canada is significantly below the rates for these five countries.[34]

Many multinationals have responded to this complexity and diversity across countries by retaining the services of international accounting firms

TABLE 7.4

Maximum Marginal Federal Tax Rates

COUNTRY	MAXIMUM MARGINAL RATE (%)
Argentina	35.00
Australia	47.00
Belgium	50.00
Brazil	27.50
Canada	29.00
China (Hong Kong)	20.00
China	45.00
France	48.09
Germany	42.00
India	33.66
Italy	43.00
Japan	37.00
Malaysia	28.00
Mexico	33.00
Netherlands	52.00
Poland	40.00
Singapore	22.00
South Africa	40.00
South Korea	35.00
Spain	29.16
Sweden	26.00
Switzerland	11.50
Taiwan	40.00
United Kingdom	40.00
United States	35.00
Venezuela	34.00

Source: Adapted from: Towers Perrin. *Worldwide Total Remuneration, 2005–2006,* 32. Go to the Towers Perrin website (www.towers.com) for further information.

to provide advice and prepare host-country and home-country tax returns for their expatriates. Increasingly, firms are also outsourcing the provisions of further aspects of the total expatriate compensation packages, including a variety of destination services in lieu of providing payment in a package.[35] When multinationals plan compensation packages, they need to consider to what extent specific practices can be modified in each country to provide the most tax-effective, appropriate rewards for PCNs, HCNs, and TCNs within the framework of the overall compensation policy of the firm.

As one international HRM manager noted, the difficulties in international compensation "are not compensation so much as benefits." Pension plans are very difficult to compare or equalize across nations, as cultural practices vary considerably. Transportability of pension plans, medical coverage, and social security benefits are very difficult to normalize[36] (see also IHRM Notebook 7.4).

Differences in national sovereignty are also at work in the area of mandated public and private pension schemes—what many nations refer to as "social security" programs. Table 7.5 highlights the differences in mandated degree of contribution (ranging from a low of zero percent to a high of over 60 percent) as well as the mix of employer–employee contribution, and puts Canada with a total contribution of 9.90 percent at the lower end of the contribution rate scale.

For many international firms, expatriate assignments are likely to increase in distance, number, and duration over an employee's career, and more and more firms may create cadres of permanent international assignees—called *globals* by some firms. The inherent complexity and dynamism of culturally embedded and politically volatile national tax and pension processes promise to tax the resources, time, and attention of international human resource managers for the foreseeable future. Seamless networks of global firms, their specialist consultants, and local and regional public and private interest are a goal, not yet a reality.

IHRM Notebook 7.4

Expatriate Benefits

Companies need to address many issues when considering benefits of employees on international assignments, including whether:

- They should maintain expatriates in home-country programs, particularly if the company does not receive a tax deduction for it.
- The companies have the option of enrolling expatriates in host-country benefit programs and/or making up any difference in coverage.

- Host-country legislation regarding termination affects benefit entitlement.
- Expatriates should receive home-country or host-country social security benefits.
- Benefits should be maintained on a home-country or host-country basis, who is responsible for the cost, whether other benefits should be used to offset any shortfall in coverage, and whether home-country benefit programs should be exported to local nationals in foreign countries.

TABLE 7.5

Social Security Contributions by Employers and Employees

COUNTRY	EMPLOYER CONTRIBUTION RATE (%)	EMPLOYEE CONTRIBUTION RATE (%)	TOTAL CONTRIBUTION RATE (%)
Argentina	17.00	17.00	34.67
Australia	0.00*	0.00*	0.00*
Belgium	34.69	13.07	47.76
Brazil	20.00	11.00	31.00
Canada	4.95	4.95	9.90
China (Hong Kong)	0.00	0.00	0.00
China	43.50	18.00	61.50
France	**	**	**
Germany	16.90	16.90	33.80
India	13.59	1.75	0.00
Italy	**	**	**
Japan	11.07	11.07	22.13
Malaysia	1.80	0.50	2.30
Mexico	29.00	4.00	33.00
Netherlands	0.00*	32.60	32.60
Poland	16.26	26.96	43.22
Singapore	0.00*	0.00*	0.00*
South Africa	1.00	1.00	2.00
South Korea	6.66	6.66	13.32
Spain	23.60	4.70	28.30
Sweden	24.26	7.00	31.26
Switzerland	5.05	5.05	10.10
Taiwan	4.55	1.30	5.85
United Kingdom	12.80	11.00	23.00
United States	6.20	6.20	12.40
Venezuela	9.00	4.00	13.00

*When the contributions are at zero, they are funded out of the General Tax Revenue and range from zero to very high values.
**Varies
Source: Adapted from: Towers Perrin. *Worldwide Total Remuneration, 2005–2006*, 32. Go to the Towers Perrin website (www.towers.com) for further information.

International Living-Cost Data

Obtaining up-to-date information on international living costs is a constant issue for multinationals. As we noted at the beginning of this chapter, the level of local knowledge required in many areas of international HRM requires specialist advice. Consequently, many multinationals retain the services of consulting firms that may offer a broad range of services or provide highly specialized services relevant to HRM in a multinational context. With regard to international living costs, a number of consulting firms offer regular surveys calculating a cost-of-living index that can be updated in terms of currency exchange rates. A recent Mercer survey of living costs including housing[37] in selected cities ranked the 10 most expensive cities as Moscow, London, Seoul, Tokyo, Hong Kong, Copenhagen, Geneva, Osaka, Zurich, and Oslo. No Canadian city was among the 50 most expensive in the world. Toronto as the most expensive city in Canada dropped 35 places to 82nd place (see IHRM Today 7.5).

MNEs using the balance-sheet approach must constantly update compensation packages with new data on living costs, which is an ongoing administrative requirement. This is an important issue to expatriate employees and forms the basis of many complaints if updating substantially lags behind any rise in living costs.

R P C 7.10

Multinationals must also be able to respond to unexpected events such as the currency and stock market crash that suddenly unfolded in a number of Asian countries in late 1997. Some countries experience devaluation of their currencies; Indonesia, for example, saw its currency (the rupiah) drop in value by over 50 percent against the U.S. dollar in a matter of weeks. This event had a dramatic impact on prices, the cost of living, and the cost of servicing debt for Indonesian firms with loans denominated in a foreign currency such as the U.S. dollar. There is also much debate about what should be in the "basket of goods" that consulting firms use as the basis for calculating living costs around the world. For example, the Swiss Bank UBS uses the "Big Mac Index" to measure living costs around the world.[38] According to Table 7.6, it takes just over three hours for the average worker in Nairobi to earn enough for a Big Mac. While in Toronto the global burger costs

IHRM Today 7.5

Living-Cost Ranking of Canadian Cities

According to the 2007 Mercer global living-cost survey, Canadian cities are not among the 50 most expensive cities in the world. Mercer's survey analyzes and measures the comparative cost of more than 200 items in 143 cities around the world. The items include housing, transportation, food, clothing, household goods, and entertainment.

In this annual survey, New York has been the base city, with an index value of 100 points. In the 2007 survey, New York retained its position as the most expensive city in North America (15th place), while Toronto dropped 35 places to 82nd place as the most expensive Canadian city, followed by Vancouver (90th) and Calgary (92nd). Ottawa

kept its position as the least expensive city in Canada in 109th place.

According to the survey: "Canadian cities have traditionally rated favourably in the worldwide rankings. The new scores reflect a low rate of inflation and stable housing prices. In addition, while it has appreciated slightly against the U.S. dollar, the Canadian dollar depreciated nearly 13% against the euro since last year's survey."

Source: *Cost of Living Survey—Worldwide Rankings, 2007* (developed and conducted by Mercer Human Resource Consulting). Retrieved August 13, 2007, from www.canadiansresidentabroad.com/issues/summer07/article05.htm

TABLE 7.6

Range of Working Times Required to Buy One Big Mac*

CITY	MINUTES
Tokyo	10
Los Angeles	11
Chicago, Miami	12
New York	13
Toronto, Sydney, Auckland	14
Zurich, Dublin	15
Frankfurt, Vienna, Geneva, London	16
Berlin, Hong Kong, Montreal, Munich	17
Oslo, Copenhagen	18
Helsinki, Amsterdam, Nicosia, Madrid	19
Taipei, Brussels, Milan	20
Stockholm, Paris	21
Singapore	22
Dubai	25
Athens	26
Vilnius	43
Kiev	55
Bucharest	69
Mumbai	70
Manila	81
Mexico City	82
Caracas	85
Jakarta, Lima	86
Nairobi	91
Bogotá	97

*Price of one Big Mac divided by weighted average hourly pay across 13 occupations.
Source: *Price and Earnings: A Comparison of Purchasing Power Around the Globe*. (2006). UBS AG, Wealth Management Research. More information is available at www.ubs.com/1/e/media_overview/media_global/search1/search10?newsId=103130

14 minutes of working time, in Tokyo, the global burger can be bought for a mere 10 minutes' effort.[39]

It is also possible to take a wider view and focus on *business costs* rather than living costs for expatriates, because the multinational firm is interested in the overall cost of doing business in a particular country as well as the more micro issue of expatriate living costs. *The Economist* Intelligence Unit calculates such indexes, which measure the relative costs of doing business in different economies by compiling statistics relating to wages, costs for expatriate staff, air travel and subsistence, corporation taxes, perceived corruption levels, office and industrial rents, and road transport. Generally, the developed countries tend to rank as being more expensive than developing countries because their wage costs are higher.

Differentiating between PCNs and TCNs

As we have indicated, one of the outcomes of the balance-sheet approach is to produce differentiation between expatriate employees of different nationalities because of the use of nationality to determine the relevant home-country base salary. In effect, this is a differentiation between PCNs and TCNs. Many TCNs have a great deal of international experience because they often move from country to country in the employ of one multinational (or several) headquartered in a country other than their own (for example, an Indian banker may work in the Singapore branch of a Canadian bank). As Reynolds[40] has observed, there is no doubt that paying TCNs according to their home-country base-salary can be less expensive than paying all expatriates on a PCN scale (particularly if the multinational is headquartered in a country such as the United States or Germany, which both have high managerial salaries and strong currencies), but justifying these differences can be very difficult. Nonetheless, it is common practice for MNEs to use a home-country balance-sheet approach for TCNs. Evidently, the reduction in expenses outweighs the difficulty of justifying any pay differentials. However, as firms expand internationally, it is likely that TCN employees will become more valuable and firms may need to rethink their approach to compensating TCNs.

As a starting point, multinational firms need to match their compensation policies with their staffing policies and general HR philosophy. If, for example, a firm has an ethnocentric staffing policy, its compensation policy should be one of keeping the expatriate *whole* (that is, maintaining relativity to PCN colleagues plus compensating for the costs of international service). If, however, the staffing policy follows a geocentric approach (that is, staffing a position with the "best person," regardless of nationality), there may be no clear "home" for the TCN, and the firm will need to consider establishing a system of *international base pay* for key managers, regardless of nationality, that is paid in a major reserve currency such as the U.S. dollar or the euro. This system allows firms to deal with considerable variations in base salaries for managers.

RPC 7.11

Tentative Conclusions: Patterns in Complexity, Challenges, and Choices

As outlined at the beginning of the chapter, international compensation administration may be more complex than its domestic counterpart, but is only slowly and fitfully evolving from a dominant domestic state of origin.[41] Domestic pay patterns—that is norms and assumptions, pay strategies and practices, as well as pay forms and administration—are increasingly challenged as executives in MNEs are exposed to alternative pay forms, varying legal and institutional contexts, and the rapidly changing realities of global competitiveness.

Recent developments in the study of global pay issues may be seen to operate at three distinct vertical levels: the basic level of cultural values and assumptions; the intermediate level of pay strategy, practices, and systems design; and the surface (artifact) level of pay administration and form[42]— see Figure 7.1. On a second, horizontal level, firms must individually determine how to strike a balance between traditional, internally based models and explanations of pay and those more externally focused models and explanations of pay that comprise a global challenge to the status quo.[43]

Figure 7.1

Complexity, Challenges, and Choices in Global Pay

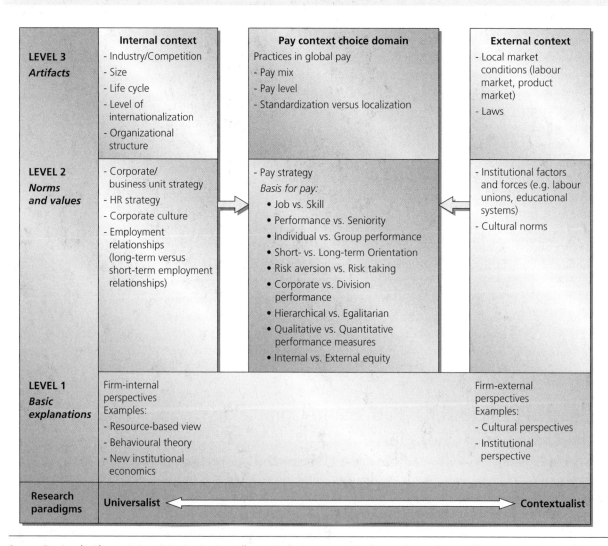

	Internal context	**Pay context choice domain**	**External context**
LEVEL 3 *Artifacts*	- Industry/Competition - Size - Life cycle - Level of internationalization - Organizational structure	Practices in global pay - Pay mix - Pay level - Standardization versus localization	- Local market conditions (labour market, product market) - Laws
LEVEL 2 *Norms and values*	- Corporate/ business unit strategy - HR strategy - Corporate culture - Employment relationships (long-term versus short-term employment relationships)	- Pay strategy *Basis for pay:* • Job vs. Skill • Performance vs. Seniority • Individual vs. Group performance • Short- vs. Long-term Orientation • Risk aversion vs. Risk taking • Corporate vs. Division performance • Hierarchical vs. Egalitarian • Qualitative vs. Quantitative performance measures • Internal vs. External equity	- Institutional factors and forces (e.g. labour unions, educational systems) - Cultural norms
LEVEL 1 *Basic explanations*	Firm-internal perspectives Examples: - Resource-based view - Behavioural theory - New institutional economics		Firm-external perspectives Examples: - Cultural perspectives - Institutional perspective
Research paradigms	Universalist ←		→ Contextualist

Source: Reprinted with permission. © Marion Festing, Allen D. Engle, Sr., Peter J. Dowling, and Bernadette Müller.

Globalizing firms must individually choose between internally and externally focused assumptions, strategies, and practices. This combined choice is the complex "context" of pay for any given global firm. Pay context is the pivotal centre column in Figure 7.1.

On the level of basic explanations, firms can choose to emphasize firm-specific theories of job worth (such as resource-based views of the firm,[44] behavioural theory,[45] or new institutional economics models[46]) or they may emphasize firm external theories of job worth (such as cultural and institutional perspectives[47]). These theories may be implicit and not articulated by pay practitioners and yet these assumptions may indirectly drive all other pay processes. On the more explicit, and more widely investigated, level of norms and values, pay strategy may be seen as some combination of internal, corporate norms (derived from and consistent with pay strategy, IHRM strategy, and traditional employment relationships—practised "psychological contracts") and external, environmental norms (derived from labour unions, educational systems, and local or regional institutional sources) that may vary significantly by geographic region.

Pay strategy may be defined in terms of a series of interlocking strategic choices on the basis of pay (job vs. skill, performance vs. seniority[48]), unit of aggregation (paying individuals, groups, organizations, short- vs. long-term orientation to pay[49]), patterns of variation in pay (variability or risk in pay, hierarchical vs. egalitarian pay orientation[50]), and an overall focus on internal equity—as captured by job evaluation systems—as opposed to external equity—as captured by market surveys.[51] "Universal" pay systems may be preferred by corporate pay planners rather than having to deal with myriad "local" systems. Ease of administration and the standardization of practices are attractive and can contribute to simplicity in global assignments, resolving disputes related to perceived inequities or policy inconsistencies, etc. However, local or regional "host contexts" and/or firm strategy may influence firms to compromise these global preferences and strategically align pay practices more or less in conformance with local or regional requirements.[52] Strategic necessity and contextual requirements may incrementally grudgingly "move" pay practices away from a universalized and toward a more localized character.[53]

Note that in the centre column of Figure 7.1, under "Pay strategy *Basis for pay*," a number of levels of analysis have emerged to supplement or augment traditional job-based pay. Firms may provide a *person* with personal "choice" in pay and pay for his or her skills or competencies.[54] Alternatively, a firm may pay at the traditional *job* level, realizing that even standard jobs may vary tremendously across geographic regions. Firms may pay at the task *group* or plant level of aggregation.[55] Finally, firms may provide "customized" pay at the *national* level, or provide standardized "core" pay for all employees in the global *firm*.[56] Increasingly, we may combine pay packages across these vertical levels of analysis and pay for a combination of personal, job, group, national, or corporate purposes.[57] These composite pay systems are more complex, but they are also more flexible and responsive to diverse employee demands and changing global business conditions.

Recall our earlier comments on global challenges to executive compensation practices and forms of corporate governance. These challenges may be seen as an ongoing debate between advocates of pay systems that value competitive individualism and result in "hierarchical" pay systems with large pay differentials for executives, market-sensitive professions and other "critical" employee groups,[58] and the advocates of pay systems that value cooperative collectivism, and result in more "egalitarian" pay systems with smaller pay differentials and more shared group or firm-wide reward practices.[59] Increasingly, multinational firms that violate corporate or local norms in one location in order to respond to local norms in a second location do so at their own risk.[60]

At the final level of pay form and administration (artifacts), we may determine that pay practices such as pay mix (between base pay, the nature and extent of benefits, use of long-term and short-term incentives, etc.), overall level of pay, and the degree to which pay is standardized across all units or customized to local conditions may be the result of internal or external influences.[61] Firm-specific realities (such as operating in a monopolistic industry, a low degree of internationalization, and simple organizational design) may mitigate for standardized pay practices. Conversely, strongly held local values, institutions, and regulations; an advanced level of internationalization; and decentralized organizational designs may mitigate for more flexible, localized pay practices.[62]

Summary

In this chapter, we have examined the complexities that arise when firms move from compensation at the domestic level to compensation in an international context. It is evident from our review that compensation policy becomes a much less precise process than is the case in the domestic HR context. To demonstrate this complexity, we first detailed the key components of an international compensation program and outlined the two main approaches to international compensation (the going-rate and the balance-sheet approaches), including the advantages and disadvantages of each approach.

We also addressed special problem areas such as taxation, obtaining valid international living-cost data, and the problems of managing TCN compensation, and presented a model of global pay that highlights the complexity and yet familiarity of pay practices in the global context. It is this combination of pay decisions based on strategic global standardization and sensitivity to changing local and regional conditions that characterizes the state of international pay practices.

We posited that a strategic yet sensitive balance can be achieved only by creating and maintaining professional networks, composed of home office and local affiliate HR practitioners, outsourcing selected activities through specialist consultants, and maintaining close cooperation with local and regional governments and other key local institutions.

Key Terms

base salary 224
global compensation 221

tax equalization 233
tax protection 233

Web Links

www 7.1   Treasury Board Secretariat:

www.tbs-sct.gc.ca

www 7.2   National Joint Council:

www.njc-cnm.gc.ca

www 7.3   ORC Worldwide specializes in compensation issues and offers a range of global, regional, and national surveys and information about expatriate compensations, benefits, and tax-related aspects:

www.orcworldwide.com

www 7.4   ECA International offers a broad range of HR services and information, including data sets relevant to HR practitioners dealing with international assignments:

www.eca-international.com

www 7.5   For the United States–Canada Income Tax Treaty, go to:

www.intltaxlaw.com/treaties/canada/p597.pdf

The Canada–United States Convention with Respect to Taxes on Income and on Capital can be found at:

www.fin.gc.ca/treaties/USA_e.html

www 7.6   Browse the Canada Revenue Agency website for more information on Canadian taxation:

www.ccra.gc.ca

www 7.7   *The Economist* Intelligence Unit website is located at:

www.eiu.com/index.asp

RPC Icons

RPC 7.1   Assesses the effectiveness of the program in achieving the organization's goals, and its competitiveness in terms of attracting and retaining qualified employees

RPC 7.2   Assesses the effectiveness of the program in achieving the organization's goals, and its competitiveness in terms of attracting and retaining qualified employees

RPC 7.3   Assesses the effectiveness of the program in achieving the organization's goals, and its competitiveness in terms of attracting and retaining qualified employees

RPC 7.4	Assesses the effectiveness of the program in achieving the organization's goals, and its competitiveness in terms of attracting and retaining qualified employees
RPC 7.5	Identifies and develops the philosophy, strategy, and policy in relation to the total compensation package that is consistent with the organization's goals. This is accomplished within the context of the legal, regulatory, taxation, and community framework.
RPC 7.6	Designs and evaluates total compensation strategies to ensure that they reflect the organization's goals, culture, structure, and external environment
RPC 7.7	Identifies and develops the philosophy, strategy, and policy in relation to the total compensation package that is consistent with the organization's goals. This is accomplished within the context of the legal, regulatory, taxation, and community framework.
RPC 7.8	Designs and evaluates total compensation strategies to ensure that they reflect the organization's goals, culture, structure, and external environment
RPC 7.9	Identifies and develops the philosophy, strategy, and policy in relation to the total compensation package that is consistent with the organization's goals. This is accomplished within the context of the legal, regulatory, taxation, and community framework.
RPC 7.10	Designs and evaluates total compensation strategies to ensure that they reflect the organization's goals, culture, structure, and external environment
RPC 7.11	Designs and evaluates total compensation strategies to ensure that they reflect the organization's goals, culture, structure, and external environment

Discussion Questions

1. What should be the main objectives for a multinational firm with regard to its compensation policies?
2. Describe the main differences in the going-rate and the balance-sheet approaches to international compensation.
3. What are the key differences in salary compensation for PCNs and TCNs? Do these differences matter?
4. What are the main points that MNEs must consider when deciding how to provide benefits?

Using the Internet

1. Browse Shell's independent network of information centres around the world (the *Outpost Network*) at **www.outpostexpat.nl** and identify and review the centres' information about Shell's compensation

benefits for Shell expatriates and their families. What do you think about this kind of website and online service? Check out Canadian MNEs such as the Seagram Company Limited and see whether you find similar expatriate online assistance or support systems. How important are such tools to expatriates?

2. Compare legally required employer benefits in Canada and another country of your choice. Search relevant Internet sources such as government websites and identify differences in benefit systems. Discuss the implications for employees moving between the two countries on international assignments.

Exercises

1. Why is it important for MNEs to understand the compensation practices of other countries? Discuss in groups the different compensation practices in the home countries represented by your group members and identify potential challenges for Canadian companies and their expatriate compensation systems when entering each of those countries.

2. Explain how balancing the interests of global and local, occupational and functional perspectives might play out in a compensation decision scenario.

3. In this chapter, we focused predominantly on long-term international assignments. Discuss in groups some of the differences in terms of compensation practices when you are dealing with short-term assignments abroad.

Case

Going to India

Geoff Smith had just celebrated his fortieth birthday when his boss, Andrew, offered him the job of managing a new multibillion project to overhaul and operate Flying India's staff catering facilities across India the following year. Andrew heads the Canadian-based multinational catering organization Murphy & Klein Canada, which manages and owns a wide range of regional and national brands and concepts across Canada, Australia, and a number of Far East Asian countries.

Geoff has been actively involved in the discussions with Flying India and the Indian government and, after almost two years of negotiations and countless trips to Delhi, Geoff and his team had just finalized an agreement with Flying India. The deal involves a complete overhaul of Flying India's canteens and staff catering services and facilities in India. It was agreed by both partners that this process should take no longer than three years and will be jointly supervised by a senior management team member of Murphy & Klein Canada and Flying India's on-board catering unit.

Throughout the negotiations, Geoff has developed strong personal ties with Flying India, based on mutual trust and respect. Thus, it did not come as a surprise to Geoff and Andrew when Flying India expressed a strong preference for Geoff to be the Canadian part of the joint supervisory team.

Geoff has been with Murphy & Klein Canada for 21 years and worked his way up from being a waiter in several brand-owned concepts to a senior management position responsible for several national brands. Geoff has been married to Linda for 19 years and they have three children, aged 11, 14, and 17. The family lives in the country between Guelph and Toronto in a nice farmhouse that Geoff and Linda expect to have paid off in five years. Every day, Geoff commutes the 72 kilometres to the headquarters of Murphy & Klein Canada.

During his time with the company, Geoff has had only three short-term international assignments—in Detroit, Philadelphia, and London, UK. Despite his limited international experience at a professional level, Geoff and his family have been true globetrotters, using every school holiday for trips outside Canada and overseas.

While Geoff's family is in general very happy for Geoff and excited by a potential move to Delhi for three years, Geoff is thinking very carefully about the advantages and disadvantages of leaving Canada and moving to India. Geoff faces a number of financial and non-financial situations and challenges that he wants to discuss with Andrew next week.

Questions

1. If Geoff's whole family will be going with him to India, should Geoff maintain or sever his residency in Canada? Put yourself in Geoff's shoes and discuss the advantages and disadvantages of both options. In making your decision, also consider taxation implications.

2. If you were Geoff, would you prefer a going-rate approach or a balance-sheet approach to negotiate your base salary? What kind of approach to determine the base salary will Andrew opt for? Why?

3. Create an expatriate compensation worksheet that outlines a package proposal, complete with details of all components, currencies, etc. In your package, you need to consider Geoff's personal circumstances and the fact that the whole family will be going to India after having sold their house in Canada.

For more information about Canadians doing business in India, refer to KPMG's White Paper: *The Canadian Experience in India*, Toronto: KPMG, 2006.

Endnotes

1. See: J. Kerr & J. Slocum. (2005). Managing Corporate Culture through Reward Systems. *Academy of Management Executive, 19*(4), 130–138; and P. Evans, V. Pucik, & J. Barsoux. (2002). *The Global Challenge. A Framework for International Human Resource Management.* Boston: McGraw-Hill, particularly 327–341.

2. E. Locke. (2004). Linking Goals to Monetary Incentives. *Academy of Management Executive, 18*(4), 130–133; F. Lufthansa & A. Stajkovic. (1999). Reinforce for Performance: The Need to Go Beyond Pay and Even Rewards. *Academy of Management Executive, 13*(2), 49–57; and A. Pomeroy. (2006, April). Executive Briefing: Global Pay for Performance. *HR Magazine, 51*(4), 18.

3. Martin Hilb presents a well-written and thorough introduction to this interesting topic area in: *New Corporate Governance: Successful Board Management Tools* (2nd ed.). (2006). Berlin: Springer Publishing; a fascinating critique of contemporary executive pay and governance is provided by: L. Bebchuk & J. Fried. (2004). in *Pay Without Performance: The Unfulfilled Promise of Executive Compensation*, Cambridge, MA: Harvard University Press.

4. D. Kirby. (2004, December). Strategies for Assessing Global Markets. *Workspan, 47*(12), 44–45.

5. A. Wright. (2004, March). Don't Settle for Less—Global Compensation Programs Need Global Compensation Tools. *Employee Benefit Plan Review*, 14–18; D. Robb. (2006, March). Unifying Your Enterprise With a Global HR Portal. *HR Magazine, 51*(3), 109–115.

6. K. Chou & H. Risher. (2005, September). Point/Counterpoint: Pay for Performance. *Workspan, 48*(9), 28–37; S. Troutman & S. Ross. (2005, August). Rationalizing Global Incentive Pay Plans: Look At the Big Picture, Part One. *Workspan, 48*(8), 18–22; S. Troutman & S. Ross. (2005, September). Rationalizing Global Incentive Pay Plans: Look At the Big Picture, Part Two. *Workspan, 48*(9), 52–56; S. Troutman & S. Ross. (2005, October). Rationalizing Global Incentive Pay Plans: Look At the Big Picture, Part Three. *Workspan, 48*(10), 30–33. Also see: E. Krell. (2005, March). Evaluating Returns on Expatriates. *HR Magazine, 50*(3), 60–65; and S. Nurney. (2005, March). The Long and the Short of It: When Transitioning From Short-Term to Long-Term Expatriate Assignments, Consider the Financial Implications. *HR Magazine, 50*(3), 91–94.

7. K. Chou & H. Risher. (2005, September). Point/Counterpoint: Pay for Performance. *Workspan, 48*(9), 28–37; D. Green. (2005, October). In the Global Reward Environment One Size Doesn't Fit All. *Workspan, 48*(10), 34–38; and P. Gooderham, M. Morley, C. Brewster, & W. Mayrhofer. (2004). Human Resource Management: A Universal Concept? In C. Brewster, W. Mayrhofer, & M. Morley (Eds.), *Human Resource Management in Europe: Evidence of Convergence?* Oxford: Elsevier Butterworth-Heinemann, 1–26.

8. See: M. Hilb. (2006). *New Corporate Governance: Successful Board Management Tools* (2nd ed.). Berlin: Springer Publishing; L. Bebchuk & J. Fried. (2004). *Pay Without Performance: The Unfulfilled Promise of Executive Compensation*. Cambridge, MA: Harvard University Press; and A. Pomeroy. (2005, November). Executive Briefing: With Executive Comp, Go Your Own Way. *HR Magazine, 50*(1), 14; E. Poutsma, P. Ligthart, & R. Schouteten. (2005). Employee Share Schemes in Europe—The Influence of U.S. Multinationals. *Management Revue, 16*(1), 99–122; New Ideas—Compensation: Institutional Investors Say Executives Are Overpaid; Need Stronger Pay-For-Performance Strategies. (2006, February). *Workspan, 49*(2), 14; M. Hovy. (2005, February). Future Global Remuneration Strategies: Compliance, Defiance or Alignment? *Workspan, 48*(2), 34–38; M. Hoppe's. "An interview with Geert Hofstede." (2004). *Academy of Management Executive, 18*(1), 75–79, includes a provocative quote from Hofstede: "A present fad is the myth of the magical powers of top executives. The importance of management in general, and top management in particular, is overrated and top managers are overpaid. In many cases top managers have been brought in who turn out to be parasites on

their corporation rather than assets to its real success. The importance of the people who do the work is underrated, although this trend differs between countries and parts of the world" (78). Challenges indeed.

9. See: M. Hilb. (2006). *New Corporate Governance: Successful Board Management Tools* (2nd ed.). Berlin: Springer Publishing; and S. Tyson & F. Bournois (Eds.). (2005). *Top Pay and Performance: International and Strategic Approach*. Oxford: Elsevier Butterworth-Heinemann; New Ideas—Compensation: U.S. CEO and Director Pay On the Rise. (2006, January). *Workspan, 49*(1), 14; M. Thompson. (February, 2006). Investors Call For Better Disclosure of Executive Compensation in Canada. *Workspan Focus: Canada* (supplement to *Workspan*), 4–6; G. Morgenstern. (2006, April 10). Advice on Boss's Pay May Not Be So Independent. *New York Times*.

10. For a recent example and discussion of transparency in pay, see: D. McHugh. (2004, August 26). Nine German Firms Reveal Executive Pay. *Lexington [Kentucky] Herald Leader*, B8, and A. Engle & P. Dowling. (2004, June). *Global Rewards: Strategic Patterns in Complexity*. Conference proceedings of the International Conference of Human Resource Management in a Knowledge-Based Economy, Ljubljana, Slovenia.

11. For example, specialized firms such as P-E International in Britain provide a survey of worldwide living costs, while PricewaterhouseCoopers offers a worldwide consulting service called Global Human Resource Solutions, which covers a broad range of international HR issues.

12. C. Reynolds. (2000). *2000 Guide to Global Compensation and Benefits*. San Diego, CA.: Harcourt Professional Publishing, 3, 15–16.

13. Ibid., Chapters 5 and 28; and Y.-S. Hsu. (2007) Expatriate Compensation: Alternative Approaches and Challenges. *WorldatWork Journal, 16*(1), 15–19.

14. See: K. Lowe, J. Milliman, H. De Cieri, & P. Dowling. (2002, Spring). International Compensation Practices: A Ten-Country Comparative Analysis. *Human Resource Management, 41*(1), 45–66; S. Overman.(2000, March). In Sync: Harmonizing Your Global Compensation Plans May Be Done More "In Spirit" Than to the Letter. *HR Magazine, 45*(3), 86–92; K. Bensky. (2002, October). Developing a Workable Global Rewards System. *Workspan, 45*(10), 44–48; and E. Scott & R. Burke. (2007, March). Taming the Beast: Aligning Global Sales Incentives. *Workspan, 50*(3), 44–49.

15. M. Bloom & G. T. Milkovich. (1999). A SHRM Perspective on International Compensation and Rewards Systems. *Research in Personnel and Human Resource Management* (Supplement 4). Greenwich, CT: JAI Press, 283–303; V. Pucik. (1997, Spring). Human Resources in the Future: An Obstacle or a Champion of Globalization? *Human Resource Management, 36*(1), 163–167.

16. G. T. Milkovich & M. Bloom. (1998). Rethinking International Compensation. *Compensation and Benefits Review, 30*(1), 15–23.

17. H. J. Ruff & G. I. Jackson. (1974). Methodological Problems in International Comparisons of the Cost of Living. *Journal of International Business Studies, 5*(2), 57–67.

18. For the website of ORC Worldwide, go to www.orcinc.com.

19. For the website of ECA International, go to www.eca-international.com.

20. Ibid.

21. The experience of the first author in his research on expatriates and their families is that for some expatriates (particularly expatriates with little international experience), using home leave allowances for foreign travel can intensify feelings of homesickness. Without the benefit of returning home to mix with employees and friends, it is possible to idealize what they remember of their experience at work and home and fail to come to a measured judgment of what is good and bad in both their host and home environments. Overall, it would seem prudent for MNEs to take the view that home leave allowances should normally be used for the purpose they are provided—to give employees and their families the opportunity to renew

family and business ties, thereby increasing the probability of reduced adjustment problems when they are repatriated.

22. It is common in Asia and many developing countries in other regions for expatriates and local businesspeople to employ maids and cooks in their houses. As stated in an earlier endnote when discussing employment of drivers, it may be expected that an expatriate would employ servants and to not do so would be judged negatively, as this would be depriving local people of employment. Not surprisingly, this is one benefit that expatriate spouses miss when they return to their home country.

23. Canadian Employee Relocation Council. (2006, February). *CERC Spousal Benefits Survey*. Retrieved September 12, 2007, from www.cerc.ca/PDFs/2006_Spousal_ben_Survey.pdf

24. Trends in Expatriate Compensation. (1990, October 18). *Bulletin to Management*, 336.

25. The material in the tables describing the two main approaches to international compensation is based on various sources—the research and consulting experience of the first author and various discussions on this topic with a range of HR managers and consultants in Australia and the United States.

26. In interviews conducted by the first author with senior management of Australian firms operating internationally, repatriation difficulties was one of the major reasons cited for not following a going-rate approach with Australian expatriates.

27. For more detailed discussions of the concept of keeping the expatriate "whole," see: B. W. Teague. (1972). *Compensating Key Personnel Overseas*. New York: The Conference Board; and J. J. Martoccho. (2004). *Strategic Compensation* (3rd ed.). (Upper Saddle River, NJ: Pearson/Prentice-Hall.

28. This discussion of the balance-sheet approach follows the presentation in Chapter 5 of: *2000 Guide to Global Compensation and Benefits*. (2000). C. Reynolds (Ed.), San Diego, CA: Harcourt Professional Publishing.

29. See Chapter 3 of: T. J. Bergmann, V. G. Scarpello, & F. S. Hills. (1998). *Compensation Decision Making* (3rd ed.). Fort Worth, TX: Dryden Press, for a review of equity theory applied to compensation.

30. R. Cui. (2006). International Compensation: The Importance of Acting Globally. *WorldatWork Journal, 15*(4), 18–23.

31. Peggy Stuart. (1991, October). Global Payroll—A Taxing Problem. *Personnel Journal*, 80–90.

32. Ibid.; tax equalization can become a potential area of familial contention and more complex when dual-career families seek tandem international assignments, as presented by: G. Aldred. Dual-Career Support: Strategies for Designing and Providing Career Support for International Assignee Partners. (2006, February) *GMAC Strategic Advisor, 2*(6), 1–4 (www.gmacglobalrelocation.com).

33. Tax Burdens. (2000, November 2). *The Economist*. Retrieved July 18, 2003, from www.economist.com.

34. Towers Perrin. *Worldwide Total Remuneration*, 2005–2006, 32. Go to the Towers Perrin website (www.towers.com) for further information.

35. *Global Relocation Trends, 2002 Survey Report*. (2002). GMAC Global Relocation Services. Accessed through the Society for Human Resource Management Global Website (www.shrmglobal.org).

36. Schuler & Dowling. (1988). *Survey of SHRM/I Members*. New York: Stern School of Business, New York University.

37. Mercer Human Resource Consulting. *Cost of Living Survey—Worldwide Rankings, 2007*. Developed and conducted by Mercer Human Resource Consulting. Retrieved August 23, 2007, from www.canadiansresidentabroad.com/issues/summer07/article05.htm.

38. UBS AG, Wealth Management Research. (2006). *Price and Earnings: A Comparison of Purchasing Power Around the Globe*.

39. Ibid., 11.

40. C. Reynolds. (1988). Cost-Effective Compensation. *Topics in Total Compensation, 2*(1), 320.

41. G. Milkovich & J. Newman. (2005). *Compensation* (8th ed.). Boston: McGraw-Hill/Irwin, Chapter 16.

42. See: E. Schein. (1985). *Organizational Culture and Leadership*. San Francisco: Jossey-Bass.

43. P. Dowling, A. Engle, M. Festing & B. Mueller. (2005, June). *Complexity in Global Pay: A Meta-Framework*. Conference Proceedings of the 8th Conference on International Human Resource Management, Cairns, Australia. CD-ROM indexed by title and first author's name; and C. Brewster. (1999). Strategic Human Resource Management: The Value of Different Paradigms. *Management International Review, 39*(3), 45–64.

44. J. Barney. (1991). Firm Performance and Sustained Competitive Advantage. *Journal of Management, 17*(1), 99–120.

45. See: J. G. March & H. A. Simon. (1958). *Organizations*. New York: Wiley and Sons, Inc.

46. O. Williamson. (1984). Efficient Labor Organization. In F. Stephens (Ed.), *Firms, Organization and Labour*. London: MacMillan, 87–118.

47. As in: M. Armstrong & H. Murlis. (1991). *Reward Management: A Handbook of Remuneration Strategy and Practice*. London: Kogan Page Limited. Also see: G. T. Milkovich & M. Bloom. (1998). Rethinking International Compensation. *Compensation and Benefits Review, 30*(1), 15–23.

48. A. Engle & M. Mendenhall. (2004). Transnational Roles, Transnational Rewards: Global Integration In Compensation. *Employee Relations, 26*(6), 613–625.

49. L. Gomez-Mejia & T. Welbourne. (1991). Compensation Strategies in a Global Context. *Human Resource Planning, 14*(1), 29–41; R. Heneman, C. von Hippel, D. Eskew, & D. Greenberger. (2002). Alternative Rewards in Unionized Environments. In R. Heneman (Ed.), *Strategic Reward Management*. Greenwich, CT: Information Age, 131–152.

50. L. Gomez-Mejia & T. Welbourne. (1991), ibid.; M. Bloom & G. T. Milkovich. (1991). A SHRM Perspective on International Compensation and Reward Systems. *Research in Personnel and Human Resource Management* (Supplement 4). Greenwich, CT: JAI Press, 283–303.

51. G. T. Milkovich & J. Newman. (2005). *Compensation* (8th ed.). Boston: McGraw-Hill/Irwin.

52. M. Festing, J. Eidems, & S. Royer. (2007, April). Strategic Issues and Local Constraints in Transnational Compensation Strategies—An Analysis of Cultural, Institutional and Political Influences. *European Management Journal, 25*(2), 118–131.

53. M. Bloom, G. T. Milkovich, & A. Mitra. (2003). International Compensation: Learning From How Managers Respond to Variations in Local Host Contexts. *International Journal of Human Resource Management, 14*, 1350–1367. Also see: A. Mitra, M. Bloom, & G. T. Milkovich. (2002). Crossing a Raging River: Seeking Far-Reaching Solutions to Global Pay Challenges. *WorldatWork Journal, 11*(2), 6–17.

54. J. Boudreau, P. Ramstad, & P. Dowling. (2003). Global Talentship: Toward a Decision Science Connecting Talent to Global Strategic Success. In W. H. Mobley & P. W. Dorfman (Eds.), *Advances in Global Leadership, 3*. Oxford: Elsevier Science, 63–99. Also see: A. Engle, M. Mendenhall, R. Powers, & Y. Stedham. (2001). Conceptualizing the Global Competency Cube: A Transnational Model of Human Resource. *Journal of European Industrial Training, 25*(7), 346–353.

55. E. E. Lawler III. (2000, May). *Rewarding Excellence*. San Francisco: Jossey-Bass; C. Garvey. (2002). Steer Teams With the Right Pay. *HR Magazine, 47*(5), 71–78.

56. G. T. Milkovich & M. Bloom. (1998). Rethinking International Compensation. *Compensation and Benefits Review, 30*(1), 15–23.

57. Ibid. Also see: A. Engle & M. Mendenhall. (2004). Transnational Roles and Transnational Rewards: Global Integration in Compensation. *Employee Relations, 26*(6), 613–625.

58. G. T. Milkovich & J. Newman. (2005). *Compensation* (8th ed.). Boston: McGraw-Hill/Irwin, 75–77, 80–81.

59. Ibid.

60. H. Timmons. (2003, May 31). Pay Debated at British Bank's Meeting. *The New York Times*.

61. A. Katsoudas, S. Olsen, & P. Weems. (2007). New Trends in Global Equity Rewards. *Workspan, 50*(3), 28–33.

62. See: P. Dowling, A. Engle, M. Festing, & B. Mueller. (2005, June). *Complexity in Global Pay: A Meta-Framework*. Conference Proceedings of the 8th Conference on International Human Resource Management, Cairns, Australia. CD-ROM indexed by title and first author's name; M. Bloom, G. T. Milkovich, & A. Mitra. (2003). International Compensation: Learning From How Managers Respond to Variations in Local Host Contexts. *International Journal of Human Resource Management, 14*, 1350–1367.

Chapter 8

Re-Entry and Career Issues

COMING HOME?

The following account by an expatriate in his own words introduces our chapter and the discussion about the challenges faced by international assignees, their families, and their companies in the post-assignment phase of international assignments. As repatriation raises issues for both the expatriate (and his or her family) and the multinational, some of which may be connected to events that occurred during the international assignment, we will treat the post-assignment stage as part of the international assignment.

In the summer of 2005 the family and I returned to Canada to begin a new chapter in our lives. The sun had inevitably set on a life of globe hopping that saw our family relocate on average every two years. . . . Ironically, a Canadian would never expect to experience culture shock in their homeland but after fifteen years abroad you wish for some of the things you left behind. The truth is: our children were not truly Canadian. Our daughter was born in Lund, Sweden, and our son was less than two years old when we set out on our odyssey.

As parents we assumed that our Canadian-passport-bearing children would adapt rather quickly but this was not the case. Our daughter was lost with the Canadian currency and the numerous nicknames for the coinage, nickel, dime, quarter, looney and toonie. Dress codes were scaled down from what they were accustomed to and some fads just seemed out of place, for instance, pyjamas in class!

The calendar was for our son the first sign that customs were different in North America. Commencing the week on Sunday rather than on Monday was a source of confusion for him for some time. The orientation of the date still stops us in our tracks when completing forms. But perhaps the most amusing observation was when our son asked us: what were the tall grey wooden buildings in the fields? "You mean the barns?" we responded in disbelief.

Language as we know can be a barrier. In this case I'm referring to mumbling teenagers! Who would have guessed that our teenage son would experience difficulty in understanding his peers? It took a hearing test to convince him that he was not going deaf, but rather his friends were not enunciating clearly enough. Our daughter was at a loss as to why the school French curriculum lagged behind that in Sweden when at least officially

Canada is a bilingual (French and English) country. We explained that an appreciation for languages comes with exposure and a desire to assimilate. So what are our children wishing for today? You guessed it, greener pastures by way of Europe to complete their studies. For ourselves: it's winter without snow!

Source: Bellefleur, D. (2007, Spring). Culture Shock in Canada. *Canadians Resident Abroad Magazine*. Retrieved August 20, 2007, from www.canadiansresidentabroad.com

Introduction

It is evident from the preceding chapters that there have been numerous advances in our understanding and knowledge of the issues surrounding the management and support of expatriates in terms of recruitment and selection, pre-departure training, and compensation. As Figure 8.1 indicates, the expatriation process also includes **repatriation**: the activities involved in bringing the expatriate back to the home country.

repatriation

activities involved in bringing the expatriate back to the home country

While it is now more widely recognized by managers and academics that repatriation needs careful managing, attention to this aspect of international assignments has been somewhat belated. In the past, the unpredictable and incremental nature of globalization led to reactive assignments, and re-entry to the firm was left unspoken or dealt with informally on an ad hoc basis. As more expatriates completed their assignments, firms were faced with organizing these returns in a more planned pattern that allowed for a more strategic and complete use of the returning employee's newfound experiences and insights, while at the same time easing the repatriates' return to their "home" country and firm.[1]

Re-entry into the home country presents new challenges. The repatriate (returning person) is coping with what has been termed re-entry shock, or reverse culture shock. While people frequently expect life in a new country to be different, they may be less prepared for homecoming to present problems

FIGURE 8.1

Expatriation Includes Repatriation

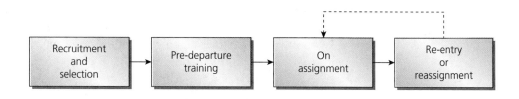

of adjustment. As a consequence, it can be a traumatic experience for some,[2] even more than what was encountered in the foreign location. From the multinational's perspective, repatriation is frequently considered as the final stage in the expatriation process (as indicated in Figure 8.1), but the multinational's ability to attract future expatriates is affected by the manner in which it handles repatriation.[3]

In this chapter, we focus on the key factors associated with re-entry, including how the repatriation process is handled by the individual and the receiving work unit, as well as family adjustment. We will also explore how repatriation affects the successful "closure" of the foreign assignment, its impact on future career paths within the multinational, and the effect on staff mobility. The reasons for the international assignment and its outcomes are assessed—that is, how the multinational recoups its investment in human capital and the process of knowledge and competence transfer on re-entry. It should be noted that what is written about the re-entry process centres on the traditional expatriate assignment, based predominantly on experiences of repatriated PCNs.

The Repatriation Process

Typically, on completion of an international assignment, the multinational brings the expatriate back to the home country, although not all international assignments end with a transfer home. Some expatriates may agree to become part of the multinational's international team of managers—as indicated by the dotted arrow in Figure 8.1—and thus have consecutive overseas assignments. In the event that one of these consecutive assignments involves the expatriate returning to the home-country operations, it will be treated as just another posting rather than re-entry or repatriation. For example, John Jones is moved from his home base in the Canadian parent operations to Japan for two years. He then spends four years in China, followed by one year in headquarters in Canada before moving on to another position in the English operations. That one-year period spent at headquarters is not treated as re-entry back into the home-country operations. In contrast, Mary Smith has spent three years working in China and is repatriated back to Canada into a defined position at headquarters.

As outlined in Figure 8.2, repatriation may be seen to encompass three phases. First, before the global assignment, MNEs may act to assign home sponsors or mentors and hold them responsible for keeping the expatriate in touch with changing conditions in the home country. Ideally, such sponsors might have relevant expatriate assignments as part of their own work history. Web-based indices of relevant national, regional, industrial, or firm websites may be provided. These ongoing communication protocols may be formal or informal.[4] By initially creating this network of personal and media links, the expatriate may be able to keep up with the changes in the home country, work unit, and the larger firm, as well as changes in the local or regional community while on assignment. This more systematic updating

FIGURE 8.2

Repatriation Activities and Practices

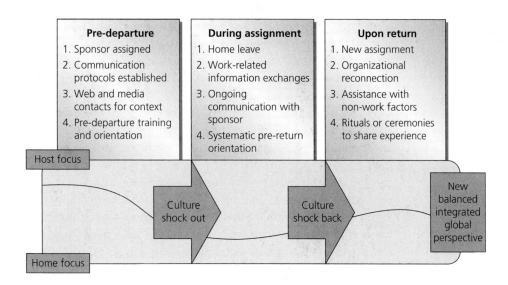

may contribute to more realistic expectations on the part of the expatriate, reducing culture shock on return.

Second, during the assignment, home leave, work-related information exchanges, sponsor communications, and a systematic pre-return orientation process can all facilitate realistic expectations and ease the return. Allowing for periodic returns to the home country will help the expatriate and her or his family to reconnect with firm employees, family, and friends and catch up with changing business conditions. Some MNEs allow their expatriates to use their holidays to visit more exotic, once-in-a-lifetime locations closer to the host country.[5] In some cases, this is not a wise policy for the employer as by doing this, some expatriates lose their perspective of how things may be changing in their home country and may develop a somewhat "rose-coloured glasses" view of life back at home.[6] Work-related information exchanges are part of any expatriate assignment. Through these regular and ongoing task-related communications, rich information about changes in home personnel, power politics, strategic developments, and less work-related updates can be passed on to the expatriate. Ongoing and regular communications with the sponsor during the assignment and a systematic pre-return orientation will be discussed in detail later in the chapter. These two activities may become more intense in the months or weeks immediately prior to the return.

Finally, on the expatriate's return, a series of immediately practical and more long-term activities combine during what is normally a very restricted time frame. Multinational firms can be less effective in their use of expatriates by either being too vague and unfocused about repatriates, or they can try to be too efficient by expecting the returning expatriate to jump back into the home assignment before the issues and processes related to return are resolved—literally before their bags are unpacked.[7] Practical issues on return relate to housing—for longer-term assignments, homes are sometimes sold and new houses and short-term accommodations must be found. Schools for children, new shopping patterns, and family survival activities in new locations are required. Expatriates must be assigned a new work space and given a whole new orientation to the MNE. The new job assignment and local work group must be introduced and understood. On a broader scale, the repatriate must reconnect with the local social network of the MNE, and personal and career dynamics may have to be adjusted in new and potentially unpredictable ways.[8] Changes and adjustments for societal, firm, and job dynamics on the personal, family, job, organizational, and career levels are involved in this final stage.

Note the two stages of culture shock represented at the bottom in Figure 8.2. The overemphasis on a home focus, at the expense of a focus on the host assignment, can lead to problems with performance on assignment and premature return, as outlined in Chapters 4 and 5. At the same time, an overemphasis on host activities, at the expense of some awareness of changes at home, can lead to a second culture shock on return. The goal of any set of expatriation/repatriation practices should result in the successful integration of home and host experiences. Achieving this more balanced set of transitions is not always easy. For example, in 1996, Harzing[9] conducted a comprehensive survey of 287 subsidiaries of nearly 100 different multinationals. She reported that 52 percent of sampled firms experienced repatriate re-entry problems. The latter could provoke staff turnover, in that repatriates may leave the organization (for more detail, see IHRM Today 8.1).

Considering the information provided in IHRM Today 8.1, it seems that an increasing number of firms are seemingly ignoring the fate of repatriates. One of the reasons may lie in the following comment by the GMAC 2004 report's authors:

> To a great extent, this [increase] can be explained by the nature of the expatriate-tracking process itself. In general, expatriates are tracked in order to apply and record specially developed payroll and benefits packages and to comply with tax-reporting requirements. Once expatriates complete their assignments, these considerations expire. Consequently the key motivation for tracking them also disappears. The concept of tracking the employment status of expatriates after they complete their assignments is nonetheless a valuable one in its own right.[10]

Given the reasons why international assignments are used, the direct and indirect costs involved, and the various roles that are assigned to expatriates—as discussed in Chapter 4—it seems important to understand why re-entry is problematic yet of seemingly less importance to researchers and practitioners than other stages of the international assignment. To this end,

Repatriate Turnover

The GMAC Global Relocation Services global surveys* provide data on repatriate turnover. Firms in the 2006 survey indicated that 23 percent of repatriates left the company within the first year. The 2004 survey reported that 13 percent of repatriates left within the first year, and 10 percent within two years. This compares with the 2002 survey, where responding firms admitted a 44 percent expatriate turnover rate, half of whom left their firms within the first year of re-entry. The 2006 survey notes that, for surveyed firms, retaining expatriate talent remains a considerable challenge. Explanations for repatriate turnover ranged, as follows:

- "Employees with international experience are more likely to leave the company" (2002 survey).
- "Most expatriates leave to pursue other expatriate assignments that they view as beneficial to their careers" (2004 survey).

- "Expatriates anticipate a lack of attractive positions to return to in the home country and seek out better opportunities outside their company" (2006 survey).

It should be remembered that 39 percent of the multinationals in the 2002 GMAC survey did not know their expatriate attrition rate, and this figure almost doubled in the 2004 survey, with 69 percent of responding firms indicating that they did not know when expatriates left. Given this, the percentage of exiting employees could be higher.

Source: *GMAC Global Relocation Services, U.S. National Foreign Trade Council, & SHRM Global Forum. *Global Relocation Trends: 2002 Survey Report*, *2004 Survey Report*, and *2006 Survey Report*. These reports are available at the GMAC Global Relocation Services website: www.gmacglobalrelocation.com/survey.html

we now examine factors that may contribute to re-entry problems, considering the process first from the individual's perspective and then from the multinational's viewpoint.

Individual Reactions to Re-Entry

As with cross-cultural adjustment, the re-entry process is a complex interaction of several factors. It is possible to group the major factors that have been identified as moderators of re-entry readjustment into two categories—job-related factors and social factors—as depicted in Figure 8.3, which we now discuss.

Job-Related Factors

Job-related factors centre around future employment prospects as a consequence of the international assignment, value being placed on the person's international experience, coping with new role demands, and the loss of status and financial benefits on re-entry. We will examine these factors in turn.

Career Anxiety

When surveyed, expatriates consistently list two motivators for accepting an international assignment: career advancement and financial gain.[11] It is not surprising then that a prime factor in re-entry is career anxiety. This can

FIGURE 8.3

Factors Influencing Repatriate Adjustment

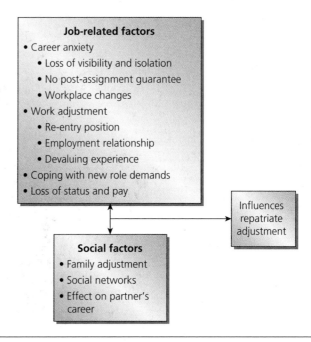

emerge prior to the physical relocation and can affect productivity during the last couple of months of the international assignment, as the person contemplates the re-entry process. So, what prompts career anxiety? The causes range among the following and are often interrelated: no post-assignment guarantee of employment, fear of a loss of visibility, and changes in the home workplace.

W(W)W 8.1

W(W)W 8.2

NO POST-ASSIGNMENT GUARANTEE OF EMPLOYMENT The lack of a guarantee of post-assignment employment is becoming a reality for the majority of those on international assignments. For example, 68 percent of multinational respondents in the 2004 GMAC survey did not provide post-assignment employment guarantees. This figure is similar to that of the 2002 survey, where 70 percent of respondents did not give a guarantee. One respondent in the 2002 survey explained: "We provide no guarantee for employment. We do guarantee to bring the person home, and if a suitable position is not readily available, they have three months."[12] In other words, repatriation more often leads to redundancy, as the 1990s trend away from re-entry job guarantees continues. A 1998 survey by Price Waterhouse (now PricewaterhouseCoopers)[13] reported a decrease in post-assignment job guarantees from 69 percent in their 1995 survey to 46 percent in 1998.

Studies that break down general trends into regions and countries reveal some differences. The Tung–Arthur Andersen 1997 survey of 49 North

American firms reported that the majority (almost 60 percent) did not guarantee a position at home on successful completion of an overseas assignment.[14] In her study of international HR practices in German and U.K. firms, Marx[15] found that the majority of German firms offered a guaranteed job on return from a foreign assignment, whereas the majority of U.K. firms admitted that they were not able to offer jobs upon repatriation. Marx suggests that Continental European firms may have to provide such guarantees in order to attract expatriates. However, a respondent in the 2002 GMAC GRS survey explained that: "Our approach depends on the base [sending] country. Europeans have a labor contract, and the U.S. does not."[16] Given the lack of job security, it is not surprising that career anxiety commences prior to homecoming and acts as a readjustment moderator upon re-entry if career outcomes are not realized.

FEAR OF A LOSS OF VISIBILITY Returning expatriates might fear that the period overseas has caused a loss of visibility and isolation—as captured by the phrase "out of sight, out of mind."[17] Again, this fear can commence toward the end of the international assignment, as the person begins to consider the re-entry process, and depends on various elements: the amount of contact that the person has had with the home organization; the position level concerned; and whether the person is aware well in advance of the availability or type of re-entry job waiting in the home country. Lack of information may increase the level of anxiety, leaving the person with a distinct impression that the company has not planned adequately, or that a mediocre or makeshift job awaits.[18] If there is no post-assignment job guarantee, the anxiety level will be understandably high.

CHANGES IN THE HOME WORKPLACE Anxiety can be exacerbated by informal communication from home-based colleagues about organizational changes. It may be that the multinational is in the process of a major restruc-turing, the aftermath of a merger or acquisition, or sale of divisions or business units. These changes are usually accompanied by job-shedding. Knowledge of such changes and potential or real job loss naturally will add to the level of anxiety, particularly if the expatriate does not have a guaranteed job upon repatriation.

Another issue here is that restructuring can affect the host-country operations—such as closure of a plant, dissolving of a joint venture, or merging of operations post-acquisition. This may leave the expatriate stranded or force an early repatriation that has not been planned.[19] If similar changes are also occurring in the home country, then availability of suitable positions will have been reduced. One repatriate who was placed in such a position explains:

> The division I worked for was reorganized, and the subsidiary I worked for was placed under stringent cost-cutting guidelines, which forced me to return earlier than anticipated. My re-entry was very cold, with little support in finding a job since previous management had been fired.[20]

Work Adjustment

Black, Gregersen, and Mendenhall[21] argue that work adjustment has an important impact on a person's intent to stay with the organization. Career anxiety is one moderating factor, but others may also lead to readjustment problems: the employment relationship, the re-entry position, and the value to the firm of overseas experience.

THE EMPLOYMENT RELATIONSHIP An individual's career expectations may be based on clear messages sent by top management to the effect that an international assignment is a condition for career progression. That is, verbal or written statements such as: "We are an international company and we need internationally oriented people who have worked in our overseas facilities." These pronouncements can be made in the context of the need for a global orientation or mindset where a definite link is made between international experience and global managers.

Perceptions regarding expected career outcomes also are influenced by comments made by HR or line managers during the recruitment and selection stage. For example, the line manager may suggest to a younger employee: "You should volunteer for that international assignment. It would be a smart career move at this stage in your life." If others have been promoted upon repatriation, it may be perceived to be the norm, thus reinforcing the perception that international assignments lead to promotion on re-entry.

For these reasons, the person believes promotion should follow based on successful performance while abroad, and if the re-entry position does not eventuate within a reasonable timeframe, then career anxiety is justified. A study by Lazarova and Caligiuri[22] of 58 repatriates from four North American-based companies found that repatriation support practices are positively related to perceptions of organizational support, and these affect repatriates' intention to stay or to leave the organization. The psychological contract is a moderator of re-entry readjustment as well as on-assignment adjustment and performance. The repatriate may believe that the performance overseas warrants promotion, that signals were given by the organization that effective performance in the international assignment would result in career advancement. When the expected promotion does not materialize, the repatriate may feel there is no option but to exit the organization. It is important to note that the psychological contract concerns perceptions and expectations, complicated by the fact that the MNE representative making statements about career outcomes prior to the international assignment is not necessarily the person who is responsible for re-entry decisions about job placement and promotion.

RE-ENTRY POSITION It would seem that, for some, promotion is a primary issue, as the following comment by a repatriate reveals:[23]

> Get a promotion before the return! You are forgotten while over-
> seas, and you start all over on the return. The promotions go to

people who have been in a position for extended periods; nothing done overseas counts in this company.

Fears surrounding future employment and career development can materialize. Peers are promoted ahead of the repatriated manager, and the repatriate sometimes is placed in a position that is, in effect, a demotion. The situation may be exacerbated if the repatriate had held a senior position in the foreign location and now finds himself (or herself) at a less senior level. As a consequence, the re-entry position is frequently judged by whether it matches the repatriate's career expectation, particularly when the international assignment has caused considerable family disruption, such as a forced break in the career of the accompanying partner, or difficulties experienced with the education of children involved. Put simply, the repatriate wants the end to justify the means, so that the family unit is fully compensated for the sacrifices it has made in expectation of career advancement. Suutari and Brewster, in their study of Finnish expatriates,[24] report that most repatriates left only after they felt that they had given the company sufficient time to find more suitable positions for them. These authors identified an "external pull factor": External recruiters were actively "headhunting" repatriates either during the assignment or on their return.

A question put to responding firms in the GMAC surveys concerned the career impact of international experience. Firms were asked to compare the careers of expatriates with those of employees without international experience, with the results shown in Table 8.1. The GMAC 2002 report's authors made the following comment:

> We find it disturbing that each year, a high percentage of respondents are not sure about the impact that an international assignment has on an expatriate's career. How can one make a convincing case for accepting an assignment if one cannot determine the impact that the assignment will have on an expatriate's career?

TABLE 8.1

Career Impacts of International Assignments

	2005 Survey	2004 Survey	2002 Survey
Expatriates were promoted faster	37 per cent	34 per cent	36 per cent
Expatriates obtained new positions in the company more easily	36 per cent	35 per cent	33 per cent
Expatriates changed employers more often	24 per cent	23 per cent	23 per cent
Not sure about the career link to international experience	40 per cent	40 per cent	35 per cent

A similar comment was made regarding the 2004 survey results: "It was disturbing that so many respondents lack the information needed to make a convincing case for accepting these assignments."[25] This sentiment was echoed in the 2005 PricewaterhouseCoopers report on global trends in policies and practices related to international assignments: "Further research into why [repatriate] assignees seek alternative employment should be high on an organizations agenda."[26]

Stroh[27] found that the best predictors of repatriate turnover were whether the company had a career development plan and whether the company was undergoing turbulence, such as downsizing. She argues that lower rates of repatriate turnover are more likely in organizations that planned for the repatriation of their employees and that provided career development planning for them. We will return to the career aspects later in this chapter.

VALUE TO THE FIRM OF OVERSEAS EXPERIENCE Career progression is important, but to be promoted on re-entry signifies that international experience is important and valued by the organization. Consider the following comments made by a number of expatriates:

> I think that our corporation can benefit from the experience I gained abroad, but no one asked me for any information. It is as if I never went.[28]

> When I came home, I was assigned to a newly created, undefined staff job, where I had no friends, no contacts, and no access to management.[29]

> The problem is when one comes back from an international assignment it may happen that there is no position for the person to return to. Sometimes it is necessary to be a supplementary person in a department and one has to wait for a job. That is not very nice to come back to.[30]

> They didn't bother to say "thank you for the job you did in [country X]." And quite frankly, it was such a tremendous job, it was a huge, huge, *huge* project, and it went quite well.[31]

As these comments reveal, the re-entry position may be in a less challenging job with reduced responsibility and status than that held either during the international assignment or prior to the period overseas; in "holding" positions, such as a task force or project team; or in temporary positions, engaged in duties that do not appear to exploit their newly gained international expertise.[32] For some, the return position is frequently a lateral move rather than a promotion.[33] The positions do not seem to be related to, nor draw on, experiences and skills the person may have acquired during the international assignment—giving the impression that such experience is devalued.

The reactions of work colleagues can further the sense of devaluation of international experience. Suggestions can be met with xenophobic responses[34] along the lines of "you are at home now," or "it won't work here." Some repatriates report a general lack of interest. For example, Stroh, Gregersen, and Black[35] quote an interviewee: "Returning repatriates should be warned about the extreme lack of interest Americans usually show in anything outside their own world."

Coping with New Role Demands

Along with career issues, a mismatch of expectations affects the repatriate's perception of the role associated with network position. A role is the organized set of behaviours that are assigned to a particular position. Although an individual may affect how a role is interpreted and performed, the role itself is predetermined and usually defined in the job description.[36] Effective role behaviour is an interaction between the concept of the role, the interpretation of expectations, the person's ambitions, and the norms inherent in the role. Figure 8.4 illustrates the elements of the repatriate's role as a focus for a discussion of the readjustment issues related to role behaviour.

Readjustment problems may occur because, although the repatriate is attempting to function back in the home country, his or her role conception remains influenced by that of the foreign assignment. The message being sent (denoted by the direction of the arrow in Figure 8.4) by the home company (the role sender) has crossed the cultural boundary. The person has been operating for some time in the foreign location, and consequently may have made significant changes to his or her role behaviour.[37] For example, a Canadian working in Indonesia may have altered his managerial style and become more authoritarian, based on messages sent by the foreign subsidiary; or it could be that the time in the Indonesian subsidiary has reinforced an authoritarian tendency.

FIGURE 8.4

The Repatriate Role

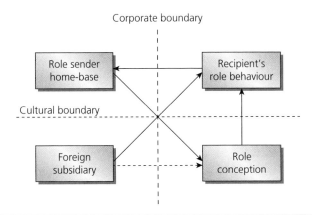

Source: Adapted from: Torbiörn, I. (1985). The Structure of Managerial Roles in Cross-Cultural Settings. *International Studies of Management & Organization, 15*(1).

Conflict is likely to occur if the repatriate does not resume the managerial behaviour appropriate to the Canadian context upon return.

Torbiörn[38] contends that as long as the repatriate's "identity and basic values are still bound up in the culture of the home country, the strain of adjusting to conditions at home will be slight." However, while the repatriate may retain the role conception and the cultural norms regarding behaviour appropriate to that role, the foreign subsidiary's influence may linger, indicated by the dotted arrow in Figure 8.4, and what is communicated to the home company, in the form of role behaviour, will not conform to the home company's expectations. As shown by the broken line between the role sender and role recipient boxes at the top of Figure 8.4, there is a "corporate boundary" to be crossed in the communication of the role conception between the role recipient (the repatriate) and the role sender (the home company). The role sender, however, may not recognize the cultural and corporate boundaries that affect the repatriate's role conception and role behaviour, and thus unwittingly contribute to readjustment problems.

While research in this area is limited, in their study of 125 repatriate managers from four large U.S. multinationals, Black and Gregersen[39] found that role clarity, rather than role conflict, was significantly related to work adjustment. Discussing these findings, the authors explain that role conflict may be an important factor in expatriate assignments due to conflicting role signals between home office and the foreign subsidiary, whereas role conflict on return most likely stems from conflicting job signals from different individuals within the home operation. They add: "While there are advantages in providing jobs that are clear and free from role conflicts, it is perhaps more important for firms to provide clear jobs upon repatriation." In other words, role clarity emerges as an aspect of healthy repatriation.

A further contribution to our understanding of repatriate readjustment comes from Black and Gregersen's finding regarding role discretion. **Role discretion** refers to the freedom to adjust the work role to fit the individual, making it easier for the person to utilize past, familiar behaviour, thus reducing the level of uncertainty in the new job, which assists adjustment. They found that, for their sample, role discretion had a positive impact on adjustment, a finding that appears to confirm earlier studies on the relationship between role discretion, role clarity, and work adjustment.[40] In a later survey of Finnish repatriates, Gregersen found fairly consistent results in terms of role clarity and role discretion with those of American repatriates. He comments:

> The consistent results between American and Finnish managers suggest that greater role discretion upon repatriation seems to facilitate repatriation adjustment. In addition, the importance of role clarity to work adjustment suggests that Finnish and American firms may want to provide clearer jobs upon repatriation.[41]

However, it would appear that, for U.S. companies at least, role clarity and role discretion remain repatriation issues. These issues emerged as being important in Baughn's[42] survey of U.S. repatriates. The category "reduced

role discretion

the freedom to adjust the work role to fit the individual

responsibility and autonomy on the job" was ranked second, after "career advancement," as a major concern upon repatriation for respondents in the Tung–Arthur Andersen survey mentioned earlier. These findings lend added support to the importance of role clarity, role conflict, and role discretion in work adjustment after re-entry.[43]

Further, the above studies suggest that the corporate boundary in Figure 8.4 may be stronger than the "cultural boundary" in terms of the repatriate role. Limited support for this conclusion comes from the results of a study by Forster,[44] who surveyed 124 employees recently repatriated back to the United Kingdom. Analysis of the responses indicated five predictors for repatriation maladjustment (in ranked order):

- Length of time abroad.
- Unrealistic expectations of job opportunities in the home company.
- Downward job mobility.
- Reduced work status.
- Negative perceptions of the help and support provided by employers during and after repatriation.

Job-related factors were found to be more important than non-work and family factors.

A point that is not directly addressed, but may help to explain the inter-relationships between the variables found significant in the above studies, is that the period overseas does alter the person. The experiences of living and working in another country can affect the person's self-efficacy (the degree to which an individual believes that he or she can execute a set of behaviours). As well, the expatriate position commonly involves a more demanding job position. Learning how to successfully cope with the various challenges encountered during the foreign assignment may give the person more self-confidence, along with a broader perspective.[45] These changes may be subtle for some people; for others, they can be profound and may be influenced by factors such as length of time spent abroad, country of assignment, and individual differences such as age and personality. As a result, the reverse culture shock experienced by the repatriate may be as much a function of the degree to which the person has altered, as to the changes that have occurred in the home country, as indicated in Figure 8.5.

Likewise identity has been recognized as an aspect linking international assignments, career development, and repatriation,[46] although there has been limited research on how a repatriate's identity construction is positively or negatively related to the international experience. What is evident from anecdotal evidence, however, is that repatriates note a change in perspective post-assignment. The process of redefining oneself is not restricted to professional competence but may include self-development aspects such as self-confidence, flexibility, and tolerance. The challenge is to align this "new self" to expectations that organization and family members have that are based on what the repatriate considers as "what I was before, not whom I have become."

FIGURE 8.5

The Readjustment Challenge

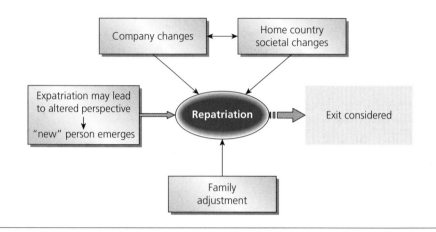

The period of time spent overseas is an important aspect. The longer the person is away from the home country, the more likely there will be readjustment problems on return.[47] Another contributing factor to re-entry adjustment may be the length of time that the repatriate is kept in a so-called "holding pattern." This may be acceptable as an interim measure, but the longer repatriates are treated as temporary, the more likely they are to become anxious about the future, and have less commitment to the home work unit and the parent organization.[48]

Other workplace changes may affect readjustment. The repatriate often encounters changes in the formal and informal information channels in the home organization, particularly if there has been widespread restructuring and downsizing. Technological advances in the multinational may render the repatriate's functional skills and knowledge outdated. Unless there was sufficient contact with the expatriate during the international assignment, the person will be unprepared for these changes. When coupled with other job-related problems, these changes make work adjustment a difficult process.

Loss of Status and Pay

Usually, at least for PCNs, the international assignment is a form of promotion. It carries greater autonomy, a broader area of responsibility (because of the smaller size of the overseas subsidiary), and, at the top-management level, a prominent role in the local community. The result is higher status. Some expatriates use the term *kingpin* to describe their positions overseas. On return, the repatriate is expected to resume his or her position within the home company, with the loss of status and autonomy. In effect, the repatriate is treated as just another company executive. This shift may cause readjustment problems. For example, a repatriate can find that, whereas in the foreign operation he was the key decision maker, now he has to seek permission from a superior.

Compounding the problem is the loss of expatriate premiums. As Conway states: "More commonly, employees are brought home to resume life on a scale that may be significantly less comfortable than what they had grown used to abroad. Pay is usually lower in absolute terms."[49] A similar finding is reported by the Tung–Arthur Andersen survey referred to earlier. However, in their study of 21 U.S. firms, Napier and Petersen[50] found that most of the repatriates in their sample felt that their personal finances were better *after* the assignment than *before*, even though they were not as favourable as before the overseas assignment. Napier and Petersen explain that the total compensation package received while on assignment was greater than before, thus allowing the person to return to the United States with increased savings.

Another contributing factor is that the returning manager may no longer be able to afford to buy a home similar to the one sold a few years before. Canadian house price surveys such as the quarterly Royal LePage reports provide average house prices and price changes to the previous year for different housing types in different markets across Canada (see IHRM Today 8.2).

A U.S. study suggests that the current practice of providing expatriates with better housing during an international assignment than they had at home may contribute to repatriation problems. That is, a drop in the standard of housing conditions has a negative impact on the adjustment of U.S.

IHRM Today 8.2

Canada's House Prices

For quite some time now, Canadians have been experiencing a major housing boom, with cumulative real price gains of more than 60 percent. Despite a "few cracks," according to the Scotiabank Group *Real Estate Trends 2007* report, Canadian housing conditions still remain solid:

> The fundamentals underpinning Canada's housing market are still quite good. Unemployment is low, immigration is high and apartment vacancy rates are tight. There is little evidence of overbuilding or speculative buying. The industry has relatively little direct exposure to subprime lending, with these loans accounting for only about 5% of domestic mortgages in recent years compared with about 20% in the United States.

Reports such as the Royal LePage second-quarter survey of Canadian house prices in 2007 show price changes over a one-year period. Take Toronto and the Greater Toronto Area as an example: The price for a standard townhouse in Toronto's Bloor West Village had risen 63.1 percent, from $260,000 in 2006 to $424,000 in April–June 2007. Many other areas in Toronto and Greater Toronto have seen price increases of between 5 to 10 percent: In 2006, a standard townhouse located in Mississauga cost $220,000—the same house was worth $231,000 a year later. Central Scarborough is one of the relatively few areas that experienced a price decrease (9.3 percent).

Sources: Royal LePage. *Survey of Canadian House Prices, Second Quarter 2007*, 40. Retrieved September 20, 2007, from http://docs.rlpnetwork.com/hps/Q2_2007_HPS_EN.pdf; and A. Warren. (2007, September 13). Real Estate Trends. *Scotia Economics*, 1–9.

repatriates.[51] This creates somewhat of a dilemma for U.S. HR managers and their counterparts in other countries where repatriates have similar adjustment experiences. As we discussed in Chapter 5, the amount of support provided for the expatriate and family is critical to adjustment and intent to stay in the foreign location, but may have a negative effect on re-entry.

Social Factors

RPC 8.2

The familiar surrounds of the home environment may ease the transition, or at least the cultural adjustment will not be as demanding as that confronted in the foreign country. However, the international experience can distance the repatriate, and his or her family, socially and psychologically. If the expatriate position gave the person a high profile, involving interaction with the social and economic elite, the return home may bring with it some measure of social disappointment, thus reinforcing the *kingpin* syndrome. The financial loss of the compensation premium, housing subsidy, and related benefits can exacerbate these feelings.

Family Adjustment

It must be stressed here that, when spouses, partners, and children are involved, each family member experiences his or her own readjustment problems. For some returnees, re-entry is a shock. It is as if they had pressed the "pause" button as they flew out of the country, and expected life at home to remain in the "freeze frame." Re-entry reminds them that life is not static. Others, as a coping behaviour in the foreign location, may have glamorized life back home and now have to come to terms with reality, to accept the negative as well as the positive aspects of home. For example, the foreign country may have appeared to be more expensive in relative terms, but on repatriation, the family is confronted with a higher level of inflation in the home country than was previously the case. Conversely, life at home may now seem dull and unexciting in contrast, and the family unit may begin to glamorize the life they left behind in the foreign location. These reactions can be compounded if the family income has been reduced on repatriation. Of course, the income level depends on whether spouses/partners worked while in the foreign location, and how quickly they find suitable jobs on repatriation.

Social Networks

Naturally, impressions generated about changes in the home country may depend on how effectively the family has been able to keep up to date with events back home. One could expect that the coverage by satellite television news channels such as CNN and BBC World, along with global-oriented newspapers, make it easier for Canadian, U.S., and U.K. expatriates to follow their home events, than those coming from smaller countries such as Australia or the Netherlands. However, with the rapid advances in Internet, wireless, and mobile phone technology, digital cameras, and e-mail, it is now significantly easier to stay in touch, although this depends on the availability of, and access to, television cable networks, computer facilities, and Internet connections in the foreign location. (See IHRM Today 8.3.)

Re-establishing social networks can also be difficult, especially if the family has been repatriated to a different province, state, or community in the home country. Families who return to their previous domestic locations often find that friends have moved away. Repatriated spouses may find their friends have re-entered the workforce and are no longer available for social activities. There can be a sense of loss as the level of attention and support from the multinational is withdrawn: "The phone does not ring. We went from a very close [expatriate] community to here where everyone is very busy with their own lives."[52] Many repatriates report that people show little interest in hearing about their expatriate experiences, which can make conversation uncomfortable.[53] As one U.S. repatriate relates: "It was very difficult discussing my experiences with my co-workers and friends because Americans refuse to accept that life somewhere else could be as good as or better than in the U.S.A."[54]

Children may also find re-entry difficult. Coming back to school, attempting to regain acceptance into peer groups, and being out of touch with current slang, sport, and fashions can cause problems. However, there are few reported studies in the literature that focus on children's repatriation. An exception is a study of 40 Japanese children that found the children faced

IHRM Today 8.3

Staying in Touch

Ever since the Sept. 11, 2001, terrorist attacks in the U.S., Josef Blumenfeld makes sure to email his wife and let her know he has arrived safely while away on business. But when he touched down at Tokyo's Narita International Airport two years ago, his BlackBerry didn't work. "It felt like being in a black hole," says Mr. Blumenfeld, 39 years old, a communications consultant from Massachusetts.

Even as options for mobile communications have proliferated, the BlackBerry—which started life as a simple-to-use, dedicated email device—has caught on all over the world, from the U.S. to Europe to India and China. Until now there has been one gaping hole in the BlackBerry universe: Japan.

That changes today, when NTT DoCoMo Inc., Japan's biggest mobile-phone operator, begins marketing the latest version of the device to business users. Research In Motion Ltd., of Canada, starts selling its new BlackBerry 8707h in Japan, with the ability to read email in both Japanese and English. At first, only this BlackBerry model will work in Japan. Overseas visitors will either have to buy one from DoCoMo—or continue their frustration until a similar version goes on sale elsewhere.

The news has brought feelings of euphoria to some expatriates who do business in Japan and want to stay closely connected to work and home. Mr. Blumenfeld says he missed being able to instantly communicate with family members and colleagues. He says he would get the new model, and then "I'd hug my BlackBerry simply for the connection to home it provides."

Source: Chozick, A. (2006, September 26). Expats delight in debut of BlackBerry in Japan. *The Wall Street Journal Asia*.

difficulties reintegrating into both their peer groups and the Japanese educational system.[55] One can speculate, though, that the more difficult the re-entry process for the children, the greater the "spillover" effect for the repatriate.

Effect on Partner's Career

Partners encounter difficulties in re-entering the workforce, particularly if the partner has not been able to work outside the home prior to, or during, the foreign assignment, but now desires to find outside employment, either as part of a re-entry coping strategy or due to altered family circumstances. Negative experiences during the job search may affect the partner's self-worth, compounding the readjustment process and even causing tension in the relationship. For those who held positions prior to the overseas assignment, difficulties in re-entering the workforce may depend on occupation,[56] length of time abroad, unemployment levels in the home country, and personal characteristics such as age and gender.[57]

There is a dearth of research into the effects of the foreign assignment and repatriation on the partner's career, and many questions surrounding this issue remain unexplored (see IHRM Notebook 8.1). Readjustment of the expatriate, whether male-led or female-led, may be linked with concerns about the effect that the foreign assignment might have on the partner's career.

Given that dual-career couples are on the increase and that more females expect overseas assignments, the issue of the partner's career is likely to

---

IHRM Notebook 8.1

Expats' Partners and Their Careers: A Research Area with Many Questions to Be Answered!

- Do new employers consider the value of the time overseas to compensate for the forced career disruption? One study reported: "being a trailing spouse during the expatriate's international assignment constitutes a damaging gap in their employment history."*

- Have those partners who were able to work during the foreign assignment found employment in career-related jobs and been able to progress on repatriation?

- Do male "trailing" partners face different challenges on repatriation than do females? In one of the few reported studies into dual-career expatriates, Harvey** found a difference between female expatriate managers' expectations prior to and after expatriation, exposing the need for support for the male trailing partner. The overseas

assignment was the focus of Harvey's study, but one could assume that the same results would hold true on repatriation. More recently, Linehan and Scullion[†] looked at the repatriation process of female expatriates working in various European companies but did not consider the career aspect of the accompanying spouse/partner.

Sources: *The Conference Board. (1997). *Managing Expatriates' Return: A Research Report* (No. 1 148-96-RR). New York: Conference Board, 40.
**Harvey, M. G. (1997). Dual-Career Expatriates: Expectations, Adjustment and Satisfaction with International Relocation. *Journal of International Business Studies, 28*(3), 627–658.
†Linehan, M., & Scullion, H. Repatriation of European Female Corporate Executives: An Empirical Study. *International Journal of Human Resource Management, 13*(2).

become a major factor in determining staff availability for future overseas assignments. A 2002 global survey by ORC Worldwide[58] found that the most common forms of spousal assistance on re-entry were job-search assistance (20 percent), curriculum vitae/résumé preparation (20 percent), and career counselling (18 percent). The report's authors comment:

> Surprisingly, the provision of these three important support mechanisms has decreased since the previous increase in the 1996 survey. Taking into account the increased recognition of the dual-career issues and their significance for successful assignments leading to the growth in pre-assignment and on-assignment spousal assistance, this decrease in the support on repatriation was unexpected.

Our analysis has revealed how various factors influence re-entry and readjustment at the individual level. These moderating factors can combine in hard–to-predict ways, creating a volatile situation that may lead to a repatriate's unforeseen and debilitating exit from a multinational.

Multinational Responses

The above sections have considered the re-entry and career issues from the perspective of the individual repatriate. We will now examine the issues from the viewpoint of the multinational. Early studies into the issue of repatriation indicated that it was somewhat neglected by multinationals. For example, Mendenhall, Dunbar, and Oddou[59] concluded that U.S. human resource professionals may be unaware of the challenges facing repatriated managers. Commenting on the results of his 1989 study, Harvey[60] noted that:

> Even though many executives have experienced difficulties upon repatriation, [U.S.] multinational companies have seemingly not addressed the issues related to repatriation with the same level of interest as preparing executives for expatriation.

A 1997 survey found that only 27 percent of responding firms indicated they held re-entry sessions to discuss issues such as career objectives, performance, and plan for re-entry. The majority of these firms indicated that they waited up to 90 days before initiating such sessions.[61] Some progress seems to have been made lately. For example, GMAC data shows that in 2002, 73 percent of responding firms held re-entry discussions, compared with 86 percent in 2004. The timing and formality of these re-entry discussions varies. For example, in 2004, 44 percent of respondents held repatriation discussions before departure, mostly on an informal basis.

The GMAC surveys do not report on spousal or family involvement in re-entry discussions, but these aspects were raised in the ORC Worldwide 2002 report. As mentioned earlier in this chapter, job-search assistance, résumé preparation, and career counselling were the most common forms of assistance. However, the report does not indicate if this was negotiated before or during the international assignment or on re-entry, or if it was part of a re-entry discussion.

Managing the process of repatriation should be of concern to multinationals that desire to maximize the benefits of international assignments and create a large internal labour market. A well-designed repatriation process is important in achieving these objectives, for three main reasons: staff availability, return on investment, and knowledge transfer. These are now discussed.

Staff Availability and Career Expectations

RPC 8.3

The way the multinational handles repatriation has an impact on staff availability for current and future needs, as indicated in Figure 8.6. Re-entry positions signal the importance given to international experience. If the repatriate is promoted or given a position that obviously capitalizes on international experience, other members of the multinational interpret international assignments as a positive career move. On the other hand, if the multinational does not reward expatriate performance, tolerates a high turnover among repatriates, or is seen to terminate a repatriate's employment on re-entry, then the workforce may interpret the acceptance of an international assignment as a high-risk decision in terms of future career progression within the organization. The multinational's ability to attract high-calibre staff for international assignments is thereby lessened, and this can have a negative effect on the multinational's activities in the long term.

Lately, there has been some discussion about international assignments and **boundaryless careers**. The term *boundaryless career* appears to have been coined in recognition of shifts occurring in the employment relationship, particularly in Western countries. The traditional hierarchical career path, with definable stages (such as junior, middle, and senior manager), assumed long-term employment within one organization—the so-called *job for life*, where one climbed the corporate ladder. Today, employees tend to voluntarily or

boundaryless career

sequence of job opportunities that go beyond the boundaries of single-employment settings

FIGURE 8.6

Linking Repatriation Process to Outcomes

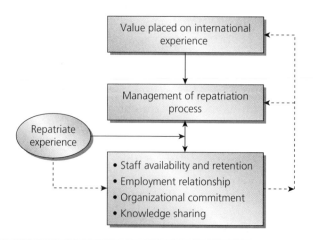

Chapter 8: Re-Entry and Career Issues

involuntarily switch jobs more frequently, as economic circumstances change, such as unemployment as a result of organizational restructuring or reskilling as jobs disappear. "The boundaryless careerist . . . is the highly qualified mobile professional who builds his or her career competencies and labor market value through transfers across boundaries."[62] Careers therefore are becoming discontinuous in the sense that the person moves between organizations and may have periods of unemployment, or self-employment, or contract work interspersed with more traditional employment arrangements. International assignments, particularly for career expatriates or global managers, are sometimes regarded as boundaryless in that the assignment places the person in another organization, most commonly a subsidiary or an international joint venture.

Accompanying this view is the notion that the individual rather than the organization is responsible for career management: The term "**protean**" (after the Greek god Proteus who could change into any form)[63] is sometimes used to reflect the idea of a self-directed career that involves continuous learning. Multinationals are reinforcing the notion of protean and boundaryless careers when they do not guarantee repatriates positions on re-entry. As Stahl et al.[64] found in their large study of 494 German managers posted to 59 countries:

> The vast majority of expatriates viewed their international assignment as an opportunity for skill development and future career advancement, even though it may not be with their current company, [which] supports the notion of boundaryless careers.

In such cases, commitment to the organization (an outcome in Figure 8.6) is replaced by commitment to one's career. Such a change may restrict the ability of the organization to attract high-calibre individuals to undertake international assignments—that is, staff availability—thus affecting the quality as well as the quantity of suitable candidates and the development of a cadre of global operators.

Similar results were found in a study of German and Singaporean expatriates. Both of these groups reported concerns with their firms' ability to facilitate their careers on their return from international assignments, provide in-company opportunities to use the new knowledge and skills they had gained during their international assignments, or provide them with new positions having the responsibility, autonomy, and compensation at levels that met their expectations. They did feel that these international assignments enhanced their opportunities among other possible employers and facilitated the development of their own intercultural and professional or managerial skills.[65]

In some instances, firms may choose to select "international itinerants"—"professional managers who over their careers are employed for their ability by at least two business organizations that are not related to each other, in at least two different countries"[66]—instead of selecting in-house candidates who will have to be repatriated to the MNE. By selecting these itinerants in lieu of internal candidates, overall costs may be reduced, ongoing support costs can be managed, and—germane to our discussion—repatriation activities can be eliminated. The two main disadvantages of using these types of assignees

protean
the idea of a self-directed career that involves continuous learning

relate to a lack of in-depth firm knowledge by the itinerants and the problems that the MNE may have in selecting and controlling itinerants.[67]

However, contradicting evidence also exists in the literature on the issue of boundaryless careers. Other researchers suggest that expatriate careers still correspond very much to the traditional model of the organizational career, especially in the case of a global corporate philosophy that includes the development of global leaders.[68] Festing and Müller[69] found in a study of 168 alumni of a European business school that when international assignments had an important strategic value for the MNE and were accompanied by a high level of IHRM activities, expatriates had rather traditional career expectations, aiming at a long-term employment relationship with their employer. In these cases, the retention rates of international managers after the international assignment were high. This indicates that the organizational context may at least partly influence the emergence of expatriate career patterns and confirms the relationships outlined in Figure 8.6 (e.g., that IHRM measures such as repatriation programs influence the outcomes in terms of the employment relationship in general and, specifically, employee retention rates and commitment to the organization).

How actively the MNE manages—as a matter of strategy or circumstances—an international assignee's career may vary substantially. Career management is conceptualized by Baruch and Peiper in an analysis of 194 U.K.-based firms as being more or less sophisticated and with more or less involvement by the firm in an employee's career. "Basic" and "formal" practices, comprising less-sophisticated career practices and low levels of involvement, are characterized by practices such as common career paths, written personal career planning, job posting, and lateral moves. More sophisticated practices with higher levels of firm involvement in an employee's career are described as "multidirectional" and "active planning" forms of careers. These models are characterized by practices related to in-depth career counselling, succession planning, a strong link between performance management systems and career planning, peer appraisals, and upward appraisal processes.[70] Little is known at this time about the factors that determine how much time, energy, and effort returning expatriates and executives in MNEs will put into career practices designed to maintain existing work relationships, as opposed to readily looking for external job opportunities on their return or seeing repatriation turnover as an inevitable cost of doing business globally.

Return on Investment

R P C 8.4

Expatriates are expensive, especially expatriates from first-world advanced economies. Where possible, multinationals try to localize positions through the employment of HCNs, but not all positions can or should be localized. As we discussed in Chapter 4, the alternative—which more companies are utilizing or experimenting with—is a short-term or non-standard assignment to replace the traditional expatriate form. Cost containment is the driver here, along with staff immobility. For example, 79 percent of firms in a 2005 global survey by PricewaterhouseCoopers[71] identified cost reduction as important or very important in the evolution of international assignment practices, and the GMAC surveys indicate that cost containment continues to drive assignment trends.

However, faced with the business reality that expatriates will always be with us, the question is how to ensure that the organization reaps the benefits of international assignments, regardless of duration and form. Black and Gregersen[72] calculate that a U.S. multinational spends around one million dollars on each expatriate over the duration of a foreign assignment. They argue that, if approximately one in four repatriates exits the firm within a year of repatriation:

> It represents a substantial financial and human capital loss to the firm, especially if the skills, knowledge, and experience that the individual gains are important to the firm and scarce in the internal or external labor markets.

Getting a return on this investment (ROI) would appear to be an important objective, but not easy to achieve. First, there is a matter of definition. Respondents in the GMAC 2002 survey were asked if ROI could be defined as "accomplishing the assignment objectives at the expected cost." A total of 96 percent of respondents agreed with this definition—a figure that dropped to 10 percent in the 2004 survey, increasing slightly to 14 percent in 2005. It is not clear whether the 2004 respondents misunderstood the question or disagreed with GMAC's definition. In one of the few articles that considered ROI on international assignments, McNulty and Tharenou[73] recognize that a meaningful definition should include a cost–benefit analysis of financial and non-financial data, measured against the purpose of the assignment. Identifying direct costs is relatively easy, as relocation expenses, an itemized compensation package, and other international assignee entitlements are accessible. The indirect, intangible, non-financial costs are more problematical. These include the non-direct costs of expatriate failure or underperformance (as identified in Chapter 5) and the opportunity cost of not using an HCN.

Placing monetary value on the benefits of the international assignment is also a challenge as the intangibles—such as knowledge and skills transfer, management development, and relationship- and network-building—are somewhat invisible, often tacit, and person-bound. It is difficult to measure intellectual, social, and human capital gains—improvements in the stock of knowledge and competence that result from a successful repatriation process. ROI analysis also focuses on the international assignment period, and can be an exercise to justify cost-reduction measures (such as replacing expatriates with HCNs) rather than considering gains that accrue to the organization through repatriated staff.

Although firms participating in the GMAC surveys tracked assignment costs, only 46 percent of respondents in the 2004 survey compared estimated with actual costs, and only 37 percent did so in the 2005 survey. Difficulties encountered in attempts to measure ROI were:

- Receiving of feedback from the business unit concerned.
- Tracking of international assignments in a systematic way.
- No formal planning.
- A lack of objective measures.
- Too many decisions being made without realizing the costs related to the international assignment.
- Globalization is a "must" for us (so the ROI almost doesn't matter).

More importantly, there is a link between value placed on the international experience and strategic outcomes (see Figure 8.6). As the authors of the GMAC *2004 Survey Report*[74] argue:

> If management is not aware of the return on investment (or lack of return) for international assignments, how can expatriates be recognized and rewarded for making signal contributions to their firm's success? Until companies sharpen their pencils and learn to measure the impact of international assignments on the corporate bottom line, they will be unable to convince international assignment candidates that acceptance of such assignments will have a positive impact on their careers.

Further, employees will perform their own ROI calculations, based on perceived and actual costs and benefits, and these calculations will influence their willingness to accept an international assignment—or repeat the experience. Aligning corporate objectives with individual expectations is not an easy task, and compounds any attempts to balance costs and benefits for both parties.

Knowledge Transfer

 8.5

A common theme in current international business that is stressed by company managers is the need for cross-fertilization of ideas and practices that assist in developing and maintaining competitive advantage. International assignments are a primary method of achieving this objective. As the PricewaterhouseCoopers 2002[75] report concludes:

> Organizations need to make sure that their business strategies are supported by sound mobility strategies. . . . The need to move key employees around the business, regardless of national boundaries, will be increasingly vital to the success of a global organization.

Given the roles played by expatriates, along with their cost, it is reasonable to expect that multinationals would endeavour to retain key staff and to extract and build on their international experience. However, as we have seen in our examination of re-entry and career issues, a relatively high turnover of repatriate staff seems acceptable. That 69 percent of responding firms in the 2004 GMAC survey do not know their expatriate attrition rate is evidence of this (a jump from 39 percent in 2002). One GMAC survey respondent commented: "There is a high level of investment with a low value on the experience."[76] More telling is the continuing trend not to guarantee post-assignment positions so that the organization has greater flexibility over employment levels.

We can draw several conclusions regarding repatriate attrition rates. First, despite the rhetoric, knowledge transfer is treated as a one-way activity. Expatriates are sent on international assignments and effectiveness is determined based on the performance of their ascribed roles and work responsibilities. Any transfer of knowledge and competence occurs in the host location and remains there. Expatriates return to their home base and are reassigned or resign (consider the comments about international assignments in IHRM Today 8.4).

More recent surveys reinforce these findings. There is no mention about an international assignment being part of transferring knowledge and competence around the organization, or even as a two-way process. The point here is that while performing their tasks in the host location, expatriates develop skills and gain experience, knowledge, and network relationships that can then be used upon repatriation in some way or another. For example, a project manager working in Russia can, on re-entry to his Canadian home base, report technical problems encountered and solutions that were developed to overcome these problems, thus sharing the experience. However, not all of the knowledge about that project is explicit. Much will remain tacit and person-bound. What is codified and made explicit often is retained within the project team, even though some of the information and knowledge could be applicable to other projects or types of business concerning Russia, such as important contacts, management styles, and some technical solutions. In addition, international assignments vary in terms of purpose, duration, location, and nature, and these differences affect the acquisition and transfer of knowledge and skills.

HCNs transferred to headquarters for developmental reasons, for example, may benefit through such exposure but the experience will remain

---

IHRM Today 8.4

Company Objectives of International Assignments

Below are some views about company objectives of international assignments volunteered by responding firms in the 2002 GMAC survey.

- The primary reason for an expatriate assignment is to go into a country and train someone who is local to do a specific job function and then return home.
- Work is project-oriented. We send expatriates to complete projects and leave.

- Expatriates develop local management talent.
- Our main reason for sending expatriates is to supplement national staff capacity, provide training and coaching, and provide professional expertise.
- We view these as developmental assignments to broaden employee experience.

Source: GMAC Global Relocation Services, U.S. National Foreign Trade Council, & SHRM Global Forum. *Global Relocation Trends: 2004 Survey Report*, 40.

Chapter 8: Re-Entry and Career Issues

person-bound if the home unit does not allow the repatriated HCN opportunities to share knowledge and information. Contacts at headquarters can be used for personal advantage. A similar case can be made for TCNs transferred back from another subsidiary. The aims of cross-fertilization of ideas and best practices given to justify cross-border movement of staff require the right environment to facilitate sharing of information and knowledge. The "not invented here" mindset (or xenophobia) can operate to devalue repatriate contributions.

What knowledge and skills are acquired through a typical international assignment? A study of 19 Austrian repatriates provides some answers. Based on in-depth interviews, Fink et al.[77] classified repatriate knowledge into five categories:

1. *Market-specific knowledge*: Local system (political, social, economic), local language, and local customs.
2. *Personal skills*: Intercultural knowledge, self-confidence (that is, ability to make quick decisions), flexibility, tolerance.
3. *Job-related management skills*: Communication, project management, problem-solving.
4. *Network knowledge*: Meeting diverse people—clients, suppliers, subsidiary personnel, other expatriates.
5. *General management capacity*: An expanded job description, broader job responsibilities, exposure to other parts of the organization.

The range of knowledge and skills listed comprise both tacit and explicit knowledge. The authors consider that the first four categories are useful for the sending organization, while the last (general management capacity) is most beneficial to the individual. Fink et al. conclude that repatriate knowledge may be useful in enhancing a firm's competitiveness, but acknowledge the difficulties in capitalizing on this, particularly if repatriates exit before such knowledge has been transferred. They also point out that the size of the firm and its stage in the internationalization process, is a critical factor. The Austrian firms in their sample were SMEs who did not have need for a large number of general managers and thus were unable to meet repatriate expectations based on their newly acquired skills and knowledge.

The trend toward not providing post-assignment position guarantees suggests that multinationals accept loss of experience, knowledge, and competence—that repatriates effectively forced to leave the organization will take with them what could be vital and valuable, allowing competing firms to reap the benefits of a substantial investment in human capital. Those who remain in the organization may not be motivated to share.[78] Perhaps this seemingly downgrading of the repatriate experience is partly due to the fact that many firms are unaware of the benefits of the international assignment to both the firm and the individual, as ROI calculations, clearly linked to the nature and purpose of the assignment, are not performed. As Downes and Thomas[79] found, multinationals that valued international experience were rewarded by loyal employees who contributed to the intellectual capital base of their companies. Unfortunately, that repatriates become an underutilized resource has been a consistent finding in studies and surveys examining repatriation.[80]

Blakeney, Oddou, and Osland[81] recommend that HR practitioners in multinational firms take a wider, more systematic view of the expatriate–repatriate cycle and focus on: (1) identifying the critical, implicitly held knowledge assets inherent in expatriation/repatriation and (2) reducing the sources of resistance to knowledge transfer inherent in the motivation and capabilities of the repatriate, as well as the structural and cultural impediments inherent in the receiving unit at home. This can be done by building trust and enhancing the shared sense of social identity between the repatriate and the receiving unit. Practically speaking, HR practices that combine a unified expatriation/repatriation cycle that explicitly emphasizes knowledge transference in each stage of the process (namely, in selection, pre-departure, and in-country training; mentoring or coaching; designing the international assignment; re-entry training; and returnee job assignment and selection, as well as the training of the returnees' own managers) will assist in the successful transfer of knowledge. More formal activities, including seminars by repatriates as post-assignment "action learning" exercises and the development of knowledge-disseminating teams and databases made up to index the expertise of repatriates, can facilitate progress.[82]

Recent empirical research by Tung points out the potential for patterns of international careers, in this case, careers in MNEs moving back and forth between China and North America, to contribute to outward foreign direct investment strategies for MNEs.[83] These humans capital flows are only now being documented, and a rudimentary understanding of the complex relationships among government policies, cultural solidarity in the face of diasporas, and personal career ambitions is beginning to emerge.

Designing a Repatriation Program

While there is no simple, quick solution, preparing the repatriate and family for re-entry appears to have some value. The potential for mismatch of expectations regarding the future may be addressed as part of pre-re-entry training before the return, and discussed during re-entry counselling sessions (sometimes referred to as *debriefing*) between the receiving organization in the home country and the repatriate. Such sessions would enable both parties to take a "reality check."

What should be covered in formal repatriation programs? IHRM Notebook 8.2 is an amalgam of the lists suggested by respondents in the various surveys referred to above.

Some MNEs assign the expatriate a mentor (also referred to as a company contact, sponsor, or "godfather"). The mentor is usually in a more senior position than the expatriate, is in the sending work unit, and knows the expatriate personally. The rationale behind the use of a mentor is to alleviate the "out of sight, out of mind" feeling discussed earlier through the provision of information (such as workplace changes) on a regular basis, so that the expatriate is more prepared for conditions faced on re-entry. A

Topics Covered by a Repatriation Program

- Preparation, physical relocation, and transition information (what the company will help with).
- Financial and tax assistance (including benefit and tax changes; loss of overseas allowance).
- Re-entry position and career path assistance.
- Reverse culture shock (including family disorientation).
- School systems and children's education and adaptation.
- Workplace changes (such as corporate culture, structure, decentralization).
- Stress management, communication-related training.
- Establishing networking opportunities.
- Help in forming new social contacts.

mentor should also ensure that the expatriate is not forgotten when important decisions are made regarding positions and promotions.

A survey of re-entry practices in 152 multinational companies in the United States, Europe, and Asia[84] found that 26 percent of respondents provided mentors for their expatriates, although this was related to various organizational factors:

- *Size of expatriate workforce*: Firms with more than 250 expatriates were more likely to assign mentors (43 percent) than those with 55–100 expatriates (15 percent).
- *Which work unit was responsible for the expatriate*: Mentors are more likely if corporate HR formulates expatriate policy (in 35 percent of cases) and when the expatriate is managed by a separate international assignments unit (in 41 percent of cases) rather than at the divisional level (18 percent).
- *Nationality of responding company*: 35 percent of Continental European firms reported the use of mentors, compared to 20 percent of U.S. firms. This result compares with findings from a study of European-based multinationals: Over a quarter used a career mentor/sponsor system, with a further 19 percent indicating that such a scheme would be introduced in the future.

Linehan and Scullion[85] found that 40 of the 50 females in their study had experienced mentoring relationships, and believed that their management positions were partially due to that relationship. The mentors provided contact and support from the home organization that also facilitated re-entry and reduced the "out of sight, out of mind" syndrome. Their experiences led them to adopt mentoring roles in their new domestic positions.

It is reasonable to suggest that the practice of mentoring, to be effective, has to be managed. For example, what happens when the mentor retires or leaves the firm—two likely events in a multinational undergoing radical restructuring? Also, who monitors the mentor's performance? Recent surveys have not specifically covered the practice of mentoring, although 12 percent of responding firms in the 2002 GMAC survey indicated that they used mentors. Firms in a 1997/1998 Price Waterhouse survey[86] defined mentoring duties to include:

- Maintaining contact with the expatriate throughout the assignment.
- Ensuring expatriates are kept up to date with developments in the home country.
- Ensuring expatriates are retained in existing management development programs.
- Assisting expatriates with the repatriation process, including helping them with a repatriation position.

It may be that having a mentor assists the expatriate to adjust during the foreign assignment but, by itself, does not necessarily help on re-entry. Stroh[87] concludes that her study "did not show that having a mentoring program would make an independent contribution to repatriate retention rate," although there was a suggested link between assignment of a mentor, career development, and repatriate retention. In other words, an effective mentor is likely to alert the firm of the imminent return of the repatriate and thus affects the re-entry position, or the practice is part of a managed repatriation program.

Caligiuri and Lazarova[88] recommend no fewer than 12 proactive strategies to maximize the likelihood that the professional, financial and emotional issues faced by repatriates and their families will be dealt with and repatriates will be able to return with an integrated and balanced set of experiences that will be available to the MNE (see the lowest segment of the right-hand column of Figure 8.2). (See IHRM Notebook 8.3.)

While recognition of the importance of repatriation programs is increasing (see also IHRM Today 8.5) and companies are experimenting with other measures such as mentors, other avenues could be explored, such as using repatriates as an important information source. Inviting repatriates to assist in developing repatriation programs may contribute to relevant and effective policies. It may also have a desirable side effect on readjustment, simply by giving participating repatriates a sense that they are not an underutilized resource and that the firm recognizes they can make a valuable contribution to the expatriation process. It is, naturally, important that wherever possible the multinational ensures equity of treatment among PCN, TCN, and HCN expatriates.

Summary

This chapter has been concerned with the repatriation process. One may conclude that in re-entry, the broader sociocultural context of the home country takes a backstage position—unlike in the expatriation adjustment phase, when the foreign culture can be overwhelming.[89] Cultural novelty has been found to affect adjustment and, for the majority of repatriates, coming home to the familiar culture may assist in readjustment. Indeed, given the more profound effect that job-related factors appear to have, *re-entry shock* is

Proactive Repatriation Strategies by the Firm

- Managing expectations via pre-departure briefings on what can be expected during the assignment and upon return.
- Multiple career planning sessions focusing on career objectives and performance indicators, carried out by HR managers or a purpose-built team of past repatriates and relevant executives.
- Written repatriate agreements when feasible to clarify the types of assignments available upon return.
- Mentoring programs that continue on into the repatriate's post-assignment career. This practice may act to notify the firm of any post-assignment dissonance and reduce turnover.
- Extended home visits to keep up with social, family, and organizational changes.
- Reorientation programs to provide the repatriate with a briefing on changes in strategy, policies, and organization.
- Personalized reorientation by the MNE so the repatriate and her or his family can better deal with the emotionally charged issues of social readjustment, schools, family dynamics, and lifestyle changes inherent in return.
- Personalized financial and tax advice, as well as access to interim financial benefits such as short-term loans—similar to the professional advice available to executives.
- Providing some kind of an adjustment period upon return that may or may not include a vacation or reduced workload.
- Improved employee satisfaction and commitment upon return will potentially translate into a more globally capable firm.* Visible and concrete expressions of the repatriate's value to the firm (in the form of promotion, public ceremonies, or a completion bonus) may be required to seal and reinforce this new, more globally encompassing relationship between the multinational firm and the repatriate.

Source: *Stroh, L., Black, J. S., Mendenhall, M., & Gregersen, H. (2005). *International Assignments: An Integration of Strategy, Research and Practice.* Mahiwah, NJ: Lawrence Erlbaum.

Repatriation Practices

In terms of empirical evidence of practices, GMAC's 2005 survey of trends in global relocation reports 81 percent of responding firms discussed repatriation upon return, while 59 percent discussed repatriation before the employee left for the assignment. At the same time, 57 percent of responding firms did not offer post-assignment guarantees, but 83 percent reported they identified a new job (via transfers) within the firm. Responding firms stated they felt the practice of highlighting opportunities for repatriates to use their international experience was useful in reducing turnover upon return (64 percent), followed by the practices of providing a variety of assignments for the repatriate to select from (50 percent) and repatriation assistance (43 percent).

Even with all of these practices, employee attrition remains a concern: 21 percent of repatriates leave during the assignment, 23 percent leave within one year of return, and 20 percent exit by the second year. These rates are twice those reported for all employees.

Source: GMAC Global Relocation Services, U.S. National Foreign Trade Council, & SHRM Global Forum. *Global Relocation Trends: 2005 Survey Report*, 15.

perhaps a more accurate term to describe the readjustment process experienced upon repatriation.

With regard to job-related aspects centred on career issues on re-entry, we identified a number of factors that affected career anxiety, including no post-assignment guarantee of employment; fear that the period overseas had caused a loss of visibility; changes in the home workplace that affect re-entry positions; and the employment relationship. The re-entry position was an important indicator of future career progression and the value placed on international experience. Coping with new role demands was another factor in readjustment, along with loss of status and pay.

We explored social factors, among them a loss of social standing—the kingpin syndrome—and the accompanying loss of the expatriate lifestyle. Family readjustment was also important. A specific aspect was the effect of the international assignment on the spouse/partner's career, such as being reemployed and having international experience recognized.

We also looked at multinational responses to repatriates' concerns and the companies' focus on re-entry procedures. Within this context, we discussed how repatriation affected staff availability, whether companies were measuring and obtaining a return on investment through international assignments, and the contribution of repatriates to knowledge transfer. The concepts of protean and boundaryless careers were introduced in terms of the international assignment and career outcomes. In the final part, we put forward recommendations regarding the designing of effective repatriation programs, including the use of mentors and available forms of technology.

While the focus of this chapter has been repatriation in the general sense, the issue of career expatriates should be raised. The repatriation literature reviewed in preparation for this chapter makes little mention of the process of managing the return of those who have been part of the international team of managers (or cadre)—those who have worked outside their home countries for lengthy periods of time. For this strategically important group of employees, at some point repatriation may coincide with retirement. One is left with the impression that those who return to retire in their home country are no longer of concern to their firms. However, one could expect that these individuals would require special counselling to assist not only the transition back to the home country, but from work to retirement as well.

Viewing repatriation as part of the expatriation process, as suggested in Figure 8.2, should remind those responsible for expatriation management of the need to prepare repatriates for re-entry and to recognize the value of the international experience to both parties.

Key Terms

boundaryless careers 274

protean 275

repatriation 255

role discretion 266

Web Links

www 8.1 For more details and information about the GMAC surveys, go to:

www.gmacglobalrelocation.com/insight_support/global _relocation.asp

www 8.2 The Canadian PricewaterhouseCoopers homepage can be found at:

www.pwc.com/ca/eng/main/home/index.html

www 8.3 To find out more about Canadian house prices, go to, for example, Royal LePage's website at:

www.royallepage.ca/CMSTemplates/GlobalNavTemplate .aspx?id=361

RPC Icons

RPC 8.1 Monitors HR activities of the organization, identifies problem areas, initiates responses, and resolves issues that stand in the way of business success

RPC 8.2 Monitors HR activities of the organization, identifies problem areas, initiates responses, and resolves issues that stand in the way of business success

RPC 8.3 Monitors HR activities of the organization, identifies problem areas, initiates responses, and resolves issues that stand in the way of business success

RPC 8.4 Develops business cases for HR activities (e.g., return on investment [ROI] evaluations, data collection and assessment)

RPC 8.5 Monitors HR activities of the organization, identifies problem areas, initiates responses, and resolves issues that stand in the way of business success

RPC 8.6 Creates procedures for researching and establishing HR policies

Discussion Questions

1. What factors contribute to re-entry shock?
2. How can multinationals assist dual-career couples' repatriation?
3. Placing value on the international assignment assists repatriate retention. Discuss this statement.
4. What are the elements of a good mentoring system for international assignees?
5. What aspects would you include in a pre-repatriation program?

Using the Internet

1. Check out the hands-on advice provided by Canadian expatriates returning home. The *Canucks* site at **www.canucks.co.uk/othersites.cfm**

provides some interesting links to, for example, a repatriation checklist and guide by an expatriate and his family, who lived for seven years in the Middle East (**http://kurucz.ca/expatrepat/index.html**). Identify and discuss some the expats' challenges and issues related to their repatriation and discuss some of the first-hand advice and recommendations they provide for each other. How do these recommendations and this advice differ from or agree with the discussion in this chapter? If there are differences, give possible reasons for this.

2. Browse the Canadian federal government's site at **www.canada.gc.ca**. Where and what are the government's policies and practices regarding its employees and their families abroad returning home from international assignments? Can we expect differences between public sector and private companies in terms of expatriate, and in particular, repatriation policies and practices?

Exercises

1. Contact an employer that you know manages a team of international assignees and arrange for a meeting or a telephone interview with an HR department representative. Explore the company's policies and practices supporting the repatriation of its international assignees. Do those company practices differ from our suggestions and recommendations? If so, why? Are repatriation programs industry-dependent?

2. Think back to a time when you returned to Canada and/or to your home from a long trip abroad or away from your family. How did it feel? Why did it feel that way? How important are close ties with your family back home? Could you imagine becoming a global manager? What would you do to avoid re-entry culture shock after a long-term international assignment?

Case

Repatriation and Loss Prevention at ISCAM

On his last day of work at ISCAM, Wayne Bullova wrote his letter of resignation, took the five weeks of vacation he was due, and walked through the February snow across the downtown Greater Sudbury street to open his own safety and security consulting firm.

Only three years earlier, Wayne had jumped at the chance to take the assignment as Loss Prevention and Safety Director at ISCAM's new regional centre in Peru. As a global mining engineering firm with decades of international activities, ISCAM had done a very good job of preparing Wayne and his family for the differences between Lima and Greater Sudbury. The children had quickly adjusted to the International School and, surprisingly, his Mexican-born wife had enjoyed being involved in both the expatriate community and the local Peruvian church group associated with the cathedral. Wayne, a former captain with the Canadian Forces, had immediately enjoyed the increased responsibilities and centrality of his new role. His security role provided occasional adrenalin rushes as he responded to Sendero Luminoso (the Communist Party of Peru) activities in mine sites around Huaneayo, and the evident success of the counterterrorism and security protocols he developed was gratifying.

His return to Greater Sudbury some six months ago was a different matter. He knew that things would be different at home after the corporate restructuring that occurred a year into his expatriate assignment. His longtime mentor and friend, Herman Balkin, had taken a reportedly very generous early retirement package after a long-simmering executive power struggle unpredictably came to a head. Several restructuring "aftershocks" relocated many of his colleagues outside of northern Ontario.

During his assignment in Peru, Wayne became more and more frustrated, as his informal corporate intelligence network dissolved and the role of his liaison was passed around among a series of increasingly junior and, to his mind, clueless, executives. Then, the assignment he was promised by the company president was "rethought," and when he returned six months ago, he spent the better part of a month trying to get an office and to understand his new job. Everyone he talked to had a different perspective on what he was being asked to do. He felt claustrophobic and, to make matters worse, the new counterterrorism and security protocols he had developed and used with great success in Peru were either systematically ignored or so modified by his supervisors that they were unrecognizable.

At a Toronto Maple Leafs game, he shared his growing frustrations with Balkin. On the home front, the new house Wayne and his family had purchased on their return—having sold their home on the advice of the HR director at the time of the international assignment—was expensive, hard to heat, and placed them in a city school district that the children were having problems with. He had looked at private schools, but the tuition fees were astronomical and his salary was not much more that it had been three years ago. Also, his wife had started to complain about northern Ontario's winters again.

At work, Wayne felt as if he had returned to a totally different world. Balkin asked if ISCAM had asked Wayne to renew his executive noncompetition agreement. Wayne replied that ISCAM had not. "Well, there you go," said Balkin. "Let's do what we have talked about for years. With your technical expertise and my industry contacts, we can work for ourselves—at least we'll know who our bosses are and what the job is."

Source: Fictionalized synthesis from several interviews.

Questions

1. What could ISCAM have done throughout Wayne's assignment and on his return to Greater Sudbury to arrange a smoother repatriation for him?

2. What could or should Wayne have done to help himself and his family to prepare for their return to Greater Sudbury? To what extent is it the company's fault that Wayne and his family are finding it difficult to adjust to their lives back in Greater Sudbury?

3. What could the company have done to help Wayne's family to overcome its readjustment problems? What are the limits of a company's responsibilities for expatriates' family members and their repatriation?

Endnotes

1. See: L. Stroh, J. S. Black, M. Mendenhall, & H. Gregersen. (2005). *International Assignments: An Integration of Strategy, Research and Practice*. Mahiwah, NJ: Lawrence Erlbaum; M. Harvey & M. Novicevic. (2006). The Evolution from Repatriation of Managers in MNEs to "Patriation" in Global Organizations. In G. Stahl & I. Björkman (Eds.), *Handbook of Research in International Human Resource Management*. Cheltenham, UK: Edward Elgar, 323–343.

2. R. Moran. (1989, December). Coping with Re-Entry Shock. *International Management*, 67; M. G. Harvey. (1989, Spring). Repatriation of Corporate Executives: An Empirical Study. *Journal of International Business Studies, 20*(1), 131–144.

3. Stroh et al. *International Assignments;* Harvey. Repatriation of Corporate Executives.

4. Y. Paik, B. Segand, & C. Malinowski. (2002). How to Improve Repatriation Management: Are Motivations and Expectations Congruent Between the Company and Expatriates? *International Journal of Management, 23*, 635–648; Stroh et al. *International Assignments*.

5. J. S. Black, H. Gregersen, & M. Mendenhall. (1992). Towards a Theoretical Framework for Repatriation Adjustment. *Journal of International Business Studies, 23*, 737–760.

6. The first author has seen a number of examples over the years where expatriate families have taken their holidays in other locations rather than returning to their home country and have subsequently developed a rather unrealistic picture, which led to difficulties when the reality of subsequent repatriation resulted in adjustment difficulties.

7. Stroh et al. *International Assignments*, 215–216.

8. W. Mayrhofer, M. Meyer, A. Iellatchitch, & M. Schiffinger. (2004). Careers and Human Resource Management: A European Perspective. *Human Resource Management Review, 14*, 473–498; Stroh et al. *International Assignments*, 199–217.

9. A-W. Harzing. (1996). *Environment, Strategy, Structure, Control Mechanisms, and Human Resource Management in Multinational Companies* (company report: University of Limburg).

10. GMAC Global Relocation Services, U.S. National Foreign Trade Council, & SHRM Global Forum. (2004). *Global Relocation Trends: 2004 Survey Report*, 54. This report, along with the 2002 and 2006 survey reports, is available at the GMAC Global Relocation Services website: www.gmacglobalrelocation.com/survey.html

11. R. L. Tung & Arthur Andersen. (1997). *Exploring International Assignees' Viewpoints: A Study of the Expatriation/Repatriation Process*. Chicago, IL: Arthur Andersen, International Executive Services; D. C. Feldman & D. C. Thomas. (1992). Career Issues Facing Expatriate Managers. *Journal of International Business Studies, 23*(2), 271–294.

12. GMAC GRS. *Global Relocation Trends: 2002 Survey Report*, 51.

13. Price Waterhouse Europe. (1997). International Assignments: European Policy and Practice. Europe: Price Waterhouse International Assignment Services.

14. R. L. Tung & Arthur Andersen. *Exploring International Assignees' Viewpoints*.

15. E. Marx. (1996). *International Human Resource Practices in Britain and Germany*. London, UK: Anglo-German Foundation for the Study of Industrial Society.

16. GMAC GRS. *Global Relocation Trends: 2002 Survey Report*, 51.

17. Harzing. *Environment, Strategy, Structure, Control Mechanisms;* D. Osborn. (1997). The International Mobility of French Managers. *European Management Journal, 15*(5), 584–590.

18. S. Black & H. B. Gregersen. (1991). When Yankee Comes Home: Factors Related to Expatriate and Spouse Repatriation Adjustment. *Journal of International Business Studies, 22*(4), 671–694.

19. M. Bolino & D.C. Feldman. (2000). Increasing the Skill Utilization of Expatriates. *Human Resource Management, 39*(4), 367–379.

20. L. K. Stroh, H. B. Gregersen, & J. S. Black. (1998). Closing the Gap: Expectations Versus Reality among Repatriates. *Journal of World Business, 33*(2), 119.

21. J. S. Black, H. B. Gregersen, & M. E. Mendenhall. (1992). Toward a Theoretical Framework of Repatriation Adjustment. *Journal of International Business Studies, 23*(4), 737–760.

22. M. Lazarova & P. Caligiuri. (2001). Retaining Repatriates: The Role of Organizational Support Practices. *Journal of World Business, 36*(4), 389–401.

23. Stroh, Gregersen, & Black. Closing the Gap, 119.

24. V. Suutari & C. Brewster. (2003). Repatriation: Empirical Evidence from a Longitudinal Study of Careers and Expectations among Finnish Expatriates. *International Journal of Human Resource Management, 14*(7), 1132–1151.

25. GMAC GRS. *Global Relocation Trends: 2004 Survey Report*, 49.

26. PricewaterhouseCoopers. *International Assignments: Global Policy and Practice Key Trends 2005*. Human Resource Services. Downloaded from PWC website: www.pwc.com

27. L. K. Stroh. (1995). Predicting Turnover among Repatriates: Can Organizations Affect Retention Rates? *International Journal of Human Resource Management, 6*(2), 450.

28. M. Lazarova & P. Caligiuri. Retaining Repatriates: The Role of Organizational Support Practices, 395.

29. Stroh, Gregersen, & Black. Closing the Gap, 120.

30. M. Linehan & H. Scullion. (2002). Repatriation of European Female Corporate Executives: An Empirical Study. *International Journal of Human Resource Management, 13*(2), 259–260.

31. A. B. Bossard & R. B. Peterson. (2005). The Repatriate Experience as Seen by American Expatriates. *Journal of World Business, 40*, 17.

32. Stroh, Gregersen, & Black. Closing the Gap. See also: R. L. Tung. (1988). Career Issues in International Assignments. *Academy of Management Executive, 2*(3), 241–244; H. B. Gregersen. (1992, Spring). Commitments to a Parent Company and a Local Work Unit during Repatriation. *Personnel Psychology, 45*(1), 29–54; R. L. Tung. (1998). A Contingency Framework Revisited. *Human Resource Management Review, 8*(1), 23–37.

33. R. L. Tung & E. L. Miller. (1990). Managing in the Twenty-First Century: The Need for Global Orientation. *Management International Review, 30*(1), 5–18; D. Allen & S. Alvarez. (1998). Empowering Expatriates and Organizations to Improve Repatriation Effectiveness. *Human Resource Planning, 21*(4), 29–39.

34. M. R. Hammer, W. Hart, & R. Rogan. (1998). Can You Go Home Again? An Analysis of the Repatriation of Corporate Managers and Spouses. *Management International Review, 38*(1), 67–86.

35. Stroh, Gregersen, & Black. Closing the Gap, 120.

36. H. Mintzberg. (1973). *The Nature of Managerial Work*. Englewood Cliffs, NJ: Prentice-Hall, 54.

37. L. Gomez-Mejia & D. B. Balkin. (1987). The Determinants of Managerial Satisfaction with the Expatriation and Repatriation Process. *Journal of Management Development, 6*(1), 7–17.

38. I. Torbiörn. (1985). The Structure of Managerial Roles in Cross-Cultural Settings. *International Studies of Management & Organization, 15*(1), 69.

39. Black & Gregersen. When Yankee Comes Home, 688.

40. H. B. Gregersen & J. S. Black. (1990). A Multifaceted Approach to Expatriate Retention in International Assignments. *Group and Organization Studies, 15*(4), 461–485; also Torbiörn, The Structure of Managerial Roles in Cross-Cultural Settings.

41. H. B. Gregersen. (1992, November). Coming Home to the Arctic Cold: Finnish Expatriate and Spouse Repatriation Adjustment and Work-Related Outcomes (paper presented at the Academy of International Business Meeting, Brussels), 23.

42. C. Baughn. (1995). Personal and Organizational Factors Associated with Effective Repatriation. In J. Selmar (Ed.), *Expatriate Management: New Ideas for International Business*. Westport, CT: Quorum Books.

43. Black, Gregersen, & Mendenhall. Toward a Theoretical Framework of Repatriation.

44. N. Forster. (1994). The forgotten employees? The experiences of expatriate staff returning to the UK. *International Journal of Human Resource Management, 5*(2), 405–425.

45. N. K. Napier & R. B. Peterson. (1991). Expatriate Re-Entry: What Do Expatriates Have to Say? *Human Resource Planning, 14*(1), 19–28.

46. For a review of this literature, see: E. Kohonen. (2005). Developing Global Leaders through International Assignments: An Identity Construction Perspective. *Personnel Review, 34*(1), 22–36.

47. Black & Gregersen. When Yankee Comes Home, 686; and Baughn. Personal and Organizational Factors.

48. Harvey. Repatriation of Corporate Executives; & Stroh. Predicting Turnover among Repatriates.

49. Conway. Reducing Expatriate Failure Rates, 38.

50. Napier & Petersen. Expatriate Re-Entry, 24.

51. Black & Gregersen. When Yankee Comes Home.

52. H. De Cieri, P. J. Dowling, & K. F. Taylor. (1991). The Psychological Impact of Expatriate Relocation on Partners. *International Journal of Human Resource Management, 2*(3), 403.

53. M. G. Harvey. (1982). The Other Side of Foreign Assignments: Dealing with the Repatriation Dilemma. *Columbia Journal of World Business, 17*(1), 52–59; R. Savich & W. Rodgers. (1988, August). Assignment Overseas: Easing the Transition Before and After. *Personnel*, 44–48.

54. Baughn. Personal and Organizational Factors Associated with Effective Repatriation, 224.

55. W. Enloe & P. Lewin. (1987). Issues of Integration Abroad and Readjustment to Japan of Japanese Returnees. *International Journal of Intercultural Relations, 11*, 223–248.

56. G. K. Stevens & S. Black. (1991). The Impact of Spouse's Career-Orientation on Managers during International Transfers. *Journal of Management Studies, 28*(4), 417–428.

57. Black & Gregersen. When Yankee Comes Home.

58. Organization Resources Counselors Inc. (now ORC Worldwide). (2002). *Dual Careers and International Assignments Survey*, 7.

59. M. Mendenhall, E. Dunbar, & G. Oddou. (1987). Expatriate Selection, Training and Career-Pathing: A Review and a Critique. *Human Resource Planning, 26*(3), 331–345.

60. Harvey. The Other Side of Foreign Assignments.

61. The Conference Board. (1997). *Managing Expatriates' Return: A Research Report* (No. 1148-96-RR). New York: Conference Board, 28.

62. D. C. Thomas, M. B. Lazarova, & K. Inkson. (2005). Global careers: New phenomenon or new perspectives? *Journal of World Business, 40*(4), 341.

63. See for example: J. M. Mezias & T. A. Scandura. (2005). A Needs-Driven Approach to Expatriate Adjustment and Career Development: A Multiple Mentoring Perspective. *Journal of International Business Studies, 36*(5), 519–539.

64. G. K. Stahl, E. L. Miller, & R. L. Tung. (2002). Toward the Boundaryless Career: A Closer Look at the Expatriate Career Concept and the Perceived Implications of an International Assignment. *Journal of World Business, 37*, 222.

65. See G. Stahl & C. Chua. (2006). Global Assignments and Boundaryless Careers: What Drives and Frustrates International Assignees? In M. Morley, N. Heraty, & D. Collins (Eds.), *International Human Resource Management and International Assignments*. Basingstoke, UK: Palgrave Macmillan, 133–152.

66. M. Banai & W. Harry. (2006). Boundaryless Global Careers: The International Itinerants. In M. Morley, N. Heraty, & D. Collins (Eds.), *International Human Resource Management and International Assignments*. Basingstoke, UK: Palgrave Macmillan, 153–180, especially 157.

67. Ibid.

68. Y. Baruch & Y. Altman. (2002). Expatriation and repatriation in MNCs: A Taxonomy. *Human Resource Management, 41*(2), 239–259.

69. M. Festing & B. Müller. (2007, August). Antecedents and Outcomes of Expatriate's Psychological Contracts—Framework and Empirical Results (paper presented at the Academy of Management Annual Meeting, Philadelphia).

70. For more on the sophistication and commitment to career management, see: Y. Baruch & M. Peiper. (2000). Career Management Practices: An Empirical Survey and Implications. *Human Resource Management, 39*(4), 347–366; J. Richardson & M. Mallon. (2005). Career Interrupted: The Case of the Self-Directed Expatriate. *Journal of World Business. 40*, 409–420; and D. Thomas, M. Lazarova, & K. Inkson. (2005). Global Careers: New Phenomenon or New Perspectives? *Journal of World Business, 40*, 340–347.

71. PricewaterhouseCoopers. (2005). *International Assignments: Global Policy and Practice Key Trends.*

72. Black & Gregersen. When Yankee Comes Home.

73. Y. M. McNulty & P. Tharenou. (2004). Expatriate Return on Investment. *International Studies of Management & Organization, 34*(3), 68–95.

74. GMAC GRS. *Global Relocation Trends: 2004 Survey Report*, 8.

75. PricewaterhouseCoopers. (2002). *International Assignments*, 28.

76. GMAC GRS. *Global Relocation Trends: 2002 Survey Report*, 56.

77. G. Fink, S. Meierewert, & U. Rohr. (2005). The Use of Repatriate Knowledge in Organizations. *Human Resource Planning, 28*(4), 30–36.

78. M. Lazarova & I. Tarique. (2005). Knowledge Transfer upon Repatriation. *Journal of World Business, 40*(4), 361–373.

79. M. Downes & A. S. Thomas. (1999). Managing Overseas Assignments to Build Organizational Knowledge. *Human Resource Planning, 22*(4), 31–48.

80. See for example: R. L. Tung & Arthur Andersen. *Exploring International Assignees' Viewpoints;* Price Waterhouse Europe. International Assignments: European Policy and Practice; M. Lazarova & P. Caligiuri. Retaining Repatriates: The Role of Organizational Support Practices.

81. R. Blakeney, G. Oddou, & J. Osland. (2006). Repatriate Assets: Factors Impacting Knowledge Transfer. In M. Morley, N. Heraty, & D. Collins (Eds.), *International Human Resource Management and International Assignments*. Basingstoke, UK: Palgrave Macmillan, 181–199.

82. As reported by R. Blakeney et al., Repatriate Assets, Colgate-Palmolive developed a database of repatriate skills, as "the company saw the value of having information on each manager's knowledge/experience with particular cultures and disseminating knowledge about local markets throughout its global operations" (194). For a more in-depth discussion of potential relationships among knowledge mapping processes, career development, and strategic activities in transnational firms, see: A. Engle, P. Dowling, & M. Mendenhall. (2007). Transnational Trajectories: Emergent Strategies of Globalization and a New Context for Strategic HRM in MNEs (working paper).

83. R. Tung. (2007, May). The Human Resource Challenge to Outward Foreign Direct Investment Aspirations from Emerging Economies: The Case of China. *International Journal of Human Resource Management, 18,* 868–889.

84. The Conference Board. (1997). *Managing Expatriates' Return: A Research Report* (No. 1 148-96-RR). New York: Conference Board.

85. M. Linehan & H. Scullion. Repatriation of European Female Corporate Executives.

86. Price Waterhouse Europe. International Assignments, 32.

87. Stroh. Predicting Turnover among Repatriates, 454.

88. P. Caligiuri & M. Lazarova. (2001). Strategic Repatriation Policies to Enhance Global Leadership Development. In M. Mendenhall, T. Kühlmann, & G. Stahl (Eds.), *Developing Global Leaders: Policies, Processes and Innovations*. Westport, CT: Quorum Books, 243–256.

89. Black & Gregersen. When Yankee Comes Home.

Chapter 9

IHRM in the Host-Country Context

Chapter Learning Objectives

After reading this chapter, you should be able to:

- discuss the most important drivers shaping the interplay between global standardization and the localization of human resource practices in a multinational context including:
    - standardization drivers such as MNE strategy and structure, maturity and age, and corporate culture
    - localization drivers such as the host-country's cultural and institutional environment, the mode of operation, and the subsidiary's role
- outline measures that support the development of a balance of globalization and the localization of HRM
- discuss the global code of conduct as a device for controlling employee behaviour worldwide
- explain the strategic importance of offshoring

"Think global, act local" has often been hailed as a successful concept for companies expanding beyond their national borders into markets and cultural contexts different from their own. A translation of this notion into action is illustrated by Four Seasons Hotels and Resorts' Antoine Corinthios, president, Europe, Middle East, and Africa, who was described as a cultural chameleon ("an Italian in Italy, French in France"), and who explained that "If you are going global, you cannot be one way."

Yet, while Four Seasons recognizes and responds to local differences [with 74 hotels in 31 countries currently] ("each hotel is tailor-made"), at the same time, the Canadian hotels and resorts company strives for global integration through globally uniform standards. Within the HR context, for example, Four Seasons' key standard has been the "Golden Rule":

> Human resource management at Four Seasons started and ended with "The Golden Rule," which stipulated that one should treat others as one would wish to be treated. "The Golden Rule is the key to the success of the firm," founder and CEO [Isadore] Sharp emphasized, "and it's appreciated in every village, town, and city around the world.

Four Seasons' approach to balanced global integration and local responsiveness requires an understanding of the importance of the various facets of the host-country context. Therefore, we now shift our discussion of international HRM from managing an international workforce and its expatriates to managing a larger group of the MNE workforce, including employees at headquarters as well as in foreign locations, and to highlighting key host-country aspects and their implications for the IHRM function.

Source: Hallowell, R., Bowen, D., & Knoop, C. I. (2003, January 8). Four Seasons Goes to Paris: 53 Properties, 24 Countries, 1 Philosophy. *Harvard Business Online*. Harvard Business School, 2, 4.

Introduction

In Chapter 2, we covered the internationalization process of the MNE and its structural implications. In Chapter 3, the focus was on cross-border alliances and the distinct situation of international SMEs. To this point, we have discussed a wide range of responses to the managerial challenges encountered in international business operations.

Yet, increasing global competition involves the need for many multinationals to realize both global integration and local responsiveness.[1] In this chapter, we discuss what this means for the HRM of MNEs in particular. The balance between these pressures will vary, depending on the extent to which a multinational adopts a more global or local approach.[2] Morris et al.[3] describe the challenge of this balance as follows:

> Multinationals develop integrative HR practices by sharing best practices from all parts of the firm to create a worldwide system that strives for consistency and to gain efficiencies of scale and scope across several different countries. At the same time each oversea affiliate has to recognize and to develop HR practices that are appropriate for their local markets, employment laws, cultural traditions and the like in order to offer local advantages.

In order to gain a better understanding of how MNEs might balance these global and local pressures in HRM systems, the host-country environment becomes relevant. As we will outline in the following sections, the cultural and institutional embedding of an organization plays an important role in this. Parent organizations, as well as subsidiaries, are each rooted in their particular country-specific environment characterized by distinct systems of norms, values, and assumptions, all of which impact organizational behaviour. Due to similar country-specific socializations, employees of the same unit usually react similarly to management practices. The parent organization must recognize that its particular way of managing human resources reflects the assumptions and values of a specific context and that these may not be appropriate abroad. Foreign affiliates may have other preferred ways of management that are more effective on a local level.

Effective multinational management requires sensitivity and adaptation to the various host-country requirements and customs regarding employment, such as hiring, reward and promotion practices, and respect for local cultural and institutional traditions. Mismatches between cultural, social, and/or political attributes of HRM practices in the parent country and in the foreign locations may result in dysfunctional effects, such as problems in attracting and retaining employees, labour relations conflicts, or ineffective employee behaviour.

The need for consistency of, and conformity to, corporate goals and objectives is driven from the strategic business orientation of the MNE, accompanied by an underlying presumption that it is possible to achieve unity of purpose if all employees worldwide adopt corporate values and codes of conduct. It is reflected in headquarters' predispositions, as we reviewed in Chapter 4, when looking at staff placement in subsidiary operations: whom to place in key positions and what positions can and should be localized. Even in mature multinationals, what has been termed "lingering ethnocentrism" is evident in the way in which the parent company approaches subsidiary management, particularly in the use of control and coordination mechanisms.[4]

How to accomplish the interplay between headquarters and foreign affiliates, however, is complicated.

These challenges of the "think global, act local" mantra are incorporated in the idea of the "transnational firm,"[5] which has driven much of multinational management thinking over the past decades.[6] The idea of the global mindset is compelling. The message is to encourage all employees to appreciate "a bigger picture"—to recognize interdependencies and interrelationships between units, and between units and headquarters, so that resource sharing and knowledge transfer succeed and are for the benefit of the corporate "whole." This is reflected in the recent intense discussion about developing global leaders and global leadership competencies.[7]

In this chapter, we will explore how an MNE's HRM practices in host-country contexts are shaped by the interaction between the various parties involved. We will also look at the tradeoffs that occur while managing people in a multinational context. Again, we recognize that the current thinking on these issues has been shaped mostly by the investigation of larger multinationals and their relationships with a network of diverse subsidiaries, but much of this research is relevant to all firms operating internationally.

Standardization and Localization of HRM Practices

Controlling cross-border operations of an MNE centres around what processes, routines, procedures, and practices can be and should be transferred abroad and to what degree these require country-specific adaptation, if any, to be effectively implemented at the local level. In the processes of transferring systems and know-how, the role of people is critical. The management of people—probably the most culture-bound resource in an international context—is faced by a high level of complexity because of the diverse cultural environment of an MNE.[8]

RPC 9.1

RPC 9.2

As discussed in previous chapters, expatriates are frequently used to oversee the successful implementation of appropriate work practices. At some point, however, multinational management replaces expatriates with local staff with the expectation that these work practices will continue as planned. This approach is based on assumptions that appropriate behaviour will have been instilled in the local workforce through training programs and hiring practices, and that the multinational's way of operating has been accepted by the local staff in the manner intended. In this way, the multinational's corporate culture will operate as a subtle, informal control mechanism—a substitution of direct supervision.

However, this depends on the willingness of the local workforce to adhere to corporate norms of behaviour, the effectiveness of expatriates as agents of socialization, and whether cost considerations have led the multinational to localize management prematurely. Here, the role of appropriate human resource management activities becomes crucial. The aim of **global standardization** of HRM practices is to reach the above-mentioned consistency and transparency, and an alignment of a geographically fragmented workforce around common principles and objectives.[9] The use of common

global standardization

alignment of a geographically fragmented workforce around common principles and objectives

management practices is intended to foster a feeling of equal treatment among managers involved in cross-border activities and, at the same time, aims at a common understanding of what is expected from the employees. Furthermore, consistent systems facilitate the administration processes by increasing operational efficiencies.[10]

The aim of realizing **local responsiveness** is to respect local cultural values and traditions, and legislation or other institutional constraints, such as government policy and/or education systems regarding HRM and work practices. As mentioned before, attempting to implement methods and techniques that have been successful in one environment can be inappropriate in another.[11]

The challenge of many multinationals is to create a *system that operates effectively in multiple countries* by exploiting local differences and interdependencies and at the same time sustaining global consistency. Unilever, for example, uses the same recruitment criteria and appraisal system on a worldwide basis to ensure a particular type of managerial behaviour in each subsidiary. However, features of the national education systems and skill levels must be considered.[12]

This discussion has shown that the standardization–localization choice that confronts the multinational in an area of operation such as marketing also applies to the management of the global workforce. This is due to the fact that HRM carries out a strategic support function within the firm. However, as has been indicated above, the extent to which HRM systems are standardized or localized depends on various interdependent factors. We call this the "HRM balance between standardization and localization." Figure 9.1 illustrates important drivers that foster either standardization or localization. To sum up, the exact balance of a firm's HRM standardization–localization choice is based on factors of influence such as strategy, structure, firm size, and maturity. The strength of corporate culture plays an important role on the standardization side, while the cultural and institutional environment, including features of the local entity such as operation mode and subsidiary role, play an important role on the localization side. As Harzing[13] confirms, there exists a continuum of both standardization and localization advantages.

Factors Driving Standardization

The factors driving the standardization of human resource management practices in MNEs were discussed in the first three chapters of this volume. *Strategic issues* are included in the model on strategic international HRM in multinational enterprises (Figure 1.5). The organizational context, including various organizational *structures* and their impact on HRM, as well as considerations about *organizational culture* are all subjects of the second chapter.

The impact of *firm size* was discussed in Chapter 3 in the context of SMEs, outlining important differences between HRM in SMEs and MNEs. Closely linked to the firm size and the *stage of maturity* is the degree of international experience.[14] For example, Motorola's or IBM's experiences in China reflect their large size and the fact that they already had a wealth of

RPC 9.3

local responsiveness

respect of local cultural values, traditions, legislation, and other institutional constraints

RPC 9.4

RPC 9.5

FIGURE 9.1

Balancing the Standardization and Localization of MNE HRM

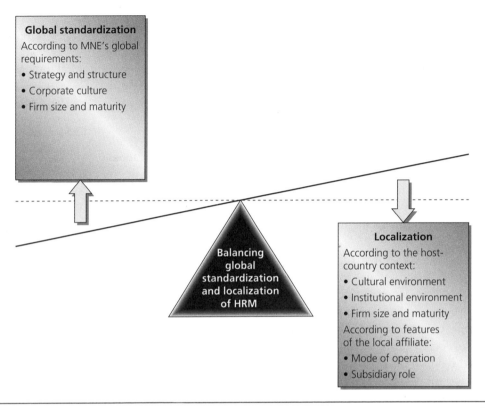

Global standardization
According to MNE's global requirements:
- Strategy and structure
- Corporate culture
- Firm size and maturity

Balancing global standardization and localization of HRM

Localization
According to the host-country context:
- Cultural environment
- Institutional environment
- Firm size and maturity

According to features of the local affiliate:
- Mode of operation
- Subsidiary role

Source: Adapted from: Festing, M., Eidems, J., & Royer, S. (2007, April). Strategic issues and local constraints in transnational compensation strategies: An analysis of cultural, institutional and political influences. *European Management Journal, 25*(2), 118–131.

international experience on which their management could draw when considering entrance into a transitional economy like China. As these firms are familiar with the great complexity of international operations, they are better prepared to cope with an additional new environment and better practised in finding appropriate HRM solutions than are other firms with less international experience. A smaller multinational or a relative newcomer to international business may not have the same level of experience, the competencies, or the needed resources with respect to HRM.

All of these factors are dependent on each other. The relationship suggested in the literature explains that a large MNE with a long international history and extensive cross-border operations:

- Pursues a multinational or transnational corporate strategy[15]
- supported by a corresponding organizational structure[16] that is
- reinforced by a shared worldwide corporate culture.[17]

However, in practice, we do not always observe perfect adherence to these factors in all MNEs. For example, a worldwide corporate culture may not be shared by all employees in all subsidiaries.[18] This factor should, nonetheless, at least be the target of many firms hoping to cope with the challenges of globalization.

In such highly internationalized organizations, we often find attempts to standardize HRM practices on a worldwide basis. Of course, this approach is not appropriate for the whole workforce but aims at a group of managers who are working at the cross-border boundaries of the firm at headquarters or in foreign locations; i.e., international boundary spanners.[19] The Schering example in IHRM Today 9.1 not only shows us that the implementation of global standards is possible but, at the same time, it also makes it clear that local adaptations and exceptions to the standards are often needed. The factors driving the localization of HRM practices are outlined in the next section.

Factors Driving Localization

As was depicted in Figure 9.1, factors driving localization include the cultural and institutional environment and features of the local entity itself. We will discuss these factors in the following paragraphs.

The Cultural Environment

In Chapter 1, we identified national culture as a moderating variable in international HRM. We explained how members of a group or society share a distinct way of life with common values, attitudes, and behaviours that are transmitted over time in a gradual, yet dynamic, process. The significance of national culture is underlined by the statement that most inhabitants of a country share the same mental program.[20] There is evidence that culture has an important impact on work and HRM practices. Sparrow, for

IHRM Today 9.1

Standardized HR Practices at Schering AG

A good example of a company that has attempted to globally standardize compensation practices is Schering AG, a German pharmaceutical company that introduced a global performance system for top managers worldwide.* Within the context of a new strategic orientation, Schering implemented a standardized bonus system for top executives that aimed at strengthening the performance culture in the company and facilitating a common orientation for all managers. The corporate element of the bonus system consisted of a standardized bonus structure. As the cultural acceptance for variable bonuses varied

across Schering's subsidiaries, the proportion between the fixed and variable parts of the total compensation package of managers was adapted to the country-specific conditions.

---

*Further details can be found in: M. Festing, J. Eidems, S. Royer, and F. Kullak. (2006). *When in Rome pay as the Romans pay? Considerations about transnational compensation strategies and the case of a German MNE* (ESCP-EAP Working Paper 22). Berlin: ESCP-EAP European School of Management. Schering AG was acquired by Bayer AG in 2006 and is now Bayer Schering Pharma AG.

example, has identified cultural influences on reward behaviour, such as "different expectations of the manager–subordinate relationship and their influence on performance management and motivational processes."[21] Triandis[22] found that cultures wherein work is based on more integrated personal social "relationships" may value a more complete balance of intrinsic and extrinsic rewards, while cultures characterized by personal independence and isolation ("individualism") as well as rapidly changing personal and social contexts may emphasize extrinsic rewards—given the absence of a strong and enduring social matrix that attributes meaning and power to intrinsic rewards. The examples indicate that the effectiveness of standardized practices might differ in various cultural contexts.

A first orientation to the features that characterize a culture is delivered by cross-cultural management studies. In Chapter 1, we pointed to the importance of the seminal work by the Dutch researcher Hofstede.[23] In addition to Hofstede's work, other intercultural studies have also made important contributions to our knowledge about cultural differences in an organizational context.[24] Here, we introduce central concepts of the most recent encompassing survey conducted by House et al.[25]—the Global Leadership and Organizational Behavior Effectiveness Research Program (GLOBE), a cooperation of 170 researchers from 62 cultures representing all major regions of the world. The study aims at explaining the impact of culture on leadership behaviour and organizational processes. The GLOBE activities started in 1991 with a long-term orientation and have developed a worldwide spread using a multi-phase, multi-method, cross-cultural research design. Three out of four research phases have been completed. At this stage, the GLOBE group has delivered data from questionnaires filled out by 17,000 middle managers active in three industries and representing 62 societies. The cultural dimensions are partly based on the dimensions identified by Hofstede and partly based on further theoretical considerations. A summary of the culture construct definitions and respective sample items is given in Table 9.1. While these dimensions are simplified and can be applied only at a societal level and not used for predicting individual behaviour, they may nevertheless give indications as to where important cultural differences can be expected. These may have an impact on the standardization–localization balance.

RPC 9.8

It is beyond the scope of this chapter to discuss the implications of all cultural dimensions identified in the GLOBE study and how conflicts between extreme culture-specific differences in values can be solved with respect to the standardization–localization balance of HRM in MNEs. However IHRM Notebook 9.1 illustrates this in relation to the decision about variable and/or fixed pay in the context of the dimension "uncertainty avoidance." The culture-based arguments outlined in IHRM Notebook 9.1 show that while an MNE may aim at a strong corporate performance orientation, local forces that do not share the same culture may alter the extent to which this is possible.[26]

It can be concluded that appropriate corporate HRM practices can help support the cohesion between different units of the MNE. Subsidiary staff may have a strong identification with the local unit, but the challenge is to

TABLE 9.1

Culture Construct Definitions and Sample GLOBE Questionnaire Items

CULTURAL CONSTRUCT DEFINITIONS	SPECIFIC QUESTIONNAIRE ITEM
Power Distance: The degree to which members of a collective expect power to be distributed equally.	Followers are (should be) expected to obey their leaders without question.
Uncertainty Avoidance: The extent to which a society, organization, or group relies on social norms, rules, and procedures to alleviate unpredictability of future events.	Most people lead (should lead) highly structured lives with few unexpected events.
Humane Orientation: The degree to which a collective encourages and rewards individuals for being fair, altruistic, generous, caring, and kind to others.	People are generally (should be generally) very tolerant of mistakes.
Collectivism I (institutional collectivism): The degree to which organizational and societal institutional practices encourage and reward collective distribution of resources and collective action.	Leaders encourage (should encourage) group loyalty even if individual goals suffer.
Collectivism II (in-group collectivism): The degree to which individuals express pride, loyalty, and cohesiveness in their organizations and families.	Employees feel (should feel) great loyalty toward this organization.
Assertiveness: The degree to which individuals are assertive, confrontational, and aggressive in their relationships with others.	People are (should be) generally dominant in their relationships with others.
Gender Egalitarianism: The degree to which a collective minimizes gender inequality.	Boys are encouraged (should be encouraged) more than girls to attain a higher education.
Future Orientation: The extent to which individuals engage in future-oriented behaviours such as delaying gratification, planning for, and investing in, the future.	More people live (should live) for the present rather than for the future.
Performance Orientation: The degree to which a collective encourages and rewards group members for performance improvement and excellence.	Students are encouraged (should be encouraged) to strive for continuously improved performance.

Source: House, R. J., Hanges, P. J., Javidan, M., Dorfman, P. W., Gupta, V. (Eds.). (2004). *Culture, Leadership and Organizations: The GLOBE Study of 62 Societies*. Thousand Oaks, CA: Sage Publications, 30.

Pay System Preferences in Different Uncertainty Avoidance Contexts

Results of a study by Lowe et al.* indicate that employees in the United States, Taiwan, Mexico, and Latin America prefer variable pay incentives, while their counterparts in Australia and Japan only moderately emphasize this kind of pay. Research shows that seniority-based pay in terms of a fixed salary is more likely to be found in countries with higher levels of uncertainty avoidance, such as Greece and Portugal.** This cultural dimension points out the extent to which people are risk-averse. Risk-taking managers are often advocates of large incentive pay-ments, while risk-adverse managers are less accepting of the high income variability that may be involved in performance-based pay.

Sources: *Lowe, K., Milliman, J., De Cieri, H., & Dowling, P. J. (2002). International compensation practices: A ten-country comparative analysis. *Human Resource Management, 41*(1), 45–66. **Schuler, R., & Rogovsky, N. (1998). Understanding compensation practice variations across firms: The impact of culture. *Journal of International Business Studies, 29*(1), 159–177.

foster employee identification at the global level through globally accepted HRM practices.[27] If the HRM practices do not match local norms and values, they must be adapted to the distinct features of the host-country culture. Multinationals might solve such culture-based divergences in the perception of the appropriateness of human resource management measures by allowing for certain well-defined exceptions that provide opportunities for local adaptation while assuring consistency with corporate guidelines. There are indications that the extent of cultural distance between headquarters and subsidiaries will also have a bearing on the degree to which human resource and work practices require adaptation.[28] The larger the cultural distance, the more important are forces for local adaptation. This is an aspect that MNEs must keep in mind when deciding on the standardization–localization balance.

The Institutional Environment

In addition to national and regional culture, institutional settings shape the behaviour and expectations in subsidiaries.[29] The institutionalism perspective[30] indicates that institutional pressures may be powerful influences on human resource practices.[31] According to Whitley,[32] institutional norms and values may be based on the features of a *national business system*. Elements that are relevant to HRM are, for example, the characteristics of the education system or the industrial relations system.

For example, in Germany, the dual vocational training system, which provides theoretical learning opportunities in part-time schools and practical experience in companies, is widespread. More than 60 percent of an age group is involved in dual vocational training for more than 350 professions.[33] This kind of training represents a well-accepted qualification in Germany, whereas in other countries this system is nonexistent or restricted to lower qualifications, such as in France. Similarly, in Canada, its disconnection to secondary education gives the Canadian apprenticeship system a negative image as a second-best option to a university or college education.[34] (For more information, see IHRM Notebook 9.2.)

The spread and reputation of such a training system has an impact on IHRM. More specifically, for example, the recruitment process and the selection criteria reflect the importance of these qualifications. Another example of institutional factors that can have HRM-related effects is that the "scope of labor legislation and its regency of codification creates new codes of conduct through issues such as sex discrimination, equal pay for equal work, and minimum wages."[35] Thus, for legitimacy reasons, it can make sense for some organizations to offer specific benefits or advantages, for example, even if they are very expensive and normally would not be offered due to efficiency considerations.

The impact of the institutional environment on IHRM is shown in the following example, which addresses staffing decisions. A study by As-Saber et al.[36] found that there was a clear preference for using HCNs in key positions by multinationals operating in India. The authors suggest that a major reason for HCN preference was the belief that an Indian would know more than an expatriate manager could learn in years on the job. As you will recall from Chapter 4, localization of HR staff positions is more likely to ensure that local customs and host-government employment regulations are followed. Khilji[37] found that, although foreign multinationals in Pakistan had formulated policies, implementation was low "because managers brought up and trained in a hierarchical and centralized set-up resist sharing power and involving employees in decision making." This occurred despite the host country's expectation that multinationals would transfer their best practices and act as a positive force in the introduction of what was regarded as desirable Western management styles. However, the multinationals in Khilji's

R P C 9.10

IHRM Notebook 9.2

Canada's Apprenticeship System

In Canada, apprenticeship programs have not had a very positive image in terms of their quality, and play only a subordinate role in the postsecondary education system. The 2002 total registration in apprenticeship programs was four times lower than university enrollment in 2001 and comprised less than half of the registrations for community college programs in 1998. One reason for their limited quality has been the lack of national standards and assessment methods Other concerns have been the limited number of trades that are appropriate for apprenticeship programs—less than 1 percent of all of the

federal government's National Occupational Classification occupations. While total registration rates for apprenticeships have increased marginally by 2.6 percent per year since 1977, completion rates are even lower and continue to decrease.

Sources: Sharpe, A., & Gibson, J. (2005, September). *The Apprenticeship System in Canada: Trends and Issues*. Ottawa: Centre for the Study of Living Standards; Bosch, G., & Charest, J. (2007). *Vocational training in five countries and its links with education and the labour market*. International Industrial Relations Association 8th European Congress, Manchester, England.

study had taken a polycentric approach, with HCNs in key positions, including that of the HR manager.

Liberman and Torbiörn,[38] in their study of eight European subsidiaries of a global firm, found variation in the degree to which employees adopted corporate norms. They suggest that at the start of a global venture, differences in management practices are attributable to cultural and institutional factors, whereas commonalities might be explained by a common corporate culture. Empirical results confirmed this. In some countries, employees agreed to wear clothing emblazoned with the company logo, as such action did not challenge their national culture. In another focus of the study, there was great resistance to the implementation of performance assessment for non-managerial positions, as it went against existing practice in one of the subsidiaries. Taylor[39] found that Chinese employees working in Japanese plants in their home country perceived team briefings and other such forums as a new form of rhetoric, replacing nationalist and Communist party propaganda of the past, and this information was consequently considered of little value by workers and managers. These examples underline the importance of finding adequate solutions for the standardization–localization balance.

These above-described effects illustrate phenomena identified by the theoretical lens of institutionalism. The **country-of-origin effect** implies that multinationals are shaped by institutions existing in their country of origin and that they attempt to introduce these parent-country HRM practices in their foreign subsidiaries.[40] This is especially the case in an ethnocentric firm. The country-of-origin effects are stronger in non-restrictive local environments than in very restrictive countries. For example, Canadian multinationals are more flexible in importing their HRM practices to British affiliates than to German units because British employment law is not as strict as that in Germany and it leaves more choices to the enterprises.[41] However, there is also evidence that MNEs tend to limit the export of practices typical for the country-of-origin to those practices that are considered to be their core competencies.[42]

The **host-country effect** refers to the extent to which HRM practices in subsidiaries are impacted by the host-country context. For example, foreign MNEs in Germany are not free in their choice of pay levels or pay mixes. This is regulated by collective wage agreements, which are typical for the German environment and must be accepted. A similar effect exists at headquarters. Here, HRM activities are influenced by the home-country environment—**home-country effects**. This differentiation reflects the discussion on home- and host-country environment, which is typical for MNEs. The home-country effect is the basis for the country-of origin effect discussed above, describing MNEs that try to transfer HRM activities shaped by their home-country environment to foreign locations.

This discussion has shown that the institutional context has an impact on HRM in several different ways. We have seen that not only the host country's institutional context can foster localization, but that forces exist from the country-of-origin, as well. Sometimes **reverse diffusion**—the transfer of

country-of-origin effect
extent to which MNEs attempt to introduce their parent-country HRM practices in foreign subsidiaries

host-country effect
extent to which HRM practices in subsidiaries are impacted by the host-country context

home-country effect
extent to which MNEs try to transfer home-country HRM activities to foreign locations

reverse diffusion
transfer of practices from foreign locations to headquarters

practices from foreign locations to headquarters—can be observed.[43] For example, there is evidence that American MNEs learn from their subsidiaries in the United Kingdom.[44] Edwards et al.[45] have reported that a "shared service" approach to organizing the HR function was developed in the United Kingdom and then introduced in the American headquarters. Relationships of the different effects between the institutional environment and the MNE units are delineated in Figure 9.2.

Conclusions for the Host-Country Environment

In the preceding two sections, we outlined how the cultural and institutional environment may influence HRM and, in particular, attempts at global standardization and local responsiveness. IHRM Notebook 9.3 summarizes these ideas and gives examples of environmental differences that could lead to problems when MNEs attempt to introduce worldwide standardized HRM practices. Within this context, it is important to recall the discussion on the convergence and divergence of HRM and work practices, as mentioned in the first chapter.

FIGURE 9.2

Institutional Effects on MNEs

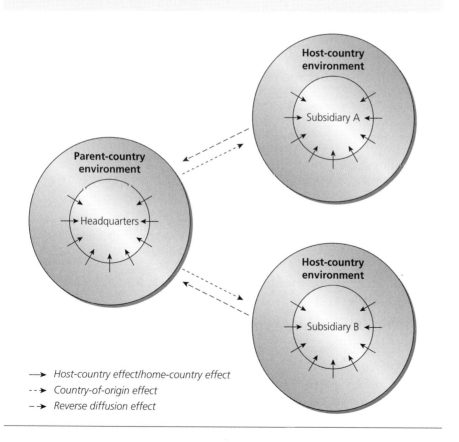

→ Host-country effect/home-country effect
--→ Country-of-origin effect
-→ Reverse diffusion effect

Impact of Cultural And Institutional Contexts on HRM Practices

HRM Practices	Impact of the Cultural Context	Impact of the Institutional Context
Recruitment and selection	• In *societies low on "in-group collectivism,"* individual achievements represent important selection criteria. • In *societies high on "in-group collectivism,"* the emphasis in the recruiting process is more on team-related skills than on individual competencies.	*Education System* The reputation of educational institutions such as public and private universities varies in different countries. This is reflected in the recruiting processes (i.e., HR marketing) and selection criteria of the firms in those countries.
Training and development	• In societies *high on gender egalitarianism,* women have the same chances for vertical career advancement as men. • In societies *low on gender egalitarianism,* female managers are rare.	*Education System* Education systems differ between different countries (existence of a dual vocational training system, quality, and reputation of higher-education institutions). This has an effect on the training needs perceived and fulfilled by MNEs.
Compensation	• In societies *high on uncertainty avoidance,* employees tend to be rather risk-averse and prefer fixed compensation packages or seniority-based pay. • In societies *low on uncertainty avoidance,* employees tend to be rather risk-taking and accept high income variability through performance-based pay.	*Legislation and Industrial Relations* Legislation such as the regulation of minimum wages or respective union agreements related to compensation has an impact on the firm's compensation choices with respect to pay mix and pay level.
Task distribution	• Societies *high on collectivism* tend to emphasize group work. • Societies *high on individualism* attribute individual responsibilities in the work system.	*Legislation and Norms* Legislation and respective norms support gender-based division of labour to a differing extent in different countries. While in some countries the percentage of female managers is relatively high, in other countries it is not common for women to work at all.

Mode of Operation Abroad

RPC 9.11

When addressing the mode of operation, it is helpful to examine this from the level of the local affiliate. Thus, we turn to firm-endogenous factors to determine the balance between global standardization and localization. Chapters 2 and 3 discussed the various modes of foreign operations and their associated HRM practices. IHRM Today 9.2 provides two examples of how the mode of operation either inhibits or facilitates work standardization.

Influence of Modes of Operation on Work Standardization

In late 1978, the Chinese government announced an open-door policy and commenced economic reforms aimed at moving the country from a centrally planned to a market economy. Western firms that entered China early were more or less forced to enter into joint ventures with state-owned enterprises (SOEs), whereas those entering later have been able to establish wholly owned subsidiaries (WOSs).

In 1983, Belgian telecommunications firm Alcatel, the Belgian government, and the Chinese Postal and Tele-communications Industries Corporation (PTIC) formed the joint venture Alcatel Shanghai Bell. There was a gradual transfer of relevant technology by the Belgian firm, with a long-term reliance on Belgian expatriates. The Belgian firm had limited control over the Chinese employees in the joint venture and was constrained by its partners' expectations and differing goals.

Nine years later, the U.S. telecommunications firm, Motorola, established a wholly owned operation in Tian-jin, China. Changing conditions in China meant that Motorola could effectively build a "transplant factory," importing production equipment and organizational pro-cesses and practices from either the parent company or other subsidiaries in its global network. This enabled Motorola to integrate the Chinese operation into the broader corporate network and to localize management.

These local managers have been supported by HRM initiatives such as a special management training program, the China Accelerated Management Program (CAMP); English language training; and transfer of Chinese employees into the U.S. operations. Motorola has been able to transfer its processes and systems, such as its Six Sigma quality control program, bringing its technology, knowledge, and work practices, supported by HRM activ-ities, into the new facilities in China relatively quickly.

Sources: Buckley, P. J., Clegg, J., & Tan, H. (2003). The art of knowl-edge transfer: Secondary and reverse transfer in China's telecommu-nications manufacturing industry. *Management International Review, 43* (Special Issue 2), 67–93; Motorola, Inc. website. Retrieved December 16, 2002, from www.motorola.com

Ownership and control are therefore important factors that need to be taken into consideration when multinationals attempt to standardize work and HRM practices. A firm's ability to independently implement processes and procedures is naturally higher in wholly owned subsidiaries, while the question of control in international joint ventures (IJV) remains a concern for multinational firms. Complementarities between IJV partners and the degree of interdependence between the IJV and other parts of the multinational have proven to be important influences on effective IJV operation and the transfer of work practices. For example, Yan's[46] study of 87 IJVs operating in China revealed the importance of defining a strategic objective for the IJV when deter-mining work practices. Yan concluded that task-related influence in an IJV plays an important role in directly shaping HRM practices.

This discussion here and in Chapter 3 indicates that the achievement of an acceptable balance in the standardization and localization of HRM prac-tices is less problematic in wholly owned subsidiaries than in cross-boarder alliances. However, in the latter, the balance also depends on many fea-tures of a particular alliance, including ownership and control issues. As we will discuss in the next section, it is important to further differentiate wholly owned subsidiaries. We will therefore now introduce the concept of a subsidiary role.

Subsidiary Role

9.12

The subsidiary role specifies the position of a particular unit in relation to the rest of the organization and defines what is expected of it in terms of contribution to the efficiency of the whole MNE. Subsidiaries can take different roles.[47] Studies have examined how subsidiary roles can differ related to subsidiary function, power and resource relationships, initiative-taking, host-country environment, the predisposition of top management, and the active championing of subsidiary managers.[48] Subsidiaries may be initiators as well as producers of critical competencies and capabilities that contribute as specific profit centres to the competitive advantage of the whole multinational. Centres of excellence at the subsidiary level can be viewed as an indication of how some network multinationals are recognizing that levels of expertise differ across the organization and that not all innovation and "best practice" originates from the centre—that is, from headquarters. The Japanese electronics firm Hitachi's establishment of an R&D centre in China is an example of building up an existing R&D facility to the status of a global centre for the development of air conditioners.[49]

We will now discuss the well-known typology of subsidiary roles by Gupta and Govindarajan.[50] Based on their interpretation of an MNE as a network of capital, product, and knowledge flows, the authors attribute the highest importance to knowledge flows. They differentiate between (a) the magnitude of knowledge flows—the intensity of the subsidiary's engagement in knowledge transfer—and (b) the directionality of transactions—whether subsidiaries are knowledge providers or recipients. The differentiation between knowledge inflows and outflows leads to the typology shown in Table 9.2.

Subsidiaries characterized as *global innovators* provide significant knowledge for other units and gain importance as MNEs move toward the transnational model. This role is reflected in an IHRM[51] orientation in which the parent firm develops HRM policies and practices that are then transferred to its overseas affiliates.[52]

The *integrated player* also creates knowledge but at the same time is the recipient of knowledge flows. Thus, a subsidiary characterized by this role can represent an important knowledge node in the MNE network.[53] This

TABLE 9.2

Gupta and Govindarajan's Four Generic Subsidiary Roles

	LOW OUTFLOW	HIGH OUTFLOW
Low inflow	Local innovator	Global innovator
High inflow	Implementer	Integrated player

Source: Adapted from: Gupta, A., & Govindarajan, V. (1991). Knowledge flows and the structure of control within multinational corporations. *Academy of Management Review, 16*(4), 768–792.

should be supported by a highly integrated HRM orientation. Thus, the HRM practices and policies between headquarters and subsidiaries are very similar, probably characterized by a high extent of global standardization and localized elements when this is needed. *Implementers* heavily rely on knowledge from the parent company or peer subsidiaries and create a relatively small amount of knowledge themselves. If the IHRM system is export-oriented (that is, global HRM decisions are mainly made in the parent company), then the local subsidiaries are responsible for the implementation process at the local level.

In the *local innovator* role, subsidiaries engage in the creation of relevant country/region-specific knowledge in all key functional areas because they have complete local responsibility. The HRM systems in such polycentric firms have only weak ties with headquarters. As every subsidiary operates independently from the parent company and from other subsidiaries, this independence results in a number of localized HRM policies and practices.

Harzing and Noorderhaven[54] recently tested this typology and found empirical support in a sample of 169 subsidiaries of MNEs headquartered in the Netherlands, France, Germany, the United Kingdom, Japan, and the United States:

> In comparison to earlier studies, our results show an increasing differentiation between subsidiaries, as well as an increase in the relative importance of both knowledge and product flows between subsidiaries, suggesting that MNCs are getting closer to the ideal type of the transnational company.[55]

A development toward the ideal type of the transnational corporation involves more subsidiaries engaging in high knowledge outflows, thus taking on the role of *global innovator* or *integrative players*. The difficulties in transferring knowledge and competence with respect to management practices from the subsidiary level—whether from a designated "centre of excellence"[56] or not—to the rest of the network are similar to the difficulties that we discussed in the context of headquarters–to-subsidiary transfer. The "sticky" nature of knowledge, for example, applies regardless of its origins, but the designated role of the subsidiary and the standing of its management are critical in determining the spread and adoption of subsidiary-initiated practices.

Stickiness represents one reason why some firms move toward an export-oriented approach to IHRM rather than an integrative management orientation.[57] Another major barrier to an integrative approach can be what Birkinshaw and Ridderstråle[58] describe as "the corporate immune system." Subsidiary initiatives are often met with significant resistance. Individuals within the organization resist change or support low-risk projects, and are wary of ideas that challenge their own power base. Michailova and Husted use the terms "knowledge-sharing hostility" and "knowledge hoarding" to explain non-sharing behaviours identified in their study of firms operating in Russia.[59]

Increasing the mobility of managers is one way to break down these barriers and produce corporate rather than subsidiary champions who are prepared to disseminate information about subsidiary initiatives and capabilities, and recommend adoption in other parts of the organization where appropriate. Tregaskis,[60] in her study of R&D centres, reports how one firm found that personal relationships formed through visits of key staff to other units facilitated information sharing and the eventual adoption of new products by other subsidiaries. Face-to-face interactions were important in building trust and exchanges of tacit knowledge, which might be possible in the context of corporate or regional meetings. Hence, frequent personal exchanges between the MNE units via individual encounters or regional or global meetings are essential in the processes of successful identification and transfer of knowledge.[61]

This discussion has indicated how the subsidiary role and related processes of knowledge transfer may impact the balance of standardization and localization in HRM. Recalling the power and resource relationships outlined at the beginning of this section, it must be stressed that powerful subsidiaries may have a stronger position in influencing the standardization–localization balance than those affiliates active in less significant markets or with rather unspecific skills.[62] Birkinshaw and Ridderstråle[63] define the structural power and resource-based power of subsidiaries vis-à-vis the corporate headquarters as two basic sources of influence within networks, and distinguish between "core" subsidiaries and "peripheral" subsidiaries. There is evidence that those subsidiaries controlling large market volumes and possessing strategically important function-specific skills within the MNE network have a strong impact on the standardization–localization balance.[64]

Creating the HRM Balance between Standardization and Localization

Various studies[65] have investigated coordination, communication, and control processes between parent organizations and subsidiaries. The analysis of these mechanisms contributes to our understanding about how the balance between globalization and localization is achieved.

RPC 9.13

Here, we will follow the differentiation between structural/formal and informal/subtle coordination mechanisms used by Martinez and Jarillo.[66] These authors define coordination as "the process of integrating activities that remain dispersed across subsidiaries."[67] The essential difference between these two groups of coordination mechanisms is that the latter is person-oriented, whereas the former is not. Martinez and Jarillo attribute the nonperson-oriented coordination mechanisms to simple strategies of internationalization. More complex strategies, however, require a higher coordination effort. A high degree of coordination is usually realized by using both: the non-person-oriented coordination mechanisms and person-oriented coordination mechanisms.[68]

In the context of corporate IHRM practices and policies, non-person-oriented coordination devices include, for example, written material on HRM practices such as handbooks or information leaflets, either provided in print or via the organization's intranet. However, as this is a one-way communication device, it can only supplement the complex process of balancing global and local needs. It does not meet the requirements of a complex transnational approach to IHRM. Here, person-oriented coordination is indispensable.

As has already been indicated in the context of knowledge transfer between subsidiaries, HR managers from headquarters, as well as from the foreign affiliates, must exchange their knowledge, expectancies, and experiences in the different local contexts. Therefore, meetings and common project work using a respective supporting infrastructure such as an intranet platform[69] are essential throughout the process of developing and implementing the standardization–localization balance in IHRM. Furthermore, powerful line managers acting as opinion leaders should be involved in the process as well, in order to achieve broad support for the transnational HRM measures. Finally, high importance placed on the respective HRM solution by the corporate top management is essential for the success of the initiative.[70]

Code of Conduct—Monitoring HRM Practices in the Host Country

An issue that has been somewhat overlooked in the IHRM literature is the need to monitor the HRM practices used in the host country. This is even more important in cases of cross-border alliances: Many multinationals, particularly in the textile, clothing, and footwear (TCF) industries, and other consumer goods industries such as electrical goods, do not establish their own manufacturing operations.

A critical issue in the management of the international supply chain is ensuring that quality standards are met. However, particularly for multinationals with well-known brands (e.g., Nike, Levi Strauss & Co., Benetton, Reebok, and Adidas), the major management challenge has been the reaction of its Western consumers to employment practices used by its subcontractors in countries such as India, China, Turkey, Indonesia, El Salvador, Honduras, the Dominican Republic, and the Philippines. (See IHRM Today 9.3.)

Various multinationals have been accused of condoning work practices such as the use of child labour, long working hours for minimal pay, and unsafe working environments—conditions that would not be permitted in their home countries. Public uproar in the 1990s resulted in various actions by governments, the United Nations, and nongovernment organizations to try to also enforce codes of conduct for subcontractors through their multinational partners.[71] Some multinationals, with corporate reputations and valuable brands at stake, quickly introduced their own codes of conduct.[72] These codes of conduct included, for example, acceptable working conditions, no child labour, and minimum-wage provisions. There is now a universal standard, similar to the ISO 9000 quality standard, called Social Accountability 8000, the principles of which are drawn from the United Nation's human rights conventions.[73]

Levi Strauss & Co. and Child Labour in Bangladesh

The following is a case study that appears on the Levi Strauss & Company website.

Shortly after our Terms of Engagement (TOE) were implemented, factory assessors discovered that two factories in Bangladesh were employing workers under the minimum working age. While a clear violation of the TOE, Levi Strauss & Co. management found itself in a difficult situation when it came to addressing the problem.

The issue of underage labor is a complicated one in Bangladesh—a country where it is not uncommon for a child (defined in the TOE as a person younger than 15 or younger than the mandatory schooling age) to support an entire family on his or her wages. Further, many children born in Bangladesh are not issued birth certificates and due to malnutrition, many people can look younger than their age.

Other companies facing the issue of child labor at the time simply instructed their contractors to fire underage workers. Levi Strauss & Co. management decided to take a different approach—one that would be informed and guided by the company's values: empathy, originality, integrity and courage.

Several Levi Strauss & Co. managers and consultants met with the contractors to develop an agreement on what to do in the immediate situation and how the contractors would operate going forward. Under the agreement, the factories agreed to continue to pay the already employed underage workers their salaries and benefits while they attended school and offer them full-time jobs when they reached the legal working age.

Levi Strauss & Co. agreed to pay for the students' tuition and books. If there was no room in the nearby public school, Levi Strauss & Co. and the factories would rent space and hire a teacher for the students.

The factories also agreed that going forward, their personnel would require any youth who applies for a job to present a school certificate stating that the applicant is 15 years old or older. In the event an applicant appears much younger, a dental examination may be used to establish the worker's age.

Our approach to this difficult situation earned Levi Strauss & Co. the praise of Bangladeshi and U.S. government officials, academics and several nongovernmental organizations (NGOs). Subsequently, the Bangladesh Garment Manufacturers and Exporters Association along with other groups set aside approximately $1 million for the education of about 75,000 underage girls who previously worked in factories.

Levi Strauss & Co. Case Study: Child Labor in Bangladesh. Retrieved September 22, 2007, from www.levistrauss.com/Downloads/CaseStudyBangladesh.pdf

While the code of conduct approach initially appeared to handle the public relations issue, ongoing enforcement has proven difficult. The role of HRM related to a global code of conduct may include the following:

- Drawing up and reviewing codes of conduct.
- Conducting a cost–benefit analysis to oversee compliance of employees and relevant alliance partners.
- Championing the need to train employees and alliance partners in elements of the code of conduct.
- Checking that performance and rewards systems take into consideration compliance to codes of conduct.

The case at the end of this chapter illustrates one example of a firm that has established a global code of conduct, and indicates some of the internal and external effects that such a code of conduct may have for an MNE.

Managing Human Resources in "Offshoring Countries"

The Concept and Strategic Importance of Offshoring

Offshoring is an important trend for reaching competitive advantage in the globalized economy.[74] In this section, we will give special emphasis to the context of host countries, which are typical recipients of the offshoring activities of MNEs. For these offshoring countries, we will discuss HRM implications[75] because this trend leads to a revolution in the global division of labour. New interfaces emerge that need to be managed.[76]

Unfortunately, there is no common and worldwide-accepted definition of the term *offshoring*. Frequently, it is used as a subcategory of **outsourcing**, which can be defined as "the act of transferring some of a company's recurring interval activities and decision rights to outside providers, as set in a contract."[77] Depending on whether these offshoring activities are equity-based, we can differentiate between captive offshoring, which involves an affiliated firm, and outsourcing, which involves a non-affiliated firm. While offshoring has a long tradition in, for example, the automobile industry, it has recently gained importance in the service industry and especially in the information technology (IT) sector.[78]

Despite some offshoring activities in the Canadian manufacturing and service sectors, Canada's industry as a whole has not been very active in terms of locating operations and productions abroad in comparison to the United States and Europe.[79] The main locations for service offshoring activities of European companies are the United Kingdom, Ireland, Spain, and Portugal in Western Europe and Poland, Hungary, and Romania in Eastern Europe. Nearly half of the projects go to Asia.[80] On a global scale, current leading beneficiaries of IT offshoring include, for example, Ireland and India. Canada has also benefited greatly from offshoring. In A. T. Kearney's 2004 *Top 12 Ranking for Offshore Location Attractiveness*, Canada ranked eighth in terms of providing information services—behind India, China, the Czech Republic, Singapore, the Philippines, and Brazil. Kearney's index sees Canada's strongest assets as its high education levels, infrastructure quality, and business-friendly environments.

According to the Canadian Chamber of Commerce, the future of Canada as an offshore destination will remain strong—in particular, in terms of its offshore relationship with its neighbour to the south.

> With a strong technological infrastructure, highly educated workforce, low telecommunications costs and a history of trading with the United States, Canada is in the ideal position to pick up even more outsourced business from the United States.[81]

9.15

outsourcing

transferring some of a company's activities and decision rights to outside providers

W W W **9.4**

W W W **9.5**

A recent PricewaterhouseCoopers survey gives an overview of foreign locations in which companies plan to begin business operations in the near future. The results show that India and China are expected to be the most important locations for future foreign business operations (see Figure 9.3). Both countries together represent 40 percent of the world's supply of labour.[82]

For example, in India the development of offshoring was a result of strong support by the government to help the country meet those requirements that have an impact on the choice of the location for offshore activities. This choice depends on costs (labour and trade costs), the quality of institutions (particularly legislation) and infrastructure (particularly telecommunications), the tax and investment regime, and the skills of the employees (particularly language and computer skills).[83] International call centres comprise a prominent example of offshore activities. "But, in fact, offshoring of services also includes more sophisticated, high value-added activities, such as accounting, billing, financial analysis, software development, architectural design, testing, and research and development."[84]

FIGURE 9.3

Target Countries for Future Foreign Business Operations

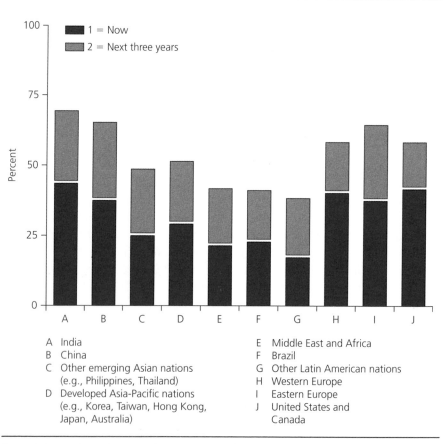

A India
B China
C Other emerging Asian nations (e.g., Philippines, Thailand)
D Developed Asia-Pacific nations (e.g., Korea, Taiwan, Hong Kong, Japan, Australia)
E Middle East and Africa
F Brazil
G Other Latin American nations
H Western Europe
I Eastern Europe
J United States and Canada

Source: PricewaterhouseCoopers (Ed.). (2006). *Technology executive connections. Successful strategies for talent management.* United States: PricewaterhouseCoopers, 43.

As mentioned previously, in this chapter we will concentrate on the two most important countries for future foreign operations: India and China. Although it is beyond the scope of this chapter to deliver an all-encompassing description and analysis of the employment relations systems and approaches to HRM, we will analyze the situation with respect to offshoring and draw implications for HRM in each country. Finally, emerging issues for HRM in offshoring countries will be discussed.

Offshoring and HRM in India

As mentioned above, India has developed a flourishing business process outsourcing (BPO) industry[85] and relevant competencies. The technological infrastructure and the qualifications as well as the motivation of the employees are perceived as benefits by Western investors and partners.

Furthermore, each year 3.1 million graduates enter the workforce and 20 percent of the population speaks English.[86] Indian graduates are prepared to work for salaries that used to be 80 percent lower than those of their Western counterparts. To capitalize on this cost advantage, U.S. firms such as IBM, Hewlett-Packard, and Electronic Data Systems have outsourced software development to Indian suppliers.[87] Other multinationals, such as General Electric, have used the availability of a highly educated yet relatively cheap labour force to establish their call centres in various parts of India. Local staff employed in these call centres are trained to speak English with accents and idioms so that U.S., U.K., and Australian customers are often unaware that their "local" call has been diverted to a call centre in India.

However, problems have also been reported from Indian BPOs and many of them are associated with HRM issues. For example, annual personnel turnover rates range from 20 to 80 percent and a shortage exists, considering the high demand for a skilled workforce, especially in middle management. As some HR managers have reported, only half of the candidates even show up for a job interview.[88] This shortage and the high demand for skilled workers have led to an annual increase in salaries of between 10 and 20 percent. Consequently, the cost advantages of offshoring to India are in danger. Additional issues are the problems of worker dissatisfaction and conflicts caused by stress, as well as cases of reported sexual and racial abuse.[89] All of these factors can lead to a decrease in productivity and thus, to further financial losses.[90]

These findings are confirmed by the results of an empirical study conducted by Mehta et al., who concluded that HRM issues are perceived as a major weakness in BPO firms.[91] This represents a challenge to the HRM of BPO firms. As reported by Sparrow and Budhwar,[92] the Indian HRM policies and practices are still very much influenced by castes, social relationships, and politics.

> At times, selection, promotion and transfer are based on ascribed status and social and political connections, so there is a strong emphasis on collectivism—family and group attainments take precedence over work outcomes. . . . Motivational tools are more likely

to be social, interpersonal, and even spiritual. In such conditions, the employee's orientation emphasizes personalized relationships rather than performance.[93]

These issues lead to an HRM system that is characterized by informalities and less rationality.[94] This might contradict the previously discussed attempts for a global standardization of HRM policies and practices by MNEs.[95] However, a study conducted in 51 BPO companies situated close to New Delhi revealed that the work settings were designed to guarantee maximum customer satisfaction. Furthermore, the authors discovered a more formal, structural, and rational approach to HRM, similar to those in developed countries. Nevertheless, with respect to HRM practices and their effects on the employees, weaknesses have also been identified. The emphasis on career development and training was lower than in Western firms.

Further HRM issues to be addressed in the future included increasing attrition rates, prevention of psychological and stress-related problems, more flexibility in the workplace (part-time jobs do not currently exist), and the creation of a more interesting work environment to help build long-term relationships with well-qualified employees.[96] Only if the employees' needs are met by HRM measures is retention possible.[97]

Offshoring and HRM in China

China is one of the fastest-growing economies in the world. It is a country well known for inexpensive manufacturing, although costs in this sector are rising.[98] Currently, salaries in China are even lower than in India. However, the total number of graduates is only half that produced by India, and the percentage of English-speaking graduates is also much lower.[99] While Chinese universities produce a high number of science and technology graduates, students come from an educational system in which they were rarely encouraged to take initiative and deliver creative solutions, although these are major requirements by MNEs.[100] Consequently, the Chinese economy suffers from a skill shortage similar to that in India, especially for those jobs that require both technical as well as management know-how.[101] Similar turnover rates and the same tendency of increasing salaries for highly skilled employees can also be observed in China.[102] Reported problems or barriers to working with local entities include not only difficulties of staff recruitment and retention, but also problems in cross-cultural communication, poor working practices in supplier firms, and corrupt staff behaviour.[103]

For Western MNEs who are planning to offshore activities to China, it is important to understand the role played by network connections called *guanxi*: dyadic personal relationships between people. Tung and Worm[104] explain that while these relationships bear similarities to the Western practice of networking, there are differences: Guanxi are contingent on conditions such as asymmetry, reciprocity, and necessity. The authors stress the importance of guanxi for successful business operations in China but recognize the difficulties this poses for Western executives. They suggest that hiring practices for key positions should take into account prospective Chinese employees' guanxi. The difficulty is being able to assess whether prospective employees have the right guanxi.

Multinationals find that they need to invest in training so that employees learn how to properly use equipment, operate systems, and the like. What actions can these firms take to gain the benefits of this investment in human capital? Obviously, it is not easy to prevent employees from leaving the operation. The poaching of skilled employees is a business reality. Shanghai Bell was an early entrant into the Chinese market and became the "academy for the industry," experiencing high staff turnover to both Chinese and foreign-owned competitors.[105]

In post-reform China, employees tend to change jobs frequently in pursuit of higher wages and not in an effort to develop their skills.[106] To a certain extent, this may be traced back to the employment system that existed prior to reforms associated with the transition to a market economy. Guaranteed continuation of employment, along with various welfare and benefits offered to employees, such as accommodation, medical treatment, child care, and pensions, has been referred to as the *"iron rice bowl."*[107] In exchange for job security, employees had little freedom to move to another work unit—that is, they were unable to quit or transfer jobs and were locked into a dependency relationship with their enterprises. By the same token, managers were deprived of their right to fire or lay off unqualified or non-productive employees.[108]

While companies operating in China are endeavouring to *reduce their attrition rates*, through the provision of additional benefits and staff development programs, Chinese employees are beginning to recognize compensation differentials and that is having an impact on job attitudes. A fair environment and good management practices are emerging as the essential tools for retaining Chinese employees, rather than above-market compensation alone. Goodall and Roberts,[109] in their study of a European oil company operating in China, cite the example of one employee who found that being part of a wider organizational network was incentive enough to stay with the multinational.

The above-mentioned recruitment, qualification, and retention problems require HRM practices that meet the needs of highly skilled human resources socialized in the Chinese context. However, HRM in China has only recently evolved and is challenging the former administrative system.[110] The transition is difficult because of the previous strong influence of the state and a current highly competitive situation:[111]

> Until quite recently, the personnel function in SOEs was confined to job allocation, personnel record filing, and the provision of welfare benefits. The primary task for personnel management was to keep the employees politically and ideologically sound. Many of the HR functions which are familiar to their western counterparts were beyond the experience of personnel staff in China.[112]

From this analysis Cooke derives key features that describe the current state of HRM in China:[113]

- There is no systematic approach for linking HRM with the business strategy.
- Despite a surplus of labour, many companies face recruiting and retention problems.
- There is no systematic link between performance management, reward, and long-term motivation.
- There is a lack in coherence and continuity of enterprise training.

However, research also shows differences between different types of enterprises.[114] Venter[115] points out that resource-rich companies, often characterized by foreign ownership, have a more encompassing approach to HRM, which includes formal education as a selection mechanism, selecting the educational elite and continuing to develop them through extensive training programs. To cope with the problem of high turnover rates, it is suggested that procedural justice as well as measures for increasing commitment to the organization may be helpful.[116] To sum up, employee needs must be met by respective HRM practices and the creation of a satisfying work environment.

Summarizing Emerging Issues

From this brief analysis of the situation in key offshore countries, important issues emerge with respect to the role of HRM as well as skill shortages and the resulting consequences. Eventually, in this context, the role of ex-host-country nationals (EHCNs) is discussed.

A Possible Role for HRM

As we have seen from the discussion above, offshoring activities can fail. Common reasons for this include the unsatisfactory quality of products or services, problems of management control, the rapid turnover of local staff, and language problems. A recent survey by the Chartered Institute of Personnel and Development (CIPD), *Offshoring and the Role of HR*, conducted in more than 600 companies in the United Kingdom, has revealed that the involvement of the HR department in offshoring decisions and processes was limited. Based on the survey results, CIPD identified the following roles for HRM.[117]

- Consulting with unions/employee representatives.
- Manpower planning, considering the scope for employee redeployment.[118]
- Contributing to the internal communication strategy.
- Identifying training needs.
- Designing new jobs that stem from offshoring operations.
- Highlighting potential risks, such as the implications of employment regulation both in the home country and in foreign locations.

This discussion clearly shows that there are still starting points for strengthening the local HRM systems in Indian and Chinese firms. This measure would be further supported if HRM played a more important role in offshoring decisions and processes.

Skill Shortage Consequences in a Broader Regional Context

Skill shortage represents a major problem in the offshoring countries of India and China. According to a recent PricewaterhouseCoopers survey,[119] 41 percent of 153 respondents from all over the world have reported problems in recruiting technical talent in emerging countries. Even more companies (47 percent) find it difficult to retain well-qualified staff. However, this is not a phenomenon that exists only in these countries. For a long time, skill shortage has also been the focus of discussion in the context of developed Western countries. Examples include Ireland[120] and Canada.[121] Table 9.3 shows the areas in which companies perceive talent to be scarce today and within the next three years.

Considering the high unemployment rates, for example, in several European Union countries, these figures might seem astonishing. But as a senior HR executive of a large technology division of Siemens Corporation, Germany, states: "For technical degrees, things are becoming more competitive. We are having greater difficulty—experiencing a longer time to hire for qualified graduates and especially for more senior positions."[122] As this example shows, the skill shortage problem prevails in other parts of the world as well. The problem threatens to increase with changing workforce demographics, as well as changes in attitudes and values.[123]

However, the consequences for the offshoring countries of India and China are striking. The scarcity of labour supply and the resulting competition between employers lead to tremendous turnover rates[124] and resulting salary increases. These factors endanger the cost advantages Western MNEs are looking for in offshoring countries. As one respondent of the above-mentioned PricewaterhouseCoopers survey stated:

> Compensation levels in many of the emerging markets are increasing to the point where we no longer view India and now even China as necessarily low-cost countries. . . . Our operations in India and China are already looking at offshoring to Indonesia and, believe it or not, Vietnam.[125]

It is interesting to note, however, that this development is also being experienced by companies originating from offshoring countries such as India and

TABLE 9.3

Where Talent Is Scarce

	OVERALL	NORTH AMERICA	EUROPE	ASIA-PACIFIC
Today	45%	33%	51%	40%
Next 3 years	66%	66%	63%	73%

Source: PricewaterhouseCoopers (Ed.). (2006). *Technology executive connections: Successful strategies for talent management*. United States: PricewaterhouseCoopers, 19.

Chapter 9: IHRM in the Host-Country Context

China. Due to the skill shortage, Chinese companies already look for offshore opportunities themselves.[126] This seems to reflect another step in the course of globalization.

Coping with Skill Shortages: The Role Of Returning HCNs

Another important issue that might be addressed when discussing skill shortages in emerging countries points to a group of people who originate from these countries, study abroad, and then return to their home countries. These individuals have been described as "ex-host-country nationals" (EHCNs) by Tung and Lazarova[127] in an empirical study of EHCNs in Central and Eastern Europe. They state that especially in these transitional economies ". . . where there is a significant shortage of local talent, EHCNs appear to be a good source of supply for much needed competencies and skills to enable these countries to survive and thrive in the global economy."[128] This is confirmed by Saxenian: She states that if those highly skilled employees decide to return home, they are accelerating the technological developments in their home countries.[129] In her research, Saxenian discusses the cases of China and India. In an empirical investigation of Chinese university students in Canada, Tung found that the majority of the students were receptive to the idea of returning to China.[130] However, in their study of Eastern European EHCNs, Tung and Lazarova report readaptation problems when EHCNs return to their home countries. This indicates that there is a risk as to whether the EHCNs will stay in their countries of origin and whether they will be as effective and successful as they are supposed to be. If they decide not to return to their home country after their studies, there is a danger of "brain drain."[131] This is critical in a situation of skill shortage in an emerging country.[132] The findings by Tung and Lazarova of reintegration problems of EHCNs have important implications for HRM practitioners because they indicate that EHCNs might expect to be treated in a similar way to expatriates, with careful reintegration into their countries of origin. According to Tung and Lazarova, returning HCNs can be regarded as a "brain gain" and represent a valuable measure to cope with the challenge of skill shortages in host-country locations.

Summary

This chapter has focused on issues relating to HRM and work practices in the host-country context. In the first part of this chapter, we explained the importance of a balance of HRM standardization and localization in MNEs. As major drivers for standardization, we referred to MNE strategy and structure, firm maturity and age, and corporate culture, issues that were discussed in previous chapters. Localization drivers included the host country's cultural and institutional environment, the mode of operation, and the subsidiary role. We also pointed out the importance of personal contacts and meetings for realizing an adequate integrative HRM approach.

We went on to discuss another measure that can have an important effect on controlling the behaviour of human resources in host countries, and with this we introduced the concept of a code of conduct (see also the case at the end of this chapter, in which we present the example of the global code of conduct at the German MNE, Degussa).

In the last part of the chapter, we addressed the special situations of both India and China—countries currently subject to massive offshoring activities, especially in the service sector. In this discussion, we stressed the implications of skill shortages and other challenges for HRM.

Key Terms

country-of-origin effect 304
global standardization 296
home-country effect 304
host-country effect 304

local responsiveness 297
outsourcing 313
reverse diffusion 304

Web Links

www 9.1   With funding from the Government of Canada's Sector Council Program, the Canadian Apprenticeship Forum's website provides information about apprenticeships or a career in the skilled trades, including links to relevant provincial websites:

www.apprenticetrades.ca

In addition, the Canada Revenue Agency website provides information about the Apprenticeship Job Creation Tax Credit— what the credit is, who qualifies, to which trades the credit is applicable, and much more:

www.cra-arc.gc.ca/whatsnew/apprenticeship-e.html#tphp

www 9.2   For more information about Levi Strauss & Co. and the company's case studies, go to:

www.levistrauss.com/Citizenship/CaseStudies.aspx

www 9.3   For more information about Social Accountability International and the SA 8000, go to:

www.sa-intl.org/index.cfm?&stopRedirect=1

www 9.4   The Conference Board of Canada discusses Canada's limited offshoring activities at:

www.conferenceboard.ca/press/2005/Offshoring.asp

www 9.5   For more information about A. T. Kearney's *Offshore Location Attractiveness Index* go to:

www.atkearney.com/shared_res/pdf/Making_Offshore_S.pdf

RPC Icons

RPC 9.1 Contributes to the development of the organization's vision, goals, and strategies, with a focus on human capital

RPC 9.2 Contributes to improvements in the organization's structures and work processes

RPC 9.3 Contributes to the development of the organization's vision, goals, and strategies, with a focus on human capital

RPC 9.4 Contributes to the development of the organization's vision, goals, and strategies, with a focus on human capital

RPC 9.5 Leads in the development of HR initiatives that support the organization's strategic directions

RPC 9.6 Leads in the development of HR initiatives that support the organization's strategic directions

RPC 9.7 Identifies the organization's HR needs

RPC 9.8 Contributes to improvements in the organization's structures and work processes

RPC 9.9 Contributes to the development of the organization's vision, goals, and strategies, with a focus on human capital

RPC 9.10 Leads in the development of HR initiatives that support the organization's strategic directions

RPC 9.11 Identifies the organization's HR needs

RPC 9.12 Identifies the organization's HR needs

RPC 9.13 Identifies the organization's HR needs

RPC 9.14 Directs the organization in ethical HR practices and application of conflict-of-interest guidelines

RPC 9.15 Contributes to the development of the organization's vision, goals, and strategies, with a focus on human capital

Discussion Questions

1. What are the determinants of the balance of standardization and localization in human resource management in MNEs?
2. How does a subsidiary's role affect its ability to transfer ideas and work practices to other parts of the global network? What is the impact of the resources controlled by the respective affiliate?
3. What contributes to the poaching of subsidiary employees? What steps can be taken to recruit and retain key employees?

Using the Internet

1. Browse the list of best employers in Canada organized by Hewitt Associates and *The Globe and Mail*'s "Report on Business" magazine at **http://was7.hewitt.com/bestemployers/canada/best.htm**. Check the websites of the top 10 firms on the list for codes of conduct. Do they have

one? If so, what do the different codes of conduct have in common? What are the differences? Why do you think these differences exist?

2. Imagine you need or want to offshore your Web design work. Where do you look for partners and how do you start? As a starting point, browse sites such as OffshoreXperts.com at **www.offshorexperts.com/index.cfm/fa/home.home**

Exercises

1. Assume you are the head of HR in an MNE. What measures would you take to develop and implement a transnational HRM strategy?
2. What are typical HRM problems in offshoring organizations? How can companies in India and China, for example, design their human resource management systems to avoid these problems?

Case

Degussa's *Global Code of Conduct*
The Firm

Degussa group* is a multinational corporation with a market leadership position in the specialty chemistry sector. The group is represented worldwide on all five continents and based in more than 300 locations. Degussa Canada Inc. has its national headquarters in Brampton, Ontario. The cornerstone for Degussa was placed in 1843 in Frankfurt, Germany; after several acquisitions, 44,000 employees today work for this company worldwide. Since June 2004, the Degussa group has been a 100 percent subsidiary of RAG AG.

Due to its important size, long history, and broad international experience, Degussa operates relatively independently from the parent company. Degussa's key production facilities, sales, and marketing offices can be found in some 60 countries, but the business activity is mainly in Europe, North America, and Asia. In 2005, Degussa generated sales of 11.8 billion euros; almost three-quarters of this sales volume was generated outside of Germany.

Firm Organization

Degussa has a decentralized organization within a global business framework. This is achieved through business units, which have full accountability for local operations. However, to maintain strategic control of its international business, strategic management decisions are mainly made at headquarters—a philosophy that is also reflected in the structure of the management board, which consists solely of German managers.

---

*As of September 12, 2007, what was Degussa became the Chemicals Business Area of the new Evonik Industries. For further information on this industrial group, see www.evonik.com.

To foster a corporate strategy and a new corporate culture known as "Blue Spirit," a set of supporting principles was developed that are incorporated into management practices (e.g., a bonus system for executives linked to corporate goals), including Degussa's *Global Social Policy* and the *Global Code of Conduct*. The aim is to bring together several different corporate cultures and to create one company in which every employee at every site feels as though he or she is part of a common whole.

The Global Code of Conduct

Degussa's *Global Code of Conduct* aims at supporting the employees in their daily work and providing them with reference points. In the course of growing globalization, the variety of relevant markets and cultures has increased. The expectations of employees as well as customers are becoming more complex, and different national and cultural backgrounds gain importance in the day-to-day work in this multinational company. The *Global Code of Conduct* is binding for every Degussa staff member and is applied in all subsidiaries as well as in the parent company. In addition, the code includes guidelines that control interactions with the corporate environment, as well as with the public and with governmental agencies or institutions. Even in regions like India, for example, where local rules and laws have other standards, the *Global Code of Conduct* is valid. In case regional requirements go beyond the Degussa code, the firm is forced to adapt to these conditions and has to include relevant deviations within the code.

Every employee worldwide is expected to comply with the *Global Code of Conduct*. Degussa has appointed various compliance officers in different units to ensure that the rules are respected. In addition, these officers can answer any related questions to assist employees in complying with these rules. Beyond this, local HR departments offer training sessions, information, and publications to ensure that all employees are familiar with the code. All employees are encouraged to name strengths and weaknesses of the code and to actively participate in the continuing further development of this *Global Code of Conduct*.

Source: Based on information obtained from Degussa's website, and Consult—*Kienbaum Kundenmagazin*, (2007, January), Kienbaum Human Resources Management Consulting, 1–7.

Questions

Although Degussa is now part of Evonik Industries, the following questions can be answered by going to www.degussa.com/degussa/en. For the first question, in the menu on the left-hand side of the page, click on "Company," then on "Employees & Management," and then on "Managing and Supervisory Board."

1. For a globally operating group such as Degussa, what would be the advantages and disadvantages of making most strategic management decisions at headquarters? Did Degussa's management and supervisory board have an HR specialist on the team? What does this tell you about the company and the strategic importance of its HR function?

2. Degussa's management board consisted solely of German managers. What are the advantages and disadvantages of having a homogeneous team such as this in terms of the nationality of the key decision makers? Check out the board members' résumés and their educational and professional backgrounds. Considering some of the board members' international experience, what meaning do passport nationalities have nowadays? Consider your own educational and work experiences: How Canadian are you? What makes you a Canadian?

To answer the following question, go to www.degussa.com/degussa/en, scroll down the right-hand side of the page to "Download Center" and click on "More." On the resulting page, under "Reports," click on "Environmental and Human Resources Reports" and then scroll down to "Global Code of Conduct" to access this document.

3. Read the code of conduct. How applicable are the different rules in the countries in which Evonik Degussa is operating? Can you see any possible misinterpretation, misunderstanding, or even conflicts when applying and implementing this code of conduct in Canada? Explain your answer.

Endnotes

1. C. A. Bartlett, S. Ghoshal, & P. W. Beamish. (2008). *Transnational management: Text, cases and readings in cross-border management.* Boston: McGraw-Hill; A.-W. Harzing & N. Noorderhaven. (2006). Knowledge flows in MNCs: An empirical test and extension of Gupta and Govindarajan's typology of subsidiary roles. *International Business Review, 15,* 195–214; and J. B. Hocking, M. Brown, & A.-W. Harzing. (2007, November 26). Balancing global and local strategic contexts: Expatriate knowledge transfer, applications and learning within a transnational organization. *Human Resource Management, 46*(4), 513–533.

2. P. Evans, V. Pucik, & J.-L. Barsoux. (2002). *The global challenge: Frameworks for international human resource management.* Boston: McGraw-Hill.

3. S. S. Morris, S. A. Snell, & P. M. Wright. (2006). A resource-based view of international human resources: Toward a framework of integrative and creative capabilities, In G. Stahl & I. Björkman (Eds.), *Handbook of research in international human resource management.* Cheltenham, UK: Edward Elgar Ltd., 433–448.

4. S. Blazejewski & W. Dorow. (2007). *Corporate cultures in global interaction: A management guide.* Gütersloh, Germany: Bertelsmann Foundation.

5. Bartlett, Ghoshal, & Beamish. *Transnational management: Text, cases and readings in cross-border management.*

6. A. Engle, M. Mendenhall, R. Powers, & Y. Stedham. (2001). Conceptualizing the global competency cube: A transnational model of human resource. *Journal of European Industrial Training, 25*(7), 346–353.

7. See, for example: A. J. Morrison. (2000). Developing a global leadership model. *Human Resource Management, 39*(2/3), 117–131; N. J. Adler. (2005). Shaping history: global leadership in the twenty-first century. In H. Scullion & M. Linehan, *International human resource management: A critical text.* Basingstoke, UK/New York: Palgrave MacMillan, 281–297; J. S. Osland, A. Bird, M. Mendenhall, & A. Osland. (2006). Developing global leadership capabilities and global mindset: A review. In G. K. Stahl & I. Björkman (Eds.), *Handbook of research in international human resource management.* Cheltenham, UK: Edward Elgar,

197–222; P. Caligiuri. (2006). Developing global leaders. *Human Resource Management Review, 16*(2), 219–228; M. E. Mendenhall, T. M. Kühlmann, & G. K. Stahl. (2000). *Developing global business leaders*. Westport CT: Greenwood Publishing Group. See also Chapter 8 in this textbook.

8. P. M. Rosenzweig & N. Nohria. (1994). Influences on human resource management practices in multinational corporations. *Journal of International Business Studies, 25*(2), 229–251.

9. P. Evans, V. Pucik, & J.-L. Barsoux. (2002). *The global challenge: Frameworks for international human resource management*. Boston: Irwin/McGraw-Hill; R. White. (2005). A strategic approach to building a consistent global rewards program. *Compensation and Benefits Review, 37*(4), 23–40.

10. M. Bloom, G. T. Milkovich, & A. Mitra. (2002). International compensation: Learning from how managers respond to variations in local host contexts. *International Journal of Human Resource Management, 14*(8), 1350–1367.

11. P. Lawrence & J. Lorsch. (1967). Differentiation and integration in complex organizations. *Administrative Science Quarterly, 12*, 1–30; N. Forster & R. Whipp. (1995). Future of European human resource management: A contingent approach. *European Management Journal, 13*(4), 434–442; P. Gunnigle, K. R. Murphy, J. N. Cleveland, N. Heraty, & M. Morley. (2002). Localization in human resource management: Comparing American and European multinational corporations. *Advances in International Management, 14*, 259–284.

12. K. Kamoche. (1996). Strategic human resource management within a resource-capability view of the firm. *Journal of Management Studies, 33*, 213–233.

13. A. W. K. Harzing. (1999). *Managing the multinationals: An international study of control mechanisms*. Cheltenham, UK: Edward Elgar.

14. For an analysis of the impact of organizational factors on global standardization with special emphasis on international experience, see: B. Myloni, A.-W. Harzing, & H. Mirza. (2007, December). The effect of corporate-level organizational factors on the transfer of human resource management practices: European and US MNCs and their Greek subsidiaries. *International Journal of Human Resource Management, 18*(12), 2057–2074.

15. N. J. Adler & F. Ghadar. (1991). Strategic human resource management: A global perspective. In R. Pieper (Ed.), *Human resource management: An international comparison*. Berlin/New York: De Gruyter, 235–260.

16. Bartlett, Ghoshal, & Beamish. Transnational management: *Text, cases and readings in cross-border management*.

17. See Chapter 2.

18. Blazejewski & Dorow. *Corporate cultures in global interaction: A management guide*.

19. J. D. Thompson. (1967). *Organizations in actions*. New York: McGraw-Hill; A. H. Aldrich. (1979). *Organizations & environments*. Englewood Cliffs, NJ: Prentice Hall.

20. G. Hofstede. (1991). *Culture and organizations—Software of the mind*. London: McGraw-Hill.

21. P. Sparrow. (2004). International rewards systems: To converge or not to converge? In C. Brewster & H. Harris (Eds.), *International HRM: Contemporary issues in Europe*. London, UK: Routledge, 102–119. See also: G. T. Milkovich & M. Bloom. (1998). Rethinking international compensation. *Compensation and Benefits Review, 30*(1), 15–23.

22. H. Triandis. (2002). Generic individualism and collectivism. In M. Gannon & K. Newman (Eds.), *The Blackwell Handbook of Cross-Cultural Management*. Oxford: Blackwell Business Pub., 16–45.

23. G. Hofstede. (1980). *Culture's consequences: International differences in work-related values*. Beverly Hills, CA: Sage.

24. E. T. Hall & M. Hall. (1990). *Understanding cultural differences*. Yarmouth: Intercultural Press; C. Hampden-Turner & F. Trompenaars. (1993). *The seven cultures of capitalism: Value systems for creating wealth in the United States, Britain, Japan, Germany, France, Sweden,*

and The Netherlands. New York: Doubleday; H. W. Lane & J. J. DiStefano. (2000). *International management behavior: From policy to practice* (4th ed.). Cambridge: Blackwell.

25. R. J. House, P. J. Hanges, M. Javidan, P. W. Dorfman, & V. Gupta (Eds.). (2004). *Culture, leadership and organizations: The GLOBE Study of 62 Societies*. Thousand Oaks, CA: Sage.

26. This example is adapted from: M. Festing, J. Eidems, & S. Royer. (2007, April). Strategic issues and local constraints in transnational compensation strategies: An analysis of cultural, institutional and political influences. *European Management Journal, 25*(2), 118–131.

27. C. Reade. (2001). Dual identification in multinational corporations: Local managers and their psychological attachment to the subsidiary versus the global organization. *International Journal of Human Resource Management, 12*(3), 405–424.

28. W. Liu. (2004). The cross-national transfer of HRM practices in MNCs: An integrative research model. *International Journal of Manpower, 25*(6), 500–517. For a general discussion of cultural distance see, for example: O. Shenkar. (2001). Cultural distance revisited: Towards a more rigorous conceptualization and measurement of cultural differences. *Journal of International Business Studies, 32*(3), 519–536.

29. A well-known definition for institutions is the following: Institutions consist of cognitive, normative, and regulative structures and activities that provide stability and meaning to social behaviour. See: W. R. Scott. (1995). *Institutions and organizations*. Thousand Oaks, CA: Sage, 33.

30. P. J. DiMaggio & W. W. Powell. (1983). The iron cage revisited: Institutional isomorphism and collective rationality in organizational fields. *American Sociological Review, 48*, 47–160; R. D. Whitley. (1992). *European business systems: Firms and markets in their national contexts*. London, UK: Sage; R. D. Whitley. (1992). *Business systems in East Asia: Firms, markets and societies*. London, UK: Sage.

31. A. Ferner. (1997). Country of origin effects and HRM in multinational companies. *Human Resource Management Journal, 7*(1), 19–37.

32. Whitley. *Business systems in East Asia: Firms, markets and societies*; Whitley. *European business systems: Firms and markets in their national context*.

33. Federal Ministry of Education and research (Ed.). (2004). *Education in Germany*. Bonn/Berlin: Federal Ministry of Education and Research.

34. A. Sharpe & J. Gibson. (2005, September). The Apprenticeship System in Canada: Trends and Issues. *Centre for the Study of Living Standards*.

35. P. Sparrow. (2004). International rewards systems: To converge or not to converge? In C. Brewster & H. Harris (Eds.) *International HRM: Contemporary issues in Europe*. London, UK: Routledge, 103.

36. S. N. As-Saber, P. J. Dowling, & P. W. Liesch. (1998). The role of human resource management in international joint ventures: A study of Australian-Indian joint ventures. *International Journal of Human Resource Management, 9*(5), 751–766.

37. S. E. Khilji. (2002). Modes of convergence and divergence: An integrative view of multinational practices in Pakistan. *International Journal of Human Resource Management, 13*(2), 232–253.

38. L. Liberman & I. Torbiörn. (2000). Variances in staff-related management practices at eight European country subsidiaries of a global firm. *International Journal of Human Resource Management, 11*(1), 37–59.

39. B. Taylor. (1999). Patterns of control within Japanese manufacturing plants in China: Doubts about Japanization in Asia. *Journal of Management Studies, 36*(6), 853–873.

40. Ferner. Country of origin effects and HRM in multinational companies.

41. A. Ferner, P. Almond, P. Butler, I. Cark, T. Colling, T. Edwards, & L. Holden. (2004). Das Human Resource Management amerikanischer Unternehmen in Großbritannien (Human resource management of US American enterprises in the United Kingdom). In H. Wächter & R. Peters (Eds.), *Personalpolitik amerikanischer Unternehmen in Europa*. München/Mering:

Hampp; A. Ferner, P. Almond, & T. Colling. (2005). Institutional theory and the cross-national transfer of employment policy: The case of "workforce diversity" in US multinationals. *Journal of International Business Studies, 36*, 304–321.

42. M. Pudelko & A.-W. Harzing. HRM practices in subsidiaries of US, Japanese and German MNCs: Country-of-origin, localization or dominance effect? *Human Resource Management* (forthcoming).

43. T. Edwards, P. Almond, I. Clark, T. Colling, & A. Ferner. (2005). Reverse diffusion in US multinationals: Barriers from the American business system. *Journal of Management Studies, 42*, 1261–1286.

44. A. Ferner, J. Quintanilla, & M. Varul. (2001). Country-of-origin effects, host-country effects, and the management of HR in multinationals. *Journal of World Business, 36*(2), 107–127.

45. T. Edwards, P. Almond, I. Clark, T. Colling, & A. Ferner. (2005). Reverse diffusion in US multinationals: Barriers from the American business system. *Journal of Management Studies, 42*, 1261–1286.

46. Y. Yan. (2003). A comparative study of human resource management practices in international joint ventures: The impact of national origin. *International Journal of Human Resource Management, 14*(4), 487–510.

47. For example: A. Gupta & V. Govindarajan. (1991). Knowledge flows and the structure of control within multinational corporations. *Academy of Management Review, 16*(4), 768–792; A. Gupta & V. Govindarajan. (1991). Organizing for knowledge flows within MNCs. *International Business Review, 3*(4), 443–458; J. Birkinshaw & A. J. Morrison. (1995). Configurations of strategy and structure in subsidiaries of multinational corporations. *Journal of International Business Studies, 26*(4), 729–754; J. Birkinshaw & N. Hood. (1998). Multinational subsidiary evolution: Capability and charter change in foreign-owned subsidiary companies. *Academy of Management Review, 23*(4), 773–795; B. Ambos & W. D. Reitsberger. (2004). Offshore centers of excellence: Social control and success. *Management International Review*, 4451–4466; K. Ferdows. (1989). Mapping international factory networks. In K. Ferdows (Ed.), *Managing International Manufacturing*. Amsterdam: North-Holland, 3–21; K. Ferdows. (1997). Making the most of foreign factories. *Harvard Business Review, 75*, 73–88.

48. See, for example: Birkinshaw & Hood. Multinational subsidiary evolution: Capability and charter change in foreign-owned subsidiary companies.

49. T. Ying. (2005, March 26–27). Electronics giant to open R&D company. *China Daily*, 4.

50. Gupta & Govindarajan. Knowledge flows and the structure of control within multinational corporations.

51. Human resource management implications are mainly based on: S. Taylor, S. Beechler, & N. Napier. (1996). Toward an integrative model of strategic international human resource management. *Academy of Management Review, 21*, 959–985.

52. A.-W. Harzing & N. Noorderhaven. Knowledge flows in MNCs: An empirical test and extension of Gupta and Govindarajan's typology of subsidiary roles.

53. Ibid.

54. Ibid.

55. Ibid., 195.

56. For a recent study on centres of excellence see: B. Ambos & W. D. Reitsperger. (2004). Offshore Centers of Excellence: Social Control and Success. *Management International Review, 44* (Special Issue 2), 51–65.

57. Morris, Snell, & Wright. A resource-based view of international human resources: Toward a framework of integrative and creative capabilities.

58. J. Birkinshaw & J. Ridderstråle. (1999). Fighting the corporate immune system: A process study of subsidiary initiatives in multinational corporations. *International Business Review, 8*(2), 154.

59. S. Michailova & K. Husted. (2003). Knowledge-sharing hostility in Russian firms. *California Management Review, 45*(3), 59–77.

60. O. Tregaskis. (2003). Learning networks, power and legitimacy in multinational subsidiaries. *International Journal of Human Resource Management, 14*(3), 431–447.

61. Taylor, Beechler, & Napier. Toward an integrative model of strategic international human resource management.

62. Festing, Eidems, & Royer. Strategic issues and local constraints in transnational compensation strategies: An analysis of cultural, institutional and political influences.

63. J. Birkinshaw & J. Ridderstråle. (1999). Fighting the corporate immune system: A process study of subsidiary initiatives in multinational corporations. *International Business Review, 8* (2), 149–180.

64. Festing, Eidems, & Royer. Strategic issues and local constraints in transnational compensation strategies: An analysis of cultural, institutional and political influences. For other resource dependence-oriented analyses, see: Y. Kim. (2002). Different subsidiary roles and international human resource management: An exploratory study of Australian subsidiaries in Asia. *Journal of Asia-Pacific Business, 4*, 39–60; B. Myloni, A.-W. Harzing, & H. Mirza. (2007, December). The effect of corporate-level organizational factors on the transfer of human resource management practices: European and US MNCs and their Greek subsidiaries. *International Journal of Human Resource Management, 18*(12), 2057–2074.

65. Gupta & Govindarajan. Knowledge flows and the structure of control within multinational corporation; Harzing. *Managing the multinationals: An international study of control mechanisms.*

66. J. I. Martinez & J. C. Jarillo. (1989). The evolution of research on coordination mechanisms in multinational corporations. *Journal of International Business Studies, 19*, 489–514.

67. J. I. Martinez & J. C. Jarillo. (1991). Coordination demands of international strategies. *Journal of International Business Studies, 21*, 431.

68. For a further discussion in the context of IHRM strategies see: M. Festing. (1997). International HRM in German MNCs. *Management International Review, 37* (Special Issue 1), 43–64.

69. A PricewaterhouseCoopers report points out that global workforce management includes the management of a respective database. For example, 70,000 employees of IBM have their profiles online: PricewaterhouseCoopers (Eds.). (2006). *Technology executive connections: Successful strategies for talent management.* United States: PricewaterhouseCoopers, 40.

70. These insights are based on an interview by one of the authors with the head of HR of a transnational organization.

71. J. P. Doh & T. R. Gay. (2004). Globalization and corporate social responsibility: How non-governmental organizations influence labor and environmental codes of conduct. *Management International Review, 44* (Special Issue 2), 7–29.

72. J. P. Sajhau. (1997). *Business ethics in the textile, clothing and footwear (TCF) industries: Codes of conduct* (working paper). Geneva: International Labour Office, Sectoral Activities Programme.

73. For standards for codes of conduct, refer also to: L. Paine, R. Deshpande, J. D. Margolis, & K. E. Bettcher. (2005, December). Up to code: Does your company's conduct meet world-class standards? *Harvard Business Review*, 122–133.

74. UNCTAD (Ed.). (2004). *World Investment Report 2004.* New York/Geneva: United Nations.

75. For a general discussion on entry mode choice including offshoring refer to: WTO (Ed.). (2005). *World Trade Report 2005, III—Thematic Essays, C—Offshoring Services: Recent Developments and Prospects.* Geneva: World Trade Organization.

76. UNCTAD. *World Investment Report 2004.* See also: S. Schmid & M. Daub. (2005). *Service Offshoring Subsidiaries—Towards a Typology* (Working Paper 12). Berlin: ESCP-EAP European School of Management.

77. WTO (Ed.). (2005). *World Trade Report 2005, III—Thematic Essays, C—Offshoring Services: Recent Developments and Prospects.* Geneva: World Trade Organization, 266.

78. Ibid., 267. See also: S. Schmid & M. Daub. *Service Offshoring Subsidiaries—Towards a Typology*.

79. P. Le Goff. (2005). Canada and Offshoring. Ottawa: *Library of Parliament*, Economic Division, PRB 04-59E.

80. UNCTAD (Ed.). (2004). *Service offshoring takes off in Europe*. Issued jointly by UNCTAD & Roland Berger Strategy Consultants. Geneva/New York: UNCTAD.

81. The Canadian Chamber of Commerce. (2005). Offshore outsourcing: Opportunities and challenges for the Canadian Economy. The Canadian Chamber of Commerce.

82. *Financial Times* [London, England], July 20, 2006.

83. UNCTAD. *Service offshoring takes off in Europe*.

84. UNCTAD (Ed.). (2004). *Offshoring—At the tipping point?* Geneva/New York: UNCTAD.

85. For different types of outsourcing in India, see: S. Bhowmik. (2004). Work in a globalizing economy: Reflections on outsourcing in India. *Labour, Capital and Society, 37*, 76–96.

86. I. Hunter. (2006). *The Indian Offshore Advantage—How Offshoring Is Changing the Face of HR*. Aldershot, UK: Gower Publishing.

87. J. Shankar. (2003, June 17). Growth surge drives subcontinent boom. *The Australian*, 34.

88. *Financial Times* [London, England], July 20, 2006.

89. With these examples, the importance of the global codes of conduct mentioned earlier in this chapter is underlined.

90. P. S. Budhwar, H. K. Luthar, & J. Bhatnagar. (2006). The dynamics of HRM systems in Indian BPO Firms. *Journal of Labor Research, 27*(3), 339–360.

91. A. Mehta, A. Armenakis, N. Mehta, & F. Irani. (2006). Challenges and opportunities of business process outsourcing in India. *Journal of Labor Research, 27*(3), 323–338.

92. P. Sparrow & P. S. Budhwar. (1997). Competition and change: Mapping the Indian HRM recipe against world wide patterns. *Journal of World Business, 32*, 224–242. See also: D. S. Sainni & P. S. Budhwar. (2004). HRM in India. In P. S. Budhwar, *Managing human resources in Asia-Pacific*. London/New York: Routledge, 113–139.

93. Budhwar, Luthar, & Bhatnagar. The dynamics of HRM systems in Indian BPO Firms, 345.

94. For further information about the Indian HRM system, refer to Sainni & Budhwar. HRM in India.

95. I. Björkman. (2004). Transfer of HRM to MNC affiliates in Asia-Pacific. In P. Budhwar (Ed.), *Managing Human resources in Asia-Pacific*. London, UK: Routledge, 253–267. For differences between Indian and foreign firms with respect to performance appraisal practices and management values, see: S. C. Amba-Rao, J. A. Petrick, J. N. D. Gupta, & T. J. Von der Embse. (2000). Comparative performance appraisal and management values among foreign and domestic firms in India. *International Journal of Human Resource Management, 11*(1), 60–89; As-Saber, Dowling, & Liesch. The role of human resource management in international joint ventures: A study of Australian–Indian joint ventures.

96. Budhwar, Luthar, & Bhatnagar. The dynamics of HRM systems in Indian BPO firms.

97. PricewaterhouseCoopers. *Technology executive connections: Successful strategies for talent management*, 42.

98. *International Herald Tribune*, April 20, 2005.

99. Budhwar, Luthar, & Bhatnagar. The dynamics of HRM systems in Indian BPO firms.

100. B. Einhorn. (2006, October 26). A dragon in R&D: China's labs may soon rival its powerhouse factories—and multinationals are flocking in for tech innovation. *Business Week*.

101. PricewaterhouseCoopers. (2006, July 20). *Technology executive connections: Successful strategies for talent management; Financial Times* [London, England].

102. *International Herald Tribune*, April 20, 2005.

103. B. Wilkinson, M. Eberhardt, J. McLaren, & A. Millington. (2005). Human resource barriers to partnership sourcing in China. *International Journal of Human Resource Management, 16*, 1886–1900.

104. R. L. Tung & V. Worm. (2001). Network capitalism: The role of human resources in penetrating the China market. *International Journal of Human Resource Management, 12*(4), 517–534.

105. P. J. Buckley, J. Clegg, & H. Tan. (2003). The art of knowledge transfer: Secondary and reverse transfer in China's telecommunications manufacturing industry. *Management International Review, 43*, 67–93.

106. C. J. Zhu. (1997). Human resource development in China during the transition to a new economic system. *Asia Pacific Journal of Human Resources, 35*(3), 19–44. The same is true in other Asian countries. Evidence is reported by: N. Kathri, C. T. Fern, & P. Budhwar. (2001). Explaining employee turnover in an Asian context. *Human Resource Management Journal, 11*(1), 54–74.

107. D. Z. Ding, K. Goodall, & M. Warner. (2000). The end of the "iron rice-bowl": Whither Chinese human resource management? *International Journal of Human Resource Management, 11*, 217–237; M. Warner. (2004). Human resource management in China revisited: Introduction. *International Journal of Human Resource Management, 15*, 617–634.

108. C. J. Zhu & P. J. Dowling. (2002). Staffing practices in transition: Some empirical evidence from China. *International Journal of Human Resource Management, 13*(4), 569–597.

109. K. Goodall & J. Roberts. (2003). Only connect: Teamwork in the multinational. *Journal of World Business, 38*(2), 150–164.

110. F. L. Cooke. (2004). HRM in China. In P. S. Budhwar, *Managing human resources in Asia-Pacific*. London/New York: Routledge, 17–34.

111. Zhu & Dowling. Staffing practices in transition: Some empirical evidence from China.

112. F. L. Cooke. (2004). HRM in China. In P. S. Budhwar, *Managing human resources in Asia-Pacific*. London/New York: Routledge, 26.

113. Cooke. HRM in China. This is confirmed by an empirical study by Glover and Siu. These authors have discussed the need for a better quality of management initiative in China. In their study, they found poor standards of training, dissatisfaction with the pay level, and inadequate communication structures: L. Glover & N. Siu. (2000). The human resource barriers to managing quality in China. *International Journal of Human Resource Management, 11*(5), 867–882.

114. See, for example: F. L. Cooke. (2004). Foreign firms in China: Modelling HRM in a toy manufacturing corporation. *Human Resource Management Journal, 14*(3), 31–52; Ding, Goodall, & Warner. The end of the "iron rice-bowl": Whither Chinese human resource management?

115. K. Venter. (2003). Building on formal education: Employers' approaches to the training and development of new recruits in the People's Republic of China. *International Journal of Training and Development, 7*(3), 186–202.

116. N. Khatri, C. T. Fern, & P. Budhwar. (2001). Explaining employee turnover in an Asian context. *Human Resource Management Journal, 11*(1), 54–74.

117. Chartered Institute of Personnel and Development. *People Management* (online magazine). Retrieved January 26, 2007, from www.peoplemanagement.co.uk.

118. Strategic decisions made at corporate headquarters, such as plant rationalization, can result in the closure of host-country operations, as multinationals divest and withdraw or de-internationalize. For example, in 2002, U.S. automobile manufacturer Ford Motor Company closed 5 of its 11 plants in Europe, resulting in job losses. The English car-assembly plant had been in operation for almost 71 years. Some staff was retained in the R&D (engine design) centre in England, but job losses are an inevitable outcome of such actions.

119. PricewaterhouseCoopers. (2006). *Technology executive connections: Successful strategies for talent management.* The survey generated responses from senior executives based in five principal regions: 30 percent Asia, 41 percent Europe, 23 percent North America, 5 percent Middle East and Africa, and 1 percent Latin America.

120. S. McGuiness & J. Bennett. (2006). Examining the link between skill shortages, training composition and productivity levels in the construction industry: Evidence from Northern Ireland. *International Journal of Human Resource Management, 17*(2), 265–279.

121. R. J. Burke & E. Ng. (2006). The changing nature of work and organizations: Implications for human resource management. *Human Resource Management Review, 16*, 86–94.

122. PricewaterhouseCoopers. *Technology executive connections: Successful strategies for talent management*, 21.

123. Burke & Ng. The changing nature of work and organizations: Implications for human resource management.

124. It is not just in China and India that a high turnover of subsidiary staff is being experienced. Firms operating in Russia have faced similar issues, as a study by Camiah and Hollinshead highlights. Demand for Russians with foreign language skills and experience working in Western companies is high, and such individuals can generally move freely between jobs. Khatri, Fern, and Budhwar report similar job-hopping behaviours in Singapore and other Asian countries: N. Camiah and G. Hollinshead. (2003). Assessing the potential for effective cross-cultural working between "new" Russian managers and Western expatriates. *Journal of World Business, 38*(3), 245–261; N. Khatri, C. T. Fern, & P. Budhwar. (2001). Explaining employee turnover in an Asian context. *Human Resource Management Journal, 11*(1), 54–74.

125. PricewaterhouseCoopers. *Technology executive connections: Successful strategies for talent management*, 40. Chinese wages and salaries are still lower than in Europe or in the United States. However, a worker in a sneaker factory earns 30 percent more than a colleague in Vietnam and 15 percent more than a colleague in Indonesia. See *International Herald Tribune*, April 20, 2005.

126. *Financial Times* [London, England], July 20, 2006.

127. R. L. Tung & M. Lazarova. (2006). Brain drain versus brain gain: An exploratory study of ex-host-country nationals in Central and Eastern Europe. *International Journal of Human Resource Management, 17*(11), 1853–1872.

128. Ibid., 1871.

129. A. Saxenian. (2005). From Brain Drain to Brain Circulation: Transnational Communities and Regional Upgrading in India and China. *Studies in Comparative International Development, 40*(2), 35–61.

130. R. Tung. (2007, May 1). The Human Resource Challenge to Outward Foreign Direct Investment Aspirations from Emerging Economies: The Case of China. *International Journal of Human Resource Management, 18*(5), 868–899.

131. Y. Baruch, P. W. Budhwar, & N. Kathri. (2007). Brain drain: Inclination to stay abroad after studies. *Journal of World Business, 42*, 99. For a critical view on brain drain, see: S. C. Carr, K. Inkson, & K. Thorn. (2005). From global careers to talent flow: Reinterpreting "brain drain." *Journal of World Business, 40*, 386–398.

132. However, as skill shortages exist in many countries, Carr et al. replace the term "brain drain" by describing "talent flows across borders," and Tung and Lazarova at least see a positive notion of brain gain: Carr, Inkson, and Thorn. From global careers to talent flow: Reinterpreting "brain drain; Tung and Lazarova. Brain drain versus brain gain: An exploratory study of ex-host-country nationals in Central and Eastern Europe.

Chapter 10

International Industrial Relations

Chapter Learning Objectives

After reading this chapter, you should be able to:

- outline the key issues in international industrial relations and the policies and practices of multinationals
- discuss the potential constraints that trade unions may have in relation to multinationals
- name key concerns for trade unions
- identify recent trends and issues in the global workforce context
- discuss the formation of regional economic zones such as the European Union and the impact of opponents to globalization

FOUR SEASONS GOES TO PARIS

For Four Seasons Hotels and Resorts, entering the French hospitality market in the late 1990s meant becoming a French employer, which implied understanding French labour laws, business culture, and national idiosyncrasies.

At that time, France's leaders remained committed to a capitalism that maintained social equity with laws, tax policies, and social spending that reduced income disparity and the impact of free markets on public health and welfare. France's tax burden, 45 percent of the GDP in 1998, was three percentage points higher than the European average—and eight points higher than the Organisation for Economic Co-operation and Development (OECD) average. A further burden on employers was the 1999 reduction of the workweek to 35 hours. Unemployment and retirement benefits were generous. Importantly, Four Seasons' management was not unfamiliar with labour-oriented government policy. "Canada has many attributes of a welfare state, so our Canadian roots made it easier to deal with such a context," Young [John Young, Fours Seasons executive vice president, HR] explained.

The country was known for its strong unions. "In France, one still finds a certain dose of antagonism between employees and management," a French manager commented. The political party of the Force Ouvrière, the union that was strongest at the Four Seasons' George V, garnered nearly 10 percent of the votes in the first round of the 2002 French presidential election with the rallying cry, "Employees fight the bosses!" "If you look at the challenges of operating in France," noted Corinthios [Four Seasons' Antoine Corinthios, president, Europe, Middle East, and Africa], "they have labor laws that are restrictive, but not prohibitive. The laws are not the same as, for example, in Chicago. You just need to be more informed about them."

The law did give employers some flexibility, allowing them to work someone a little more during peak business periods and less during a lull. A housekeeper, for example, might work 40–hour weeks in the summer in exchange for a few 30–hour weeks in the late fall. Furthermore, French employers could hire 10 percent to 15 percent of staff on a "temporary," seasonal basis. A particularly tricky area of labour management in France involved terminations. "Wherever we operate in the world," a Four Seasons manager explained, "we do not fire at will. There is due process. There is no surprise. There is counseling. So, Paris isn't that different, except to have the termination stick is more challenging because you really need a very, very good cause and to document everything carefully. If you have one gap in the documentation, you will have to rehire the terminated employee."

Four Seasons' expansion into new markets and countries such as France illustrates some of the challenges to be met and decisions to be made regarding the management of, or approach toward local labour unions. As this chapter shows, much of the success of foreign operations depends on the right policies and practices in relation to international industrial labour relationships. Besides an exploration of the MNEs' perspectives of international industrial labour relations, this chapter will also discuss the concerns and views of local and internationally organized trade unions.

Source: Hallowell, R., Bowen, D., & Knoop, C. (2002). Four Seasons goes to Paris. *Academy of Management Executive*, 16(4), 7.

Introduction

In this chapter we will use the more traditional term *industrial relations* to describe the broad field of study that looks at broader issues of work and employment. We recognize that newer terms such as *employee relations* and *employment relations* are also used in the literature, but prefer to use the traditional term in the global context as do organizations such as the International Organisation of Employers and the International Labour Organization.[1]

Before we examine the key issues in industrial relations as they relate to multinational firms, we need to consider some general points about the field of international industrial relations.[2] First, it is important to realize that it is difficult to compare industrial relations systems and behaviour across national boundaries; an industrial relations concept may change considerably when translated from one industrial relations context to another.[3] The concept of collective bargaining in Canada, for example, is understood to mean negotiations between a local trade union and management; in Sweden and Germany, the term refers to negotiations between an employers' organization and a trade union at the industry level. Cross-national differences also emerge as to the objectives of the collective bargaining process and the enforceability of collective agreements. Many European unions continue to view the collective bargaining process as an ongoing class struggle between labour and capital, whereas in Canada and the United States, union leaders tend toward a pragmatic economic view of collective bargaining rather than an ideological view. Second, it is very important to recognize in the international industrial relations field that no industrial relations system can be understood without an appreciation of its historical origin.[4] As Schregle[5] has observed:

> A comparative study of industrial relations shows that industrial relations phenomena are a very faithful expression of the society

in which they operate, of its characteristic features and of the power relationships between different interest groups. Industrial relations cannot be understood without an understanding of the way in which rules are established and implemented and decisions are made in the society concerned.

An interesting example of the effect of historical differences may be seen in the structure of trade unions in various countries. Poole[6] has identified several factors that may underlie these historical differences:

- The mode of technology and industrial organization at critical stages of union development.
- Methods of union regulation by government.
- Ideological divisions within the trade union movement.
- The influence of religious organizations on trade union development.
- Managerial strategies for labour relations in large corporations.

As Table 10.1 shows, union structures differ considerably among Western countries. These include industrial unions, which represent all grades of employees in an industry; craft unions, which are based on skilled occupational groupings across industries; conglomerate unions, which represent members in more than one industry; and general unions, which are open to almost all employees in a given country. These differences in union structures have had a major influence on the collective bargaining process in Western countries. Some changes in union structure are evident over time; for example, enterprise unions are increasingly evident in industrialized nations. Enterprise unions are common in Asia–Pacific nations, although

TABLE 10.1

Trade Union Structure in Leading Western Industrial Societies

Australia	general, craft, industrial, white-collar
Belgium	industrial, professional, religious, public sector
Canada	**industrial, craft, conglomerate**
Denmark	general, craft, white-collar
Finland	industrial, white-collar, professional and technical
Great Britain	general, craft, industrial, white-collar, public sector
Japan	enterprise
The Netherlands	religious, conglomerate, white-collar
Norway	industrial, craft
Sweden	industrial, craft, white-collar and professional
Switzerland	industrial, craft, religious, white-collar
USA	industrial, craft, conglomerate, white-collar
West Germany	industrial, white-collar

Source: Poole, M. (1986). *Industrial Relations: Origins and Patterns of National Diversity*. London, UK: Routledge & Kegan Paul, 79.

there are national variations in their functions and in the proportion of enterprise unions to total unions.

The less one knows about how a structure came to develop in a distinctive way, the less likely one is to understand it. As Prahalad and Doz[7] note, the lack of familiarity of multinational managers with local industrial and political conditions has sometimes needlessly worsened a conflict that a local firm would have been likely to resolve. Increasingly, MNEs are recognizing this shortcoming and admitting that industrial relations policies must be flexible enough to adapt to local requirements. This is evidently an enduring approach, even in firms that follow a non-union labour relations strategy where possible, as the case at the end of the chapter points out; although the case is some years old, the key points made remain relevant to current international industrial relations.

Key Issues in International Industrial Relations

The focus of this chapter is on the industrial relations strategies adopted by multinationals rather than the more general topic of comparative industrial relations.[8] We have already covered the emerging topic of "offshoring of labour" in Chapter 9. In this chapter, we examine the central question for industrial relations in an international context that concerns the orientation of MNEs to organized labour.

Industrial Relations Policies and Practices of Multinational Firms

Because national differences in economic, political, and legal systems produce markedly different industrial relations systems across countries, multinationals generally delegate the management of industrial relations to their foreign subsidiaries. However, a policy of decentralization does not keep corporate headquarters from exercising some coordination over industrial relations strategy. Generally, corporate headquarters will become involved in or oversee labour agreements made by foreign subsidiaries because these agreements may affect the international plans of the firm and/or create precedents for negotiations in other countries. Further, Marginson et al.[9] found that the majority of the firms in their study monitored labour performance across units in different countries. Comparison of performance data across national units of the firm creates the potential for decisions on issues such as unit location, capital investment, and rationalization of production capacity. The use of comparisons would be expected to be greatest where units in different countries undertake similar operations. For recent reviews of the literature in this area, see the work of Gunnigle and his colleagues.[10]

Much of the literature on the industrial relations practices of multinationals tends to be at a more cross-national or comparative level. There is, however, some research on industrial relations practices at the firm level. Empirical research has identified a number of differences in multinational approaches to industrial relations. Indeed, a number of studies have examined differences in the propensity of multinational headquarters to intervene in, or to centralize control over, matters such as industrial relations in host locations. Multinational headquarters involvement in industrial relations is influenced by several factors, as detailed below: the degree of inter-subsidiary production integration, nationality of ownership of the subsidiary, international human resource management approach, MNE prior experience in industrial relations, subsidiary characteristics, characteristics of the home product market, and management attitudes toward unions.

The Degree of Inter-Subsidiary Production Integration

According to Hamill,[11] a high degree of integration was found to be the most important factor leading to the centralization of the industrial relations function within the firms studied. Industrial relations throughout a system become of direct importance to corporate headquarters when transnational sourcing patterns have been developed; that is, when a subsidiary in one country relies on another foreign subsidiary as a source of components or as a user of its output.[12] In this context, a coordinated industrial relations policy is one of the key factors in a successful global production strategy.[13] One early example of the development of an international policy for industrial relations can be seen in the introduction of employee involvement across the Ford Motor Company's operations.[14]

Nationality of Ownership of the Subsidiary

There is evidence of differences between European and U.S. firms in terms of headquarters involvement in industrial relations.[15] A number of studies have revealed that U.S. firms tend to exercise greater centralized control over labour relations than do British or other European firms.[16] U.S. firms tend to place greater emphasis on formal management controls and a close reporting system (particularly in the area of financial control) to ensure that planning targets are met. In his review of empirical research of this area, Bean[17] showed that foreign-owned multinationals in Britain prefer single-employer bargaining (rather than involving an employer association), and are more likely than British firms to assert managerial prerogative on matters of labour utilization. Further, Hamill[18] found U.S.-owned subsidiaries to be much more centralized in labour relations decision making than British-owned ones. Hamill attributed this difference in management procedures to the more integrated nature of U.S. firms, the greater divergence between British and U.S. labour relations systems than between British and other European systems, and the more ethnocentric managerial style of U.S. firms.

International Human Resource Management Approach

RPC 10.1

In earlier chapters, we discussed the various international human resource management approaches utilized by multinationals; these have implications for international industrial relations. Interestingly, an ethnocentric predisposition is more likely to be associated with various forms of industrial relations conflict.[19] Conversely, it has been shown that more geocentric firms will have more influence on host-country industrial relations systems, due to the geocentric firms' greater propensity to participate in local events.[20]

MNE Prior Experience in Industrial Relations

European firms have tended to deal with industrial unions at the industry level (frequently via employer associations) rather than at the firm level. The opposite is more typical for Canadian and U.S. firms. In both countries, employer associations have not played a key role in the industrial relations system, and firm-based industrial relations policies are the norm.[21]

Subsidiary Characteristics

Research has identified a number of subsidiary characteristics to be relevant to centralization of industrial relations. First, subsidiaries that are formed through acquisition of well-established indigenous firms tend to be given much more autonomy over industrial relations than are greenfield sites set up by a multinational firm.[22] Second, according to Enderwick, greater intervention would be expected when the subsidiary is of key strategic importance to the firm and the subsidiary is young.[23] Third, where the parent firm is a significant source of operating or investment funds for the subsidiary (that is, where the subsidiary is more dependent on headquarters for resources), there will tend to be increased corporate involvement in industrial relations and human resource management.[24] Finally, poor subsidiary performance tends to be accompanied by increased corporate involvement in industrial relations. Where poor performance is due to industrial relations problems, multinationals tend to attempt to introduce parent-country industrial relations practices aimed at reducing industrial unrest or increasing productivity.[25]

Characteristics of the Home Product Market

An important factor is the extent of the home product market[26]—an issue that was discussed in detail in Chapter 1. If domestic sales are large relative to overseas operations (as is the case with, for example, many U.S. firms), it is more likely that overseas operations will be regarded by the parent firm as an extension of domestic operations. This is not the case for many European firms, whose international operations represent the major part of their business. Lack of a large home market is a strong incentive to adapt to host-country institutions and norms. There is evidence of change in the European context: Since the implementation of the single European market in 1993, there has been growth in large European-scale companies (formed via acquisition or joint ventures) that centralize management organization and strategic decision making. However, processes of operational decentralization with regard to industrial relations are also evident.[27]

Management Attitudes Toward Unions

An additional important factor is that of management attitudes or ideology concerning unions.[28] Knowledge of management attitudes concerning unions may provide a more complete explanation of multinational industrial relations behaviour than could be obtained by relying solely on a rational economic model. Thus, management attitudes should also be considered in any explanation of managerial behaviour, along with such factors as market forces and strategic choices. This is of particular relevance to U.S. firms, since union avoidance appears to be deeply rooted in the value systems of American managers.[29]

Despite its strong historical ties with the United States, in terms of union origins and developments and its adversarial union–management relations, Canada's private and in particular public sectors have been highly unionized in comparison to the United States. Table 10.2 shows that, of the 10 developed economies listed, Canada has the second-highest level of union membership, after Sweden, while the United States, France, and Korea have low levels of union density. Hence, managers from the latter countries may be less likely to have extensive experience with unions than may managers in Canada and many other countries.

Overall, Table 10.2 shows that union density growth has declined in many countries, which might be explained by economic factors such as reduced public sector employment and reduced employment in manufacturing industries as a share in total employment. In Canada, the once strong growth of union density has been largely attributed to the unionization of the public sector. However, budgetary constraints at all levels of Canada's government and its broader public sector (e.g., education, health care, and social services) have resulted in significant employment decreases.[30] The overall union density decline is also suggested to be associated with increased competition,

TABLE 10.2

Union Membership in Selected Countries

	Union Density (%)		Union Density Growth (%)
	1995	2000	1990–2000
Australia	35	25	−39
Canada	**34**	**31**	**−11**
France	10	10	stable
Germany	29	24	−25
Italy	38	36	−8
Japan	24	21	−16
Korea	14	12	−29
Sweden	83	79	−1
UK	32	29	−24
USA	15	13	−19

Source: Adapted from: Bamber, G., Ryan, S., & Wailes, N. (2004). Globalization, employment relations and human resources indicators in ten developed market economies: International data sets. *International Journal of Human Resource Management, 15*(8), Table 18.

decentralization of industrial relations to business unit-level, changes in governance, and legislative changes. Union membership decline is also linked to the introduction of new forms of work organization, globalization of production, and changes in workforce structure.[31]

Although several problems are inherent in data collection for a cross-national comparison of union density rates, several theories have been suggested to explain the variations among countries. Such theories consider economic factors such as wages, prices, and unemployment levels; social factors such as public support for unions; and political factors. In addition, studies indicate that the strategies utilized by labour, management, and governments are particularly important.[32]

Industrial disputes comprise another key issue in international industrial relations. Hamill[33] examined the strike-proneness of multinational subsidiaries and indigenous firms in Britain across three industries. Strike-proneness was measured via three variables—strike frequency, strike size, and strike duration. There was no difference across the two groups of firms with regard to strike frequency, but multinational subsidiaries did experience larger and longer strikes than local firms. Hamill suggests that this difference indicates that foreign-owned firms may be under less financial pressure to settle a strike quickly than local firms—possibly because they can switch production out of the country.

Overall, it is evident that international industrial relations are influenced by a broad range of factors. Commenting on the overall results of his research, Hamill concluded that:

> . . . general statements cannot be applied to the organization of the labor relations function within MNEs. Rather, different MNEs adopt different labor relations strategies in relation to the environmental factors peculiar to each firm. In other words, it is the type of multinational under consideration which is important rather than multinationality itself.[34]

Trade Unions and International Industrial Relations

Trade unions may limit the strategic choices of multinationals in three ways: (1) by influencing wage levels to the extent that cost structures may become uncompetitive; (2) by constraining the ability of multinationals to vary employment levels at will; and (3) by hindering or preventing global integration of the operations of multinationals.[35] We will briefly examine each of these potential constraints.

Influencing Wage Levels

Although the importance of labour costs relative to other costs is decreasing, labour costs still play an important part in determining cost competitiveness in most industries. The influence of unions on wage levels is therefore important. Multinationals that fail to successfully manage their wage levels will suffer labour cost disadvantages that may narrow their strategic options.

Constraining the Ability of Multinationals to Vary Employment Levels at Will

For many multinationals operating in Western Europe, Japan, and Australia, the inability to vary employment levels at will may be a more serious problem than wage levels. Many countries now have legislation that limits considerably the ability of firms to carry out plant closure, redundancy, or layoff programs unless it can be shown that structural conditions make these employment losses unavoidable. Frequently, the process of showing the need for these programs is long and drawn-out. Plant closure or redundancy legislation in many countries also frequently specifies that firms must compensate redundant employees through specified formulas, such as two weeks' pay for each year of service. In many countries, payments for involuntary terminations can be quite substantial.

Trade unions may influence this process in two ways: by lobbying their own national governments to introduce redundancy legislation, and by encouraging regulation of multinationals by international organizations such as the OECD. (Later in this chapter we describe the Badger case, which forced Raytheon to finally accept responsibility for severance payments to employees made redundant by the closing down of its Belgian subsidiary.) Multinational managers who do not take these restrictions into account in their strategic planning may well find their options severely limited. In fact, recent evidence shows that multinationals are beginning to consider the ability to dismiss employees to be one of the priorities when making investment location decisions.[36]

Hindering or Preventing Global Integration of Multinational Operations

In recognition of these constraints, many multinationals make a conscious decision not to integrate and rationalize their operations to the most efficient degree, because to do so could cause industrial and political problems. Prahalad and Doz[37] cite General Motors as an example of this "sub-optimization of integration." GM was alleged in the early 1980s to have undertaken substantial investments in Germany (matching its new investments in Austria and Spain) at the demand of the German metalworkers' union (one of the largest industrial unions in the Western world) in order to foster good industrial relations in Germany. One observer of the world auto industry suggested that car manufacturers were sub-optimizing their manufacturing networks partly to placate trade unions and partly to provide redundancy in sources to prevent localized social strife from paralyzing their network. This sub-optimization led to unit manufacturing costs in Europe that were 15 percent higher, on average, than an economically optimal network would have achieved. Prahalad and Doz drew the following conclusion from this example:

> Union influence thus not only delays the rationalization and integration of MNEs' manufacturing networks and increases the cost of such adjustments (not so much in the visible severance payments

and "golden handshake" provisions as through the economic losses incurred in the meantime), but also, at least in such industries as automobiles, permanently reduces the efficiency of the integrated MNC network. Therefore, treating labour relations as incidental and relegating them to the specialists in the various countries is inappropriate. In the same way as government policies need to be integrated into strategic choices, so do labour relations.[38]

Response of Trade Unions To Multinationals

Trade union leaders have long seen the growth of multinationals as a threat to the bargaining power of labour because of the considerable power and influence of large multinational firms. While it is recognized that multinationals are "neither uniformly anti-union nor omnipotent and monolithic bureaucracies,"[39] their potential for lobbying power and flexibility across national borders creates difficulties for employees and trade unions endeavouring to develop countervailing power. There are several ways in which multinationals have an impact on trade union and employee interests. Kennedy[40] has identified seven characteristics of MNEs as the source of trade union concern about multinationals, as outlined in IHRM Notebook 10.1.

Many of the points made by Kennedy would now be recognized as characteristics of the process now described as *offshoring* (also discussed in Chapter 9). This topic will remain a key issue within the broader debate concerning globalization and the employment consequences of globalization. For recent reviews of offshoring, see Auer et al.,[41] Cooke,[42] and Pyndt and Pedersen.[43]

Another issue reported by trade unions is their claim that they have difficulty accessing decision makers located outside the host country and obtaining financial information. For example, according to Martinez Lucio and Weston:

> Misinformation has been central to the management strategy of using potential investment or disinvestment in seeking changes in certain organizations. . . . For example, in companies such as Heinz, Ford, Gillette and General Motors, workers have established that they had on occasions been misinformed by management as to the nature of working practices in other plants.[44]

A final, and to some extent unusual, union concern is illustrated in IHRM Today 10.1.

The response of labour unions to multinationals has been threefold: to form international trade secretariats; to lobby for restrictive national legislation; and finally, to try and achieve regulation of multinationals by international organizations.

International Trade Secretariats

International trade secretariats (ITSs) function as loose confederations to provide worldwide links for the national unions in a particular trade or industry (e.g., metals, transport, and chemicals). The secretariats have mainly

international trade secretariats

loose confederations providing worldwide links for national unions in a particular trade or industry

Trade Union Concerns about MNEs

1. *Formidable financial resources*—This includes the ability to absorb losses in a particular foreign subsidiary that is in dispute with a national union and still show an overall profit on worldwide operations. Union bargaining power may be threatened or weakened by the broader financial resources of a multinational. This is particularly evident where a multinational has adopted a practice of transnational sourcing and cross-subsidization of products or components across different countries. "The economic pressure which a nationally based union can exert upon a multinational is certainly less than would be the case if the company's operations were confined to one country."*

2. *Alternative sources of supply*—This may take the form of an explicit "dual sourcing" policy to reduce the vulnerability of the multinational to a strike by any national union. Also, temporary switching of production in order to defeat industrial action has been utilized to some extent in, for example, the automotive industry.**

3. *Ability to move production facilities to other countries*—A reported concern of employees and trade unions is that job security may be threatened if a multinational seeks to produce abroad what could have, or previously has, been manufactured domestically. National relative advantages provide MNEs with choice as to location of units. Within the European Union, for example, evidence suggests that multinational management is locating skill-intensive activities in countries with national policies promoting training and with relatively high labour costs. Conversely, semi-skilled, routinized activities are being located in countries with lower labour costs.† Threats by multinationals, whether real or perceived, to reorganize production factors internationally, with the accompanying risk of plant closure or rationalization, will have an impact on management–labour negotiations at a national level. However, technical and economic investments would reduce a multinational's propensity to relocate facilities.

4. *Remote locus of authority (i.e., corporate head office management of a multinational firm)*—While many multinationals report decentralization and local responsiveness of HRM and industrial relations, trade unions and works councils have reported that the multinational decision-making structure is opaque and the division of authority obscured. Further, employee representatives may not be adequately aware of the overall MNE organizational strategy and activities.‡

5. *Production facilities in many industries*—As Vernon§ has noted, most multinationals operate in many product lines.

6. *Superior knowledge and expertise in industrial relations.*

7. *Capacity to stage an "investment strike"*—The multinational could refuse to invest any additional funds in a plant, thus ensuring that the plant will become obsolete and economically non-competitive.

Source: *Bean, R. (1985). Comparative Industrial Relations: An Introduction to Cross-National Perspectives. New York: St. Martin's Press, 191.
**Ibid.
†Marginson, P., Armstrong, P., Edwards, P. K., & Purcell, J. (1995). Extending Beyond Borders: Multinational Companies and the International Management of Labour. International Journal of Human Resource Management, 6(3).
‡Mahnkopf, B., & Altvater, E. (1995). Transmission Belts of Transnational Competition? Trade Unions and Collective Bargaining in the Context of European Integration. European Journal of Industrial Relations, 1(1), 101–117.
§Vernon, R. (1977). Storm Over the Multinationals: The Real Issues. Cambridge, MA: Harvard University Press.

operated to facilitate the exchange of information.[45] The long-term goal of each ITS is to achieve transnational bargaining with each of the multinationals in its industry. Each ITS has followed a similar program to achieve the goal of transnational bargaining.[46] The elements of this program are (1) research and

Unions Oppose TTCL Expat Management

The hiring of expatriates to run large utilities on behalf of the government is facing union opposition as a Canadian firm appears poised to take over the management of the country's only fixed-line operator, the Tanzania Telecommunications Company Ltd (TTCL). The opposition to SaskTel International is led by trade unions and opposition politicians. It comes just months after the government cancelled a contract under which South African expatriates have been managing the country's power utility, Tanesco.

Cabinet approval is awaited for appointment of the Canadian company, which is already running a project to upgrade TTCL's infrastructure. Tanzania has not achieved any tangible success with the contracted managers —hired under the country's privatisation programme, which is overseen by the Presidential Parastatal Sector Reform Commission. Critics allege a long-term conspiracy to weaken the country's only fixed-line business and eventually destroy it. Already, the Telecommunications Workers Union of Tanzania (Tewuta) has written to President Jakaya Kikwete asking him to suspend the takeover by the Canadian firm. Kewuta has called on Members of Parliament to scrutinise the proposal by the Canadians to ensure that the country's national interests are not compromised.

Tenders for the management of TTCL were advertised openly with seven companies submitting bids. Three bids were then selected for the prequalification stage. These were Equity Telecom BV, Netherland Telecom and SaskTel International. Word soon filtered out that the Canadians had clinched the deal. According to a draft of the contract, the scope of the work which the expatriate managers will do will include installations, operations and maintenance in areas that include public Internet access facility, public data telecommunication and public telecommunication system. It also includes installation of international gateways, in partnership with other stakeholders. SaskTel will undertake installation of fibre optic cables and information and communications technology (ICT) backbone. It will also participate in regional and global connectivity projects such as the East African Submarine Cable System (EASSy) and the East African Internet Exchange Point.

The union claims that the expatriates will be paid a minimum of up to Tsh37 billion ($29.4 million) in management fees and that payment will be made monthly in arrears based on actual levels of effort and expenses incurred during that month up to the maximum amount set out in the budget.

Source: Edwin, Wilfred. (2006, July 18). Unions oppose TTCL expat management. *The East African*.

information, (2) calling of company conferences, (3) establishing of company councils, (4) companywide union–management discussions, and (5) coordinated bargaining. Overall, the ITSs have met with limited success, the reasons for which Northrup[47] attributes to (1) the generally good wages and working conditions offered by multinationals, (2) strong resistance from multinational firm management, (3) conflicts within the labour movement, and (4) differing laws and customs in the industrial relations field.

Lobbying for Restrictive National Legislation

On a political level, trade unions have for many years lobbied for restrictive national legislation in Europe and the United States. The motivation for trade unions to pursue restrictive national legislation is based on a desire to prevent the export of jobs via multinational investment policies. For example, in the United States, the AFL-CIO has lobbied strongly in this area.[48] The strong trend for direct investments by foreign MNEs into Canadian businesses could provoke similar calls for restrictive legislative measures. A major difficulty for unions when pursuing this strategy is the reality of conflicting national economic interests. In times of economic downturn, this factor may become an insurmountable barrier for trade union officials. To date, these attempts have largely been unsuccessful and, with the increasing internationalization of business, it is difficult to see how governments will be persuaded to legislate in this area.

Regulation of Multinationals by International Organizations

W W W 10.1–10.5

Attempts by trade unions to exert influence over multinationals via international organizations have met with some success. Through trade union federations such as the European Trade Union Confederation (ETUC) and the International Confederation of Free Trade Unions (ICFTU), the labour movement has been able to lobby the International Labour Organization (ILO), the United Nations Conference on Trade and Development (UNCTAD),[49] the Organisation for Economic Co-operation and Development (OECD), and the European Union (EU). The ILO has identified a number of workplace-related principles that should be respected by all nations: freedom of association, the right to organize and collectively bargain, abolition of forced labour, and non-discrimination in employment. In 1977, the ILO adopted a code of conduct for multinationals (Tripartite Declaration of Principles Concerning MNEs and Social Policy).[50] The ILO code of conduct, which was originally proposed in 1975, was influential in the drafting of the OECD guidelines for multinationals, which were approved in 1976. These voluntary guidelines cover disclosure of information, competition, financing, taxation, employment and industrial relations, and science and technology.[51]

chapeau clause

key section of the voluntary OECD guidelines for multinationals

A key section of these guidelines is the umbrella or **chapeau clause** (the latter is the more common term in the literature) that precedes the guidelines themselves. This clause states that multinationals should adhere to the guidelines "within the framework of law, regulations and prevailing labor relations and employment practices, in each of the countries in which they operate." Campbell and Rowan[52] state that employers have understood the chapeau clause to mean compliance with local law supersedes the guidelines, while labour unions have interpreted this clause to mean that the guidelines are a "supplement" to national law. The implication of this latter interpretation is significant: A firm could still be in violation of the OECD guidelines even though its activities have complied with national law and practice.

Given the ambiguity of the chapeau clause and the fact that the OECD guidelines are voluntary, it is likely that this issue will remain controversial.

There is also some controversy in the literature as to the effectiveness of the OECD guidelines in regulating multinational behaviour.[53] This lack of agreement centres on assessments of the various challenges to the guidelines. The best known of these challenges is the Badger case described in IHRM Today 10.2.

Blanpain[54] concludes that the Badger case made clear the responsibility of the parent company for the financial liability of its subsidiary, but that this responsibility is not unqualified. As to whether the Badger case proved the "effectiveness" of the OECD guidelines, Jain[55] and Campbell and Rowan[56] point out that the Belgian unions devoted considerable resources to make this a test case and had assistance from both American unions (which, through the AFL-CIO, lobbied the U.S. Department of State) and the Belgian government in their negotiations with the OECD and Badger executives. Liebhaberg[57] is more specific in his assessment:

> Despite an outcome which those in favour of supervision consider to be positive, the Badger Case is a clear demonstration of one of the weaknesses in the OECD's instrument, namely that it does not represent any sort of formal undertaking on the part of the twenty-four member states which are signatories to it. The social forces of each separate country must apply pressure on their respective governments if they want the guidelines applied.

A recent development with the OECD guidelines (which are addressed by 36 OECD and non-OECD governments) has been the follow-up procedures: National Contact Points. The system of National Contact Points promotes observance of the guidelines by MNEs operating in or from the governments' territories. It appears that this system is now having some

IHRM Today 10.2

The Badger Case*

The Badger Company was a subsidiary of Raytheon, a U.S.-based multinational. In 1976, the Badger Company decided to close its Belgian subsidiary, and a dispute arose concerning termination payments. Since Badger (Belgium) NV had filed for bankruptcy, the Belgian labour unions argued that Raytheon should assume the subsidiary's financial obligations. Raytheon refused, and the case was brought before the OECD by the Belgian government and the International Federation of Commercial, Clerical, Professional and Technical Employees (FIET), an international trade secretariat. The OECD's Committee on Interna-tional Investment and Multinational Enterprises (CIME) indicated that paragraph six of the guidelines (concerned with plant closures) implied a "shared responsibility" by the subsidiary and the parent in the event of a plant closing. Following this clarification by the CIME and a scaling down of initial demands, Badger executives and Belgian government officials negotiated a settlement of this case.

*For a detailed account of this case see: Blanpain, R. (1977). *The Badger Case and the OECD Guidelines for Multinational Enterprises*. Deventer, Netherlands: Kluwer.

influence on MNE behaviour in the industrial relations area. As the chair of the 2005 Annual Meeting of the National Contact Points (NCPs) noted:

> The NCPs' reports suggest that many adhering governments have deepened their use of the Guidelines in the context of a "whole of government" approach to corporate responsibility. They have expanded their promotion with and through embassy networks, export credit and investment guarantee programs and other specialized agencies and Ministries. Taken together, the NCP reports on promotion attest to the ongoing vigour of adhering countries' commitment to the Guidelines.[58]

Recognizing the limitations of voluntary codes of conduct, European trade unions have also lobbied the European Commission to regulate the activities of multinationals.[59] Unlike the OECD, the European Commission can translate guidelines into law, and has developed a number of proposals concerning disclosure of information to make multinationals more "transparent."[60] These are discussed in more detail in the next section.

Regional Integration: The European Union (EU)

Regional integration such as the development of the European Union (EU) has had significant implications for industrial relations.[61] In the Treaty of Rome (1957), some consideration was given to social policy issues related to the creation of the European Community. In the EU, the terms *social policy* or *social dimension* are used to cover a number of issues, including in particular labour law and working conditions, aspects of employment and vocational training, and social security and pensions.

A number of significant developments have taken place in EU social policy over the past four decades. The Social Charter of the Council of Europe (or, simply, the European Social Charter) came into effect in 1965. In 1987, the major objective of the implementation of the Single European Act was to establish the Single European Market (SEM) on December 31, 1992, in order to enhance the free movement of goods, money, and people within the SEM. The social dimension aims to achieve a large labour market by eliminating the barriers that restrict the freedom of movement and the right of domicile within the SEM. The European Community Charter of the Fundamental Social Rights of Workers (often referred to simply as the Social Charter) was introduced in 1989, and has guided the development of social policy in the 1990s.[62] Naturally, the social dimension has been the subject of much debate: Proponents defend the social dimension as a means of achieving social justice and equal treatment for EU citizens, while critics see it as a kind of "social engineering."[63]

At the signing of the Treaty on European Union in Maastricht in February 1992, Britain was allowed to opt out of the social policy agreements. The other 11 member states were party to a protocol (the Social Policy Protocol), which allows them to agree their own directives without Britain's participation.[64] With the election of the Blair Labour government in Britain in 1997, this anomaly was resolved when all members of the EU signed the Treaty of Amsterdam on June 17, 1997. This means that a single coherent legal basis now exists for action by the EU member states with regard to social policy.

The "Social Provisions" chapter of the Treaty of Amsterdam opens with a general statement of objectives.[65] Its first article (Article 117 of the EC Treaty), drawn largely from Article 1 of the Maastricht Social Agreement, begins with a reference to fundamental social rights such as those in the European Social Charter of 1961 and the Social Charter of 1989. It then sets out the objectives for the EU: to support and complement the activities of the member states in a number of listed areas. These include improvement of working conditions and of the working environment in the interest of workers' health and safety, information and consultation of workers, integration of persons excluded from the labour market, and equality of opportunity, and at work, between men and women. However, the Treaty excludes matters of pay, the right of association, and the right to strike or to lock out. The European Commission department responsible for social policy is known as the Directorate General for Employment, Social Affairs & Equal Opportunities.[66]

Disclosure of Information and European Works Councils

The EU has introduced a range of directives related to the social dimension. Of the directives concerned with multinationals, the most contentious has been the Vredeling Directive (associated with Henk Vredeling, a former Dutch member of the EU Commission).[67] The Seventh (Vredeling) Directive's requirement of disclosure of company information to unions faced strong opposition, led by the then Conservative British government and employer representatives. They argued that employee involvement in consultation and decision making should be voluntary. The European Works Councils (EWC) Directive was approved on September 22, 1994, and implemented two years later. Under the terms of the Treaty of Amsterdam, this directive applies to all EU member states. This was the first pan-European legislation that regulated collective relationships between multinationals and employees. The directive requires EWCs to be established in multinationals with at least 1,000 employees, having 100 or more employees in each of two member states. According to Chesters, more than 1,000 multinationals, including around 200 U.S.-based firms, are affected by the EWC directive.[68] The directive is designed to provide coverage to all employees, whether unionized or not. The EWC directive aims to enhance employees' rights to information and consultation in general and provide rights to information regarding international corporate decisions that would significantly affect workers' interests.[69] Partly in response to the EWC directive, firms such as General Motors and Heinz have subsidized visits of worker representatives to other plants and provided information and forums for discussion at the European level.[70]

Obviously, all firms operating in the EU will need to become familiar with EU directives and keep abreast of changes. While harmonization of labour laws can be seen as the ultimate objective, Michon[71] argues that the notion of a European social community does not mean a unification of all social conditions and benefits or, for that matter, of all social systems. However, the EU does aim to establish minimal standards for social conditions that will safeguard the fundamental rights of workers. A study on European Works Councils by Gilman and Marginson[72] summarized these somewhat conflicting trends in the following way:

> The salience of both country and sector influences on the provisions of EWC agreements places a question mark against the perspective that sees EWCs as primarily international extensions of national structures of information and consultation. The influence of national systems of industrial relations on the provisions of EWC agreements is important, but the similarities within particular sectors, which cross national borders, reflects a more general process of "converging divergences" (Katz and Darbishire, 2000) under which growing divergence in industrial relations arrangements and practice within national systems is occurring alongside increased cross-border convergence of practices within given sectors.

The Issue of Social "Dumping"

One of the concerns related to the formation of the SEM was its impact on jobs. There was alarm that those member states that have relatively low social security costs would have a competitive edge and that firms would locate in those member states that have lower labour costs. The counter-alarm was that states with low-cost labour would have to increase their labour costs, to the detriment of their competitiveness.[73] There are two industrial relations issues here: the movement of work from one region to another and its effect on employment levels, and the need for trade union solidarity to prevent workers in one region from accepting pay cuts to attract investment, at the expense of workers in another region. There is some, although not as much as was expected, evidence of social "dumping" in the EU.[74] It is likely that this issue will be a contentious one in Europe for some time, and multinationals need to be aware of this debate when doing business in Europe.[75]

One of the key reasons that the question of social dumping will probably remain a live issue is the acceptance into the EU in 2004 and 2007 of 12 members that are mostly relatively low-income states, some of which have not fully completed their transition from a communist system. The EU, through the Lisbon Strategy, has recommitted itself to the European Employment Strategy, with ambitious targets to be achieved by 2010. As Ingham et al.[76] concluded, however, the likelihood of the EU being able to meet the targets set out in the European Employment Strategy is remote.

In line with the OECD guidelines, Canada has created a National Contact Point, represented by an interdepartmental committee of the federal government that includes the departments of Foreign Affairs and International Trade, Industry, Human Resources and Social Development, Environment, Natural Resources, and Finance, along with the Canadian International

Development Agency. External key business and labour partners include the Canadian Labour Congress and the Confédération des syndicates nationaux. The overall aim of Canada's National Contact Point is the promotion of awareness of the OECD guidelines and their successful implementation. While Canada's NCP points out that the guidelines are not a substitute for, nor do they override, Canadian law, the committee emphasizes the guidelines' salient role in the government's promotion of corporate social responsibility (CSR). Activities and results include national round tables, conferences, and CSR reports for, for example, Canadian mining firms operating in developing countries.

Summary

The literature reviewed in this chapter and the discussion surrounding the formation of regional economic zones such as the European Union and the Asia–Pacific Economic Cooperation (APEC)[77] supports the conclusion that transnational collective bargaining has yet to be attained by trade unions.[78] As Enderwick[79] noted:

> The international operations of MNEs do create considerable impediments in effectively segmenting labour groups by national boundaries and stratifying groups within and between nations. Combining recognition of the overt segmentation effects of international business with an understanding of the dynamics of direct investment yields the conclusion that general multinational collective bargaining is likely to remain a remote possibility.

Enderwick argues that trade unions should opt for less-ambitious strategies in dealing with multinationals, such as (1) strengthening national union involvement in plant-based and company-based bargaining; (2) supporting research on the vulnerability of selective multinationals; and (3) consolidating the activities of company-based ITSs. Despite setbacks, especially with the regional economic integration issues discussed in this chapter, it is likely that trade unions and the ILO will pursue these strategies and continue to lobby where possible for the regulation of multinationals via the European Commission and the United Nations.

It is also likely that opponents of globalization will continue to attempt to influence public opinion in the developed economies with campaigns against selected MNEs, with industrial relations policies and practices being a particular target. The 2005 campaign against Wal-Mart, utilizing the documentary film *Wal-Mart: The High Cost of Low Price*,[80] is an example of such a campaign. One of the key points made in the film is that Wal-Mart employees have either poor medical coverage or none at all. However, as the business magazine *Fortune* astutely pointed out, in a globalized economy:

> American companies can't continue paying the world's highest health-care costs. Don't blame Wal-Mart; blame America's inability to devise a national health care plan that takes the burden off employers.[81]

With globalization, what was once a domestic issue has now become in part an international issue and, in turn, raises public policy questions as to what health care costs U.S. firms can be expected to fund in a globalized economy. It is likely that the impact of globalization on international industrial relations will be an ongoing issue in the foreseeable future.

Key Terms

chapeau clause 346   international trade secretariats 343

Web Links

www 10.1 European Trade Union Confederation (ETUC):

www.etuc.org

www 10.2 International Trade Union Confederation (ITUC):

www.ituc-csi.org

www 10.3 International Labour Organization (ILO):

www.ilo.org

www 10.4 United Nations Conference on Trade and Development (UNCTAD):

www.unctad.org

www 10.5 Tripartite Declaration of Principles Concerning MNEs and Social Policy:

www.ilo.org/public/english/employment/multi/download/english.pdf

www 10.6 European Commission Directorate General for Employment, Social Affairs & Equal Opportunities:

http://ec.europa.eu/dgs/employment_social/index_en.htm

www 10.7 Canada's National Contact Point for the OECD Guidelines for Multinational Enterprises:

www.ncp-pcn.gc.ca

RPC Icons

RPC 10.1 Creates procedures for researching and establishing HR policies
RPC 10.2 Creates procedures for researching and establishing HR policies

Discussion Questions

1. Why is it important to understand the historical origins of national industrial relations systems?

2. In what ways can trade unions constrain the strategic choices of multinationals?
3. Identify four characteristics of MNEs that give trade unions cause for concern.
4. What is "social dumping" and why should unions be concerned about it?
5. Can you give examples of documentary films like the one about Wal-Mart that are critical of large multinational firms?

Using the Internet

1. How are trade unions responding to MNE employment practices? Take a look at foreign-based car manufacturing MNEs operating in Canada (e.g., GM or Ford in Ontario) and explore their industrial relations policies and practices with the Canadian Auto Workers Union. Browse through online company documents and press releases and daily and weekly Canadian and international business publications.
2. Check out the International Trade Union Confederation (ITUC) website and find out how this organization is involved in the campaigns it promotes. Go to the ITUC home page at **www.ituc-csi.org** and click on "Campaigns."

Exercises

1. Compare the historical origins of the national industrial relations systems of Canada and a country of your choice. How have the historical developments of these systems in Canada and your country of choice influenced current labour relations in those two countries? Identify labour relations policies and practices illustrating those influences.
2. In groups, select a country of your choice and explore its labour relations, structures, policies, and practices. With your group, discuss how these aspects might affect your staffing decisions when expanding in the country you have chosen.

Case

Advice for Companies Going Global

The key to successfully expanding overseas is to become one with the culture of the location, even if it means unionization of employees, Michael R. Quinlan, [then] chairman and chief executive officer of McDonald's Corp., tells conferees at a meeting of the Human Resources Management Association of Chicago.

After opening fast-food restaurants in 53 nations, McDonald's has learned that it must follow the established practices of a foreign country to succeed there, Quinlan says. For example, a number of European countries and Australia have very strict unionization standards, and operations there are unionized as a condition of doing business. Acknowledging that McDonald's has had some "horrible union fights around the world," Quinlan advises employers considering expansion into other nations to "do it their way, not your way."

The main implication of dealing with unions is the increased cost of wages and benefits, according to Quinlan. Still, he adds that he does not feel unionization has interfered with employees' loyalty to McDonald's or to the company's philosophy of service and employee motivation. Declaring that unions do not "bring much to the equation" of the employee/employer relationship, Quinlan says McDonald's is "basically a non-union company" and intends to stay that way.

Another source of difficulty for McDonald's in its expansion overseas lies in the fact that fast-food restaurants are unfamiliar in most nations. Opening the first McDonald's inside the Communist-bloc, in Yugoslavia, took 12 years, Quinlan notes. He also points out that the company's policy is to staff its restaurants, from crew through management, only with nationals—for the 3,300 foreign outlets, the corporation employs only 35 expatriate U.S. citizens, and its goal is to have 100 percent local employees within five years.

Source: Bureau of National Affairs. (1991, March 7). *Bulletin to Management*, 66–67.

Questions

1. In groups, discuss the different approaches and strategies that global players such as McDonald's can select to deal with local labour unions when entering a new country.
2. Do you agree with Quinlan's statement that unions do not "bring much to the equation" of the employee/employer relationship? Explain!
3. Considering McDonald's relatively standardized products and service, does it come as a surprise to you that McDonald's employs so relatively few expatriates?
4. If McDonald's achieves its goal of having 100 percent local employees, what are the advantages and disadvantages of having solely local management negotiating with the local labour unions?

Endnotes

1. For the International Organisation of Employers, go to www.ioe-emp.org, click on "Policy Areas" and then on "International Industrial Relations." For the International Labour Organization, go to www.ilo.org.
2. These introductory comments are drawn from: J. Schregle. (1981). Comparative Industrial Relations: Pitfalls and Potential. *International Labour Review, 120*(1), 15–30.

3. This point is also referred to as the *emic–etic* problem. See Chapter 1 for a detailed discussion of this point.

4. O. Kahn-Freund. (1979). *Labour Relations: Heritage and Adjustment*. Oxford: Oxford University Press. Also see: R.B. Peterson & J. Sargent. (1997). Union and Employer Confederation Views on Current Labour Relations in 21 Industrialized Nations. *Relations Industrielles, 52*(1), 39–59.

5. J. Schregle. Comparative Industrial Relations, 28.

6. M. Poole. (1986). *Industrial Relations: Origins and Patterns of National Diversity*. London: Routledge.

7. C. K. Prahalad & Y. L. Doz. (1987). *The Multinational Mission: Balancing Local Demands and Global Vision*. New York: The Free Press.

8. For general reviews of the comparative industrial relations literature, see: T. Kennedy. (1980). *European Labour Relations*. Lexington, MA: Lexington Books; R. Bean. (1985). *Comparative Industrial Relations: An Introduction to Cross-National Perspectives*. New York: St. Martin's Press; Poole. *Industrial Relations*; G. Bamber, R. Lansbury & N. Wailes (Eds.). *International and Comparative Employment Relations* (4th ed.). London, UK: Sage. 2004.

9. P. Marginson, P. Armstrong, P. K. Edwards & J. Purcell. (1995). Extending Beyond Borders: Multinational Companies and the International Management of Labour. *International Journal of Human Resource Management, 6*(3), 702–719; and M. Martinez Lucio & S. Weston. (1994). New Management Practices in a Multinational Corporation: The Restructuring of Worker Representation and Rights. *Industrial Relations Journal, 25*, 110–121.

10. See the following publications by Gunnigle and his colleagues: P. Gunnigle, D. G. Collings, & M. J. Morley. (2006). Accommodating global capitalism: Industrial relations in American MNCs in Ireland. In A. Ferner, J. Quintanilla, & C. Sanchez-Runde (Eds.), *Multinationals and the Construction of Transnational Practices: Convergence and Diversity in the Global Economy*. London, UK: Palgrave Macmillan; P. Gunnigle, D. Collings, & M. Morley. (2005). Exploring the dynamics of industrial relations in US multinationals: Evidence from the Republic of Ireland. *Industrial Relations Journal, 36*(3), 241–256; P. Almond, T. Edwards, T. Colling, A. Ferner, P. Gunnigle, M. Muller-Camen, J. Quintanilla, & H. Waechter. (2005). Unraveling home and host country effects: An investigation of the HR policies of an American multinational in four European countries. *Industrial Relations, 44*(2), 276–306; and I. Clark, P. Almond, P. Gunnigle, & H. Waechter. (2005). The Americanisation of the European business system? *Industrial Relations Journal, 36*(6), 494–517.

11. J. Hamill. (1984). Labour Relations Decision Making within Multinational Corporations. *Industrial Relations Journal, 15*(2), 30–34.

12. S. H. Robock & K. Simmonds. (1989). *International Business and Multinational Enterprises* (4th ed.). Homewood, IL: Irwin; Marginson, Armstrong, Edwards, & Purcell. Extending Beyond Borders.

13. D. F. Hefler. (1981). Global Sourcing: Offshore Investment Strategy for the 1980s. *Journal of Business Strategy, 2*(1), 7–12.

14. K. Starkey & A. McKinlay. (1993). *Strategy and the Human Resource: Ford and the Search for Competitive Advantage*. Oxford, UK: Blackwell.

15. B. C. Roberts & J. May. (1974). The Response of Multinational Enterprises to International Trade Union Pressures. *British Journal of Industrial Relations, 12*, 403–416; and R. Hyman & A. Ferner. (1992) (cited in Bean, *Comparative Industrial Relations*).

16. See: J. La Palombara & S. Blank. (1976). *Multinational Corporations and National Elites: A Study of Tensions*. New York: The Conference Board; A. B. Sim. (1977). Decentralized Management of Subsidiaries and Their Performance: A Comparative Study of American, British and Japanese Subsidiaries in Malaysia. *Management International Review, 17*(2), 45–51; and Y. K. Shetty. (1979). Managing the Multinational Corporation: European and American Styles. *Management International Review, 19*(3), 39–48.

17. Bean. *Comparative Industrial Relations*.

18. Hamill. Labour Relations Decision Making.

19. See: P. Marginson. (1992). European Integration and Transnational Management–Union Relations in the Enterprise. *British Journal of Industrial Relations, 30*(4), 529–545.

20. Martinez Lucio & Weston. New Management Practices in a Multinational Corporation.

21. See: Bean. *Comparative Industrial Relations*; D. Bok. (1971). Reflections on the Distinctive Character of American Labor Law. *Harvard Law Review, 84*, 1394–1463; J. P. Windmuller & A. Gladstone (Eds.). (1984). *Employers Associations and Industrial Relations: A Comparative Study*. Oxford: Clarendon Press.; and L. R. Gomez-Mejia, D. Balkin, R. Cardy, D. Dimick, & A. Templer. (2004). *Managing Human Resources*. Toronto: Pearson Prentice Hall.

22. Hamill. Labour Relations Decision Making.

23. P. Enderwick. (1984). The Labour Utilization Practices of Multinationals and Obstacles to Multinational Collective Bargaining. *Journal of Industrial Relations, 26*(3), 354–364.

24. P. M. Rosenzweig & N. Nohria. (1994). Influences on Human Resource Management Practices in Multinational Corporations. *Journal of International Business Studies, 25*(2), 229–251.

25. Hamill. Labour Relations Decision Making.

26. Also see: Bean. *Comparative Industrial Relations*.

27. P. Marginson & K. Sisson. (1994). The Structure of Transnational Capital in Europe: The Emerging Euro-Company and Its Implications for Industrial Relations. In R. Hyman & A. Ferner (Eds.), *New Frontiers in European Industrial Relations*. Oxford: Blackwell; K. Williams & M. Geppert. (2006). The German model of employee relations on trial: Negotiated and unilaterally imposed change in multi-national companies. *Industrial Relations Journal, 37*(1), 48–63.

28. For an interesting discussion of the importance of understanding ideology, see: G. C. Lodge. (1985). Ideological Implications of Changes in Human Resource Management. In D. R. E. Walton & P. R. Lawrence, *HRM Trends and Challenges*. Boston: Harvard Business School Press.

29. T. A. Kochan, R. B. McKersie, & P. Cappelli. (1984). Strategic Choice and Industrial Relations Theory. *Industrial Relations, 23*(1), 16–39.

30. L. R. Gomez-Mejia, D. Balkin, R. Cardy, D. Dimick, & A. Templer. *Managing Human Resources*. Toronto: Pearson Prentice Hall, 405–406.

31. See: V. Frazee. (1998). Trade Union Membership Is Declining Globally. *Workforce, 3*(2), 8; *World Labour Report: Industrial Relations, Democracy and Social Stability*, 1997–98. Geneva: ILO; W. Groot & A. van den Berg. (1994). Why Union Density Has Declined. *European Journal of Political Economy, 104*, 749–763.

32. See: Bean. *Comparative Industrial Relations*; Poole. *Industrial Relations*; and J. Visser. (1988). Trade Unionism in Western Europe: Present Situation and Prospects. *Labour and Society, 13*(2), 125–182.

33. J. Hamill. (1984). Multinational Corporations and Industrial Relations in the U.K. *Employee Relations, 6*(5), 12–16.

34. Hamill. Labour Relations Decision Making, 34.

35. This section is based in part on: Prahalad & Doz. *The Multinational Mission*, Chapter 5, The Impact of Organized Labour.

36. For example, the decision by Hoover to shift some of its production from France to Scotland in the early 1990s appeared to be influenced by the ease with which the employer could implement layoffs. See: D. Goodhart. (1993, February 15). Ground rules for the firing squad. *Financial Times*, 8.

37. Prahalad & Doz. *The Multinational Mission*.

38. Ibid., 102.

39. M. Allen. (1993). Worldly Wisdom. *New Statesman and Society, 6*, xii.

40. Kennedy. *European Labour Relations*.

41. P. Auer, G. Besse, & D. Meda (Eds.). (2006). *Offshoring and the internationalization of employment: A challenge for a fair globalization?* Geneva: International Labour Organization.

42. W. Cooke. (2005). Exercising power in a prisoner's dilemma: Transnational collective bargaining in an era of corporate globalization? *Industrial Relations Journal, 36*(4), 283–302.

43. J. Pyndt & T. Pedersen. (2006). *Managing Global Offshoring Strategies*. Copenhagen. Copenhagen Business School Press.

44. M. Martinez Lucio & S. Weston. (1995). Trade Unions and Networking in the Context of Change: Evaluating the Outcomes of Decentralization in Industrial Relations. *Economic and Industrial Democracy,16*, 244.

45. For a detailed analysis of ITSs, see: R. Neuhaus. (1982). *International Trade Secretariats: Objectives, Organization, Activities* (2nd ed.). Bonn: Friedrich-EbertStiftung. For an overview of international labour politics and organizations, see: T. Boswell & D. Stevis. (1997). Globalisation and International Labour Organizing: A World-System Perspective. *Work and Occupations, 24*(3), 288–308.

46. N. Willatt. (1974). *Multinational Unions: A Study*. London, UK: Financial Times.

47. H. R. Northrup. (1978). Why Multinational Bargaining Neither Exists Nor Is Desirable. *Labour Law Journal, 29*(6), 330–342. Also see: J. Gallagher. (1997). Solidarity Forever. *New Statesman & Society*, 10.

48. See: Kennedy. *European Labour Relations;* and R. B. Helfgott. (1983). American Unions and Multinational Enterprises: A Case of Misplaced Emphasis. *Columbia Journal of World Business, 18*(2), 81–86.

49. Until 1993, there was a specialized UN agency known as the United Nations Centre on Transnational Corporations (UNCTC), which had published a number of reports on MNEs (see, for example, *Transborder Data Flows: Transnational Corporations and Remote-sensing Data*, (1984), New York, and *Transnational Corporations and International Trade: Selected Issues*, (1985), New York. Since 1993, the responsibilities of the UNCTC have been assigned to UNCTAD. For further information, see the UNCTAD website at www.unctad.org. For more information, see Boswell & Stevis, Globalisation and International Labour Organizing.

50. See: B. Leonard. (1997, August). An interview with Anthony Freeman of the ILO. *HR Magazine, 42*(8), 104–109. For coverage of the ongoing debate on international labour standards and globalisation, see: E. Lee. (1997). Globalisation and Labour Standards: A Review of Issues. *Management International Review, 136*(2), 173–189; and R. N. Block, K. Roberts, C. Ozeki, & M. J. Roomkin. (2001, April). Models of International Labour Standards. *Industrial Relations, 40*(2), 258–286.

51. For a detailed description and analysis of the *OECD Guidelines for Multinational Enterprises*, see: D. C. Campbell & R. I Rowan. (1983). *Multinational Enterprises and the OECD Industrial Relations Guidelines*. Philadelphia: The Wharton School, Industrial Research Unit, University of Pennsylvania; and R. Blanpain. (1985). *The OECD Guidelines for Multinational Enterprises and Labour Relations. 1982–1984: Experiences and Review*. Deventer, Netherlands: Kluwer.

52. Campbell & Rowan. *Multinational Enterprises and OECD*.

53. J. Rojot. (1985). The 1984 Revision of the OECD Guidelines for Multinational Enterprises. *British Journal of Industrial Relations, 23*(3), 379–397.

54. R. Blanpain. (1979). *The OECD Guidelines for Multinational Enterprises and Labour Relations, 1976–1979: Experience and Review*. Deventer, Netherlands: Kluwer.

55. H. C. Jain. (1980). Disinvestment and the Multinational Employer—A Case History from Belgium. *Personnel Journal, 59*(3), 201–205.

56. Campbell & Rowan. *Multinational Enterprises and OECD*.

57. B. Liebhaberg. (1980), *Industrial Relations and Multinational Corporations in Europe*. London, UK: Cower, 85.

58. OECD Guidelines to Multinational Enterprises: 2005 Annual Meeting of the National Contact Points (report by the chair, meeting held in June 2005), 3; OECD "Investment" page: www.oecd.org/investment. See also the special issue of *Transnational Corporations Journal*, (2005, December), *14*(3), Voluntary Codes of Conduct for Multinational Corporations: Promises and Challenges.

59. C. S. Jensen, J. S. Madsen, & J. Due. (1995). A Role for a Pan-European Trade Union Movement? Possibilities in European IR-regulation. *Industrial Relations Journal, 26*(1), 4–18; and Mahnkopf & Altvater. Transmission Belts of Transnational Competition?

60. G. W. Latta & J. R. Bellace. (1983). Making the Corporation Transparent: Prelude to Multinational Bargaining. *Columbia Journal of World Business, 18*(2), 73–80; J. T. Addison & W. S. Siebert. (1994). Recent Developments in Social Policy in the New European Union. *Industrial and Labour Relations Review, 48*(1), 5–27; and N. Donnelly & C. Rees. (1995). Industrial Relations and Multinational Companies in the European Community: The Work of the International Companies Network. *Warwick Papers in Industrial Relations, 54*. Coventry, UK: Warwick Business School.

61. See, for example: P. Teague. (1994). EC Social Policy and European Human Resource Management. In C. Brewster & A. Hegewisch (Eds.), *Policy and Practice in European Human Resource Management*. London, UK: Routledge; and L. Ulman, B. Eichengreen, & W. T. Dickens (Eds.), (1993), *Labour and an Integrated Europe*. Washington, DC: The Brookings Institution.

62. Commission of the European Communities. (1990). *Community Charter of the Fundamental Social Rights of Workers*. Luxembourg: Office for Official Publications of the European Communities.

63. See, for example: J. Lodge. (1989). Social Europe: Fostering a People's Europe? In J. Lodge (Ed.), *European Community and the Challenge of the Future*. London, UK: Pinter; J. Addison & S. Siebert. (1991). The Social Charter of the European Community: Evolution and Controversies. *Industrial and Labour Relations Review, 44*(4), 597–625; and M. Hall. (1994). Industrial Relations and the Social Dimension of European Integration: Before and After Maastricht. In R. Hyman & A. Ferner (Eds.), *New Frontiers in European Industrial Relations*. Oxford, UK: Blackwell.

64. J. Pickard. (1992, January). Maastricht Deal Worries the Multinationals. *PM Plus*, 4; B. Fitzpatrick. (1992). Community Social Law after Maastricht. *Industrial Law Journal, 21*(3), 199–213; and B. Bercusson & J. J. Van Dijk. (1995). The Implementation of the Protocol and Agreement on Social Policy of the Treaty on European Union. *The International Journal of Comparative Labour Law and Industrial Relations, 11*(1), 3–30.

65. The Treaty of Amsterdam revised the treaties on which the European Union was founded. For further information, go to the European Union website at http://europa.eu.int/abc/obj/amst/en/index.htm and www.europarl.eu.int/basicdoc/en/default.htm.

66. Go to the European Union website at http://europa.eu.int/comm/dgs/employment_social/index_en.htm.

67. For a detailed analysis of the Vredeling Directive, see D. Van Den Bulcke. (1984). Decision Making in Multinational Enterprises and the Information and Consultation of Employees: The Proposed Vredeling Directive of the EC Commission. *International Studies of Management and Organization, 14*(1), 36–60.

68. See: M. Gold & M. Hall. (1994). Statutory European Works Councils: The Final Countdown? *Industrial Relations Journal, 25*(3), 177–186; and Marginson. European Integration and Transnational Management–Union Relations in the Enterprise.

69. Addison & Siebert. Recent Developments in Social Policy; P. Knutsen. (1997). Corporatist Tendencies in the Euro-Polity: The EU Directive of 22 September 1994, on European Works Councils. *Economic and Industrial Democracy, 18*(2), 289–323.

70. Martinez Lucio & Weston. Trade Unions and Networking in the Context of Change.

71. F. Michon. (1990). The "European Social Community": A Common Model and Its National Variations? Segmentation Effects, Societal Effects. *Labour and Society, 15*(2), 215–236. Also see: E. Szyszczak. (1995). Future Directions in European Union Social Policy Law. *Industrial Law Journal, 24*(1), 19–32.

72. M. Gilman & P. Marginson. (2002). Negotiating European Works Councils: Contours of Constrained Choice. *Industrial Relations Journal, 33*(1), 36–51.

73. W. Nicoll & T. C. Salmon. (1990). *Understanding the European Community*. Hertfordshire, UK: Philip Allan, 191.

74. C. L. Erickson & S. Kuruvilla. (1994). Labour Costs and the Social Dumping Debate in the European Union. *Industrial and Labour Relations Review, 48*(1), 28–47.

75. For further reading, see: M. Muller-Camen, P. Almond, P. Gunnigle, J. Quintanilla, & A. Tempel. (2001). Between Home and Host Country: Multinationals and Employment Relations in Europe. *Industrial Relations Journal, 32*(5), 435–448.

76. M. Ingham, H. Ingham, H. Bicak, & M. Altinay. (2005). The impact of (more) enlargement on the European Employment Strategy. *Industrial Relations Journal, 36*(6), 456–477. See also: P. Marginson & G. Meardi. (2006). European Union enlargement and the foreign direct investment channel of industrial relations transfer. *Industrial Relations Journal, 37*(2), 92–110.

77. M. Zanko. (2003). Change and Diversity: HRM Issues and Trends in the Asia-Pacific Region. *Asia Pacific Journal of Human Resources, 41*(1), 75–87.

78. See: H. Ramsey. (1997). Solidarity at Last? International Trade Unionism Approaching the Millennium. *Economic and Industrial Democracy, 18*(4), 503–537; and Jensen, Madsen, & Due. A Role for a Pan-European Trade Union Movement?

79. Enderwick. The Labour Utilization Practices of Multinationals, 357.

80. See *Wal-Mart: The High Cost of Low Cost* (film): www.walmartmovie.com.

81. G. Colvin. (2005, November 28). Don't blame Wal-Mart: The giant retailer isn't evil—just caught up in the global economy. *Fortune*, 41.

Chapter 11

Performance Management

Chapter Learning Objectives

After reading this chapter, you should be able to:

- discuss multinational performance management at the global and local level, including aspects such as non-comparable data, the volatility of the global environment, the effect of distance, and level of subsidiary maturity
- describe performance management as part of an MNE's control system
- identify factors associated with expatriate performance, including compensation package, task and role, headquarters' support, host-environment factors, and cultural adjustment
- discuss performance management of expatriates and non-expatriates, and of those on non-standard tasks and assignments (e.g., commuter and virtual)
- list issues related to the performance appraisal of international employees

The following case illustrates some of the challenges that expatriate managers could face when it comes to the management and, in particular, the evaluation of their performances by their home-country organizations.

[A U.S. expatriate executive operating in Chile] had almost single-handedly stopped a strike that would have shut down their factory completely for months and worsened relations between the Chileans and the parent company in the United States. In a land where strikes are commonplace, such an accomplishment was quite a coup, especially for an American. The numerous meetings and talks with labor representatives, government officials, and local management required an acute understanding of their culture and a sensitivity beyond the ability of most people. However, because of exchange rate fluctuations with its primary trading partners in South America, the demand for their ore temporarily decreased by 30 percent during the expatriate's tenure. Rather than applauding the efforts this expatriate executive made to avert a strike and recognizing the superb negotiation skills he demonstrated, the home office saw the expatriate as being only somewhat better than a mediocre performer. In other words, because for home office management the most visible criterion of the expatriate's performance was somewhat negative (sales figures), it was assumed that he had not performed adequately. And though the expatriate's boss knew a strike had been averted, the bottom-line concern for sales dollars overshadowed any other significant accomplishments.

The aim of this chapter is to draw together the relevant literature on performance management in the international context as it relates to IHRM, particularly in the subsidiary context. The focus is on identifying those aspects imposed by international operations that require a substantial modification of traditional performance management (especially appraisal criteria, the roles of various actors in the processes, and the processes themselves).

Source: Oddou, Gary, & Mendenhall, Mark. (2000). Expatriate Performance Appraisal: Problems and Solutions. In Mark Mendenhall and Gary Oddou (Eds.), *Readings and Cases in International Human Resource Management*. Scarborough: Nelson Canada, 213–223.

Introduction

The complexities of managing performance in a firm's various globally distributed facilities have received a great deal of professional and academic attention in the last decade. As presented in Chapters 2 and 3, diversity in productions and operations, geographical dispersal, and varieties in modes of operations all combine to make performance measurement and the creation of performance management processes that are simultaneously locally relevant and globally comparable a major challenge for HRM practitioners.[1] Monitoring performance and ensuring conformity to agreed-on standards are significant elements in the managerial control system of a multinational firm and yet, as Cascio has stated, "the terrain of global performance management systems is largely uncharted."[2]

In this chapter, we differentiate between *performance management* and *performance appraisal*. **Performance management** is a process that enables the multinational to evaluate and continuously improve individual, subsidiary unit, and corporate performance against clearly defined, pre-set goals and targets. Figure 11.1 illustrates the major issues, actors, and decision processes related to performance management in the international context. This model will allow us to investigate the complex interaction between local and global

performance management

the process that enables evaluation and improvement of individual, subsidiary, and corporate performance

FIGURE 11.1

MNE Performance Management: Perspectives, Issues, Actions, and Consequences

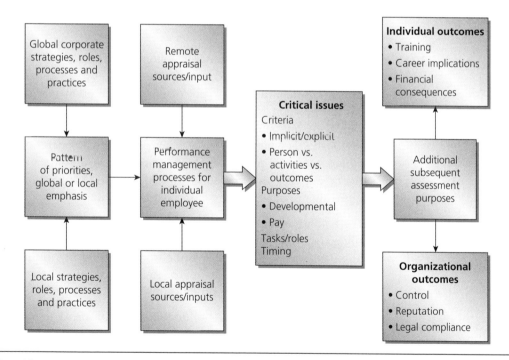

Source: Adapted from: Engle, A., and Dowling, P. (2006, September). *State of Origin: Research in Global Performance Management—Progress or a Lost Horizon?* Conference proceedings of the VIIIth World Congress of the International Federation of Scholarly Associations of Management, Berlin.

contexts for performance and the tasks of the actors, performance criteria, and purposes for, and timing of, performance management as these elements relate to individual and firm outcomes. It provides a convenient starting point for our exploration of the link between the multinational's internationalization strategies, its goals for individual units in terms of contribution to global profitability, and the performance management of individual employees, whether PCN, TCN or HCN. The aspects of these relationships are critical, as an individual's performance is appraised (or evaluated) according to expectations of appropriate outcomes and behaviour that contribute to organizational goal attainment.

Multinational Performance Management

While its general strategic position may be international, multinational, global, or transnational[3] (depending on, for instance, its size, industry, and geographic dispersal), a multinational makes strategic choices based on economic and political imperatives. Within this context, as indicated in Figure 11.1, the MNE has specific expectations for each of its foreign subsidiaries, cooperative ventures, and other forms of operation modes, in terms of market performance and contribution to total profits and competitiveness. When evaluating subsidiary performance against these expectations, however, it is important to recognize various constraints that may affect goal attainment. These constraints include: the importance of the whole versus a part, non-comparable data, volatility of the global environment, separation by time and distance, and variable levels of subsidy maturity.

Whole vs. Part

By its very nature, a multinational is a single entity that faces a global environment, which means that it simultaneously confronts differing national environments. Integration and control imperatives often place the multinational in the position where it decides that the good of the whole is more important than one subsidiary's short-term profitability. An example, provided by Pucik,[4] is where a multinational establishes an operation in a particular market where its main global competitor has a dominant position. The objective of entering the market is to challenge the competitor's cash flow with aggressive pricing policies. Pucik explains that:

> The balance sheet of this particular subsidiary might be continually in the red, but this strategy, by tying up the competitor's resources, may allow substantially higher returns in another market. The difficulties in quantifying such a global strategy in terms of the usual return-on-investment objectives are obvious.

Another situation is where the multinational establishes a joint venture in a particular market in order to have a presence there, even though it has low expectations in the short term and may provide minimum resources to the venture. Therefore, the consequences of such global decisions for subsidiary management must be taken into consideration for performance appraisal.

Non-Comparable Data

Frequently, the data obtained from subsidiaries may be neither interpretable nor reliable, as the following examples illustrate:[5]

> Sales in Brazil may be skyrocketing, but there are reports that the Brazilian government may impose tough new exchange controls within a year, thus making it impossible for the multinational to repatriate profits. Does this mean that the MNE is performing effectively? Is the subsidiary performing effectively?

> Sales in Peru may be booming, but headquarters management was unaware that under Peruvian accounting rules, sales on consignment are counted as firm sales. How should the headquarters accounting system handle these sales relative to sales from other subsidiaries, which do not consider sales on consignment as firm sales?

As Garland et al.[6] explain, physical measures of performance may be easier to interpret than in the above examples, but difficulties may still arise. For instance, notions of what constitutes adequate quality control checks can vary widely from one country to another, import tariffs can distort pricing schedules, or a dock strike in one country can unexpectedly delay supply of necessary components to a manufacturing plant in another country. Further, local labour laws may require full employment at plants that are producing at below capacity. These factors can make an objective appraisal of subsidiary performance problematic, and may complicate the appraisal of individual subsidiary managers.

Volatility of the Global Environment

The turbulence of the global environment requires that long-term goals be flexible in order to respond to potential market contingencies. According to Pucik,[7] an inflexible approach may mean that subsidiaries could be pursuing strategies that no longer fit the new environment. Consider, for example, the impact on international business of major events such as the collapse of communist rule in the late 1980s in Eastern Europe and the former Soviet Union; the adoption of the euro (€) as the single currency by most of the European Union countries; Chinese market reforms; the severe acute respiratory syndrome (SARS) and bird flu epidemics; the spread of international terrorism; the Gulf Wars; rising oil prices; high-profile corporate collapses; and the adoption of international accounting standards.

Each of these events has had profound implications for the global and local strategies of multinationals. Because subsidiaries operate in a state of such volatility and fluctuation, they must tailor long-term goals to the specific situation in a given market. Problems arise when subsidiary managers perceive that goals and deadlines set by a distant headquarters strategy team are unrealistic and inflexible, due to a failure to take into account local conditions that change as a result of a volatile environment. Obviously, involving regional and subsidiary managers in strategic planning assists in overcoming this perception.

Separation by Time and Distance

Judgments concerning the congruence between the multinational and local subsidiary activities are further complicated by the physical distances involved; time-zone differences; the frequency of contact between the corporate head office staff and subsidiary management; and the cost of the reporting system.[8] Developments in sophisticated worldwide communications systems (such as fax machines, video telephone conferences, and e-mail) do not fully substitute for face-to-face contacts between subsidiary managers and corporate staff. In some areas, the telecommunications system may be so overloaded, or underdeveloped, that reliable telephone, fax services, and Internet connections cannot be assumed. It is often necessary to meet personally with a manager to fully understand the problems that managers must deal with. For this reason, many multinational corporate managers spend a considerable amount of time travelling in order to meet expatriate and local managers in foreign locations. It is then possible for HR corporate staff, when designing performance management systems, to take account of country-specific factors.

Alternatively, the growing use of Web-based human resource information systems that include performance management modules may be seen as a response—by larger, more sophisticated, and well-funded multinationals—to the separations of time, distance, and culture experienced by multinational firms. These strategies may be driven by the complexity and inherent uncertainty of global performance and a sense that successfully competing in the global marketplace will require increased efficiency of operations. And yet the potential of these technical systems to control and coordinate activities and actors within the firm may be limited by unspoken or badly articulated roles, processes, practices, criteria, and purposes.[9]

Variable Levels of Maturity

According to Pucik,[10] without the supporting infrastructure of the parent, market development in foreign subsidiaries is generally slower and more difficult to achieve than at home, where established brands can support new products and new business areas can be cross-subsidized by other divisions. As a result, more time may be needed to achieve results than is customary in a domestic market, and this fact ought to be recognized in the performance management process. Further, variations in customs and work practices between the parent country and the foreign subsidiary need to be considered. For example:

> One does not fire a Mexican manager because worker productivity is half the American average. In Mexico, that would mean that this manager is working at a level three or four times as high as the average Mexican industrial plant. Here we need relevant comparative data, not absolute numbers; our harassed Mexican manager has to live with Mexican constraints, not European or American ones, and these can be very different. The way we measure worker productivity is exactly the same, but the numbers come out differently because of that environmental difference.[11]

In summary, there are a number of significant constraints that must be taken into account when considering foreign subsidiary performance. Because performance measurement is primarily based on strategic factors, it affects the appraisal and success of the subsidiary's chief executive (or managing director) most directly.

Control and Performance Management

Although it is not often described as such, performance management is a part of a multinational's control system. You may recall from the discussion of control mechanisms in Chapter 2 that performance targets are a part of formal control. Through formal control mechanisms and communication through the feedback and appraisal aspects, performance management also contributes to shaping corporate culture, both formally and informally,[12] thereby acting as an informal control mechanism as well as part of the bureaucratic control system. Employees are rewarded for adopting appropriate work behaviours and this in turn reinforces normative control. Figure 11.2 illustrates the performance–behaviour–outcomes linkage. It is through formal and informal control mechanisms that the multinational achieves the consistency, coordination, and compliance of desired behaviour and outcomes to implement its global strategy. These behaviours and outcomes are expected at all levels and areas—at headquarters as well as in subsidiary operations.

In a sense, by adopting a performance management approach, MNEs are drawing on a number of human resource management activities to realize performance goals set during the performance appraisal process. Its proponents argue, somewhat convincingly, that effective performance management is beneficial to both the individual and the firm. As Tahvanainen[13] points

FIGURE 11.2

MNE Control and Performance

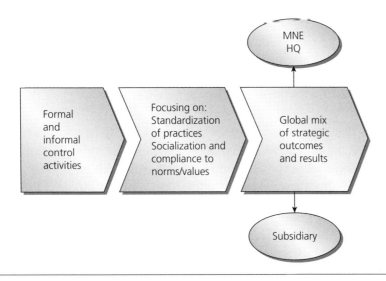

out, strong goal-setting and appraisal are key elements of an individual performance management system that also may include training and development, and performance-related pay.

Performance Management of International Employees

Having considered the broader context, we now turn our attention to individual performance management. Consistent with our general approach, we use the term *expatriate* to cover PCNs, TCNs, and those HCNs on assignment to headquarters. We also address performance management issues relating to those on non-standard and short-term assignments (such as commuter and virtual assignments) and non-expatriates (international business travellers). Given the broad scope and the fact that often issues are common to both expatriates and non-expatriates, we have decided to use the term *international employees* when all of these various groups are involved.

As discussed in Chapter 4, international assignments vary in terms of the duration and scope of physical relocation required. That is, from traditional expatriate assignments when expatriates and, usually, their family members relocate, to virtual assignments, where no physical relocation by employees or their families is required. When attempting to manage the performance of staff working across the multinational, it is essential to consider all of these variables in relation to the nature of the international assignment. The following sections also identify some performance management issues associated with expatriate and non-expatriate international assignments.

Expatriate Performance Management

As noted in Chapters 4 and 5, expatriation remains a key dimension of multinational enterprise and performance. When attempting to determine expatriate performance, it is important to consider the impact of the following variables, and their interrelationship.

- The compensation package.
- The task—the assignment task variables and the role of the expatriate.
- Headquarters' support.
- The environment in which performance occurs—the subsidiary or foreign facility.
- Cultural adjustment—of the individual and the accompanying family members.

Figure 11.3 depicts these variables and forms the basis on which we will explore the nature of the international assignment, how performance is managed, the criteria for assessment, and the other elements that comprise an effective performance management system.

Compensation Package

We examined the issues surrounding compensation in Chapter 7. However, it is essential that we recognize the importance of remuneration and reward in the performance equation. Perceived financial benefits, along with the

FIGURE 11.3

Variables Affecting Expatriate Performance

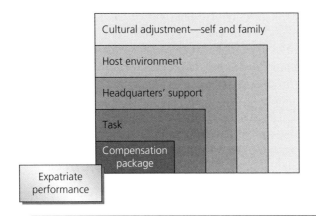

career progression potential associated with an overseas assignment, are often important motives for accepting a posting. If these expectations are not realized during the assignment, the level of motivation and commitment is likely to decrease, thus affecting performance.

Task

As outlined earlier, expatriates are assigned to foreign operations to fulfill specific tasks (see also IHRM Notebook 11.1). Interesting presentations on executive performance management have recently been provided as part of

IHRM Notebook 11.1

Expatriate Task Forms

Hays identified four tasks that expatriates are assigned to carry out in foreign operations:

1. The *chief executive officer*, or subsidiary manager, who oversees and directs the entire foreign operation.
2. The *structure reproducer* has the assignment of building or reproducing in a foreign subsidiary a structure similar to one that he or she knows from another part of the company. The structure reproducer could be building a marketing framework, implementing an accounting and financial reporting system, or establishing a production plant, for example.

3. The *troubleshooter* is the individual who is sent to a foreign subsidiary to analyze and solve a particular operational problem.
4. The *operative* is the individual whose assignment is to perform functional job tasks in an existing operational structure, generally in lower level, supervisory positions.

Sources: Hays, Richard. (1974). Expatriate Selection: Insuring Success and Avoiding Failure. *Journal of International Business Studies,* 5(1), 25–37. Tung appears to have based her initial studies on these categories (see: Tung, R. (1981). Selection and Training of Personnel for Overseas Assignments. *Columbia Journal of World Business, 16*(1), 68–78).

a wider discussion of "corporate governance." Issues of performance criteria (an over-reliance on "shareholder value" models of executive performance) and the evolving roles, responsibilities, and institutional safeguards to assure a complete, accurate, and unbiased assessment of top-level managers are widely cited for this critical task group.[14]

In a recent review of cross-cultural performance management systems, Caligiuri identifies four basic types of international assignments: *technical assignments*—short-term knowledge transference activities, said to make up 5 to 10 percent of expatriate assignments; *developmental assignments*—focusing on in-country performance and the acquisition of local or regional understanding by the assignee, said to make up 5 to 10 percent of assignments; *strategic assignments*—high-profile activities that focus on developing a balanced global perspective, said to make up 10 to 15 percent of assignments; and *functional assignments*—described as more enduring assignments with local employees that involve the two-way transfer of existing processes and practices, said to make up between 55 and 80 percent of assignments.[15] Accurately assessing performance in the tasks inherent in technical and functional assignments may well involve a limited number of sources and focus on more concrete output criteria (projects completed, contracts signed, etc.). Assessing progress in developmental and strategic assignments, given their more complex, subjective tasks, are likely to involve a wider variety of local and global participants and perspectives.[16]

Task variables are generally considered to be more under a multinational's control than environmental factors. Because of this relative control, task variables can be better assessed and more easily changed, depending, of course, on the level of position and the nature of the task assignment. Along with the specifics of the task, the multinational, like any other organization, determines the role that accompanies each task position. A role is the organized set of behaviours that are assigned to a particular position. Although an individual may affect how a role is interpreted and performed, the role itself is predetermined.[17] For the expatriate (role recipient), the parent company (role sender) predetermines his or her role in the foreign assignment, and role expectations may be clearly communicated to the expatriate before departure. Black and Porter[18] found that American expatriates working in Hong Kong exhibited managerial behaviour similar to those remaining in the United States. In their discussion of this finding, these authors suggest that the U.S. multinationals involved communicated role expectations by omitting to provide cross-cultural training before departure. In the absence of incentives to modify their role behaviour when abroad, it is not surprising that the expatriates involved performed as they did. This study reminds us that the transmission of expatriate role conception is culturally bound. As Torbiörn[19] explains:

> The content of the managerial role, as perceived by both the individual manager and the parent company, is affected by organizational norms, in terms of parent-company expectations of the manager, and by the set of cultural norms that the manager holds

in relation to other cultural and organizational norms that may be represented by other role senders. Organizational and cultural norms thus interactively determine the role content of the manager.

The difficulty this presents for the expatriate manager is that the role is defined in one country but performed in another. That is, the cultural norms regarding the set of behaviours that define "a manager in the United States" may not be the same as those considered appropriate for a manager's role in Indonesia.

Communication of role conception from the multinational to the expatriate is indicated by the straight arrows in Figures 11.4 and 11.5. Role conception is

FIGURE 11.4

PCN Role Conception

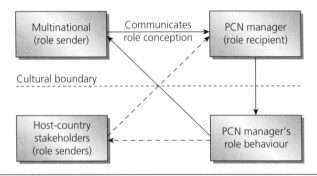

Source: Adapted from: Torbiörn, I. (1985). The Structure of Managerial Roles in Cross-Cultural Settings. *International Studies of Management & Organization, 15*(1), 60.

FIGURE 11.5

TCN Role Conception

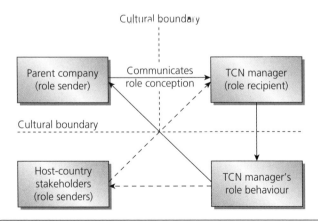

Source: Adapted from: Torbiörn, I. (1985). The Structure of Managerial Roles in Cross-Cultural Settings. *International Studies of Management & Organization, 15*(1), 60.

also communicated to the role recipient by host-country stakeholders (e.g., subsidiary employees, host-government officials, customers, suppliers, etc.), as shown by the dashed arrows. This, however, crosses a cultural boundary. Role behaviour provides the feedback loop, again at two levels: the parent-company and the host-country stakeholders. Trying to perform to differing expectations may cause role conflict. If the PCN manager adapts his role behaviour according to the role conception communicated in the host environment, it may conflict with that predetermined at headquarters. Janssens'[20] study of expatriate performance indicated that role conflict is likely to result in situations where the international manager has an understanding of the host-country culture and realizes that the use of headquarters' procedures or actions may lead to ineffective management. She postulates that the higher the degree of intercultural interaction, the more problems the expatriate has with role conflict.

From the perspective of headquarters, commitment to the parent is perceived as important, given the part that the PCN plays in transferring know-how and "the company way of doing things" into the subsidiary. This helps to explain the preference for using headquarters' standards in expatriate performance appraisal as a control mechanism.[21] If the PCN is perceived to identify too closely with host-subsidiary concerns, he or she may be recalled (the term *going native* has, in the past, often been used to describe this perception). Some MNEs will restrict the length of stay to no more than three years to avoid the possibility of PCN identification with local concerns. Because of the importance given to the parent as role sender in performance appraisal, a PCN may elect to ignore role communication sent from the host-country stakeholders if they consider that performance appraisal is determined by how role behaviour conforms to headquarters' expectation. After all, the expatriate's career is with the parent, not the host subsidiary.

Some empirical support for such a view comes from work by Gregersen and Black[22] in their study of U.S. expatriate retention and dual commitments (to the parent and the local organizations). They found, at the correlational level, commitment to the parent and to the local operation were both positively related to intent to stay. However, "regression analysis indicated that when controlling for certain demographic and attitudinal variables, commitment to the parent company appears to be slightly more relevant to expatriates' intention to stay." Role conflict was found to affect commitment to the parent company, but was unrelated to commitment to the host company.

Another intervening variable may be that of role autonomy. For example, job discretion emerged as an important aspect from a survey of 115 U.S. expatriates working in various countries by Birdseye and Hill.[23] They found that: "Foreign work methods may be more structured than their American counterparts (perhaps more procedures and protocols) and that individuals have less discretion in how they approach tasks and problems." These authors conclude that individuals are likely to blame this lack of discretion on the organization, the job, and the location—in that order. A similar finding emerged from a study of U.S. domestic and international relocation by Feldman and Tompson.[24] The degree of change in job duties was positively related to adjustment, while the degree of change in the organization was negatively related to adjustment. Thus, role conflict and role autonomy appear to be important elements in job satisfaction and task performance.

Role clarity emerged as an important variable in a meta-analysis of expatriate adjustment and performance. Integrating studies on expatriate adjustment, Bhaskar-Shrinivas et al.[25] found that:

> . . . role clarity and work adjustment was the second largest effect . . . suggesting that the uncertainty regarding objectives, goals, and role requirements is the strongest stressor in expatriates' overseas work environments. In addition, role clarity also has a moderate potential to spill over and minimize nonwork difficulties.

Role expectations are likely to be more complex for the TCN than the PCN, as the role is defined by and performed in two different countries. That is, role conception crosses two cultural boundaries, as shown in Figure 11.5. Parent-company and host-country role senders may have differing expectations of role behaviour that, in turn, are different from the accepted managerial behaviour defined by the prevailing norms in the TCN's own country. For example, a Canadian manager working for a Dutch multinational posted as a TCN in Indonesia may face added difficulties. The Canadian's role behaviour may be deemed inappropriate by both the parent (Dutch multinational) and the host nationals (Indonesians). As Torbiörn[26] points out:

> The task of the PCN manager could be described as one of realizing the expectations of a psychologically close, but physically distant stakeholder [parent] in an environment containing other role senders [host-country stakeholders] who are psychologically distant, but physically close. . . . The TCN manager must try to meet the expectations of role senders who are all psychologically distant in a context that is also psychologically distant.

However, as you may recall from our discussion of the rationale for using TCNs, often the country of assignment is perceived by headquarters as culturally close, and this may be an important factor that influences the decision to use a TCN (e.g., a German multinational decides to transfer a Canadian to the United States rather than a German). As there are very few studies that specifically examine TCN performance management issues,[27] we can only assume that many of the aspects relating to PCNs discussed above will apply to the TCN situation. A Canadian manager working in Indonesia, for instance, whether as a PCN or TCN, may encounter lack of job discretion—with perhaps the same effect in terms of performance—depending on the strength of other intervening variables. For example, differing role senders may exacerbate the situation through conflicting role expectations.

The preceding discussion demonstrates the importance of considering the role that accompanies each task position. Given that task performance is a core component of expatriate appraisal, it is also necessary to recognize that it does not occur in isolation. Many individuals and firms rank job ability as the primary ingredient relating to their expected probability of success in the international assignment, as discussed in Chapter 5. Certain types of tasks, however, require significantly more interaction with host-country stakeholders. Thus, the task variables should not be evaluated in isolation from the subsidiary environment context.

Another factor relating to task variables that warrants consideration is how similar the job to which the individual is assigned abroad is to the job that the person held domestically. Some types of tasks require an individual to operate within a given structure, while other tasks demand the creation of the structure. Individuals vary greatly in their ability to conceive and implement a system and in their tolerance for lack of structure and ambiguity. Some multinationals have experienced failure abroad because they assumed that an individual could be effective in setting up a structure, such as a marketing system, based on evidence of good performance within the existing marketing structure in the domestic corporation.[28]

Headquarters' Support

The expatriate assignment differs from a domestic relocation because it involves the transfer of the individual and accompanying family members into a foreign environment, outside their normal cultural comfort zones. The individual's primary motivation for accepting the assignment may be career or financially orientated, but this is often mixed with a genuine feeling of loyalty and commitment to the sending organization. As mentioned previously, the process of adjustment to the foreign location typically produces, to varying degrees, a range of emotional and psychological reactions to unfamiliar situations encountered over the period of the stay in the host country. The level of headquarters' support provided to the individual and the family is an important performance variable.

Host Environment

The environment has an impact on any job, but it becomes of primary importance with regard to expatriate management. According to Gregersen et al.,[29] the international context—with its differing societal, legal, economic, technical, and physical demands—can be a major determinant of expatriate performance. Consequently, expatriate performance should be placed within its international as well as its organizational context. Therefore, the five major constraints identified in the previous section in terms of multinational strategy and goal-setting for the subsidiary are important considerations for expatriate performance management.

The type of operation to which the expatriate is assigned is important. For instance, it may be relatively easier to perform in a wholly owned subsidiary than in a joint venture with a state-owned enterprise in China. Conflicting goals between the parent companies are a common problem within international joint ventures and can make the expatriate's job more difficult. An expatriate IJV manager may have difficulty trying to serve two masters and may experience a high level of uncertainty regarding the effect of differing goal expectations for the IJV on their performance appraisal. Similarly, the stage of the international business will influence the success of the expatriate. An expatriate overseeing the establishment of a new facility in a foreign country, especially in a developing or emerging market, will face different challenges and constraints than will an expatriate who is posted into a mature operation.

Cultural Adjustment

The process of cultural adjustment may be a critical determinant of expatriate job performance. Indeed, much of the literature reviewed in our discussion of the cause of expatriate "failure" covers the process of adjustment. It is likely that expatriates and their families will have some difficulty adjusting to a new environment, and this will impact on the manager's work performance. The dilemma is that adjustment to a foreign culture is multifaceted, and individuals vary in terms of their reaction and coping behaviours. Determining the relevance of adjustment to the new environment when assessing expatriate work performance may be problematical.

The five variables—compensation package, task, headquarters' support, host environment, and cultural adjustment—reviewed above, and shown in Figure 11.3, are not mutually exclusive, but interact in a way that has significant implications for the appraisal of international employees' performance. Designers and users of performance management systems need to be conscious of, and responsive to, the impact of these variables.

A Cross-Cultural Context for Performance Management

As noted in Figure 11.1, corporate and local strategies and role expectations create much of the potential for complexity and conflict in the definitions underlying criteria, processes, and standards that make up performance management. Regional and national institutional, regulatory, and historical contexts can impact the character of the criteria selected, task definitions, the timing, and even the purposes of performance management. We present three European examples of the relationship between national context and firm-level practices. Nordic performance management (particularly Danish, Finnish, and Swedish firms) have been described as decentralized, based on a broad range of hard and soft criteria (the "balanced scorecard"), and strategically linked to identify and support changes in operational-level activities.[30]

In France, legal and cultural factors combine to create a performance management system characterized by administrators with a high level of legal expertise—even though France's labour laws allow some flexibility in assessing performance within a merit-based and nondiscriminatory framework. It is seen as a system linked to motivation and developing intellectual capital via coaching and competency-based assessments, with tasks often facilitated by the acceptance of advanced forms of technology. Centralization in processes, implicit or nontransparent procedures, a propensity to have more or less favourable impressions of individuals based on the prestige of their previous university–corporate–governmental experiences, and a strong link between assessment and hierarchical remuneration may be seen to result from widely held cultural norms and values within certain segments of French society.[31] As with any national assessment, care must be taken not to overgeneralize. Practices in France vary by size of the firm—with larger firms being more open to a wider variety of performance management practices and criteria than smaller firms—as well as by industry, level of internationalization, and occupational level of employee.[32]

By contrast, and with the same caveats against overgeneralization, performance management in Germany must adjust to a much more precisely delineated set of legal and institutional factors. A strong tradition of collective bargaining—be it on the plant, firm, or industry level—plant-level co-determination, and a centuries-old tradition of vocational training all contribute to performance management systems characterized by a high level of worker input via works councils, consensus-building processes and activities, a long-term career focus, the valuing of flexibility in task capability to enhance long-term job security, and the placing of a high value on specialized technical knowledge.[33]

Processes tend to be more consensual, explicit, ongoing, and informal in a day-to-day setting, yet roles, standards, criteria, purposes, schedules, and consequences are explicitly formalized and regulated via co-determination. Performance-based pay, as a consequence or outcome of the performance management system, has been much slower to gain widespread acceptance among German firms. This may be due to the use of short-term performance criteria to trigger British and U.S. models of performance-based pay. German firms tend to focus on linking performance management results to drive long-term training and development activities.[34]

According to the Conference Board of Canada and its *Compensation Planning Outlook 2003* survey, many Canadian organizations have been dissatisfied with their performance management programs. Commentators in the Canadian HR field highlight the performance management system or program as an important concept that leads to improvement in the quality of employees and, thus, improvement in the overall organizational performance. So far, however, only 5 percent of participants in the Conference Board's survey described their performance management systems as being very effective.[35]

Performance Management of Non-Expatriates

In Chapter 4, non-expatriates (i.e., the international business traveller, or "frequent flyer") were described as employees whose work involves international travel but who are not considered international assignees because they do not relocate to another country. Performance management issues may also impact on the performance of another group: commuters. This is a form of non-standard assignment outlined in Chapter 4, where the person does not completely relocate but commutes between the home country and an office in another country. An example is an executive who considers "home" to be a suburb of Windsor but who, from Monday morning to Friday night, lives and works in Detroit while the family remains in Windsor[36]—or the daily commuters who make up a large part of the 260,000 businesspeople and tourists travelling between Canada and the United States on a daily basis.[37]

In Chapter 4, we also discussed the trend toward the use of virtual assignments to overcome staff immobility. Instead of moving into the host environment, the person manages the international position from the home country, using a combination of regular communication linkups and frequent trips to the foreign location.

As yet, little is known about the implications for individual performance assessment of such international business travel, whether as part of a non-standard assignment or as a component of a specific job. However, as IHRM Notebook 11.2 outlines, it is possible to suggest some performance management challenges.

IHRM Notebook 11.2

Potential Performance Management Challenges: International and Virtual Assignees

- How to determine performance criteria and goals related to the effective conduct of non-standard assignments, especially virtual assignees. As indicated in Figure 11.1, agreement on performance criteria is an important component of the performance management process. This requires the link between each employee's performance and the achievement of the multinational's strategic goals and objectives to be clearly established and understood. However, as the role conceptions in Figures 11.4 and 11.5 show, shared conceptions of roles and expectations are complicated by the numbers of cultures and organizational contexts involved. With virtual assignees, monitoring and evaluating a physically and geographically distant group of employees is problematical. It is "management by remote control." In addition, the virtual assignee may be faced with dual goals—that of the domestic-located job and the virtual work group. Therefore, the perennial challenge of effectively communicating the strategic links between the assignee's performance and organizational strategy is likely to be magnified.*

- An understanding of the criteria for performance is generally advocated as a highly participative process between supervisor and employee.** As with the traditional expatriate assignment, work conducted through non-standard assignments and international travel still is conducted across cultural and national boundaries, and thereby subject to cultural differences in norms about acceptable or preferred levels of participation.

- Isolating the international dimensions of job performance might not be as straightforward as in traditional expatriate assignments. It may depend on the level of difficulty inherent in the performance criteria set and how individual performance levels are determined.

- Outstanding performance, underperformance, or failure in non-expatriate and non-assignments will challenge the performance appraisal process.

- As we will explore in a later section of this chapter, regular feedback on progress toward those performance goals is usually provided through the performance appraisal activity. Performance feedback for assignees will be relevant only if it reflects the international contexts in which tasks

(continued)

Chapter 11: Performance Management

Potential Performance Management Challenges: International and Virtual Assignees (continued)

are performed.[†] The enduring concerns of who should conduct performance appraisals, how the appraisals should be conducted, and on what performance data the appraisals should be based may be intensified when it involves increasing numbers of others outside head office with whom the assignee is working.

- One key function of performance appraisal feedback is that it provides opportunities to improve performance by identifying performance gaps that might be eliminated with training and development. Cross-cultural awareness and competence training will still be relevant for non-expatriates. However, a detailed analysis of other pre-departure and ongoing training that might be required for non-expatriate assignments is yet to be conducted.

- Employee expectations about rewards for performance and as elements of their working conditions, together with motivation, are important aspects of individual performance. In multinationals, the management of links between performance and rewards is already complex due to the specialized local knowledge required across

multiple employment and legal environments. The challenges for IHRM are to determine what to reward when dealing with non-expatriate assignments, and the way in which compensation for each type of international assignment fits with global compensation strategy.

- The impact of non-standard assignments on host-country national co-workers should also be considered—particularly in terms of the impact on these staff of international business travellers and commuters who "drop in, drop out."

Sources: *Welch, D., Worm, V., & Fenwick, M. (2003). Are Virtual Assignments Feasible? *Management International Review, 43* (Special Issue 1), 95–114; Caligiuri, P. (2006). Performance Measurement in a Cross-Cultural Context. In W. Bennett, C. Launce, & J. Woehr (Eds.), *Performance Management: Current Perspectives and Future Challenges*. Mahwah, NJ: Lawrence Erlbaum Associates.
**See, for example: Armstrong, M. (1994). *Performance Management*. London, UK: Kogan; and Stiles, P., Gratton, L., Truss, C., Hope-Hailey, V., & McGovern, P. (1997). Performance Management and the Psychological Contract. *Human Resource Management Journal, 7*(1), 57–66.
†Harvey, M. (1997). Focusing the International Personnel Performance Appraisal Process. *Human Resource Development Quarterly, 8*(1), 41–62.

Performance Appraisal of International Employees

RPG 11.1

Now that we have an understanding of the variables likely to influence performance, including the nature of the international assignment being performed, we can discuss the criteria by which performance is to be appraised (or evaluated—the terms are used interchangeably in the relevant literature). We note that the focus on expatriate management is also reflected in the literature about the performance appraisal of international staff, and much of the following discussion reflects that emphasis. However, aspects of expatriate performance appraisal are also relevant to the appraisal of non-expatriates and these, along with the aspects that distinguish between the two categories of international staff, will be highlighted.

As shown in Figure 11.1, individual performance management involves a set of decisions on the dimensions and level of performance criteria, task and role definitions, and the timing of the formal and informal aspects of the appraisal. Traditionally, it comprises a formal process of goal-setting, performance appraisal, and feedback. Data from this process are often used to determine pay and promotion, and training and development requirements. Company goals influence the individual's salient task set, against which job goals and standards are established and measured. There are differences in the way this process is handled within companies. For example, in Germany and Sweden, it is common for employees to have input into job goal-setting, whereas in other countries such as the United States, job goals tend to be assigned.[38] In addition, the type and length of assignment appear to influence how performance management is handled. For example, a study of Finnish firms revealed that those on short-term assignments were treated the same as any other employee in the company, and there was more flexibility in the timing of the performance review for those assigned to projects.[39]

Performance Criteria

The global firm's ability to measure an employee's individual contribution to performance and to assess the aggregate contribution of human capital to strategic progress is a complex and timely topic in organizational studies.[40] Goals tend to be translated into performance appraisal criteria, so specificity and measurability issues are important aspects; also, we need to recognize that hard, soft, and contextual goals are often used as the basis for performance criteria. **Hard goals** are objective, quantifiable, and can be directly measured—such as return on investment (ROI), market share, etc. **Soft goals** tend to be relationship- or trait-based, such as leadership style or interpersonal skills. **Contextual goals** attempt to take into consideration the factors that result from the situation in which performance occurs. For example, MNEs commonly use arbitrary transfer pricing and other financial tools for transactions between subsidiaries to minimize foreign-exchange risk exposure and tax expenditures.

hard goals

goals that are objective and quantifiable, and can be directly measured

soft goals

goals that tend to be relationship- or trait-based

contextual goals

goals that attempt to take assignment characteristics into consideration

Another consideration is that all financial figures are generally subject to the problem of currency conversion, including sales and cash positions. Further complications arise because host governments can place restrictions on repatriation of profits and currency conversion. The nature of the international monetary system and local accounting differences may preclude an accurate measurement of results. The dilemma this poses is that the use of transfer pricing and other financial tools is necessary because of the complexity of the international environment. Multinationals cannot allow subsidiaries to become autonomous in financial management terms, and place controls on subsidiary managers. Thus, the financial results recorded for any particular subsidiary do not always reflect accurately its contribution to the achievements of the corporation as a whole, so such results should not be used as a primary input in performance appraisal.[41] For this reason, a performance management approach is now advocated, rather than traditional performance appraisal, as it allows clarification of goals and expectations of performance against those goals.

Janssens[42] suggests that performance appraisal of subsidiary managers against hard criteria is often supplemented by frequent visits by headquarter staff and meetings with executives from the parent company. Soft criteria can be used to complement hard goals, and take into account areas that are difficult

W W W 11.1

W W W 11.2

to quantify, such as leadership skills. Appraisal of these areas is somewhat subjective, however, and, in the context of both expatriate and non-expatriate assignments, more complicated due to cultural exchanges and clashes. However, relying on hard criteria such as financial data to evaluate how well a manager operates a foreign subsidiary does not take into account the way results are obtained and the behaviours used to obtain these results.[43] Concern with questionable ethical practices led to, for example, the enactment of the OECD's Convention on Combating Bribery of Foreign Public Officials in International Business Transactions, the Corruption of Foreign Public Officials Act in Canada, and the U.S. Foreign Corrupt Practices Act, which may prompt an increased use of behavioural as well as results data to appraise the performance of managers in foreign subsidiaries.[44]

An appraisal system that uses hard, soft, and contextual criteria, however, builds on the strengths of each while minimizing their disadvantages.[45] Using multiple criteria wherever possible is therefore recommended in the relevant literature. In addition, job analysis must, as Harvey[46] suggests, generate criteria that adequately capture the nature of international work as opposed to the domestic context, in order to provide valid appraisal information.

Who Conducts the Performance Appraisal?

Another issue is who conducts the performance appraisal. Typically, employees are appraised by their immediate superiors, and this can pose problems for subsidiary chief executive officers (or managers). They work in countries geographically distant, yet are evaluated by superiors back at headquarters who are not in the position to see on a day-to-day basis how the expatriate performs in the particular situation. Consequently, subsidiary managers tend to be assessed according to subsidiary performance, with a reliance on hard criteria similar to that applied to heads of domestic units or divisions. Of course, there is a danger that a subsidiary manager will make decisions and implement local strategies that favour short-term performance, to the detriment of longer-term organizational goals.

Appraisal of other employees is likely to be conducted by the subsidiary's CEO or the immediate host-country supervisor, depending on the nature and level of the position concerned.[47] With regard to expatriate performance appraisal, host-country managers may have a clearer picture of expatriate performance and can take into consideration contextual criteria. However, they may have culturally bound biases (e.g., about role behaviour) and lack an appreciation of the impact of the expatriate's performance in the broader organizational context. As the case at the end of this chapter shows, some expatriates may prefer to have parent-company evaluators, given that their future career progression may depend on how the appraisal data is utilized back at headquarters. This may be particularly true in cases where foreign operations are considered to be relatively less important than domestic operations.[48] Others may prefer host-country appraisal if they perceive it as a more accurate reflection of their performance.

Multiple raters are sometimes used in the domestic context—such as the technique referred to as "360-degree feedback." It has been argued that, given the cross-cultural complexity of the foreign assignment, a team of evaluators should be used for performance appraisal. For example, Gregersen et al.[49] found that most firms (81 percent) in their survey of HR directors in 58 U.S. multinationals used more than one rater when assessing expatriate performance. The immediate superior (in either the home or host country), the expatriate as self-rater, and the HR manager (either home country- or host country-based) were commonly used as multiple evaluators of U.S. expatriate performance. Likewise, a survey of 99 Finnish internationally operating companies reported that, for 79 percent of respondents, expatriate performance appraisal was conducted by the superior located in Finland.[50] Often, though, this was simply because there was no suitable person in the host country to conduct such appraisals.

The GMAC Global Relocation Services surveys, mentioned in previous chapters, include questions regarding expatriate performance. Host-country performance reviews were used by 69 percent of responding firms in the 2004 survey, compared to 65 percent in 2002; home country-based reviews were used by 50 percent and 43 percent in 2004 and 2002, respectively (the numbers do not total as respondents were allowed multiple answers—some firms combine both home- and host-country reviews). For the virtual assignment situation, the use of multiple appraisers would most likely be the most accurate way to determine performance. However, the availability of knowledgeable, trained raters may constrain the approach taken in the international context.

Standardized or Customized Performance Appraisal Forms

Domestic companies commonly design performance appraisal forms for each job category, particularly those using a traditional performance appraisal approach rather than performance management. Such standardization assists in the collection of accurate performance data on which personnel decisions can be made, and allows for cross-employee comparisons. The question often posed is: Should these standardized forms be adapted when used for appraising international managers? As Gregersen et al.[51] argue:

> In principle, performance appraisal systems are designed carefully and often presumed to be static. Valid reasons exist for maintaining standard, traditionally used appraisals (e.g., when the system has been tested, has identified baselines, and reduces future development costs). These reasons are valid as long as the context of the performance does not change. In the expatriate setting, however, the performance context does change, and sometimes it changes dramatically. Given a global context, previous testing and established baselines grounded in domestic situations can become meaningless.

Despite this, they found in their sample of U.S. firms that 76 percent in fact used the same standardized appraisal forms for expatriate appraisal.[52] Employees who relocate within the multinational and non-expatriate assignees who also cross cultural boundaries in their performance context do not always feel that headquarters-based appraisal forms allow for consideration of the critical success factors of their performance, such as cross-cultural competence.[53]

Frequency of Appraisal

In practice, formal appraisal is commonly on a yearly basis, and this appears to extend to international performance systems even though the domestic-oriented literature on this topic recommends an ongoing combination of formal and informal performance appraisal and feedback. For example, the majority of the U.S. companies in the Gregersen et al. study referred to above reported annual appraisal practices. It is interesting to note that the U.S. companies using annual appraisal systems were more likely to use standard appraisal forms and hard criteria. In their discussion of this finding, Gregersen et al. comment that replicating domestic practices requires less effort in collecting and interpreting the data, and that the preference for following the domestic system might reflect lack of international experience within the companies in the sample. As only 28 percent of the HR respondents in their study reported having been on international assignments themselves, they might not be aware of the need to take contextual criteria into consideration, or see a need for the customization of their expatriate performance systems.

Performance Feedback

An important aspect of an effective performance management system is the provision of timely feedback of the appraisal process. One of the problems with annual appraisal is that employees do not receive the consistent, frequent feedback considered critical in order to maintain or improve their performance. The performance literature also suggests that regular feedback is an important aspect in terms of meeting targets and revising goals, as well as assisting in motivation of work effort. The difficulty for the expatriate who is being evaluated by a geographically distant manager is that timely, appropriate feedback is viable only against hard criteria.

For virtual assignees, this is further complicated when geographic dispersion dictates reliance on e-mail communication (see IHRM Today 11.1). Interpersonal relations and an effective choice of communication medium are two factors influencing virtual workgroup relations.[54]

Appraisal of HCN Employees

The discussion so far has omitted the issue of appraising the performance of HCN employees. To a certain extent, this reflects the limited research on the topic in the context of IHRM, although there is a growing body of literature on comparative HRM practices. What is important to mention here is that the practice of performance appraisal itself confronts the issue of cultural applicability.[55] Performance appraisal in different nations can be interpreted as a

Miscommunication in Virtual Assignments

Milliman et al. reported two critical incidents involving miscommunication between managers working on a virtual assignment in the United States and Malaysia. E-mail feedback about his Malaysian counterpart's good performance provided to the Malaysian by the American head of the project generated a cycle of cross-cultural conflict. This threatened the virtual team's performance when the Malaysian sought to transfer out of the team.

Adopting an organizational learning approach, the researchers analyzed the miscommunication and its consequences. They concluded that the two managers concerned had different views about what constituted "the primary source of job performance, how performance feedback is provided, what role the subordinate will have in communicating with a superior, how conflict is handled, and what communication styles are expected." The approach used to analyze these incidents provides a useful IHRM starting point for developing effective cross-cultural performance feedback communication skills.

Source: Milliman, J., Taylor, S., & Czaplewski, A. (2002). Cross-Cultural Performance Feedback in Multinational Enterprises: Opportunity for Organizational Learning. *Human Resource Planning, 25*(3), 29–43.

signal of distrust or even an insult. In Japan, for instance, it is important to avoid direct confrontation to "save face," and this custom affects the way in which performance appraisal is conducted. A Japanese manager cannot directly point out a work-related problem or error committed by a subordinate:

> Instead, he is likely to start discussing with the subordinate about the strong points of that person's work, continuing with a discussion about the work on a relatively general level. Then he might continue to explain the consequences of the type of mistake committed by the subordinate, still without directly pointing out the actual mistake or the individual employee. From all this, the subordinate is supposed to understand his mistake and propose how to improve his work.[56]

One way to overcome the dilemma of cultural adaptation is to use host-country nationals to assist in devising a suitable system for appraising subsidiary employees and to advise on the conduct of the appraisal. The need for local responsiveness may affect the multinational's ability to effectively implement a standardized approach to performance management at all levels within the global operation.[57]

As we discussed in relation to PCNs and TCNs, the level of position involved is an important consideration. If a multinational appoints an HCN as its subsidiary manager, then much of what we covered in terms of goals (particularly hard goals) and performance measures could be expected to apply to the HCN. In terms of task performance and potential role conflict, as can be seen from Figure 11.6, Torbiörn[58] recognizes that HCN managers face particular role concerns that are different from those of the PCN and TCN manager. The HCN manager is expected to perform a role that is conceptualized by a psychologically and physically distant parent company, but

FIGURE 11.6

HCN Role Conception

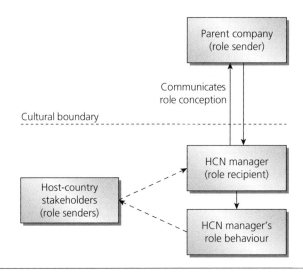

Source: Adapted from: Torbiörn, I. (1985). The Structure of Managerial Roles in Cross-Cultural Settings. *International Studies of Management and Organization, 15*(1), 61.

enacted in an environment with other role senders who are both psychologically and physically close.

Parent-company role conception is communicated to the HCN, but it crosses the cultural boundary, as does feedback expressed as the HCN's role behaviour (the straight arrows in Figure 11.6). Input from host-country role senders, though, does not cross a cultural boundary. The HCN receives role expectations and enacts role behaviours in his or her own cultural environment (as depicted by the shading the Figure 11.6). For subsidiary staff below the top-management level, one would expect that the performance management system would be localized to take into consideration local behavioural norms of work behaviour. Torbiörn's model depicts only HCN managerial role conception and communication.

Conflict may arise when HCNs report to a PCN expatriate manager who also conducts their performance appraisal. In a way, this is the reverse of the discussion surrounding local managers appraising the performance of expatriates in terms of cultural bias. The difference, of course, is the impact that parent-company standards have on the performance management system and the degree to which localization is permitted in a standardized approach.[59] It may not be culturally sensitive to use appraisal techniques such as 360-degree feedback, for instance. In practice, multinationals from, for example, the United States have often used the same appraisal form for HCNs as for their domestic employees. Sometimes the forms are translated from English, sometimes they are not. Both approaches have drawbacks. As discussed above, while some companies are developing information systems to assist in performance appraisal, the widespread use of computer-generated data is hampered by the legal constraints imposed by some host governments or by concerns about personal privacy.

An aspect that is overlooked in the limited literature is the potential for role conflict for those HCNs transferred into the parent's operations.[60] For that period, the HCN may be evaluated according to role behaviour expectations communicated by role senders that are physically close but psychologically distant, in an environment that is also psychologically distant. The HCN is then transferred, usually back to his or her home country, and may experience difficulties in readjusting role behaviour.

In relation to performance appraisal generally, it seems that the process remains problematic, irrespective of cultural impacts. For example, a study by Gerringer et al. reported a common finding across 10 countries/regions—the failure of performance appraisal to fulfill its development purpose. The study formed part of the Best Practices in International HRM project, a multiple-year, multiple-researcher, multi-national project.[61] The 10 countries/regions were Australia, Canada, China, Indonesia, Japan, Korea, Latin America, Mexico, Taiwan, and the United States. Researchers noted: "It appears that the potential of appraisal is not fully realized in current practice, not only (as widely believed) in the U.S., but also in most other countries."[62]

Recent reviews of global performance management indicate more and more widespread use of performance management systems by multinational firms, that formal reviews tend to be annual or biannual, and that online systems are still in the minority (20 percent of responding firms), although one-third of the firms stated they had plans to move to online systems. Objective and subjective criteria are used, and training based on the results of the performance management process is growing. Systems capabilities related to consistency within the far-flung system in the firm, integrating performance management into other HR activities (such as succession planning and compensation), and linking performance management to strategic planning while incorporating the leadership of senior management are seen as critical if performance management is to contribute to the control of MNEs.[63]

The criticality of balancing global (parent) processes, practices, roles, and norms with local or regional equivalents is of ongoing interest to students of global performance management. Investigating the impact of high-context cultures on selecting and valuing implicit, explicit-subjective, or explicit-objective forms of performance criteria is an ongoing activity. The effects of legal and regulatory contexts on the aforementioned processes, practices, and norms, and the widening range of tasks and assignments required of employees in multinational firms all combine to make performance management a complex, yet critical area of human resource management.

Summary

Technical competence is a necessary but not sufficient condition for successful international performance. Cross-cultural interpersonal skills, sensitivity to foreign norms and values, and ease of adaptation to unfamiliar environments are just a few of the managerial characteristics that most multinational firms seek when selecting international managers. The added challenge is the effective management and appraisal of performance across all of the multinational's operations. In this regard, we have identified the basic components of the performance management system that is conscious of, and responds to, the organizational, national, and international elements. We explored a range of multinational performance aspects, including whole (global) versus part (subsidiary); non-comparable data; the volatility of the global environment; the effect of distance; and the level of maturity, and briefly discussed performance management as a control mechanism.

In addition, we presented factors associated with expatriate performance, including the compensation package; task and role; headquarters' support; host-environment factors; and cultural adjustment. This was followed by a discussion about the performance management of non-expatriates and those on non-standard assignments. We used virtual assignment as an illustration of some of the aspects that need to be considered in these non-traditional assignment types. In the final part of this chapter, we discussed key issues relating to the performance appraisal of international employees, and the appraising of HCN managers and employees in subsidiary operations.

Broadening out the discussion to the multinational level, and addressing performance management and appraisal concerns related to non-expatriates and those on non-standard assignments, has been useful to remind us that there are many dimensions to international business operations that need to be considered when designing an effective performance management system in the multinational context.

Key Terms

contextual goals 379

hard goals 379

performance management 363

soft goals 379

Web Links

www 11.1   Detailed information about Canada's Corruption of Foreign Public Officials Act can be found at:

www.justice.gc.ca/en/dept/pub/cfpoa/guide5.html

www 11.2   The OECD's Convention on Combating Bribery of Foreign Public Officials in International Business Transactions located at:

**www.oecd.org/document/21/0,3343,en_2649
_201185_2017813_1_1_1_1,00.html**

RPC Icon

RPC 11.1   Identifies, evaluates, and implements measurement systems for current and future job/team performance

Discussion Questions

1. Discuss the major factors associated with the appraisal of expatriate managerial performance.
2. Why is it important to include hard, soft, and contextual goals when assessing managerial performance?
3. In what ways would the role of a manager working in a non-standard international assignment arrangement differ from that of a typical expatriate manager?

Using the Internet

1. Go to Geert Hofstede's homepage at **www.geert-hofstede.com/ geert_hofstede_contrarian_position.shtml** and read his article "Cultural Dimensions," which explains the meaning of cultural dimension and their implications for managers. From the menu for "Hofstede Scores," located on the same Web page, choose a country and compare it to Canada. What do the different countries' scores tell you about the potential challenges and opportunities for managers and their performances if they were sent to the country of your choice for an international assignment?
2. Go to the University of Western Ontario's Web page **www.lib.uwo.ca/ business/50bestwork.html** and select a range of internationally operating companies from the list of the 2006 Best Employers in Canada, choosing from either (or both) of the lists of large and medium-sized companies. Do the performance management systems of these companies differ? If so, in what areas? Why?

Exercises

1. In the section on the volatility of the global environment, several world events were listed that have had profound implications for the global and local strategies of MNEs. Select a recent world event, identify the specific HR implications that may arise from this, and devise policies as to how these may be handled.
2. "One of the dangers of performance appraisal is that, because the focus is so much on a particular individual, the teamwork aspect gets lost. In an international location, it is perhaps desirable to focus more on how the PCN has settled in and is operating as part of a team, rather than as an individual to the possible detriment of the team." Do you agree with this statement? Discuss it with your classmates.

Case

A Rainy Expatriate Performance Appraisal

Richard Hoffman, a Québécois chemical engineer working for a Canadian-based energy firm, was given a three-year expatriate assignment in Venezuela as a technical liaison and environmental protection project manager. His local project supervisor was Jean, a French engineer who had lived in French Guiana and then Venezuela for over 20 years. Richard thought that as a Francophone from Quebec, he and Jean would be able to build a working relationship quickly.

At the beginning of the project, Richard sent Jean an e-mail (in French, and not the usual corporate English) containing what he thought of as the five most significant goals associated with his assignment—similar to the "management by objectives" section of the more or less standard performance appraisal forms he had filled out for years during earlier assignments in Edmonton, Toronto, and at corporate headquarters in Montreal.

After several months with no response from Jean, Richard ran into Jean in the hallway between meetings and asked him about the e-mail and his progress to date. "Don't worry about that," Jean responded blandly. "Just keep working to meet the deadlines and I will check with your co-workers and the other project managers on your work. Where did you go to engineering school by the way?"

Richard waited another six months and was becoming increasingly anxious as the firm's annual review week approached. He finally caught up with Jean on a rainy Friday in the lobby of the office building as they both waited for their drivers to arrive. When asked about the upcoming performance review, Jean snorted and said. "C'est tout fini—it's all been taken care of. Make an appointment with my assistant Louisa next week and we can go over the report we have sent to Montreal." As Jean stepped gingerly into the rainy Caracas parking lot, Richard thought back to the last few weeks with his team, the sometimes loud disagreements with the other project managers, and wondered if it was too late in the day to call his old supervisor in Toronto.

Source: Based on the synthesis of a series of expatriate experiences.

Questions

1. At the very beginning of his expatriate assignment, what could and/or should Richard have done differently in terms of formulating and discussing his objectives?
2. What went wrong with Richard's appraisal process?
3. Does this case illustrate a need for standardized appraisal forms and processes? Why?

Endnotes

1. Excellent overviews of research in this area are provided by: P. Caligiuri. (2006). Performance Measurement in a Cross-Cultural Context. In W. Bennett, C. Launce, & J. Woehr (Eds.), *Performance Management: Current Perspectives and Future Challenges*. Mahwah, NJ: Lawrence Erlbaum Associates, 227–244; and W. Cascio. (2006). Global Performance Management Systems. In G. Stahl & I. Björkman (Eds.), *Handbook of Research in International Human Resource Management*. Cheltenham, UK: Edward Elgar, 176–196.

2. W. Cascio. Global Performance Management Systems, 193.

3. C. A. Bartlett & S. Ghoshal. (1987, Summer). Managing Across Borders: New Strategic Requirements. *Sloan Management Review*, 7–17.

4. V. Pucik. (1985). Strategic Human Resource Management in a Multinational Firm. In H. V. Wortzel & L. H. Wortzel (Eds.), *Strategic Management of Multinational Corporations: The Essentials*. New York: John Wiley, 429, 430.

5. J. Garland, R. N. Farmer, & M. Taylor. (1990). *International Dimensions of Business Policy and Strategy* (2nd ed.). Boston: PWS-KENT, 193.

6. Ibid.

7. Pucik. Strategic Human Resource Management in a Multinational Firm, 430.

8. Ibid.

9. A. Engle & P. Dowling. (2006, September). *State of Origin: Research in Global Performance Management—Progress or a Lost Horizon?* Conference proceedings of the VIIIth World Congress of the International Federation of Scholarly Associations of Management, Berlin; J. Kochanski & A. Sorensen. (2006). Managing Performance Management. *Workspan, 48*(9), 20–27; and J. Ryder. (2005). The Future of HR Technology. *HR Magazine, 50*(3), 67–69.

10. Pucik. Strategic Human Resource Management in a Multinational Firm.

11. Garland, Farmer, & Taylor, 193.

12. M. Fenwick, H. De Cieri, & D. Welch. (1999). Cultural and bureaucratic control in MNEs: The role of expatriate performance management. *Management International Review, 39* (Special Issue 3), 107–124.

13. M. Tahvanainen. (1998). *Expatriate Performance Management*. Helsinki: Helsinki School of Economics Press.

14. M. Hilb. (2006). *New Corporate Governance: Successful Board Management Tools* (2nd ed.). Berlin: Springer Publishing; and F. Malik. (2006). *Effective Top Management*. Frankfurt: Wiley-VCH.

15. P. Caligiuri. Performance Measurement in a Cross-Cultural Context.

16. For more on how the purposes and roles inherent in assignment may impact on the characteristics of performance management systems, see: A.Engle & P. Dowling. State of Origin.

17. H. Mintzberg. (1973). *The Nature of Managerial Work*. Englewood Cliffs, NJ: Prentice-Hall, 54.

18. J. S. Black & L. W. Porter. (1991). Managerial Behaviors and Job Performance: A Successful Manager in Los Angeles May Not Succeed in Hong Kong. *Journal of International Business Studies, 22*(1), 99–113.

19. I. Torbiörn. (1985). The Structure of Managerial Roles in Cross-Cultural Settings. *International Studies of Management & Organization, 15*(1), 52–74.

20. M. Janssens. (1994). Evaluating International Managers' Performance: Parent Company Standards as Control Mechanism. *International Journal of Human Resource Management, 5*(4), 853–573.

21. Ibid.

22. H. B. Gregersen & J. S. Black. (1990). A Multifaceted Approach to Expatriate Retention in International Assignments. *Group & Organization Studies, 15*(4), p. 478.

23. M. G. Birdseye & J. S. Hill. (1995). Individual, Organization/Work and Environmental Influences on Expatriate Turnover Tendencies: An Empirical Study. *Journal of International Business Studies, 26*(4), 800.

24. D. C. Feldman & H. B. Tompson. (1993). Expatriation, Repatriation, and Domestic Geographical Relocation: An Empirical Investigation of Adjustment to New Job Assignments. *Journal of International Business Studies, 24*(3), 507–529.

25. P. Bhaskar-Shrinivas, M. A. Shaffer, & D. M. Luk. (2005). Input-Based and Time-Based Models of International Adjustment: Meta-Analytic Evidence and Theoretical Extensions. *Academy of Management Journal, 48*(2), 272.

26. I. Torbiörn. The Structure of Managerial Roles in Cross-Cultural Settings, 59.

27. For example, in one of the few articles on this topic, Chadwick looks at the TCN assignment in general, and does not specifically address performance. Rather, the focus is on fair treatment and equity regarding compensation: W. F. Chadwick. (1995). TCN Expatriate Manager Policies. In Jan Selmer (Ed.), *Expatriate Management: New Ideas for International Business.* Westport, CT: Quorum Books.

28. M. Conway. (1984, July). Reducing Expatriate Failure Rates. *Personnel Administrator*, 31–37.

29. H. B. Gregersen, J. M. Hite, & J. S. Black. (1996). Expatriate Performance Appraisal in U.S. Multinational Firms. *Journal of International Business Studies, 27*(4), 711–738.

30. See: F. Nilsson & M. Kald. (2002). Recent Advances in Performance Management: The Nordic Case. *European Management Journal, 20*(3), 235–245; V. Suutari & M. Tahvanainen. (2002). The Antecedents of Performance Management amongst Finnish Expatriates. *International Journal of Human Resource Management, 13*(1), 55–75; and M. Tahvanainen. (2000). Expatriate Performance Management: The Case of Nokia Telecommunications. *Human Resource Management, 39*(2), 267–276.

31. M. Festing & C. Bartzantny. (2008). Performance Management in Germany and France. In A. Varma, P. Budhwar, & A. DeNisi (Eds.), *Performance Management Systems: A Global Perspective.* London, UK: Routledge; and P. Gooderham, O. Nordhaug, & K. Ringdal. (1999). Institutional and Rational Determinants of Organizational Practices: Human Resource Management in European Firms. *Administrative Science Quarterly, 44*, 507–531.

32. Festing & Bartzantny. Performance Management in Germany and France; and M. Tahvanainen & V. Suutari. (2005). Expatriate Performance Management in MNCs. In H. Scullion & M. Lineham (Eds.), *International HRM: A Critical Text.* Basingstoke, UK: Macmillan, 91–113.

33. M. Dickmann. (2003). Implementing German HRM Abroad: Desired, Feasible, Successful? *International Journal of Human Resource Management, 34*(2), 265–283.

34. For more on Anglo-Saxon approaches to performance-based pay, see: H. Aguinis. (2007). *Performance Management.* Upper Saddle River, NJ: Pearson Education, particularly Chapter 10. For more information related to German performance management, see: Festing & Bartzantny. Performance Management in Germany and France; and M. Pudelko. (2006). A Comparison of HRM Systems in the USA, Japan and Germany in Their Socioeconomic Context. *Human Resource Management Journal, 16*(2), 123–153.

35. D. Brown. (2002, December 2). HR improving at performance management. *Canadian HR Reporter, 15*(2)1; and D. Brown. (2003, March 10). Performance management separates wheat from chaff. *Canadian HR Reporter, 16*(5).

36. M. Fenwick. (2003). On International Assignment: Is Expatriation the Only Way to Go? *Asia Pacific Journal of Human Resources, 42*(3), 365–377.

37. London [Ontario] Chamber of Commerce. (2007, June 1). *Delays at US/Canadian border addressed.* London, ON: London Chamber of Commerce.

38. Tahvanainen. *Expatriate Performance Management.*

39. M. Tahvanainen, D. Welch, & V. Worm. (2005). Implications of Short-Term International Assignments. *European Management Journal, 23*(6), 663–673.

40. For a well-presented and far-reaching discussion of the relationship between strategic purpose and talent management, see: J. Boudreau & P. Ramstad. (2007). *Beyond HR: The New Science of Human Capital*. Boston: Harvard Business School Press.

41. Pucik. Strategic Human Resource Management.

42. Janssens. Evaluating International Managers' Performance.

43. R. W. Beatty. (1989). Competitive Human Resource Advantages Through the Strategic Management of Performance. *Human Resource Planning, 12*(3), 179–194.

44. K. F. Brickley. (1992). *Corporate Criminal Liability: A Treatise on the Criminal Liability of Corporations, Their Officers and Agents* (cumulative supplement). Deerfield, IL: Clark Boardman Callaghan. Enacted in 1977, the FCPA addresses the problem of questionable foreign payments by U.S. multinationals and their managers. The act was amended by Congress in 1988 to include substantial increases in the authorized criminal fines for organizations and new civil sanctions for individuals violating the FCPA.

45. Tahvanainen. *Expatriate Performance Management*; and Gregersen, Hite, & Black. Expatriate Performance Appraisal in U.S. Multinational Firms.

46. M. Harvey. (1997). Focusing the International Personnel Performance Appraisal Process. *Human Resource Development Quarterly, 8*(1), 41–62.

47. Tahvanainen. *Expatriate Performance Management*.

48. E. Naumann. (1993). Organizational Predictors of Expatriate Job Satisfaction. *Journal of International Business Studies, 24*(1), 61–80.

49. Gregersen, Hite, & Black. Expatriate Performance Appraisal in U.S. Multinational Firms.

50. Tahvanainen. *Expatriate Performance Management*.

51. Gregersen, Hite, & Black. Expatriate Performance Appraisal in U.S. Multinational Firms, 716.

52. It should be remembered that these authors take a traditional performance appraisal approach, rather than utilizing the newer performance management literature that we discuss in this chapter. It may be that the goal-setting stressed in the performance management literature will assist standardization.

53. Cascio. Global Performance Management Systems; and Engle and Dowling. State of Origin.

54. See: W. Cascio & S. Shurygailg. (2003). E-leadership in Virtual Firms. *Organizational Dynamics, 31*, 362–375.

55. See, for example: N. J. Adler. (2002). *International Dimensions of Organizational Behavior* (4th ed.). Cincinnati, OH: South Western/Thomson; S. Schneider. (1988). National vs. Corporate Culture: Implications for Human Resource Management. *Human Resource Management, 27*, 231–246; and G. P. Latham & N. K. Napier. (1989). Chinese Human Resource Management Practices in Hong Kong and Singapore: An Exploratory Study. In G. Ferrls, K. Rowland, & A. Nedd (Eds.), *Research in Personnel and Human Resource Management, 6*. Greenwich, CT: JAI.

56. J. V. Koivisto. (1992, November 23–24). Duality and Japanese Management: A Cosmological View of Japanese Business Management (paper presented at the European Institute of Advanced Studies in Management Workshop, *Managing in Different Cultures*, Cergy, Group Essec, France).

57. Caligiuri. Performance Measurement in a Cross-Cultural Context; and Engle & Dowling. State of Origin.

58. Torbiörn. The Structure of Managerial Roles in Cross-Cultural Settings.

59. Engle & Dowling. State of Origin.

60. The performance appraisal of inpatriates is briefly covered in: M. Harvey & M. Buckley. (1997). Managing Inpatriates: Building a Global Core Competency. *Journal of World Business, 32*(1), 35–52. For a more general overview of the role of inpatriates in control processes for multinational firms, see: M. Harvey & M. Novicevic. (2006). The Evolution from Repatriation of Managers in MNEs to "Inpatriation" in Global Organizations. In G. Stahl & I. Björkman

(Eds.), *Handbook of Research in International Human Resource Management*. Cheltenham: Edward Elgar, 323–346.

61. J. Gerringer, C. Frayne, & J. Milliman. (2002). In Search of "Best Practices" in International Human Resource Management: Research Design and Methodology. *Asia Pacific Journal of Human Resources, 40*(1), 9–37.

62. J. Milliman, S. Nason, C. Zhu, & H. De Cieri. (2002). An Exploratory Assessment of the Purposes of Performance Appraisals in North and Central America and the Pacific Rim. *Asia Pacific Journal of Human Resources, 40*(1), 117.

63. See W. Cascio's discussion (2006) as well as a survey of 278 firms from 15 countries reported in: P. Bernthal, R. Rogers, & A. Smith. (2003). *Managing Performance: Building Accountability for Organizational Success*. Pittsburgh, PA: Development Dimensions International.

Chapter 12

IHRM Trends: Complexity, Challenges, and Future Choices

Chapter Learning Objectives

After reading this chapter, you should be able to:

- discuss international business ethics and HRM
- describe modes of operation other than wholly owned subsidiaries and the required IHRM activities
- outline ownership issues relating to IHRM requirements of organizations other than large multinationals, such as:
    - family-owned firms
    - nongovernment organizations (NGOs)
- identify safety and security issues and the assessment and planning activities required
- understand that research is still required to unravel the intricacies and interrelationships among the IHRM function and activities, firm internationalization, and strategic directions and goals

Terrorists tried to blow up an apartment complex in Kuwait housing 59 Canadians last winter but the bombing was disrupted by local security authorities, says a newly declassified intelligence report. The government report, marked "secret," reveals that the lives of a large number of Canadians may have been spared when the Kuwaiti Security Services broke up a terrorist cell in January and February. The cell intended to attack the Alia Ghaliya apartment complex, also known as Fintas Towers, a pair of high-rise buildings that overlook the Persian Gulf and are popular among Western expatriates. . . .

"There are over 3,800 Canadians registered with the Canadian embassy in Kuwait," the report says. "The terrorist threat to them and other Westerners in the country has probably diminished somewhat, as a consequence of these counter-terrorism efforts. Nevertheless, extremist attacks of lesser sophistication, such as drive-by shootings, may still occur." Fintas Towers is located south of Kuwait City and houses mainly expatriate oil workers. Al-Qaeda has made repeated strikes against Western housing complexes in neighbouring Saudi Arabia. In October 2001, Canadian Luc Ethier was gunned down in Kuwait. His friends believe the attack was the work of local extremists responding to a call by bin Laden to kill Americans. Yesterday, the Department of Foreign Affairs was advising Canadians that "there are credible reports indicating that terrorists may be planning attacks, possibly against Westerners and/or Western interests" in Kuwait.

Since 9/11, the continuous worldwide terrorist attacks and attempted attacks highlight the increasing importance of developing company policies and practices ensuring the safety and security of employees on international assignments. Aside from the salient role it has to play in this process, IHRM faces a number of other challenges that have emerged from developments that, so far, have received limited attention in the IHRM literature and that, as a result, will be addressed in greater detail in this chapter.

Source: Bell, Stewart. (2005, October 28). Failed terror strike targeted Canadians: Thwarted by Kuwait. *National Post*, A11.

Introduction

In this book, we have explored the international HRM issues related to managing people in a multinational context. To that end, we have focused on the implications that the process of internationalization has for HRM activities and policies. We now turn our attention to developments that have not previously been emphasized in the general IHRM literature and the challenges they present to IHRM: international business ethics, modes of operation other than wholly owned subsidiaries, family-owned firms, nongovernment organizations (NGOs), and the developing role of IHRM in contributing to safety and security and dealing with global terrorism. In a sense, these topics reflect what some Japanese MNE's refer to as the "general affairs" aspect of IHRM: the expectation that the human resource function will be the first line of defence in dealing with unpredictable and emergent issues from the many and varied environments and constituency groups that make up the complexity of MNEs.[1]

In the sections that follow, we return to a discussion of some issues that distinguish HRM in MNEs. Revisiting the model of strategic HRM in MNEs presented in Chapter 1, Figure 12.1 contains highlights (boldfaced) of those issues and topics that are unique or distinct for MNEs. These topics include ethical issues associated with *external factors* such as regional characteristics; *internal factors* such as mode of operation; *external factors* related to safety,

FIGURE 12.1

Returning to Topics of Strategic HRM in Multinational Enterprises

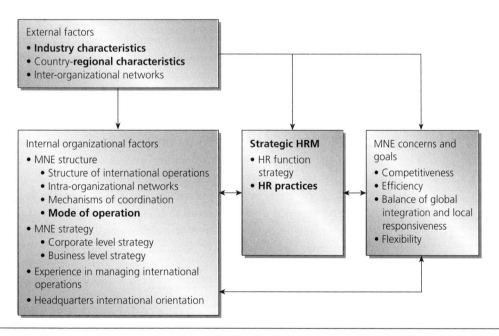

Source: Adapted from: De Cieri, H., & Dowling, P. J. (1999). Strategic Human Resource Management in Multinational Enterprises: Theoretical and Empirical Developments. In P. M. Wright et al. (Eds.), *Research in Personnel and Human Resource Management: Strategic Human Resources in the 21st Century* (Supplement 4). Stamford, CT: JAI Press.

security, and terrorism as industry or regional characteristics; and trends in research on the HR function and practices as these issues relate to *strategic HRM* and HR practices among MNEs.

External Factors: International Business Ethics and HRM

Global organizations face a challenge: Should they apply their own values everywhere they do business, irrespective of the cultural context and standard of local practices? To appreciate the dilemma, take the situation of a multinational that has assigned a PCN to manage its operations in a host country where bribery is commonly practised, child labour is used, and workplace safety measures are lacking. Whose standards should prevail? Those of the MNE's parent country or those of the host country?

There are three main responses to this question. The first involves ethical relativism, the second ethical absolutism, and the third, ethical universalism. For the **ethical relativist**, there are no universal or international rights and wrongs; it all depends on a particular culture's values and beliefs. For the ethical relativist, when in Rome, one should do as the Romans do. Unlike the relativist, the **ethical absolutist** believes that when in Rome, one should do what one would do at home, regardless of what the Romans do. This view of ethics gives primacy to one's own cultural values. Opponents of this view argue that ethical absolutists are intolerant individuals who confuse respect for local traditions with ethical relativism. It must be noted that while some behaviours are wrong wherever they are practised (e.g., bribery of government officials), other behaviours may be tolerated in their cultural context (e.g., the practice of routine gift-giving between Japanese businesspeople). In contrast to the ethical relativist, the **ethical universalist** believes there are fundamental principles of right and wrong that transcend cultural boundaries and that MNEs must adhere to these fundamental principles or global values.

The existence of universal ethical principles can also be seen in the agreements that exist among nations that are signatories to the United Nations Declaration of Human Rights and a number of international accords such as the Guidelines for Multinational Enterprises adopted by the Organisation of Economic Co-operation and Development (OECD). The need for international accords and corporate codes of conduct has grown commensurately with the spread of international business and the considerable growth of offshoring (as outlined in Chapter 9), but translating ethical principles and values into practice in the international business domain is an enormous task in the absence of a supranational legislative authority. Efforts to make progress in this area have centred on regulation, the development of international accords, and the use of education and training programs.

New Global Developments on the Criminalization of Bribery

Bribery and corruption tends to top the list of the most frequent ethical problems encountered by international managers.[2] **Bribery** involves the payment of agents to do things that are inconsistent with the purpose of their position or office in order to gain an unfair advantage.

ethical relativist
believes "when in Rome, do as the Romans do"

ethical absolutist
believes home-country values and practices should rule, regardless of host-country beliefs

ethical universalist
believes the fundamental principles of right and wrong transcend cultural boundaries

W W W 12.1

W W W 12.2

bribery
a practice that involves payment or gifts to gain an unfair advantage

Bribery can be distinguished from so-called gifts and "facilitating" or "grease" payments. The latter are payments to motivate agents to complete a task they would routinely do in the normal course of their duties. While most people do not openly condone bribery, many argue for a lenient approach based on the view that bribery is necessary to do business (the ethical relativist's argument). However, it is now generally agreed that bribery undermines equity, efficiency, and integrity in the public service; undercuts public confidence in markets and aid programs; adds to the cost of products; and may affect the safety and economic well-being of the general public.

For these reasons, there has been an international movement to criminalize the practice of bribery. In 1977, the United States enacted the Foreign Corrupt Practices Act (FCPA) to prohibit U.S.-based firms and U.S. nationals from making bribery payments to foreign government officials. In addition, payments to agents violate the act if it is known that the agent will use those payments to bribe a government official. The act was amended in 1988 to permit "facilitating" payments but mandates record-keeping provisions to help ensure that illegal payments are not disguised as entertainment or business expenses. The FCPA has in the past been criticized for placing U.S. firms at a competitive disadvantage, since European and Asian firms did not face criminal prosecution for paying bribes to foreign officials.[3] But the evidence on the competitive disadvantage of the FCPA is mixed. The FCPA has also been criticized by some for being ethnocentric, while others saw it as moral leadership on the part of the United States.[4]

In the absence of adequate international self-regulation to control bribery and corruption, the United States lobbied other nation-states for almost two decades to enact uniform domestic government regulation to provide a level playing field. Finally, in December 1996, the United Nations adopted the Declaration Against Corruption and Bribery in International Commercial Transactions that committed UN members to criminalize bribery and deny tax deductibility for bribes. A year later, the declaration was endorsed by 30 member nations, and four non-member nations of the OECD adopted the Convention on Combating Bribery of Foreign Public Officials in International Business Transactions (OECD Convention). Under the OECD convention, members agreed to establish domestic legislation by the end of 1998, criminalizing the bribing of foreign public officials on an extraterritorial basis. The OECD convention came into force in February 1999, and as of 2007, had been ratified by 36 countries. Each member state is required to undergo a peer review and to provide a report reviewing its implementation of the convention.

 RPC 12.1

WWW 12.3

Canada responded to the OECD convention with its Corruption of Foreign Public Officials Act, which entered into force on February 14, 1999. The Corruption of Foreign Public Officials Act focuses on three main offence areas: bribing a foreign public official, laundering property and proceeds, and possession of property and proceeds.

 WWW 12.4

Given the seriousness of offences and penalties at national levels and in the OECD convention, it is imperative that enterprises involved in global business take active steps to manage their potential exposure. Also, although the OECD convention currently addresses the supply side of corruption in the public sector, it is likely that the ambit of the convention will be expanded to include bribery in the private sector as well as the demand side of bribery. HR professionals have an important role to play in instituting a strategic plan for legal compliance and developing corporate codes for voluntary compliance. They can also provide training in understanding the difference between corrupt bribery payments, gifts, and allowable facilitation payments, and also training in the development of negotiation skills to handle problem situations that may arise in sensitive geographical regions and industries. The debate over payments to foreign officials is likely to continue for many years to come.

The Berlin-based nongovernment lobby group Transparency International (TI) publishes an annual *Corruption Perceptions Index*. The index measures perceptions—not actual levels of corruption—for over 50 countries and is based on international surveys of businesspeople and financial journalists. The ranking is scored from zero (most corrupt) to ten (least corrupt). Table 12.1 shows the

TABLE 12.1

Transparency International *Corruption Perceptions Index 2006*

COUNTRY RANK	COUNTRY/TERRITORY	2006 CPI SCORE*
1	Finland	9.6
	Iceland	9.6
	New Zealand	9.6
4	Denmark	9.5
5	Singapore	9.4
6	Sweden	9.2
7	Switzerland	9.1
8	Norway	8.8
9	Australia	8.7
	Netherlands	8.7
11	Austria	8.6
	Luxembourg	8.6
	United Kingdom	8.6
14	Canada	8.5
15	Hong Kong	8.3
16	Germany	8.0
17	Japan	7.6
18	France	7.4
	Ireland	7.4
20	Belgium	7.3
	Chile	7.3
	USA	7.3

*CPI Score relates to perceptions of the degree of corruption as seen by businesspeople and risk analysts, and ranges between 10 (highly clean) and 0 (highly corrupt).

Source: Adapted from: Transparency International *Corruption Perceptions Index 2006* (www.transparency .org/policy_research/surveys_indices/cpi/2006/CPI_2006_presskit_eng[1].pdf). For the most up-to-date TI *Corruption Perceptions Index*, go to www.transparency.org.

Chapter 12: IHRM Trends: Complexity, Challenges, and Future Choices

2006 TI index country rank of the top 22 least-corrupt countries in descending order. Finland, Iceland, and New Zealand (all small-population, advanced economies) were the top equal-ranked three least-corrupt countries, while Canada ranked fourteenth. The countries perceived to be the most corrupt (not shown in Table 12.1) were Guinea, Iraq, Myanmar, and Haiti, which were ranked at the bottom of the list of 163 countries[5] (see also IHRM Today 12.1).

The public and financial consequences of a bribery scandal can be significant for an MNE. The case at the end of this chapter provides a sense of the actual and reputational costs of unethical conduct for an MNE.

Challenges for the Multinational's HR Function

Managers involved in international business activities face many of the same ethical issues as those in domestic business, but the issues are more complex because of the different social, economic, political, cultural, and legal environments in which MNEs operate. Firms that opt consciously or by default to leave ethical considerations up to individual employees not only contribute to the pressures of operating in a foreign environment (and perhaps contribute to poor performance or early recall of the expatriate), but also allow internal inconsistencies that affect total global performance.

When MNEs select international assignees, the assignees' ability to manage with integrity could be a job-relevant criterion, and any pre-departure training or orientation program should include an ethics component that discusses ethical dilemmas that expatriates may encounter. In designing training programs to meet the challenges of multinational business, the HR function

RPC 12.2

IHRM Today 12.1

Doing Business in South Korea

When doing business in countries such as South Korea, an international assignee has to be aware of bribery and corruption as potentially common business practices:

> Throughout the 40-odd years of South Korea's industrialization, the fastest way to get ahead in politics or business has often been with the help of brown envelopes of cash. Such practices were supposed to become a thing of the past with the arrival of Roh Moo-hyun as president five years ago. . . . A slew of bribery scandals, some of them involving Mr Roh's aides, has underlined the extent to which money still talks in Asia's third largest economy. "The Roh Moo-hyun government introduced systems to cut down on corruption but they are still very unstable," says

Kim Chong-su, secretary of the Council for the Korean Pact on Anti-Corruption and Transparency, a government-linked body. Corruption remains endemic in Korean society. Company executives describe entertaining government officials on the golf course and adhering to a custom of betting on—and conveniently losing—each hole. Mothers, meanwhile, are known to pay teachers to seat their children at the front of the class. And watchdog Transparency International ranked South Korea 25th out of the world's 30 developed economies in its latest corruption perceptions index.

Sources: Fifield, Anna. (2007, November 10/11). Spectre of corruption returns to haunt Korea. *Financial Times*, 5.

should not only raise the issue of cultural relativities but also discuss the extent to which moral imperatives transcend national and cultural boundaries. To avoid the temptation to cut ethical corners, expatriates should not be placed under unreasonable pressure to deliver good financial results, and they must be given feedback and reinforcement. Performance appraisals, compensation programs, and regular trips home are important instruments in developing and maintaining ethical cultures.

WWW 12.5

WWW 12.6

WWW 12.7

The difficulties involved when massive, highly standardized firms attempt to be sensitive to local customs and values while becoming more international is personified by Wal-Mart, the giant U.S. retailer. The highly successful low-cost strategy (with its attendant standardization, scale, and scope economies) that characterizes this would-be MNE has become a magnet for concerns, protests, and social commentary all over the world. Issues related to offshoring procurement (especially from China); the consequences of a relentless low-cost strategy in relation to direct employee and contractor wages, health care benefits, working conditions, and job security; and the competitive impact of Wal-Mart's "super-stores" on traditional local retail establishments, city centre infrastructure, and small-population communities have initiated a worldwide discussion of the economic, social, and political consequences of global business[6] (see, for example, IHRM Today 12.2).

IHRM Today 12.2

Wal-Mart Entering India

As the following article reports, many of the concerns raised by North American communities when Wal-Mart opens stores in their areas were expressed by merchants in India when Wal-Mart's plans to enter their country became known. Wal-Mart's first store in India was scheduled to open in August 2008.

Demonstrators waving banners and shouting slogans marched on government buildings here Thursday to protest the entry of Wal-Mart, the world's largest retailer, into India. Wal-Mart and a venture partner, Bharti Enterprises, are working on a deal that could change the face of the country's $300 billion retail sector and has aroused fears of mass job losses. In New Delhi, more than 100 protesters shouted "Go back Wal-Mart" and waved placards saying "Save Small Retailers." Some broke through police barricades and burned an effigy of a dummy with "Wal-Mart Down" scrawled on it.

But there were no protesters Thursday in a suburb of Mumbai where Michael T. Duke, vice chairman of Wal-Mart Stores, accompanied by Rajan B. Mittal of Bharti Enterprises, visited a mall and a hypermarket. Wal-Mart and Bharti plan a joint venture in a retail market that is forecast to more than double by 2015. Retailing in India, now dominated by small family-run stores, has also attracted the interest of other top global retailers like Tesco and Carrefour.

But owners of small shops are concerned at what they call Wal-Mart's "backdoor entry." Foreign multibrand retailers in India are restricted to cash-and-carry and franchise operations, the route chosen by Metro of Germany, Shoprite Holdings of South Africa and Marks & Spencer of Britain. "We believe Wal-Mart is going to ruin this country and millions of people will lose their jobs," said Dharmendra Kumar,

Little is presently known about the evolving roles and responsibilities for HRM in balancing the economic imperatives of cost control and global standardization with the social and institutional realities of citizenship in a widening range of diverse contexts—particularly in terms of the development of labour sourcing, compensation, and employee relations strategies.[7] However, it seems clear that these are likely to remain dominant issues in international business in the 21st century.

Internal Factors: Mode of Operation and IHRM

We have stressed the need to broaden the scope of IHRM beyond that of subsidiary operations. While not downplaying its importance, for many MNEs, managing and staffing subsidiary units is only one aspect of international business operations, although the weighting given to subsidiary management will vary significantly according to the nature of international activities and the size of the internationalizing firm (see Chapter 1). The fact that external parties are involved in contractual modes, joint ventures, and strategic alliances imposes management and HR constraints that are not usually present in wholly owned operations. While the HR implications of international joint ventures have received considerable attention in the literature,[8] there remains a need for studies that consider the HR implications of contractual modes where the firm is operating at arm's length. Training, for instance, is often an important part of contractual modes, playing a key role in the transfer of technology and systems and inculcation of company culture, and acting as a screening process (for example, in selecting suitable franchisees). As a result, staff may be primarily involved in short-term assignments to deliver training in foreign locations, rather than as traditional expatriates.

Family-Owned Firms

Often, family-owned firms are treated as a subset of SMEs (which we discussed in Chapter 3). However, large multinationals can be family-owned, although the definition of what constitutes family ownership varies across countries. An excellent example of a large MNE that remains family-owned is the Bechtel Corporation, a global engineering, construction, and project management company that is headquartered in San Francisco.[9] Firms that later become publicly owned often retain members of the founding family as major stockholders. The long involvement of the Ford family in the management of the U.S. automobile company, the Ford Motor Company, is an example of a situation in which family concerns have received wide media coverage in the context of international business decision making.

A factor that may contribute to the demise or takeover of a family firm is the way in which management succession is handled. Replacing top management is often seen as a challenge, but handing over control can be fraught with conflict and turmoil when family businesses are involved. HR planning takes on a different dimension in the context of family-owned firms and gives rise to much speculation in high-profile MNEs such as Aldi (German supermarket chain) and News Corporation (Murdoch's media group, including the U.K.'s *The Times* (London), the *New York Post*, international *The Wall Street Journal*, Sky Channel, and the Fox network). Another aspect is the way the internationalization process is handled in family-owned firms. There has been a suggestion that Asian family firms try to keep as much control as possible within the immediate or at least the extended family. A study by Yeung[10] of the internationalization of three Chinese family-owned Hong Kong firms found that these firms were able to meet the challenges of growth while still preserving their family management and structure, although control through socialization was used when nonfamily managers were placed in key positions. As Yeung points out, the globalization of family firms has been a remote topic in international business studies.

Nongovernment Organizations

The globalization of trade and business has provoked a vigorous debate within national states, and often is expressed in anti-globalization rallies and protests. The activities of environmental groups such as Greenpeace highlight how these organizations have also become internationalized. They tend to have national "managers" in various countries, and variations of structural forms for coordination and accountability. Aid agencies such as the Red Cross, the Red Crescent, World Vision, and Médecins Sans Frontières (Doctors Without Borders) are prominent examples of NGOs. Compared with for-profit multinationals, NGOs may utilize different organizational structures and have members who may internalize to a greater degree the shared values and beliefs due to the nature of the organization's mission and activities. Nonetheless, in terms of global control and operations, NGOs may have similar managerial concerns to those of, for instance, oil companies. Physical risk—such as the danger of staff being taken hostage and of having property damaged—is common to firms operating in hostile contexts (see, for example, IHRM Today 12.3).

As Fenwick[11] identifies, non-profit organizations have been largely ignored in IHRM research, possibly because IHRM "reflects the traditional management ethos of effectiveness and efficiency rather than the non-profit ethos of values-driven, charitable and philanthropic ideals."[12] It would seem that the need to broaden the focus of the IHRM field to include NGOs will be necessary, as the impact and influence of NGOs is more than likely to continue well into the 21st century.

External Factors: Challenges in an Uncertain World—Safety, Security, and Counterterrorism[13]

Traditionally, many domestic and international human resource managers have been responsible for legal compliance and training issues related to safety in the workplace.[14] As national and international regulations related to workplace safety expanded, specific professional standards of practice, reporting mechanisms, and roles were specified in the area of corporate risk management.[15] Risk categories associated with natural disaster protocols, emergency and disaster preparedness plans for MNE plant and facilities, workplace violence policies, industrial theft and sabotage protocols, and "hardening" of individual facilities to enhance in-house security have emerged, and a growing body of professional and academic literature exists.

Less clear are the particular roles, expectations, and portfolios of responsibilities that IHRM managers and directors have been called on to incorporate into their existing responsibilities. Intuitively, in smaller MNEs—operating in less-sensitive industries and less-turbulent markets—the IHRM generalists will be called on to incorporate these protocols by outsourcing technical security systems and personnel as required.[16] In larger organizations, particularly MNEs operating in more public and sensitive industries and/or more socially and politically turbulent regions of the world, significant investment in developing integrated, coordinated, and specialized risk management practices within the HR function is warranted. Many MNEs have developed their own idiosyncratic systems and processes in response to a history of "critical incidents" that the firm has experienced over years or even decades (e.g., the kidnapping of an executive, a natural disaster impacting a key facility, or an airline or private aircraft disaster that decimated the executive cadre of the MNE).

R P C 12.3

Not surprisingly, executives in most MNEs are unwilling to discuss the protocols processes, systems, and structures that they have in place in this sensitive area. More recently, emerging risk categories relate to cyberterrorism, political terrorist groups targeting specific firms and industries, and the risks inherent in pandemics such as SARS, avian flu, and airborne contaminants (as discussed in Chapter 1). IHRM Notebook 12.1 provides a starting point for an MNE-specific audit, outlining a working set of corporate risk assessment categories in six areas.

Analytically, according to Czinkota et al., IHRM managers may be able to assess the potential risk from terrorist threats at three levels of analysis:

IHRM Notebook 12.1

Corporate Risk Assessment Categories

- *In-facility emergency and disaster preparedness*—including being in compliance with local safety laws and standards (e.g., the Canada Labour Code at a federal level and the Occupational or Workplace Health and Safety Acts at a provincial level in Canada); creating a command centre and triage area; and establishing protocols for transport-evacuation and the systematic location of employees, liaison with public sector emergency workers, and media relations.

- *In-facility security*—comprising perimeter security, search protocols into and out of facilities (truck inspections, deliveries, etc.), internal search protocols (lockers, etc.), bomb threat procedures, risk control for violence in the facility and threats to management (including training on warning signs, protection of property and equipment, and safeguarding executives), protection and lighting in parking areas, and the use of cameras in the workplace.

- *Industrial espionage, theft, and sabotage*—activities to secure internal communications (e-mails, telephones, etc.), open records protection, employee privacy regulations, clearly defined physical inspections and search processes.

- *Cyberterrorism*—hardware, software, and human systems to deal with hacking, information theft, internal sabotage, sabotage of software systems, and the development and maintenance of an architecture of backup systems and multiple independent operations for information systems.

- *Out-of-facility fire and travel risks*—providing travelling managers with portable five-minute air packs, travel policies prohibiting employees from staying in hotel rooms above the seventh floor (most aerial ladder trucks only reach to the sixth floor), policies prohibiting top-level managers from travelling on the same airline flight/private aircraft, hotel evacuation training if travelling teams of employees are staying at the same hotel.

Sources: Personal correspondence and interview with Tom Schneid, February 12, 2007. Also see: Schneid, T., & Collins, L. (2001). *Disaster Management and Preparedness*. Boca Raton, FL: Lewis Publishers/CRC Press. For a similar discussion on the dimensions of risk management practices and the degree to which multinational enterprises are viewing security and terrorism as critical strategic issues, planning for these forms of risks, and allocating resources for training and protocol enhancements, see: Wernick, D. (2006). Terror Incognito: International Business in an Era of Heightened Geopolitical Risk. In G. Suder (Ed.), *Corporate Strategies under International Terrorism and Adversity*. Cheltenham, UK: Edward Elgar, 59–82.

primary—"at the level of the individual person and firm"; *micro*—"specific regions, industries or levels in international value chains"; and *macro*—"the effect of a terrorist attack on the global environment . . . the world economy, consumer demand for goods and services, and reactions by supranational organizations such as the United Nations."[17] As an example of micro level risk analysis, the travel/hospitality industry is particularly sensitive to terrorist events or natural disasters that may inhibit travel in general, travel to a certain region or country, or to specific travel destinations.[18] On the primary and micro levels:

> It is useful to distinguish the most vulnerable links in firm's value chains. . . . From the individual [firm's] perspective, it is more useful to view terrorism at the micro level wherein input sourcing, manufacturing, distribution, and shipping and logistics are likely to be the most vulnerable areas.[19]

Surveys of multinational chief executives in 2004 by PricewaterhouseCoopers and the RAND Corporation–Europe report that terrorism is perceived as one of the five greatest threats to business growth and a significant threat to their organizations.[20] Other research and survey results report that CEOs and CFOs have increased their investments in risk management and security systems in the range of 10 percent per year since 2001 and expect those increases to continue.[21] By systematically analyzing people and processes, IHRM professionals may contribute to "stabilizing risk"[22] through recommendations that "harden" processes in the value chain, recruit people with capabilities and skills relevant for these kinds of processes, and train employees in these processes and systems.

WWW 12.8

In a similar vein, Gillingham presents risk analysis in terms of partitioning security risk into an external environmental dimension (geographic region of operation) and an internal company dimension (industry, firm media profile, national affiliation associated with the company). Low-risk companies in low-risk environments do not need to invest as heavily in security systems and protocols. High-risk companies in low-risk environments should follow security strategies that focus on hardening individual sites. Low-risk companies in high-risk environments can follow security strategies that disperse activities across the region and build redundant infrastructure, so that value chain activities in the high-risk region can be provided by out-of-region units. High-risk companies in high-risk environments must invest much more in quite elaborate risk management strategies.[23] Much remains to be understood in this rapidly evolving area, and the expectations, standards, and practices of IHRM executives and professionals as they relate to safety and security are in flux. According to Czinkota et al.:

> In-depth case studies on firms directly affected by terrorism will also serve to provide grounded information as to the nature of the relationships between types of terrorism and their specific effects, and facilitate the development of models and theory.[24]

A similar conclusion can be reached in terms of the need for a better understanding of these challenges facing IHRM in MNEs.

Strategic HRM: Research Issues and Theoretical Developments

The field of IHRM has been slow to develop a rigorous body of theory. There are a number of reasons for this:

- Major methodological problems are involved in the area of international management and IHRM. These problems greatly increase the

---

IHRM Notebook 12.2

Key International Management and IHRM Methodological Challenges

- *Defining culture and the emic–etic distinction:* The problems of defining culture and the emic–etic distinction were discussed in Chapter 1.
- *Static group comparisons:* An enduring issue in international research is that virtually all cross-cultural comparisons are based on "static group designs."[*] The difficulty with static group comparisons in inter-national research is that subjects are not randomly assigned from a superordinate population to different levels of a treatment variable. In practice, it is impossible for cross-cultural researchers to avoid this methodological problem. This difficulty is further compounded by ill-defined notions of culture as an independent variable. As Malpass[**] observed:

  No matter what attribute of culture the investigator prefers to focus upon or to interpret as the causative variable, any other variable correlated with the alleged causative variable could potentially serve in an alternative explanation of a mean difference between two or more local populations.

  As a practical solution to this problem, Malpass recommends that investigators should attempt to obtain data on as many rival explanations as possible and then demonstrate that they are less plausible (by conducting post hoc statistical

analyses, for example) than the investigator's favoured interpretation.[†]

- *Translation and stimulus equivalence:* Researchers need to be aware that problems may arise when translating concepts central to one culture into the language of another culture. Triandis and Brislin[‡] argue that translation problems should be a starting point for research, rather than a data collection frustration. The decentring technique—translating from the original to the target language and back again through several iterations—is advocated. This technique allows the researcher to test if there is any emic colouring of the concepts under investigation. A related point is that non-native speakers need to translate research findings into English for publication in English-language journals.

Sources: [*]See: Bhagat, R. S., & McQuaid, S. J. (1982). Role of Subjective Culture in Organizations: A Review and Directions for Future Research. *Journal of Applied Psychology, 67,* 653–685; Campbell, D. T., & Stanley, J. (1966). *Experimental and Quasi-Experimental Design for Research.* Chicago: Rand-McNally; and Malpass, R. S. (1977). Theory and Method in Cross-Cultural Psychology. *American Psychologist, 32,* 1069–1079.
[**]Malpass. Theory and Method, 1071.
[†]For further discussion on this point, see: Kelly, L., & Worthley, R. (1981). The Role of Culture in Comparative Management: A Cross-Cultural Perspective. *Academy of Management Journal, 24,* 164–173; and Dowling, P. J., & Nagel, T. W. (1986). Nationality and Work Attitudes: A Study of Australian and American Business Majors. *Journal of Management, 12,* 121–128.
[‡]Triandis, H. C., & Brislin, R. W. (1984). Cross-Cultural Psychology. *American Psychologist, 39,* 1006–1016.

complexity of doing international research and, as Adler[25] noted some years ago, it is often quite difficult to solve these problems with the rigour usually required of within-culture studies by journal editors and reviewers (see also IHRM Notebook 12.2).

- International studies are invariably more expensive than domestic studies. International research takes more time, involves more travel, and frequently requires the cooperation of host-country organizations, government officials, and researchers. Developing a stream of research is consequently much more difficult. An example, though, of how academics can overcome some of these difficulties is the "best practice" country/regional study and analysis of 10 countries approaches to HRM, involving a diverse team of academics from various countries.[26]

Until relatively recently, many management and HR researchers have regarded the IHRM field as a marginal academic area. This attitude was reflected in the relatively small number of stand-alone business school courses in IHRM—a situation that is changing, particularly in Canada, Europe, and the Asia–Pacific region, but less so in the United States. A strong positive development was the establishment of a dedicated journal in the field (*International Journal of Human Resource Management*) in 1990 by Professor Michael Poole at Cardiff University in Wales that has had a significant impact on the development of research in the field of international HRM. An increasing number of books that have focused on HRM in particular regions such as Latin America,[27] Central and Eastern Europe,[28] the Middle-East,[29] Europe,[30] Africa,[31] and the Asia-Pacific[32] have also made a valuable contribution to the IHRM literature.

The Human Resource Function in MNEs

As presented in Chapter 1, the sheer complexity of the IHRM function in MNEs has led to a fundamental reexamination of the purposes, actors, roles, and relationships between line managers and staff HR specialists, between subsidiary HR staff and corporate HR specialists, between MNE employees and outsourced contractors, and between the various HR actors within the MNE hierarchy (e.g., HR members on the board of directors, at vice president level or reporting directly to a board member).[33] An analysis of HR staffing practices in 17 European countries and Japan by Brewster et al.[34] led to the following conclusions:

- Larger MNEs have proportionately smaller HR departments (measured by ratio of HR staff to total headcount), while smaller firms, perhaps more engaged in transactional administration and reacting to daily issues, have proportionately larger HR departments.
- HR ratio varies with industry sector, such that firms with lower levels of internal and external interdependence and standardized work outputs require less HR activity, while sectors characterized by more external networking and more organic and unpredictable, non-routine work outputs are associated with a greater HR headcount.

- National regulatory heritage, in the form of regulatory complexity, creates a context for HR activities. Japan, characterized by mandatory transactions, has larger HR staffs, while the former communist nations of Central and Eastern Europe, reacting to the deregulation associated with changes from planned economies and the widespread acceptance of "market forces," have smaller HR staffs. Beyond these patterns, how transactional or strategic HR becomes is not clearly related to the size of the HR staff.
- More resources spent on training and employee development, HR presence on the board of directors, and the absence of unions are all associated with larger HR staffs.
- Institutionally, where roles and relationships are more formally established by bureaucratic systems, trade union contracts, or government mandates, HR departments are smaller.[35]

Clearly, disentangling the complex relationships among those institutional, industrial, and historical contingencies that may contribute to the pattern of IHRM philosophies, strategies, policies, practices, and capabilities of an MNE, industry, or nation remains a rich area for future research.[36]

Summary and Concluding Remarks

Throughout this book, we have endeavoured to highlight the challenges faced by firms as they confront human resource management concerns related to international business operations. This chapter has been concerned with identified trends and future challenges—both managerial and academic—that are likely to have an impact on IHRM, both as a function and as a scientific field of study. We specifically addressed international business ethics and HRM, modes of operation other than wholly owned subsidiaries, and the IHRM activities that are required, such as training for contractual and project operations.

Furthermore, we have discussed ownership issues relating to family-owned firms and nongovernment organizations (NGOs), along with the IHRM challenges specific to these organizations as they grow internationally. These challenges have remained relatively under-identified, despite their continuing importance in international business and global activities.

This chapter also addressed the complex assessment and planning activities related to safety, security, and counterterrorist efforts, and we discussed research issues in IHRM and developments that are endeavouring to assist in understanding the intricacies and interrelationships between the IHRM function and IHR activities, firm internationalization, and strategic directions and goals.

A consistent theme throughout this book has been the way in which IHRM requires a broader perspective of what operating internationally involves, and a clear recognition of the range of issues pertaining to all categories of staff operating in different functional, task, and managerial capacities is essential.

As Poole[37] stated in his editorial in the first issue of the *International Journal of Human Resource Management* in 1990:

> International human resource management archetypically involves the world-wide management of people in the multinational enterprise.

Key Terms

bribery 396
ethical absolutist 396

ethical relativist 396
ethical universalist 396

Web Links

www 12.1   United Nations Universal Declaration of Human Rights:
           www.un.org/Overview/rights.html

www 12.2   Guidelines for Multinational Enterprises adopted by the Organisation of Economic Co-operation and Development:
           www.oecd.org/dataoecd/56/36/1922428.pdf

www 12.3   OECD Anti-Bribery Convention—Country monitoring reports are available on the OECD website at:
           www.oecd.org/topic/0,2686,en_2649_34859_1_1_1_1_37447,00 .html

www 12.4   Canada's Corruption of Foreign Public Officials Act:
           www.justice.gc.ca/en/dept/pub/cfpoa/guide5.html

www 12.5   Film criticizing Wal-Mart:
           www.walmartmovie.com

www 12.6   Website criticizing Wal-Mart:
           www.wakeupwalmart.com

www 12.7   Wal-Mart's response to this criticism:
           www.walmartfacts.com

www 12.8   For more information about the RAND Corporation, go to:
           www.rand.org

RPC Icons

RPC 12.1   Directs the organization in ethical HR practices and application of conflict-of-interest guidelines

RPC 12.2   Directs the organization in ethical HR practices and application of conflict-of-interest guidelines

RPC 12.3 Monitors company's programs in the areas of health, safety, security, and workers' compensation, and responds to serious injury or fatality in the workplace

Discussion Questions

1. Identify a number of HRM problems that typically arise with expatriate assignments. In what ways might the core ethical values and guidelines identified in this chapter apply to them?
2. Why is management succession frequently an issue for family-owned firms?
3. Beyond checklists and systematic analysis, what actions can MNEs take to reduce risks related to terrorism? What roles can HRM take in these processes?

Using the Internet

1. Browse the Médecins Sans Frontières Canadian website at **www .msf.ca** and find out about some of the key themes and challenges with which this NGO is dealing. How and in which areas can companies and internationally businesses develop initiatives and programs related to corporate social responsibility that support or cooperate with NGOs such as Médecins Sans Frontières?
2. Canadian organizations in industries such as mining have many international operations—often located in developing countries and remote regions. Browse the Natural Resources Canada website at **www.nrcan .gc.ca/mms/sociprac/pol_e.htm** and explore some of the corporate policies and social practices of companies in Canada's minerals and metals industry. Discuss the role HR could or has to play in developing, implementing, and controlling such activities.

Exercises

1. Form culturally diverse groups and discuss each participant's view on bribery and international initiatives to criminalize foreign bribery. Discuss and explain why bribery is in some cultural contexts a common business practice, while in other cultural contexts, bribery is seen as wrong and unethical.
2. Discuss in groups which IHRM activities would be pertinent to the assignment by Médecins Sans Frontières of a medical team to a country such as Bangladesh? Contact this NGO's Canadian base and compare your suggestions with the NGO's actual international HR policies and processes supporting Médecins Sans Frontières assignees operating internationally.

Case

Too Little, Too Late? Siemens Belatedly Wakes Up to Reputation Risk

Frankfurt, Germany—It is a tense, dramatic account of police raids, arrests and the investigation into allegations that at least Euro200m ($265m) was siphoned out of secret bank accounts in Liechtenstein, Austria and Switzerland. A page-turning airport thriller? No, the 20-F filing submitted by Siemens, a German conglomerate, to the Securities and Exchange Commission in Washington, D.C., on December 11th. At the same time, the firm restated its earnings to take account of uncertainties over transactions being investigated by state prosecutors in at least three countries.

The purpose of these murky dealings remains unclear: was it a case of self-enrichment by crooked employees or something more sinister—carefully laundered bribes to win Siemens business in some of the 190 countries in which it operates? Siemens insists that it was a victim of crime not an accessory to it. It is investigating Euro420m of suspicious payments to consultants over the past seven years. Meanwhile, six present and former employees, including one former board member arrested on December 12th, are in custody.

In the flow of adverse publicity since police raided 30 of its offices a month ago, Siemens has tried to show that it is taking appropriate action. It announced the formation of a "task force" to clarify and standardize its employees' business practices. It also appointed an ombudsman to encourage internal whistleblowing. But for Transparency International (TI), an anti-corruption campaign group, this was not enough. It had already suspended Siemens's membership of its German chapter in 2004 because of the company's reluctance to be transparent about an unresolved bribery case in Italy. (The case was settled last month without admission of guilt.) Siemens's sluggish reaction to investigations in Liechtenstein triggered a letter last month from TI warning that the firm's membership would be liable for termination after December 15th.

At an emergency board meeting this week, Siemens announced new measures to show how determined it is to change its culture. It appointed a law firm to investigate the company's compliance and control systems. And it appointed Michael Hershman, an anti-corruption expert and one of the founders of TI (a nice touch), to review anti-corruption controls and training at Siemens. But will this be enough to save the company's reputation or its planned joint venture, Nokia Siemens Networks, which is due to start business on January 1st? The reputation risk could give Nokia grounds to pull out.

Some of Siemens' problems stem from the 1990s, before Germany and other nations signed the OECD's anti-bribery convention in 1999. Yet the Italian case post-dates the convention and another case in Greece concerns preparations for the 2004 Olympics. Siemens and the Munich prosecutors point to evidence that in the latest shenanigans the suspects "banded together" to defraud the firm. There is only so much one can do, sighs a Siemens spokesman, against "criminal energy."

But even poor supervision and control, rather than connivance with bribery, are bad enough. It cannot help appearances that Heinrich von Pierer, who was chief executive of Siemens in the 1990s before bribery was outlawed, still heads the supervisory board. He was supposed to steer the company through its transition to OECD anti-bribery rules and compliance with America's Sarbanes-Oxley Act, which requires greater disclosure and personal responsibility from executives. Worst of all for Germany's reputation as export champion of the world is the suspicion that it may owe some of its prowess to secret bank accounts and slush funds.

Klaus Kleinfeld, Siemens's chief executive since January 2005, may escape the full wrath of shareholders. But he still has plenty to do to reach self-imposed profit targets for some of the group's worse-performing divisions such as business systems, which is loss-making, and communications, where profits are sliding. The constant bad publicity cannot help.

Source: *The Economist*. (2006, December 13), *381*(8508), 65–66.

Questions

1. Imagine you are in your first serious management job. How would you react if you were being pressured by your company to win an international multimillion-dollar order, knowing that you can get the deal only by bribing local authorities (your superiors would provide you with the necessary financial and non-financial resources)? Why would you have that reaction? Be honest with yourself!
2. Browse Siemens' home page. Where and how does Siemens state its stance against bribery and corruption?
3. In groups, discuss recommendations for ways in which Siemens could change its organizational culture in the area of anti-corruption. What has Siemens done so far?
4. Where does Siemens stand today in its fight against bribery and corruption? What has changed since December 2006 in terms of Siemens' personnel politics at a senior management level? What have been the consequences of these HR actions for Siemens' fight against bribery and corruption?

Endnotes

1. See: T. Jackson. (2002). *International HRM: A Cross-cultural Approach* (Chapter 5, The Motivating Organization: The Japanese Model). London, UK: Sage, 107–126; E. Ikegami. (1995). *The Taming of the Samurai: Honorific Individualism and the Making of Modern Japan*. Cambridge: Harvard University Press; and J. Abegglen & G. Stalk. (1985). *Kaisha: The Japanese Corporation*. New York: Basic Books.
2. See the Organisation for Economic Co-operation and Development (OECD) website page "Bribery in International Business" for a comprehensive list of OECD resources: www.oecd.org/topic/0,2686,en_2649_34855_1_1_1_1_37447,00.html.

3. Carson, T. L. (1984). Bribery, Extortion, and the Foreign Corrupt Practices Act. *Philosophy and Public Affairs*, 66–90. See also the United States Department of Justice website at www.usdoj .gov/criminal/fraud/fcpa.html for up-to-date information on the Foreign Corrupt Practices Act (FCPA).

4. W. Bottiglieri, M. Marder, & E. Paderon. The Foreign Corrupt Practices Act: Disclosure Requirements and Management Integrity. *SAM Advanced Journal*. (1991, Winter), 21–27.

5. Transparency International *Corruption Perceptions Index 2006*: www.transparency.org/policy _research/surveys_indices/cpi/2006/CPI_2006_presskit_eng[1].pdf.

6. W. Cascio. (2006). The High Cost of Low Wages. *Harvard Business Review, 84*(12), 23; W. Cascio. (2006). Decency Means More Than "Always Low Prices": A Comparison of Costco to Wal-Mart's Sam's Club. *Academy of Management Perspectives, 20*(3), 26–37; P. Ghemawat. (2006). Business, Society and the "Wal-Mart Effect." *Academy of Management Perspectives, 20*(3), 41–43; A. Harrison & M. McMillan. (2006). Dispelling Some Myths About Offshoring. *Academy of Management Perspectives, 20*(4), 6–22; and D. Farrell, M. Laboissiere, & J. Rosenfeld. (2006). Sizing the Emerging Global Labor Market. *Academy of Management Perspectives, 20*(4), 23–34.

7. H. De Cieri & P. Dowling. (2006). Strategic International Human Resource Management in Multinational Enterprises: Developments and Directions. In G. Stahl & I. Björkman (Eds.), *Handbook of Research in International Human Resource Management*. Cheltenham, UK: Edward Edgar, 15–35; P. Rosenzweig. (2006). The Dual Logics Behind International Human Resource Management: Pressures for Global Integration and Local Responsiveness. In G. Stahl & I. Björkman (Eds.), *Handbook of Research in International Human Resource Management*. Cheltenham, UK: Edward Elgar, 36–48; and P. Stiles & J. Trevor. (2006). The Human Resource Department: Roles, Coordination and Influence. In G. Stahl & I. Björkman (Eds.), *Handbook of Research in International Human Resource Management*. Cheltenham, UK: Edward Elgar, 49–67.

8. R. Schuler & I. Tarique. (2006). International Joint Venture System Complexity and Human Resource Management. In G. Stahl & I. Björkman (Eds.), *Handbook of Research in International Human Resource Management*. Cheltenham, UK: Edward Elgar, 385–404.

9. Go to the Bechtel Corporation's website for details: www.bechtel.com/overview.htm.

10. H. W. C. Yeung. (2000). Limits to the Growth of Family-Owned Business? The Case of Chinese Transnational Corporations from Hong Kong. *Family Business Review, XIII*(1), 55–70.

11. M. Fenwick. (2005). Extending Strategic International Human Resource Management Research and Pedagogy to the Non-Profit Multinational. *International Journal of Human Resource Management, 16*(4), 497–512.

12. Ibid., 508.

13. The authors would like to acknowledge the assistance of Tom Schneid, Professor of Loss Prevention and Safety, and Larry Collins, Associate Professor of Loss Prevention and Safety and Chair of the Department of Loss Prevention and Safety, in the College of Justice and Safety at Eastern Kentucky University, Richmond, Kentucky, in the preparation of this section of Chapter 12.

14. Although much of this material is specific to national or industry regulations, for a U.S. perspective, see: R. Mathis & J. Jackson. (2006), *Human Resource Management* (11th ed.). Mason, OH: South-Western/Thomson, Chapter 15.

15. M. Schumann & T. Schneid. (1997). *Legal Liability: A Guide for Safety and Loss Prevention Professionals*. Gaithersburg, MD: Aspen Publishers.

16. For a review of the range of services available to firms, see: 2007 Loss Prevention Resource Guide. (2007). *Loss Prevention: The Magazine for LP Professionals, 6*(1), 67–98.

17. M. Czinkota, G. Knight, & P. Liesch. (2004). Terrorism and International Business: Conceptual Foundations. In G. Suder (Ed.), *Terrorism and the International Business Environment: The Security-Business Nexus*. Cheltenham, UK: Edward Edgar, 48.

18. F. Dimanche. (2004). The Tourism Sector. In G. Suder (Ed.), *Terrorism and the International Business Environment: The Security-Business Nexus*. Cheltenham, UK: Edward Elgar, 157–170.

19. Czinkota et al. Terrorism and International Business: Conceptual Foundations, 55. For a very similar analysis specific to SARS, see: W.-J. Tan & P. Enderwick. (2006). Managing Threats in the Global Era: The Impact and Responses to SARS. *Thunderbird International Business Review, 48*(4), 515–536. J. McIntyre & E. Travis (2006) provide a thorough albeit general discussion of MNE practices related to hardening global supply chains in: Global Supply Chain Under Conditions of Uncertainty: Economic Impacts, Corporate Responses and Strategic Lessons. In G. Suder (Ed.), *Corporate Strategies under International Terrorism and Adversity*. Cheltenham, UK: Edward Elgar, 128–160.

20. D. Wernick. (2006). Terror Incognito: International Business in an Era of Heightened Geopolitical Risk. In G. Suder (Ed.), *Corporate Strategies under International Terrorism and Adversity*. Cheltenham, UK: Edward Elgar, 68.

21. G. Hulme. (2004, July 5). Under Attack. *Information Week*: www.informationweek.com/shared/printableArticle.jhtlm?articleID=22103493; D. Wernick. Terror Incognito, 68–69.

22. Czinkota et al. Terrorism and International Business: Conceptual Foundations, 55.

23. D. Gillingham. (2006). Managing in an Era of Terrorism. In G. Suder (Ed.), *Corporate Strategies under International Terrorism and Adversity*. Cheltenham, UK: Edward Elgar, 196–203, particularly Table 1.2, 199.

24. Ibid., 55–56.

25. N. Adler. (1983). Cross-Cultural Management Research: The Ostrich and the Trend. *Academy of Management Review, 8*, 226–232.

26. For a review and related articles, see: M. A. Von Glinow (guest editor). (2002). Best Practices in IHRM: Lessons Learned from a Ten-Country/Regional Analysis. *Asia Pacific Journal of Human Resources, 40*(1) (special issue).

27. M. Elvira & A. Davila (Eds.). (2005). *Managing Human Resources in Latin America*. London, UK: Routledge.

28. M. Morley, N. Heraty, & S. Michailova (Eds.). (2007). *Managing Human Resources in Central and Eastern Europe*. London, UK: Routledge.

29. P. Budhwar & K. Mellahi (Eds.). (2006). *Managing Human Resources in the Middle-East*. London, UK: Routledge.

30. H. Larsen & W. Mayrhofer (Eds.). (2006). *Managing Human Resources in Europe*. London, UK: Routledge.

31. K. Kamoche, Y. Debrah, F. Horwitz, & G. Nkombo Muuka (Eds.). (2003). *Managing Human Resources in Africa*. London, UK: Routledge.

32. P. Budhwar (Ed.). (2004). *Managing Human Resources in Asia-Pacific*. London, UK: Routledge.

33. See: P. Sparrow. (2006). Globalization of HR at Function Level: Exploring the Issues Through International Recruitment, Selection and Assessment Processes (International Programs, Visiting Fellow Working Papers). Cornell University: http://digitalcommonsilr.cornell.edu/intlvf/25; I. Björkman & J. Lervik. (2006, September). Transferring HRM Practices Within Multinational Corporations (working paper); I. Björkman, A. Smale, J. Sumelius, V. Suutari, & Y. Lu. (2006). Changes in Institutional Context and MNC Operations in China: Subsidiary HRM Practices in 1996 versus 2006 (working paper); and P. Buckley, J. Clegg, N. Forsans, & K. Reilly. (2001). Increasing the Size of the "Country": Regional Economic Integration and Foreign Direct Investment in a Globalised World Economy. *Management International Review, 41*(3), 251–274. For more on the nature and significance of an international HR perspective at various vertical levels in the MNE, see: S. Gibb. (2003). Line Manager Involvement in Learning and Development:

Small Beer or Big Deal? *Employee Relations, 25*(3), 281–293; P. Magnusson & D. Boggs. (2006). International Experience and CEO Selection: An Empirical Study. *Journal of International Management, 12*, 107–125; and M. Svoboda & S. Schroder. (2001). Transforming Human Resources in the New Economy: Developing the Next Generation of Global HR Managers at Deutsche Bank AG. *Human Resource Management, 40*(3), 261–273.

34. C. Brewster, G. Wood, M. Brookes, & J. Van Ommeren. (2006). What Determines the Size of the HR Function? A Cross-National Analysis. *Human Resource Management, 45*(1), 3–21.

35. Ibid., 13–16.

36. Z. Aycan. (2005). The Interplay Between Cultural and Institutional/Structural Contingencies in Human Resource Management Practices. *International Journal of Human Resource Management, 16*(7), 1083–1119; H. De Cieri & P. Dowling. (2006). Strategic International Human Resource Management in Multinational Enterprises: Developments and Directions; S. Taylor & N. Napier. (2005). International HRM in the Twenty-First Century: Crossing Boundaries, Building Connections. In H. Scullion & M. Linehan (Eds.), *International Human Resource Management: A Critical Text.* Basingstoke, UK: Palgrave/Macmillan, 298–318; and C. Brewster. (2006). Comparing HRM Policies and Practices Across Geographical Borders. In G. Stahl & I Björkman (Eds.), *Handbook of Research in International Human Resource Management.* Cheltenham, UK: Edward Elgar, 68–90.

37. M. Poole. (1990). Editorial: Human Resource Management in an International Perspective. *International Journal of Human Resource Management, 1*(1), 1–15.

Cases

Case 1

Spanning the Globe

Allen D. Engle, Sr.[1]

Eric Christopher, Associate Director for Global HR Development at Tex-Mark, was sitting in his car in an early morning traffic jam. He had thought that by leaving his home at 7:00 a.m. he would have been ahead of the heavy commuter traffic into San Antonio's city centre. The explanation for the long queue was announced by the radio traffic service: A large, portable crane, used to set up concrete barriers around road work, had overturned, and inbound and outbound traffic would be at a dead stop for at least an hour.

Eric had ended up at Tex-Mark, a computer input–output manufacturer and supplier, through an indirect career route. Brought up in the Hill Country Village district of San Antonio, Eric had graduated from Churchill High School and Baylor University in Waco, Texas, with a major in History and a minor in Spanish. His maternal grandmother lived in Tennessee, but was born and grew up in Edinburgh, Scotland, and Eric had spent several summers while in high school and at university backpacking around Europe.

His facility for languages was impressive and he had an excellent working use of Spanish, French, Italian, and German. He could converse in Cantonese, as the result of working in a noodle restaurant during university and had started a tutorial course in Mandarin last fall.

Upon graduation, Eric backpacked around Europe and South America until his money ran out. Returning to Dallas he took a ticketing job with Southwest Airlines and was quickly moved to the training unit. After four successful years at Southwest, he was contacted by a headhunter about a position as Global Development–Assistant with Tex-Mark. The promised combination of global travel, more money, and a return to San Antonio proved irresistible, and Eric had been with Tex-Mark for five years now. His career progress to date was outstanding, despite the extra workload self-imposed by undertaking M.B.A. studies at the University of Texas, San Antonio, as a part-time student.

Tex-Mark had started out as a spinoff firm from Dell Computers in the late 1970s. Patents combined with an excellence in engineering, an outstanding institutional sales staff, cost-sensitive production, and pricing all combined to make Tex-Mark a major force in the printer and optical scanner industry. Tex-Mark inherited a production facility in San Antonio from Dell, but the company also had international production facilities operating in three countries: Monterrey, Mexico; Leith, Scotland; and more recently in Jaipur,

India. A major new facility was scheduled to start production in Wuhu, China, late next year.

Research and new product development activities were split between the home offices in San Antonio, a printer centre in Durham, North Carolina, and an optical research "centre of excellence" in Edinburgh, Scotland. Major sales, distribution, and customer service centres had recently expanded into Asia and are now located in Rheims in France; in Memphis, Tennessee; in Sydney, Australia; in Rio de Janeiro, Brazil; in Hong Kong; and in Tel Aviv, Israel.

Faced with the long delay, Eric turned the radio volume down, turned up the air conditioning, and telephoned his office on his hands-free car phone to advise them of his situation. Fortunately, his personal assistant was already at work so Eric was able to rearrange his schedule. He asked that the 10:30 a.m. meeting with Fred Banks, a plant engineer recently repatriated from Jaipur, be pushed back an hour. His major concern was a teleconference meeting at 2:00 p.m. with his director, who was currently visiting the sales centre in Memphis, and the other four members of the executive career development team in San Antonio. The general topic was a review and evaluation of training and development strategies for expatriate professionals and managers resulting from Tex-Mark's growth and the new production shift to Asia. Eric had indirectly heard that Juanita Roberto, the Vice President for HR, wanted costs cut and her delegates on the team would be pushing for streamlined (Eric had mentally translated that as "cheaper") training programs, shorter expatriate assignments, and faster appointment of HCNs whenever possible. While Eric had prepared for this crucial meeting, he needed to incorporate some information from his office files.

The radio announcer broke into Eric's thoughts, commenting that overextension or carrying too much weight probably caused the crane to overturn. "I can identify with that," Eric thought to himself.

Eric's meeting with Fred Banks had not gone well. Fred was one of the last of the "Dell legacies," a Dell engineer who had stayed on with Tex-Mark after the spinoff in 1978. Fred had been a bright and promising young engineer back then, and was one of the first people chosen to go to Scotland in 1983. He was so successful in bringing that facility on line in an eleven-month assignment that he was made lead engineer of the team that went into Mexico in 1989. The three-year Mexican project did not go as smoothly. Certainly there were many unavoidable economic uncertainties during that period.

Reviewing the files, Eric felt a large part of the problem was that Fred's team did not relate well to their Mexican counterparts. Furthermore, the Tex-Mark team did not treat the local and national government agencies with enough respect and sensitivity. Eric noted that permits and authorizations that should have taken weeks instead took six months or more.

After the Mexican project, Fred stayed in San Antonio, with occasional trips to Durham, North Carolina. His assignment to India in 1999 was by sheer chance, as a last-minute replacement for another engineer whose father was diagnosed with a serious cancer some two weeks before the family was to set off on assignment. Eric had helped design the pre-departure training program for the original candidate and had even included a one-week visit for the candidate and his wife.

Today, Fred was angry and disappointed that an eighteen-month assignment in India had turned into a three-year assignment, and that a research position in Durham "promised" to him by a previous VP (two VPs ago) was filled by a younger Durham resident employee. Eric bluntly countered that the eighteen-month assignment had become a three-year assignment largely due to Fred's unwillingness to train and hand over responsibilities to local engineers and his inability to work constructively with district and federal regulators in India.

The conversation took a hostile turn and although Eric did not lose his temper, he was troubled by Fred's final comment: "If this is how you treat the people willing to go abroad, you'll never get your best engineers to leave San Antonio."

Preparing for the 2:00 p.m. meeting, Eric reviewed the unofficial, yet "standard" expatriate training program he had been instrumental in developing over the last three years (see Figure 1). Although Eric recommended that all pre-departure activities should be undertaken, this was not compulsory.

Figure 1

Tex-Mark Corporation Policy for Expatriate Preparation and On-Assignment Support

Pre-Departure Activities

1. *Country briefings:* Outsourced to a consulting firm in San Antonio that had experience dealing with the countries in which Tex-Mark operated. Tex-Mark was prepared to pay for four sessions, each lasting one hour.
2. *Reading assignments:* Three to four books (depending on region of assignment) on national or regional culture and/or doing business in the focal region. Accompanying spouses/partners had access to a similar library.
3. *Interviews and conversations* with Tex-Mark employees with foreign country experiences.
4. *Language courses:* Attendance at elective "survival level" language classes. These courses last from eight to twelve weeks, with three course meetings a week. Tex-Mark will pay for spouses/partners as well.

In-Country Training and Development

Upon arrival, Tex-Mark staff in the local operation will assist the accompanying spouse/partner with job-search activities. They will assist with finding children acceptable schooling situations. Where possible, Tex-Mark staff will endeavour to provide a social support network.

Repatriation

Upon return, all expatriates are required to go through a debriefing and career counselling session with HR staff. This should be held within two months of the person's re-entry to the home location.

With the Chinese operation adding to the number of expatriate destinations, Eric realised Tex-Mark should have a more formal policy regarding international assignments. Feedback regarding the interviews and conversations with Tex-Mark employees with foreign country experiences was mixed. Some had developed into longer term mentoring arrangements but other expatriates had found it not useful. Still, it was a low-cost way of providing information. Language courses were problematical. On too many occasions, there was not the time—employees left the country midway through their language courses. He recalled the idea of more "extensive" assignments requiring more "complete" and "rigorous" preparation from an M.B.A. course he took last year. Obviously, China is a more challenging and difficult assignment than France, but can we differentiate treatment on the grounds of cultural difficulty?

More importantly, Eric asked himself, how can I suggest we make our training more rigorous given Juanita Roberto's focus on cost? Even if I win on this point, what will I answer when asked what methods or activities make up more "rigorous" training? Finally, what is the role of language training? Eric knew that not everyone took to languages the way he did, and that Mandarin is not Spanish.

Finally, is now the time to raise the issue of repatriation? The meeting with Fred had been disturbing. Eric knew that the current debriefing and counselling sessions had a reputation for being more "tell and sell" than a meaningful exchange of ideas and insights. Top management had recently signalled this as a growing "problem." Eric had planned to gather data on repatriate turnover. Perhaps this should be given a higher priority. After all, how could Tex-Mark decide to plan for international assignments, involving more TCN movements, and the transfer of HCNs into its U.S. operations for training and development, without considering repatriation?

Questions

In the Role of Eric:

1. Summarize your thoughts on the problems at hand, alternative solutions, and your strategy on how to proceed at the forthcoming meeting.
2. How will your proposal solve the problems you have defined?
3. How can you defend your solution from budgetary concerns? In what way is your approach both a solution to the problems of expatriates at Tex-Mark and a good economic investment?

In Your Opinion:

1. Does Eric's personal background assist in his assessment of the problems he faces?
2. Would you have approached this situation differently? If so, what benefits would your different approach provide for Tex-Mark?

Endnote

1. Allen D. Engle, Sr. © 2004

Case 2

Quality Compliance at the Hawthorn Arms

Allen D. Engle, Sr.[1]

Sitting in his room at the Hawthorn Arms Hotel in Shannon, Ireland, waiting for a morning flight to London and then on to Marseilles, Alistair Mackay reflects on how uninspiring hotel rooms are. He had just completed a series of meetings with Irish officials in Limerick, concluding with a debriefing session over a Guinness with his Irish colleagues to plan their next move. Negotiations over a potential contract were proceeding well but there would labour implications that would require a formal response. Consequently, Alistair had missed the last evening flight out to London. "Another night away from the family. Thank goodness I am not missing our wedding anniversary tomorrow. I must remember to find something really special in the duty-free shop."

Six months ago, Alistair was appointed Director of Personnel Development, European Division, for Trianon, an Anglo-French avionics firm. Trianon had begun as a subcontractor for the Concorde, and gradually had gained a reputation in the 1970s and 1980s as a high-quality, if sometimes undependable, subcontractor for major French and British aerospace defence contractors. Attempts to expand into civilian markets by gaining contracts for the original European Airbus were unsuccessful, although today nearly 30 percent of Trianon's sales are through civilian contracts. Now, under new executive management, Trianon is focused on major navigational display contracts for the next generation of Airbus production. Prior to joining Trianon, Alistair had worked in the legal department of a Scottish bank. European Union employment requirements had become his specialty, and provided a springboard into his current position.

His cell phone rings, and he receives an unexpected call from his colleague Henri Genadry, General Director of Joint Ventures, Mergers, and Acquisitions, Display Division. Henri informs him that the expected outright purchase of a scanner-cathode ray tube production facility in Veceses, outside of Budapest, Hungary, was not going ahead. Instead, the decision had been made at corporate headquarters in Marseilles for a ten-year joint venture with a Hungarian government-backed firm.

Henri goes on to explain that the Hungarian control and equity interests in this project are expected to make ministry officials in Budapest happy. Henri was hopeful the decision will make executives and administrators at Malev, the state supported airline, friendly to Trianon in the long term. "We will now need a 'quality compliance manager' for a three-year assignment in Hungary. It is an important position as we will need to keep tight control on this joint venture operation. There will be some travel to France and Germany—at least in the first year—until we see how things are working out with these new partners."

Alistair asks, "When do you expect this 'quality compliance manager' to be available?" There is a pause on the other end of the line, after which Henri blandly responds, "Five or six weeks if we are to meet corporate timetables. We expect the person to be in on the ground, so to speak. We will need a realistic assessment of current processes for a start. The person will need to be familiar with the joint venture's objectives and targets. We have some details through the due diligence process but skills audits were somewhat rushed." Alistair then asks that details, including a job description, be e-mailed to his intranet address.

"Well," Henri admits, "this is the first joint venture the firm has been involved in outside of the U.K., Germany, or France. The job description will be very precise on the technical—"quality" side, but vague on the administrative —"compliance" side. You may need to fill in the missing pieces as you see fit."

After a few more minutes of general chatting, Henri finishes the phone call. Alistair plugs his laptop into the telephone port on his room's desk, and after a few false starts, logs on to the secure corporate Web site and accesses three personnel files from a folder he had prepared some weeks ago in expectation that he would be asked for a decision. Of course, he had expected the position to be that of project engineer in an operation of which the firm would have 100 percent ownership. Now he was looking for a quality compliance manager in a joint venture.

Alistair doesn't like making these kinds of decisions when feeling so remote and "disconnected" from the firm. He considers calling his friend and mentor, Gunther Heinrich, in Frankfurt, Germany, and asking him about the Hungarian project, as the German-based divisions had more experience dealing with Hungarian issues. He looked at his watch. It was 22.30. "Not a civilized time to call anyone, let alone Gunther." Alistair knew that Gunther's wife Britt had presented them with a son three weeks ago, and they were having trouble getting the child to sleep through the night. "I will call him from the airport and set up a meeting. I will have the job description by then."

Alistair is also feeling uncomfortable with the process he is going through. "Surely we can do better than react like this after the event. Why were we not part of the decision-making process on the Hungarian venture?"

Questions

1. Consider the three candidates in Figure 1. If forced to make a decision tomorrow, which candidate should Alistair choose for the job? What major factors should determine his choice?

2. We are told nothing of the process that Trianon uses to recruit candidates for this level of final selection. Given what you know about the firm from the case, outline a general recruitment and selection process for Trianon. Describe how your proposed process fits with "best" selection practices as well as the strategic needs of this company.
3. Should HR staff be involved in strategic decisions relating to international business operations such as finalizing a joint venture agreement?

Figure 1

Alistair Mackay's Short List of Possible Candidates

First Candidate

Marie Erten-Loiseau. Born in Prague, her family moved to Toulon when Marie was twelve years old. Brought up in France, she was educated as an aeronautical engineer in France and Germany. Marie worked for Trianon for thirteen years in two divisions in France and Germany, with increasing levels of project responsibility. Her leadership of two projects over the last three years in Lodz, Poland, and two sites in Czechoslovakia has been marked by remarkable success. Married, her husband is semi-retired. They have one child in university.

Second Candidate

Janos Gabor. Born in Gyor, Hungary, Janos was educated at University of Pécs, Hungary. He has a good background in the production of cathode ray tube and display systems technologies, albeit from the central European perspective. He has worked at Trianon for nearly four years, and has just been transferred into the cathode ray tube division as a senior engineer. His family is reportedly very well connected with national government officials, particularly the old, ex-party members of multiple ministerial bureaucracies. Janos is single.

Third Candidate

Sinead Marrinan-McGuire, a production engineer on loan to Trianon's London office for joint venture analyses and "due diligence" reviews on technical and legal grounds. She has spent three years on the R&D development team in Dublin and London, working on the very technologies to be applied in this Hungarian joint venture project. Alistair met and talked with her today in Limerick and was very impressed with her understanding of corporate-level concerns and strategic issues. Most of her career has been in Ireland and around London, with only short, tactical trips to France. Married, her husband is a solicitor in Dublin. They have three children, ages 7, 9 and 13.

Endnote

1. Allen D. Engle, Sr. © 2004

Jaguar or Bluebird? (A) Mark Chan's Decision: Stay Overseas or Return Home after His Expatriate Assignment?[1]

Günter K. Stahl[2], Chei Hwee Chua[3], and Rebekah France[4]

Sitting in a field filled with yellow buttercups, Mark Chan took in a deliberate deep breath of the fresh English country air and felt a sense of contentment as he basked in the warm summer sunshine. He and his family were having a Sunday picnic with their neighbours, the Howards, in their neighbourhood park. Some distance away, his wife Linda was happily chatting with the Howards, while his two children and the little Howards played with their dog.

Looking at them brought back fond memories of their time in England so far. Almost five years ago, Mark accepted an expatriate assignment and moved to England from Singapore with his family. Mark was glad that his family had settled down happily. They made new friends and assimilated well into the English culture and lifestyle.

Mark gave a sigh. The thought of having to decide on his next career move hit him again. His international assignment in England was coming to an end in three months' time and he could either continue pursuing an international career or return to Singapore. Mark felt that deciding on his next career move had never been so difficult. This time, he had a lot more to consider. He not only had to take into account his own career development needs, but also the needs of his wife and children. Mark knew that his company was expecting his answer within the next few days, but the numerous discussions he had with Linda in weighing the pros and cons of each career option could just never come to a decisive conclusion. The more Mark thought about it, the more confused and frustrated he got.

Mark's thoughts triggered his memory back to the critical career decisions that he had made in the past and the series of events that led to his current predicament.

A Bachelor on the Road: An Initial String of International Assignments

Mark started his career at the Singapore subsidiary of a Japanese consulting company and embarked on a string of international assignments that lasted about one year each. These international assignments took him to Japan, Thailand, Indonesia, Vietnam, and Malaysia. His job was to help foreign companies to scout and evaluate merger or acquisition opportunities in Asia, as well as the negotiation and closing of the deals. Deciding on taking up these international assignments was easy. He had always liked the idea of living and working overseas and learning about new cultures. He was a bachelor and his parents were not too old then and could take care of themselves. There was nothing to tie him down.

Homeward Bound: Starting a New Job and Family

After working overseas for six years, Mark got married and decided that it was time for him to settle down back in Singapore and start a family. He joined the Singapore subsidiary of Energem,[5] a diversified, global company with market-leading positions in a number of industries, including specialty chemicals, polymers, health care, and gases and related products. Headquartered in the United Kingdom, Energem employs over 60,000 people worldwide and has extensive operations in Europe, North and South America, and Asia–Pacific. Joining Energem at mid-career, Mark was offered a position as a marketing manager at its Specialty Chemicals division, with responsibilities for corporate accounts of multinational companies in Southeast Asia. Based on Energem's global management ranking structure,[6] it was a level 4 middle-management position. Mark was attracted to Energem because it offered international career prospects and had a well-known leadership development program for "high potentials," including those who had been recruited locally.

A year later, Mark had a job change and a promotion to level 3. He accepted the offer by Energem's corporate unit, Group Mergers & Acquisitions (M&A), to join its team as M&A manager and analyst for Asia–Pacific. Energem was starting to embark on M&A activities in this region and Mark's past experience fitted well with the requirements of the job. Mark reported directly to the global M&A Vice President who was based in the U.K. and Mark's responsibilities included scouting for M&A opportunities, conducting due diligence, and negotiations and liaison with Energem's various country heads and global business line heads.

An International Assignment Opportunity

At the end of his third year at Energem, Mark was offered a three-year international assignment opportunity at the corporate headquarters in London by Energem's Group Information Technology (IT) unit. Mark was very excited about the offer. The job was to conduct M&A activities for the strategic IT needs of Energem's joint ventures globally. Accepting the offer would mean another promotion for Mark and he would enter Energem's senior management category. He would report directly to the Chief Information Officer and would be close to the "gods" at corporate headquarters. Mark also relished the challenge of living and working overseas, and the salary and expatriate benefits package were very attractive. Mark remembered that although making the decision to accept the assignment was not as easy as it had been during his bachelor days, he did not find himself in a huge dilemma. Although Linda would have to give up her job as a private banker to follow him on the assignment and they had two children, they both agreed that it was a small window of opportunity for them to go overseas since their children were still very young and Linda could take a break from her career and spend more time with the children.

An Expatriate Again

Mark recalled his first day at work in the London office. He felt comfortable and settled into his new office easily. Since he had been to the London office rather often in the past, he knew the place well and also knew a number of colleagues based there through past projects. By early evening, he was already having a beer with a few colleagues in the pub near the office.

Despite the initial friendliness, Mark soon realized that there were some colleagues who felt that he got the job because Energem needed a "token Asian" on the team to show that it valued diversity. Since Energem's M&A activities in Asia were of a smaller scale compared with those in Europe and the United States, they did not think that someone from a subsidiary in Asia would have the knowledge and ability required for the job. Mark knew that there was nothing much that he could do about this perception, except to prove them wrong. Leveraging on his expertise in conducting due diligence and consummating M&As gained within Energem and through his six years as an M&A consultant prior to joining Energem, Mark learned quickly and performed well on the job. As time went by, he earned the respect of those colleagues who initially had their doubts. Mark also used the expatriate assignment opportunity to hone his cross-cultural skills and expand his network of contacts within and outside Energem. When his three-year contract came to an end, he was offered an extension of two years. He had a promotion to level 1 and was now responsible for special M&A projects within Group IT that were confidential and of a larger scale.

On the home front, Mark and his family had settled down in England happily and found the English lifestyle appealing. Energem provided them with a large house with a big garden in the countryside, less than an hour by train to Mark's office in London. They also bought an old English sheepdog—something that they had always wanted but were unable to do, as their apartment in Singapore could not accommodate such a big dog. As Mark and his family were Christians, they got to know the people in their neighbourhood quickly through attending church services and activities. Some colleagues also lived in the same neighbourhood. Mark and his family found it relatively easy to integrate into the local community. They became close friends with several neighbours and often had dinner parties or Sunday picnics together.

After having been a working mom, Linda was thrilled at her new "occupation" as a full-time homemaker. Linda found herself busier than when she was working. She had always felt guilty for not spending enough time with the children and was glad to make it up to them during their time in London. She felt that it was important to spend as much time as she could with them during their formative years. Linda made friends with the other homemakers in the neighbourhood quickly and often met up with them for afternoon teas to exchange gardening tips and cooking recipes. Linda was fascinated by the gardens of their neighbours and became interested in gardening. Soon, their garden was as lovely as those of their neighbours and Linda was especially proud of her plot of red roses, which bloomed beautifully in spring and summer.

As Mark continued to reminisce about how they had spent their time in England so far, he realized that the time they spent together as a family had been much more than when they were back home in Singapore and they had became more close-knit. Being away from relatives and friends in Singapore and having to travel a lot during the week, Mark made it a point not to work during the weekends and often took the family out on weekend excursions and holidays. Back in Singapore, Mark's family led a typical Singaporean lifestyle. When they went out, they would shop, eat, and watch movies at the various large shopping malls found in the city. Hence, Mark and Linda found the typical English countryside lifestyle a refreshing change and eagerly adopted it. They especially enjoyed the long walks in the parks nearby, the drives around the English countryside, visits to the castles, and the horse rides on the hilly greens. The family also often went on weekend holidays to the neighbouring countries. Moreover, compared with the year-round hot and humid climate in Singapore, they preferred the English temperate climate and were fascinated by the changes in seasons.

Being a car enthusiast, Mark was thrilled by the affordability of cars in England. Owing to the Singapore government's efforts at preventing traffic congestion in the small city state, even ordinary cars are luxury items. In Singapore, he could only afford a Nissan Bluebird. But in England, Mark had two cars and they were a Jaguar and a Triumph convertible. With an expatriate salary and benefit package, a temperate climate, a large house with a big garden in the countryside, and two fancy cars, Mark's family found themselves living a life that they could only dream of in Singapore.

A Bugle Call for Return

At the end of their fourth year in England, Linda's father passed away unexpectedly after a heart attack. After the funeral, Linda stayed in Singapore with the children for a month to take care of her mother. The months after her return to England proved to be very difficult. Although she had a younger brother who could take care of their mother and she had always been happy and satisfied with life in England, she was often worried about her mother and felt the need to return to Singapore permanently to take care of her.

An International Career or Return Home to Singapore?

Seeing that Linda was yearning to return home, Mark started to look for a position back at the Singapore subsidiary of Energem. After eight months of searching, Mark was beginning to lose hope when he learned that the Regional General Manager (Asia–Pacific) for the Specialty Chemicals division had unexpectedly left for a job at one of their competitors, and Energem had to fill his position quickly with a manager who was familiar with the Asia–Pacific markets. Given his familiarity with the markets in this region and his extensive international experience, Mark thought that he was the natural candidate for this position. He was prepared to accept it on the spot.

Mark remembered clearly the Monday morning when he received the phone call from the Global Vice-President of the Specialty Chemicals division telling him that although nobody doubted his qualification, they had offered the job to one of his former colleagues who was based at Energem's Singapore subsidiary.

The memory of that phone conversation and the resulting emotions of anger, disbelief, and betrayal all came back to him. "It's ridiculous," he told Linda when he informed her about the bad news. "They selected someone with zero international experience! What happened to all that talk about being a global player and the importance of international experience? It's all crap!"

Having the door closed on this option, Mark was left with the offer of a middle-management position in the Polymers Division to consider. The Global Vice-President of the Polymers Division told Mark that he was impressed with his track record and that he valued his international experience. However, there were simply no senior management positions available at the moment and he could only offer Mark the position of regional marketing manager for its rubber and coatings business in Asia–Pacific. He added that this would be a temporary position and that Mark would be given first-priority consideration as soon as a senior management position became available at the Singapore organization.

The other option that Mark had was to continue pursuing his international career. Having proved his abilities in handling global M&A activities, Mark was offered a three-year international assignment at Energem's subsidiary in the Netherlands, where they were about to relocate the headquarters of the corporate unit, Group Mergers & Acquisitions, reflecting Energem's attempts to decentralize critical functions and units. Mark was offered the position of Global Strategy Manager for Energem's special M&A projects. This would mean a promotion to level D. Naturally, the promotion would also mean a higher salary and he would continue to enjoy the perks as an expatriate. On the other hand, taking the regional marketing manager position in Singapore would essentially mean a demotion. He would have to accept a salary cut and would lose all the expatriate benefits.

The question that Mark continually wrestled with was: "Does it make sense to give up an attractive international career and a good life in Europe for a return to Singapore at a lower rank position?" Career-wise, the answer was clearly "No." On the other hand, Linda had been pressuring him to return to Singapore. Moreover, looking at things on a long-term basis, Mark knew that moving back to Singapore now would be the best option for Linda and possibly also the children. If they stayed abroad too long, Linda would find it even more difficult to continue her banking career. As for the children, they had started to go to school. Unlike England's educational system, on which the Singapore's system is based, the Netherlands is Dutch-speaking and has a very different educational system. Mark thought, "If we don't move back now, it will be even harder for everybody in the future. But I have worked so hard to be where I am now! I don't want to throw my career away."

Having been absorbed in his thoughts for some time, Mark suddenly heard giggling and felt a tiny hug from behind. It was his younger son, John. "Daddy! It's time to eat now! The shepherd's pie that Mrs. Howard brought looks really delicious!" As Mark walked toward the rest of his family and the Howards, he felt torn between his career aspirations and the long-term needs of his family. Mark knew that whichever decision he made, either his career or his family would suffer.

Endnotes

1. This case was written by Günter K. Stahl, Assistant Professor of Asian Business & Comparative Management at INSEAD and Chei Hwee Chua, Doctoral Student, Moore School of Business, University of South Carolina, with research support from Rebekah France, INSEAD MBA 03J. It is intended to be used as a basis for class discussion rather than to illustrate either effective or ineffective handling of an administrative situation.

   The authors gratefully acknowledge financial support for the project "Expatriate Careers" (INSEAD research grant #2010-502 R). We would also like to thank the Overseas Singapore Clubs, Singapore International Foundation, Contact Singapore, and Singapore National Employers Federation for support.

   Copyright © 2003 INSEAD Singapore.

2. INSEAD Singapore.

3. University of South Carolina.

4. INSEAD.

5. This is a fictitious name.

6. Energem's global management ranking structure is as follows: levels 9, 8, 7, 6, and 5 are junior management positions, levels 4 and 3 are middle-management positions, and levels 2, 1, D, C, B, and A are senior management positions.

Jaguar or Bluebird? (B) Mark Chan Returns Home after His Expatriate Assignment[1]

Günter K. Stahl[2], Chei Hwee Chua[3], and Rebekah France[4]

Home Sweet Home

After several more rounds of long discussions with Linda, they finally decided to move back to Singapore. The needs of his wife, children, and mother-in-law were the overriding factors in his decision.

The following months were spent packing and shipping their things and bidding farewells. Other than that, they did not have much time to think about their return to Singapore until the day of the departure. In fact, it did not cross their mind that it was something that they had to be mentally prepared for. "After all, Singapore is home," they thought.

Reality Bites

It had been half a year since Mark and his family moved back to Singapore. To their surprise, adapting back to life in Singapore turned out to be not as easy as they had imagined. After getting used to living in a large house with a big garden in the countryside for five years, their apartment in Singapore seemed much smaller than before. Although they lived in a luxurious condominium complex with facilities such as swimming pools, Jacuzzis, saunas, gym, and tennis courts, they simply missed the vastness of the English countryside and the lifestyle that they led in England. Mark no longer had his fancy cars and drove a Nissan Bluebird, as he used to do five years ago, before he left Singapore. Linda had to give up her gardening. The children missed their teachers and friends at school. And they all missed their dog terribly. It was impossible to bring it back since it would have been too large for their apartment.

While the whole family was having dinner one evening, Mark's elder son, Jeremy, suddenly blurted out, "I really *don't* want to go to school *anymore*!" "*Me, too!*" John, the younger one, followed.

Total silence fell on the dining room. Tears started to trickle down Linda's face and she began sobbing uncontrollably. She, too, was unhappy. All the tensions and unhappiness that had built up over the past six months suddenly came out in the open. She could no longer pretend that it was great to move home. She knew that all of them were, in one way or another, unhappy with their new life back in Singapore.

Five months ago, Jeremy and John went to school on the first day with bright and cheery faces, but came back quiet and gloomy. Especially Jeremy; he hadn't been quite his usual chirpy self since then. Except for the weekends, the boys were either tired or felt ill every morning, and wanted to skip school. Mark and Linda found out that they did not like going to school because they felt out of place and were unable to make new friends. They said that, very often, their teachers and classmates could not understand what they were saying and neither could they fully understand what their teachers and classmates were saying. Having lived in England since they were two and three years old, respectively, both boys grew up speaking English with a clear British accent. So, being in an environment where their new teachers and classmates spoke "Singlish"—English with a Singaporean accent and Singaporean slang words—communication became a problem. Sometimes, their classmates made fun of their accent by imitating them. They also found Mandarin classes tough since they did not have Mandarin classes in England and they spoke English at home. Therefore, Linda engaged a private tutor to give the boys additional Mandarin classes. Linda and Mark consoled them and told them that they should give school a try and that things would get better. The sudden outburst at the dinner table showed that things obviously did not get better.

Linda and Mark could empathize with their children. Although Linda was happy to be back in Singapore so that she could take care of her mother, she found her life back in Singapore less satisfying than she had imagined while she was in England. In the beginning, her friends were glad to have her back and listened to her about her life in England with interest. However, this interest waned and they started switching topics whenever she mentioned England. Soon, Linda found it difficult to identify with her friends. Sometimes, she couldn't help feeling that some of them who had always lived in Singapore were rather myopic and uninteresting, whereas at other times, she felt left out when they talked about their jobs and office politics. Another problem was job search. Linda was keen to start working again, but with the economic downturn in Singapore, there were few suitable job openings. The application letters that Linda sent either had no replies or were rejected.

For Mark, he began to regret his decision to accept the job in Singapore. When he accepted the position, he knew that it would be a demotion in rank and the scope of his responsibilities would be less. However, he did not expect that he would be feeling bored with the job after just a few months.

Mark started asking the Global Vice-President of the division about more senior positions, but was told that such positions were not available at the moment and that he should be patient. With the downturn of the global economy, there was no growth in the division's business, particularly in Asia–Pacific. And nobody at the senior management level was leaving or retiring soon. Mark also got the same answer from the other divisions. After six months, Mark realized that his "temporary" position might not be temporary after all, since senior management positions in Singapore would not be available for quite a while. He felt trapped.

The outbursts by his two children and his wife reminded Mark of his own frustration with his current job situation and his anger at being not offered the Regional General Manager position in the Specialty Chemicals Division. "This is simply unfair! What's the point of getting international experience when it doesn't get you a decent job back home?" he thought, bitterly. "How long am I supposed to wait? I've had enough! There must be companies out there that value international experience."

After consoling his wife and children, Mark went to his home office and dialled the mobile phone number of his friend Nigel, who was head of the local office of an international executive search firm.

Endnotes

1. This case was written by Günter K. Stahl, Assistant Professor of Asian Business & Comparative Management at INSEAD and Chei Hwee Chua, Doctoral Student, Moore School of Business, University of South Carolina, with research support from Rebekah France, INSEAD MBA 03J. It is intended to be used as a basis for class discussion rather than to illustrate either effective or ineffective handling of an administrative situation.

   The authors gratefully acknowledge financial support for the project "Expatriate Careers" (INSEAD research grant #2010-502 R). We would also like to thank the Overseas Singapore Clubs, Singapore International Foundation, Contact Singapore, and Singapore National Employers Federation for support.

2. INSEAD Singapore.
3. University of South Carolina.
4. INSEAD.

Case 5

Wolfgang's Balancing Act: Rewarding *Healthcare* Executives in a Dispersed Yet Integrated Firm[1]

Marion Festing and Allen Engle

Healthcare—A Successful Global Player in the Pharmaceutical Market

Healthcare is one of the largest European pharmaceutical companies. The headquarters is situated in Hamburg, Germany, and today there are about 200 subsidiaries all over the world. In 2005, around the globe 30,000 people were working for *Healthcare*. Net sales amounted to €5,9m [approximately CDN$9.5 million], with a net profit of €750m [about $1.2 million].

The company was founded more than 100 years ago. It started in a small shop in Elmshorn, a little town north of Hamburg. In the beginning, the main business was retailing, with only a small part of the product range resulting from in-house production. The founder himself had a background in pharmaceutics. He was very dedicated to science, and naturally interested in research and the development of new drugs.

Over the years, in-house-production was expanded and soon the founder distributed his products all over Germany and later on in many European countries. Overseas, the activities started in the United States with a small affiliate in New York. Over time, *Healthcare* acquired several local pharmaceutical companies, which later became 100 percent subsidiaries. Today, the U.S. market is one of the core markets for *Healthcare*. However, the first affiliate in the United States was only the beginning of the firm's globalization. After this initial success, *Healthcare* began to enter other lucrative markets of the world—such as Japan, China, Latin America, and Australia.

Over time, the headquarters in Germany grew dramatically. Headquarters activities centred on research and the production and distribution of pharmaceutical products that were now largely developed within the firm.

While in the past the product range was highly differentiated, today *Healthcare* concentrates on a few business areas such as oncology and dermatology. Within these business areas, the firm is now recognized globally as one of the industry's leaders. The firm intends to continue to build and extend this leading position in these worldwide specialized markets.

Discontinuous changes in the environment—such as increasing costs for research and development and increasing pressure on prices due to cost containment by national authorities, and generic competition—have forced innovative pharmaceutical companies such as *Healthcare* to operate their key business processes globally. The firm has developed a multi-centred company in order to ensure effective utilization of resources and provide nimble market penetration and product ramp-up. Critical capabilities include corporate-wide R&D processes, a concentration on a few production sites with worldwide supply responsibility, and a fast penetration of the key markets. These capabilities will allow *Healthcare* to ensure the faster and more cost-effective development of innovative products, reduce production costs, and thereby provide for significant sales growth and increased profitability.

In the past, *Healthcare*'s situation was characterized by worldwide activities but mainly local business processes (e.g., development and production focusing on local/regional markets). Local issues were aggregated to the four significant regions in which *Healthcare* has organized operations. These regions are Europe, United States/Canada, Latin America, and Asia–Pacific. Consequently, the human resource management (HRM) processes were adapted to country- or region-specific conditions, and global integration was not a major issue. For example, executives and high potentials were recruited, selected, assessed, and compensated based on different regional standards. International human resource activities concentrated on only a few international managers who acted as coordination agents.

Wolfgang Hansen: The New HR Manager

Wolfgang Hansen has been recruited as a new HR manager at *Healthcare*. Wolfgang holds a master's degree in International Management from the University of Hamburg. During his studies, he participated in a study-abroad program, spending a year in London. He has specialized in human resource management and compensation strategies. Wolfgang's initial assignment upon graduation was in the HR department of a medium-sized German technical company. However, he missed the international dimension in this job and decided to pursue an executive M.B.A. with a transnational orientation in order to prepare for this ideal career. His first job after having completed his transnational M.B.A. program was at *Healthcare*.

Wolfgang has been with *Healthcare* for one year, beginning as an HR manager. Three months ago, he was placed in charge of global compensation policies, with the newly created title of *Personalreferent für globale Vergütungsstrategien*. His first project is reviewing existing policies and practices. He has been asked to make a series of recommendations on further coordination of global pay systems at the next meeting of the board of directors in Frankfurt in January. Preparing for the board meeting, Wolfgang reviews a series of documents such as recent annual reports, the Leadership Competency Set, the new Global Performance Management System, and firm-internal strategic documents on the development of the corporate and HRM strategies. Each document set has been placed in its own folder. These six folders contain the following items.

Folder One: The *Healthcare Group*

In 2005, *Healthcare* again had a very successful year and reached records for key financial ratios (see Table 1). Thus, the firm was well prepared for reaching new ambitious targets for 2006. The *Healthcare Group*'s very positive business development is based on the sustained growth of its top products in all important markets (see Table 2). Both the strategic reorientation and the improvement in

TABLE 1

Key Data on the *Healthcare Group* (values expressed in €m)

	2005	2004	CHANGE
Net sales	6,34	5,83	+ 8%
Gross profit	3,951	3,625	+ 9%
R&D costs	981	916	+ 7%
Operating profit	891	736	+ 21%
Net profit	750	577	+ 23%
Return on sales	12.5%	11.2%	+ 1.3%
Cash flows from operating activities	982	702	+ 40%
Basic earnings per share (€)	3.33	2.52	+ 23%
Total equity	3,134	2,725	+ 15%
Equity ratio	52.6%	47.5%	+ 5.1%
Personnel costs	1,376	1,336	+ 3%
Number of employees (Annual average)	30,680	29,875	+ 2.7%

TABLE 2

Net Sales by Region of the *Healthcare Group*

	In €m		% of Total	
	2005	2004	2005	2004
Europe	2,512	2,394	42%	44%
United States/Canada	2,079	1,856	35%	34%
Asia–Pacific	308	275	5%	5%
Latin America	667	565	11%	10%
Other activities	365	326	6%	6%
Total	**5,931**	**5,416**	**100%**	**100%**

operational efficiency have contributed to the growth of its business. *Healthcare*'s aim is to create a solid basis in order to further improve the company's profitability by optimizing the cost structure.

Folder Two: Personnel Structure of the *Healthcare Group*

The *Healthcare Group* employed 32,185 people worldwide as of December 31, 2005, which was an increase of more than 10 percent compared to the previous year (28,854). The number of employees working for the headquarters of *Healthcare* decreased by 232 and now accounts for roughly 33 percent of the Group's worldwide personnel, while the number of employees worldwide increased by 3,331 employees (see Table 3). Personnel costs have risen accordingly, amounting to €1,699m in 2005 Table 4).

TABLE 3

Healthcare Group Employees by Region in 2005

	2005	2004
Healthcare headquarters	9,853	9,621
Europe	8,732	7,956
United States/Canada	4,869	4,523
Asia–Pacific	2,569	1,956
Latin America	3,706	2,944
Other employees	2,456	1,854
Total	**32,185**	**28,854**

TABLE 4

Healthcare Group Personnel Costs

	In €m	
	2005	2004
Wages and salaries	1,365	1,266
Social security and support payments	272	269
Pensions	62	61
Total	**1,699**	**1,596**

Folder Three: The Leadership Competence Set of the *Healthcare Group*

The corporate Leadership Competency Set defines the critical competencies managers need to possess to master the future challenges of the *Healthcare Group*. They have been developed based on an analysis of the business needs and by asking key players and HR people in nearly all locations of the company worldwide for their contributions. They are the basis for all HR practices and policies and are intended to ensure consistency across businesses and locations. They comprise business-related competencies, people-related competencies, and personal competencies.

Business-Related Competencies

- *Achievement orientation*: Sets and works toward achieving challenging business objectives and targets and delivers outstanding results for the *Healthcare Group*.
- *Innovation and change*: Identifies the need for change and generates novel ideas to create or improve processes, systems, or products. Builds commitment to change.
- *Decision making*: Makes sound, timely, and courageous decisions while balancing the risks and benefits to the *Healthcare Group*.

People-Related Competencies

- *Team leadership*: Inspires team members to maximize team output by providing clear direction, empowering them, establishing oneself as a leader, and balancing team resources with assignments.
- *Capability development*: Develops people and the organization to ensure that the *Healthcare Group* has the capabilities needed for future success.
- *Relationship-building*: Establishes mutually trusting relationships with people both inside and outside of the *Healthcare Group* in order to foster open communication and advance the goals and business.
- *Impact and influence*: Influences others to gain their support for driving the *Healthcare Group*'s strategy and goals forward and enters conflicts if necessary.

Personal Competencies

- *Business understanding*: Demonstrates an understanding of the implications of the *Healthcare Group*'s strategies, industry dynamics, market trends, the competitive environment, and one's function/profession in the accomplishment of business objectives.
- *Analytical thinking*: Approaches situations by identifying the best information available and systematically assessing it for meaning and impact.

- *Self-development*: Maintains a critical awareness of one's own working style and performance. Takes steps to build strengths and addresses development needs in line with the strategic objectives of the *Health-care Group*.

Folder Four: Corporate Human Resource Policies

The corporate human resource policies, which centre around these leadership competencies, are outlined in Table 5. These policies have triggered changes in the structures and processes of HR as practised across the firm's regions.

Folder Five: The Global Performance System

Within the context of the new strategic orientation, *Healthcare* has also implemented a *global performance system*, composed of common standards for individual performance management, as well as a bonus system common to all executives. With this new global performance system, *Healthcare* intends to strengthen the performance culture within the company and facilitate a common orientation for all managers.

The individual performance management system contains two elements:

1. *Goal-setting and appraisal*: The new system ensures that every manager gets a precise orientation on expectations and priorities, clear feedback on individual achievements, and contingent rewards.

TABLE 5

HR Policies of the *Healthcare Group*

HR AREA	POLICY DIRECTION
Recruitment of key talents	Good recruitment practices
	Strategic workforce planning
Management development	Corporate management development system based on corporate Leadership Competency Set
Transfer/mobility	Enhanced cross-functional mobility
	Well-balanced cross-regional mobility
Executive compensation	Attractive and competitive compensation
	Aligned bonus system
Pension system	Move to define contribution systems
Organizational development	Clear structures, efficient processes
	Corporate announcements on managerial and structural changes
Performance management	Balanced goal-setting
	Measuring performance
	Clear feedback
	Linkage to variable pay

2. *Leadership feedback*: In order to ensure the systematic development of each manager, the system envisages a differentiated feedback on leadership behaviour (based on the corporate leadership competencies), identification of development needs, and a real consensus built for targeted development activities.

The individual performance management is based on consistent goal categories, a rating scale, a template, and a performance management cycle that is standardized at all sites and coordinated to critical corporate processes. To ensure equal application, all managers belonging to the target group are trained on the system, its philosophy, procedures, and goals.

Closely linked to the individual performance system is the *compensation policy* of the firm and the newly developed bonus system. The compensation policy is characterized by a balance of corporate standards and local applications for cash-related compensation. Fringe benefits are organized solely on a local or regional level.

The most centralized compensation element is *long-term incentives*. Following traditional industry practice, *Healthcare* grants share options to its managers. The size of the options is largely dependent on the level of management the position holds in the hierarchy. For every level, a possible range of options is defined.

With respect to base pay and *short-term incentives*, the situation is different. Global standards define an orientation for the level of total cash (fixed pay plus variable pay) to local/regional market standards. This means that the total cash a manager receives depends mainly on his or her local/regional compensation levels. Corporate standards define the market standards (based on target benchmark firms and target quartile positions). Pay level is largely defined according to local standards, while taking into consideration *Healthcare*'s industry-specific positioning targets.

The bonus of managers at *Healthcare* is based on three components:

1. *Individual component*: Based on results of six to ten individual objectives in the respective area of responsibility. The weight of this component is 50 percent.
2. *"My unit" component for regions, countries, global business units, or regional business units*: Reflects the performance of the organizational unit that a manager is responsible for or working in. The weight of this component is 25 percent. The goal achievement is measured by deviation between contribution margin and net sales goals and the actual numbers. Note that for headquarter functions (e.g., controlling or HR) that have no profit and loss account, the "my unit" component is replaced by an additional individual component, which accounts for 25 percent as well.
3. *"Broader context" component*: This reflects the joint responsibility for performance of a higher organizational level (i.e., the corporate level). The weight of this component is 25 percent. The evaluation of goal achievement on the corporate level is based on the degree of corporate

goal achievement. Corporate goals are decided by the board each year; the leading parameter is corporate contribution margin.

Both the "Broader context" and the "My unit" components are leveraged. As a consequence, a goal achievement of, for example, 120 percent will lead to 200 percent payout for this component. On the other hand, a goal achievement of less than 100 percent will decrease the payout for the respective component significantly. In this manner, unit and broad context components have potential variance in payoffs and/or shortfall that are disproportionate to their simple weights. For every component, a payout is calculated; the sum of the three components is the total bonus a manager receives.

Folder Six: An Overview of the Corporate and HRM Strategy

As stated above, the competitive situation in the pharmaceutical industry has required *Healthcare* executives to redesign cross-border activities. While the company has always been active in a large number of foreign markets, business processes were traditionally locally orientated in the past. Wolfgang recalls a typology of international firms developed by Christopher Bartlett and the late Sumantra Ghoshal. Thinking in student terms, realigning or rebalancing *Healthcare*'s pay system means increasing global integration. In an abstract sense, *Healthcare* is attempting to develop a transnational strategy now by globally integrating certain activities while leaving room for local responsiveness. Figure 1 shows the developments in *Healthcare*'s cross-border strategy.

This tendency is reflected in the HR strategy. While recruitment, selection, performance management, and compensation policies for executives were designed according to local standards in the past, these processes are

FIGURE 1

Recent Developments in *Healthcare*'s Internationalization Strategy

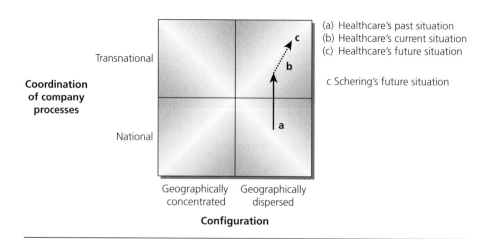

(a) Healthcare's past situation
(b) Healthcare's current situation
(c) Healthcare's future situation

c Schering's future situation

replaced by new solutions. These solutions focus on furthering global consistency of HR systems in order to respond to strategic changes on the corporate level. The overall goal is to strengthen an aligned performance orientation and to support global coordination, which is essential for globally integrated business processes. Elements indicating a stronger global integration include the above-mentioned common set of leadership competencies. This concept has been developed by the headquarters' HR department in cooperation with local HR representatives and managers from different regions and business units.

Bumps on the Road to International Coordination at *Healthcare Group*

Some of his colleagues in the HR department have told Wolfgang about problems with a standardized compensation model, which was supposed to be implemented two years ago. *Healthcare*'s aim was to have the same compensation system in each country. The company wanted to have the highest possible degree of standardization in order to make transnational processes easier and more efficient. It planned to split the salary in two parts: 65 percent fixed income and 35 percent variable income, depending on individual performance. The plan was to introduce this system not only for managers but for all employees.

Shortly after announcing the new plans, several of *Healthcare*'s regional HR managers and employees vocally opposed the new system. In France, managers even called for a strike. In Germany, the situation was difficult as well because the worker's council (Betriebsrat) did not agree to the new system and many negotiations followed. Many employees were frightened by the new system as they were dependent on a high percentage of fixed (guaranteed) income. They panicked at the thought of losing nearly half of their income and were afraid that they would never reach the 100 percent they gained before.

As a consequence, the implementation of this system was never realized. In designing the new compensation system, *Healthcare*'s management board had considered only economic issues, disregarding existing yet unspoken cultural frames of reference and perceptions. Wolfgang knew he had to be careful to avoid oversimplification and an overstandardization, and develop a more country-specific system that could be adjusted to local characteristics.

From his international background, Wolfgang knew how important it is to include his HR counterparts from the different countries and regions in the process of further developing the HR policies and systems. This would allow him to more accurately understand the cultural and legal particularities at hand as well as ensure him a higher level of political support in *Healthcare*'s regions and countries.

For example, as a first step, Wolfgang has been in close contact with the HR representatives in the most important strategic markets, which currently are the United States and Japan. Here, he has negotiated exceptions for the standardized currency base of performance-based pay elements. He has learned that the local currency is most important because local managers are not used to considering a foreign currency and would not accept this as a major element of the compensation system.

Another issue for discussion was the percentage dedicated to fixed and variable pay. Wolfgang had problems understanding the Japanese opposition to the new global performance management system. During *Healthcare*'s yearly HR conference, he felt that Mr. Okubayashi, the Japanese head of HR at *Healthcare*, was not happy with the global performance system but did not really engage in discussions about how to improve or adapt the system. Thus, one evening Wolfgang invited him for dinner in a nice sushi bar in Düsseldorf, where *Healthcare*'s yearly HR conference took place. Over innumerable cups of saki, Okubayashi patiently outlined traditional compensation systems in Japan. On sobering up the next day, Wolfgang slowly realized that, given culture and firm traditions, it would be very difficult to introduce a high level of variable pay based on individual performance in Japan. He attributed this to a higher level of risk-aversion characterizing the Japanese culture as compared to many other cultures. From his studies he knew about the Hofstede's dimensions describing cultural differences. As he recalled, one of them was uncertainty avoidance. This points out the extent to which people are risk-averse or are prepared to take risks. He thought that risk-taking managers were probably ready to accept large incentive payments, while risk-averse managers were not prepared to accept a high income variability, which may be involved in performance-based pay. The latter may be the case in Japan.

When Wolfgang talked to the American head of HR at *Healthcare*, Thomas Miller, in a very late afternoon video conference, he received a different message. Miller loudly and repeatedly asserted that, from an American perspective, the global performance management system suggested by the headquarters was "wimpy" and would not reward the outstanding achievements of "franchise player" star managers. Compared to the big U.S. pharmaceutical companies, the percentage of variable pay for top managers, Thomas declared the monetary incentive system of *Healthcare* "ridiculous" and demanded a higher proportion of variable pay. Wolfgang had to turn the video link sound down twice by the end of the Web-enabled teleconference meeting. Was this a sign of a higher level of risk-taking as a result of the underlying culture in the United States?

Step by step, Wolfgang learned how important it is to ensure acceptance in the important strategic markets and to consider local labour market regulations. He came to realize that country-specific determinants such as cultural values or the legal environment of the firm must be considered if cultural acceptance problems or legal conflicts are to be minimized. This newly acquired awareness made his mandate even more complicated. While through the international orientation of his M.B.A. program he had some ideas about the situation in some countries, he was unaware of the conditions in other countries. Implementing a new system always runs the risk of losing political support and insulting the perspectives of the local HR administrators and the business unit heads.

Thinking about the positive effects of the international HR conference as well as his individual discussions with Okubayashi and Miller, Wolfgang took the opportunity of visiting some of *Healthcare*'s subsidiaries and taking out the HR managers for lunch. He diligently tried to identify their relative positions as to the strengths and weaknesses of the current compensation system and collected ideas for his presentation to the board.

Conclusion: A Not-So-Happy Christmas

It is Christmas Eve. Wolfgang is sitting in a newly built ski hotel in Garmisch-Partenkirchen, overlooking the snowy mountains and preparing the final draft of his presentation for the management board meeting at the beginning of January. The six file folders lay spread out across the large blonde ash table and even across the oak floor, as thick, heavy snowflakes silently fall outside. He is thinking about reorganizing *Healthcare*'s compensation system. His task is to find the right mixture of standardization and flexibility. On the one hand, he has to implement a new compensation system in order to reduce costs. On the other hand, he has to take into account the traditional local HR practices. As he considers all he has learned at *Healthcare* over the last few months, he asks himself a series of questions. A visual learner, Wolfgang prepares a chart that captures his sense of integration and local responsiveness at *Healthcare* (see Figure 2).

Questions

Block A: Standardization vs. Local Responsiveness of Compensation Systems

Wolfgang reconsiders the degree of global standardization and local responsiveness of the current global compensation system.

1. Should he move some of the existing pay elements across the T-account in Figure 2, shifting them from "Global consistency" to "Localization"?
2. Should he add or delete some existing practices from the T-account?
3. Should he change the weights or emphases (percentages) of existing elements of the pay system?

Block B: Job-Based vs. Competency-Based Compensation

Furthermore Wolfgang considers whether *Healthcare*'s job-based pay dominates the existing system, while other avenues such as competency-based compensation have not been pursued.

1. How can the firm communicate to the geographically dispersed executives the need to acquire and maintain those management competencies that have been defined in the competency set (in Folder Three)?
2. Would a purely competency-based pay system be somehow more flexible?
3. But then what about the standardization *Healthcare* has just achieved through standardizing the job descriptions across units?
4. How would Wolfgang take these three competency categories and use them to develop a series of measurable, behavioural indicators to be

FIGURE 2

Balancing Global Integration and Local Responsiveness in *Healthcare*'s Compensation Strategy

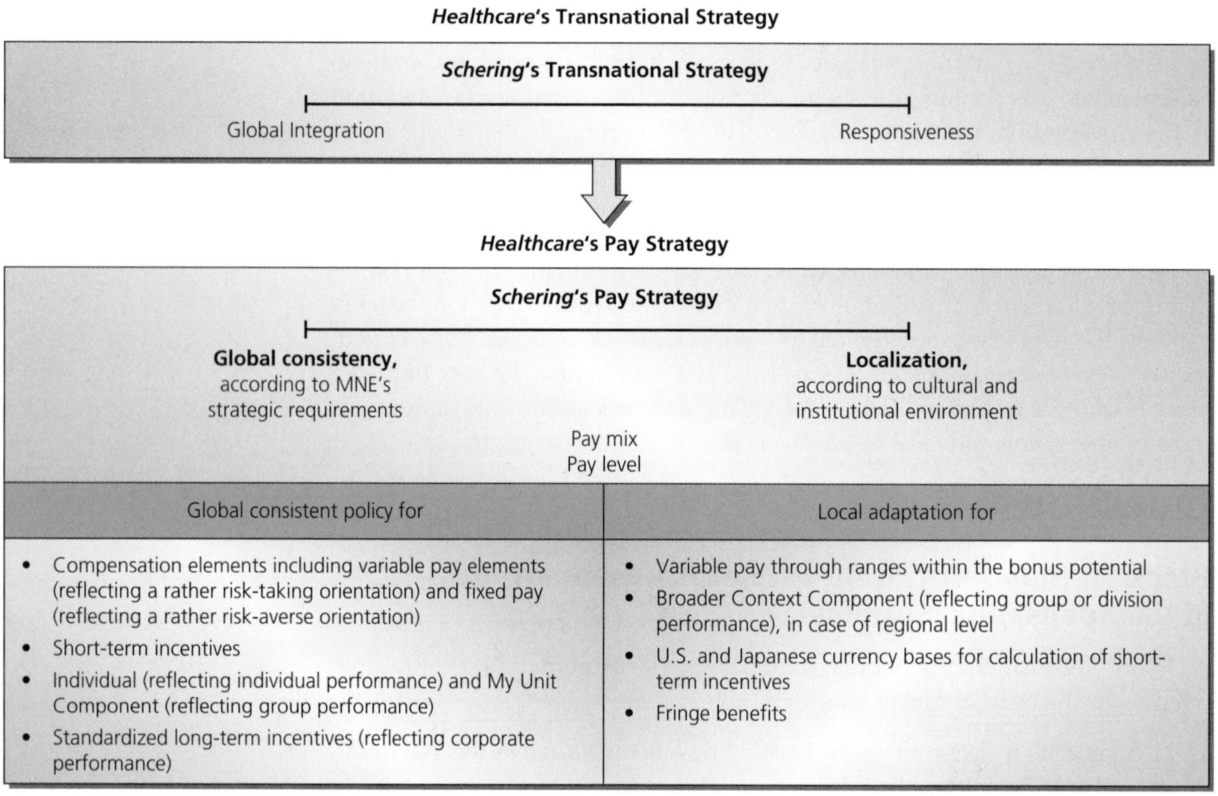

Healthcare's Transnational Strategy

Schering's Transnational Strategy	
Global Integration	Responsiveness

Healthcare's Pay Strategy

Schering's Pay Strategy	
Global consistency, according to MNE's strategic requirements	**Localization,** according to cultural and institutional environment

Pay mix
Pay level

Global consistent policy for	Local adaptation for
• Compensation elements including variable pay elements (reflecting a rather risk-taking orientation) and fixed pay (reflecting a rather risk-averse orientation) • Short-term incentives • Individual (reflecting individual performance) and My Unit Component (reflecting group performance) • Standardized long-term incentives (reflecting corporate performance)	• Variable pay through ranges within the bonus potential • Broader Context Component (reflecting group or division performance), in case of regional level • U.S. and Japanese currency bases for calculation of short-term incentives • Fringe benefits

used to assess an executive's contributions to *Healthcare*? In what sense should these new behavioural indicators be customized to local (regional) contexts? How can Wolfgang go about this process to ensure a balance of organizational standardization and local relevance?

Frustrated with the complexities he is facing, Wolfgang is planning a telephone conference with regional compensation administrators and other executives in order to expand his analysis with this group and to build political support for a new policy. Does he have the time to deal with all of the inevitable differing perspectives that will emerge, and can they together create a systematic set of recommendations before his report is due to the *Healthcare* board? As a member of Wolfgang's telephone conference, please comment on the Question Blocks A and B.

Endnote

1. The authors would like to thank Frank Kullak, Judith Eidems, Susanne Royer, Andrea Nägel, and Sinnet Lorenzen for their support.

Strategic Forecasts and Staffing Formulation: Executive and Managerial Planning for Bosch–Kazakhstan[1]

Marion Festing[2] and Manfred Froehlecke[3]

Introduction

Personnel planning and staffing issues are critical success factors in foreign subsidiaries of multinational enterprises. They must be designed in the context of corporate goals and issues and the specific situation in the host country. From a firm-internal perspective, personnel planning and staffing are related to a company's corporate strategy and embedded in the corporate human resource strategy. Thus, planning and staffing decisions must be coordinated with other HR activities within the MNE, such as human resource development. This perspective must then be balanced with a careful consideration of the particularities in the host-country context and the availability of qualified personnel within the external labour market.

In this case study, we will first outline the company background and then describe the situation in the country of interest, which is Kazakhstan. Based on this information, you are to take the role of a Bosch corporate HR manager. You are supposed to analyze both the company- and country-specific context, and outline a proposed model for personnel planning and staffing of the Bosch subsidiary in Kazakhstan. If you perceive any further information needs, please explicitly define a realistic set of supporting assumptions.

Company Background: Robert Bosch Group[4]

The Bosch Group is a leading global manufacturer of automotive and industrial technology, consumer goods, and building technology. In fiscal 2006, some 260,000 employees generated sales of 43.7 billion euros. Set up in Stuttgart, Germany, in 1886 by Robert Bosch (1861–1942) as "Workshop of

Precision Mechanics and Electrical Engineering," the Bosch Group today comprises a manufacturing, sales, and after-sales service network of some 300 subsidiaries and more than 13,000 Bosch service centres in over 140 countries. One statement by the founder Robert Bosch is important to an understanding of the HR philosophy characterizing this MNE: "It is my intention, apart from the alleviation of all kinds of suffering, to promote the moral, physical, and intellectual development of the people."

Executive and Managerial Planning

The international executive and managerial planning (EMP) at Bosch is part of the strategic planning process of the company. Once a year, the global executive staffing needs for selected countries are derived from each division's long-term strategic planning activities. Starting from the current local structure, the required number of managerial positions is determined within the parameters of an eight-year forecast. Various measures are taken to meet the managerial staffing needs. They can be short term (e.g., hiring of managerial staff from the external labour market, assignment of expatriates) or medium or long term (e.g., development of high-potential employees—see the employee development discussion below) or special programs like the Junior Managers Programs (JUMP).

The EMP is carried out using a standardized tool from the divisional HR department in cooperation with regional HR departments. Aggregated results are analyzed from division, regional, and Robert Bosch World (corporate) levels. Continuous comparisons of the planned versus actual labour staffing situations provide feedback on those assignments that have to be initiated or redefined.

The planning period of eight years consists of two parts: The input for the first four years stems from business plans and succession planning. Forecast for the last four years is based on more global, macro assumptions (e.g., changes in the leadership projected at a figure of 5 percent). Therefore, EMP is linked to employee development instruments in the Bosch Group.

Employee Development in the Bosch Group

Bosch understands employee development as a continuous process of maintaining and further developing employees' qualifications needed to cope with present and future challenges. A major principle in this respect is the promotion of employees from within Bosch rather than the acquisition of new hires from outside.

HR departments support employees and managers by providing tools and programs and giving guidance. The universally standardized systems and processes for employee development are depicted in Figure 1.

An important procedure for the development of employees is the Management Potential Review (MED; see Figure 1)[5], which is conducted on a worldwide level. It pursues the following objectives:

FIGURE 1

Employee Development Instruments

Performance discussion with each associate	Results
Once a year between associate and supervisor	Goal achievement over the past year
	Goal agreement for the coming year
	Feedback on performance measures: maintaining/improving performance

Individual development discussion upon request of	Results
Associate, supervisor, or HR department at greater intervals	Associate's personal development goals over the next three to five years
	Strengths and growth potential
	Developmental activities

Management potential review (MED), all associates	Results
Once a year between supervisors and HR department	Evaluating potential
	Supplemental development activities
	Planning for staffing needs

Decision on admission to manager development plan (MDP)

Leadership development centre new members of MDP	Results
	Potential analysis
	Advice on strength and growth potential
	Suggestions for development and career activities

Career advancement discussion only with members of MDP	Results
Subsequent to admission to MDP and (if possible) subsequent to participation in leadership development centre	Agreement of career advancement goals and suitable measures over a period of up to four years

- Full utilization of the company's reserves of high-potential employees without compromising on performance standards.
- Staffing requirements and development planning (middle and upper management) for the upcoming four years (succession planning—see EMP section above).
- Consistency in planning and tracking of employee development and career advancement measures.

- Use of overseas assignments, project tasks, and cross-functional moves as common development measures.

Employees who show above-average development potential with regard to specialist and management positions will be systematically prepared for the next management level by way of the Manager Development Plan (MDP). Besides outstanding performance, Bosch expects a task- or role-relevant personality profile, preparedness to take on new tasks and greater responsibilities, and mobility potential, as well as a willingness to take on international assignments. MDP is a prerequisite for promotion into the managerial ranks.

The preparation of MDP candidates is a mixture of on-the-job and off-the-job measures, with the target being to bring the employees into the next management level in no more than four years. In many cases, the achievement of the career advancement objective is connected with the transfer to a new assignment.

Talent Management

As stated before, Bosch mainly relies on hiring and developing talent from within the firm. Consequently, it is important to focus on the acquisition of qualified university graduates and professionals to meet a wider range of potential future managerial requirements. Besides direct entries and local programs, Bosch has a standardized Bosch-wide entry program for junior managers (JUMP).[6] The goal of the program is to recruit junior managers (master's degree with up to three years of professional experience) with the potential to assume a middle management position in six to eight years.

The program lasts one and a half to two years and is composed of three to four stages, including a six-month stay abroad as well as a cross-divisional assignment. This form of training emphasizes a common set of worldwide standards, experiences, and activities, and is designed to permit more rigorous and systematic preparations for a range of management tasks.

Expatriates

Currently more than 2,000 expatriates are working for Bosch worldwide. An expatriate, as defined by Bosch, is an employee working for more than 18 months outside his or her home country with special contractual conditions (contract in the host country for a limited period of time—normally three to five years—special allowances for hardship, cost-of-living allowance, etc.). Over 1,100 Germans are working in more than 40 countries; approximately 500 employees from Bosch subsidiaries are working in Germany (inpatriates); and roughly 400 third-country nationals (TCNs) are assigned to locations outside their home countries for limited periods of time. A majority of these employees were assigned due to technical and process expertise, yet some assignments were made for career development or training reasons. Two-thirds of the expatriates are assigned in the managerial ranks.

Bosch requires all top managers, beside their other experiences, to have at least two years of international working experience. This international experience is an explicit prerequisite for promotion.

Country-Specific Features of Kazakhstan[7]

Kazakhstan is located in Central Asia, with China, Russia, Kyrgyzstan, Turkmenistan, and Uzbekistan as neighbour states (see Figure 2). It covers a total of 2,717,300 square kilometres. The climate is continental, with cold winters and hot summers.

The population is 15,233,244 (July 2006 estimate), including a wide ethnic diversity (53.4 percent Kazakhs, 30 percent Russians, 3.7 percent Ukrainians, 2.4 percent Germans and some other ethnic minorities). The main religions are Islam (47 percent) and Russian Orthodox (44 percent). The state language is Kazakh but Russian is used in everyday business by most of the people. Kazakhstan became independent from the former Soviet Union in 1991 and is now is a republic characterized by an authoritarian presidential rule. The capital is Astana, with 538,000 inhabitants.

FIGURE 2

Kazakhstan's Geographic Location

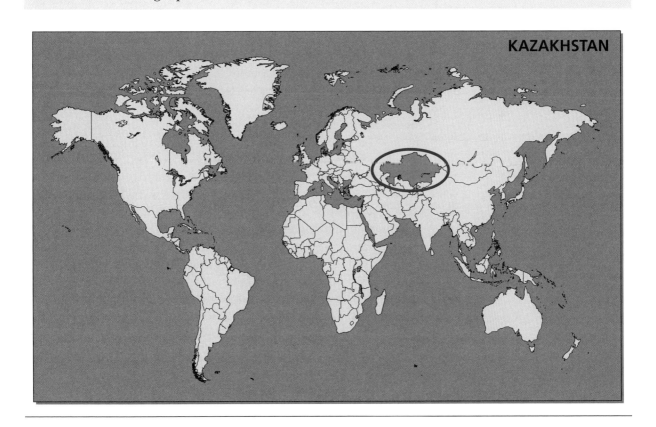

The economic situation of the country can be described by a GDP real growth rate of 8.5 percent (2006 estimate), an unemployment rate of 7.4 percent (2006 estimate), and a comparably low labour cost, averaging 86 cents (U.S.) per hour. Main exports include oil, ferrous and nonferrous metals, machinery, chemicals, grain, wool, meat, and coal.

The education system is one of the major concerns of the country. Public expenditure for education amounted to 2.4 percent of GDP in 2006 but the education system is widely privatized. Nearly 4 percent of the population holds a university degree. Due to a lack of public funding, academic research is largely dependent on foreign aid.

Your Task: Executive and Managerial Planning for a Subsidiary in Kazakhstan[8]

The board of management of the Bosch Group has requested executive and managerial planning (EMP) for Kazakhstan in line with the yearly strategic long-term-planning (eight years' forecast—see the EMP section above). The plan should predict the demand for executive staffing at all levels and for all divisions. It should also specify how the demand will be met, including staffing sources such as the use of expatriates, local management development plans (MDPs), special programs (e.g., JUMP), or external hires.

As seen from Bosch's corporate perspective, the situation in Kazakhstan is as follows:

- There are four production sites in different rural locations. Each one belongs to a different product division: gasoline, Bosch–Rexroth, security systems, and diesel motors.
- The organizations are characterized by different market/product maturity stages: gasoline, Bosch–Rexroth, and security systems are consolidated. Only small or no growth in headcount is planned over the next ten years. In contrast, diesel is still growing fast (headcount plus 30 percent in the next three years).
- The labour market for qualified managers and specialists is very small. External hires in Kazakhstan will take much longer than equivalent processes in Germany. Local candidates have very little mobility and largely lack broader national or international experiences.
- Bosch's major production sites are by and large not attractive locations to most qualified employees.
- The high numbers of expatriates were the result of the rapid in-country growth, especially for the diesel site. Higher management positions are currently solely filled by expatriates.

Taking the role of HR manager at Bosch you must address the following three questions:

1. Analyze the company- and country-specific situation by using the steps outlined in Figure 3.

FIGURE 3

Form for Situation Analysis

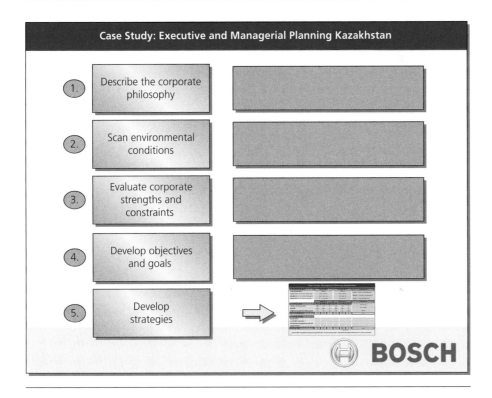

2. Plan the number and nature of short/medium-term (2009–2012) as well as long-term (2013–2016) staffing requirements on the basis of the figures in the chart below and the described situation. Use your figures to fill in the blanks in the chart in Figure 4.
3. Finally, prepare an action plan describing how you will meet managerial staffing targets. Look especially at information provided in the "Employee Development" and "Talent Management" sections of the case for activities and timetables. Write your full action plan.[9]

List of Bosch-Specific Abbreviations and Definitions

EMP: Executive and managerial planning

MED: Management Potential Review (MED is the abbreviation for the German term *Mitarbeiterentwicklungs-Durchsprache*)

MDP: Manager Development Plan

Figure 4

Planning Chart

Case Study: Executive and Managerial Planning Kazakhstan							
1. Personnel structure	**Actual 2007**		**Forecast 2014***			**Comments**	
Total headcount	7,632		8,523				
Lower (# / as % of total employees)	115 / 1,50 %		151 / 1,77 %			Lower = Lower management	
Middle (# / as % of total employees)	54 / 0,71 %		70 / 0,82 %			Middle = Middle management	
Upper (# / as % of total employees)	3 / 0,04 %		3 / 0,04 %			Upper = Top management	
2. Staffing needs	**2007–2010**			**2011–2014**			**Comments**
	low	middle	upper	low	middle	upper	
Headcount fluctuation	34	11	0	4	0	0	Further need because of growth
Backfill	40	24	2	50	36	2	Replacement because of e.g. expatriate return, retirement
Additional needs from M&A projects	0	0	0	0	0	0	To simplify the case we left this point out
Total staffing needs	74	35	2	54	36	2	= 203
3. Staffing sources	**2007–2010**			**2011–2014**			**Comments**
Expatriates							
Local MDP members							
Programs, e.g., JUMP							
External hires							
Staffing total	74	35	2	54	36	2	= 203

* 01.01.FY

BOSCH

Endnotes

1. The case study is imaginary. Bosch has no such activities in Kazakhstan. However, the described HR measures reflect current practices within this MNE.
2. Professor of Human Resource Management and Intercultural Leadership, ESCP-EAP European School of Management, Berlin, Germany.
3. Vice President, Corporate Department Human Resources Management—Executives, Robert Bosch GmbH, Stuttgart, Germany.
4. See also www.bosch.com.
5. MED is the abbreviation for the German term *Mitarbeiterentwicklungs-Durchsprache* or, in English, Management Potential Review.
6. The standardized entry program JUMP is still in the implementation phase. Other comparable programs (e.g., Management Trainee Program) have been in place for some time.
7. This section is mainly based on www.cia.gov(cia/publications/factbook/geos/kz.html and http://service.spiegel.de/digas/servlet/jahrbuch?L=KAZ. Accessed March 15, 2007.

8. The case study is imaginary. Bosch has no such activities in Kazakhstan.
9. The case study is simplified. A detailed planning of functional areas is not our intention. The student should learn to ask the right questions about how to source manpower, what challenges the company faces in a difficult environment, and what measures must be taken to meet future demands.

7

Norge Electronics (Portugal), SA[1]

Stephen J. J. McGuire[2]

Executive Summary

The case begins with the protagonist, João Silva, in Oslo for a meeting of personnel directors of the subsidiaries of a large Scandinavian multinational, Norge Electronics. Silva is the administrative director (finance and administration, HR, legal) of the division's smallest subsidiary—Norge Electronics Portugal. Silva had been asked by the vice president of human resources to present to the personnel directors what has been achieved in Portugal. The evening before his presentation, Silva received a fax from a consultant he hired in Portugal with the preliminary results of a climate study. The consultant's report is not what Silva expected and, in fact, raises questions about the effectiveness of a series of change actions implemented over the past two years. The case describes in detail the actions taken by Silva to "professionalize" HR management in the Portuguese subsidiary.

The Annual Meeting of Personnel Directors

In his hotel room in the city of Oslo, João Silva reviewed the presentation he would make the following day. Although he felt prepared, he was somewhat apprehensive. He had just received by fax from a consultant in Lisbon the preliminary results of a climate study of Norge Portugal. He had commissioned the consultant's study on the advice of Norge's vice president of human resources, with the understanding that the results would be included in his presentation, as initial evidence of the progress made in HR management in his country.

The next day, the annual meeting of Norge's personnel directors would take place. Silva would meet the personnel directors of the other Norge subsidiaries for the first time. He hadn't participated in the meeting before, mainly because Norge Portugal was a small subsidiary and Silva was not technically a personnel manager. His title was Administrative Director; he was accountable for finance, control and accounting, personnel, legal, and diverse administrative matters. In addition, the electronics division was one of the smallest divisions within the Norwegian multinational.

Each year, the personnel directors of the Norge subsidiaries met to hear the president of the conglomerate's vision of the company's future and the vice president for human resources' ideas for the HR function. Silva suspected that the VP of HR's speech might trigger a whole new stream of projects in some countries. After the speeches, there would be presentations by Silva and three other personnel directors about what had been done in their countries during the past year, issues encountered, and results achieved. On the second day, the group would split up, with people going to different workshops. Silva had chosen the workshop on management development for the morning and pension plans for the afternoon.

Silva had been selected by the VP of HR to be one of the four directors presenting to the general audience. The VP had told many people, "They do a lot of HR management in Portugal." Silva had agreed with the VP of HR to provide an overview of the actions he had taken for the past two years and finish his presentation with the results of the climate study.

Background: Norge Electronics (Portugal), SA

Norge Portugal was founded nine years earlier, with headquarters in Lisbon. Its business purpose was the sale, installation, and maintenance of sophisticated equipment for textile manufacturers. The Portuguese subsidiary endorsed a philosophy of "total service" to its customers. Although its customer base was small, it was highly profitable and had an excellent reputation with the majority of its customers, many of whom were going through tough times. Norge's revenue came from four sources:

1. Sale of Norge equipment.
2. Fees from maintenance/service contracts.
3. Sale of spare parts (durable equipment as well as consumables).
4. Commissions on the sale of other equipment and spare parts from other manufacturers—mostly, but not exclusively, from other Norge companies.

Lars Jorgensen, the managing director, described the mission of the Portuguese firm the following way:

- "Never sell to anyone who is not committed to increasing productivity."
- "Prove to the customer, and prove it again, that the textile industry, if well managed, can be profitable in Portugal."

- "Our prices should be a function of our added value to customers, not our costs."
- "Never hesitate to help a customer with a problem with a competitor's equipment . . . tomorrow the customer will remember who was there when help was needed."

Jorgensen had an excellent reputation as a technician. An engineer, he also had a graduate degree in business administration from a leading international business school in Barcelona. The customers liked Jorgensen, who spent most of his time doing public relations and generating new sales. Silva also liked his boss very much, partly because Jorgensen rarely "interfered" in the Administration Department.

The technicians at Norge Portugal liked to make their service calls accompanied by Jorgensen. They knew that he wouldn't hesitate to take off his jacket and tie (on those few occasions when he actually wore them) and get his hands dirty adjusting a machine or replacing a bit of wire. It was sometimes said that the best training that the firm had to offer was a service call with Jorgensen.

To service the maintenance contracts that nearly all customers had, the firm sent a team of technicians to the customer at least once per quarter to inspect the equipment and identify potential productivity problems. Technicians did preventive maintenance work, verified stock levels of spare parts and consumables, and so on. The team often spent time helping the factory's production manager with equipment that hadn't been sold by Norge. At first, Silva had thought that Norge went too far to satisfy a customer but gradually he changed his opinion. Customer loyalty was very high, and the commission that Norge earned on the sale of complementary equipment was one of the reasons that the Portuguese firm was so profitable.

Norge's Unique Selling Proposition

Although many customers considered Norge's fees to be high, the monthly maintenance/service charge was generally accepted. The margin on the sale of equipment was high. The upcoming fiscal year promised to be good, since some customers expressed interest in upgrading equipment. Norge's unique selling proposition (USP) was its guaranteed increase in productivity. Before selling any equipment, Norge scrupulously studied the customer's current productivity levels. Although this was by no means an easy task, after nine years in the market, Norge had learned a great deal. Everything was documented carefully, and a complete report was prepared for the customer. Each semester, the customer controller produced a report on each customer's productivity level (per line of equipment) and compared it with a baseline, or starting point. Productivity was expressed as one number, the Norge Productivity Index (NPI). Naturally, the monthly report contained a breakdown of partial measures and a complete explanation, but Silva knew that the customers' general managers paid far more attention to the NPI number than anything else in the report. He also suspected they paid more attention to the NPI than to anything their own production managers might report.

TABLE 1

GUIMTEX's NPI Evolution

Equipment: SA 4000; TXT 3.8: REV 47

(Model III)

Installation: February 1999

Baseline	2/99:	100
NPI	6/99:	83
NPI	12/99:	143
NPI	5/00:	161
NPI	11/00:	180
NPI	5/01:	199
NPI	11/01:	206
NPI	6/02:	219
NPI	12/02:	229
NPI	6/03:	238
NPI	11/03:	244
NPI	5/04:	246
NPI	11/04:	269

This simple measurement approach had proven to be highly effective. GUIMTEX, for example, was a customer that followed Norge's advice scrupulously and was ready to add an additional line of equipment. GUIMTEX's current line had the NPI evolution shown in Table 1.

Norge Portugal's Structure

Norge Portugal had only 57 employees, although it did use technicians from other subsidiaries for major installation projects, usually from Norge Spain. Norge's departments were Sales, Service and Maintenance, Customer Control, and Administration.

Sales Department ("Departamento Comercial")

This department was accountable for the sale of new equipment and upgrades, pricing of products and services, and importing equipment and parts. The warehouse manager reported to the commercial director, Ole Halvorsen.

Service and Maintenance Teams ("Equipas")

Three intervention teams reported to the director, Henrique Fonseca. Lars Jorgensen considered the team concept to be strategic. Each team had between four and seven members: technicians and clerical employees. The North 1 Team was headed by Mario Pronto, North 2 Team by Ze Serra, and Centre/South Team by Pedro Paiva. In theory, each technician on the team could do all regular activities, although the team leader was the most experienced. Team members substituted for each other often to ensure that each customer got "total service" even on weekends and holidays, if needed. Rarely would a technician go alone to a customer, and quite frequently the whole team would descend on a customer, especially when a new line was installed.

Norge technicians had traditionally been classified in five categories, from Level I (the lowest) to Level V, basically according to their experience. Norge was not unionized (and thus had no collective bargaining agreement); however, the technicians found it practical to use these categories. It took between two and three years to train a good technician. Since technicians also sold, technical knowledge was necessary but insufficient. Customer relations, budgeting, teamwork skills, and persuasion were all important aspects of the job.

Customers were assigned to teams based on geographic location and type of equipment. Fonseca tried to ensure that the amount of work done by the teams was similar. Some teams had to travel more than others did. Team Ni, for example, concentrated more on the Greater Oporto area, although it also had one customer in the Lisbon area and GUIMTEX in Guimarães (between Oporto and Braga).

Team N2 had to travel somewhat more, servicing customers south of Oporto in Aveiro, near Braga, Guimarães, and Vila Nova de Famalicão, as well as customers near the Spanish border in Covilhã and Fundão. Team N2 had FEMIFA in V.N. Famalicão (north of Braga) but also TEXIWEAR in Aveiro. (See Appendix 7A.)

Team Centre/South had customers in the greater Lisbon and Coimbra areas and still others scattered around the country, including one in the Azores Islands. This team also serviced two customers in Africa, although the maintenance agreement with African textile manufacturers was not identical to the agreements with domestic customers.

Customer Control Department ("Depto. De Controlo De Clientes")

The customer controller was a young man, Nuno Abrantes, who had a special aptitude for this kind of work. According to Jorgensen, Abrantes was "underpaid," but Silva knew that Abrantes wouldn't find any other work like this in Portugal. Abrantes's department had only four people, two of whom were administrative assistants. The fourth was a Level III technician, who hoped to return to a service team but for now was happy to learn as much as he could with Abrantes. This department was accountable for invoicing, collection of receivables, documentation of customer productivity levels, and preparation of NPIs based on information provided by technicians. Abrantes also played an important informal role in training technicians: Abrantes was Norge's IT troubleshooter, not because of his formal job duties, but rather because he was good with computers.

Administration Department ("Departamento Administrativo")

Silva's department was accountable for finance management, treasury, general and cost accounting, legal, and personnel. Outside counsel was retained to review all contracts and to provide general legal support.

The Norge Family

According to Jorgensen, Norge's customers made up part of the "Norge family." Most were in the northern part of the country, which is why there were two teams for the North and only one for the South/Centre. Silva saw no need to change the team structure or assignments, but Fonseca (director of "Equipas") thought that another team was needed in the North. Team N2, according to Fonseca, travelled too much. Within the "family," 18 customers contributed approximately 65 percent of Norge's revenue, with the top four customers representing around 35 percent of the business.

The current average NPI was 169 for all customers, not considering the year of installation. Jorgensen and Fonseca considered 169 to be "good." It was true that many Portuguese textile firms were "behind" those in other European countries in terms of modern management. Silva felt that some of Norge Portugal's customers could compete in the global textile market, whereas others probably would not survive in the long term. Jorgensen was proud of his "family" and prompted customers to expand their businesses. Although in theory all members of the "Norge family" were supposed to get equal support, the technicians were more committed to some customers than to others.

Silva was mostly worried about FEMIFA, an important customer in Vila Nova de Famalicão. FEMIFA's NPI (about 138) was not outstanding, but Silva knew that these things took time—and more time for some customers than for others. Because Silva had set up separate profit-and-loss accounts per customer, he knew that the FEMIFA account was highly profitable—if only Norge could collect its money in a timely and regular way. FEMIFA had one complete line installed but had also purchased supplementary equipment that brought high commissions to Norge. A good customer in all aspects except prompt payment, he thought.

Evolution of the Personnel Function at Norge Portugal

During his first year at Norge, Silva did little more than process pay. At that time, it had been important to establish basic procedures and routines and to "legalize" the pay system. Before his arrival, some payments (for example, lunch subsidies and technicians' expense reimbursement) had been made in a disorganized way, and laws were being ignored; he had soon corrected that situation.

During his second year, Silva received Norge's VP of HR in Lisbon. The Electronics Division did not have a central HR staff. The VP of HR for the conglomerate directly took care of this division. During his visit, and through phone and written contact afterward, Silva developed an agreed-upon set of priorities for the Personnel function in Portugal. Most of the ideas came from the VP of HR, but Silva implemented them without much support (or interference) from the MNC (multinational corporation) or from his managing director. Silva considered the VP of HR to be an "ideas man" and Lars to be a "customer man." On the other hand, Silva considered himself to be a "man of action," pragmatic, ready for any challenge, hardworking, and business-minded. He approached the personnel function the same way he approached accounting: with an analytical mind and an orientation toward results.

Organization Chart and Job Descriptions

Silva's first personnel project had been to put on paper the firm's organization chart. Although the company was small, Silva thought it necessary to document the structure. (See Appendix 7B.) The organization chart was presented to the directors, who agreed that it was an accurate depiction of the organization.

His second project was to obtain written descriptions of the tasks and responsibilities of all jobs. With Jorgensen's approval, he got each manager to describe the jobs of their subordinates on one side of a piece of paper. The next level of supervisors then described their subordinates' jobs, until all jobs below the directors were documented. To demonstrate that he took the matter seriously, Silva requested delivery of all documents by a certain date in December, and ensured that the deadline was achieved. He informed his colleagues that if documents were late, he would delay the payment of that month's expense reimbursement claims and the 14th salary.[3] Although there were a few complaints, he received all job descriptions within the deadline.

Job-Evaluation Project

With the job descriptions completed, Silva proceeded to job evaluation. He got from the VP of HR a manual with job-evaluation charts of an analytical point method of job evaluation used by firms in Scandinavia but unknown in Portugal. This method had been used by some of Norge's other subsidiaries, although references from these firms were not available. The system didn't seem very complex to Silva, who after a few phone calls to the VP of HR managed to determine the points corresponding to each job description. He also evaluated the director-level jobs in the company, based on his knowledge of what they were accountable for, although job descriptions had not been prepared for directors.

When he had completed the exercise, he prepared a report for Lars and requested a meeting. They discussed this off-site over a long lunch at the Clube de Empresdrios[4] in order to maintain confidentiality. After explaining the methodology to Jorgensen, Silva showed him the points corresponding to the Norge jobs. Jorgensen made very few comments about the actual points that resulted but was concerned that there were too many job grades. He recommended fewer grades and fewer distinctions between jobs. Silva had argued that the *purpose* of the exercise was to differentiate the jobs! After some discussion, they agreed that instead of using the actual points corresponding to each job, they would "round off" the numbers and use only one number (the midpoint) for all jobs in a given grade (see Appendix 7C). They agreed to communicate to the directors only the grades—the points would not be disclosed. No information would be given to the employees at this point; it was "too early."

After the meeting, Silva prepared a "map" showing the company's grading structure and the distribution of jobs in the grades (see Appendix 7D). He wrote a memo to the other directors explaining that these grades had been approved by Jorgensen and should be used henceforth as guidelines in personnel decisions. The directors were instructed to discuss this matter only among themselves and not to communicate grades to the employees just yet.

When new employees were admitted or when promotions occurred, Silva updated the grade "map" and sent copies to the directors.

Dynamic Human Resources Management

Silva's fourth area of concern was called "dynamic HR." The general idea had come from the VP of HR, who had asked Silva to think ahead about the HR needs of the firm in the years to come. In the job description project, Silva had come to the conclusion that certain functions were not really being taken care of by anyone in the company. It also seemed to him that some employees actually did very little. Silva described the long-term objective of this project as "equipping the firm with the stocks of human resources needed to face the challenges ahead."[5] To implement "dynamic HR," he proceeded with two projects: staffing and pay-for-performance.

Staffing

Silva's first hire was Nuno Abrantes for the job of Client Controller. Previously, Fonseca had been accountable for this function. Although Fonseca had done a good job preparing the NPIs and reports, he had been overworked. Plus, Silva knew that Fonseca preferred to spend time with the customers, particularly some of the smaller customers—to show them that they were indeed part of the "Norge family." Fonseca didn't have a college degree but was an excellent technical engineer. Silva also hired an accountant, thus freeing his own time considerably. He hired secretaries for each director, so that they would have the support they needed to get the work done in a more orderly fashion. Although Jorgensen continued to claim that he didn't need a secretary, Silva knew that the increased size of the firm simply wouldn't permit that the directors continued to share one secretary. At Fonseca's insistence, more technical and clerical people were hired to fill out the teams.

Pay-for-Performance

Silva knew that a staff increase would not necessarily lead to a more dynamic use of the company's human capital. Each employee, he felt, should be treated as an investment and therefore must provide an appropriate return. When he introduced the pay-for-performance system, he had four objectives in mind:

1. *To increase the pay of those employees with superior performance.* One thing that Jorgensen said sounded right to Silva: "Good people are never expensive."
2. *To reduce upward pressure on base salaries.* Without a system, salaries had tended to "creep up" without any logic or justification. With a system, employees could look forward to increases as well as year-end bonuses in accordance with their performance.
3. *To detect those employees whose performance was unacceptable and take steps to remove them from the organization.* Firing in Portugal was a complex, messy affair to be avoided except in extreme cases. However, Silva knew that if an employee did not receive any increase a couple of years in a row, then he or she would start reading the *Expresso*[6] very carefully.
4. *To rationalize the process of determining salary increases.* For many years, increases had been given for criteria that no one could explain logically.

Although it was true that very few employees had complained about pay, Silva felt that this was not necessarily a good sign. When the good performers complained, one needed to listen. When the poor performers didn't complain, one needed to listen even more carefully!

The Results Evaluation System

Because Silva had access to all of the company's information on sales and profit margins per customer, it was possible for him to establish a system of remuneration for performance based on actual results—in other words, sales, profit margins per customer, and so on. The accounting system allowed Silva to know exactly which employee sold what product or service, how many hours each technician had spent at each customer's, and what margin each product or service provided. Silva called the new performance appraisal system the "Results Evaluation System," which was implemented according to the following steps.

1. The administrative director reviewed the results of the year just completed, comparing actuals with the budget. For the Commercial Department, he calculated sales minus departmental cost of sales, not including any sales made by the service teams ("equipas"). This margin was compared against the budgeted figure. For the customer controller, he examined two aspects: day's receivables and promptness in delivering NPI reports (percentage on time). For each equipa, he calculated the team's margin (revenues from sales, service,

maintenance, spare parts, and the like, minus product costs and cost of sales and service). All results were compared with the corresponding budget figures. This type of analysis was done for all departments, including his own.

2. With the results of these analyses prepared, he approached Jorgensen and asked the managing director to attribute a performance rating to each director. Jorgensen would review Silva's analyses but was free to consider mitigating circumstances. Jorgensen met with each director to discuss how the year had gone. After these meetings, he informed Silva of his performance rating of each director.

3. Based on his own analyses and the directors' performance ratings, Silva defined a "recommended distribution" of ratings for each department. The idea was to allow the departments with better overall performance to have more "excellent" and "very good" performers and the departments with lower results to have fewer high evaluations. Silva informed each director of the expected distribution for his department. At first, there were some protests, but Silva explained that the director should use the recommended distribution as a guideline, and deviate from it if necessary.

4. The director of each department would then evaluate the performance of his department's employees. Because the firm was small, this was a manageable task. The director was free to use whatever system he felt appropriate; Silva asked only for the final results expressed in numerical form ("1" = poor; "5" = excellent).

5. Based on the best information he had, Silva prepared a theoretical performance score for each employee. Naturally, he didn't know the employees well enough to evaluate their performance, but he was able to get a good idea of each person's actual results. He was concerned that those employees who really added value to the company were not properly rewarded and that "free riders" went undetected. For many employees, he could calculate what he called a "personal gross margin," an estimate of the value they added to the firm. The personal gross margin was calculated by revenue (sales, service fees, etc.) less salary, benefits costs, and other personnel costs. This margin was then translated into a theoretical performance score on a one to five scale, according to the relative contribution of each person in the department. Silva's theoretical scores also took into account overall departmental performance—the number of 5s, 4s, 3s, 2s, and 1s corresponded to each department's "recommended distribution" of ratings.

6. When Silva received the results from each director, he compared each person's performance score with the theoretical performance score. If the two scores did not match, Silva met with the evaluator to discuss the discrepancy. Well prepared with facts and numbers, Silva usually convinced the directors to change their evaluations, although this did not always happen. There were occasional disagreements with fellow directors, and some tension with Fonseca.

7. With the final list of performance ratings, Silva simulated salary increases within the limits of the next year's budget. When calculating the new salary and benefits budget, Silva always left some "fat" for unplanned merit increases during the year, although he disliked doing so. He recognized that both Jorgensen and Fonseca would pressure him for increases during the year and he wanted to make sure that there was some room within the budget to allow him to comply.

8. After he had simulated the salary increases, Silva calculated potential bonuses. The amounts would vary according to what money was available in the budget. For the current year, the system was designed to pay a bonus of about 20 percent of base salary to the highest ("5") performers, about 10 percent for "very good" ("4") performers, 5 percent to 7 percent for "good" ("3") performers, but no bonus for performance below "good" ("2" or "1").

9. After numerous iterations, the administrative director would meet with the managing director to explain the proposed increases and bonuses, and get approval of the proposal. Typically, Jorgensen would make some minor changes to Silva's plan, but he accepted the overall framework.

Based on this system, Silva had introduced some order into the salary administration process. Although personnel costs had increased significantly, some costs had become variable, which would provide the organization with greater flexibility in case of a business downturn.

Pay Market Surveys

In order to understand how Norge Portugal paid its employees in relation to other firms in the country, Silva purchased two salary surveys. One survey provided data per function (sales, marketing, etc.) for "typical" jobs in large, medium, and small firms. This data contained no information on industry-sector differences. Silva believed that this survey was useful for comparing the salaries of Norge's directors, salespeople, and secretaries with the general Portuguese pay market.

The second survey provided data for different job sizes, according to a certain job-evaluation method. Data were broken down by industry sector, firm size, and ownership (foreign or Portuguese, state-owned or private). To use the data, Silva correlated the Norge points that he had obtained in the job-evaluation exercise with the benchmark jobs used as references in the survey. Thus, he obtained an estimate of comparable market pay for each Norge grade, aware that there was some margin for error. He chose as the reference point foreign-owned companies, which in Portugal tended to pay at a higher level than did domestic firms.

The Climate Survey

Based on a strong recommendation from the VP of HR, Silva hired a management consultant to carry out a study of Norge Portugal's climate. The VP of HR believed that Silva should present the study results at the Oslo meeting, thus providing some evidence of the progress that had been accomplished. Working together, the consultant, Silva, and Jorgensen had customized a questionnaire that the consultant had used successfully elsewhere. The questionnaire was distributed to all Norge Portugal's employees, along with a cover letter signed by Jorgensen and a pre-stamped envelope addressed to the consultant. Because of the small sample size, no demographic data on respondents were requested. All responses were strictly confidential. The consultant would report to Norge only the aggregate response. In addition, the consultant interviewed six Norge employees, in order to understand the firm better and be able to interpret the survey results. (See Appendix 7E for the climate study factors.)

As Silva was about to leave for Oslo, the consultant informed him that 48 questionnaires had been returned. He promised to send Silva a preliminary report with the quantitative survey results as soon as possible (see Appendix 7F). The consultant would also prepare a report with his conclusions after analysis of the results and interviews, but this report would be available only after Silva returned to Lisbon.

Endnotes

1. Stephen J. J. McGuire "Norge Electronics (Portugal)" Thunderbird International Business Review, 4(91), Jan/Feb 2007. Copyright © 2007 Wiley Periodicals Inc. Reprinted with permission of John Wiley & Sons, Inc.

2. Stephen J. J. McGuire, Ph.D., is an associate professor of management and director of the CSULA Entrepreneurship Institute at California State University, Los Angeles. He taught at Georgetown University, the Catholic University of Portugal, Moscow University Touro, and the George Washington University, where he was awarded the Bender Prize for Teaching Excellence. He is a former partner of the Hay Group, where he worked as a management consultant for major organizations in 23 countries.

3. According to Portuguese law, employees at all levels receive 14 monthly payments per year. The "13th" month is provided when the employee takes his or her vacation (usually one month in the summer) and the "14th" is paid before the Christmas holidays.

4. The Business Managers Club, an upscale Lisbon restaurant typically frequented by executives.

5. A somewhat literal translation of the original Portuguese.

6. The *Expresso* is the Lisbon newspaper with the largest job advertisement listings.

Appendix A

Map of Portugal

Appendix

Appendix B

Organization Chart: Norge Electronics (Portugal), SA

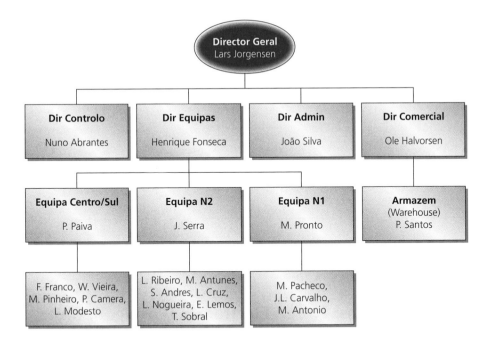

Appendix C

Norge Electronics (Portugal) Grades

Grade 20 is the highest and corresponds to the managing director's job; grade 1 is the lowest.

NORGE GRADE	GRADE MIDPOINT	NUMBER OF EMPLOYEES
20	1500	1
19	1300	
18	1130	1
17	980	2
16	850	
15	740	
14	645	1
13	560	1
12	490	2
11	420	3

Norge Grade	Grade Midpoint	Number of Employees
10	370	1
9	330	2
8	300	9
7	260	4
6	230	6
5	200	5
4	175	7
3	150	3
2	130	3
1	100	6
	Total	57

Appendix D

Job Evaluations: Norge Electronics (Portugal), SA

Position	Incumbents	Grade	Grade Midpoint
Director Geral	L. Jorgensen	20	1500
Director Comercial	O. Halvorsen	18	1130
Director Administrativo	J. Silva	17	980
Director Equipas	H. Fonseca	17	980
Director Controlo Clientes	N. Abrantes	15	740
Accounting Supervisor	P. Pereira	13	560
Treasurer	A.P. Argento	12	490
Leader Equipa N2	J. Serra	11	420
Leader Equipa N1	M. Pronto	11	420
Leader Equipa C/S	P. Paiva	11	420
Tech Rep Level V	L. Ribeiro, M. Pacheco, F. Franco	8	300
Tech Rep Level IV	M. Antunes, J.L. Carvalho	8	300
Tech Rep Level III	L. Nogeira, S. Andres, W. Vieira, M. Pinheiro	8	300
Tech Rep Level II	T. Sobral	8	300
Import/Export Clerk	R. Ferreira	8	300

Appendix D (cont.)

Position	Incumbents	Grade	Grade Midpoint
Tech Rep Level I	P. Camara, L. Modesto, M. Antonio, E. Lemos, J. Cruz	7	260
Bookkeeper	P. Costa	7	260
Senior Sales Clerk	S. Jesus	6	230
Warehouse Manager	P. Santos	6	230
Clerk (N1)	J.L. Reis, R. Coutinho	5	200
Clerk (N2)	H. Castelhano, C.J. Gouveia	5	200
Clerk (C/S)	P. Santos Silva	5	200

Appendix E

Climate Study Factors

SAT—JOB SATISFACTION
The degree to which employees are satisfied with their current jobs.

CLAR—CLARITY OF MISSION AND OBJECTIVES
The degree to which employees understand and accept the organization's mission and objectives.

ESTRUT—STRUCTURE
The degree to which the organizational structure supports, rather than interferes with, getting information, making decisions and getting the work done.

SIN—SYNERGY WITHIN THE ORGANIZATION
The degree to which people in different parts of the organization work together, support each other and do not duplicate activities.

AMB—BUSINESS AMBITIOUSNESS
The degree to which the mission and objectives are perceived as lofty and challenging.

ESTILO—MANAGEMENT STYLE
The degree to which managers' styles are supportive of employees and helpful in getting the work done.

REMUN—REMUNERATION

The degree to which remuneration is perceived as (a) internally equitable, (b) competitive with other organizations, and (c) supportive of individual and team performance.

IDENT—CORPORATE IDENTITY

The degree to which employees (a) perceive the organization as having a unique identity and (b) accept and support the identity.

EMPOW—EMPOWERMENT OF EMPLOYEES

The degree to which employees feel empowered to take the actions and decisions they need to take in order to get the job done. Also, the perception of how much the organization empowers, rather than controls, employees.

RH—HUMAN RESOURCE POLICIES

The degree to which human resource policies and practices are perceived as (a) supportive of getting the work done, (b) appropriate to employee needs, and (c) appropriate to prepare the organization for the future.

Appendix F

Preliminary Results of the Climate Survey

The chart shows the percentage of favorable responses by all respondents (48) on the questions in 10 climate categories.

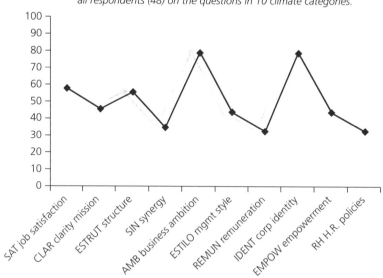

Index

Note: Bold page numbers refer to figures, tables, and boxed material.

Ulrich, D., 78
UNCTAD. *See* United Nations Conference on Trade and Development (UNCTAD)
Unilever, 297
United Kingdom
    country-of-origin effect and, 304
    domestic market and, 20
    English language and, 202
    expatriate failure and, 165
    expatriate selection and, 175
    foreign direct investment and, **54**
    industrial relations and, 338
    mergers and acquisitions, 80
    offshoring and, 313, 318
    repatriation and, 261, 267
    reverse diffusion and, 305
    selection tests and, 173
    Social Policy Protocol and, 348–349
    subsidiaries and, 309
    subsidiary performance and, 123
    trade unions and, 341
United Nations
    codes of conduct and, 311
    Declaration Against Corruption and Bribery in International Commercial Transactions, 397
    Declaration of Human Rights, 396
    terrorism and, 405
United Nations Conference on Trade and Development (UNCTAD)
    cross-border mergers and acquisitions, 71
    labour movement lobbying, 346
    small and medium-sized companies and, 90–91
    transnationality index, 19–21, **20**, **21**
United Parcel Service (UPS), **34**
United States
    bribery and, 397
    commuter assignments, 376–377
    compensation and, 223, 228, 232
    cultural adjustment and, 162, 165
    English language and, 202
    equal employment opportunity issues and, **174**
    expatriate failure and, 159, 160, 165
    expatriate gender and, 181

foreign direct investment and, **54**
housing conditions, 269–270
IHRM theory and, 407
industrial relations and, 338, 339
language study in, 171–172
mergers and acquisitions, 72, 80
offshoring and, 313
organizational structures and, 51, 52, **52**, 53
pay system preferences, 302
pre-departure training and, 194, 195
preliminary visits and, 201
repatriation and, 261, 266–267, 271, 273, 282
reverse diffusion and, 305
selection tests and, 172–173
small and medium-sized companies and, 90
social security, 226
subsidiaries and, 309
trade unions and, 340, 346
transnationality index and, 20–21, 22
Universality assumptions, 15
Universal management myth, 156
Universal pay systems, 241
U.S. National Foreign Trade Council, 194

Value-chain model, 18
Values
    expatriate as agent of socialization and, 130
    hierarchy of, 197, **197**
    standardization and localization and, 295
Valy-Durbin, S. J., 181
Van Daak, Rainer, 115
Varma, A., 181
Venter, K., 318
Vernon, R., 344
Vietnam, 319
Villinger, R., 78–79
Virtual assignments
    advantages and disadvantages of, 179
    geographic distance and, 129
    mobility and, 157
    performance feedback and, 382, **383**
    performance management and, 368, 377, **377–378**

as type of international assignment, 128
Visibility, loss of, 261
Vodafone, 21, 117
Vredeling, Henk, 349
Vredeling Directive, 349

Wade, Rod, 197
Wal-Mart, 400, **400–401**
Wang, G., 212
Wang, J., 212
Warner, M., 12
Watanabe, Katsuaki, 147
Web-based programs, 207
Weber, W., 93, 95
Welch, D., 118, 128, 161, 165, 207
Wells, L., 51
Weston, S., 343
Wholly owned subsidiaries (WOSs), 307
Williamson, P., 50
Willis, H. L., 172
Wilson, Red, 73
Wong, May M. L., 125
Work arrangements
    non-expatriates and, 134
    performance and, 165–166
    repatriation and, 262–265, 266, 268
World Investment Report, 72
World Vision, 402
Worldwide Business Operations, **57**
World Wide Web, 221
Worm, V., 128, 207, 316
Wright, C., 202
Wright, S., 202
Wyatt, T., 16, 17

Xenophobia, 280

Yan, Y., 307
Yeung, H. W. C., 402
Yorke, Richard, 122
Young, John, 334

Zeira, Y., 81, 114
Zhang, D., 212
Zhao, C., 212
Zhu, C., 212

Additional Credits

Chapter 1. 13: P.J. Dowling. 1999. Completing the Puzzle: Issues in the Development of the Field of International Human Resource Management.*Management International Review*, Special Issue No. 3, p. 31. **20:** The data in this Table is based on the World Investment Report, 2006; FDI from Developing and Transition Economies: Implications for Development. United National Conference on Trade and Development (UNCTAD), 2006. **21:** The data in this Table is based on the World Investment Report, 2006; FDI from Developing and Transition Economies: Implications for Development. United National Conference on Trade and Development (UNCTAD), 2006. **27:** Luis Gomez-Mejia, David B. Balkin and Robert L. Cardy, Managing Human Resources, p. 486. Copyright © 2004 Pearson Education Canada Inc. Reprinted with permission by Pearson Education Canada Inc.

Chapter 2. 43: E. Crooks "Hayward set for his first BP challenge", Financial Times, July 24, 2007, p. 20. **60:** Martin Fackler, New York Times News Service, Lexington Herald Leader, Lexington, Kentucky, February 19, 2007, pp. C1 and C7.

Chapter 3. 72: UNCTAD (ed.), World Investment Report 2006, New York and Geneva, United Nations, 2006. **75:** J. Birkinshaw, H. Bresman, and L. Hakanson, "Managing the post-acquisition integration process: How the human interaction and task integration processes interact to foster value creation", Journal of Management Studies, Vol. 37, No. 3 (2000), pp. 395-425. **79:** Adapted from P. Sparrow and P. Budhwar, "Competition and change: Mapping the Indian HRM recipe against worldwide patterns", Journal of World Business, Vol. 32 (3), 1997, p. 233. Copyright © Elsevier 1997. **80:** Quoted from P. Sparrow and P. Budhwar, "Competition and change: Mapping the Indian HRM recipe against worldwide patterns", Journal of World Business, Vol. 32 (3), 1997, p. 230-231. Copyright © Elsevier 1997. **82:** Table 11.2 (p. 172) from The Management of International Acquisitions by Child, John et al, Oxford University Press, 2001. By permission of Oxford University Press.

Chapter 4. 122: Geoff Dyer "HSBC highlights China staffing woes", Financial Times, 3 April 2007, p. 17.**127:** Adapted from M. Tahvanainen, D. Welch and V. Worm, "Implications of Short-Term International Assignments", European Management Journal, Vol. 23 (6), 2005, p. 669. Copyright © Elsevier 2005. **131:** Thomas A. Stewart and Anand P. Raman, "Lessons from Toyota's Long Drive" Harvard Business Review, Jul-Aug 2007, p. 74-83. Reprinted with permission of Harvard Business Review. Copyright © 2007 by HBS Publishing, all rights reserved. **139:** Reprinted with permission from The Globe and Mail.

Chapter 5. 154: Lang, Gretchen. (2004, March 27). Dual career couples : Trailing spouse's job needs start to get more company time. International Herald Tribune. Retrieved 21, 2005, from www.iht.com/articles/2004/03/27/rspouse_ed3__1.php **176:** H. Harris and C. Brewster, "The Coffee-Machine System: How International Selection Really Works", International Journal of Human Resource Management, Vol. 10, No.3 (1999) p. 493. Reprinted with permission of the publisher (Taylor & Francis Ltd, http://www.informaworld.com). **176:** S. Cryne, "Avoiding the perils of foreign assignments", Canadian HR Reporter, 12 March 2007. **177:** CERC, "2007 Employee Relocation Policy Survey-Executive Summary", CERC, 2007, pp. 11-12. **181:** Based on the literature reviewed in I.C. Fischlmayr, "Female Self-Perception as Barrier to International Careers?", International Journal of Human Resource Management, Vol. 13, No. 5 (2002), pp. 773-783. Reprinted with permission of the publisher (Taylor & Francis Ltd, http://www.informaworld.com). **186:** From Maclean's, 25 January 1999. Reprinted with permission of Maclean's Magazine.

Chapter 6. 195: Global Relocation Trends Survey(GRTS), 2003-2004, by GMAC Global Relocation Services, LLC. All Rights Reserved. **198:** M. Mendenhall, E. Dunbar and G. Oddou, "Expatriate Selection, Training and Career-Pathing: A Review and Critique", Human Resource Management, Vol. 26 (1987), pp. 338. Reprinted with permission **208:** Global Relocation Trends Survey (GRTS), 2003-2004, by GMAC Global Relocation Services, LLC. All Rights Reserved.

Chapter 7. 238: UBS, Prices and Earnings: A Comparison of Purchasing Power Around the Globe, 2005. Published by UBS AG, Wealth Management Research. <http://www.ubs.com/e/ ubs_ch/bb_ch/market_information.Referenz.0002.File.dat /3.9_PL_e.pdf 240:** Reprinted with permission. © Marion Festing, Allen D. Engle, Sr., Peter J. Dowling and Bernadete Muller.

Chapter 8. 254: Courtesy of Dean Bellefleur, D-idea. **271:** Choszick, A. "Expats delight in debut of Blackberry in Japan" The Wall Street Journal Asia, 26 September 2006.

Chapter 9. 294: R. Hallowell, D. Bowen, and C.I. Knoop, "Four Seasons goes to Paris: 53 Properties, 24 Countries, 1 Philosophy", Harvard Business Review, 8 January 2003, p. 2. Reprinted with permission of Harvard Business School Publishing. **301:** R. J. House, P. J. Hanges, M. Javidan, P.W. Dorfman, V. Gupta, V. (eds.): Culture, Leadership and Organizations. The GLOBE Study of 62 Societies, p. 30, copyright 2004 by Sage Publications, Inc.. Reprinted by permission of Sage Publications, Inc. **312:** Reprinted by permission of Levi Strauss & Co. **314:** PriceWaterhouseCoopers (eds.), Technology executive connections: Successful strategies for talent management, (USA: PriceWaterhouseCoopers, 2006), p. 43. **319:** PriceWaterhouseCoopers (eds.), Technology executive connections: Successful strategies for talent management, (USA: PriceWaterhouseCoopers, 2006), p. 19.

Chapter 10. 336: M. Poole, Industrial Relations: Origins and Patterns of National Diversity (London: Routledge & Kegan Paul, 1986), p. 79. **353:** Reproduced with permission from Bulletin to Management, a weekly report of news and trends for HR managers, Vol. 42, No. 9 (March 7, 1991) pp. 66, 71. Copyright 1991 by the Bureau of National Affairs, Inc. Free trials and subscription info: (800)-372-1033 or http://www.bna.com/products/hr

Chapter 11. 362: From Readings and Cases in International Human Resource Management, 3/e, South-Western College Publishing, 2000. Reprinted by permission of Mark Mendenhall and Gary Oddou. **362:** From Readings and Cases in International Human Resource Management, 3/e, South-Western College Publishing, 2000. Reprinted by permission of Mark Mendenhall and Gary Oddou.

Chapter 12. 394: Material reprinted with the express permission of: #National Post Company", a CanWest Partnership. **400:** Copyright 2007 Reuters. Reprinted with permission from Reuters. Reuters content is the intellectual property of Reuters or its third party content providers. Any copying, republication or redistribution of Reuters content is expressly prohibited without the prior written consent of Reuters. Reuters shall not be liable for any errors or delays in content, or for any actions taken in reliance thereon. Reuters and the Reuters Sphere Logo are registered trademarks of the Reuters group of companies around the world. For additional information about Reuters content and services, please visit Reuters website at www.reuters.com. License # REU-4224-JJM. **410:** "Too Little Too Late?

Siemens belatedly wakes up to reputation risk" The Economist, Vol. 381, Issue 8508, 16 December 2006, p. 65-66. Permission by CCC.

Cases

418: Allen D. Engle, Sr. © 2004. **423:** Allen D. Engle, Sr. © 2004. **426:** Copyright © 2003 INSEAD Singapore. **432:** Copyright © 2003 INSEAD Singapore. **435:** Reprinted with permission. © Marion Festing and Allen D. Engle, Sr. **437:** Reprinted with permission. © Marion Festing and Allen D. Engle, Sr. **437:** Reprinted with permission. © Marion Festing and Allen D. Engle, Sr. **438:**

Reprinted with permission. © Marion Festing and Allen D. Engle, Sr. **438:** Reprinted with permission. © Marion Festing and Allen D. Engle, Sr. **440:** Reprinted with permission. © Marion Festing and Allen D. Engle, Sr. **442:** Reprinted with permission. © Marion Festing and Allen D. Engle, Sr. **446:** Reprinted with permission. © Marion Festing and Allen D. Engle, Sr. **447:** Reprinted with permission. © Marion Festing and Manfred Froehlecke. **456:** Stephen J. J. McGuire "Norge Electronics (Portugal)" Thunderbird International Business Review, 4(91), Jan/Feb 2007. Copyright (c) 2007 Wiley Periodicals Inc. Reprinted with permission of John Wiley & Sons, Inc.